# Casebook on Torts

# Casebook on

# Torts

*Ninth Edition*

## Richard Kidner

MA, BCL

*Professor of Law, University of Wales, Aberystwyth*

OXFORD

UNIVERSITY PRESS

# OXFORD

UNIVERSITY PRESS

Great Clarendon Street, Oxford OX2 6DP

Oxford University Press is a department of the University of Oxford.
It furthers the University's objective of excellence in research, scholarship,
and education by publishing worldwide in

Oxford New York

Auckland Cape Town Dar es Salaam Hong Kong Karachi
Kuala Lumpur Madrid Melbourne Mexico City Nairobi
New Delhi Shanghai Taipei Toronto

With offices in

Argentina Austria Brazil Chile Czech Republic France Greece
Guatemala Hungary Italy Japan Poland Portugal Singapore
South Korea Switzerland Thailand Turkey Ukraine Vietnam

Oxford is a registered trade mark of Oxford University Press
in the UK and in certain other countries

Published in the United States
by Oxford University Press Inc., New York

© Richard Kidner, 2006

First edition, 1990      Reprinted, 1999
Second edition, 1992     Sixth edition, 2000
Third edition, 1994      Seventh edition, 2002
Fourth edition, 1996     Eighth edition, 2004
Reprinted, 1997          Ninth edition, 2006
Fifth edition, 1998

British Library Cataloguing in Publication Data

Data available

Library of Congress Cataloging in Publication Data

Data available

Typeset by RefineCatch Limited, Bungay, Suffolk
Printed in Great Britain
on acid-free paper by
Ashford Colour Press, Gosport, Hampshire

ISBN 0-19-928788-0   978-0-19-928788-8

3 5 7 9 10 8 6 4 2

# OUTLINE CONTENTS ·

# DETAILED CONTENTS

# PREFACE

This book has been written mainly for use by undergraduates or those taking professional courses in law, and is intentionally fairly traditional in character. The object is to provide, within a small compass and at a relatively low cost, those cases which students will commonly be referred to in their courses. It is not intended that the book should constitute a complete course in itself, for it ought to be used in conjunction with a textbook. Furthermore, it is not intended to supplant the role of the lecturer or tutor, so while I have given a number of subsidiary examples of the application of the principal cases, I have refrained from extensive comment, believing that to be more the role of the teacher in conjunction with the student.

The law of tort is almost entirely based on case law, and a thorough knowledge of the leading cases is essential to understanding it. In addition, it is useful to know about other cases which apply those leading cases in order to understand their application, to illustrate the limits of liability, and to appreciate distinctions. Also the cases provide a useful peg upon which to hang one's knowledge, and they can give an instant insight into the proper analysis of a problem.

The selection has been based on what I regard as the standard cases, and the extracts attempt to provide the essence of the reasoning and the decision. If the extract is too short it is inadequate, but if it is too long it may not be read at all, and I hope I have found the right balance. Statutory materials have been included where they are necessary to understanding the subject.

In a book of this size some subjects have regrettably had to be omitted, and these include employer's liability, proof of negligence, and the 'industrial' torts such as inducing breach of contract, but I hope that what has been covered represents what is commonly included in a tort course.

The main changes for this edition are the new design, the addition of an introductory chapter and a re-organization of the order of the chapters. New cases include *Gregg* v *Scott* (Chapter 4) on causation and the loss of a chance and *Von Hannover* v *Germany* and *Campbell* v *MGN* (Chapter 26) on the protection of privacy. In addition numerous other cases have been mentioned in the notes to the principal cases. There have been few statutory changes, the main ones relating to the consequences of the Civil Partnerships Act 2004.

The new order of the chapters (beginning with negligence rather than trespass) reflects what is now the common form of presentation in law schools, although no doubt some lecturers may prefer to continue beginning with the analytical training provided by the trespass actions. I have retained the idea of splitting up the treatment of negligence so that the basic issues are dealt with first (duty, breach and remoteness) in order that students can understand the structure of negligence, and this is followed by treatment of the more sophisticated duty issues, such as economic loss.

This book contains materials available to me up to the beginning of February 2006.

*Richard Kidner*

# ACKNOWLEDGEMENTS

The publishers and author would like to thank the following for permission to reproduce extracts from the publications listed below:

The Incorporated Council of Law Reporting for England and Wales—The Law Reports, The Weekly Law Reports and the Industrial Cases Reports.

Butterworths—The All England Law Reports.

The Estates Gazette Ltd—The Estates Gazette Law Reports.

New Zealand Council of Law Reporting  New Zealand Law Reports.

Supreme Court of Canada—Canada Supreme Court Reports, reproduced with the permission of the Minister of Public Works and Government Services Canada.

Keith Stanton 'The Modern Law of Torts', (Sweet and Maxwell 1994) pp. 11–12, reproduced by permission of Sweet and Maxwell.

Every effort has been made to clear the necessary permissions. If notified, the publisher will undertake to rectify any errors or omissions at the earliest opportunity.

# TABLE OF CASES

Where extracts from cases are reproduced, the cases and the relevant page numbers are shown in **bold**.

# TABLE OF STATUTES

Where part of a Statute is reproduced, the page number appears in **bold**.

# TABLE OF STATUTORY INSTRUMENTS

# TABLE OF FOREIGN LEGISLATION

Where part of a Statute is reproduced, the page number appears in **bold**.

# TABLE OF TREATIES AND CONVENTIONS

Where part of a Statute is reproduced, the page number appears in **bold**.

# TABLE OF EUROPEAN SECONDARY LEGISLATION

Where part of a Statute is reproduced, the page number appears in **bold**.

# 1

# Introduction

There is no definition of the Law of Torts, at least not one which will help anyone understand what a tort is. While in general it deals with the liability to pay damages to someone who has suffered a loss, it is not possible to be more specific than that because tort deals with a wide range of activities and many different types of loss. It doesn't often matter whether a right of action is a tort or not, although it may do where procedural matters are concerned, for example to determine whether this country has jurisdiction if a wrong occurs abroad. Perhaps all one can say is that tort is what is in the tort textbooks, although even that is not strictly accurate as the action for breach of privacy is often included in tort books but is technically an equitable obligation.

Nevertheless some examples can indicate the wide range of torts which covers such obvious things as negligent or intentional personal injury, damage to goods or invasion of land, but also such things as the protection of reputation or of privacy, the control of strikes, the prevention of unfair trade or the control of pollution. Not all these areas can be covered in this book, but it does contain material on what are commonly regarded as the core areas of tort.

## SECTION 1: EXAMPLES OF TORTS

The book begins with negligence which covers a wide range of human activity dealing as it does with carelessly causing injury to the person, to chattels, or even to economic interests. A road accident is the simplest example of a negligence action and this raises the difficult question of whether tort is the best way to deal with compensation for personal injuries (a matter dealt with later in this chapter). But negligence can give rise to difficult legal and social issues. For example to what extent should a person be protected from psychiatric injury, as in the Hillsborough disaster case (*Alcock* v *Chief Constable of South Yorkshire* in Chapter 7), where people claimed for psychiatric problems arising from seeing or hearing of the death of a relative? This raises the issue of what you can be expected to put up with and what is so out of the ordinary that an action should be allowed.

What about economic interests? For some years tort has been struggling with the problem of negligent advice. Should you be able to sue for a negligently written reference which means you don't get a job, or should a referee be allowed considerable latitude to express a personal opinion? (*Spring* v *Guardian Assurance* in Chapter 8). What about protection of profits? For example, if a lorry damages a bridge between a village and its pub so that the road is closed and the villagers don't go to the pub, should the owner be able to sue for lost profits or is that one of the risks of being in business? (*Star Tavern* v *Nield* in Chapter 9).

Other issues concern the occupiers of land. For example, should they be required to treat trespassers in the same way as visitors with permission, or are trespassers less deserving? For example, if a person in a public park ignores a notice saying 'Dangerous Water. No Swimming' and he dives in (thereby becoming a trespasser to the lake), can he sue if he hurts his head on a rock? (*Tomlinson* v *Congleton Borough Council* in Chapter 18). This raises the issue of the extent to which people should be responsible for the consequences of their own choices.

These are only some of the questions which arise when asking what interests should be protected by the law of negligence. But even if an interest is protected other issues arise. For example, what happens when a claimant is partially at fault for his own injury, for example by not wearing a seat belt when involved in a road accident? (*Froom* v *Butcher* in Chapter 13). Causation can also be a very difficult problem—how do we separate a legally relevant act from one which is merely the background to the event? (see Chapter 4). Another related and difficult problem is whether a defendant should be liable for all the consequences of his act or for only some of them. For example if a stevedore carelessly drops a plank into the hold of a ship from which one might expect a dent in the plates of the hold, what should we do if unexpectedly the hold contains petrol fumes and the ship blows up? Should he be liable for the total loss of the ship or only for the notional dent? (*Re Polemis* in Chapter 4).

Another principal area of tort deals with rights between neighbouring land-owners in the tort of Nuisance. This can cover not only direct interference such as overhanging trees or encroaching roots, but also things which interfere with the use of the property such as noise, smoke, or obnoxious smells. This raises the issue of what rights ownership of land gives to a landowner. For example is he entitled to be free from interference with his television reception (*Hunter* v *Canary Wharf*), or be free from prostitutes perambulating outside his premises (*Thompson-Schwab* v *Costaki* in Chapter 19)?

Tort also covers intentional wrongs such as trespass to the person, to land, or to goods. The aim here is often to protect the right itself rather than to provide compensation, as in an action to determine who owns a piece of land. These intentional torts also raise questions about what interests are being protected. For example, false imprisonment is a tort and this often raises issues about the powers of the police and the liberty of the individual. Another question is whether it covers not only 'imprisonment' or all freedom of movement. For example, if a person is told that he cannot move forwards but is free to go back where he came, is that a tort? (*Bird* v *Jones* in Chapter 22). Other forms of trespass to the person protect a person not only against being struck, but also against any unwarranted contact, and thus this tort is often used to resolve matters of consent to medical treatment (*Chatterton* v *Gerson* in Chapter 22).

Again the tort of conversion protects a person from being deprived of his goods and thus protects him not only against his goods being stolen or destroyed but it can also be used to determine who owns the goods. For example, if a 'rogue' has fraudulently induced the owner to sell him goods but does not pay for them and then sells them to a third party, is the third party required to return the goods to the original owner? (*Hollins* v *Fowler* in Chapter 24). Students of the law of contract may recognize this situation as cases of 'mistake' in contract are actually brought in tort to determine ownership and that depends on the effect of the contract. This raises the issue of whether the law should protect original owners or those who have bought under a contract.

Strict liability also plays a role in tort. Are there activities which are so dangerous that a person who engages in them should be liable for any damage caused by the activity even if he is not at fault? Examples might be reservoirs which burst (*Rylands* v *Fletcher*) or nuclear power plants which leak radioactivity (see Chapter 20).

Thus issues in tort revolve around a mixture of ideas, basically in two categories. The first is 'what interests should be protected'? We are fairly clear that a person should be protected against personal injury or damage to goods, but are less sure about reputation (defamation) or privacy, where a balance has to be struck between freedom of speech and freedom from interference. Here the Human Rights Act is having considerable influence and this has been the liveliest area of tort in recent years (see Chapters 25 and 26). Economic interests are less well protected, that is where the claimant loses money but suffers no physical damage. The limits of liability here are very uncertain and have been the subject of a number of House of Lords cases in recent years. (see Chapters 8 and 9).

The other question is about the mind of the defendant. Should liability be limited to intentional acts or is fault sufficient? If so what do we mean by fault? This raises not only the issue of what society regards as unreasonable behaviour, but also what level of safety from the acts of others we are entitled to and what kind of things we have to put up with. Finally, there are cases where a person should be liable even if he is not at fault, but the scope of this form of liability has been restricted in recent years.

Even once liability is established there is the vital question of who should pay? One way tort has dealt with this is to identify a defendant with sufficient money to pay the damages. This led to the doctrine of 'vicarious liability' whereby an employer is liable for the torts of his employee if they are committed in the course of his employment. But what are the limits to this? There are problems of time and space—is he in the right place at the right time (*Compton* v *McClure*), and the closeness of the connection between the act and what the employee is employed to do (see Chapter 15). For example, what if the employee is doing something extremely stupid such as filling a tin with petrol while smoking a cigarette (*Jefferson* v *Derbyshire Farmers*), or is committing a criminal act? Should a school be liable if one of its teachers sexually abuses a pupil, that being entirely contrary to what he was employed to do? (*Lister* v *Hesley Hall*). These all involve issues of whether the act can be seen to be done by the enterprise or by the individual.

However beyond this there is the fundamental matter of insurance. Sometimes the law requires a person engaging in an activity to acquire compulsory insurance, as in motor vehicle cases, in order to ensure that there is always a suitable defendant, and often individuals will voluntarily insure themselves against liability, as with house insurance. As will be seen in the next section the existence of insurance is essential to the operation of the tort system, for without it defendants would be unable to pay and claimants would go uncompensated. However, it is now beginning to be asked whether the cost of insurance (or self insurance) is now, as in the case of the NHS, too high and thus inhibiting businesses and organizations from functioning efficiently. This had led to calls, not only here but also in many other countries, either to limit liability or compensation, or to find another way other than tort to deal with personal injury compensation. This will be dealt with in the next section.

## SECTION 2: THE AIMS OF THE LAW OF TORTS

Stanton, in *The Modern Law of Tort* (1994, pp. 11–12), explains the aims of the tort system.

Considerable effort has been expended in attempts to identify the aims of the law of tort. A justification ought to exist for the existence of a system which consumes resources in transferring money from one person (the injurer) to another (the victim). However, the range of interests protected by the law of tort makes any search for a single aim underlying the law a difficult one. Actions for wrongful interference with goods or trespasses to land serve fundamentally different ends from an action seeking compensation for a personal injury. In practice much of the discussion concerning the aims of the law of tort has concentrated on accidents and compensation for personal injuries.

The different aims which have been suggested seem to be capable of classification under a number of heads. Those who have studied tort from the perspective of economic theory have tended to favour the 'deterrent' aim of tort. This sees tort as a system which is designed to reduce the frequency and the severity of accidents. Fear of legal liability and the resulting awards of damages provides an incentive to persons, both injurers and potential victims, to indulge in safer conduct, both by avoiding hazardous activities and by increasing the level of safety precautions they provide. In practice, the 'deterrent' approach will choose to sacrifice the interests of the victim in favour of those of the defendant by leaving injured plaintiffs to bear their own losses if the damage could not have been avoided by the use of cost-justified precautions.

In contrast, the 'compensation' aim, which became very dominant among academic lawyers in the 1970s, sees the primary aim of tort as being to reduce the disruption which accidents cause to the lifestyles of victims and those dependent upon them. Victims may lose their income and may require expensive nursing care. An award of compensation alleviates this disruption and any attendant social problems. The whole thrust of the compensation aim is the protection of victims: the defendant is merely an agent by which this is achieved.

Additionally, the tort system can be seen as a mechanism for retribution and the appeasement of the injured person's feelings, as providing a mechanism for the protection of rights and as a technique whereby society is able to express judgment on the injurer's conduct. Recent practice, particularly in the context of 'disaster' litigation seems to have brought this judgmental role of tort back to prominence, even if it has failed to attract academic support.

A subsidiary aim to those already mentioned is that any compensation system should be efficient in the sense of providing an effective mechanism for distributing the money paid into it to the victims of accidents. A large percentage of this money should not be consumed by the operating costs of the system.

The difficulty presented by the law of tort is that it has developed with only limited reference to these aims and that it may fail to achieve any of them properly. In addition, the deterrence and compensation aims are almost certainly incompatible with each other.

Of the functions mentioned above the most significant are deterrence and compensation for they will often help us not only to justify the existence of liability but also guide us to determining the extent of the tort. However, as mentioned by Stanton, these objectives are often in conflict, and a judicial decision may have to effect a compromise between various objectives. Thus we may want to award compensation to a deserving claimant and yet not want to deter people from engaging in the activity. A simple example would be school trips. We may feel sympathy for a child injured on a school trip, but not want to deter schools engaging in them for fear of being sued. Fear of liability ('the compensation culture') often prevents people from engaging in perfectly sensible activities, just as a too rigid an application of health and safety rules does. Which is better—some acceptable level of risk, or stopping the activity altogether? What is an acceptable level of risk?

## Deterrence

Part of the justification for a tort is that it *identifies* what actions should be avoided and deters people from engaging in them. It is essential that we should know what action is wrongful, but a tort action may over-deter or under-deter. It may over-deter where the perception of the chance of liability is exaggerated, as in the case of school trips mentioned above. It may under-deter where either the chances of somebody suing to enforce their rights are small, such as where the matter may be one of principle but the damage is slight, or where the consequences to the individual tortfeasor may be slight, such as where he is insured. How is a driver deterred (apart from a small rise in premiums) when it will be his insurance company who pays and not himself? However, most of us do at least try to drive carefully, and it is suggested that this is not because we fear potential damages or a rise in premiums, but because the law sets a standard identified by the law of tort which as ordinary members of society we accept and adhere to.

If deterrence is the objective it may be that the criminal law is a more effective way of doing this. For example, the wearing of seat belts by car passengers is regarded as desirable. First we had Jimmy Saville exhorting us on television to 'clunk click every trip', but this had little effect. Next tort law decided that damages would be reduced by 25% for passengers injured when not wearing a set belt, but few people knew about this and again it was ineffective. Finally it was made a criminal offence and now everybody wears a seat belt. So the question arises as to how effective tort can be at accident prevention. (See also on this *Thompson v Smith Ship Repairers* in Chapter 3).

One theory allied to deterrence but based on economic ideas is that in general commercial enterprises which cause damage will have to compete with those which do not, and accordingly market forces will drive the accident causing companies out of business because having to pay compensation will make them less competitive. However, this will only work in a world where risks are covered by insurance if the insurance company distinguishes sufficiently between 'negligent' companies and those that are not. For example if an insurer demands the same premium from all tyre manufacturers because this is administratively easier than to examine the accident record of each, then the 'negligent' manufacturer will not be less competitive. Even if a distinction is made, it is unlikely that insurance premiums would be such a large proportion of costs as to make a competitive difference. Furthermore even if a higher premium is charged it may still be more profitable to pay that higher premium and continue to 'cut corners'.

Allied to deterrence is retribution and appeasement. This is becoming more common as the media stoke up public anger and strong emotions are put on public display. One example of this is bereavement. Does A have a personal *right* that his friend B should not be killed in a road accident? A may feel hurt and angry that his friend has been killed, but is it the function of tort to assuage those feelings? What good would it do to give A money? (It is right of course that the *dependants* of B should be compensated if they have lost financially as a result of the death.) Is not the criminal law more appropriate to deal with this by concentrating not on the views of A, but rather on the view of society as a whole on the wrongfulness of the actions of the person who caused the death?

Another factor, somewhat loosely related to deterrence, is that tort can sometimes raise a debate about what kind of conduct we want to control. There is often discussion about whether legislation is the better vehicle for a change in the law, but tort has the advantage that it can take an incremental approach to new developments and can engage the public in considering how to handle change. For example, there has been considerable debate over recent years about consent in medical cases and the validity of 'advance directives' given by a person about how they want to be treated if they are no longer able to decide for themselves. The public were very interested in this and a number of cases over several years developed the law, so that there now may be general agreement about how to deal with these matters.

## Compensation

Originally tort was about 'shifting' or 'transferring' the loss from the victim to the defendant. The defendant himself paid by compensating the victim. However those days are gone and we are now in an era of 'loss distribution'. In other words it is not the defendant himself who pays, but it will be his, or his employer's, insurer. Thus, nobody suffers too great a penalty but rather the loss is spread or distributed amongst all the premium payers. If the insurance fund is large enough the cost to each premium payer will be minimal. As it was no longer a question of who should suffer (A, the victim or B, the defendant), this led to the main emphasis being on whether A deserved compensation as normally no one individual would have to pay. This made it easier to expand the area of liability and has led to the so-called 'compensation culture' where the need for there to be a justification for requiring the payment of damages seems to have been lost or minimized. Thus the perception is that a person should be compensated for an injury whether it was caused by fault or was a 'pure' accident, or even caused by the victim himself. This has now led to questions being asked about whether the economy as a whole can afford this level of compensation and whether it is an efficient way of dealing with personal injuries.

However it has been said that the 'compensation culture' has been exaggerated and that the introduction of 'no win, no fee' arrangements has not had the deleterious effects sometimes claimed. As usual in tort, nothing is certain. In any event studies in the past have shown that one difficulty with tort is that while some claimants may receive large sums in damages (often widely reported), many people get nothing at all. The social security system, especially disability benefit, is intended to provide a floor of support for those who fall outside the tort system.

If losses are to be distributed via insurance across a large number of people, this must be done efficiently. However, it has been shown that the tort system is not as efficient as, for example, the social security system. In 1967 Terence Ison in 'The Forensic Lottery' showed that the cost of delivering £1 compensation to a victim could be as much as 96p, as against only a few pence for social security. Other studies, such as the Pearson Commission in 1978 have shown similar figures. Thus the tort system is very expensive to operate and needs justification other than compensation to justify its high cost. A further problem has been delay in claimants receiving compensation. While there have been a number of procedural reforms in recent years to alleviate this, delay is probably inherent in a system based on liability and which is necessarily adversarial.

One answer has been the introduction of 'no fault' systems, mainly for motor vehicle accidents. This began in Saskatchewan in Canada 1946 and has now spread to other Provinces of Canada and to American and Australian States. The system is theoretically simple. Every car driver pays a premium (usually via the road tax system), and every person injured by a motor vehicle is compensated regardless of the fault of the driver. (There are usually limits on the amounts recovered and the amounts insured but potential victims or defendants can take out additional private insurance.) It has been argued that this does away with the incentive to drive carefully, but often the criminal law is better at this and anyway the amount of premium paid can be adjusted in line with such things as motoring convictions. Also it is said that a person who does not take care for his own safety is unlikely to care about the safety of others.

The ultimate such no fault scheme is the accident compensation scheme of New Zealand, introduced in 1972, which covers virtually *all* accidents, motor related or not, and results in tort actions for personal injury being unnecessary. One criticism of such a scheme is that it raises the question of why we should compensate for accidents but not for naturally acquired diseases. (What is the difference to the sufferer between being made blind and becoming blind?) Another problem is that although fault is no longer relevant, causation still needs to be established, and this often raises similar issues to fault.

An alternative is for potential *victims* to insure themselves against being injured. (This is common for example in holiday insurance where travellers insure themselves against being injured or losing their property.) The present system is based on potential *defendants* being insured against causing loss, but as has been seen the process of transferring the loss from the victim to the defendant is expensive and time consuming. However, the 'loss insurance' alternative is not generally acceptable as it is felt that there should be a universal system protecting everybody rather than just those who select themselves by buying insurance. But if potential damages are to be capped, additional self insurance may be useful for those who want greater protection.

Finally the overall cost of compensation has become an issue. 'Tort reform' has become a political issue in the United States where compensation costs have been a significant burden for both individuals and businesses, and the issue is also being discussed here. Not only might some worthwhile activities cease, for example school trips supervised by teachers, but also insurers might refuse to cover certain professions or commercial activities. If insurance is not available that rather defeats the object of tort as a distributor of losses and may result in no compensation being available at all.

Various suggestions have been made to cap the overall burden of compensation, especially in personal injury cases, or to limit the range of potential liability. One example from this country is the Nuclear Installations Act 1965 whereby the total payout for any one nuclear event is limited in exchange for strict liability on the licensee. (The limit was necessary because the insurance industry could not provide cover for the potential catastrophic loss which might follow a nuclear escape.)

Another method has been adopted in Australia where much of tort has been 'codified' and in the process the range of liability has been limited. This prevents the tendency of tort to expand the range of activities for which there can be liability and even retrenches on some existing forms of liability, for example such statutes have restricted recovery for psychiatric injury.

Most of what has been said above is relevant to the tort of negligence, for it is here that the problems are greatest. Other torts perform slightly different functions, for example trespass to the person is often used not just to receive compensation but to determine the rights of the individual in relation to the state e.g. on the question of powers of arrest.

Nobody doubts that tort plays an essential role in regulating the conduct of people in society. Human activity means that there will inevitably be losses and tort tries to determine whether the victim or the person who caused the damage should bear the loss. However this eminently sensible objective is much more complicated than appears at first sight. The rest of this book attempts to illustrate the rules we use to achieve this aim, but it should always be asked whether that is the right objective and how well it is being achieved.

## SECTION 3: STUDYING TORTS

The cases are everything! Torts is almost wholly a case driven subject and therefore a good knowledge of the cases and what they stand for is essential. A textbook can *describe* the law, but the law itself is in the cases and their interpretation. It is intended that this book should be used in conjunction with a textbook for that can provide a structure for the law and explain what is going on. Much of the difficulty in tort is classification and structure: in other words it is the function of academic authors to find a way of explaining the cases by finding a structure of the subject which will contain and explain them. Different authors have different ideas about how to do this, and thus not only will the titles and contents of chapters in a tort textbook be different, but also cases may be placed in different chapters by different authors. Nevertheless the object is to provide an overall description of the law which appears to be coherent. However often the law is not coherent and often contains contradictions and muddle. Sometimes new developments try to make order out of disorder and this may require a complete re-evaluation of the basis of the tort. An example is Chapter 8 on liability for negligent statements where the doctrinal basis of the law is now quite different from what it was when the tort was 'invented' in 1963. 'Duty of care' in Chapter 1 is another example of continuing doctrinal change.

There are really three steps in studying the cases. The first is analytical and is common to most subjects. The objective is to identify what is relevant about a case.

What is background and what is material? How does it differ from previous cases? What is the essential element in the decision? This will usually involve a good understanding of the facts, but may involve a re-interpretation of previous cases. That is why some exam questions ask 'Would it make any difference if . . .' This is aimed to test analytical ability in identifying the crucial elements of a case.

The second step is to understand the history of the development of the tort. Nobody would sit down and invent the law as we have it today. The present law is a jumble of earlier competing ideas and compromises and these need to be unraveled. A good example is Chapter 7 on liability for psychiatric damage. It is impossible to understand the present position without knowing how we got here, how the tort developed and what compromises have been made. The present law is unsatisfactory but represents a compromise between the desire to compensate deserving cases and the need to limit the range of potential liability.

This leads to the final point. Tort is not a purely abstract subject. Decisions matter, not only to the individuals concerned, but also in the wider context. Accordingly it is necessary, certainly at the appellate level, to understand what each decision is trying to achieve and how it fits in with the aims of tort described in section 2. The courts are now much more willing to discuss these issues and recent House of Lords speeches often contain statements about the social and economic factors behind the decision. (See, for example, the speech of Lord Hobhouse in *Tomlinson* v *Congleton Borough Council* in Chapter 18, or on economic issues the speech of Lord Steyn in *Marc Rich* v *Bishop Rock Marine* in Chapter 1). It thus becomes apparent that each tort case presents considerable scope for choice, whether based on analytical, historical or policy reasons. Tort is constantly changing and the study of the subject is intended to enable students to understand 'what is going on' and to take a view about how the law should or might develop.

# 2

# Negligence: The Basic Principles of Duty of Care

## The arrangement of this and subsequent chapters

Negligence is a large and amorphous subject, and all parts of the law on it are interlocking. It is often difficult to understand one part without having studied the whole, and therefore in arranging the material I have decided to set out the basic principles first, leaving the more sophisticated developments until later. Accordingly the next three chapters on duty, standard of care, causation and remoteness of damage aim to explain the basic negligence action, principally in relation to an action for personal injuries or property damage where the concepts are easiest to understand. More difficult duty problems, such as liability for statements or for pure economic loss, will be dealt with later.

Duty is but one element in the tort of negligence, for it must be shown that not only was the defendant under a duty towards the claimant to be careful, but also that he failed to achieve the required standard of care and that that failure caused the damage, and finally that the damage was not too remote a consequence of the act.

Duty is about relationships, and it must be shown that the particular defendant stood in the required relationship to the claimant such that he came under an obligation to use care towards him. This relationship is sometimes referred to as 'proximity'. In cases of personal injury or damage to property the necessary relationship is established if the defendant ought to have foreseen damage to the claimant whereas in other cases a closer relationship may be required. Thus, duty means 'proximity' in the legal sense (this has nothing to do with geographical proximity), and proximity means the level of closeness of relationship required for the particular kind of damage. Thus, a closer relationship than mere foresight will be required for some kinds of damage, such as damage caused by statements (this will be dealt with later). Foresight of damage is a necessary ingredient in all cases of negligence and finally there is a policy element which is expressed by the view that it must be just and reasonable to impose a duty in that class of case.

Accordingly, in order to establish a duty of care it must be shown that:

(a) some damage was foreseeable to a foreseeable claimant;

(b) there is a sufficiently close relationship between the parties to establish a duty in that class of case (proximity); and

(c) that it is just and reasonable to impose a duty.

Duty of care is one of the ways in which risks can be allocated in society, i.e. should potential claimants or potential defendants bear the risk of injury occurring? This will have both social and economic implications, and hence the technical criteria of duty or the other concepts in negligence should not be taken too literally. They are merely mechanical devices for performing and expressing something deeper, that is a decision or an understanding about how risks should be allocated. This point was well expressed by McDonald J in *Nova Mink* v *Trans Canada Airlines* [1951] 2 DLR 241 when he said:

> When upon analysis of the circumstances and application of the appropriate formula, a court holds that the defendant was under a duty of care, the court is stating as a conclusion of law what is really a conclusion of policy as to responsibility for conduct involving unreasonable risk. It is saying that such circumstances presented such an appreciable risk of harm to others as to entitle them to protection against unreasonable conduct by the actor. It is declaring also that a cause of action can exist in other situations of the same type, and *pro tanto* is moving in the direction of establishing further categories of human relationships entailing recognised duties of care. . . . Accordingly there is always a large element of judicial policy and social expediency involved in the determination of the duty problem, however it may be obscured by the use of the traditional formulae. . . .

This chapter explains these formulae, but one must always bear in mind the purpose they fulfil.

## SECTION 1: PROXIMITY

### Donoghue v Stevenson
House of Lords [1932] AC 562; 1932 SC 31; 147 LJ 281

At about 8.50 p.m. on 26 August 1928, Mrs May Donoghue (whose maiden name was Mc'Alister) went to a cafe owned by Francis Minchella, known as the Wellmeadow Cafe, in Wellmeadow Road, Paisley. A friend of hers (probably a female friend) bought a bottle of ginger beer and an ice cream. The bottle was made of opaque glass. Minchella poured part of the contents into a tumbler containing the ice cream. Mrs Donoghue drank some of this and the friend then poured the remainder of the ginger beer into the glass. It was said that a decomposed snail floated out of the bottle and the pursuer claimed that she suffered shock and gastro-enteritis, and asked for £500 damages from the manufacturer of the ginger beer, David Stevenson of Paisley. The pursuer claimed that a manufacturer of products was liable in negligence to a person injured by the product, but the defendant claimed that there could be no liability as there was no contract between himself and the pursuer. Held: on the point of law involved, that such a defendant could be liable to such a claimant in negligence.

> LORD ATKIN: We are solely concerned with the question whether, as a matter of law in the circumstances alleged, the defender owed any duty to the pursuer to take care.
>
> It is remarkable how difficult it is to find in the English authorities statements of general application defining the relations between parties that give rise to the duty. The Courts are concerned with the particular relations which come before them in actual litigation, and it is sufficient to say whether the duty exists in those circumstances. The result is that the Courts have been engaged upon an elaborate classification of duties as they exist in respect of property, whether real or personal, with further divisions as to ownership, occupation or control, and distinctions based on the particular relations of the one side or the other, whether manufacturer, salesman or landlord, customer, tenant, stranger, and so on. In this way it can be ascertained at any time whether the law recognizes a duty, but only where the case can be referred to some particular species which has been examined

and classified. And yet the duty which is common to all the cases where liability is established must logically be based upon some element common to the cases where it is found to exist. To seek a complete logical definition of the general principle is probably to go beyond the function of the judge, for the more general the definition the more likely it is to omit essentials or to introduce non-essentials. The attempt was made by Brett MR in *Heaven* v *Pender* (1883) 11 QBD 503, 509, in a definition to which I will later refer. As framed, it was demonstrably too wide, though it appears to me, if properly limited, to be capable of affording a valuable practical guide.

At present I content myself with pointing out that in English law there must be, and is, some general conception of relations giving rise to a duty of care, of which the particular cases found in the books are but instances. The liability for negligence, whether you style it such or treat it as in other systems as a species of 'culpa,' is no doubt based upon a general public sentiment of moral wrongdoing for which the offender must pay. But acts or omissions which any moral code would censure cannot in a practical world be treated so as to give a right to every person injured by them to demand relief. In this way rules of law arise which limit the range of complainants and the extent of their remedy. The rule that you are to love your neighbour becomes in law, you must not injure your neighbour; and the lawyer's question, Who is my neighbour? receives a restricted reply. You must take reasonable care to avoid acts or omissions which you can reasonably foresee would be likely to injure your neighbour. Who, then, in law is my neighbour? The answer seems to be—persons who are so closely and directly affected by my act that I ought reasonably to have them in contemplation as being so affected when I am directing my mind to the acts or omissions which are called in question. This appears to me to be the doctrine of *Heaven* v *Pender*, as laid down by Lord Esher (then Brett MR) when it is limited by the notion of proximity introduced by Lord Esher himself and A. L. Smith LJ in *Le Lievre* v *Gould* [1893] 1 QB 491. Lord Esher says: 'That case established that, under certain circumstances, one man may owe a duty to another, even though there is no contract between them. If one man is near to another, or is near to the property of another, a duty lies upon him not to do that which may cause a personal injury to that other, or may injure his property.' So A. L. Smith LJ: 'The decision of *Heaven* v *Pender* 11 QBD 503, 509 was founded upon the principle, that a duty to take due care did arise when the person or property of one was in such proximity to the person or property of another that, if due care was not taken, damage might be done by the one to the other.' I think that this sufficiently states the truth if proximity be not confined to mere physical proximity, but be used, as I think it was intended, to extend to such close and direct relations that the act complained of directly affects a person whom the person alleged to be bound to take care would know would be directly affected by his careless act. . . .

. . . I venture to say that in the branch of the law which deals with civil wrongs, dependent in England at any rate entirely upon the application by judges of general principles also formulated by judges, it is of particular importance to guard against the danger of stating propositions of law in wider terms than is necessary, lest essential factors be omitted in the wider survey and the inherent adaptability of English law be unduly restricted. For this reason it is very necessary in considering reported cases in the law of torts that the actual decision alone should carry authority, proper weight, of course, being given to the dicta of the judges. . . .

LORD MACMILLAN: It humbly appears to me that the diversity of view which is exhibited in such cases as *George* v *Skivington* LR 5 Ex 1 on the one hand and *Blacker* v *Lake & Elliot, Ld* 106 LT 533, on the other hand—to take two extreme instances —is explained by the fact that in the discussion of the topic which now engages your Lordships' attention two rival principles of the law find a meeting place where each has contended for supremacy. On the one hand, there is the well established principle that no one other than a party to a contract can complain of a breach of that contract. On the other hand, there is the equally well established doctrine that negligence apart from contract gives a right of action to the party injured by that negligence—and here I use the term negligence, of course, in its technical legal sense, implying a duty owed and neglected. The fact that there is a contractual relationship between the parties which may give rise to an action for breach of contract, does not exclude the co-existence of a right of action founded on negligence as between the same parties, independently of the contract, though arising out of the relationship in fact brought about by the contract. Of this the best illustration is the right of the injured railway passenger to sue the railway company either for breach of the contract of safe carriage or for negligence in carrying him. And there is no reason why the same set of facts should not give one person a right of action in contract and another person a right of action in tort. . . .

Where, as in cases like the present, so much depends upon the avenue of approach to the question, it is very easy to take the wrong turning. If you begin with the sale by the manufacturer to the retail dealer, then the consumer who purchases from the retailer is at once seen to be a stranger to the contract between the retailer and the manufacturer and so disentitled to sue upon it. There is no contractual relation between the manufacturer and the consumer; and thus the plaintiff, if he is to succeed, is driven to try to bring himself within one or other of the exceptional cases where the strictness of the rule that none but a party to a contract can found on a breach of that contract has been mitigated in the public interest, as it has been in the case of a person who issues a chattel which is inherently dangerous or which he knows to be in a dangerous condition. If, on the other hand, you disregard the fact that the circumstances of the case at one stage include the existence of a contract of sale between the manufacturer and the retailer, and approach the question by asking whether there is evidence of carelessness on the part of the manufacturer, and whether he owed a duty to be careful in a question with the party who has been injured in consequence of his want of care, the circumstance that the injured party was not a party to the incidental contract of sale becomes irrelevant, and his title to sue the manufacturer is unaffected by that circumstance . . .

. . . Having regard to the inconclusive state of the authorities in the Courts below and to the fact that the important question involved is now before your Lordships for the first time, I think it desirable to consider the matter from the point of view of the principles applicable to this branch of law which are admittedly common to both English and Scottish jurisprudence.

The law takes no cognizance of carelessness in the abstract. It concerns itself with carelessness only where there is a duty to take care and where failure in that duty has caused damage. In such circumstances carelessness assumes the legal quality of negligence and entails the consequences in law of negligence. What, then, are the circumstances which give rise to this duty to take care? In the daily contacts of social and business life human beings are thrown into, or place themselves in, an infinite variety of relations with their fellows; and the law can refer only to the standards of the reasonable man in order to determine whether any particular relation gives rise to a duty to take care as between those who stand in that relation to each other. The grounds of action may be as various and manifold as human errancy; and the conception of legal responsibility may develop in adaptation to altering social conditions and standards. The criterion of judgment must adjust and adapt itself to the changing circumstances of life. The categories of negligence are never closed. The cardinal principle of liability is that the party complained of should owe to the party complaining a duty to take care, and that the party complaining should be able to prove that he has suffered damage in consequence of a breach of that duty. Where there is room for diversity of view, it is in determining what circumstances will establish such a relationship between the parties as to give rise, on the one side, to a duty to take care, and on the other side to a right to have care taken.

NOTE

The ruling of the House of Lords was on a point of law only, on the assumption that the facts alleged were true. The trial of the actual action was set down for 10 January 1932, but by then Stevenson had died and the case was settled for £200. For the family history of Mrs Donoghue and other interesting points about the case, see Rodger, 'Mrs Donoghue and Alfenus Varus' [1988] CLP 1 and W. McBryde, '*Donoghue* v *Stevenson*: the story of the snail in the bottle case' in *Obligations in Context*, A. Gamble (ed.) (1990). See also Heuston, '*Donoghue* v *Stevenson* in retrospect' (1957) 20 MLR 1.

### *Anns* v *Merton London Borough Council*
House of Lords [1978] AC 728; [1977] 2 All ER 492; [1977] 2 WLR 1024

Following *Donoghue* v *Stevenson* there was little development of the duty concept until it was suggested in *Dorset Yacht* v *Home Office* in 1970 that a duty should exist whenever damage was foreseeable. This was refined in *Anns* but this idea has now been abandoned and the dictum below has been disapproved. The remarks of Lord Wilberforce are reproduced here for ease of reference because this passage is often referred to in later cases.

The case itself concerned the potential liability of a local authority towards a lessee of a building for failure to ensure that the building complied with deposited plans, particularly in relation to the depth of the foundations. The actual decision has been overruled in *Murphy* v *Brentwood District Council* [1991] 1 AC 398 (see below).

LORD WILBERFORCE: Through the trilogy of cases in this House—*Donoghue* v *Stevenson* [1932] AC 562, *Hedley Byrne & Co. Ltd* v *Heller & Partners Ltd* [1964] AC 465, and *Dorset Yacht Co. Ltd* v *Home Office* [1970] AC 1004, the position has now been reached that in order to establish that a duty of care arises in a particular situation, it is not necessary to bring the facts of that situation within those of previous situations in which a duty of care has been held to exist. Rather the question has to be approached in two stages. First one has to ask whether, as between the alleged wrongdoer and the person who has suffered damage there is a sufficient relationship of proximity or neighbourhood such that, in the reasonable contemplation of the former, carelessness on his part may be likely to cause damage to the latter—in which case a prima facie duty of care arises. Secondly, if the first question is answered affirmatively, it is necessary to consider whether there are any considerations which ought to negative, or to reduce or limit the scope of the duty or the class of person to whom it is owed or the damages to which a breach of it may give rise. . . .

NOTE

For discussion of the retreat from the *Anns* principle see Kidner, 'Resiling from the *Anns* principle: the variable nature of proximity in negligence' (1987) 7 LS 319.

---

### *Caparo* v *Dickman*
House of Lords [1990] 2 AC 605; [1990] 1 All ER 568

This case concerned the liability of auditors for negligent misstatement, and the substantive issues are dealt with in Chapter 10. The extracts below deal with general issues as to duty of care.

LORD BRIDGE: . . . since the *Anns* case a series of decisions of the Privy Council and of your Lordships House, notably in judgments and speeches delivered by Lord Keith of Kinkel, have emphasised the inability of any single general principle to provide a practical test which can be applied to every situation to determine whether a duty of care is owed and, if so what is its scope: see *Governors of Peabody Donation Fund* v *Sir Lindsay Parkinson & Co. Ltd* [1985] AC 210, 239F–241C, *Yuen Kun Yeu* v *Attorney-General of Hong Kong* [1988] AC 175, 190E–194F; *Rowling* v *Takaro Properties Ltd* [1988] AC 473, 501D–G; *Hill* v *Chief Constable of West Yorkshire* [1989] AC 53, 60B–D. What emerges is that, in addition to the foreseeability of damage, necessary ingredients in any situation giving rise to a duty of care are that there should exist between the party owing the duty and the party to whom it is owed a relationship characterised by the law as one of 'proximity' or 'neighbourhood' and that the situation should be one in which the court considers it fair, just and reasonable that the law should impose a duty of a given scope upon the one party for the benefit of the other. But it is implicit in the passages referred to that the concepts of proximity and fairness embodied in these additional ingredients are not susceptible of any such precise definition as would be necessary to give them utility as practical tests, but amount in effect to little more than convenient labels to attach to the features of different specific situations which, on a detailed examination of all the circumstances, the law recognises pragmatically as giving rise to a duty of care of a given scope. Whilst recognising, of course, the importance of the underlying general principles common to the whole field of negligence, I think the law has now moved in the direction of attaching greater significance to the more traditional categorisation of distinct and recognisable situations as guides to the existence, the scope and the limits of the varied duties of care which the law imposes. We must now, I think, recognise the wisdom of the words of Brennan J in the High Court of Australia in *Sutherland Shire Council* v *Heyman* (1985) 60 ALR 1, 43–44, where he said:

> It is preferable, in my view, that the law should develop novel categories of negligence incrementally and by analogy with established categories, rather than by a massive extension of a prima facie duty of care restrained only by indefinable 'considerations which ought to negative, or to reduce or limit the scope of the duty or the class of person to whom it is owed.'

One of the most important distinctions always to be observed lies in the law's essentially different approach to the different kinds of damage which one party may have suffered in consequence of the acts or omissions of another. It is one thing to owe a duty of care to avoid causing injury to the person or property of others. It is quite another to avoid causing others to suffer purely economic loss. . . .

LORD ROSKILL: . . . I agree with your Lordships that it has now to be accepted that there is no simple formula or touchstone to which recourse can be had in order to provide in every case a ready answer to the questions whether, given certain facts, the law will or will not impose liability for negligence or in cases where such liability can be shown to exist, determine the extent of that liability. Phrases such as 'foreseeability,' 'proximity,' 'neighbourhood,' 'just and reasonable,' 'fairness,' 'voluntary acceptance of risk,' or 'voluntary assumption of responsibility' will be found used from time to time in the different cases. But, as your Lordships have said, such phrases are not precise definitions. At best they are but labels or phrases descriptive of the very different factual situations which can exist in particular cases and which must be carefully examined in each case before it can be pragmatically determined whether a duty of care exists and, if so, what is the scope and extent of that duty. If this conclusion involves a return to the traditional categorisation of cases as pointing to the existence and scope of any duty of care, as my noble and learned friend Lord Bridge of Harwich, suggests, I think this is infinitely preferable to recourse to somewhat wide generalisations which leave their practical application matters of difficulty and uncertainty. This conclusion finds strong support from the Judgment of Brennan J in *Sutherland Shire Council* v *Heyman*, 60 ALR 1, 43–44 in the High Court of Australia in the passage cited by my noble and learned friends.

LORD OLIVER: . . . Thus the postulate of a simple duty to avoid any harm that is, with hindsight, reasonably capable of being foreseen becomes untenable without the imposition of some intelligible limits to keep the law of negligence within the bounds of common sense and practicality. Those limits have been found by the requirement of what has been called a 'relationship of proximity' between plaintiff and defendant and by the imposition of a further requirement that the attachment of liability for harm which has occurred be 'just and reasonable.' But although the cases in which the courts have imposed or withheld liability are capable of an approximate categorisation, one looks in vain for some common denominator by which the existence of the essential relationship can be tested. Indeed it is difficult to resist a conclusion that what have been treated as three separate require-ments are, at least in most cases, in fact merely facets of the same thing, for in some cases the degree of foreseeability is such that it is from that alone that the requisite proximity can be deduced, whilst in others the absence of that essential relationship can most rationally be attributed simply to the court's view that it would not be fair and reasonable to hold the defendant responsible. 'Proximity' is, no doubt, a convenient expression so long as it is realised that it is no more than a label which embraces not a definable concept but merely a description of circumstances from which, pragmatically, the courts conclude that a duty of care exists.

There are, of course, cases where, in any ordinary meaning of the words, a relationship of proximity (in the literal sense of 'closeness') exists but where the law, whilst recognising the fact of the relationship, nevertheless denies a remedy to the injured party on the ground of public policy. *Rondel* v *Worsley* [1969] 1 AC 191 was such a case, as was *Hill* v *Chief Constable of West Yorkshire* [1989] AC 53, so far as concerns the alternative ground of that decision. But such cases do nothing to assist in the identification of those features from which the law will deduce the essential relation-ship on which liability depends and, for my part, I think that it has to be recognised that to search for any single formula which will serve as a general test of liability is to pursue a will-o'-the-wisp. The fact is that once one discards, as it is now clear that one must, the concept of foreseeability of harm as the single exclusive test —even a prima facie test—of the existence of the duty of care, the attempt to state some general principle which will determine liability in an infinite variety of circumstances serves not to clarify the law but merely to bedevil its development in a way which corresponds with practicality and common sense. In *Sutherland Shire Council* v *Heyman*, 60 ALR 1, 43–44, Brennan J in the course of a penetrating analysis, observed:

> Of course, if foreseeability of injury to another were the exhaustive criterion of a prima facie duty to act to prevent the occurrence of that injury, it would be essential to introduce some kind of restrictive qualification—perhaps a qualification of the kind stated in the second stage of the general proposition in *Anns* [1978] AC 728. I am unable to accept that approach. It is preferable, in my view, that the law should develop novel categories of negligence incrementally and by analogy with established categories, rather than by a massive extension of a prima facie duty of care restrained only by indefinable 'considerations which ought to negative, or to reduce or limit the scope of the duty or the class of person to whom it is owed.'

Perhaps, therefore, the most that can be attempted is a broad categorisation of the decided cases according to the type of situation in which liability has been established in the past in order to found an argument by analogy. Thus, for instance, cases can be classified according to whether what is complained of is the failure to prevent the infliction of damage by the act of the third party (such as *Dorset Yacht Co. Ltd* v *Home Office* [1970] AC 1004, *P. Perl (Exporters) Ltd* v *Camden London Borough Council* [1984] QB 342, *Smith* v *Littlewoods Organisation Ltd* [1987] AC 241 and, indeed, *Anns* v *Merton London Borough Council* [1978] AC 728 itself), in failure to perform properly a statutory duty claimed to have been imposed for the protection of the plaintiff either as a member of a class or as a member of the public (such as the *Anns* case, *Ministry of Housing and Local Government* v *Sharp* [1970] 2 QB 223, *Yuen Kun Yeu* v *Attorney-General of Hong Kong* [1988] AC 175) or in the making by the defendant of some statement or advice which has been communicated, directly or indirectly, to the plaintiff and upon which he has relied. Such categories are not, of course, exhaustive. Sometimes they overlap as in the *Anns* case, and there are cases which do not readily fit into easily definable categories (such as *Ross* v *Caunters* [1980] Ch 297). Nevertheless, it is, I think, permissible to regard negligent statements or advice as a separate category displaying common features from which it is possible to find at least guidelines by which a test for the existence of the relationship which is essential to ground liability can be deduced.

NOTES
1. The essential point of this case is that all cases of negligence need the requisite level of 'proximity' between the parties: i.e. a sufficient level of relationship. In cases of personal injury or damage to property this requirement will be satisfied by foreseeability, but in other cases, such as psychiatric injury (Chapter 7) economic loss (Chapter 9), closer relationships between the parties will be necessary to establish liability.
2. Although the idea of proximity was developed in Australia, it seems that the High Court there may now be rejecting proximity as applicable to solve all new duty issues. In *Perre* v *Apand* (1999) 164 ALR 606, McHugh J said that 'neither proximity nor the categories approach or any synthesis of them has gained the support of a majority of justices of this court. Indeed since the fall of proximity, the court has not made any authoritative statement as to what is to be the correct approach for determining the duty of care question. Perhaps none is possible.' Again in *Sullivan* v *Moody* (2001) 207 CLR 562 the court said that proximity 'expresses the nature of what is in issue and in that respect gives focus to the enquiry, but as an explanation of a process of reasoning leading to a conclusion its utility is limited'. The court said that different classes of case give rise to different problems and that the relevant 'problem' will then become the focus of attention in a judicial evaluation of the factors which tend for or against a conclusion, to be arrived at as a matter of principle. Here the issues were the relationship between negligence and defamation, and the extent and indeterminacy of potential liability.

3.  For many years the Supreme Court of Canada continued to use the *Anns* principle in cases of a proposed new duty of care, but they too have now embraced proximity. See *Cooper* v *Hobart* [2001] 3 SCR 537. This is seen as a method of limiting the potential range of liability.

---

### *Murphy* v *Brentwood*
House of Lords [1991] 1 AC 398; [1990] 3 WLR 414; [1990] 2 All ER 908

This case involved a local authority negligently approving a design for a concrete raft foundation for a house, which subsequently caused defects in the house. The substantive issues are dealt with in Chapter 11 and the extracts below deal only with general issues relating to the duty of care.

LORD OLIVER: . . . The critical question, as was pointed out in the analysis of Brennan J in his judgment in *Council of the Shire of Sutherland* v *Heyman*, 157 CLR 424, is not the nature of the damage in itself, whether physical or pecuniary, but whether the scope of the duty of care in the circumstances of the case is such as to embrace damage of the kind which the plaintiff claims to have sustained: see *Caparo Industries Plc* v *Dickman* [1990] 2 AC 605. The essential question which has to be asked in every case, given that damage which is the essential ingredient of the action has occurred, is whether the relationship between the plaintiff and the defendant is such—or, to use the favoured expression, whether it is of sufficient 'proximity'—that it imposes upon the latter a duty to take care to avoid or prevent that loss which has in fact been sustained. That the requisite degree of proximity may be established in circumstances in which the plaintiff's injury results from his reliance upon a statement or advice upon which he was entitled to rely and upon which it was contemplated that he would be likely to rely is clear from *Hedley Byrne* and subsequent cases, but *Anns* [1978] AC 728 was not such a case and neither is the instant case. It is not, however, necessarily to be assumed that the reliance cases form the only possible category of cases in which a duty to take reasonable care to avoid or prevent pecuniary loss can arise. *Morrison Steamship Co. Ltd* v *Greystoke Castle (Cargo Owners)*, for instance, clearly was not a reliance case. Nor indeed was *Ross* v *Caunters* [1980] Ch 297 so far as the disappointed beneficiary was concerned. Another example may be *Ministry of Housing and Local Government* v *Sharp* [1980] 2 QB 223, although this may, on analysis, properly be categorised as a reliance case.

   Nor is it self-evident logically where the line is to be drawn. Where, for instance, the defendant's careless conduct results in the interruption of the electricity supply to business premises adjoining the highway, it is not easy to discern the logic in holding that a sufficient relationship of proximity exists between him and a factory owner who has suffered loss because material in the course of manufacture is rendered useless but that none exists between him and the owner of, for instance, an adjoining restaurant who suffers the loss of profit on the meals which he is unable to prepare and sell. In both cases the real loss is pecuniary. The solution to such borderline cases has so far been achieved pragmatically (see *Spartan Steel & Alloys Ltd* v *Martin & Co. (Contractors) Ltd* [1973] QB 27) not by the application of logic but by the perceived necessity as a matter of policy to place some limits—perhaps arbitrary limits—to what would otherwise be an endless, cumulative causative chain bounded only by theoretical foreseeability.

   I frankly doubt whether, in searching for such limits, the categorisation of the damage as 'material,' 'physical,' 'pecuniary' or 'economic' provides a particularly useful contribution. Where it does, I think, serve a useful purpose is in identifying those cases in which it is necessary to search for and find something more than the mere reasonable foreseeability of damage which has occurred as providing the degree of 'proximity' necessary to support the action. In his classical exposition in *Donoghue* v *Stevenson* [1932] AC 562, 580–581, Lord Atkin was expressing himself in the context of the infliction of direct physical injury resulting from a carelessly created latent defect in a manufactured product. In his analysis of the duty in those circumstances he clearly, equated 'proximity' with the reasonable foresight of damage. In the straightforward case of the direct infliction of physical injury by the act of the plaintiff there is, indeed, no need to look beyond the foreseeability by the defendant of the result in order to establish that he is in a 'proximate' relationship with the plaintiff. But, as was pointed out by Lord Diplock in *Dorset Yacht Co. Ltd* v *Home Office* [1970]

AC 1004, 1060, Lord Atkin's test, though a useful guide to characteristics which will be found to exist in conduct and relationships giving rise to a legal duty of care, is manifestly false if misused as a universal; and Lord Reid, in the course of his speech in the same case, recognised that the statement of principle enshrined in that test necessarily required qualification in cases where the only loss caused by the defendant's conduct was economic. The infliction of physical injury to the person or property of another universally requires to be justified. The causing of economic loss does not. If it is to be categorised as wrongful it is necessary to find some factor beyond the mere occurrence of the loss and the fact that its occurrence could be foreseen. Thus the categorisation of damage as economic serves at least the useful purpose of indicating that something more is required and it is one of the unfortunate features of *Anns* that it resulted initially in this essential distinction being lost sight of.

NOTE

Recent examples of proximity cases include the following:

(a) In *Capital and Counties* v *Hants CC* [1997] 2 All ER 865 a number of cases concerning fire brigades were heard together. In one (the *London Fire Brigade* case) a fire had been started on some wasteland by a special effects crew. By the time the fire brigade arrived the main fire had been put out but they took no steps to see that there was no residual danger and they failed to inspect the claimant's premises which adjoined the wasteland. Later a fire broke out on the claimant's premises but it was held that the fire brigade was not liable as there was not sufficient proximity. They did not create the danger and merely by attending (which they were not required to do) they had not undertaken any duty to the claimant. The court also rejected the idea of reliance by the claimant and regarded the fire brigade as being in the same situation as a rescuer who will not be liable unless he has made the victim's position worse than it otherwise would have been. This is what happened in another case (the *Hampshire* case) where the fire officer had turned off the sprinklers: he was held liable. These cases adopted principles used in relation to exercise of statutory powers (for which see Chapter 6). See further below for an extract on the 'fair and reasonable' test.

(b) Similar principles were adopted in relation to coastguards in *OLL Ltd* v *Secretary of State for Transport* [1997] 3 All ER 897 where a party of canoeists got into difficulties near Lyme Regis and four children died. It was alleged that the coastguards had failed to co-ordinate rescue attempts properly and had misdirected the rescue helicopter. It was held that the coastguards were not liable on the same reasoning as in the *Capital and Counties* cases.

(c) In *Watson* v *British Boxing Board* [2001] 2 WLR 1256 the claimant boxer collapsed during the final round of his fight with Chris Eubank. He was attended to at the ringside and taken to hospital where he was given resuscitation treatment. However, he suffered permanent brain damage and claimed that if the defendants had required resuscitation equipment to be available at the ringside his damage would have been less severe. The defendants were held liable. The police and fire brigade cases were distinguished because those were cases of protecting the public at large, but here there was sufficient proximity since injury to boxers was a foreseeable and inevitable consequence of an activity which the defendants regulated. (It was also held to be fair and reasonable to impose a duty because the board had complete control of boxing, including control of medical provision. Boxers could reasonably rely on the board to look after their safety.) But note *Agar* v *Hyde* (2000) 201 CLR 552, in the High Court of Australia, where two rugby players suffered spinal injuries and claimed against members of the International Rugby Football Board alleging that the rules relating to scrums exposed them to unnecessary risks and it was held there was no duty. It was said that to impose a duty would diminish the autonomy of those who voluntarily participate in games and would deter regulators from continuing to supervise the game lest they be held liable for an individual's free choice.

## SECTION 2: THE UNFORESEEABLE CLAIMANT

Duty of care operates on two levels. There is the question of whether, in the class of case in issue, there is a legal duty or not (for example whether there is a duty not to make careless statements). This might be regarded as the 'House of Lords' level of the issue. There is also the question which arises in every case of negligence of whether this particular defendant owes a duty to this particular claimant—the unforeseeable claimant problem. That is, it is known that the law puts the defendant under a general obligation to take care in the particular situation, but the question is whether there is a sufficient relationship between the particular defendant and the particular claimant for that defendant to owe a duty to that claimant. The problem usually arises where the defendant is known to be or could be liable to A for his loss, but the question is whether he is also liable to B for his loss. Although this is called the unforeseeable claimant problem the same issue arises where the degree of proximity required is closer than that of mere foreseeability. Thus, the question really is whether this claimant is sufficiently proximate to this defendant, and perhaps this section should more properly be entitled 'the non-proximate claimant'.

### Bourhill v Young
House of Lords [1943] AC 92; 1942 SC 78; [1942] 2 All ER 396

Mrs Euphemia Bourhill was an Edinburgh fishwife who was travelling on a tram along Colinton Road, Edinburgh. She got off the tram and picked up her fish basket from the far side. John Young was a motorcyclist who passed the tram on the near side, and some 50 feet further on crashed into a car and was killed. John Young was negligent in that he was travelling too fast. After John Young's body had been removed Mrs Bourhill approached the site and saw the blood on the road. She alleged that she suffered 'nervous shock' as a result of the accident and gave birth to a stillborn child about a month later. Assuming John Young would have been liable to the owner of the car into which he crashed, could he also be liable to Mrs Bourhill? The case is relevant for two points: (1) whether the claimant was a foreseeable claimant; and (2) the extent to which psychiatric damage is recoverable. This latter point is discussed later. Held: dismissing the appeal, that no duty was owed to the claimant.

LORD RUSSELL: A man is not liable for negligence in the air. The liability only arises 'where there is a duty to take care and where failure in that duty has caused damage': see per Lord Macmillan in *Donoghue* v *Stevenson*. In my opinion, such a duty only arises towards those individuals of whom it may be reasonably anticipated that they will be affected by the act which constitutes the alleged breach.

Can it be said that John Young could reasonably have anticipated that a person, situated as was the appellant, would be affected by his proceeding towards Colinton at the speed at which he was travelling? I think not. His road was clear of pedestrians. The appellant was not within his vision, but was standing behind the solid barrier of the tramcar. His speed in no way endangered her. In these circumstances I am unable to see how he could reasonably anticipate that, if he came into collision with a vehicle coming across the tramcar into Glenlockhart Road, the resultant noise would cause physical injury by shock to a person standing behind the tramcar. In my opinion, he owed no duty to the appellant, and was, therefore, not guilty of any negligence in relation to her. . . .

LORD WRIGHT: My Lords, that damage by mental shock may give a cause of action is now well established and it not disputed in this case, but as Phillimore J pointed out in his admirable judgment in *Dulieu* v *White & Sons* [1901] 2 KB 669, the real difficulty in questions of this kind is to decide whether there has been a wrongful act or breach of duty on the part of the defendant vis-à-vis the plaintiff. That being the prior question, if it is answered against the plaintiff the matter is concluded. I shall, therefore, consider that issue in the first place.

This general concept of reasonable foresight as the criterion of negligence or breach of duty (strict or otherwise) may be criticized as too vague, but negligence is a fluid principle, which has to be applied to the most diverse conditions and problems of human life. It is a concrete, not an abstract, idea. It has to be fitted to the facts of the particular case. Willes J defined it as absence of care according to the circumstances: *Vaughan* v *Taff Vale Ry Co.* (1860) 157 ER 1351. It is also always relative to the individual affected. This raises a serious additional difficulty in the cases where it has to be determined, not merely whether the act itself is negligent against someone, but whether it is negligent vis-à-vis the plaintiff. This is a crucial point in cases of nervous shock. Thus, in the present case John Young was certainly negligent in an issue between himself and the owner of the car which he ran into, but it is another question whether he was negligent vis-à-vis the appellant. In such cases terms like 'derivative' and 'original' and 'primary' and 'secondary' have been applied to define and distinguish the type of the negligence. If, however, the appellant has a cause of action it is because of a wrong to herself. She cannot build on a wrong to someone else. Her interest, which was in her own bodily security was of a different order from the interest of the owner of the car. That this is so is also illustrated by cases such as have been called in the United States 'rescue' or 'search' cases. This type has been recently examined and explained in the Court of Appeal in *Haynes* v *Harwood* [1935] 1 KB 146, where the plaintiff, a police constable, was injured in stopping runaway horses in a crowded street in which were many children. His act was due to his mental reaction, whether instinctive or deliberate, to the spectacle of others' peril. Maugham LJ in the court of Appeal approved the language used by the trial judge, Finaly J ([1934] 2 KB 240, 247), when he held that to leave the horses unattended was a breach of duty not only to any person injured by being run over (in fact, no one was so injured), but also to the constable. Finlay J's words were: 'It seems to me that if horses run away it must be quite obviously contemplated that people are likely to be knocked down. It must also, I think, be contemplated that persons will attempt to stop the horses and try to prevent injury to life or limb.' . . . This again shows how the ambit of the persons affected by negligence or misconduct may extend beyond persons who are actually subject to physical impact . . . There is no dispute about the facts. Upon these facts, can it be said that a duty is made out, and breach of that duty, so that the damage which is found is recoverable? I think not. The appellant was completely outside the range of the collision. She merely heard a noise, which upset her, without her having any definite idea at all. As she said: 'I just got into a pack of nerves and I did not know whether I was going to get it or not.' She saw nothing of the actual accident, or, indeed, any marks of blood until later. I cannot accept that John Young could reasonably have foreseen, or, more correctly, the reasonable hypothetical observer could reasonably have foreseen, the likelihood that anyone placed as the appellant was, could be affected in the manner in which she was. In my opinion, John Young was guilty of no breach of duty to the appellant, and was not in law responsible for the hurt she sustained. I may add that the issue of duty or no duty is, indeed, a question for the court, but it depends on the view taken of the facts. In the present case both courts below have taken the view that the appellant has, on the facts of the case, no redress, and I agree with their view. . . .

LORD PORTER: In the case of a civil action there is no such thing as negligence in the abstract. There must be neglect of the use of care towards a person towards whom the defendant owes the duty of observing care, and I am content to take the statement of Lord Atkin in *Donoghue* v *Stevenson* [1932] AC 562, 580, as indicating the extent of the duty. 'You must take,' he said, 'reasonable care to avoid acts or omissions which you can reasonably foresee would be likely to injure your neighbour. Who, then, in law is my neighbour? The answer seems to be – persons who are so closely and directly affected by my act that I ought reasonably to have them in contemplation as being so affected when I am directing my mind to the acts or omissions which are called in question.' Is the result of this view that all persons in or near the street down which the negligent driver is progressing are potential victims of his negligence? Though from their position it is quite impossible that any injury should happen to them and though they have no relatives or even friends who might be endangered, is a duty of care to them owed and broken because they might have been but were not in a spot exposed to the errant driving of the peccant car? I cannot think so. The duty is not to the world at large. It must be tested by asking with reference to each several complainant: Was a duty owed to him or her? If no one of them was in such a position that direct physical injury could reasonably be anticipated to them or their relations or friends normally I think no duty would be owed, and if, in addition, no shock was reasonably to be anticipated to them as a result of the defender's negligence, the defender might, indeed, be guilty of actionable negligence to others but not of negligence towards them. In the present case the appellant was never herself in any bodily danger nor reasonably in fear of danger either for herself or others. She was merely a person who, as a result of the action, was emotionally disturbed and rendered physically ill by that emotional disturbance. The question whether emotional disturbance or shock, which a defender ought reasonably to have anticipated as likely to follow from his reckless driving, can ever form the basis of a claim is not in issue . . .

## NOTES

1. A good example of the unforeseeable claimant rule is *Palsgraf* v *Long Island Railroad Co.* (1928) 248 NY 339. The claimant, Helen Palsgraf, was waiting on a platform for a train to Rockaway Beach. Another train stopped and two men ran to get it, and a guard pushed one of them from behind to help him in. In doing so he dislodged a parcel, which turned out to contain fireworks. The fireworks exploded when they fell, and this was alleged to have upset some scales some distance away which fell upon the claimant. It is unlikely that this fantastic scenario actually occurred, but, even assuming the facts to be true, it was said that while a duty may have been owed to the two men in the train, no duty was owed to the claimant. Cardozo CJ quoted *Pollock on Torts*, saying 'Proof of negligence in the air so to speak will not do.' He pointed out that a claimant must have an original and primary duty owed to her, and not one simply derived from a wrong to someone else, and that the orbit of the danger as disclosed to the eye of reasonable vigilance is the orbit of the duty. 'Negligence, like risk, is thus a term of relation.' In other words, the fact that a duty was owed by the guard to the men he was pushing onto the train, did not necessarily mean that a duty was owed to Mrs Palsgraf. She was outside the orbit of the risk, and therefore was an unforeseeable claimant.

   For a full discussion of *Palsgraf*, see Prosser, 'Palsgraf Revisited' in Prosser, *Selected Topics on the Law of Torts* or 52 Mich LR 1.

2. A recent example of the unforeseeable claimant rule is *Maguire* v *Harland and Wolff* [2005] EWCA (Civ) 1 where the wife of a man who worked for the defendants and who came into contact with asbestos, sued when she contracted mesothelioma as a result of washing his work clothes which had been contaminated. It was held that even though a duty was owed to the husband, no duty was owed to the wife as at the time (in the 1960s) it was not foreseeable that anyone could contract the disease from such low level exposure from 'secondary' contact with asbestos. Accordingly she was not a foreseeable claimant.

3. In *Marx* v *Attorney General* [1974] 1 NZLR 164, an attempt was made to extend the ambit of duty beyond the individual likely to be injured so as to include his family, but the rule that actions must not be derivative was upheld. In that case the defendants, New Zealand Railways, had injured the claimant causing him brain damage, and this caused him to become hyper-sexual. As a result of this condition he injured his wife, but it was held that she could not sue, for she was an unforeseeable claimant and her action was derivative.

   For commentary upon this case see Binchy, (1975) 38 MLR 468, where it is argued that the wife's action was not derivative, but rather she was in the same position as a person who was injured by an inanimate object which had been rendered dangerous by the defendant. A conclusion similar to *Marx* is implicit in *Meah* v *McCreamer (No. 2)* [1986] 1 All ER 943, where it was said that where a car driver caused a person to suffer a personality change, as a result of which he raped two women, the rape victims would not be able to sue the driver.

■ QUESTION

X, a surgeon, negligently removes Y's only kidney. Who, apart from Y, would be a foreseeable claimant? See *Urbanski* v *Patel* (1978) 84 DLR 3d 650.

---

### *Videan* v *British Transport Commission*
Court of Appeal [1963] 2 QB 640; [1963] 2 All ER 860; [1963] 2 WLR 347

North Tawton is a small railway station on the edge of Dartmoor on the ex-London South Western Railway line to Plymouth. On 26 July 1959 the stationmaster, Dennis Videan, was going to take his family to Exeter when it was realised that his son Richard, aged 2, was missing. He was seen sitting on the railway line, and at the same time a motorised trolley, driven by one Souness, was approaching. Souness did not see the child until very late, and in an effort to save his son, Dennis Videan threw himself in front of the trolley and was killed. Richard was saved, but injured. The court held that as Richard was a trespasser he was unforeseeable and therefore could not sue. In an action by Mr Videan's widow it was held, allowing her appeal, that a duty was owed to her husband.

LORD DENNING MR: I turn now to the widow's claim in respect of the death of her husband. In order to establish it, the widow must prove that Souness owed a duty of care to the stationmaster, that he broke that duty, and that, in consequence of the breach, the stationmaster was killed. Mr Fox-Andrews says that the widow can prove none of these things. All depends, he says, on the test of foreseeability; and, applying that test, he puts the following dilemma: If Souness could not reasonably be expected to foresee the presence of the child, he could not reasonably be expected to foresee the presence of the father. He could not foresee that a trespasser would be on the line. So how could he be expected to foresee that anyone would be attempting to rescue him? Mr Fox-Andrews points out that, in all the rescue cases that have hitherto come before the courts, such as *Haynes* v *Harwood & Son* [1935] 1 KB 146, and *Baker* v *T. E. Hopkins & Sons Ltd* [1954] 1 WLR 966, the conduct of the defendant was a wrong to the victim or the potential victim. How can he be liable to the rescuer when he is not liable to the rescued?

I cannot accept this view. The right of the rescuer is an independent right and is not derived from that of the victim. The victim may have been guilty of contributory negligence—or his right may be excluded by contractual stipulation—but still the rescuer can sue. So also the victim may, as here, be a trespasser and excluded on that ground, but still the rescuer can sue. Foreseeability is necessary, but not foreseeability of the particular emergency that arose. Suffice it that he ought reasonably to foresee that, if he did not take care, some emergency or other might arise, and that someone or other might be impelled to expose himself to danger in order to effect a rescue. Such is the case here. Souness ought to have anticipated that some emergency or other might arise. His trolley was not like an express train which is heralded by signals and whistles and shouts of 'Keep clear.' His trolley came silently and swiftly upon the unsuspecting quietude of a country station. He should have realised that someone or other might be put in peril if he came too fast or did not keep a proper look-out; and if anyone was put in peril, then someone would come to the rescue. As it happened, it was the stationmaster trying to rescue his child; but it would be the same if it had been a passer-by. Whoever comes to the rescue, the law should see that he does not suffer for it. It seems to me that, if a person by his fault creates a situation of peril, he must answer for it to any person who attempts to rescue the person who is in danger. He owes a duty to such a person above all others. The rescuer may act instinctively out of humanity or deliberately out of courage. But whichever it is, so long as it is not wanton interference, if the rescuer is killed or injured in the attempt, he can recover damages from the one whose fault has been the cause of it. . . .

PEARSON LJ: I now come to the appeal of the widow, who claims damages for the death of her husband caused, as she contends, by the negligence of Souness acting as the servant of the defendant Commission. It is clear from the evidence and the judge's findings that Souness in his approach to the station was acting negligently in relation to anyone to whom he owed a duty of care, and that the conduct of Souness in this respect caused the accident. The only disputable question is whether Souness owed any relevant duty of care to the deceased. The Commission's argument, evidently accepted by the judge, has been that the position of the rescuer could not be any better than the position of the person rescued, and that, as the infant plaintiff's trespass was unforeseeable, so the act of his father in trying to rescue him was unforeseeable, and therefore both the infant plaintiff and his father were outside the zone of reasonable contemplation and the scope of duty. That would no doubt have been a formidable argument if the deceased had been only a father rescuing his son. But the deceased was the stationmaster, having a general responsibility for dealing with any emergency that might arise at the station. It was foreseeable by Souness that if he drove his vehicle carelessly into the station he might imperil the stationmaster, as the stationmaster might well have some proper occasion for going on the track in the performance of his duties. For this purpose it is not necessary that the particular accident which happened should have been foreseeable. It is enough that it was foreseeable that some situation requiring the stationmaster to go on the line might arise, and if any such situation did arise, a careless approach to the station by Souness with his vehicle would be dangerous to the stationmaster. On that ground I hold that Souness's careless approach to the station was a breach of a duty owing by him to the deceased as stationmaster, and it caused the accident, and consequently the Commission is liable to the widow and her appeal should be allowed.

### ■ QUESTION

Harman LJ in *Videan* said 'Whether if the rescuer had been a member of the public there would have been liability, I leave out of account.' What would have been the result in such a case according to (a) Lord Denning and (b) Pearson LJ?

NOTE

'Danger invites rescue' (per Cardozo CJ in *Wagner* v *International Rly Co.* (1921) 232 NY 176). Hence, it is not unforeseeable that when a person puts another (or himself) in a position of peril, someone will attempt a rescue. In *Haynes* v *Harwood* [1935] 1 KB 146, a horse van was negligently left unattended and the horses bolted. The claimant was a police officer who was injured when attempting to stop the runaway horses. The defendant was liable and could not argue that the claimant was unforeseeable.

Why did not this case automatically resolve the problem in *Videan*?

## SECTION 3: POLICY FACTORS—'FAIR AND REASONABLE'

Policy factors have always been present in the formulation of the duty issue but have been variously expressed. Nowadays policy issues can be present at two levels. Clearly in determining the level of proximity required to establish a duty policy elements will be present, usually of the 'floodgates' variety. In addition, overt policy arguments can be used to deny liability by determining whether it is 'fair and reasonable' that a duty should be imposed, and *Hill* v *Chief Constable of West Yorkshire* and *Marc Rich* v *Bishop Rock Marine* are good examples of this approach. In recent years, however, it seems there is a greater reluctance to use this technique and to rely instead on limiting proximity. This confuses the issue. It would be preferable in defining proximity to limit policy to general issues arising from that area of the law, e.g. nervous shock, and to leave to the fair and reasonable test arguments which are specific to the defendant, e.g. the police.

## Hill v Chief Constable of West Yorkshire
House of Lords [1989] AC 53; [1988] 2 All ER 238; [1988] 2 WLR 1049

Between 1975 and 1980 Peter Sutcliffe committed 13 murders and 8 attempted murders in the West Yorkshire area. The mother of the last victim, Jacqueline Hill, sued the police on behalf of the estate of her daughter for alleged negligence in failing to catch Sutcliffe earlier than they did. Held: no duty was owed as there was insufficient proximity, but the House also held that the action was barred on grounds of public policy.

LORD KEITH: . . . there is another reason why an action for damages in negligence should not lie against the police in circumstances such as those of the present case, and that is public policy. In *Yuen Kun Yeu* v *Attorney-General of Hong Kong* [1988] AC 175, 193, I expressed the view that the category of cases where the second stage of Lord Wilberforce's two stage test in *Anns* v *Merton London Borough Council* [1978] AC 728, 751–752 might fall to be applied was a limited one, one example of that category being *Rondel* v *Worsley* [1969] 1 AC 191. Application of that second stage is, however, capable of constituting a separate and independent ground for holding that the existence of liability in negligence should not be entertained. Potential existence of such liability may in many instances be in the general public interest, as tending towards the observance of a higher standard of care in the carrying on of various different types of activity. I do not, however, consider that this can be said of police activities. The general sense of public duty which motivates police forces is unlikely to be appreciably reinforced by the imposition of such liability so far as concerns their function in the investigation and suppression of crime. From time to time they make mistakes in the exercise of that function, but it is not to be doubted that they apply their best endeavours to the performance of it. In some instances the imposition of liability may lead to the exercise of a function being carried on in a detrimentally defensive frame of mind. The possibility of this happening in relation to the investigative operations of the police cannot be excluded. Further it would be reason-able to expect that if potential liability were to be imposed it would be not uncommon for actions to be raised against police forces on the ground that they had failed to catch some criminal as soon as they might have done, with the result that he went on to commit further crimes. While some such actions might involve allegations of a simple and straightforward type of failure—for example that a police officer negligently tripped and fell while pursuing a burglar—others would be likely to enter deeply into the general nature of a police investigation, as indeed the present action would seek to do. The manner of conduct of such an investigation must necessarily involve a variety of decisions to be made on matters of policy and discretion, for example as to which particular line of inquiry is most advantageously to be pursued and what is the most advantageous way to deploy the available resources. Many such decisions would not be regarded by the courts as appropriate to be called in question, yet elaborate investigation of the facts might be necessary to ascertain whether or not this was so. A great deal of police time, trouble and expense might be expected to have to be put into the preparation of the defence to the action and the attendance of witnesses at the trial. The result would be a significant diversion of police manpower and attention from their most important function, that of the suppression of crime. Closed investigations would require to be reopened and retraversed, not with the object of bringing any criminal to justice but to ascertain whether or not they had been competently conducted. I therefore consider that Glidewell LJ, in his judgment in the Court of Appeal [1988] QB 60, 76 in the present case, was right to take the view that the police were immune from an action of this kind on grounds similar to those which in *Rondel* v *Worsley* [1969] 1 AC 191 were held to render a barrister immune from actions for negligence in his conduct of proceedings in court.

NOTES
1. A similar approach was taken in *Hughes* v *National Union of Mine Workers* [1991] 4 All ER 278 where the claimant police officer was injured by striking miners and he alleged that the Chief Constable had deployed the police force negligently, thus exposing the claimant to a greater

risk of injury. The action was struck out on the ground that critical decisions have to be made with little or no time for considered thought, and accordingly public policy required that senior police officers should not be liable for on the spot operational decisions taken in the course of attempts to control serious public disorder. See also *Mulcahy* v *Ministry of Defence* [1996] 2 All ER 758 where a soldier was injured during the Gulf War when a howitzer was fired while he was standing in front of it. It was held that 'on grounds of common sense and policy' no duty was owed in battle conditions.

2. In *Elguzouli-Daf* v *Commissioner of Police* [1995] 1 All ER 833, the claimant had been held in custody for 85 days before the Crown Prosecution Service dropped the charges. It was held that the CPS owed no duty to the claimant, as such a duty would lead prosecutors to take a defensive attitude and the welfare of the community amounted to sufficient policy reason to preclude a duty. (But see *Welsh* v *Chief Constable of Merseyside* [1993] 1 All ER 692 where it was said that the CPS had *voluntarily* assumed a responsibility to the claimant—the CPS had told the claimant that certain offences would be taken into consideration in another case and would not be charged separately. They were taken into consideration in the other case but the magistrates were not told of this and the claimant was arrested for failing to answer to bail.)

3. *Hill* has been confirmed in *Brooks* v *Commissioner of Police of the Metropolis* [2005] 1 WLR 1495. In that case Duwayne Brooks was a witness to the murder in 1993 of his friend Stephen Lawrence. The subsequent investigation was badly conducted and the claimant alleged that he thereby suffered post traumatic stress disorder. Lord Steyn supported *Hill* (although Lord Bingham had doubts about its extent) and accordingly *Hill* prevented liability to a witness where the alleged breaches of duty were inextricably bound up with the investigation of the case.

4. A further ground of public policy is that there will be no duty of care if the claimant has an adequate alternative remedy: for example in *Jones* v *Department of Employment* [1988] 1 All ER 725 the claimant was denied unemployment benefit but subsequently successfully appealed to the Social Security Appeal Tribunal. It was held that he could not sue the original adjudicating officer for negligently denying him benefit and causing him distress as he was limited to his statutory right of appeal.

5. In *Osman* v *UK* [2000] EHRR 245, the European Court of Human Rights said that the application of the 'immunity' for the police was a breach of Article 6 which requires that in the determination of his civil rights everyone is entitled to a hearing by a tribunal. The court said that in *Osman* v *Ferguson* [1993] 4 All ER 344 (which applied *Hill*) the application of a blanket immunity was an unjustifiable restriction on the applicant's right to have a determination of the merits of his or her claim. The argument was that the public policy in restricting claims against the police must be balanced against the interests of the *particular* claimant, whereas the common law was balancing the interests of the police against potential claimants as a whole, and this amounted to a blanket immunity. (On this point see Lord Browne-Wilkinson in *Barrett* v *Enfield LBC* [1999] 3 WLR 79.) However, the European Court has now reconsidered its view in *Z* v *UK* (below).

### Z v United Kingdom

European Court of Human Rights (2002) 34 EHRR 3

This case arose out of *X* v *Bedfordshire CC* [1995] 2 AC 633 (see Chapter 6), in particular that the defendants had failed to prevent abuse of the applicant. The House of Lords had held that the action should be struck out as it was not fair and reasonable to impose a duty. Held: this was not a breach of Article 6 which requires that in the determination of his civil rights everyone is entitled to a hearing by a tribunal.

THE COURT:

**94** It is contended by the applicants in this case that the decision of the House of Lords, finding that the local authority owed no duty of care, deprived them of access to court as it was effectively an exclusionary rule, or an immunity from liability, which prevented their claims being decided on the facts.

**95** The Court observes, firstly, that the applicants were not prevented in any practical manner from bringing their claims before the domestic courts. Indeed, the case was litigated with vigour up to the House of Lords, the applicants being provided with legal aid for that purpose. Nor is it the case that any procedural rules or limitation periods were invoked. The domestic courts were concerned with the application brought by the defendants to have the case struck out as disclosing no reasonable cause of action. This involved the pre-trial determination of whether, assuming the facts of the applicants' case as pleaded were true, there was a sustainable claim in law. The arguments before the courts were therefore concentrated on the legal issues, primarily whether a duty of care in negligence was owed to the applicants by the local authority.

**96** Moreover, the Court is not persuaded that the House of Lords' decision that as a matter of law there was no duty of care in the applicants' case may be characterised as either an exclusionary rule or an immunity which deprived them of access to court. As Lord Browne-Wilkinson explained in his leading speech, the House of Lords was concerned with the issue whether a novel category of negligence, that is a category of case in which a duty of care had not previously been held to exist, should be developed by the courts in their law-making role under the common law (see paragraph 46 above). The House of Lords, after weighing in the balance the competing considerations of public policy, decided not to extend liability in negligence into a new area. In so doing, it circumscribed the range of liability under tort law.

**97** That decision did end the case, without the factual matters being determined on the evidence. However, if as a matter of law, there was no basis for the claim, the hearing of evidence would have been an expensive and time-consuming process which would not have provided the applicants with any remedy at its conclusion. There is no reason to consider the striking out procedure which rules on the existence of sustainable causes of action as *per se* offending the principle of access to court. In such a procedure, the plaintiff is generally able to submit to the court the arguments supporting his or her claims on the law and the court will rule on those issues at the conclusion of an adversarial procedure (see paragraphs 66 to 68 above).

**98** Nor is the Court persuaded by the suggestion that, irrespective of the position in domestic law, the decision disclosed an immunity in fact or practical effect due to its allegedly sweeping or blanket nature. That decision concerned only one aspect of the exercise of local authorities' powers and duties and cannot be regarded as an arbitrary removal of the courts' jurisdiction to determine a whole range of civil claims. . . . As it has recalled above in paragraph 87 it is a principle of Convention case-law that Article 6 does not in itself guarantee any particular content for civil rights and obligations in national law, although other Articles such as those protecting the right to respect for family life (Article 8) and the right to property (Article 1 of Protocol No. 1) may do so. It is not enough to bring Article 6 §1 into play that the non-existence of a cause of action under domestic law may be described as having the same effect as an immunity, in the sense of not enabling the applicant to sue for a given category of harm.

**99** Furthermore, it cannot be said that the House of Lords came to its conclusion without a careful balancing of the policy reasons for and against the imposition of liability on the local authority in the circumstances of the applicants' case. Lord Browne-Wilkinson in his leading judgment in the House of Lords acknowledged that the public policy principle that wrongs should be remedied required very potent counter considerations to be overridden (see paragraph 46 above). He weighed that principle against the other public policy concerns in reaching the conclusion that it was not fair, just or reasonable to impose a duty of care on the local authority in the applicants' case. It may be noted that in subsequent cases the domestic courts have further defined this area of law concerning the liability of local authorities in child care matters, holding that a duty of care may arise in other factual situations, where, for example, a child has suffered harm once in local authority care or a foster family has suffered harm as a result of the placement in their home by the local authority of an adolescent with a history of abusing younger children (see *W and Others* v *Essex County Council and Barrett* v *Enfield LBC*, cited above, paragraphs 62 to 65).

**100** The applicants, and the Commission in its report, relied on the *Osman* case (cited above) as indicating that the exclusion of liability in negligence, in that case concerning the acts or omissions of the police in the investigation and prevention of crime, acted as a restriction on access to court. The Court considers that its reasoning in the *Osman* judgment was based on an understanding of the law of negligence (see, in particular, paragraphs 138 and 139 of the *Osman* judgment) which has to be reviewed in the light of the clarifications subsequently made by the domestic courts and notably the House of Lords. The Court is satisfied that the law of negligence as developed in the domestic courts since the case of *Caparo* (cited above, paragraph 58) and as recently analysed in the case of *Barrett* v *Enfield LBC* (*loc. cit.*) includes the fair, just and reasonable criterion as an intrinsic element of the duty of care and that the ruling of law concerning that element in this case does not disclose the operation of an immunity. In the present case, the Court is led to the conclusion that the inability of the applicants to sue the local authority flowed not from an immunity but from the applicable principles governing the substantive right of action in domestic law. There was no restriction on access to court of the kind contemplated in the *Ashingdane* judgment (cited above, *loc. cit.*).

**101** The applicants may not therefore claim that they were deprived of any right to a determination on the merits of their negligence claims. Their claims were properly and fairly examined in light of the applicable domestic legal principles concerning the tort of negligence. Once the House of Lords had ruled on the arguable legal issues that brought into play the applicability of Article 6 §1 of the Convention (see paragraphs 87 to 89 above), the applicants could no longer claim any entitlement under Article 6 §1 to obtain any hearing concerning the facts. As pointed out above, such a hearing would have served no purpose, unless a duty of care in negligence had been held to exist in their case. It is not for this Court to find that this should have been the outcome of the striking out proceedings since this would effectively involve substituting its own views as to the proper interpretation and content of domestic law.

NOTES
1. Despite the ruling on Article 6, the court held that there was a breach of Article 3 (no one shall be subjected to torture or degrading treatment or punishment) and of Article 13 (everyone shall have an effective remedy before a national authority for violation of the Convention). On this point it is argued that the Human Rights Act 1998 now provides an effective remedy, even where (as here) the extrajudicial remedies were inadequate.
2. *Z* v *UK* accepts that the fair and reasonable test is an integral part of the duty issue and that the striking out procedure is not a breach of Article 6. (On this see *Kent* v *Griffiths* [2000] 2 All ER 475 at 485 per Lord Woolf.)

---

### *Capital and Counties* v *Hampshire CC*
Court of Appeal [1997] QB 1004; [1997] 3 WLR 331; [1997] 2 All ER 865

A number of cases concerning fire brigades were heard together. In one (the *London Fire Brigade* case) the defendants had attended a fire but failed to check a neighbouring property where a fire started later. It was held that there was insufficient proximity and so no liability (see Section 2 above). In another case (the *Hampshire* case) the fire officer had ordered the sprinklers to be turned off and, because he had made the situation worse than it would otherwise have been, there was sufficient proximity and thus liability. The extracts below deal only with the subsequent question of whether, assuming there is sufficient proximity, it would be 'fair and reasonable' to impose liability. It was held that fire brigades would have no immunity on this ground.

STUART-SMITH LJ: *Is it just, fair and reasonable to impose a duty of care?*

*Public, policy immunity*

. . . We consider first, therefore, whether there is any reason of policy why the Hampshire Fire Authority should not be liable. The starting point is that 'the public policy consideration which has first claim on the loyalty of the law is that wrongs should be remedied, and that very potent considerations are required to override that policy': *per* Lord Browne-Wilkinson in *X (Minors)* v *Bedfordshire County Council* [1995] 2 AC 633, 749.

Counsel for the fire brigades placed much reliance on the police cases, on the basis that there is a similarity between fire brigades answering rescue calls and the police answering calls for help and protection from the public. But it is clear from the leading case of *Hill* v *Chief Constable of West Yorkshire* [1989] AC 53 that the police do not enjoy blanket immunity. Lord Keith of Kinkel said, at p. 59:

> There is no question that a police officer, like anyone else, may be liable in tort to a person who is injured as a direct result of his actions or omissions. So he may be liable in damages for assault, unlawful arrest, wrongful imprisonment and malicious prosecution, and also for negligence. Instances where liability for negligence has been established are *Knightley* v *Johns* [1982] 1 WLR 349 and *Rigby* v *Chief Constable of Northamptonshire* [1985] 1 WLR 1242.

Other examples would be *Alcock* v *Chief Constable of South Yorkshire Police* [1992] 1 AC 310 (the Hillsborough case) and *Marshall* v *Osmond* [1983] QB 1034. These are cases, as we have already pointed out, where the police created danger and are closely analogous to the *Hampshire* case.

In the *East Suffolk* case, it is clear that the board would have been liable if through their negligence they had added to the damage the plaintiff would otherwise have suffered. The dividing line between liability and non-liability is thus defined and there is no need to pray in aid any concept of public policy. We agree with Mr Sumption that the courts should not grant immunity from suit to fire brigades simply because the judge may have what he describes as a visceral dislike for allowing possibly worthless claims to be made against public authorities, whose activities involve the laudable operation of rescuing the person or property of others in conditions often of great danger. Such claims may indeed be motivated by what is sometimes perceived to be the current attitude to litigation: 'If you have suffered loss and can see a solvent target, sue it.' None the less, if a defendant is to be immune from suit such immunity must be based upon principle.

It seems to us that in those cases where the courts have granted immunity or refused to impose a duty of care it is usually possible to discern a recognition that such a duty would be inconsistent with some wider object of the law or interest of the particular parties. Thus, if the existence of a duty of care would impede the careful performance of the relevant function, or if investigation of the allegedly negligent conduct would itself be undesirable and open to abuse by those bearing grudges, the law will not impose a duty. Some cases on either side of the line illustrate this.

Judges and arbitrators whilst involved in the judicial process are immune, but not mutual professional valuers: *Arenson* v *Arenson* [1977] AC 405. In the *Marc Rich & Co.* case [1996] AC 211 an independent and non-profit-making entity, created and operating for the sole purpose of promoting collective welfare, namely, the safety of lives and ships at sea, 'would [not] be able to carry out their functions as efficiently if they became the ready alternative target for cargo owners:' *per* Lord Steyn, at p. 241 . . .

In *Ancell* v *McDermot* [1993] 4 All ER 355 it was held that the imposition of a duty of care on the police to protect road users from hazards caused by others would be so extensive as to divert the police from the proper functions of detecting and preventing crime. And in *Osman* v *Ferguson* [1993] 4 All ER 344, although the majority of the court considered that it was arguable that there was sufficient proximity between the plaintiff's family and investigating police officers, the imposition of a duty of care towards a potential victim might result in the significant diversion of police resources from the investigation and suppression of crime and was therefore contrary to public policy.

On the other hand liability has been imposed when, in the course of carrying out their duties, the police have themselves created the danger: see *Rigby* v *Chief Constable of Northamptonshire* [1985]

1 WLR 1242; *Knightley* v *Johns* [1982] 1 WLR 349; *Alcock* v *Chief Constable of South Yorkshire* [1992] 1 AC 310 and *Marshall* v *Osmond* [1983] QB 1034.

In our judgment there is no doubt on which side of the line a case such as the *Hampshire* case falls. It is one where the defendants, by their action in turning off the sprinklers, created or increased the danger. There is no ground for giving immunity in such a case.

Rougier J in the *London Fire Brigade* case, after citing from the speeches of Lord Keith of Kinkel and Lord Templeman in *Hill's* case [1989] AC 53, set out a number of reasons why in his judgment it was not appropriate to impose a common law duty to take care on fire brigades. He said [1996] 3 WLR 988, 1003:

> I think that as regards the fire brigade many of these considerations are applicable and militate on grounds of public policy against the imposition of any common law duty. In particular, I would single out the following. (1) I do not think that any extra standard of care would be achieved. (2) Rather the reverse, if a common law duty of care can lead to defensive policing, by the same token it can lead to defensive fire-fighting. Fearful of being accused of leaving the scene too early, the officer in charge might well commit his resources when they would have been better employed elsewhere. He would be open to criticism every time there was a balance to be struck or that sort of operational choice to be made. (3) If the efficiency of the emergency services is to be tested, it should be done not in private litigation but by an inquiry instituted by national or local authorities who are responsible to the electorate. This follows the reasoning of Lord Templeman in *Hill's* case [1989] AC 53. (4) *Marc Rich & Co. AG* v *Bishop Rick-Marine Co. Ltd* [1996] AC 211 suggests that the fact that a defendant in the position of the fire brigade acts for the collective welfare is one that should be taken into account. (5) Last, and to my mind by far the most important consideration, is what is sometimes referred to as the 'floodgates' argument.

Judge Crawford QC in the *West Yorkshire* case added a number of others—we continue the numbering from that set out in the passage above. (6) The distraction that court cases would involve from the proper task of fire-fighting. (7) It might create massive claims which would be an unreasonable burden on the taxpayer. (8) It is for the individual to insure against fire risks.

These reasons have been subjected to considerable criticism by counsel for the plaintiffs on the following lines.

### (1) and (2):  No improvement in standard of care; defensive fire-fighting

It seems hardly realistic that a fire officer who has to make a split second decision as to the manner in which fire-fighting operations are to be conducted will be looking over his shoulder at the possibility of his employers being made vicariously liable for his negligence. If there can be liability for negligence, it is better to have a high threshold of negligence established in the *Bolam* test and for judges to remind themselves that fire officers who make difficult decisions in difficult circumstances should be given considerable latitude before being held guilty of negligence. It is not readily apparent why the imposition of a duty of care should divert the fire brigade resources from other fire-fighting duties.

### (3):  Private litigation unsuitable for discovering failures of service

As to this reason, counsel for the plaintiffs in the *Hampshire* case pointed out that, although there was a very extensive internal inquiry in that case starting on the day of the fire, it was only the litigation that uncovered the serious shortcomings of the service.

### (4):  Undesirability of actions against authorities operating for collective welfare

It was said that the fact that the defendant is a public authority acting for the collective welfare of the community such as the National Health Service has never been regarded as a ground for immunity; in any event the benefit is also for the individual householder.

*(5): Floodgates*

Having regard to the extreme paucity of recorded cases against fire brigades in spite of the fact that for over 40 years *Halsbury's Laws of England* have indicated that an action would lie, this argument should be disregarded. Again, the *Bolam* test should afford sufficient protection.

*(6): Distraction from fire-fighting*

In any action against a public authority officers and employees will be distracted from their ordinary duties; that should not be regarded as a valid ground for granting immunity.

*(7): Massive claims against the taxpayer*

This is ultimately an argument for the immunity from suit of government departments and all public authorities.

*(8): Insurance*

The general rule in English law is that in determining the rights inter se of A and B, the fact that one them is insured is to be disregarded: see *per* Viscount Simonds in *Lister* v *Romford Ice and Cold Storage Co. Ltd* [1957] AC 555, 576, 577. Insurance premiums are calculated having regard to the existence and likely response of the fire brigade; very substantial reductions in premiums are granted where buildings are protected by sprinklers; there may be underinsurances and absence of insurance, particularly in the lower end of the property market. Further, it would be unusual for there to be effective insurance against personal injury. Finally, there is nothing to prevent fire brigades insuring against their liability. Indeed the London and West Yorkshire brigades are insured.

In our judgment there is considerable force in the criticisms made. If we had found a sufficient relationship of proximity in the *London Fire Brigade* and *West Yorkshire* cases, we do not think that we would have found the arguments for excluding a duty of care on the ground that it would not be just, fair and reasonable convincing. The analogy with the police exercising their functions of investigating and suppressing crime is not close. The floodgates argument is not persuasive; nor is that based on insurance. Many of the other arguments are equally applicable to other public services, for example, the National Health Service. We do not think that the principles which underlie those decisions where immunity has been granted can be sufficiently identified in the case of fire brigades.

. . .

NOTES
1.  This is a complicated set of decisions and the case is much bound up with issues which relate to public bodies, for which see Chapter 6. There now seems to be some confusion between factors which limit proximity and those which will be relevant for the fair and reasonable test. It is suggested that policy will be relevant for proximity in so far as the court is trying to set a rule for a category of case such as negligent misstatement or economic loss, and the main part of *Capital and Counties* may be regarded as limiting proximity in cases where a public body has a power but not a duty to act. The 'fair and reasonable' part of the judgments set out above deals with public interest matters such as whether liability would hamper fire brigades in the execution of their duties. In other words, this test relates not to the category of liability but rather to the class of defendants.
2.  *Capital and Counties* was distinguished in *Kent* v *Griffiths* [2000] 2 All ER 474 where the claimant suffered an asthma attack and her doctor ordered an ambulance which took 40 minutes to arrive. She had a respiratory arrest. No explanation was given for the delay. In holding the defendants liable it was said that the ambulance service was part of the health service and not like the police or fire services whose function was to protect the public generally. There was no conflict between the interests of the public at large and the claimant, and no issue of allocation of resources or a conflict of priorities. If there had been a more

urgent case needing attention that would have been different, but that would have been a matter of the standard of care (i.e. to respond in a reasonable time in the circumstances) rather than a question of whether a duty was owed at all.

### Marc Rich & Co. AG v Bishop Rock Marine Co. Ltd (The Nicholas H)
House of Lords [1996] 1 AC 211; [1995] 3 WLR 227; [1995] 3 All ER 307; [1995] 2 Lloyd's Rep 299

The *Nicholas H* was on a voyage from Chile to Italy when cracks developed in her hull and she put into San Juan in Puerto Rico. A Mr Ducat was employed by NKK, a classification society, whose role is to certify ships as fit for sea for the purposes of insurance. Such societies are independent non-profit making organisations. Initially, Mr Ducat recommended permanent repairs but the shipowners objected and he was finally persuaded to allow temporary repairs. After the ship put to sea the temporary welds cracked and the ship sank with total loss of the cargo. The contract between the shipowners and the cargo owners incorporated the Hague Rules, an international convention which limited the liability of the shipowners. The claim by the cargo owners against the shipowners was settled for the amount of the limited liability ($500,000), and the cargo owners then sued NKK for the remainder of their loss ($5.7 million) on the assumption that Mr Ducat was negligent in allowing temporary repairs. Held: dismissing the appeal, that NKK was not liable.

LORD STEYN: . . . The dealings between shipowners and cargo owners are based on a contractual structure, the Hague Rules, and tonnage limitation, on which the insurance of international trade depends: Dr Malcolm Clarke, 'Misdelivery and Time Bars' [1990] LMCLQ 314. Underlying it is the system of double or overlapping insurance of cargo. Cargo owners take out direct insurance in respect of the cargo. Shipowners take out liability risks insurance in respect of breaches of their duties of care in respect of the cargo. The insurance system is structured on the basis that the potential liability of shipowners to cargo owners is limited under the Hague Rules and by virtue of tonnage limitation provisions. And insurance premiums payable by owners obviously reflect such limitations on the shipowners' exposure.

If a duty of care by classification societies to cargo owners is recognised in this case, it must have a substantial impact on international trade. In his article Mr Cane described the likely effect of imposing such duty of care as follows [1994] LMCLQ 363, 375:

> Societies would be forced to buy appropriate liability insurance unless they could bargain with shipowners for an indemnity. To the extent that societies were successful in securing indemnities from shipowners in respect of loss suffered by cargo owners, the limitation of the liability of shipowners to cargo owners under the Hague-Visby Rules would effectively be destroyed. Shipowners would need to increase their insurance cover in respect of losses suffered by cargo owners; but at the same time, cargo owners would still need to insure against losses above the Hague-Visby recovery limit which did not result from actionable negligence on the part of a classification society. At least if classification societies are immune from non-contractual liability, they can confidently go without insurance in respect of third-party losses, leaving third parties to insure themselves in respect of losses for which they could not recover from shipowners.

Counsel for the cargo owners challenged this analysis. On instructions he said that classification societies already carry liability risks insurance. That is no doubt right since classification societies do not have a blanket immunity from all tortious liability. On the other hand, if a duty of care is held to exist in this case, the potential exposure of classification societies to claims by cargo owners will be large. That greater exposure is likely to lead to an increase in the cost to classification societies of obtaining appropriate liability risks insurance. Given their role in maritime trade classification societies are likely to seek to pass on the higher cost to owners. Moreover, it is readily predictable that classification societies will require owners to give appropriate indemnities. Ultimately, ship-owners will pay.

The result of a recognition of a duty of care in this case will be to enable cargo owners, or rather their insurers, to disturb the balance created by the Hague Rules and Hague-Visby Rules as well as by tonnage limitation provisions, by enabling cargo owners to recover in tort against a peripheral party to the prejudice of the protection of shipowners under the existing system. For these reasons I would hold that the international trade system tends to militate against the recognition of the claim in tort put forward by the cargo owners against the classification society.

. . .

### The position and role of NKK

The fact that a defendant acts for the collective welfare is a matter to be taken into consideration when considering whether it is fair, just and reasonable to impose a duty of care: *Hill* v *Chief Constable of West Yorkshire* [1989] AC 53; *Elguzouli-Daf* v *Commissioner of Police of the Metropolis* [1995] 2 WLR 173. Even if such a body has no general immunity from liability in tort, the question may arise whether it owes a duty of care to aggrieved persons, and, if so, in what classes of case, e.g. only in cases involving the direct infliction of physical harm or on a wider basis.

In *W Angliss and Co. (Australia) Proprietary Ltd* v *Peninsular and Oriental Steam Navigation Co.* [1927] 2 KB 456, 462, Wright J (later to become Lord Wright)—a great judge with special expertise in maritime law and practice—described classification societies, such as Lloyd's, as occupying 'a public and quasi-judicial position.' There is a refrain of this idea to be found in Singh & Colinvaux, (British Shipping Laws), (1967), vol. 13, pp. 167–169, paras 391–394, where the editors describe a classification society as an impartial critic and arbiter (as opposed to arbitrator). These observations are helpful but not definitive. Nowadays one would not describe classification societies as carrying on quasi-judicial functions. But it is still the case that (apart from their statutory duties) they act in the public interest. The reality is simply that NKK—and I am deliberately reverting to the evidence about NKK—is an independent and non-profit-making entity, created and operating for the sole purpose of promoting the collective welfare, namely the safety of lives and ships at sea. In common with other classification societies NKK fulfils a role which in its absence would have to be fulfilled by states. And the question is whether NKK, and other classification societies, would be able to carry out their functions as efficiently if they become the ready alternative target of cargo owners, who already have contractual claims against shipowners. In my judgment there must be some apprehension that the classification societies would adopt, to the detriment of their traditional role, a more defensive position.

### Policy factors

Counsel for the cargo owners argued that a decision that a duty of care existed in this case would not involve wide ranging exposure for NKK and other classification societies to claims in tort. That is an unrealistic position. If a duty is recognised in this case there is no reason why it should not extend to annual surveys, docking surveys, intermediate surveys, special surveys, boiler surveys, and so forth. And the scale of NKK's potential liability is shown by the fact that NKK conducted an average of 14,500 surveys per year over the last five years.

At present the system of settling cargo claims against shipowners is a relatively simple one. The claims are settled between the two sets of insurers. If the claims are not settled, they are resolved in arbitration or court proceedings. If a duty is held to exist in this case as between the classification society and cargo owners, classification societies would become potential defendants in many cases. An extra layer of insurance would become involved. The settlement process would inevitably become more complicated and expensive. Arbitration proceedings and court proceedings would often involve an additional party. And often similar issues would have to be canvassed in separate proceedings since the classification societies would not be bound by arbitration clauses in the contracts of carriage. If such a duty is recognised, there is a risk that classification societies might be unwilling from time to time to survey the very vessels which most urgently require independent examination. It will also divert men and resources from the prime function of classification societies, namely to save life and ships at sea. These factors are, by themselves, far from decisive. But in an overall assessment of the case they merit consideration.

*Is the imposition of a duty of care fair, just and reasonable?*

Like Mann LJ in the Court of Appeal [1994] 1 WLR 1071, 1085H, I am willing to assume (without deciding) that there was a sufficient degree of proximity in this case to fulfil that requirement for the existence of a duty of care. The critical question is therefore whether it would be fair, just and reasonable to impose such a duty. For my part I am satisfied that the factors and arguments advanced on behalf of cargo owners are decisively outweighed by the cumulative effect, if a duty is recognised, of the matters discussed in paragraphs [above] i.e. the outflanking of the bargain between shipowners and cargo owners; the negative effect on the public role of NKK; and the other considerations of policy. By way of summary, I look at the matter from the point of view of the three parties concerned. I conclude that the recognition of a duty would be unfair, unjust and unreasonable as against the shipowners who would ultimately have to bear the cost of holding classification societies liable, such consequence being at variance with the bargain between shipowners and cargo owners based on an internationally agreed contractual structure. It would also be unfair, unjust and unreasonable towards classification societies, notably because they act for the collective welfare and unlike shipowners they would not have the benefit of any limitation provisions. Looking at the matter from the point of view of cargo owners, the existing system provides them with the protection of the Hague Rules or Hague-Visby Rules. But that protection is limited under such Rules and by tonnage limitation provisions. Under the existing system any shortfall is readily insurable. In my judgment the lesser injustice is done by not recognising a duty of care. It follows that I would reject the primary way in which counsel for the cargo owners put his case.

NOTES
1. Lord Steyn assumes (without deciding) that there was sufficient proximity and decides the case on the basis of policy considerations. In the Court of Appeal it had been questioned whether 'proximity' and the fair and reasonable test are really separate issues, but the judgment above shows that they should be dealt with separately.
2. The essential point about *Marc Rich* was that there was a 'self-contained' system whereby everybody knew where they stood. The shipowners and the cargo owners knew the limits of liability and could avoid the consequences in advance by insuring themselves against their own loss. Accordingly the principle would not apply to someone outside the system, such as a member of the crew.
3. There was a vigorous dissent by Lord Lloyd. He argued (1) that the existence of the Hague Rules in the contract between the shipowners and the cargo owners was irrelevant as it would be nonsense if NKK were liable if the rules were not incorporated but not liable if they were. Further, the Hague Rules are purely a matter between shipowners and cargo owners and have nothing to do with the potential liability of third parties. (2) There was no evidence that, if liable, classification societies would pass on the cost to shipowners. (3) The fact that classification societies are charitable non-profit-making organisations was irrelevant. He pointed out that hospitals are charitable non-profit-making organisations but are often held liable in tort.
4. For a comment on the decision in the Court of Appeal (where NKK was also held not liable) see Cane, 'The liability of classification societies' [1994] LMCLR 363. He concludes that 'if we view the law of tort as a mechanism for allocating responsibility for losses on the basis of judgements of personal morality in the absence of agreement between the litigating parties as to how those losses should be borne, the decision rests on shaky foundations. But in terms of promoting economic efficiency in the international markets in ship classifications and carriage of goods by sea, there are good arguments in favour of the Court of Appeal decision.'
5. *Marc Rich* was distinguished in *Perrett* v *Collins* [1998] Lloyd's Rep 255, where the first defendant constructed a light plane from a kit and in doing so substituted a different gearbox but failed to change the propeller to suit. The second defendant certified the aircraft as airworthy. It was held that the inspector owed a duty to the claimant passenger who was

injured when the plane crashed. *Marc Rich* was distinguished on the grounds that it does not apply to personal injury cases and a passenger was entitled to rely on careful certification; and the defendant had undertaken a statutory duty for the protection of the public, rather than simply for the purposes of the insurance industry. And see note 2 above.

■ QUESTIONS

1. Is it essential to the 'waste of resources' argument and the 'defensive attitude' point that the organisation should carry out a *public* role?

2. If the ship repairer had been negligent would he have been liable? If so, how would that differ from the case of the ship surveyor?

# 3

# Breach of Duty: The Standard of Care

Once it has been established that there is a sufficient relationship between the parties to establish a duty, the question then arises whether the defendant has been in breach of this duty. This involves a number of issues, many of which are obscured by resort to the judgement of the 'reasonable man'. That fictitious being is no more than the 'anthropomorphic conception of justice', and justice is a complicated concept. The 'reasonable man' may give the impression of certainty where there is none, for whether it is reasonable to take a certain risk involves questions of economic and social policy which are rarely expressed in the law reports. For example, how strong a sea wall should be involves balancing considerations of cost and safety; where a known risk is undertaken for good reasons (as in a police chase) who should bear the risk?

It is important to note, however, that we cannot be protected by the law against all risks: we must put up with the 'vicissitudes of life' and can only expect to be compensated for damage caused by unreasonable activities. The issue of the standard of care can be put in two ways: on the one hand we can ask whether the defendant created an unreasonable risk, and on the other we can ask what level of safety a potential claimant is entitled to expect. These are two sides of the same coin and will usually, but not always, lead to the same result. However, we also know that damage is going to occur as a result of human activity, and who should bear the risk of that damage is an important matter of social policy. To a great extent that question is answered by the fact that we have a fault rather than a no-fault system of compensation, but even within the fault system, how losses are distributed is to some extent governed by our understanding of what risks are unreasonable.

In recent years there has been a tendency to be oversensitive about safety and we have become very 'risk averse'. This has led to the so-called 'compensation culture' whereby people sue for quite ordinary risks with the result that many worthwhile activities, such as school trips, are curtailed for fear of legal action. In November 2005 the Government published a Bill which tries to address part of this problem.

---

## COMPENSATION BILL 2006

### 1. Deterrent effect of potential liability

A court considering a claim in negligence may, in determining whether the defendant should have taken particular steps to meet the standard of care (whether by taking precautions against a risk or otherwise), have regard to whether a requirement to take those steps might—

(a) prevent a desirable activity from being undertaken at all, to a particular extent or in a particular way, or

(b) discourage persons from undertaking functions in connection with a desirable activity.

## SECTION 1: THE REASONABLE MAN—THE LEVEL OF REASONABLE RISK

The standard which the law requires a person to attain must be objectively determined. A person will be regarded as negligent if he fails to act according to that standard, even if it is more difficult for him as an individual to do so than for others. The reason is that we are all entitled to expect a certain level of protection from the acts of others. So the concept of the 'reasonable man' does two things: it judges whether the defendant was careless, but also defines the level of safety a claimant is entitled to expect. This is a social and not a moral judgement.

### Glasgow Corporation v Muir
House of Lords [1943] AC 448; [1943] 2 All ER 44; 169 LT 53

The Corporation owned the old mansion in King's Park, Glasgow, in which there were tea rooms managed by Mrs Alexander. A picnic party of 30–40 people from the Milton Street Free Church asked her if they could take shelter in the old mansion and eat their tea there. Mrs Alexander agreed, and a tea urn weighing 100lbs was carried in by George McDonald and a boy called Taylor. As they entered the tea rooms George McDonald inexplicably dropped his side of the urn and six children were scalded by hot tea. The corridor was five feet wide, narrowing to three feet three inches, and a number of children were in there buying sweets. The claimants alleged that the manageress was negligent in allowing the urn to be carried into the tea rooms. Held: allowing the appeal, that the manageress was not negligent.

LORD MACMILLAN: My Lords, the degree of care for the safety of others which the law requires human beings to observe in the conduct of their affairs varies according to the circumstances. There is no absolute standard, but it may be said generally that the degree of care required varies directly with the risk involved. Those who engage in operations inherently dangerous must take precautions which are not required of persons engaged in the ordinary routine of daily life. It is, no doubt, true that in every act which an individual performs there is present a potentiality of injury to others. All things are possible, and, indeed, it has become proverbial that the unexpected always happens, but, while the precept alterum non laedere requires us to abstain from intentionally injuring others, it does not impose liability for every injury which our conduct may occasion. In Scotland, at any rate, it has never been a maxim of the law that a man acts at his peril. Legal liability is limited to those consequences of our acts which a reasonable man of ordinary intelligence and experience so acting would have in contemplation. 'The duty to take care,' as I essayed to formulate it in *Bourhill* v *Young* ([1943] AC 92, 104), 'is the duty to avoid doing or omitting to do anything the doing or omitting to do which may have as its reasonable and probable consequence injury to others, and the duty is owed to those to whom injury may reasonably and probably be anticipated if the duty is not observed.' This, in my opinion, expresses the law of Scotland and I apprehend that it is also the law of England. The standard of foresight of the reasonable man is, in one sense, an impersonal test. It eliminates the personal equation and is independent of the idiosyncrasies of the particular person whose conduct is in question. Some persons are by nature unduly timorous and imagine every path beset with lions.

Others, of more robust temperament, fail to foresee or nonchalantly disregard even the most obvious dangers. The reasonable man is presumed to be free both from over-apprehension and from over-confidence, but there is a sense in which the standard of care of the reasonable man involves in its application a subjective element. It is still left to the judge to decide what, in the circumstances of the particular case, the reasonable man would have had in contemplation, and what, accordingly, the party sought to be made liable ought to have foreseen. Here there is room for diversity of view, as, indeed, is well illustrated in the present case. What to one judge may seem far-fetched may seem to another both natural and probable.

With these considerations in mind I turn to the facts of the occurrence on which your Lordships have to adjudicate. . . . The question, as I see it, is whether Mrs Alexander, when she was asked to allow a tea urn to be brought into the premises under her charge, ought to have had in mind that it would require to be carried through a narrow passage in which there were a number of children and that there would be a risk of the contents of the urn being spilt and scalding some of the children. If, as a reasonable person, she ought to have had these considerations in mind, was it her duty to require that she should be informed of the arrival of the urn, and, before allowing it to be carried through the narrow passage, to clear all the children out of it in case they might be splashed with scalding water? . . .

In my opinion, Mrs Alexander had no reason to anticipate that such an event would happen as a consequence of granting permission for a tea urn to be carried through the passage way where the children were congregated, and, consequently, there was no duty incumbent on her to take pre-cautions against the occurrence of such an event. I think that she was entitled to assume that the urn would be in charge of responsible persons (as it was) who would have regard for the safety of the children in the passage (as they did have regard), and that the urn would be carried with ordinary care, in which case its transit would occasion no danger to bystanders. The pursuers have left quite unexplained the actual cause of the accident. The immediate cause was not the carrying of the urn through the passage, but McDonald's losing grip of his handle. How he came to do so is entirely a matter of speculation. He may have stumbled or he may have suffered a temporary muscular failure. We do not know, and the pursuers have not chosen to enlighten us by calling McDonald as a witness. Yet it is argued that Mrs Alexander ought to have foreseen the possibility, nay, the reasonable probability of an occurrence the nature of which is unascertained. Suppose that McDonald let go his handle through carelessness. Was Mrs Alexander bound to foresee this as reasonably probable and to take precautions against the possible consequences? I do not think so. . . .

NOTE

The reasonable man has been described as 'the man on the Clapham omnibus' and as 'the man who mows his lawn in his shirtsleeves'. A.P. Herbert in *Uncommon Law* described him as follows:

All solid virtues are his, save only that peculiar quality by which the affection of other men is won. . . . Devoid in short of any human weakness, with not one single saving vice, sans prejudice, procrastination, ill nature, avarice, and absence of mind, as careful for his own safety as he is for that of others, this excellent but odious character stands like a monument in our Courts of Justice, vainly appealing to his fellow citizens to order their lives after his own example.

### Bolton v Stone

House of Lords [1951] AC 850; [1951] 1 All ER 1078

The claimant, Miss Stone, was struck by a cricket ball hit out of a cricket ground at Cheetham Hill, Manchester. The ground was surrounded by a fence whose top, due to the slope of the ground, was 17 feet above the level of the pitch. The fence was 78 yards from the striker, and the claimant, when hit, was 100 yards away. One member of the club said that he thought that about six balls had been hit out of the ground in 28 years, none causing any injury. Held: allowing the appeal, that the club was not negligent.

LORD REID: Counsel for the respondent in this case had to put his case so high as to say that, at least as soon as one ball had been driven into the road in the ordinary course of a match, the appellants could and should have realized that that might happen again and that, if it did, someone might be injured; and that that was enough to put on the appellants a duty to take steps to prevent such an occurrence. If the true test is foreseeability alone I think that must be so. Once a ball has been driven on to a road without there being anything extraordinary to account for the fact, there is clearly a risk that another will follow, and if it does there is clearly a chance, small though it may be, that someone may be injured. On the theory that it is foreseeability alone that matters it would be irrelevant to consider how often a ball might be expected to land in the road and it would not matter whether the road was the busiest street, or the quietest country lane; the only difference between these cases is in the degree of risk.

It would take a good deal to make me believe that the law has departed so far from the standards which guide ordinary careful people in ordinary life. In the crowded conditions of modern life even the most careful person cannot avoid creating some risks and accepting others. What a man must not do, and what I think a careful man tries not to do, is to create a risk which is substantial. . . . In my judgment the test to be applied here is whether the risk of damage to a person on the road was so small that a reasonable man in the position of the appellants, considering the matter from the point of view of safety, would have thought it right to refrain from taking steps to prevent the danger.

In considering that matter I think that it would be right to take into account not only how remote is the chance that a person might be struck but also how serious the consequences are likely to be if a person is struck; but I do not think that it would be right to take into account the difficulty of remedial measures. If cricket cannot be played on a ground without creating a substantial risk, then it should not be played there at all. I think that this is in substance the test which Oliver J applied in this case. He considered whether the appellants' ground was large enough to be safe for all practical purposes and held that it was. This is a question not of law but of fact and degree. It is not an easy question and it is one on which opinions may well differ. I can only say that having given the whole matter repeated and anxious consideration I find myself unable to decide this question in favour of the respondent. But I think that this case is not far from the borderline. If this appeal is allowed, that does not in my judgment mean that in every case where cricket has been played on a ground for a number of years without accident or complaint those who organize matches there are safe to go on in reliance on past immunity. I would have reached a different conclusion if I had thought that the risk there had been other than extremely small, because I do not think that a reasonable man considering the matter from the point of view of safety would or should disregard any risk unless it is extremely small. . . .

LORD RADCLIFFE: My Lords, I agree that this appeal must be allowed. I agree with regret, because I have much sympathy with the decision that commended itself to the majority of the members of the Court of Appeal. I can see nothing unfair in the appellants being required to compensate the respondent for the serious injury that she has received as a result of the sport that they have organized on their cricket ground at Cheetham Hill. But the law of negligence is concerned less with what is fair than with what is culpable, and I cannot persuade myself that the appellants have been guilty of any culpable act or omission in this case.

I think that the case is in some respects a peculiar one, not easily related to the general rules that govern liability for negligence. If the test whether there has been a breach of duty were to depend merely on the answer to the question whether this accident was a reasonably foreseeable risk, I think that there would have been a breach of duty, for that such an accident might take place some time or other might very reasonably have been present to the minds of the appellants. It was quite foreseeable, and there would have been nothing unreasonable in allowing the imagination to dwell on the possibility of its occurring. But there was only a remote, perhaps I ought to say only a very remote, chance of the accident taking place at any particular time, for, if it was to happen, not only had a ball to carry the fence round the ground but it had also to coincide in its arrival with the presence of some person on what does not look like a crowded thoroughfare and actually to strike that person in some way that would cause sensible injury.

Those being the facts, a breach of duty has taken place if they show the appellants guilty of a failure to take reasonable care to prevent the accident. One may phrase it as 'reasonable care' or 'ordinary care' or 'proper care'—all these phrases are to be found in decisions of authority—but the fact remains that, unless there has been something which a reasonable man would blame as falling beneath the standard of conduct that he would set for himself and require of his neighbour, there has been no breach of legal duty. And here, I think, the respondent's case breaks down. It seems to me that a reasonable man, taking account of the chances against an accident happening, would not have felt himself called upon either to abandon the use of the ground for cricket or to increase the height of his surrounding fences. He would have done what the appellants did: in other words, he would have done nothing. Whether, if the unlikely event of an accident did occur and his play turn to another's hurt, he would have thought it equally proper to offer no more consolation to his victim than the reflection that a social being is not immune from social risks, I do not say, for I do not think that that is a consideration which is relevant to legal liability.

## ■ QUESTION

Does the nature of the activity matter? Is cricket 'a good thing'? X is in the habit of holding all-night parties. The guests habitually throw bottles into the garden. One night at 3.00 a.m., Y throws a bottle out of the window, which strikes Z, standing 20 yards away in the road. Only twice before have bottles reached the road. Is X liable for holding the party?

---

### *Blyth* v *Proprietors of the Birmingham Waterworks*
Court of Exchequer (1856) 11 Ex 781; 156 ER 1047

The defendant had laid a water main 18 inches deep, and in the main was a 'fire plug'. This was a neck in the main stopped by a wooden plug, which when released allowed water to flow up a cast iron tube to street level. On 24 February 1855 water escaped from the main and forced its way through the ground into the claimant's house, the cast iron tube above the plug being stopped up with ice. It seemed that on 15 January 1855 there was a severe frost, and this may have caused the wooden plug to be dislodged by the expansion of water. Held: the defendants were not negligent.

ALDERSON, B: I am of opinion that there was no evidence to be left to the jury. The case turns upon the question, whether the facts proved show that the defendants were guilty of negligence. Negligence is the omission to do something which a reasonable man, guided upon those considerations which ordinarily regulate the conduct of human affairs, would do, or doing something which a prudent and reasonable man would not do. The defendants might have been liable for negligence, if, unintentionally, they omitted to do that which a reasonable person would have done, or did that which a person taking reasonable precautions would not have done. A reasonable man would act with reference to the average circumstances of the temperature in ordinary years. The defendants had provided against such frosts as experience would have led men, acting prudently, to provide against; and they are not guilty of negligence, because their precautions proved insufficient against the effects of the extreme severity of the frost of 1855, which penetrated to a greater depth than any which ordinarily occurs south of the polar regions. Such a state of circumstances constitutes a contingency against which no reasonable man can provide. The result was an accident, for which the defendants cannot be held liable.

NOTES
1. This case introduces a very important problem. If the mains had been a foot lower they might have escaped the effects of the frost, but that would have been more expensive. Hence, the

'standard of care' involves difficult economic issues: how much should be paid for safety? At what level of cost is a potential defendant entitled to say that the proposed safety measure is too expensive? In *US* v *Carroll Towing* (1947) 159 F 2d 169, Judge Learned Hand said that if the probability of the damage occurring is called P, the extent of the potential damage (i.e. the liability) is called L and the cost of preventing the damage (i.e. the burden) is called B, then liability depends on whether B is less than L multiplied by P: i.e. whether B < PL. This may be a useful guide in some cases but is really too simplistic as other values may be relevant. For example, could the formula be used on its own to justify the possibility of cancer being contracted by workers in a chemical factory?

2. The particular issue in *Blyth* has now been determined by statute: under the Water Industry Act 1991, s. 209 a water undertaker is strictly liable for the escape of water from any pipe which is vested in it.

## SECTION 2: THE SKILL OF THE DEFENDANT

People have varying degrees of skill, but the test of liability must be objective. Nevertheless, the degree of skill which a potential claimant is entitled to expect from a potential defendant will not necessarily be that of the 'ordinary man', but rather the skill of the reasonable example of that kind of person. Thus, doctors must conform to the level of skill of the 'reasonable doctor' and not that of the 'man on the Clapham omnibus'.

## A: The safety we are entitled to expect

### *Wells* v *Cooper*
[1958] 2 QB 265; [1958] 2 All ER 527; [1958] 3 WLR 1128

The claimant, Albert Wells, was delivering fish to the defendant's house. As he was leaving he pulled the back door to close it and the door handle came away in his hand, and he lost his balance and fell. The door needed quite a strong pull as a draught excluder was fitted to the bottom of it and there was quite a strong wind blowing against the door. The handle had been put on by the defendant himself a few months earlier, and consisted of a lever type handle fixed by a base plate which was held to the door by four ¾ inch screws. The defendant had some experience as an amateur carpenter. Held, allowing the appeal, that the defendant was not liable for using ¾ inch screws.

JENKINS LJ: As above related, the defendant did the work himself. We do not think the mere fact that he did it himself instead of employing a professional carpenter to do it constituted a breach of his duty of care. No doubt some kinds of work involve such highly specialized skill and knowledge, and create such serious dangers if not properly done, that an ordinary occupier owing a duty of care to others in regard to the safety of premises would fail in that duty if he undertook such work himself instead of employing experts to do it for him. See *Haseldine* v *C. A. Daw & Son Ltd*, per Scott LJ, [1941] 2 KB 343. But the work here in question was not of that order. It was a trifling domestic replacement well within the competence of a householder accustomed to doing small carpentering jobs about his home, and of a kind which must be done every day by hundreds of householders up and down the country.

Accordingly, we think that the defendant did nothing unreasonable in undertaking the work himself. But it behoved him, if he was to discharge his duty of care to persons such as the plaintiff, to do the work with reasonable care and skill, and we think the degree of care and skill required of him must be measured not by reference to the degree of competence in such matters which he personally happened to possess, but by reference to the degree of care and skill which a reasonably competent carpenter might be expected to apply to the work in question. Otherwise, the extent of the protection that an invitee could claim in relation to work done by the invitor himself would vary according to the capacity of the invitor, who could free himself from liability merely by showing that he had done the best of which he was capable, however good, bad or indifferent that best might be.

Accordingly, we think the standard of care and skill to be demanded of the defendant in order to discharge his duty of care to the plaintiff in the fixing of the new handle in the present case must be the degree of care and skill to be expected of a reasonably competent carpenter doing the work in question. This does not mean that the degree of care and skill required is to be measured by reference to the contractual obligations as to the quality of his work assumed by a professional carpenter working for reward, which would, in our view, set the standard too high. The question is simply what steps would a reasonably competent carpenter wishing to fix a handle such as this securely to a door such as this have taken with a view to achieving that object.

In fact the only complaint made by the plaintiff in regard to the way in which the defendant fixed the new handle is that three-quarter inch screws were inadequate and that one inch screws should have been used. The question may, therefore, be stated more narrowly as being whether a reasonably competent carpenter fixing this handle would have appreciated that three-quarter inch screws such as those used by the defendant would not be adequate to fix it securely and would accordingly have used one inch screws instead. . . .

In relation to a trifling and perfectly simple operation such as the fixing of the new handle we think that the defendant's experience of domestic carpentry is sufficient to justify his inclusion in the category of reasonably competent carpenters. The matter then stands thus. The defendant, a reasonably competent carpenter, used three-quarter inch screws, believing them to be adequate for the purpose of fixing the handle. There is no doubt that he was doing his best to make the handle secure and believed that he had done so. Accordingly, he must be taken to have discharged his duty of reasonable care, unless the belief that three-quarter inch screws would be adequate was one which no reasonably competent carpenter could reasonably entertain, or, in other words, an obvious blunder which should at once have been apparent to him as a reasonably competent carpenter. The evidence adduced on the plaintiff's side failed, in the judge's view, to make that out. He saw and heard the witnesses, and had demonstrated to him the strength of attachment provided by three-quarter inch screws. We see no sufficient reason for differing from his conclusion. Indeed, the fact that the handle remained secure during the period of four or five months between the time it was fixed and the date of the accident, although no doubt in constant use throughout that period, makes it very difficult to accept the view that the inadequacy of the three-quarter inch screws should have been obvious to the defendant at the time when he decided to use them.

■ QUESTION

In order to decide whether the use of ¾ inch screws was negligent, who should you ask—the reasonable man, the reasonable householder, the reasonable handyperson, or the reasonable carpenter? What question should you ask? (Incidentally, at first instance the judge, Stable J, ignored the evidence of two expert witnesses to the effect that a reasonably competent carpenter would have thought ¾ inch screws to be inadequate.)

## B: The under-skilled

### *Nettleship* v *Weston*
[1971] 2 QB 691; [1971] 3 All ER 581; [1971] RTR 425

The claimant, Eric Nettleship, was teaching a friend of his, Lavinia Weston, to drive. She negligently hit a lamp post and the claimant suffered a broken knee cap. Held: allowing the appeal, that the defendant was liable. (Note: the extracts below deal only with the issue of standard of care. The case also raised the issue whether the claimant consented to the risk of injury, and it was held that he did not.)

LORD DENNING MR:

*The Responsibility of the Learner Driver towards Persons on or near the Highway*

Mrs Weston is clearly liable for the damage to the lamp post. In the civil law if a driver goes off the road on to the pavement and injures a pedestrian, or damages property, he is prima facie liable. Likewise if he goes on to the wrong side of the road. It is no answer for him to say: 'I was a learner driver under instruction. I was doing my best and could not help it.' The civil law permits no such excuse. It requires of him the same standard of care as of any other driver. 'It eliminates the personal equation and is independent of the idiosyncrasies of the particular person whose conduct is in question': see *Glasgow Corporation* v *Muir* [1943] AC 448, 457 by Lord Macmillan. The learner driver may be doing his best, but his incompetent best is not good enough. He must drive in as good a manner as a driver of skill, experience and care, who is sound in mind and limb, who makes no errors of judgment, has good eyesight and hearing, and is free from any infirmity: see *Richley (Henderson)* v *Faull, Richley, Third Party* [1965] 1 WLR 1454 and *Watson* v *Thomas S. Whitney & Co. Ltd* [1966] 1 WLR 57.

The high standard thus imposed by the judges is, I believe, largely the result of the policy of the Road Traffic Acts. Parliament requires every driver to be insured against third party risks. The reason is so that a person injured by a motor car should not be left to bear the loss on his own, but should be compensated out of the insurance fund. The fund is better able to bear it than he can. But the injured person is only able to recover if the driver is liable in law. So the judges see to it that he is liable, unless he can prove care and skill of a high standard: see *The Merchant Prince* [1982] P 179 and *Henderson* v *Henry E. Jenkins & Sons* [1970] AC 282. Thus we are, in this branch of the law, moving away from the concept: 'No liability without fault.' We are beginning to apply the test: 'On whom should the risk fall?' Morally the learner driver is not at fault; but legally she is liable to be because she is insured and the risk should fall on her.

*The responsibility of the Learner Driver towards Passengers in the Car*

Mrs Weston took her son with her in the car. We do not know his age. He may have been 21 and have known that his mother was learning to drive. He was not injured. But if he had been injured, would he have had a cause of action?

I take it to be clear that if a driver has a passenger in the car he owes a duty of care to him. But what is the standard of care required of the driver? Is it a lower standard than he or she owes towards a pedestrian on the pavement? I should have thought not. But, suppose that the driver has never driven a car before, or has taken too much to drink or has poor eyesight or hearing: and, furthermore, that the passenger *knows* it and yet accepts a lift from him. Does that make any difference? Dixon J thought it did. In *The Insurance Commissioner* v *Joyce* (1948) 77 CLR 39, 56, he said:

If a man accepts a lift from a car driver whom he *knows* to have lost a limb or an eye or to be deaf, he cannot complain if he does not exhibit the skill and competence of a driver who suffers from no defect. . . . If he knowingly accepts the voluntary services of a driver affected by drink, he cannot complain of improper driving caused by his condition, because it involved no breach of duty.

That view of Dixon J seems to have been followed in South Australia: see *Walker* v *Turton-Sainsbury* [1952] SASR 159; but in the Supreme Court of Canada Rand J did not agree with it: see *Car and General Insurance Co.* v *Seymour and Maloney* (1956) 2 DLR (2d) 369, 375.

We have all the greatest respect for Sir Owen Dixon, but for once I cannot agree with him. The driver owes a duty of care to every passenger in the car, just as he does to every pedestrian on the road: and he must attain the same standard of care in respect of each. If the driver were to be excused according to the knowledge of the passenger, it would result in endless confusion and injustice. One of the passengers may know that the learner driver is a mere novice. Another passenger may believe him to be entirely competent. One of the passengers may believe the driver to have had only two drinks. Another passenger may know that he has had a dozen. Is the one passenger to recover and the other not? Rather than embark on such inquiries, the law holds that the driver must attain the same standard of care for passengers as for pedestrians. The knowledge of the passenger may go to show that he was guilty of contributory negligence in ever accepting the lift—and thus reduce his damages—but it does not take away the duty of care, nor does it diminish the standard of care which the law requires of the driver: see *Dann* v *Hamilton* [1939] 1 KB 509 and *Slater* v *Clay Cross Co. Ltd* [1956] 2 QB 264, 270.

*The Responsibility of a Learner Driver towards his Instructor*

The special factor in this case is that Mr Nettleship was not a mere passenger in the car. He was an instructor teaching Mrs Weston to drive.

Seeing that the law lays down, for all drivers of motor cars, a standard of care to which all must conform, I think that even a learner driver, so long as he is the sole driver, must attain the same standard towards all passengers in the car, including an instructor. But the instructor may be debarred from claiming for a reason peculiar to himself. He may be debarred because he has voluntarily agreed to waive any claim for any injury that may befall him. Otherwise he is not debarred. He may, of course, be guilty of contributory negligence and have his damages reduced on that account. He may, for instance, have let the learner take control too soon, he may not have been quick enough to correct his errors, or he may have participated in the negligent act himself: see *Stapley* v *Gypsum Mines Ltd* [1953] AC 663. But, apart from contributory negligence, he is not excluded unless it be that he has voluntarily agreed to incur the risk. . . .

MEGAW LJ: . . . The important question of principle which arises is whether, because of Mr Nettleship's knowledge that Mrs Weston was not an experienced driver, the standard of care which was owed to him by her was lower than would otherwise have been the case.

In *The Insurance Commissioner* v *Joyce* (1948) CLR 39, 56–60, Dixon J stated persuasively the view that there is, or may be, a 'particular relation' between the driver of a vehicle and his passenger resulting in a variation of the standard of duty owed by the driver. He said, at p.56:

> The case of a passenger in a car differs from that of a pedestrian not in the kind or degree of danger which may come from any want of care or skill in driving but in the fact that the former has come into a more particular relation with the driver of the car. It is because that relation may vary that the standard of duty or of care is not necessarily the same in every case. . . . the gratuitous passenger may expect prima facie the same care and skill on the part of the driver as is ordinarily demanded in the management of a car. Unusual conditions may exist which are apparent to him or of which he may be informed and they may affect the application of the standard of care that is due. If a man accepts a lift from a car driver whom he knows to have lost a limb or an eye or to be deaf, he cannot complain if he does not exhibit the skill and competence of a driver who suffers from no defect.

He summarised the same principle in these words, at p. 59:

It appears to me that the circumstances in which the defendant accepts the plaintiff as a passenger and in which the plaintiff accepts the accommodation in the conveyance should determine the measure of duty . . .

Theoretically, the principle as thus expounded is attractive. But, with very great respect, I venture to think that the theoretical attraction should yield to practical considerations.

As I see it, if this doctrine of varying standards were to be accepted as part of the law on these facts, it could not logically be confined to the duty of care owed by learner drivers. There is no reason in logic why it should not operate in a much wider sphere. The disadvantages of the resulting unpredictability, uncertainty and, indeed, impossibility of arriving at fair and consistent decisions outweigh the advantages. The certainty of a general standard is preferable to the vagaries of a fluctuating standard . . .

Again, when one considers the requisite standard of care of the learner driver, if this doctrine were to apply, would not logic irresistibly demand that there should be something more than a mere, single, conventional, standard applicable to anyone who falls into the category of learner driver: that is, of anyone who has not yet qualified for (or perhaps obtained) a full licence? That standard itself would necessarily vary over a wide range, not merely with the actual progress of the learner, but also with the passenger's knowledge of that progress; or, rather, if the passenger has in fact over-estimated the driver's progress, it would vary with the passenger's reasonable assessment of that progress at the relevant time. The relevant time would not necessarily be the moment of the accident.

The question, what is the relevant time, would itself have to be resolved by reference to some principle. The instructor's reasonable assessment of the skill and competence of the driver (and also the driver's assessment of the instructor's skill and competence) might alter drastically between the start of the first lesson and the start of a later lesson, or even in the course of one particular spell of driving. I suppose the principle would have to be that the relevant time is the last moment when the plaintiff (whether instructor or driver) could reasonably have refused to continue as passenger or driver in the light of his then knowledge. The factor in itself would introduce yet another element of difficulty, uncertainty and, I believe, serious anomaly.

I, for my part, with all respect, do not think that our legal process could successfully or satis-factorily cope with the task of fairly assessing or applying to the facts of a particular case such varying standards, depending on such complex and elusive factors, including the assessment by the court, not merely of a particular person's actual skill or experience, but also of another person's knowledge or assessment of that skill or experience at a particular moment of time.

NOTES
1. In *Philips* v *Whiteley Ltd* [1938] 1 All ER 566, the claimant had her ears pierced by a jeweller and subsequently suffered an infection. It was decided that the infection was probably not due to the ear piercing, but, even if it was, the jeweller would not have been liable as he had taken all reasonable precautions that a jeweller would take and could not be expected to conform to the standards of a surgeon. Is this view consistent with *Nettleship* v *Weston*? What level of care was Mrs Philips entitled to? See also *Shakoor* v *Situ* [2000] 4 All ER 181 where it was held that a practitioner of Chinese herbal medicine was not to be judged by the standard of the reasonable general practitioner but rather by the reasonable practitioner of that art, on the grounds that the defendant had not held himself out as skilled in orthodox medicine and the claimant had chosen to use the 'alternative' medical system.

   In *Wilsher* v *Essex Area Health Authority* [1987] QB 730, at p. 750, it was argued that a junior inexperienced doctor owed a lower duty of care: Mustill LJ rejected this, saying:

   this notion of a duty tailored to the actor, rather than to the act which he elects to perform, has no place in the law of tort. . . . To my mind it would be a false step to subordinate the legitimate expectation of the patient that he will receive from each person concerned with his care a degree of skill appropriate to the task which he undertakes to an understandable wish to minimise the psychological and financial pressures on hard pressed young doctors.

   (The case was reversed on appeal on a different point: [1988] AC 1074.)

2.  In *Cook* v *Cook* (1986) 162 CLR 376, the High Court of Australia refused to follow *Nettleship* v *Weston*, preferring the views of Dixon J in *Insurance Commissioner* v *Joyce* (mentioned in *Nettleship*). The court said that the standard of care should be derived from the relationship between the parties, so that where the claimant knows of an incapacity of the defendant the standard will be lower. In this case the claimant encouraged the defendant to drive even though she knew that the defendant did not have even a provisional driving licence, and it was held that the appropriate standard was that of the inexperienced driver. Are such problems better dealt with by the defence of contributory negligence? See Kidner, 'The variable standard of care, contributory negligence and *volenti*' (1991) 11 LS 1.

## C: Special skills

### *Bolam* v *Friern Hospital Management Committee*
Queen's Bench Division [1957] 1 WLR 582; [1957] 2 All ER 118

The claimant suffered a fracture of the pelvis while he was undergoing electro-convulsive therapy. The issue was whether the doctor was negligent in failing to give a relaxant drug before the treatment, or in failing to provide means of restraint during it. Evidence was given of the practices of various doctors in this regard, and the extracts below deal with the appropriate test to be applied in assessing the conduct of the defendant. Held: the defendants were not liable.

MCNAIR J, *addressing the jury*: Before I turn to that, I must tell you what in law we mean by 'negligence.' In the ordinary case which does not involve any special skill, negligence in law means a failure to do some act which a reasonable man in the circumstances would do, or the doing of some act which a reasonable man in the circumstances would not do; and if that failure or the doing of that act results in injury, then there is a cause of action. How do you test whether this act or failure is negligent? In an ordinary case it is generally said you judge it by the action of the man in the street. He is the ordinary man. In one case it has been said you judge it by the conduct of the man on the top of a Clapham omnibus. He is the ordinary man. But where you get a situation which involves the use of some special skill or competence, then the test as to whether there has been negligence or not is not the test of the man on the top of a Clapham omnibus, because he has not got this special skill. The test is the standard of the ordinary skilled man exercising and professing to have that special skill. A man need not possess the highest expert skill; it is well established law that it is sufficient if he exercises the ordinary skill of an ordinary competent man exercising that particular art. I do not think that I quarrel much with any of the submissions in law which have been put before you by counsel. Mr Fox-Andrews put it in this way, that in the case of a medical man, negligence means failure to act in accordance with the standards of reasonably competent medical men at the time. That is a perfectly accurate statement, as long as it is remembered that there may be one or more perfectly proper standards; and if he conforms with one of those proper standards, then he is not negligent. Mr Fox-Andrews also was quite right, in my judgment, in saying that a mere personal belief that a particular technique is best is no defence unless that belief is based on reasonable grounds. That again is unexceptionable. But the emphasis which is laid by the defence is on this aspect of negligence, that the real question you have to make up your minds about on each of the three major topics is whether the defendants, in acting in the way they did, were acting in accordance with a practice of competent respected professional opinion. Mr Stirling submitted that if you are satisfied that they were acting in accordance with a practice of a competent body of professional opinion, then it would be wrong for you to hold that negligence was established. In a recent Scottish case, *Hunter* v *Hanley*, 1955 SLT 213, Lord President Clyde [at p. 217] said:

> In the realm of diagnosis and treatment there is ample scope for genuine difference of opinion and one man clearly is not negligent merely because his conclusion differs from that of other professional men, nor because he has displayed less skill or knowledge than others

would have shown. The true test for establishing negligence in diagnosis or treatment on the part of a doctor is whether he has been proved to be guilty of such failure as no doctor of ordinary skill would be guilty of, if acting with ordinary care.

If that statement of the true test is qualified by the words 'in all the circumstances,' Mr Fox-Andrews would not seek to say that that expression of opinion does not accord with the English law. It is just a question of expression. I myself would prefer to put it this way, that he is not guilty of negligence if he has acted in accordance with a practice accepted as proper by a responsible body of medical men skilled in that particular art. I do not think there is much difference in sense. It is just a different way of expressing the same thought. Putting it the other way round, a man is not negligent, if he is acting in accordance with such a practice, merely because there is a body of opinion who would take a contrary view. At the same time, that does not mean that a medical man can obstinately and pig-headedly carry on with some old technique if it has been proved to be contrary to what is really substantially the whole of informed medical opinion. Otherwise you might get men today saying: 'I do not believe in anaesthetics. I do not believe in antiseptics. I am going to continue to do my surgery in the way it was done in the eighteenth century.' That clearly would be wrong.

Before I get to the details of the case, it is right to say this, that it is not essential for you to decide which of two practices is the better practice, as long as you accept that what the defendants did was in accordance with a practice accepted by responsible persons; if the result of the evidence is that you are satisfied that this practice is better than the practice spoken of on the other side, then it is really a stronger case. Finally, bear this in mind, that you are now considering whether it was negligent for certain action to be taken in August, 1954, not in February, 1957; and in one of the well-known cases on this topic it has been said you must not look with 1957 spectacles at what happened in 1954.

NOTES

1. This case has been approved by the House of Lords in *Sidaway* v *Bethlem Royal Hospital* [1985] AC 871 and in *Whitehouse* v *Jordan* [1981] 1 WLR 246. In the latter case Lord Denning, in the Court of Appeal, attempted to argue that there was a difference between error of judgment and negligence, saying 'When I give a judgment and it is afterwards reversed by the House of Lords, is it to be said that I was negligent?' He duly was reversed by the House of Lords, Lord Edmund Davies saying that the phrase 'error of judgment' was wholly ambiguous, 'for while some such errors may be completely consistent with the due exercise of professional skill, other acts or omissions in the course of exercising clinical judgment may be so glaringly below proper standards as to make a finding of negligence inevitable'.

2. In *Bolitho* v *City and Hackney Health Authority* [1997] 4 All ER 771 the House of Lords said that in rare cases a doctor could be held to be negligent even if the treatment was sanctioned by a body of professional opinion. Lord Browne-Wilkinson noted that McNair J had referred to a *responsible* body of medical men and that the practice should be regarded as proper by a competent *reasonable* body of opinion, and said that expert evidence could be ignored if it could not be shown that such opinion had a logical basis, or if the experts had not reached a defensible opinion. To what extent is this a satisfactory control over the profession?

---

### *Sidaway* v *Governors of the Bethlem Royal Hospital*
House of Lords [1985] AC 871; [1985] 2 WLR 480; [1985] 1 All ER 643

Mrs Sidaway suffered persistent pain in her right arm and shoulder and a surgeon employed by the defendants recommended an operation to her spine to which Mrs Sidaway consented. The operation involved a risk, put at less than one per cent, of damage to the spine and Mrs Sidaway was not informed of this risk. The operation was properly conducted but unfortunately the risk materialised and the claimant became severely disabled. She sued the defendants on the ground that the surgeon had failed to inform her of the risk. Held: dismissing the appeal, that the defendants were not liable.

LORD BRIDGE: . . . The important question which this appeal raises is whether the law imposes any, and if so what, different criterion as the measure of the medical man's duty of care to his patient when giving advice with respect to a proposed course of treatment. It is clearly right to recognise that a conscious adult patient of sound mind is entitled to decide for himself whether or not he will submit to a particular course of treatment proposed by the doctor, most significantly surgical treatment under general anaesthesia. This entitlement is the foundation of the doctrine of 'informed consent' which has led in certain American jurisdictions to decisions, and in the Supreme Court of Canada, to dicta, on which the appellant relies, which would oust the *Bolam* test and substitute an 'objective' test of a doctor's duty to advise the patient of the advantages and disadvantages of undergoing the treatment proposed and more particularly to advise the patient of the risks involved.

There are, it appears to me, at least theoretically, two extreme positions which could be taken. It could be argued that, if the patient's consent is to be fully informed, the doctor must specifically warn him of *all* risks involved in the treatment offered, unless he has some sound clinical reason not to do so. Logically, this would seem to be the extreme to which a truly objective criterion of the doctor's duty would lead. Yet this position finds no support from any authority, to which we have been referred, in any jurisdiction. It seems to be generally accepted that there is no need to warn of the risks inherent in all surgery under general anaesthesia. This is variously explained on the ground that the patient may be expected to be aware of such risks or that they are relatively remote. If the law is to impose on the medical profession a duty to warn of risks to secure 'informed consent' independently of accepted medical opinion of what is appropriate, neither of these explanations for confining the duty to special as opposed to general risks seems to me wholly convincing.

At the other extreme it could be argued that, once the doctor has decided what treatment is, on balance of advantages and disadvantages, in the patient's best interest, he should not alarm the patient by volunteering a warning of any risk involved, however grave and substantial, unless specifically asked by the patient. I cannot believe that contemporary medical opinion would support this view, which would effectively exclude the patient's right to decide in the very type of case where it is most important that he should be in a position to exercise that right and, perhaps even more significantly, to seek a second opinion as to whether he should submit himself to the significant risk which has been drawn to his attention. I should perhaps add at this point, although the issue does not strictly arise in this appeal, that, when questioned specifically by a patient of apparently sound mind about risks involved in a particular treatment proposed, the doctor's duty must, in my opinion, be to answer both truthfully and as fully as the questioner requires.

The decision mainly relied on to establish a criterion of the doctor's duty to disclose the risks inherent in a proposed treatment which is prescribed by the law and can be applied independently of any medical opinion or practice is that of the District of Columbia Circuit Court of Appeals in *Canterbury* v *Spence*, 464 F. 2d 772. The judgment of the Court (Wright, Leventhal and Robinson JJ), delivered by Robinson J, expounds the view that an objective criterion of what is a sufficient disclosure of risk is necessary to ensure that the patient is enabled to make an intelligent decision and cannot be left to be determined by the doctors. He said, at p. 784:

> Respect for the patient's right of self-determination on particular therapy demands a standard set by law for physicians rather than one which physicians may or may not impose upon themselves.

In an attempt to define the objective criterion it is said, at p. 787, that 'the issue on non-disclosure must be approached from the viewpoint of the reasonableness of the physician's divulgence in terms of what he knows or should know to be the patient's informational needs'. A risk is required to be disclosed 'when a reasonable person, in what the physician knows or should know to be the patient's position, would be likely to attach significance to the risk or cluster of risks in deciding whether or not to forgo the proposed therapy'; 464 F. 2d 772, 787. The judgment adds, at p. 788 'Whenever non-disclosure of particular risk information is open to debate by reasonable-minded men, the issue is for the finder of facts.'

I recognise the logical force of the *Canterbury* doctrine, proceeding from the premise that the patient's right to make his own decision must at all costs be safeguarded against the kind of medical paternalism which assumes that 'doctor knows best'. But, with all respect, I regard the doctrine as quite impractical in application for three principal reasons. First, it gives insufficient weight to the realities of the doctor/patient relationship. A very wide variety of factors must enter into a doctor's clinical judgment not only as to what treatment is appropriate for a particular patient, but also as to how best to communicate to the patient the significant factors necessary to enable the patient to make an informed decision whether to undergo the treatment. The doctor cannot set out to educate the patient to his own standard of medical knowledge of all the relevant factors involved. He may take the view, certainly with some patients, that the very fact of his volunteering, without being asked, information of some remote risk involved in the treatment proposed, even though he describes it as remote, may lead to that risk assuming an undue significance in the patient's calculations. Secondly, it would seem to me quite unrealistic in any medical negligence action to confine the expert medical evidence to an explanation of the primary medical factors involved and to deny the court the benefit of evidence of medical opinion and practice on the particular issue of disclosure which is under consideration. Thirdly, the objective test which *Canterbury* propounds seems to me to be so imprecise as to be almost meaningless. If it is to be left to individual judges to decide for themselves what 'a reasonable person in the patient's position' would consider a risk of sufficient significance that he should be told about it, the outcome of litigation in this field is likely to be quite unpredictable.

Having rejected the *Canterbury* doctrine as a solution to the problem of safeguarding the patient's right to decide whether he will undergo a particular treatment advised by his doctor, the question remains whether that right is sufficiently safeguarded by the application of the *Bolam* test without qualification to the determination of the question what risks inherent in a proposed treatment should be disclosed. The case against a simple application of the *Bolam* test is cogently stated by Laskin CJC, giving the judgment of the Supreme Court of Canada in *Reibl* v *Hughes*, 114 DLR (3d) 1, 13:

> To allow expert medical evidence to determine what risks are material and, hence, should be disclosed and, correlatively, what risks are not material is to hand over to the medical profession the entire question of the scope of the duty of disclosure, including the question whether there has been a breach of that duty. Expert medical evidence is, of course, relevant to findings as to the risks that reside in or are a result of recommended surgery or other treatment. It will also have a bearing on their materiality but this is not a question that is to be concluded on the basis of the expert medical evidence alone. The issue under consideration is a different issue from that involved where the question is whether the doctor carried out his professional activities by applicable professional standards. What is under consideration here is the patient's right to know what risks are involved in undergoing or forgoing certain surgery or other treatment.

I fully appreciate the force of this reasoning, but can only accept it subject to the important qualification that a decision what degree of disclosure of risks is best calculated to assist a particular patient to make a rational choice as to whether or not to undergo a particular treatment must primarily be a matter of clinical judgment. It would follow from this that the issue whether non-disclosure in a particular case should be condemned as a breach of the doctor's duty of care is an issue to be decided primarily on the basis of expert medical evidence, applying the *Bolam* test. But I do not see that this approach involves the necessity 'to hand over to the medical profession the entire question of the scope of the duty of disclosure, including the question whether there has been a breach of that duty'. Of course, if there is a conflict of evidence as to whether a responsible body of medical opinion approves of non-disclosure in a particular case, the judge will have to resolve that conflict. But even in a case where, as here, no expert witness in the relevant medical field condemns the non-disclosure as being in conflict with accepted and responsible medical practice, I am of opinion that the judge might in certain circumstances come to the conclusion that disclosure of a particular risk was so obviously necessary to an informed choice on the part of the patient that no reasonably prudent medical man would fail to make it. The kind of case I have in mind would be an operation involving a substantial risk of grave adverse consequences, as, for example, the ten per cent risk of a stroke from the operation which was the subject of the Canadian case of *Reibl* v *Hughes*, 114 DLR (3d) 1. In such a case, in the absence of some cogent clinical reason why the patient should not be informed, a doctor, recognising and respecting his patient's right of decision, could hardly fail to appreciate the necessity for an appropriate warning.

In the instant case I can see no reasonable ground on which the judge could properly reject the conclusion to which the unchallenged medical evidence led in the application of the *Bolam* test. The trial judge's assessment of the risk at one to two per cent covered both nerve root and spinal cord damage and covered a spectrum of possible ill effects 'ranging from the mild to the catastrophic'. In so far as it is possible and appropriate to measure such risks in percentage terms—some of the expert medical witnesses called expressed a marked and understandable reluctance to do so—the risk of damage to the spinal cord of such severity as the appellant in fact suffered was, it would appear, certainly less than one per cent. But there is no yardstick either in the judge's findings or in the evidence to measure what fraction of one per cent that risk represented. In these circumstances, the appellant's expert witness's agreement that the non-disclosure complained of accorded with a practice accepted as proper by a responsible body of neuro-surgical opinion afforded the respondents a complete defence to the appellant's claim.

## NOTE

This case established that the *Bolam* test applied as much to the question of whether a patient should be informed of the risk as it does to diagnosis and treatment, and it rejects the doctrine of informed consent. However, in *Rogers* v *Whitaker* (1992) 175 CLR 479 the High Court of Australia has declined to follow *Sidaway* and has followed the Supreme Court of Canada in *Reibl* v *Hughes* (1980) 114 DLR 3d 1. In *Rogers* the court said (at p. 490) that 'the law should recognise that a doctor has a duty to warn a patient of a material risk inherent in the proposed treatment; a risk is material if, in the circumstances of the particular case, a reasonable person in the patient's position, if warned of the risk, would be likely to attach significance to it or if the medical practitioner is or should reasonably be aware that the particular patient, if warned of the risk, would be likely to attach significance to it'. (It was noted that there is an exception to this principle where it can be shown that the information would harm an unusually nervous, volatile or disturbed patient.)

If the *Bolam* test applies why should a doctor not disclose what a reasonable patient would want to know?

## D: Children

### *Mullin* v *Richards*
Court of Appeal [1998] 1 WLR 1304; [1998] 1 All ER 920

The claimant and defendant, both 15-year-old schoolgirls, were fighting with plastic rulers, using them as swords, when one of the rulers broke and a fragment of plastic entered the claimant's eye. Held: the defendant was not liable.

HUTCHISON LJ: . . . The test of foreseeability is an objective one; but the fact that the first defendant was at the time a 15-year-old schoolgirl is not irrelevant. The question for the judge is not whether the actions of the defendant were such as an ordinarily prudent and reasonable adult in the defendant's situation would have realised gave rise to a risk of injury, it is whether an ordinarily prudent and reasonable 15-year-old schoolgirl in the defendant's situation would have realised as much. In that connection both counsel referred us to, and relied upon, the Australian decision in *McHale* v *Watson* (1966) 115 CLR 199 and in particular, the passage in the judgment of Kitto J, at pp. 213–214. I cite a portion of the passage I have referred to, all of which was cited to us by Mr Lee on behalf of the appellant, and which Mr Stephens has adopted as epitomising the correct approach:

> The standard of care being objective, it is no answer for him [that is a child], any more than it is for an adult, to say that the harm he caused was due to his being abnormally slow-witted,

quick-tempered, absent-minded or inexperienced. But it does not follow that he cannot rely in his defence upon a limitation upon the capacity for foresight or prudence, not as being personal to himself, but as being characteristic of humanity at his stage of development and in that sense normal. By doing so he appeals to a standard of ordinariness, to an objective and not a subjective standard.

Mr Stephens also cited to us a passage in the judgment of Owen J at p. 234:

> . . . the standard by which his conduct is to be measured is not that to be expected of a reasonable adult but that reasonably to be expected of a child of the same age, intelligence and experience.

I venture to question the word 'intelligence' in that sentence, but I understand Owen J to be making the same point essentially as was made by Kitto J. It is perhaps also material to have in mind the words of Salmon LJ in *Gough* v *Thorne* [1966] 1 WLR 1387, 1391, which is cited also by Mr Stephens, where he said:

> The question as to whether the plaintiff can be said to have been guilty of contributory negligence depends on whether any ordinary child of 13½ can be expected to have done any more than this child did. I say 'any ordinary child'. I do not mean a paragon of prudence; nor do I mean a scatter-brained child; but the ordinary girl of 13½.

I need say no more about that principle as to the way in which age affects the assessment of negligence because counsel are agreed upon it and, despite the fact that we have been told that there has been a good deal of controversy in other jurisdictions and that there is no direct authority in this jurisdiction, the approach in *McHale* v *Watson* seems to me to have the advantage of obvious, indeed irrefutable, logic . . .

BUTLER-SLOSS LJ: I agree with both judgments and since there has been little authority on the proper approach to the standard of care to be applied to a child, I would like to underline the observations of Hutchison LJ and rely upon two further passages in the persuasive judgment of Kitto J in the High Court of Australia in *McHale* v *Watson* (1966) 115 CLR 199 starting at p. 213:

> In regard to the things which pertain to foresight and prudence, experience, understanding of causes and effects, balance of judgment, thoughtfulness—it is absurd, indeed it is a misuse of language, to speak of normality in relation to persons of all ages taken together. In those things normality is, for children, something different from what normality is for adults; the very concept of normality is a concept of rising levels until 'years of discretion' are attained. The law does not arbitrarily fix upon any particular age for this purpose, and tribunals of fact may well give effect to different views as to the age at which normal adult foresight and prudence are reasonably to be expected in relation to particular sets of circumstances. But up to that stage the normal capacity to exercise those two qualities necessarily means the capacity which is normal for a child of the relevant age; and it seems to me that it would be contrary to the fundamental principle that a person is liable for harm that he causes by falling short of an objective criterion of 'propriety' in his conduct—propriety, that is to say, as determined by a comparison with the standard of care reasonably to be expected in the circumstances from the normal person—to hold that where a child's liability is in question the normal person to be considered is someone other than a child of corresponding age.

I would respectfully endorse those observations as entirely appropriate to English law and I would like to conclude with another passage of Kitto J particularly relevant to today, at p. 216:

> . . . in the absence of relevant statutory provision, children, like everyone else, must accept as they go about in society the risks from which ordinary care on the part of others will not suffice to save them. One such risk is that boys of twelve may behave as boys of twelve . . .

—and I would say that girls of 15 playing together may play as somewhat irresponsible girls of 15. I too would allow this appeal.

### ■ QUESTION

Should the standard of care be looked at from the point of view of the defendant or the claimant? In other words, is it a question of asking whether the defendant acted carelessly or of asking whether the claimant was entitled to expect a greater degree of safety?

NOTES

1. *Children*. In *Ryan* v *Hickson* (1974) 55 DLR 3d 196, a 12-year-old boy was held liable for carelessly driving a snowmobile over rough terrain so as to throw his 9-year-old passenger into the path of a following snowmobile. One reason for holding him liable was that if children engage in adult activities, they must live up to the adult standard of care. Further, the defendant's father was also held liable for failing to exercise adequate supervision or to provide adequate instruction.

2. *The insane*. In *Buckley* v *Smith Transport* [1946] 4 DLR 721 the claimant was driving a tram along Queen Street in Toronto when he was run into by a lorry driven by one Taylor, who was suffering from syphilis of the brain and was under the delusion that he was under remote control from head office. The Ontario Court of Appeal held him not liable, saying that the question is whether or not he understood and appreciated the duty upon him to take care and whether he was disabled, as a result of any delusion, from discharging that duty. Is being struck by a syphilitic truck driver one of the risks of life one must be expected to put up with?

3. *Mental diseases*. In *Morris* v *Marsden* [1952] 1 All ER 925 the defendant was a schizophrenic who attacked the claimant. Stable J held him liable, saying that a person suffering from mental disease will be liable in intentional torts such as battery if he knew the nature and quality of his act even if he did not know it was wrong. See also *White* v *White* [1950] P 39, per Denning LJ.

4. *Impaired functions*. It seems that a person will not be liable if he is suffering from impaired ability but is unaware of that fact. (If he was aware he would be liable.) In *Mansfield* v *Weetabix* [1998] 1 WLR 1263, the defendant driver suffered from starvation of glucose which meant that his brain did not function properly and he crashed into the claimant's shop. The Court of Appeal held that he was not at fault and distinguished *Nettleship* v *Weston* [1971] 2 QB 691 on the ground that that case did not deal with the situation where the actor was unaware of his disability; but was the learner driver there any more to blame than the defendant here? The Court thought that to impose liability would amount to strict liability, but are not the public entitled to expect that they will not be injured by erratic driving whatever the cause?

## SECTION 3: OTHER RELEVANT FACTORS IN THE STANDARD OF CARE OWED

Whether a defendant is in breach of duty requires a decision whether a reasonable man would foresee the danger and regard the risk as unreasonable. This can be a complicated and difficult question, and some of the factors which may be relevant in making such a judgment are outlined below.

---

### *Thompson* v *Smith Shiprepairers Ltd*
Queen's Bench Division [1984] QB 405; [1984] 2 WLR 522; [1984] 1 All ER 881

The claimants worked in the defendants' shipbuilding yard and were subjected to excessive noise in their work, as a result of which they suffered impaired hearing. They had been employed since 1944 or earlier. The defendants knew of the excessive noise, but this was generally regarded as an inescapable feature of shipyard work and the industry did not take the problem seriously. There was no common practice of providing ear protection, and it was not until the early 1960s that effective protection was available, and in 1963 the Ministry of Labour published a pamphlet 'Noise and the Worker' on the dangers of noise for workers. The claimants were not given ear protection until the 1970s. Held: the defendants were liable for the extent by which the hearing problems of the claimants had been exacerbated after 1963. There was no breach before 1963 because of common practice in the industry not to provide protection, and lack of social awareness of the dangers of noise.

MUSTILL J: The plaintiffs allege that the defendants were negligent in the following respects—(i) in failing to recognise the existence of high levels of noise in their shipyards, and the fact that such noise created a risk of irreversible damage to hearing; (ii) in failing to provide any or sufficient ear protection devices, or to give the necessary advice and encouragement for the wearing of such devices as were provided; (iii) in failing to investigate and take advice upon the noise levels in their yards; (iv) in failing to reduce the noise created by work in their yards; (v) in failing to organise the layout and timing of the work so as to minimise the effect of noise. In the first instance I will concentrate on items (i) and (ii), since these are by far the most substantial.

There was general agreement that the principles to be applied when weighing-up allegations of this kind are correctly set out in the following passage from the judgment of Swanwick J in *Stokes* v *Guest, Keen and Nettlefold (Bolts and Nuts) Ltd* [1968] 1 WLR 1776, 1783:

From these authorities I deduce the principles, that the overall test is still the conduct of the reasonable and prudent employer, taking positive thought for the safety of his workers in the light of what he knows or ought to know; where there is a recognised and general practice which has been followed for a substantial period in similar circumstances without mishap, he is entitled to follow it, unless in the light of common sense or newer knowledge it is clearly bad; but, where there is developing knowledge, he must keep reasonably abreast of it and not be too slow to apply it; and where he has in fact greater than average knowledge of the risks, he may be thereby obliged to take more than the average or standard precautions. He must weigh up the risk in terms of the likelihood of injury occurring and the potential consequences if it does; and he must balance against this the probable effectiveness of the precautions that can be taken to meet it and the expense and inconvenience they involve. If he is found to have fallen below the standard to be properly expected of a reasonable and prudent employer in these respects, he is negligent.

I shall direct myself in accordance with this succinct and helpful statement of the law, and will make only one additional comment. In the passage just cited, Swanwick J drew a distinction between a recognised practice followed without mishap, and one which in the light of common sense or increased knowledge is clearly bad. The distinction is indeed valid and sufficient for many cases. The two categories are not, however, exhaustive; as the present actions demonstrate. The practice of leaving employees unprotected against excessive noise had never been followed 'without mishap.' Yet even the plaintiffs have not suggested that it was 'clearly bad,' in the sense of creating a potential liability in negligence, at any time before the mid-1930s. Between the two extremes is a type of risk which is regarded at any given time (although not necessarily later) as an inescapable feature of the industry. The employer is not liable for the consequences of such risks, although subsequent changes in social awareness, or improvements in knowledge and technology, may transfer the risk into the category of those against which the employer can and should take care. It is unnecessary, and perhaps impossible, to give a comprehensive formula for identifying the line between the acceptable and the unacceptable. Nevertheless, the line does exist, and was clearly recognised in *Morris* v *West Hartlepool Steam Navigation Co. Ltd* [1956] AC 552. The speeches in that case show, not that one employer is exonerated simply by proving that other employers are just as negligent, but that the standard of what is negligent is influenced, although not decisively, by the practice in the industry as a whole. In my judgment, this principle applies not only where the breach of duty is said to consist of a failure to take precautions known to be available as a means of combating a known danger, but also where the omission involves an absence of initiative in seeking out knowledge of facts which are not in themselves obvious. The employer must keep up to date, but the court must be slow to blame him for not ploughing a lone furrow.

NOTES

1. In times of fierce competition, when costs must be kept down, there is little incentive to spend money on safety. Mustill J said that there was general apathy about the problems of noise, and it was not until government advice became available that he felt that the employers should have taken action. Does this suggest that the common law is not an effective tool for promoting safety?

2. In *Thompson* the employers were liable for hearing loss caused since 1963, but in *Baxter* v *Harland and Wolff* [1990] IRLR 516, the Northern Ireland Court of Appeal took the period back to 1952 on the ground that the employers should have thought about the issue of noise and sought advice even before the Ministry of Labour's pamphlet of 1963. MacDermott LJ cited *McCafferty* v *Metropolitan Police Receiver* [1977] 2 All ER 756, where it was said that the duty was to take reasonable care to protect the claimant from dangers to safety or health of which the employer knew or ought to have known, and the employer must take steps to keep informed of developments and increased knowledge in the sphere in which he or she operates.

### Latimer v AEC Ltd
Court of Appeal [1952] 2 QB 701; [1952] 1 TLR 1349; [1952] 1 All ER 1302

The defendants owned a factory, and in the floor was cut a channel or conduit in which there flowed an oily cooling agent known as mystic. One day there was a heavy rainstorm and the factory was flooded: the oil rose out of the channel and mixed with the water, and when the flood subsided the whole floor was covered with a thin film of the oily mixture. The defendants put sawdust down on most, but not all, of the floor. The claimant slipped and fell on an untreated part of the floor. It was argued that the defendants should have closed the factory. Held: allowing the appeal, that the defendants were not liable as they had acted as a reasonable employer would have acted.

DENNING LJ: . . . it seems to me that [Pilcher J] has fallen into error by assuming it would be sufficient to constitute negligence that there was a foreseeable risk which the defendants could have avoided by some measure or other, however extreme. That is not the law. It is always necessary to consider what measures the defendant ought to have taken, and to say whether they could reasonably be expected of him. In a converse case, for example, a brave man tries to stop a runaway horse. It is a known risk and a serious risk, but no one would suggest that he could reasonably be expected to stand idly by. It is not negligence on his part to run the risk. So here the employers knew that the floor was slippery and that there was some risk in letting the men work on it; but, still, they could not reasonably be expected to shut down the whole works and send all the men home. In every case of foreseeable risk, it is a matter of balancing the risk against the measures necessary to eliminate it. It is only negligence if, on balance, the defendant did something which he ought not to have done, or omitted to do something which he ought to have done. In this case, in the circumstances of this torrential flood, it is quite clear the defendants did everything they could reasonably be expected to do. It would be quite unreasonable, it seems to me, to expect them to send all the men home. I agree, therefore, that there was no negligence at common law.

■ **QUESTION**

Why should the employers be entitled to make the employees bear the risk of injury? The court assumes there were only two choices open to the employers, but surely there were three:

(a) to close the factory;

(b) to keep it open, without compensation for any injury; and

(c) to keep it open, agreeing to pay compensation to anyone who slipped.

Which choice would a reasonable employer have made?

NOTES

1. A risk of greater damage than normal may increase the obligations of a potential defendant. In *Paris* v *Stepney Borough Council* [1951] AC 367 the claimant was a garage hand with only one eye, who was struck in his only eye by a splinter from a bolt. He was not wearing goggles. The House of Lords, by a majority, held that although the disability did not increase the risk of injury, it did increase the risk of the injury being more serious (i.e. becoming blind rather than one-eyed), and therefore the employers should have supplied him with goggles, even though they need not have done so for a person with two eyes.

2. An increased risk of injury to particular individuals may also be relevant; for example, if children are likely to be present, special precautions may be necessary. In *Haley* v *London Electricity Board* [1965] AC 778 the defendants had dug a trench along a pavement, and as a barrier had placed a punner hammer across it with one end resting on the ground and the other about two feet above it. The claimant was blind and his stick failed to touch the barrier, and he fell and was rendered deaf. The House of Lords held that the presence of blind persons was foreseeable, and the increased likelihood of injury to them obliged the defendants to take precautions which would not be necessary in the case of sighted persons.

---

### *Watt* v *Hertfordshire C.C.*
Court of Appeal [1954] 1 WLR 835; [1954] 2 All ER 368

An accident occurred and a woman was trapped under a heavy lorry about 200–300 yards from a fire station. The fire station had a heavy jack for lifting, but the vehicle (an Austin) which was equipped to carry it was elsewhere, and the jack was loaded onto a Fordson lorry which had no means of securing the jack. On the way to the accident the lorry had to brake suddenly and the jack moved forward, injuring the claimant's ankle. Held: dismissing the appeal, that the defendants were not negligent in sending out the jack unsecured.

SINGLETON LJ: Would the reasonably careful head of the station have done anything other than that which the sub-officer did? I think not. Can it be said, then, that there is a duty on the employers here to have a vehicle built and fitted to carry this jack at all times, or if they have not, not to use the jack for a short journey of 200 or 300 yards? I do not think that that will do.

Asquith LJ, in *Daborn* v *Bath Tramways Motor Co. Ltd*, said, [1946] 2 All ER 333, 336:

In determining whether a party is negligent, the standard of reasonable care is that which is reasonably to be demanded in the circumstances. A relevant circumstance to take into account may be the importance of the end to be served by behaving in this way or in that. As has often been pointed out, if all the trains in this country were restricted to a speed of five miles an hour, there would be fewer accidents, but our national life would be intolerably slowed down. The purpose to be served, if sufficiently important, justifies the assumption of abnormal risk.

The purpose to be served in this case was the saving of life. The men were prepared to take that risk. They were not, in my view, called on to take any risk other than that which normally might be encountered in this service. I agree with Barry J that on the whole of the evidence it would not be right to find that the employers were guilty of any failure of the duty which they owed to their workmen. In my opinion the appeal should be dismissed.

DENNING LJ: It is well settled that in measuring due care you must balance the risk against the measures necessary to eliminate the risk. To that proposition there ought to be added this: you must balance the risk against the end to be achieved. If this accident had occurred in a commercial enterprise without any emergency there could be no doubt that the servant would succeed. But the commercial end to make profit is very different from the human end to save life or limb. The saving of life or limb justifies taking considerable risk, and I am glad to say that there have never been wanting in this country men of courage ready to take those risks, notably in the fire service.

In this case the risk involved in sending out the lorry was not so great as to prohibit the attempt to save life. I quite agree that fire engines, ambulances and doctors' cars should not shoot past the traffic lights when they show a red light. That is because the risk is too great to warrant the incurring of the danger. It is always a question of balancing the risk against the end. I agree that this appeal should be dismissed.

### *Wooldridge* v *Sumner*

Court of Appeal [1963] 2 QB 43; [1962] 2 WLR 616; [1962] 2 All ER 978

The claimant, Edmund Wooldridge, was a photographer who was attending the National Horse Show at White City. The perimeter of the arena was marked by a line of tubs with shrubs in them, and the claimant was standing just behind these. The defendant owned a horse called 'Work of Art' which was ridden by Ronald Holladay. The judge found that in attempting to take a corner the horse was going too fast, and it plunged through the line of tubs, injuring the claimant. Held: allowing the appeal, that the defendant was not liable as, in the heat of the moment, Mr Holladay had merely made an error of judgment and was not negligent.

DIPLOCK LJ: To treat Lord Atkin's statement 'You must take reasonable care to avoid acts or omissions which you can reasonably foresee would be likely to injure your neighbour', [1932] AC 562, 580, as a complete exposition of the law of negligence is to mistake aphorism for exegesis. It does not purport to define what is reasonable care and was directed to identifying the persons to whom the duty to take reasonable care is owed. What is reasonable care in a particular circumstance is a jury question and where, as in a case like this, there is no direct guidance or hindrance from authority it may be answered by inquiring whether the ordinary reasonable man would say that in all the circumstances the defendant's conduct was blameworthy.

The matter has to be looked at from the point of view of the reasonable spectator as well as the reasonable participant; not because of the maxim volenti non fit injuria, but because what a reasonable spectator would expect a participant to do without regarding it as blameworthy is as relevant to what is reasonable care as what a reasonable participant would think was blameworthy conduct in himself. The same idea was expressed by Scrutton LJ in *Hall* v *Brooklands* [1933] 1 KB 205, 214: 'What is reasonable care would depend upon the perils which might be reasonably expected to occur, *and the extent to which the ordinary spectator might be expected to appreciate and take the risk of such perils.*'

A reasonable spectator attending voluntarily to witness any game or competition knows and presumably desires that a reasonable participant will concentrate his attention upon winning, and if the game or competition is a fast-moving one, will have to exercise his judgment and attempt to exert his skill in what, in the analogous context of contributory negligence, is sometimes called 'the agony of the moment.' If the participant does so concentrate his attention and consequently does exercise his judgment and attempt to exert his skill in circumstances of this kind which are inherent in the game or competition in which he is taking part, the question whether any mistake he makes amounts to a breach of duty to take reasonable care must take account of those circumstances.

The law of negligence has always recognised that the standard of care which a reasonable man will exercise depends upon the conditions under which the decision to avoid the act or omission relied upon as negligence has to be taken. The case of the workman engaged on repetitive work in the noise and bustle of the factory is a familiar example. More apposite for present purposes are the collision cases, where a decision has to be made upon the spur of the moment. 'A's negligence makes collision so threatening that though by the appropriate measure B could avoid it, B has not really time to think and by mistake takes the wrong measure. B is not to be held guilty of any negligence and A wholly fails.' (*Admiralty Commissioners* v *S.S. Volute*, [1922] 1 AC 129, 136) A fails not because of his own negligence; there never has been any contributory negligence rule in Admiralty. He fails because B has exercised such care as is reasonable in circumstances in which he has not really time to think. No doubt if he has got into those circumstances as a result of a breach of duty of care which he owes to A, A can succeed upon this antecedent negligence; but a participant in a game or competition gets into the circumstances in which he has no time or very little time to think by his decision to take part in the game or competition at all. It cannot be suggested that the participant, at any rate if he has some modicum of skill, is, by the mere act of participating, in breach of his duty of care to a spectator who is present for the very purpose of watching him do so. If, therefore, in the course of the game or competition, at a moment when he really has not time to think, a participant by mistake takes a wrong measure, he is not, in my view, to be held guilty of any negligence.

Furthermore, the duty which he owes is a duty of care, not a duty of skill. Save where a consensual relationship exists between a plaintiff and a defendant by which the defendant impliedly warrants his skill, a man owes no duty to his neighbour to exercise any special skill beyond that which an ordinary reasonable man would acquire before indulging in the activity in which he is engaged at the relevant time. It may well be that a participant in a game or competition would be guilty of negligence to a spectator if he took part in it when he knew or ought to have known that his lack of skill was such that even if he exerted it to the utmost he was likely to cause injury to a spectator watching him. No question of this arises in the present case. It was common ground that Mr Holladay was an exceptionally skilful and experienced horseman.

The practical result of this analysis of the application of the common law of negligence to participant and spectator would, I think, be expressed by the common man in some such terms as these: 'A person attending a game or competition takes the risk of any damage caused to him by any act of a participant done in the course of and for the purposes of the game or competition notwithstanding that such act may involve an error of judgment or a lapse of skill, unless the participants' conduct is such as to evince a reckless disregard of the spectator's safety.'

■ QUESTION

A horse show is being held in a local field. X takes a corner too fast and the horse ploughs through the hedge bordering the field. Y was leaning on the inside of the hedge watching the show. Z is a passer-by. Both are injured. Who can sue X?

NOTE

For an example of the 'heat of the moment' defence applied to the police, see *Marshall* v *Osmond* [1983] QB 1034, where a police car was chasing a suspect car and, in drawing up alongside it, braked too hard and skidded into it. This was held to be an error of judgement but not negligence.

---

SECTION 4: **A STATUTORY VERSION**

In Australia many states have enacted statutes with the aim of controlling the limits of tort liability. The extract below is from New South Wales and is a general statement of the duty principle. Other parts of the Act deal with causation, voluntary assumption of risk, recreational activities, warnings, contributory negligence, and the calculation of damages.

---

### NEW SOUTH WALES CIVIL LIABILITY ACT 2002

**Division 2 Duty of care**

**5B General principles**

(1) A person is not negligent in failing to take precautions against a risk of harm unless:

    (a) the risk was foreseeable (that is, it is a risk of which the person knew or ought to have known), and

    (b) the risk was not insignificant, and

    (c) in the circumstances, a reasonable person in the person's position would have taken those precautions.

(2) In determining whether a reasonable person would have taken precautions against a risk of harm, the court is to consider the following (amongst other relevant things):

    (a) the probability that the harm would occur if care were not taken,

    (b) the likely seriousness of the harm,

    (c) the burden of taking precautions to avoid the risk of harm,

    (d) the social utility of the activity that creates the risk of harm.

**5C Other principles**

In proceedings relating to liability for negligence:

    (a) the burden of taking precautions to avoid a risk of harm includes the burden of taking precautions to avoid similar risks of harm for which the person may be responsible, and

    (b) the fact that a risk of harm could have been avoided by doing something in a different way does not of itself give rise to or affect liability for the way in which the thing was done, and

    (c) the subsequent taking of action that would (had the action been taken earlier) have avoided a risk of harm does not of itself give rise to or affect liability in respect of the risk and does not of itself constitute an admission of liability in connection with the risk.

# 4

# Causation and Remoteness of Damage

Causation and remoteness of damage are separate but related topics. Once it has been shown that a defendant owed the claimant a duty to take care and was in breach of that duty, liability can still be avoided if it can be shown that the breach did not cause the damage or that the damage was too remote a consequence of the breach.

A causation problem usually occurs when we look at the damage and see that it was actually caused by a number of different factors, or, to put it another way, that a number of factors combining together brought about the damage. The problem is to determine which, if any, of these factors were legally relevant, so as to be able to say that the person responsible for that factor should be liable, perhaps to the exclusion of people responsible for other factors.

A remoteness problem can arise in two different situations: that is where the claimant is a foreseeable claimant and the damage has in fact been caused by the defendant's act, but where the damage is either unpredictable in extent or unpredictable in nature. Injury to a haemophiliac might be an example of the former, and *Re Polemis* (below), where the dropping of a plank into the hold of a ship caused it to explode, is an example of the latter.

## SECTION 1: CAUSATION

There is no simple formula which can test whether an act or event is a legally relevant cause of the damage, and many books and cases content themselves with asking whether the act was a 'substantial' factor in bringing about the harm. The solution is pragmatic rather than theoretical, and is founded as much on social policy as on logic. However, one test which will solve a number of cases, but not all, is the 'but for' test, illustrated by the first case.

### Barnett v Chelsea and Kensington Hospital
Queen's Bench Division [1969] 1 QB 428; [1968] 1 All ER 1068; [1968] 2 WLR 422

The claimant, William Barnett, and two other men were nightwatchmen at the Chelsea College of Science and Technology. At 5.00 a.m. on the morning of New Year's Day 1966, all three shared some tea, and about 20 minutes later they began vomiting. At 8.00 a.m. they went to the defendant hospital and were seen by a nurse who telephoned the doctor on duty. He replied 'Well, I am vomiting myself and I have not been drinking. Tell them to go home and go to bed and call their own doctors . . .'. The three men returned to the college but continued to feel ill, and by 2.00 p.m. the claimant had died. It was shown that he had been poisoned with arsenic, and a coroner's verdict of murder by persons unknown was returned. His widow said the hospital failed to treat her husband. Held: the hospital was not liable.

NEILD J: Without doubt the casualty officer should have seen and examined the deceased. His failure to do either cannot be described as an excusable error as has been submitted. It was negligence. It is unfortunate that he was himself at the time a tired and unwell doctor, but there was no one else to do that which it was his duty to do. Having examined the deceased I think the first and provisional diagnosis would have been one of food poisoning. . . .

It remains to consider whether it is shown that the deceased's death was caused by that negligence or whether, as the defendants have said, the deceased must have died in any event. In his concluding submission Mr Pain submitted that the casualty officer should have examined the deceased and had he done so he would have caused tests to be made which would have indicated the treatment required and that, since the defendants were at fault in these respects, therefore the onus of proof passed to the defendants to show that the appropriate treatment would have failed, and authorities were cited to me. I find myself unable to accept that argument, and I am of the view that the onus of proof remains upon the plaintiff, and I have in mind (without quoting it) the decision cited by Mr Wilmers in *Bonnington Castings Ltd* v *Wardlaw* [1956] AC 613. However, were it otherwise and the onus did pass to the defendants, then I would find that they have discharged it, as I would proceed to show.

There has been put before me a timetable which I think is of much importance. The deceased attended at the casualty department at five or 10 minutes past eight in the morning. If the casualty officer had got up and dressed and come to see the three men and examined them and decided to admit them, the deceased (and Dr Lockett agreed with this) could not have been in bed in a ward before 11 a.m. I accept Dr Goulding's evidence that an intravenous drip would not have been set up before 12 noon, and if potassium loss was suspected it could not have been discovered until 12.30 p.m. Dr Lockett, dealing with this, said: 'If this man had not been treated until after 12 noon the chances of survival were not good.'

Without going in detail into the considerable volume of technical evidence which has been put before me, it seems to me to be the case that when death results from arsenical poisoning it is brought about by two conditions; on the one hand dehydration and on the other disturbance of the enzyme processes. If the principal condition is one of enzyme disturbance—as I am of the view it was here—then the only method of treatment which is likely to succeed is the use of the specific antidote which is commonly called B.A.L. Dr Goulding said in the course of his evidence:

The only way to deal with this is to use the specific B.A.L. I see no reasonable prospect of the deceased being given B.A.L. before the time at which he died—and at a later point in his evidence—I feel that even if fluid loss had been discovered death would have been caused by the enzyme disturbance. Death might have occurred later.

I regard that evidence as very moderate, and it might be a true assessment of the situation to say that there was no chance of B.A.L. being administered before the death of the deceased.

For those reasons, I find that the plaintiff has failed to establish, on the balance of probabilities, that the defendants' negligence caused the death of the deceased.

NOTE

The 'but for' test is perhaps the simplest, and should be tried first, but it cannot solve all problems. For example, Fleming (*Law of Torts*, 9th edn) puts the case of two people carrying candles independently and simultaneously approaching a leaking gas pipe, causing an explosion. Can each claim that the explosion would have happened anyway, even if he or she had not been there?

### *Fairchild* v *Glenhaven Funeral Services*
House of Lords [2003] 1 AC 32; [2002] 3 WLR 89; [2002] 3 All ER 305; [2002] UKHL 22

The claimants developed mesothelioma by exposure to asbestos dust. The disease could be caused by exposure to even a small number of asbestos fibres. The claimants had worked for a number of employers successively and were unable to prove during which employment the disease had been contracted. Held that each employer had materially increased the risk of contracting the disease and all were liable.

LORD BINGHAM

**2** The essential question underlying the appeals may be accurately expressed in this way. If

(1) C was employed at different times and for differing periods by both A and B, and

(2) A and B were both subject to a duty to take reasonable care or to take all practicable measures to prevent C inhaling asbestos dust because of the known risk that asbestos dust (if inhaled) might cause a mesothelioma, and

(3) both A and B were in breach of that duty in relation to C during the periods of C's employment by each of them with the result that during both periods C inhaled excessive quantities of asbestos dust, and

(4) C is found to be suffering from a mesothelioma, and

(5) any cause of C's mesothelioma other than the inhalation of asbestos dust at work can be effectively discounted, but

(6) C cannot (because of the current limits of human science) prove, on the balance of probabilities, that his mesothelioma was the result of his inhaling asbestos dust during his employment by A or during his employment by B or during his employment by A and B taken together,

is C entitled to recover damages against either A or B or against both A and B? To this question (not formulated in these terms) the Court of Appeal (Brooke, Latham and Kay LJJ), in a reserved judgment of the court reported at [2002] 1 WLR 1052, gave a negative answer. It did so because, applying the conventional 'but for' test of tortious liability, it could not be held that C had proved against A that his mesothelioma would probably not have occurred but for the breach of duty by A, nor against B that his mesothelioma would probably not have occurred but for the breach of duty by B, nor against A and B that his mesothelioma would probably not have occurred but for the breach of duty by both A and B together. So C failed against both A and B. The crucial issue on appeal is whether, in the special circumstances of such a case, principle, authority or policy requires or justifies a modified approach to proof of causation.

**33** The present appeals raise an obvious and inescapable clash of policy considerations. On the one hand are the considerations powerfully put by the Court of Appeal ([2002] 1 WLR 1052 at 1080, para 103) which considered the claimants' argument to be not only illogical but

also susceptible of unjust results. It may impose liability for the whole of an insidious disease on an employer with whom the claimant was employed for quite a short time in a long working life, when the claimant is wholly unable to prove on the balance of probabilities that that period of employment had any causative relationship with the inception of the disease. This is far too weighty an edifice to build on the slender foundations of *McGhee* v *National Coal Board* [1973] 1WLR 1, and Lord Bridge has told us in *Wilsher* v *Essex Area Health Authority* [1988] AC 1074 that *McGhee* established no new principle of law at all. If we were to accede to the claimants' arguments, we would be distorting the law to accommodate the exigencies of a very hard case. We would be yielding to a contention that all those who have suffered injury after being exposed to a risk of that injury from which someone else should have protected them should be able to recover compensation even when they are quite unable to prove who was the culprit. In a quite different context Lord Steyn has recently said in *Frost* v *Chief Constable of Yorkshire* [1999] 2 AC 455, 491 that our tort system sometimes results in imperfect justice, but it is the best the common law can do.

The Court of Appeal had in mind that in each of the cases discussed in paras 14–21 above (*Wardlaw, Nicholson, Gardiner, McGhee*) there was only one employer involved. Thus there was a risk that the defendant might be held liable for acts for which he should not be held legally liable but no risk that he would be held liable for damage which (whether legally liable or not) he had not caused. The crux of cases such as the present, if the appellants' argument is upheld, is that an employer may be held liable for damage he has not caused. The risk is the greater where all the employers potentially liable are not before the court. This is so on the facts of each of the three appeals before the House, and is always likely to be so given the long latency of this condition and the likelihood that some employers potentially liable will have gone out of business or disappeared during that period. It can properly be said to be unjust to impose liability on a party who has not been shown, even on a balance of probabilities, to have caused the damage complained of. On the other hand, there is a strong policy argument in favour of compensating those who have suffered grave harm, at the expense of their employers who owed them a duty to protect them against that very harm and failed to do so, when the harm can only have been caused by breach of that duty and when science does not permit the victim accurately to attribute, as between several employers, the precise responsibility for the harm he has suffered. I am of opinion that such injustice as may be involved in imposing liability on a duty-breaking employer in these circumstances is heavily outweighed by the injustice of denying redress to a victim. Were the law otherwise, an employer exposing his employee to asbestos dust could obtain complete immunity against mesothelioma (but not asbestosis) claims by employing only those who had previously been exposed to excessive quantities of asbestos dust. Such a result would reflect no credit on the law. It seems to me, as it did to Lord Wilberforce in *McGhee* [1973] 1 WLR 1 at 7, that

> the employers should be liable for an injury, squarely within the risk which they created and that they, not the pursuer, should suffer the consequence of the impossibility, foreseeably inherent in the nature of his injury, of segregating the precise consequence of their default.

*Conclusion*

**34** To the question posed in paragraph 2 of this opinion I would answer that where conditions (1)–(6) are satisfied C is entitled to recover against both A and B. That conclusion is in my opinion consistent with principle, and also with authority (properly understood). Where those conditions are satisfied, it seems to me just and in accordance with common sense to treat the conduct of A and B in exposing C to a risk to which he should not have been exposed as making a material contribution to the contracting by C of a condition against which it was the duty of A and B to protect him. I consider that this conclusion is fortified by the wider jurisprudence reviewed above. Policy considerations weigh in favour of such a conclusion. It is a conclusion which follows even if either A or B is not before the court. It was not suggested in argument that C's entitlement against either A or B should be for any sum less than the full compensation to which C is entitled, although A and B could of course seek contribution against each other or any other employer liable in respect of the same damage in the ordinary way. No argument on apportionment was addressed to the House. I would in conclusion emphasise that my opinion is directed to cases in which each of the conditions specified in (1)–(6) of paragraph 2 above is satisfied and to no other case. It would be unrealistic to suppose that the principle here affirmed will not over time be the subject of incremental and analogical development. Cases seeking to develop the principle must be decided when and as they arise. For the present, I think it unwise to decide more than is necessary to resolve these three appeals which, for all the foregoing reasons, I concluded should be allowed.

NOTES

1. It is noteworthy that the result means that although one defendant did cause the injury, the other did not and yet both are liable. The occasions when this would be justified must be very rare (for an example see *Cook* v *Lewis* in note 4 *below*) and as Lord Nicholls pointed out (para. 43) considerable restraint is called for in any relaxation of the threshold, and it certainly does not apply merely because a claimant has difficulty in surmounting the burden of proof. The matter is one of judgment and policy, and here the point was that both defendants have been

in breach of their duty to the claimant and it would be unjust if both were exonerated even though one of the negligent parties did injure the claimant.

2. When does the principle in *Fairchild* apply? Need both acts be wrongful? Lord Rogers thought (para. 170) that the principle would apply where, as in *McGhee* v *NCB* [1973] 1 WLR 1, the other possible source of the injury is a similar but lawful act of the same defendant, but he reserved his opinion on whether the principle applies where the other possible source is a similar but lawful act of someone else or is a natural event.

3. The House of Lords did not discuss the question of how to apportion the damages between the defendants. Should it be based on relative length of service with each, or relative density of asbestos dust, or what? An interesting approach to this problem can be seen in the American case of *Sindell* v *Abbott Laboratories* (1980) 2 ALR 4th 1061 where the claimant suffered a malignant tumour, allegedly caused by a drug called DES. This drug was manufactured by a large number of companies and the claimant could not prove who manufactured the pills she had taken. The Supreme Court of California said that each manufacturer should be liable for the proportion of the damages reflected by its market share of the drug. However, if one company had made 51 per cent of the pills on the market could it be liable alone on the basis that it is more likely than not that it was its pills which caused the damage?

4. A case which is much discussed in *Fairchild* is *Cook* v *Lewis* [1952] 1 DLR 1 (and its American equivalent *Summers* v *Tice* (1948) P 2d 1). In *Cook* the claimant, Lewis, while out shooting grouse, was shot by either Cook or his companion Aikenhead. The jury found that one of the two had shot the claimant but were unable to decide which. The Supreme Court of Canada said that both could be liable, arguing that the person who did not shoot the claimant had deprived him of a remedy against the person who did shoot him by carelessly confusing the situation, and was thus required to prove that he was not the person who shot the claimant. In *Fairchild* Lord Nicholls referred to this case saying, 'The unattractive consequence, that one of the hunters will be held liable for an injury he did not in fact inflict, is outweighed by the even less attractive alternative, that the innocent plaintiff should receive no recompense even though one of the negligent hunters injured him. It is this balance . . . which justifies a relaxation in the standard of causation required. Insistence on the normal standard of causation would work an injustice.'

---

### *Gregg* v *Scott*
House of Lords [2005] 2 AC 176; [2005] 2 WLR 268; [2005] 4 All ER 812; [2005] UKHL 2

The claimant went to see Dr Scott about a lump under his arm which the doctor thought was a collection of fatty tissue. Some time later the claimant went to another doctor and he was then diagnosed as suffering from non-Hodgkin's lymphoma (a cancer). The claimant argued that the misdiagnosis by Dr Scott had delayed his treatment for cancer by nine months. Expert evidence showed that the effect of the delay was to reduce his chances of surviving for more than 10 years from 42% to 25%, and the defendant accordingly argued that even if there had been no delay the probability was that the claimant would not have survived anyway. Held: the defendant was not liable as the claimant was unable to show that on a balance of probabilities he would have been cured if the doctor had not been negligent.

LORD HOFFMANN:

*Loss of a chance*

72. The alternative submission was that reduction in the prospect of a favourable outcome ('loss of a chance') should be a recoverable head of damage. There are certainly cases in which it is. *Chaplin* v *Hicks* [1911] 2 KB 786 is a well-known example. The question is whether the principle of that case can apply to a case of clinical negligence such as this.

73. The answer can be derived from three cases in the House of Lords: *Hotson* v *East Berkshire Area Health Authority* [1987] AC 750, *Wilsher* v *Essex Area Health Authority* [1988] AC 1074 and *Fairchild* v *Glenhaven Funeral Services Ltd* [2003] 1 AC 32.

74. In *Hotson* the claimant was a boy who broke his hip when he fell out of a tree. The hospital negligently failed to diagnose the fracture for five days. The hip joint was irreparably damaged by the loss of blood supply to its cartilage. The judge found that the rupture of the blood vessels caused by the fall had probably made the damage inevitable but there was a 25% chance that enough had remained intact to save the joint if the fracture had been diagnosed at the time. He and the Court of Appeal awarded the claimant damages for loss of the 25% chance of a favourable outcome.

75. The House of Lords unanimously reversed this decision. They said that the claimant had not lost a chance because, on the finding of fact, nothing could have been done to save the joint. The outcome had been determined by what happened when he fell out of the tree. Either he had enough surviving blood vessels or he did not. That question had to be decided on a balance of probability and had been decided adversely to the claimant.

76. In *Wilsher* a junior doctor in a special care baby unit negligently put a catheter in the wrong place so that a monitor failed to register that a premature baby was receiving too much oxygen. The baby suffered rentrolental fibroplasia ('RLF'), a condition of the eyes which resulted in blindness. The excessive oxygen was a possible cause of the condition and had increased the chances that it would develop but there were other possible causes: statistics showed a correlation between RLF and various conditions present in the Wilsher baby. But the causal mechanism linking them to RLF was unknown.

77. The Court of Appeal awarded damages for the reduction in the chance of a favourable outcome. Again this was reversed by the House of Lords. The baby's RLF was caused by lack of oxygen or by something else or a combination of causes. The defendant was liable only if the lack of oxygen caused or substantially contributed to the injury. That had to be proved on a balance of probability.

78. In *Fairchild*, the claimant had contracted mesothelioma by exposure to asbestos. The medical evidence was that the condition was probably the result of a cell mutation caused by a single fibre. The claimant had worked with asbestos for more than one employer and could not prove whose fibre had caused his disease. The Court of Appeal said that the cause of the disease was not indeterminate. It had either been caused by the defendant's fibre or it had not. It was for the claimant to prove causation on a balance of probability. The House of Lords accepted that the disease had a determinate cause in one fibre or other but constructed a special rule imposing liability for conduct which only increased the chances of the employee contracting the disease. That rule was restrictively defined in terms which make it inapplicable in this case.

79. What these cases show is that, as Helen Reece points out in an illuminating article ('Losses of Chances in the Law' (1996) 59 MLR 188) the law regards the world as in principle bound by laws of causality. Everything has a determinate cause, even if we do not know what it is. The blood-starved hip joint in *Hotson*, the blindness in *Wilsher*, the mesothelioma in *Fairchild*; each had its cause and it was for the plaintiff to prove that it was an act or omission for which the defendant was responsible. The narrow terms of the exception made to this principle in *Fairchild* only serves to emphasise the strength of the rule. The fact that proof is rendered difficult or impossible because no examination was made at the time, as in *Hotson*, or because medical science cannot provide the answer, as in *Wilsher*, makes no difference. There is no inherent uncertainty about what caused something to happen in the past or about whether something which happened in the past will cause something to happen in the future. Everything is determined by causality. What we lack is knowledge and the law deals with lack of knowledge by the concept of the burden of proof.

80. Similarly in the present case, the progress of Mr Gregg's disease had a determinate cause. It may have been inherent in his genetic make-up at the time when he saw Mr Scott, as *Hotson*'s fate was determined by what happened to his thigh when he fell out of the tree. Or it may, as Mance LJ suggests, have been affected by subsequent events and behaviour for which Dr Scott was not responsible. Medical science does not enable us to say. But the outcome was not random; it was governed by laws of causality and, in the absence of a special rule as in *Fairchild*, inability to establish

that delay in diagnosis caused the reduction in expectation in life cannot be remedied by treating the outcome as having been somehow indeterminate.

81.  This was the view of the Supreme Court of Canada in *Laferrière* v *Lawson* (1991) 78 DLR (4th) 609, a case very like the present. A doctor negligently failed in 1971 to tell a patient that a biopsy had revealed a lump in her breast to be cancerous. She first learned of the cancer in 1975, when the cancer had spread to other parts of the body and died in 1978 at the age of 56. The judge found that earlier treatment would have increased the chances of a favourable outcome but was not satisfied on a balance of probability that it would have prolonged her life. Gonthier J said that although the progress of the cancer was not fully understood, the outcome was determined. It was either something capable of successful treatment or it was not.

> 'Even though our understanding of medical matters is often limited, I am not prepared to conclude that particular medical conditions should be treated for purposes of causation as the equivalent of diffuse elements of pure chance, analogous to the non-specific factors of fate or fortune which influence the outcome of a lottery.' (p. 656)

82.  One striking exception to the assumption that everything is determined by impersonal laws of causality is the actions of human beings. The law treats human beings as having free will and the ability to choose between different courses of action, however strong may be the reasons for them to choose one course rather than another. This may provide part of the explanation for why in some cases damages are awarded for the loss of a chance of gaining an advantage or avoiding a disadvantage which depends upon the independent action of another person: see *Allied Maples Group Ltd* v *Simmons & Simmons* [1995] 1 WLR 1602 and the cases there cited.

83.  But the true basis of these cases is a good deal more complex. The fact that one cannot prove as a matter of necessary causation that someone would have done something is no reason why one should not prove that he was more likely than not to have done it. So, for example, the law distinguishes between cases in which the outcome depends upon what the claimant himself (*McWilliams* v *Sir William Arrol & Co* [1962] 1 WLR 295) or someone for whom the defendant is responsible (*Bolitho* v *City and Hackney Health Authority* [1998] AC 232) would have done, and cases in which it depends upon what some third party would have done. In the first class of cases the claimant must prove on a balance of probability that he or the defendant would have acted so as to produce a favourable outcome. In the latter class, he may recover for loss of the chance that the third party would have so acted. This apparently arbitrary distinction obviously rests on grounds of policy. In addition, most of the cases in which there has been recovery for loss of a chance have involved financial loss, where the chance can itself plausibly be characterised as an item of property, like a lottery ticket. It is however unnecessary to discuss these decisions because they obviously do not cover the present case.

84.  Academic writers have suggested that in cases of clinical negligence, the need to prove causation is too restrictive of liability. This argument has appealed to judges in some jurisdictions; in some, but not all, of the States of the United States and most recently in New South Wales and Ireland: *Rufo* v *Hosking* (1 November 2004) [2004] NSWCA 391); *Philp* v *Ryan* (17 December 2004) [2004] 1 IESC 105. In the present case it is urged that Mr Gregg has suffered a wrong and ought to have a remedy. Living for more than 10 years is something of great value to him and he should be compensated for the possibility that the delay in diagnosis may have reduced his chances of doing so. In effect, the appellant submits that the exceptional rule in *Fairchild* should be generalised and damages awarded in all cases in which the defendant may have caused an injury and has increased the likelihood of the injury being suffered. In the present case, it is alleged that Dr Scott may have caused a reduction in Mr Gregg's expectation of life and that he increased the likelihood that his life would be shortened by the disease.

85.  It should first be noted that adopting such a rule would involve abandoning a good deal of authority. The rule which the House is asked to adopt is the very rule which it rejected in *Wilsher*'s case [1988] AC 1074. Yet *Wilsher*'s case was expressly approved by the House in *Fairchild* [2003] 1 AC 32. *Hotson* [1987] AC 750 too would have to be overruled. Furthermore, the House would be dismantling all the qualifications and restrictions with which it so recently hedged the *Fairchild* exception. There seem to me to be no new arguments or change of circumstances which could justify such a radical departure from precedent.

NOTES

1. Lord Nicholls dissented by accepting the 'loss of a chance' argument. He said 'In order to achieve a just result in such cases the law defines the claimant's actionable damage more narrowly by reference to the *opportunity* the claimant lost, rather than by reference to the loss of the desired *outcome* which was never within his control. In adopting this approach the law does not depart from the principle that the claimant must prove actionable damage on the balance of probability. The law adheres to this principle but defines actionable damage in different, more appropriate terms. The law treats the claimant's loss of his opportunity or chance as itself actionable damage. The claimant must prove this loss on balance of probability. The court will then measure this loss as best it may.' Lord Hope also dissented on similar grounds, adding that once liability had been established damages would need to be reduced. This should be done by calculating what the damages would have been if the claimant would have made a full recovery and reduce this on the basis of the claimant's condition (i.e. his chances of recovery) at the time of the negligence. In this case the judge at first instance thought a reduction of 80% to be appropriate.

2. One difficulty raised by this case is the task of assessing the chances of something happening in the future. Here the court found that the chances of survival had reduced from 42% to 25%. How can such precise figures be arrived at? Expert witnesses would clearly have considerable power and responsibility. However one advantage of the decision is that the courts do not have to make such precise findings, but only have to decide whether there was a more than 50% chance—i.e. a balance of probabilities.

3. Another problem is that a person who establishes a 51% chance gets full damages whereas someone with a 49% chance gets nothing. Should the damages of the former be reduced? (But this would raise the issue in note 2). However the sense of the majority judgments is that the House is rejecting the idea of proportional damages based on the precise degree of probability, both in respect of liability and measurement of damages.

4. For a comment on this case see Stapleton, 'Loss of a chance of cure from cancer' (2005) 68 MLR 996.

---

### Smith v Littlewoods
House of Lords [1987] AC 241; [1987] 1 All ER 710; [1987] 2 WLR 480

The Littlewoods Organisation purchased the Regal Cinema in Dunfermline, with right of entry from 31 May 1976. Thereafter the cinema remained empty, but by the middle of June it was regularly being broken into, mainly by children, and damage was being caused. On one occasion a small fire had been started. Contractors employed by Littlewoods knew about the vandalism but Littlewoods did not. On 5 July 1976 a fire was deliberately started by vandals inside the cinema, and the fire spread to the property of the two pursuers, owners of the Maloco Cafe, and the minister of St Paul's Church. It was alleged that the defenders should have prevented the vandals gaining access to the cinema. Held: dismissing the appeal, that the defenders were not liable as they did not know of the earlier acts of vandalism and were thus not under any duty to the pursuers.

LORD GOFF: My Lords, the Lord President founded his judgment on the proposition that the defenders, who were both owners and occupiers of the cinema, were under a general duty to take reasonable care for the safety of premises in the neighbourhood.

Now if this proposition is understood as relating to a general duty to take reasonable care *not to cause damage* to premises in the neighbourhood (as I believe that the Lord President intended it to be understood) then it is unexceptionable. But it must not be overlooked that a problem arises when the pursuer is seeking to hold the defender responsible for having failed to *prevent* a third party from causing damage to the pursuer or his property by the third party's own deliberate wrongdoing. In such a case, it is not possible to invoke a general duty of care: for it is well recognised that there is no *general* duty of care to prevent third parties from causing such damage. The point is expressed very clearly in *Hart and Honoré, Causation in the Law*, 2nd ed. (1985), when the authors state, at pp. 196–197:

> The law might acknowledge a general principle that, whenever the harmful conduct of another is reasonably foreseeable, it is our duty to take precautions against it . . . But, up to now, no legal system has gone so far as this . . .

The same point is made in *Fleming, The Law of Torts*, 6th ed. (1983), where it is said, at p. 200: 'there is certainly no *general* duty to protect others against theft or loss.' I wish to add that no such general duty exists even between those who are neighbours in the sense of being occupiers of adjoining premises. There is no general duty upon a householder that he should act as a watchdog, or that his house should act as a bastion, to protect his neighbour's house . . .

Another statement of principle, which has been much quoted, is the observation of Lord Sumner in *Weld-Blundell* v *Stephens* [1920] AC 956, when he said, at p. 986: 'In general . . . even though A is in fault he is not responsible for injury to C which B, a stranger to him, deliberately chooses to do.' This dictum may be read as expressing the general idea that the voluntary act of another, independent of the defender's fault, is regarded as a novus actus interveniens which, to use the old metaphor, 'breaks the chain of causation.' But it also expresses a general perception that we ought not to be held responsible in law for the deliberate wrongdoing of others. Of course, if a duty of care is imposed to guard against deliberate wrongdoing by others, it can hardly be said that the harmful effects of such wrongdoing are not caused by such breach of duty. We are therefore thrown back to the duty of care. But one thing is clear, and that is that liability in negligence for harm caused by the deliberate wrongdoing of others cannot be founded simply upon foreseeability that the pursuer will suffer loss or damage by reason of such wrongdoing. There is no such general principle. We have therefore to identify the circumstances in which such liability may be imposed.

That there are special circumstances in which a defender may be held responsible in law for injuries suffered by the pursuer through a third party's deliberate wrongdoing is not in doubt. For example, a duty of care may arise from a relationship between the parties, which gives rise to an imposition or assumption of responsibility upon or by the defender, as in *Stansbie* v *Troman* [1948] 2 KB 48, where such responsibility was held to arise from a contract. In that case a decorator, left alone on the premises by the householder's wife, was held liable when he went out leaving the door on the latch, and a thief entered the house and stole property. Such responsibility might well be held to exist in other cases where there is no contract, as for example where a person left alone in a house has entered as a licensee of the occupier. . . .

These are all special cases. But there is a more general circumstance in which a defender may be held liable in negligence to the pursuer although the immediate cause of the damage suffered by the pursuer is the deliberate wrongdoing of another. This may occur where the defender negligently causes or permits to be created a source of danger, and it is reasonably foreseeable that third parties may interfere with it and, sparking off the danger, thereby cause damage to persons in the position of the pursuer. The classic example of such a case is, perhaps, *Haynes* v *Harwood* [1935] 1 KB 146, where the defendant's carter left a horse-drawn van unattended in a crowded street, and the horses bolted when a boy threw a stone at them. A police officer who suffered injury in stopping the horses before they injured a woman and children was held to be entitled to recover damages from the defendant. There, of course, the defendant's servant had created a source of danger by leaving his horses unattended in a busy street. Many different things might have caused them to bolt—a sudden noise or movement, for example, or, as happened, the deliberate action of a mischievous boy. But all such events were examples of the very sort of thing which the defendant's servant ought reasonably to have foreseen and to have guarded against by taking appropriate precautions. In such a case, Lord Sumner's dictum (*Weld-Blundell* v *Stephens* [1920] AC 956, 986) can have no application to exclude liability.

*Haynes* v *Harwood* was a case concerned with the creation of a source of danger in a public place. We are concerned in the present case with an allegation that the defenders should be held liable for the consequences of deliberate wrongdoing by others who were trespassers on the defenders' property. In such a case it may be said that the defenders are entitled to use their property as their own and so should not be held liable if, for example, trespassers interfere with dangerous things on their land. But this is, I consider, too sweeping a proposition. It is well established that an occupier of land may be liable to a trespasser who has suffered injury on his land; though in *Herrington* v *British Railways Board* [1972] AC 877, in which the nature and scope of such liability was reconsidered by your Lordships' House, the standard of care so imposed on occupiers was drawn narrowly so as to take proper account of the rights of occupiers to enjoy the use of their land. It is, in my opinion, consistent with the existence of such liability that an occupier who negligently causes or permits a source of danger to be created on his land, and can reasonably foresee that third parties may trespass on his land and, interfering with the source of danger, may spark it off, thereby causing damage to the person or property of those in the vicinity, should be held liable to such a person for damage so caused to him. It is useful to take the example of a fire hazard, not only because that is the relevant hazard which is alleged to have existed in the present case, but also because of the intrinsically dangerous nature of fire hazards as regards neighbouring property. Let me give an example of circumstances in which an occupier of land might be held liable for damage so caused. Suppose that a person is deputed to buy a substantial quantity of fireworks for a village fireworks display on Guy Fawkes night. He stores them, as usual, in an unlocked garden shed abutting onto a neighbouring house. It is well known that he does this. Mischievous boys from the village enter as trespassers and, playing with the fireworks, cause a serious fire which spreads to and burns down the neighbouring house. Liability might well be imposed in such a case; for, having regard to the dangerous and tempting nature of fireworks, interference by naughty children was the very thing which, in the circumstances, the purchaser of the fireworks ought to have guarded against.

But liability should only be imposed under this principle in cases where the defender has negligently caused or permitted the creation of a source of danger on his land, and where it is foreseeable that third parties may trespass on his land and spark it off, thereby damaging the pursuer or his property. Moreover it is not to be forgotten that, in ordinary households in this country, there are nowadays many things which might be described as possible sources of fire if interfered with by third parties, ranging from matches and firelighters to electric irons and gas cookers and even oil-fired central heating systems. These are commonplaces of modern life; and it would be quite wrong if householders were to be held liable in negligence for acting in a socially acceptable manner. No doubt the question whether liability should be imposed on defenders in a case where a source of danger on his land has been sparked off by the deliberate wrongdoing of a third party is a question to be decided on the facts of each case, and it would, I think, be wrong for your Lordships' House to anticipate the manner in which the law may develop: but I cannot help thinking that cases where liability will be so imposed are likely to be very rare.

There is another basis upon which a defender may be held liable for damage to neighbouring property caused by a fire started on his (the defender's) property by the deliberate wrongdoing of a third party. This arises where he has knowledge or means of knowledge that a third party has created or is creating a risk of fire, or indeed has started a fire, on his premises, and then fails to take such steps as are reasonably open to him (in the limited sense explained by Lord Wilberforce in *Goldman* v *Hargrave* [1967] 1 AC 645, 663–664) to prevent any such fire from damaging neighbouring property. If, for example, an occupier of property has knowledge, or means of knowledge, that intruders are in the habit of trespassing upon his property and starting fires there, thereby creating a risk that fire may spread to and damage neighbouring property, a duty to take reasonable steps to prevent such damage may be held to fall upon him. He could, for example, take reasonable steps to keep the intruders out. He could also inform the police; or he could warn his neighbours and invite their assistance. If the defender is a person of substantial means, for example a large public company, he might even be expected to employ some agency to keep a watch on the premises. What is reasonably required would, of course, depend on the particular facts of the case. I observe that, in *Goldman* v *Hargrave*, such liability was held to sound in nuisance; but it is difficult to believe that, in this respect, there can be any material distinction between liability in nuisance and liability in negligence. . . .

I wish to emphasise that I do not think that the problem in these cases can be solved simply through the mechanism of foreseeability. When a duty *is* cast upon a person to take precautions against the wrongdoing of third parties, the ordinary standard of foreseeability applies and so the possibility of such wrongdoing does not have to be very great before liability is imposed. I do not myself subscribe to the opinion that liability for the wrongdoing of others is limited because of the unpredictability of human conduct. So, for example, in *Haynes* v *Harwood* [1935] 1 KB 146, liability was imposed although it cannot have been at all likely that a small boy would throw a stone at the horses left unattended in the public road; and in *Stansbie* v *Troman* [1948] 2 KB 48, liability was imposed although it cannot have been at all likely that a thief would take advantage of the fact that the defendant left the door on the latch while he was out. Per contra, there is at present no general duty at common law to prevent persons from harming others by their deliberate wrongdoing, however foreseeable such harm may be if the defender does not take steps to prevent it.

NOTES
1. In *Stansbie* v *Troman* [1948] 2 KB 48, mentioned above, a decorator (Stansbie) was working alone in Mr Troman's house, and he left to get some wallpaper, leaving the door unlocked. While he was away a thief entered the property and stole £334. The decorator was held liable on the basis that he had increased the risk of theft. The chances of a thief appearing at that time were presumably small, and anyway, even if the door had been locked, a persistent thief could have broken in. Would this case be decided the same way today and, if so, on what basis? If a guest of the householder had property stolen could the guest sue?
2. There have been a number of other cases on this problem of liability for the intervening act of a third party. See *Lamb* v *Camden Borough Council* [1981] QB 625 and *Knightley* v *Johns* [1982] 1 WLR 349.

## SECTION 2: REMOTENESS OF DAMAGE

Even if the defendant's act caused the damage, liability can still be excluded if the damage was too remote, that is if the *kind* of damage was an unforeseeable consequence of the act. There has been a great deal of argument about this subject, but it may be that the different theories do not lead to very different results.

One problem is the relationship between this concept and duty of care, for some cases can be decided by application of either concept (e.g. *Tremain* v *Pike* [1969] 3 All ER 1303), and a number of cases on such topics as economic loss and nervous shock were once regarded as remoteness cases, whereas now they are seen as duty cases. One way to illustrate the difference is by the facts (but not the decision) in *Smith* v *London South Western Rly* (1870) LR 6 CP 14. The defendant's employees had cut some hedge trimmings which were laid in heaps alongside a railway line, and a passing locomotive set fire to one of the heaps. The fire spread across a stubble field 200 yards wide, across a road, and finally burnt the claimant's cottage. If we assume that the fire at the cottage was unforeseeable, for example because the road would have acted as a fire break, the position is this: if the claimant did *not* own the field there is no liability because no duty was owed to him since he was not a foreseeable claimant, having no property that was likely to be damaged. But if he *did* own the field he becomes a foreseeable claimant, and the question becomes one of remoteness: for how much damage can he recover?

### Re Polemis
Court of Appeal [1921] 3 KB 560; 90 LJKB 1353; 126 LJ 154

Messrs Polemis and Boyazides chartered a ship called the *Thrasyvoulos* to Furness, Withy & Co. At Lisbon the ship loaded cargo for Casablanca, which included a number of drums of petrol, some of which leaked on the voyage due to heavy weather. At Casablanca some stevedores negligently dislodged a plank which fell into the hold, and a spark ignited the petrol vapour from the drums and a fire started, which ultimately destroyed the ship. The arbitrators found that 'the causing of the spark could not reasonably have been anticipated from the falling of the board, though some damage to the ship might reasonably have been anticipated'. Held: dismissing the appeal, that the charterers (as employers of the stevedores) were liable for the destruction of the ship.

BANKES LJ: In the present case the arbitrators have found as a fact that the falling of the plank was due to the negligence of the defendants' servants. The fire appears to me to have been directly caused by the falling of the plank. Under these circumstances I consider that it is immaterial that the causing of the spark by the falling of the plank could not have been reasonably anticipated. The appellants' junior counsel sought to draw a distinction between the anticipation of the extent of damage resulting from a negligent act, and the anticipation of the type of damage resulting from such an act. He admitted that it could not lie in the mouth of a person whose negligent act had caused damage to say that he could not reasonably have foreseen the extent of the damage, but he contended that the negligent person was entitled to rely upon the fact that he could not reasonably have anticipated the type of damage which resulted from his negligent act. I do not think that the distinction can be admitted. Given the breach of duty which constitutes the negligence, and given the damage as a direct result of that negligence, the anticipations of the person whose negligent act has produced the damage appear to me to be irrelevant. I consider that the damages claimed are not too remote . . .

SCRUTTON LJ: The second defence is that the damage is too remote from the negligence, as it could not be reasonably foreseen as a consequence. On this head we were referred to a number of well known cases in which vague language, which I cannot think to be really helpful, has been used in an attempt to define the point at which damage becomes too remote from, or not sufficiently directly caused by, the breach of duty, which is the original cause of action, to be recoverable. For instance, I cannot think it useful to say the damage must be the natural and probable result. This suggests that there are results which are natural but not probable, and other results which are probable but not natural. I am not sure what either adjective means in this connection; if they mean the same thing, two need not be used; if they mean different things, the difference between them should be defined. And as to many cases of fact in which the distinction has been drawn, it is difficult to see why one case should be decided one way and one another . . . To determine whether an act is negligent, it is relevant to determine whether any reasonable person would foresee that the act would cause damage; if he would not, the act is not negligent. But if the act would or might probably cause damage, the fact that the damage it in fact causes is not the exact kind of damage one would expect is immaterial, so long as the damage is in fact directly traceable to the negligent act, and not due to the operation of independent causes having no connection with the negligent act, except that they could not avoid its results. Once the act is negligent, the fact that its exact operation was not foreseen is immaterial. . . . In the present case it was negligent in discharging cargo to knock down the planks of the temporary staging, for they might easily cause some damage either to workmen, or cargo, or the ship. The fact that they did directly produce an unexpected result, a spark in an atmosphere of petrol vapour which caused a fire, does not relieve the person who was negligent from the damage which his negligent act directly caused.

NOTES
1. This case is no longer regarded as law following the decision in *The Wagon Mound* (below), but it is necessary to know about it because of the extensive debate on the subject of remoteness and the various tests which have been adopted. Note also the dictum of Lord Sumner in *Weld Blundell* v *Stephens* [1920] AC 956, where he said that foresight 'goes to culpability, not to compensation', a view which was condemned in *The Wagon Mound*. For a discussion of the *Polemis* rule see Davies, 'The Road from Morocco' (1982) 45 MLR 534.

2. This test required *some* damage to be foreseeable and to have occurred, for otherwise there would be no duty or breach of duty. Thus, the charterers were at least liable for the dent in the steel plating in the hold when the plank fell, but the question was whether they were liable for more. It would not have applied if the claimants had suffered no foreseeable damage at all. For a discussion of this problem, see Goodhart, 'The imaginary necktie and the rule in *Re Polemis'* (1952) 68 LQR 514.

---

### The Wagon Mound (No. 1)
Privy Council [1961] AC 388; [1961] 1 All ER 404; [1961] 2 WLR 126

The defendants, Overseas Tankship (UK) Ltd, were charterers of the *SS Wagon Mound*, which was moored at the Caltex Wharf in Sydney Harbour. On 30 October 1951 they negligently allowed a quantity of bunkering oil to spill into the harbour, and some of this drifted over to the Sheerlegs Wharf which was owned by the claimants, Morts Dock and Engineering Co. The manager of the wharf asked the manager of Caltex Oil whether it was safe to continue welding operations and was told that the flammability of bunkering oil in sea water was such that it was. However, later that day a fire broke out at the wharf, apparently caused by molten metal falling on some cotton waste which was lying on a piece of debris, which set fire to the surrounding oil. The trial judge found that the defendant could not reasonably be expected to have known that the oil was capable of being set on fire when spread on water. The claimants not only suffered loss by fire, but also suffered foreseeable loss caused by oil congealing on their slipways. Held: allowing the appeal, that the defendants were not liable.

VISCOUNT SIMONDS: Enough has been said to show that the authority of *Polemis* has been severely shaken though lip-service has from time to time been paid to it. In their Lordships' opinion it should no longer be regarded as good law. It is not probable that many cases will for that reason have a different result, though it is hoped that the law will be thereby simplified, and that in some cases, at least, palpable injustice will be avoided. For it does not seem consonant with current ideas of justice or morality that for an act of negligence, however slight or venial, which results in some trivial foreseeable damage the actor should be liable for all consequences however unforeseeable and however grave, so long as they can be said to be 'direct.' It is a principle of civil liability, subject only to qualifications which have no present relevance that a man must be considered to be responsible for the probable consequences of his act. To demand more of him is too harsh a rule, to demand less is to ignore that civilised order requires the observance of a minimum standard of behaviour.

This concept applied to the slowly developing law of negligence has led to a great variety of expressions which can, as it appears to their Lordships, be harmonised with little difficulty with the single exception of the so-called rule in *Polemis*. For, if it is asked why a man should be responsible for the natural or necessary or probable consequences of his act (or any other similar description of them) the answer is that it is not because they are natural or necessary or probable, but because, since they have this quality, it is judged by the standard of the reasonable man that he ought to have foreseen them. Thus it is that over and over again it has happened that in different judgments in the same case, and sometimes in a single judgment, liability for a consequence has been imposed on the ground that it was reasonably foreseeable or, alternatively, on the ground that it was natural or necessary or probable. The two grounds have been treated as conterminous, and so they largely are. But, where they are not, the question arises to which the wrong answer was given in *Polemis*. For, if some limitation must be imposed upon the consequences for which the negligent actor is to be held responsible—and all are agreed that some limitation there must be—why should that test (reasonable foreseeability) be rejected which, since he is judged by what the reasonable man ought to foresee, corresponds with the common conscience of mankind, and a test (the 'direct' consequence) be substituted which leads to nowhere but the never-ending and insoluble problems of causation. 'The lawyer,' said Sir Frederick Pollock, 'cannot afford to adventure himself with philosophers in the logical and metaphysical controversies that beset the idea of cause.' Yet this is just what he has most unfortunately done and must continue to do if the rule in *Polemis* is to prevail. A conspicuous example occurs when the actor seeks to escape liability on the ground that the 'chain of causation' is broken by a 'nova causa' or 'novus actus interveniens.' . . .

At an early stage in this judgment their Lordships intimated that they would deal with the proposition which can best be stated by reference to the well-known dictum of Lord Sumner: 'This however goes to culpability not to compensation.' It is with the greatest respect to that very learned judge and to those who have echoed his words, that their Lordships find themselves bound to state their view that this proposition is fundamentally false.

It is, no doubt, proper when considering tortious liability for negligence to analyse its elements and to say that the plaintiff must prove a duty owed to him by the defendant, a breach of that duty by the defendant, and consequent damage. But there can be no liability until the damage has been done. It is not the act but the consequences on which tortious liability is founded. Just as (as it has been said) there is no such thing as negligence in the air, so there is no such thing as liability in the air. Suppose an action brought by A for damage caused by the carelessness (a neutral word) of B, for example, a fire caused by the careless spillage of oil. It may, of course, become relevant to know what duty B owed to A, but the only liability that is in question is the liability for damage by fire. It is vain to isolate the liability from its context and to say that B is or is not liable, and then to ask for what damage he is liable. For his liability is in respect of that damage and no other. If, as admittedly it is, B's liability (culpability) depends on the reasonable foreseeability of the consequent damage, how is that to be determined except by the foreseeability of the damage which in fact happened—the damage in suit? And, if that damage is unforeseeable so as to displace liability at large, how can the liability be restored so as to make compensation payable?

But, it is said, a different position arises if B's careless act has been shown to be negligent and has caused some foreseeable damage to A. Their Lordships have already observed that to hold B liable for consequences however unforeseeable of a careless act, if, but only if, he is at the same time liable for some other damage however trivial, appears to be neither logical nor just. This becomes more clear if it is supposed that similar unforeseeable damage is suffered by A and C but other foreseeable damage, for which B is liable, by A only. A system of law which would hold B liable to A but not to C for the similar damage suffered by each of them could not easily be defended. Fortunately, the attempt is not necessary. For the same fallacy is at the root of the proposition. It is irrelevant to the question whether B is liable for unforeseeable damage that he is liable for foreseeable damage, as irrelevant as would the fact that he had trespassed on Whiteacre be to the question whether he has trespassed on Blackacre. Again, suppose a claim by A for damage by fire by the careless act of B. Of what relevance is it to that claim that he has another claim arising out of the same careless act? It would surely not prejudice his claim if that other claim failed: it cannot assist it if it succeeds. Each of them rests on its own bottom, and will fail if it can be established that the damage could not reasonably be foreseen. We have come back to the plain common sense stated by Lord Russell of Killowen in *Bourhill* v *Young* [1943] AC 92, 101. As Denning LJ said in *King* v *Phillips* [1953] 1 QB 429: 'there can be no doubt since *Bourhill* v *Young* that the test of *liability for shock* is foreseeability of *injury by shock*.' Their Lordships substitute the word 'fire' for 'shock' and endorse this statement of the law.

NOTES

1. For a discussion of this and the following case, see Dias, 'Remoteness of Damages and Legal Policy' [1962] CLJ 178, and 'Trouble on Oiled Waters' [1967] CLJ 62. For a modern analysis see Staunch, 'Risk and Remoteness of Damage in Negligence' (2001) 64 MLR 191.

2. It may be that foreseeability by itself is not the whole story, for other, often unexpressed, factors may also be relevant (see below). Thus, in *March* v *Stramare* (1991) ALR 423, McHugh J said (in a minority judgment):

Once it is recognised that foreseeability is not the exclusive test of remoteness and that policy-based rules, disguised as causation principles, are also being used to limit responsibility for occasioning damage, the rationalisation of the rules concerning remoteness of damage requires an approach which incorporates the issue of foreseeability but also enables other policy factors to be articulated and examined.

One such approach, and the one I favour, is the 'scope of the risk' test which has much support among academic writers as well as the support of Denning LJ in *Roe* v *Minister of Health* [1954] 2 QB 66 at 85, where his Lordship said:

'Starting with the proposition that a negligent person should be liable, within reason, for the consequences of his conduct, the extent of his liability is to be found by asking the one question: Is the consequence *fairly* to be regarded as within the risk created by the negligence? If so, the negligent person is liable for it: but otherwise not' (my emphasis).

Damage will be a consequence of the risk if it is the kind of damage which should have been reasonably foreseen. However, the precise damage need not have been foreseen. It is sufficient if damage of the kind which occurred could have been foreseen in a general way: *Hughes* v *Lord Advocate* [1963] AC 837. But the 'scope of the risk' test enables more than foreseeability of damage to be considered. As Fleming points out (*The Law of Torts*, 7th ed, p. 193), it also enables allowance to:

'. . . be made to such other pertinent factors as the purpose of the legal rule violated by the defendant, analogies drawn from accepted patterns of past decisions, general community notions regarding the allocation of "blame" as well as supervening considerations of judicial policy bearing on accident prevention, loss distribution and insurance.'

3. The Privy Council left open the question whether the foresight test applies to torts of strict liability, and there is some doubt whether it applies in trespass. In the Canadian case of *Allen* v *Mount Sinai Hospital* (1980) 109 DLR 3d 634 (a case of medical battery), Linden J said 'In battery, however, any and all damage is recoverable, if it results from the wrongful act, whether it is foreseeable or not.' However, in the New Zealand case of *Mayfair* v *Pears* [1987] 1 NZLR 459, the Court of Appeal agreed that the foresight test may in some cases be too benevolent to a trespasser, but refused to lay down any hard and fast rule of remoteness, saying the rules of remoteness are intended to 'limit the amounts recoverable by the plaintiff [claimant] to those that are not only connected to the act but which are reasonable having regard to its nature and the interests of the parties and society'. (The defendant was held not liable for a fire which burnt down a building owned by the claimant. The fire started accidentally in the defendant's car which was unlawfully parked on the claimant's land.)

---

### The Wagon Mound (No. 2)
Privy Council [1967] 1 AC 617; [1966] 1 All ER 709; [1966] 3 WLR 498

This case arose out of the same fire as in *The Wagon Mound No. 1*, but the claimant here, Miller Steamship Pty, was the owner of the ships, *The Corrimal* and *The Audrey D.*, which were lying alongside Sheerlegs Wharf. The trial judge in this action made significantly different findings of fact, and the Privy Council held the defendants were liable.

LORD REID: The findings of the learned trial judge are as follows:

(1) Reasonable people in the position of the officers of the *Wagon Mound* would regard the furnace oil as very difficult to ignite upon water. (2) Their personal experience would probably have been that this had very rarely happened. (3) If they had given attention to the risk of fire from the spillage, they would have regarded it as a possibility, but one which could become an actuality only in very exceptional circumstances. (4) They would have considered the chances of the required exceptional circumstances happening whilst the oil remained spread on the harbour waters as being remote. (5) I find that the occurrence of damage to the plaintiff's property as a result of the spillage was not reasonably foreseeable by those for

whose acts the defendant would be responsible. (6) I find that the spillage of oil was brought about by the careless conduct of persons for whose acts the defendant would be responsible. (7) I find that the spillage of oil was a cause of damage to the property of each of the plaintiffs. (8) Having regard to those findings, and because of finding (5), I hold that the claim of each of the plaintiffs, framed in negligence, fails.

. . .

The crucial finding of Walsh J in this case is in finding (5): that the damage was 'not reasonably foreseeable by those for whose acts the defendant would be responsible.' That is not a primary finding of fact but an inference from the other findings, and it is clear from the learned judge's judgment that in drawing this inference he was to a large extent influenced by his view of the law. The vital parts of the findings of fact which have already been set out in full are (1) that the officers of the *Wagon Mound* [1961] AC 388 'would regard furnace oil as very difficult to ignite upon water'—not that they would regard this as impossible; (2) that their experience would probably have been 'that this had very rarely happened'—not that they would never have heard of a case where it had happened, and (3) that they would have regarded it as a 'possibility, but one which could become an actuality only in very exceptional circumstances'—not, as in *The Wagon Mound (No. 1)*, that they could not reasonably be expected to have known that this oil was capable of being set afire when spread on water. The question which must now be determined is whether these differences between the findings in the two cases do or do not lead to different results in law.

In *The Wagon Mound (No. 1)* the Board were not concerned with degrees of foreseeability because the finding was that the fire was not foreseeable at all. So Lord Simonds had no cause to amplify the statement that the 'essential factor in determining liability is whether the damage is of such a kind as the reasonable man should have foreseen.' But here the findings show that some risk of fire would have been present to the mind of a reasonable man in the shoes of the ship's chief engineer. So the first question must be what is the precise meaning to be attached in this context to the words 'foreseeable' and 'reasonably foreseeable.'

Before *Bolton* v *Stone* [1951] AC 850 the cases had fallen into two classes: (1) those where, before the event, the risk of its happening would have been regarded as unreal either because the event would have been thought to be physically impossible or because the possibility of its happening would have been regarded as so fantastic or far-fetched that no reasonable man would have paid any attention to it—'a mere possibility which would never occur to the mind of a reasonable man' (*per* Lord Dunedin in *Fardon* v *Harcourt-Rivington*) (1932) 146 LT 391—or (2) those where there was a real and substantial risk or chance that something like the event which happens might occur, and then the reasonable man would have taken the steps necessary to eliminate the risk.

*Bolton* v *Stone* [1951] AC 850 posed a new problem. There a member of a visiting team drove a cricket ball out of the ground onto an unfrequented adjacent public road and it struck and severely injured a lady who happened to be standing in the road. That it might happen that a ball would be driven onto this road could not have been said to be a fantastic or far-fetched possibility: according to the evidence it had happened about six times in 28 years. And it could not have been said to be a far-fetched or fantastic possibility that such a ball would strike someone in the road. people did pass along the road from time to time. So it could not have been said that, on any ordinary meaning of the words, the fact that a ball might strike a person in the road was not foreseeable or reasonably foreseeable—it was plainly foreseeable. But the chance of its happening in the foreseeable future was infinitesimal. A mathematician given the data could have worked out that it was only likely to happen once in so many thousand years. The House of Lords held that the risk was so small that in the circumstances a reasonable man would have been justified in disregarding it and taking no steps to eliminate it.

But it does not follow that, no matter what the circumstances may be, it is justifiable to neglect a risk of such a small magnitude. A reasonable man would only neglect such a risk if he had some valid reason for doing so, e.g., that it would involve considerable expense to eliminate the risk. He would weigh the risk against the difficulty of eliminating it. If the activity which caused the injury to Miss Stone had been an unlawful activity, there can be little doubt but that *Bolton* v *Stone* would have been decided differently. In their Lordships' judgment *Bolton* v *Stone* did not alter the general principle that a person must be regarded as negligent if he does not take steps to eliminate a risk which he knows or ought to know is a real risk and not a mere possibility which would never influence the mind of a reasonable man. What that decision did was to recognise and give effect to the qualification that it is justifiable not to take steps to eliminate a real risk if it is small and if the circumstances are such that a reasonable man, careful of the safety of his neighbour, would think it right to neglect it.

In the present case there was no justification whatever for discharging the oil into Sydney Harbour. Not only was it an offence to do so, but it involved considerable loss financially. If the ship's engineer had thought about the matter, there could have been no question of balancing the advantages and disadvantages. From every point of view it was both his duty and his interest to stop the discharge immediately. . . .

In their Lordships' view a properly qualified and alert chief engineer would have realised there was a real risk here and they do not understand Walsh J to deny that. But he appears to have held that if a real risk can properly be described as remote it must then be held to be not reasonably foreseeable. That is a possible interpretation of some of the authorities. But this is still an open question and on principle their Lordships cannot accept this view. If a real risk is one which would occur to the mind of a reasonable man in the position of the defendant's servant and which he would not brush aside as far-fetched, and if the criterion is to be what that reasonable man would have done in the circumstances, then surely he would not neglect such a risk if action to eliminate it presented no difficulty, involved no disadvantage, and required no expense.

NOTES
1. The reason for the different evidence and findings of fact may be that when *No. 1* was decided the contributory negligence rules in New South Wales meant that if a claimant was contributorily negligent at all the claimant lost his or her case entirely: naturally, therefore, the claimants would have been wary of saying that the fire was foreseeable. By the time of *No. 2* the rules had changed, so that in a case of contributory negligence the damages could be apportioned between the parties, thus providing less risk to the claimant.
2. The procedure in *No. 2* was complex, and in the event the Privy Council found the defendants were liable in negligence but not in nuisance. The explanation for this is complicated, and is discussed by Hoffman in (1967) 83 LQR 13.
3. The oddest case on remoteness is *Falkenham* v *Zwicker* (1979) 90 DLR 3d 289. On 1 February 1977 the defendant was driving her car in Nova Scotia when she slammed on her brakes to avoid a cat in the road. The car left the road and ran into wire fencing alongside the road. This caused the fence to 'unzip', in that a number of staples sprung out of the fence into the field. There were no cows in the field at the time. On 24 May the claimant put his cows into the field: they ate the staples. The staples caused the cows to contract 'hardware disease'. The vet put magnets in their stomachs, but five of the cows never recovered and were sent to the meat packer. MacIntosh J, in the Supreme Court of Nova Scotia, held the defendant liable for the reduced value of the cows. How could this be?

## A: Subsequent interpretations—the egg shell skull rule

*The Wagon Mound* changed the theory of remoteness of damage, but did it make any practical difference? One area where this arose was the so-called 'egg shell skull' rule, whereby, in personal injury cases at least, you take your victims as you find them—i.e. if the claimant has a thin skull and therefore suffers extensive injury, a defendant is liable for the whole loss and not just for the damage which might have been expected to occur to a normal person.

## Robinson v Post Office

Court of Appeal [1974] 1 WLR 1176; [1974] 2 All ER 737; 16 KIR 12

The claimant slipped on an oily ladder and cut his shin. He went to a doctor who gave him an anti-tetanus injection. The claimant was allergic to the serum and contracted encephalitis. Held: dismissing the appeal, that the defendants were liable for the entire damage.

ORR LJ: Mr Newey's main argument, however, was that the onset of encephalitis was not reasonably foreseeable and that on the basis of the decision of the Privy Council in *Overseas Tankship (UK) Ltd* v *Morts Dock and Engineering Co. Ltd (The Wagon Mound)* [1961] AC 388, the Post Office should not be held liable for that consequence of the injury. In answer t ) this argument the plaintiff relied on the judgment of Lord Parker C J in *Smith* v *Leech Brain & Co. Ltd* [1962] 2 QB 405. In that case an employee already suffering from premalignant changes had, as a result of his employers' negligence, sustained a burn which the judge found to have been the promoting agent in the development of cancer from which the employee died, and in a fatal accident claim by his widow it was argued for the defendant employers that the development of cancer was unforeseeable and that on the basis of *The Wagon Mound* decision the claim should be dismissed. Lord Parker CJ, however, rejected this argument in the following passages from his judgment, at pp. 414–415, which are quoted in the judgment now under appeal:

> For my part, I am quite satisfied that the Judicial Committee in *The Wagon Mound* case did not have what I may call, loosely, the thin-skull cases in mind. It has always been the law of this country that a tortfeasor takes his victim as he finds him . . . The test is not whether these employers could reasonably have foreseen that a burn would cause cancer and that he would die. The question is whether these employers could reasonably foresee the type of injury he suffered, namely, the burn. What, in the particular case, is the amount of damage which he suffers as a result of that burn, depends upon the characteristics and constitution of the victim.

It is to be noted, as pointed out in the judgment under appeal, that the last of these passages is supported by very similar language used by Lord Reid in the later case of *Hughes* v *Lord Advocate* [1963] AC 837, 845.

On this appeal Mr Newey did not challenge the correctness of Lord Parker CJ's reasoning and conclusion in the *Leech Brain* case and accepted that some at least of the subsequent decisions fell within the same principle, but he claimed that an essential link which was missing in the present case was that it was not foreseeable that administration of a form of anti-tetanus prophylaxis would itself give rise to a rare serious illness. In our judgment, however, there was no missing link and the case is governed by the principle that the Post Office had to take their victim as they found him, in this case with an allergy to a second dose of ATS. . . . In our judgment the principle that a defendant must take the plaintiff as he finds him involves that if a wrongdoer ought reasonably to foresee that as a result of his wrongful act the victim may require medical treatment he is, subject to the principle of novus actus interveniens, liable for the consequences of the treatment applied although he could not reasonably foresee those consequences or that they could be serious.

### ■ QUESTION

The claimant was here suffering from a 'pre-existing susceptibility' to greater damage than normal. Was the ship in *Re Polemis* also suffering from such a defect?

### NOTE

This case is also a good example of the application of the 'but for' test of causation. The claimant also sued the doctor. When the claimant saw the doctor he was given a test to see if there would be adverse reaction to the serum. The doctor was supposed to wait half an hour, but in fact waited only half a minute to see if there was a reaction. Thus, although negligent, the doctor was not liable because the reaction did not become apparent for nine days. The test, even if performed properly, would have made no difference.

### Stephenson v Waite Tileman Ltd
New Zealand Court of Appeal [1973] 1 NZLR 153

The claimant cut his hand on a wire rope. Medical evidence was given that an 'unknown virus' had entered the wound, causing brain damage. Held: allowing the appeal, the defendants were liable for the whole damage.

RICHMOND J: It would seem to me that if the principle of the eggshell skull cases is still part of English law, then it must follow both on grounds of logic and practical policy that the principle of new risk created by injury must also be part of the law. It would be illogical to allow recovery in respect of disease latent in the plaintiff's body but activated by physical injury and at the same time to deny recovery in respect of illness caused by an infection entering the plaintiff's system as the result of a wound. On the more practical side, it may in any given case be quite impossible to decide in which category a particular consequence of an accident lies. Thus in the case of the present appeal, it is common ground that an infection entered the appellant's system through the wound caused by the wire rope. It is not however possible to say whether the virus was of an unusually virulent kind against which the appellant put up a normal resistance or whether the virus was one to which the appellant was unusually susceptible. . . .

The result of this lengthy review of the authorities is to disclose the existence of a very strong body of judicial opinion both in England and in Commonwealth jurisdictions in favour of the view that the eggshell skull rule remains part of our law notwithstanding the decision in *The Wagon Mound (No. 1)*. As already indicated, I accept that view myself and for reasons which I have endeavoured to express I am also satisfied that similar principles must be applied to cases where a foreseeable kind of physical injury gives rise to some new risk or state of susceptibility in the victim. I have also found it helpful to consider the various fact situations which have arisen in the reported cases while endeavouring to arrive at some general principle which may be fairly and properly applied. I now summarise my conclusions:

1   In cases of damage by physical injury to the person the principles imposing liability for consequences flowing from the pre-existing special susceptibility of the victim and/or from new risk or susceptibility created by the initial injury remain part of our law.
2   In such cases the question of foreseeability should be limited to the initial injury. The tribunal of fact must decide whether that injury is of a kind, type or character which the defendant ought reasonably to have foreseen as a real risk.
3   If the plaintiff establishes that the initial injury was within a reasonably foreseeable kind, type or character of injury, then the necessary link between the ultimate consequences of the initial injury and the negligence of the defendant can be forged simply as one of cause and effect— in other words by establishing an adequate relationship of cause and effect between the initial injury and the ultimate consequence.

■ QUESTION

In this case the claimant was *not* suffering from a pre-existing susceptibility, and therefore it is not strictly an 'egg shell skull' case at all. Does the view of Richmond J mean that the *Polemis* test now applies to personal injuries?

## B: Subsequent interpretations—the kind of damage

In *The Wagon Mound No. 1* Viscount Simonds said that 'the essential factor in determining liability is whether the damage is of such a kind as the reasonable man should have foreseen'. Obviously the answer to such a question will often depend on how wide a category of 'kind of damage' is adopted as the test.

### *Hughes* v *Lord Advocate*
House of Lords [1963] AC 837; [1963] 2 WLR 779; [1963] 1 All ER 705

Some Post Office employees erected a shelter tent over a utility hole in Russell Road, Edinburgh. At about 5.30 p.m. they went for their tea, leaving the tent unattended. It had four red paraffin lamps, one at each corner, and the men pulled the ladder out of the utility hole. The pursuer, aged eight, and his uncle, aged ten, approached the shelter. They picked up one of the paraffin lamps and took the ladder into the shelter. They tied the lamp to a rope and lowered it into the hole and they followed. When they emerged from the hole, the lamp was knocked back into it and there was an enormous explosion, causing flames to reach 30 feet. The pursuer fell back into the hole and was badly burnt. It was thought that when the lamp fell into the hole, some paraffin escaped and vaporised. This was so unlikely as to be unforeseeable. Held: allowing the appeal, that the defendant was liable.

LORD REID: This accident was caused by a known source of danger, but caused in a way which could not have been foreseen, and, in my judgment, that affords no defence. I would therefore allow the appeal.

LORD JENKINS: It is true that the duty of care expected in cases of this sort is confined to reasonably foreseeable dangers, but it does not necessarily follow that liability is escaped because the danger actually materialising is not identical with the danger reasonably foreseen and guarded against. Each case much depends on its own particular facts. For example (as pointed out in the opinions), in the present case the paraffin did the mischief by exploding, not burning, and it is said that while a paraffin fire (caused, for example, by the upsetting of the lighted lamp or otherwise allowing its contents to leak out) was a reasonably foreseeable risk so soon as the pursuer got access to the lamp, an explosion was not.

To my mind, the distinction drawn between burning and explosion is too fine to warrant acceptance. Supposing the pursuer had on the day in question gone to the site and taken one of the lamps, and upset it over himself, thus setting his clothes alight, the person to be considered responsible for protecting children from the dangers to be found there would presumably have been liable. On the other hand, if the lamp, when the boy upset it, exploded in his face, he would have had no remedy because the explosion was an event which could not reasonably be foreseen. This does not seem to me to be right.

LORD MORRIS: My Lords, in my view, there was a duty owed by the defenders to safeguard the pursuer against the type or kind of occurrence which in fact happened and which resulted in his injuries, and the defenders are not absolved from liability because they did not envisage 'the precise concatenation of circumstances which led up to the accident.' . . .

LORD GUEST: In dismissing the appellant's claim the Lord Ordinary and the majority of the judges of the First Division reached the conclusion that the accident which happened was not reasonably foreseeable. In order to establish a coherent chain of causation it is not necessary that the precise details leading up to the accident should have been reasonably foreseeable; it is sufficient if the accident which occurred is of a type which should have been foreseeable by a reasonably careful person . . . or as Lord Mackintosh expressed it in the *Harvey* case, 1960 SC 155, the precise concatenation of circumstances need not be envisaged. Concentration has been placed in the courts below on the explosion which, it was said, could not have been foreseen because it was caused in a unique fashion by the paraffin forming into vapour and being ignited by the naked flame of the wick. But this, in my opinion, is to concentrate on what is really a non-essential element in the dangerous situation created by the allurement. The test might better be put thus: Was the igniting of paraffin outside the lamp by the flame a foreseeable consequence of the breach of duty? In the circumstances, there was a combination of potentially dangerous circumstances against which the Post Office had to protect the appellant. If these formed an allurement to children it might have been foreseen that they would play with the lamp, that it might tip over, that it might be broken, and that when broken the paraffin might spill and be ignited by the flame. All these steps in the chain of causation seem to have been accepted by all the judges in the courts below as foreseeable. But because the explosion was the agent which caused the burning and was unforeseeable, therefore the accident, according to them, was not reasonably foreseeable. In my opinion, this reasoning is fallacious. An explosion is only one way in which burning can be caused. Burning can also be caused by the contact between liquid paraffin and a naked flame. In the one case paraffin vapour and in the other case liquid paraffin is ignited by fire. I cannot see that these are two different types of accident. They are both burning accidents and in both cases the injuries would be burning injuries. Upon this view the explosion was an immaterial event in the chain of causation. It was simply one way in which burning might be caused by the potentially dangerous paraffin lamp. . . .

LORD PEARCE: The obvious risks were burning and conflagration and a fall. All these in fact occurred, but unexpectedly the mishandled lamp instead of causing an ordinary conflagration produced a violent explosion. Did the explosion create an accident and damage of a different type from the misadventure and damage that could be foreseen? In my judgment it did not. The accident was but a variant of the foreseeable.

■ QUESTION

What was foreseeable?

   (a) damage by paraffin? (in which case would the defendants have been liable if the boys had drunk the paraffin?);
   (b) damage by lamp? (in which case would the defendants have been liable if the claimant had dropped the lamp on his foot?);
   (c) damage by burning? (how was the claimant supposed to have burnt himself?). If it is supposed that there was a risk that the boy might touch the lamp and burn himself (how badly?) is that a variant of being sucked into the hole by an unforeseeable explosion?

NOTES

1. *Hughes* is not inconsistent with the theory behind *The Wagon Mound*, that is that remoteness should be tested by probability rather than by cause; nevertheless, it is based on probability of result rather than probability of the method of bringing about the result.

2. In *Jolley* v *Sutton London BC* [2000] 3 All ER 409, an old boat had been left on land belonging to the defendants for some time. The claimant (aged 14) and a friend decided to try to repair it and raised it up by using a jack. Some six weeks later the boat collapsed, injuring the claimant who was underneath it. The Court of Appeal had held that the defendants were not liable as even though interference by children was foreseeable, it was not foreseeable that a child would try to jack the boat up. It was said that this was not a foreseeable kind of *accident* and *Hughes* was distinguished. However, the House of Lords held the defendants liable saying that the appropriate risk was that of children meddling with the boat and that risk had materialised.

3. In *Tremain* v *Pike* [1969] 3 All ER 1303, the defendant operated a farm at Beer in Devon, where there were too many rats. The claimant, a herdsman employed by the defendant, contracted a rare disease, Weil's Disease, from contact with rats' urine. Payne J held, *inter alia*, that this was different from the foreseeable damage such as injury by rat bites, and therefore it was too remote. Injury by rat bites is foreseeable: injury by rats' urine is not. But if the test was injury by rats the result might have been different. Which is the appropriate category?

---

*Doughty* v *Turner Manufacturing Co.*
Court of Appeal [1964] 1 QB 518; [1964] 1 All ER 98; [1964] 2 WLR 248

The defendants had two cauldrons containing sodium cyanide powder, which became liquid when heated to 800C by electrodes. Each bath had a cover made of an asbestos compound. What was not known was that the compound, when heated above 500C underwent a chemical change and emitted steam. Due to negligence one of the covers slid into the liquid, which then erupted, injuring the claimant who was standing near the bath. Held: allowing the appeal, that the defendants were not liable.

HARMAN LJ: The plaintiff's argument most persuasively urged by Mr James rested, as I understood it, on admissions made that, if this lid had been dropped into the cauldron with sufficient force to cause the molten material to splash over the edge, that would have been an act of negligence or carelessness for which the defendants might be vicariously responsible. Reliance was put upon *Hughes* v *Lord Advocate* [1963] AC 837, where the exact consequences of the lamp overturning were not foreseen, but it was foreseeable that, if the manhole were left unguarded, boys would enter and tamper with the lamp, and it was not unlikely that serious burns might ensue for the boys. Their Lordships' House distinguished *The Wagon Mound* case [1961] AC 388 on the ground that the damage which ensued, though differing in degree, was the same in kind as that which was foreseeable. So it is said here that a splash causing burns was foreseeable and that this explosion was really only a magnified splash which also caused burns and that, therefore, we ought to follow *Hughes* v *Lord Advocate* and hold the defendants liable. I cannot accept this. In my opinion, the damage here was of entirely different kind from the foreseeable splash. Indeed, the evidence showed that any disturbance of the material resulting from the immersion of the hard-board was past an appreciable time before the explosion happened. This latter was caused by the distintegration of the hard-board under the great heat to which it was subjected and the consequent release of the moisture enclosed within it. This had nothing to do with the agitation caused by the dropping of the board into the cyanide. I am of opinion that it would be wrong on these facts to make another inroad on the doctrine of foreseeability which seems to me to be a satisfactory solvent of this type of difficulty.

■ QUESTION

If an explosion is a variant of fire, why is not an eruption a variant of a splash?

NOTE

A better solution to this case is that taken by Diplock LJ, and is based on duty. The foreseeable risk was burning people by splashing if the cover was dropped from a height into the bath. However, as the chemical change in the cover was unknown, there was no duty to prevent the cover being *in* the bath: thus, if the cover slides gently in, the defendants are not in breach of any duty. Note also that if the claimant had been outside the range of potential splashing (said to be about one foot) he would have been an unforeseeable claimant anyway.

# 5

## Special Duty Problems: Omissions

The common law took the view that it would be too great a burden to impose liability upon a person for a mere omission. The law could not require a person to love his neighbour, but could only ask that he should avoid injuring him, and so there is, for example, no liability for failing to prevent a blind person walking over a cliff. For a general discussion of these issues see the *Stovin* v *Wise* (below). Given the general position, the next problem was whether a person who volunteers to help, although under no duty to do so, is liable if that person assists negligently? For example, can a doctor who voluntarily assists at a road accident be liable for negligent medical attention?

Even though the common law took the view that mere inaction did not give rise to liability, duties can in fact be imposed in two ways. The first is terminological, that is interpreting an omission as a negligent act. Thus, in *Kelly* v *Metropolitan Rly* [1895] 1 QB 944 the claimant was injured in a railway accident where a train was driven into a wall at Baker Street station. The defendants admitted this was a breach of contract, but claimed that it was not a tort because there was only an omission, in that the engine driver had merely failed to turn off the steam. The court naturally held that this amounted to the positive act of driving the train negligently.

The second way of imposing a duty is by the reliance of the claimant upon the defendant. This can come about either by the previous conduct of the defendant, which induces reliance by the claimant that the defendant will continue to act in that way, or by reliance which comes out of a relationship of dependence between the parties.

---

### Stovin v Wise
House of Lords [1996] AC 923; [1996] 3 WLR 388; [1996] 3 All ER 801

For the facts and decision in this case see Chapter 6. The extract below deals with the general issue of liability for omissions.

LORD HOFFMANN

*4. Acts and omissions*

The judge made no express mention of the fact that the complaint against the council was not about anything which it had done to make the highway dangerous but about its omission to make it safer. Omissions, like economic loss, are notoriously a category of conduct in which Lord Atkin's generalisation in *Donoghue* v *Stevenson* [1932] AC 562 offers limited help. In the High Court of Australia in *Hargrave* v *Goldman* (1963) 110 CLR 40, 66, Windeyer J drew attention to the irony in Lord Atkin's allusion, in formulating his 'neighbour' test, to the parable of the Good Samaritan [1932] AC 562, 580:

> The priest and the Levite, when they saw the wounded man by the road, passed by on the other side. He obviously was a person whom they had in contemplation and who was closely and directly affected by their action. Yet the common law does not require a man to act as the Samaritan did.

A similar point was made by Lord Diplock in *Dorset Yacht Co. Ltd* v *Home Office* [1970] AC 1004, 1060. There are sound reasons why omissions require different treatment from positive conduct. It is one thing for the law to say that a person who undertakes some activity shall take reasonable care not to cause damage to others. It is another thing for the law to require that a person who is doing nothing in particular shall take steps to prevent another from suffering harm from the acts of third parties (like Mrs Wise) or natural causes. One can put the matter in political, moral or economic terms. In political terms it is less of an invasion of an individual's freedom for the law to require him to consider the safety of others in his actions than to impose upon him a duty to rescue or protect.

A moral version of this point may be called the 'why pick on me?' argument. A duty to prevent harm to others or to render assistance to a person in danger or distress may apply to a large and indeterminate class of people who happen to be able to do something. Why should one be held liable rather than another? In economic terms, the efficient allocation of resources usually requires an activity should bear its own costs. If it benefits from being able to impose some of its costs on other people (what economists call 'externalities,') the market is distorted because the activity appears cheaper than it really is. So liability to pay compensation for loss caused by negligent conduct acts as a deterrent against increasing the cost of the activity to the community and reduces externalities. But there is no similar justification for requiring a person who is not doing anything to spend money on behalf of someone else. Except in special cases (such as marine salvage) English law does not reward someone who voluntarily confers a benefit on another. So there must be some special reason why he should have to put his hand in his pocket.

In *Hargrave* v *Goldman*, 110 CLR 40, 66, Windeyer J. said:

> The trend of judicial development in the law of negligence has been . . . to found a duty to take care either in some task undertaken, or in the ownership, occupation, or use of land or chattels.

There may be a duty to act if one has undertaken to do so or induced a person to rely upon one doing so. Or the ownership or occupation of land may give rise to a duty to take positive steps for the benefit of those who come upon the land and sometimes for the benefit of neighbours. In *Hargrave* v *Goldman* the High Court of Australia held that the owner and occupier of a 600-acre grazing property in Western Australia had a duty to take reasonable steps to extinguish a fire, which had been started by lightning striking a tree on his land, so as to prevent it from spreading to his neighbour's land. This is a case in which the limited class of persons who owe the duty (neighbours) is easily identified and the political, moral and economic arguments which I have mentioned are countered by the fact that the duties are mutual. One cannot tell where the lightning may strike and it is therefore both fair and efficient to impose upon each landowner a duty to have regard to the interests of his neighbour. In giving the advice of the Privy Council affirming the decision (*Goldman* v *Hargrave* [1967] 1 AC 645) Lord Wilberforce underlined the exceptional nature of the liability when he pointed out that the question of whether the landowner had acted reasonably should be judged by reference to the resources he actually had at his disposal and not by some general or objective standard. This is quite different from the duty owed by a person who undertakes a positive activity which carries the risk of causing damage to others. If he does not have the resources to take such steps as are objectively reasonable to prevent such damage, he should not undertake that activity at all.

NOTE

On the general issue see also *Smith* v *Littlewoods* [1987] AC 241 (parts of which are extracted in Chapter 4). There Lord Goff said that the general proposition of there being no duty for omissions may one day need to be reconsidered as it is said to provoke an invidious comparison with affirmative duties of good-neighbourliness in most countries outside the common law orbit. However, if that were to be done there would need to be strict limits on any such affirmative duty. On this see Markesinis, 'Negligence, Nuisance and Affirmative Duties of Action' (1989) 105 LQR 104.

### *Mercer* v *South Eastern and Chatham Rly*
Queen's Bench Division [1922] 2 KB 549; 92 LJKB 25; 127 LT 723

The claimant was a jogger who approached a level crossing near Slade Green in Kent. The main gates were closed and he waited for a train (the down train) to pass. He then found that the small gate at the side for pedestrian use was unlocked, and he passed through and was knocked down by a train going the other way (the up train). The claimant used the crossing two or three times a week and was accustomed to finding the small gate locked if a train was due. Held: the defendants owed the claimant a duty and were liable.

LUSH J: What in the present case is the true inference to be drawn from the facts as I have stated them?

I should certainly hesitate to hold that if in a case of this kind a person wishing to use the level crossing were, merely because he found the gate unlocked, to omit to look and see whether the way was clear when there was nothing to prevent him from doing so, and were to walk on, reading a newspaper, for example, he could make the company liable if he were run down by a train that he could easily have seen or heard. The railway company may have tacitly invited him to cross the line, but they did not invite him to leave his common sense behind him. There are however special circumstances in this case, inasmuch as, owing to the position of the down train, the plaintiff could neither see nor hear the up train.

I come to the conclusion on these facts that the plaintiff got in front of the up train because he was thrown off his guard by what the signalman did, that the danger was not an obvious one, and that he was injured while taking what was in the circumstances ordinary and reasonable care . . .

In this case I think that the defendants gave a tacit invitation, and that it was in consequence of his acting upon that invitation that the plaintiff was injured.

It may seem a hardship on a railway company to hold them responsible for the omission to do something which they were under no legal obligation to do, and which they only did for the protection of the public. They ought, however, to have contemplated that if a self-imposed duty is ordinarily performed, those who know of it will draw an inference if on a given occasion it is not performed. If they wish to protect themselves against the inference being drawn they should do so by giving notice, and they did not do so in this case.

### *R* v *Instan*
Court for Crown Cases Reserved [1893] 1 QB 450

Kate Instan lived with her aunt, who was 73. Towards the end of her life the aunt suffered from gangrene in the leg, but the defendant failed to give her any medical or nursing attention, nor did she give her any food. The cause of death was gangrene, accelerated by neglect and lack of food. Held: the defendant was guilty of manslaughter.

LORD COLERIDGE CJ: We are all of opinion that this conviction must be affirmed. It would not be correct to say that every moral obligation involves a legal duty; but every legal duty is founded on a moral obligation. A legal common law duty is nothing else than the enforcing by law of that which is a moral obligation without legal enforcement. There can be no question in this case that it was the clear duty of the prisoner to impart to the deceased so much as was necessary to sustain life of the food which she from time to time took in, and which was paid for by the deceased's own money for the purpose of the maintenance of herself and the prisoner, it was only through the instrumentality of the prisoner that the deceased could get the food. There was, therefore, a common law duty imposed upon the prisoner which she did not discharge.

NOTE

Although this is a criminal case, there is no doubt the defendant would have been liable in tort for a breach of duty arising from the relationship of dependence by the aunt upon the niece. For a discussion of the liability of the operator of a boat towards a passenger who falls overboard, see *The Ogopogo (Horsley* v *MacLaren)* [1971] 2 Lloyd's Rep 410. (A passenger fell overboard without any negligence by the defendant operator: the operator owed a duty to rescue him. Also, the operator could have been liable to a person who attempted to rescue the passenger in the water, if the operator's method of going about the rescue had been negligent, which it had not.)

■ QUESTION

A enters B's bar and becomes drunk. B ejects A from the bar because he is becoming a nuisance. B knows that A will be walking home, and on the way home A is run over by a car. Is B liable to A for failing to call a taxi or the police? See *Jordan House Ltd* v *Menow* (1974) 38 DLR 3d 105 and *Hunt* v *Sutton Group* (2001) 196 DLR 4th 738 where liability was imposed in such circumstances. Note however that in Australia such liability has been rejected: see *Cole* v *South Tweed Heads Rugby League Football Club* (2004) 78 ALJR 933 where the High Court said that control would be impractical and would interfere with the customer's autonomy, privacy and freedom of action. How should such cases be resolved here? Also, on policy grounds a 'social' host would not be liable: *Childs* v *Dersormeaux* (2002) 217 DLR 4th 217. Compare *Barrett* v *Ministry of Defence* [1995] 3 All ER 87 where the Ministry was not liable for failing to prevent a naval airman becoming so drunk at a naval base that he eventually died.

# 6

## Special Duty Problems:
## Exercise of Statutory Powers

Public bodies are provided with extensive powers to act for the public benefit but often have limited resources. Difficult decisions have to be made, and if those decisions are wholly unreasonable they may be corrected by judicial review, i.e. by public law remedies. A more difficult question is whether failure by a public body provides a *private* right of action to someone harmed (or not benefited) by the decision. The *Anns* case (below) introduced a distinction between policy and operational matters but it is now recognized that this cannot provide a touchstone of liability. While the general principles of duty of care apply (i.e. proximity and whether it is fair and just to impose liability) there are several limitations on the liability of public bodies in negligence as illustrated by *X* v *Bedfordshire CC* and *Stovin* v *Wise* (below). For example, in relation to the exercise of statutory powers Lord Hoffmann said in *Stovin* v *Wise* that in addition to the decision of the public body being unreasonable, there must be 'exceptional grounds for holding that the policy of the statute requires compensation to be paid to persons who suffer loss because the power was not exercised'. This brings into account not only what were the obligations of the public body to act for the public benefit but also, more particularly, whether the statutory structure envisaged payment of compensation to individuals rather than leaving the matter to be dealt with by public law remedies. For a modern analysis of the issues, see Buckley, 'Negligence in the public sphere: is clarity possible?' (2000) 5I NILQ 25.

---

### *Anns* v *Merton London Borough Council*
House of Lords [1978] AC 728; [1977] 2 WLR 1024; [1977] 2 All ER 492

The claimants were lessees of flats in a building in Wimbledon, and in 1970 there were structural movements which caused walls to crack. This was due to inadequate foundations. In 1962 the builders had deposited plans with the predecessors of the defendant local authority, which showed that the foundations would be at least three feet deep, but in fact they were only two feet six inches. The claimants sued the local authority on the ground that their predecessors' inspectors had either not inspected the foundations, or, if they had, had done so negligently. The Public Health Act 1936 required the local authority to pass building regulations, and they had the power to inspect any foundations to see if they complied with the regulations. Held: dismissing the appeal, that the local authority owed a duty of care. (This case has now been overruled by the House of Lords in *Murphy* v *Brentwood District Council* [1991] 1 AC 398, and the validity of the dicta of Lord Wilberforce relating to the exercise of powers has now been doubted, but is included here for reference purposes.)

LORD WILBERFORCE: What then is the extent of the local authority's duty towards these persons? Although, as I have suggested, a situation of 'proximity' existed between the council and owners and occupiers of the houses, I do not think that a description of the council's duty can be based upon the 'neighbourhood' principle alone or upon merely any such factual relationship as 'control' as suggested by the Court of Appeal. So to base it would be to neglect an essential factor which is that the local authority is a public body, discharging functions under statute: its powers and duties are definable in terms of public not private law. The problem which this type of action creates, is to define the circumstances in which the law should impose, over and above, or perhaps alongside, these public law powers and duties, a duty in private law towards individuals such that they may sue for damages in a civil court. It is in this context that the distinction sought to be drawn between duties and mere powers has to be examined.

Most, indeed probably all, statutes relating to public authorities or public bodies, contain in them a large area of policy. The courts call this 'discretion' meaning that the decision is one for the authority or body to make, and not for the courts. Many statutes also prescribe or at least pre-suppose the practical execution of policy decisions: a convenient description of this is to say that in addition to the area of policy or discretion, there is an operational area. Although this distinction between the policy area and the operational area is convenient, and illuminating, it is probably a distinction of degree; many 'operational' powers or duties have in them some element of 'discretion.' It can safely be said that the more 'operational' a power or duty may be, the easier it is to superimpose upon it a common law duty of care.

I do not think that it is right to limit this to a duty to avoid causing extra or additional damage beyond what must be expected to arise from the exercise of the power or duty. That may be correct when the act done under the statute *inherently* must adversely *affect* the interest of individuals. But many other acts can be done without causing any harm to anyone—indeed may be directed to preventing harm from occurring. In these cases the duty is the normal one of taking care to avoid harm to those likely to be affected.

Let us examine the Public Health Act 1936 in the light of this. Undoubtedly it lays out a wide area of policy. It is for the local authority, a public and elected body, to decide upon the scale of resources which it can make available in order to carry out its functions under Part II of the Act—how many inspectors, with what expert qualifications, it should recruit, how often inspections are to be made, what tests are to be carried out, must be for its decision. It is no accident that the Act is drafted in terms of functions and powers rather than in terms of positive duty. As was well said, public authorities have to strike a balance between the claims of efficiency and thrift (du Parcq LJ in *Kent* v *East Suffolk Rivers Catchment Board* [1940] 1 KB 319, 338): whether they get the balance right can only be decided through the ballot box, not in the courts. It is said—there are reflections of this in the judgments in *Dutton* v *Bognor Regis Urban District Council* [1972] 1 QB 373—that the local authority is under no duty to inspect, and this is used as the foundation for an argument, also found in some of the cases, that if it need not inspect at all, it cannot be liable for negligent inspection: if it were to be held so liable, so it is said, councils would simply decide against inspection. I think that this is too crude an argument. It overlooks the fact that local authorities are public bodies operating under statute with a clear responsibility for public health in their area. They must, and in fact do, make their discretionary decisions responsibly and for reasons which accord with the statutory purpose; see *Ayr Harbour Trustees* v *Oswald* (1883) 8 App Cas 623, 639, *per* Lord Watson:

> the powers which [section 10] confers are discretionary . . . But it is the plain import of the clause that the harbour trustees . . . shall be vested with, and shall avail themselves of, these discretionary powers, whenever and as often as they may be of opinion that the public interest will be promoted by their exercise.

If they do not exercise their discretion in this way they can be challenged in the courts. Thus, to say that councils are under no duty to inspect, is not a sufficient statement of the position. They are under a duty to give proper consideration to the question whether they should inspect or not. Their immunity from attack, in the event of failure to inspect, in other words, though great is not absolute. And because it is not absolute, the necessary premise for the proposition 'if no duty to inspect, then no duty to take care in inspection' vanishes.

Passing then to the duty as regards inspection, if made. On principle there must surely be a duty to exercise reasonable care. The standard of care must be related to the duty to be performed—namely to ensure compliance with the byelaws. It must be related to the fact that the person responsible for construction in accordance with the byelaws is the builder, and that the inspector's function is supervisory. It must be related to the fact that once the inspector has passed the foundations they will be covered up, with no subsequent opportunity for inspection. But this duty, heavily operational though it may be, is still a duty arising under the statute. There may be a discretionary element in its exercise—discretionary as to the time and manner of inspection, and the techniques to be used. A plaintiff complaining of negligence must prove, the burden being on him, that action taken was not within the limits of a discretion bona fide exercised, before he can being to rely upon a common law duty of care. But if he can do this, he should, in principle, be able to sue.

Is there, then, authority against the existence of any such duty or any reason to restrict it? It is said that there is an absolute distinction in the law between statutory duty and statutory power—the former giving rise to possible liability, the latter not, or at least not doing so unless the exercise of the power involves some positive act creating some fresh or additional damage.

My Lords, I do not believe that any such absolute rule exists . . .

NOTES
1. For a full discussion of this case, see Bailey and Bowman, 'The policy/operational dichotomy—a cuckoo in the nest' [1986] CLJ 430. See also *Sutherland Shire Council* v *Heyman* (1985) 157 CLR 424, where, on similar facts to *Anns*, the High Court of Australia held that a local authority did owe a duty to take care, but on the facts was not in breach of it. The court differed from *Anns* in saying that the ordinary principles of negligence applied to public bodies, and that the issue was one of proximity or reliance.
2. For the subsequent history of the *Anns* distinction between policy and operational matters, see *X* v *Bedfordshire CC* and *Stovin* v *Wise* (below) where it was noted that the distinction is difficult to apply and does not provide a hard and fast principle in determining liability. There is now a greater awareness that whatever the merits or otherwise of the decision of the public body, there need to be special circumstances over and above unreasonableness to justify allowing a *private* right of action to someone harmed by the decision or to someone the public body has failed to benefit.
3. In *Sheppard* v *Glossop Corporation* [1921] 3 KB 132 a local authority had power to put up street lights. The defendants did so, but resolved to extinguish the light at 9.00 p.m. The claimant was injured by falling over a retaining wall at 11.30 p.m. The court held the defendants not liable as they were not obliged to light the streets. How would this be regarded now? Was this a policy or an operational decision? Would it matter what the reasons were for turning off the lights at 9.00 p.m.?
4. The distinction between private and public law has not been worked out, but it seems clear that if the issue is classified as one of public law, a claimant may not evade the restrictions placed upon public law remedies by bringing a private action. In *O'Reilly* v *Mackman* [1983] 2 AC 237, at p. 285, Lord Diplock said:

it would in my view as a general rule be contrary to public policy, and as such an abuse of the process of the court, to permit a person seeking to establish that a decision of a public authority infringed rights to which he was entitled to protection under public law to proceed by way of an ordinary action and by this means to evade the provision of Order 53 for the protection of such authorities.

An example of this principle is *Cocks* v *Thanet DC* [1983] 2 AC 286, where the claimant claimed to be homeless and requested the defendants to house him under the Housing (Homeless Persons) Act 1977. He was turned down and began an action for a declaration and damages, alleging the council were in breach of their duty under the Act. The House of Lords held that he could only use public law remedies to quash the council's decision, and could not use private law remedies. See also *Jones* v *Department of Employment* [1988] 1 All ER 725, where a person who was turned down for unemployment benefit successfully appealed to a Social Security Appeal

Tribunal and was allowed benefit. He then tried to sue the adjudicating officer for negligently denying him benefit, claiming expenses and damages for distress. It was held that he had no action in negligence.

However, in *Roy* v *Kensington and Chelsea Family Practitioner Committee* [1992] 1 All ER 705 the House of Lords warned that the *O'Reilly* v *Mackman* principles should not be applied too strictly. Lord Bridge said 'It is appropriate that an issue which depends exclusively on the existence of a purely public law right should be determined in judicial review proceedings and not otherwise. But where a litigant asserts his entitlement to a subsisting right in private law, whether by way of a claim or defence, the circumstance that the existence and the extent of the private right asserted may incidentally involve the examination of a public law issue cannot prevent the litigant from seeking to establish his right by action commenced by writ or originating summons . . .' (The defendants had reduced the claimant's 'basic practice allowance' as they believed he was not devoting a substantial amount of his time to the NHS. The claimant was permitted to sue on the basis that the defendants were in breach of contract and was not limited to a public law claim that they had acted *ultra vires* or unreasonably.)

---

## *X* v *Bedfordshire C.C.*

House of Lords [1995] 2 AC 633; [1995] 3 WLR 152; [1995] 3 All ER 353

This case involved a number of actions against various local authorities. In the 'abuse' cases (*Bedfordshire* and *Newham*) it was alleged that the authorities had, in one case, failed to diagnose abuse, and in the other had identified the wrong person as the abuser. In the 'education' cases (*Dorset, Hampshire* and *Bromley*) it was alleged that the authorities had failed properly to identify and provide for the special educational needs of the claimants. Held: that no duty was owed in either the abuse or education cases in pursuance of the authorities' statutory obligations.

LORD BROWNE-WILKINSON: . . .

*Discretion: justiciability and the policy/operational test*

*(a) Discretion*

Most statutes which impose a statutory duty on local authorities confer on the authority a discretion as to the extent to which, and the methods by which, such statutory duty is to be performed. It is clear both in principle and from the decided cases that the local authority cannot be liable in damages for doing that which Parliament has authorised. Therefore if the decisions complained of fall within the ambit of such statutory discretion they cannot be actionable in common law. However if the decision complained of is so unreasonable that it falls outside the ambit of the discretion conferred upon the local authority, there is no a priori reason for excluding all common law liability.

That this is the law is established by the decision in the *Dorset Yacht* case [1970] AC 1004 and by that part of the decision in *Anns* v *Merton London Borough Council* [1978] AC 728 which, so far as I am aware, has largely escaped criticism in later decisions. In the *Dorset Yacht* case Lord Reid said [1970] AC 1004, 1031:

> Where Parliament confers a discretion the position is not the same. Then there may, and almost certainly will, be errors of judgment in exercising such a discretion and Parliament cannot have intended that members of the public should be entitled to sue in respect of such errors. But there must come a stage when the discretion is exercised so carelessly or unreasonably that there has been no real exercise of the discretion which Parliament has conferred. The person purporting to exercise his discretion has acted in abuse or excess of his power. Parliament cannot be supposed to have granted immunity to persons who do that.

. . .

Exactly the same approach was adopted by Lord Wilberforce in *Anns* v *Merton London Borough Council* [1978] AC 728 who, speaking of the duty of a local authority which had in fact inspected a building under construction, said, at p. 755:

> But this duty, heavily operational though it may be, is still a duty arising under the statute. There may be a discretionary element in its exercise—discretionary as to the time and manner of inspection, and the techniques to be used. A plaintiff complaining of negligence must prove, the burden being on him, that action taken was not within the limits of a discretion bona fide exercised, before he can begin to rely upon a common law duty of care.

It follows that in seeking to establish that a local authority is liable at common law for negligence in the exercise of a discretion conferred by statute, the first requirement is to show that the decision was outside the ambit of the discretion altogether: if it was not, a local authority cannot itself be in breach of any duty of care owed to the plaintiff.

In deciding whether or not this requirement is satisfied, the court has to assess the relevant factors taken into account by the authority in exercising the discretion. Since what are under consideration are discretionary powers conferred on public bodies for public purposes the relevant factors will often include policy matters, for example social policy, the allocation of finite financial resources between the different calls made upon them or (as in *Dorset Yacht*) the balance between pursuing desirable social aims as against the risk to the public inherent in so doing. It is established that the courts cannot enter upon the assessment of such 'policy' matters. The difficulty is to identify in any particular case whether or not the decision in question is a 'policy' decision.

### (b) Justiciability and the policy/operational dichotomy

. . . As Lord Wilberforce [in *Anns*] appreciated, this approach did not prove a hard and fast test as to those matters which were open to the court's decision. In *Rowling* v *Takaro Properties Ltd* [1988] AC 473 the Privy Council reverted to the problem. In that case the trial judge had found difficulty in applying the policy/operational test, but having classified the decision in question as being operational, took the view that as a result there was a common law duty of care. Commenting on the judge's view, Lord Keith of Kinkel said, at p. 501:

> Their Lordships feel considerable sympathy with Quilliam J's difficulty in solving the problem by reference to this distinction. They are well aware of the references in the literature to this distinction (which appears to have originated in the United States of America), and of the critical analysis to which it has been subjected. They incline to the opinion, expressed in the literature, that this distinction does not provide a touchstone of liability, but rather is expressive of the need to exclude altogether those cases in which the decision under attack is of such a kind that a question whether it has been made negligently is unsuitable for judicial resolution, of which notable examples are discretionary decisions on the allocation of scarce resources or the distribution of risks: see especially the discussion in *Craig on Administrative Law* (1983), pp. 534–538. If this is right, classification of the relevant decision as a policy or planning decision in this sense may exclude liability; but a conclusion that it does not fall within that category does not, in their Lordships' opinion, mean that a duty of care will *necessarily* exist. (Emphasis added.)

From these authorities I understand the applicable principles to be as follows. Where Parliament has conferred a statutory discretion on a public authority, it is for that authority, not for the courts, to exercise the discretion: nothing which the authority does within the ambit of the discretion can be actionable at common law. If the decision complained of falls outside the statutory discretion, it *can* (but not necessarily will) give rise to common law liability. However, if the factors relevant to the exercise of the discretion include matters of policy, the court cannot adjudicate on such policy matters and therefore cannot reach the conclusion that the decision was outside the ambit of the statutory discretion. Therefore a common law duty of care in relation to the taking of decisions involving policy matters cannot exist.

*If justiciable, the ordinary principles of negligence apply*

If the plaintiff's complaint alleges carelessness, not in the taking of a discretionary decision to do some act, but in the practical manner in which that act has been performed (e.g. the running of a school) the question whether or not there is a common law duty of care falls to be decided by applying the usual principles i.e. those laid down in *Caparo Industries Plc* v *Dickman* [1990] 2 AC 605, 617–618. Was the damage to the plaintiff reasonably foreseeable? Was the relationship between the plaintiff and the defendant sufficiently proximate? Is it just and reasonable to impose a duty of care? See *Rowling* v *Takaro Properties Ltd* [1988] AC 473; *Hill* v *Chief Constable of West Yorkshire* [1989] AC 53.

However the question whether there is such a common law duty and if so its ambit, must be profoundly influenced by the statutory framework within which the acts complained of were done. The position is directly analogous to that in which a tortious duty of care owed by A to C can arise out of the performance by A of a contract between A and B. In *Henderson* v *Merrett Syndicates Ltd* [1994] 3 WLR 761 your Lordships held that A (the managing agent) who had contracted with B (the members' agent) to render certain services for C (the Names) came under a duty of care to C in the performance of those services. It is clear that any tortious duty of care owed to C in those circumstances could not be inconsistent with the duty owed in contract by A to B. Similarly, in my judgment a common law duty of care cannot be imposed on a statutory duty if the observance of such common law duty of care would be inconsistent with, or have a tendency to discourage, the due performance by the local authority of its statutory duties.

NOTES

1. One valuable point is the separation of public and private law and that it is unhelpful 'to introduce public law concepts as to the validity of a decision into the question of liability at common law'. The question is solely whether the decision is properly within the discretion of the public body, but there can be liability if the decision is so unreasonable as to take it outside the ambit of that discretion so long as there are other special circumstances justifying a private right of action. If the decision tends more to the 'operational' end of the spectrum there can be liability so long as it is fair and reasonable to impose a duty (see *Barrett* v *Enfield*, below).

2. This was an application to strike out the statements of claim and much remained to be proved. The end result was that even if the cases were justiciable, and some may not have been, nevertheless in the main educational cases and all the abuse cases it was not fair and reasonable to impose a duty. The only potential liability which remained was for cases of negligent advice given by professional employees.

3. There have been a number of cases following on from the *Bedfordshire* case but the parameters for liability in relation to children are still unclear. In *A* v *Essex CC* [2004] 1 WLR 1881 the claimants adopted a child who proved to be very aggressive. It was said that there was no duty to the adopting parents on the part of the professionals involved in compiling reports on the child, although there may be a duty to the child. (In fact the adopters won here as it was intended that they should receive various reports which due to an administrative error were not passed on to them.) In *JD* v *East Berkshire Community Health Trust*, [2005] 2 AC 373; [2005] UKHL 23, the assumed facts were that a doctor had misdiagnosed a child's illness and had wrongly concluded that the cause was abuse by the parents. The action was brought by the parents for psychiatric injury caused by this wrongful allegation. It was held that no duty was owed by the doctor to the parents. The main reason was that owing a duty both to the child and the parents would produce a conflict of interest. Lord Rodger said at para 110 'The duty to the children is simply to exercise reasonable care and skill in diagnosing and treating any condition from which they may be suffering. In carrying out that duty the doctors have regard only to the interests of the children. Suppose, however, that they were also under a duty to the parents not to cause them psychiatric harm by concluding that they might have abused their child. Then, in deciding how to proceed, the doctors would always have to take account of the risk that they might harm the parents in this way. There would be not one but

two sets of interests to be considered. Acting on, or persisting in, a suspicion of abuse might well be reasonable when only the child's interests were engaged, but unreasonable if the interests of the parents had also to be taken into account. Of its very nature, therefore, this kind of duty of care to the parents would cut across the duty of care to the children.'

### Barrett v Enfield London Borough Council
House of Lords [2001] 2 AC 550; [1999] 3 WLR 79; [1999] 3 All ER 193

The claimant was born in 1972, and in 1973 he was taken into care and he remained in care with various foster parents and institutions until 1990. He alleged that the various placings were unsatisfactory and that the defendants failed to have him adopted. He claimed that as a result of the defendants' failure to exercise due care he suffered a psychiatric illness which caused him to harm himself, he became involved in criminal activities, he could not find work and had an alcohol problem. Held: the action would not be struck out.

LORD SLYNN: . . . In summary the *Bedfordshire* case establishes that decisions by local authorities whether or not to take a child into care with all the difficult aspects that involves and all the disruption which may come about are not ones which the courts will review by way of a claim for damages in negligence, though there may be other remedies by way of judicial review or through extra judicial routes such as the Ombudsman.

The question in the present case is different, since the child was taken into care; it is therefore necessary to consider whether any acts or omissions and if so what kind of acts or omissions can ground a claim in negligence. The fact that no completely analogous claim has been accepted by the courts previously points to the need for caution and the need to proceed 'incrementally' and 'by analogy with decided cases.'

. . .

It is obvious from previous cases and indeed is self-evident that there is a real conflict between on the one hand the need to allow social welfare services exercising statutory powers to do their work in what they as experts consider is the best way in the interests first of the child, but also of the parents and of society, without an unduly inhibiting fear of litigation if something goes wrong, and on the other hand the desirability of providing a remedy in appropriate cases for harm done to a child through the acts or failure to act of such services.

It is no doubt right for the courts to restrain within reasonable bounds claims against public authorities exercising statutory powers in this social welfare context. It is equally important to set reasonable bounds to the immunity such public authorities can assert. . . .

The position is in some respects clear; in others it is far from clear. Thus it is clear that where a statutory scheme *requires* a public authority to take action in a particular area and injury is caused, the authority taking such action in accordance with the statute will not be liable in damages unless the statute expressly or impliedly so provides. Nor will the authority be liable in damages at common law if its acts fall squarely within the statutory duty. Where a statute *empowers* an authority to take action in its discretion, then if it remains within its powers, the authority will not normally be liable under the statute, unless the statute so provides, or at common law. This, however, is subject to the proviso that if it purports to exercise its discretion to use, or it uses, its power in a wholly unreasonable way, it may be regarded as having gone outside its discretion so that it is not properly exercising its power, when liability in damages at common law may arise. It can no longer rely on the statutory power or discretion as a defence because it has gone outside the power.

. . .

On this basis, if an authority acts wholly within its discretion—i.e. it is doing what Parliament has said it can do, even if it has to choose between several alternatives open to it, then there can be no liability in negligence. It is only if a plaintiff can show that what has been done is outside the discretion and the power, then he can go on to show the authority was negligent. But if that stage is reached, the authority is not exercising a statutory power but purporting to do so and the statute is no defence.

This, however, does not in my view mean that if an element of discretion is involved in an act being done subject to the exercise of the overriding statutory power, common law negligence is necessarily ruled out. Acts may be done pursuant and subsequent to the exercise of a discretion where a duty of care may exist—as has often been said even knocking a nail into a piece of wood involves the exercise of some choice or discretion and yet there may be a duty of care in the way it is done. Whether there is an element of discretion to do the act is thus not a complete test leading to the result that, if there is, a claim against an authority for what it actually does or fails to do must necessarily be ruled out.

Another distinction which is sometimes drawn between decisions as to 'policy' and as to 'operational acts' sounds more promising. A pure policy decision where Parliament has entrusted the decision to a public authority is not something which a court would normally be expected to review in a claim in negligence. But again this is not an absolute test. Policy and operational acts are closely linked and the decision to do an operational act may easily involve and flow from a policy decision. Conversely, the policy is affected by the result of the operational act: see *Reg.* v *Chief Constable of Sussex, Ex parte International Trader's Ferry Ltd* [1998] 3 WLR 1260.

Where a statutory power is given to a local authority and damage is caused by what it does pursuant to that power, the ultimate question is whether the particular issue is justiciable or whether the court should accept that it has no role to play. The two tests (discretion and policy/operational) to which I have referred are guides in deciding that question. The greater the element of policy involved, the wider the area of discretion accorded, the more likely it is that the matter is not justiciable so that no action in negligence can be brought. It is true that Lord Reid and Lord Diplock in the *Dorset Yacht* case accepted that before a claim can be brought in negligence, the plaintiffs must show that the authority is behaving so unreasonably that it is not in truth exercising the real discretion given to it. But the passage I have cited was, as I read it, obiter, since Lord Reid made it clear that the case did not concern such a claim, but rather was a claim that Borstal officers had been negligent when they had disobeyed orders given to them. Moreover, I share Lord Browne-Wilkinson's reluctance to introduce the concepts of administrative law into the law of negligence, as Lord Diplock appears to have done. But in any case I do not read what either Lord Reid or Lord Wilberforce in the *Anns* case (and in particular Lord Reid) said as to the need to show that there has been an abuse of power before a claim can be brought in negligence in the exercise of a statutory discretion as meaning that an action can never be brought in negligence where an act has been done pursuant to the exercise of the discretion. A claim of negligence in the taking of a decision to exercise a statutory discretion is likely to be barred, unless it is wholly unreasonable so as not to be a real exercise of the discretion, or if it involves the making of a policy decision involving the balancing of different public interests; acts done pursuant to the lawful exercise of the discretion can, however, in my view be subject to a duty of care, even if some element of discretion is involved. Thus accepting that a decision to take a child into care pursuant to a statutory power is not justiciable, it does not in my view follow that, having taken a child into care, an authority cannot be liable for what it or its employees do in relation to the child without it being shown that they have acted in excess of power. It may amount to an excess of power, but that is not in my opinion the test to be adopted: the test is whether the conditions in the *Caparo* case [1990] 2 AC 605 have been satisfied.

In *Rowling* v *Takaro Properties Ltd* [1988] AC 473, 501 Lord Keith of Kinkel, said in giving the opinion of the Privy Council in relation to the policy/operational test:

> They incline to the opinion, expressed in the literature, that this distinction does not provide a touchstone of liability, but rather is expressive of the need to exclude altogether those cases in which the decision under attack is of such a kind that a question whether it has been made negligently is unsuitable for judicial resolution, of which notable examples are discretionary decisions on the allocation of scarce resources or the distribution of risks: see especially the discussion in *Craig on Administrative Law* (1983), pp. 534–538. If this is right, classification of the relevant decision as a policy or planning decision in this sense may exclude liability; but a conclusion that it does not fall within that category does not, in their Lordships' opinion, mean that a duty of care will necessarily exist.

Both in deciding whether particular issues are justiciable and whether if a duty of care is owed, it has been broken, the court must have regard to the statutory context and to the nature of the tasks involved. The mere fact that something has gone wrong or that a mistake has been made, or that someone has been inefficient does not mean that there was a duty to be careful or that such duty has been broken. Much of what has to be done in this area involves the balancing of delicate and difficult factors and courts should not be too ready to find in these situations that there has been negligence by staff who largely are skilled and dedicated.

. . .

In the Court of Appeal in the present case [1998] QB 367, Lord Woolf MR makes it clear that he does not suggest that a social services authority has a total immunity for whatever happens when it is acting or purporting to act pursuant to statutory powers or duties. He accepts, at p. 378 the principle assumed in *Capital & Counties Plc* v *Hampshire County Council* [1997] QB 1004, 1040**a** namely, 'there is no general immunity for professionals or others carrying out difficult tasks in stressful circumstances.' The staff of the local authority exercising its functions should be in no better or worse a position. He accepts that social workers and staff 'could however be negligent in an operational manner' and he gives as examples, carelessness in looking after a child's property, in failing to carry out instructions carefully in the way they report or fail to report what they have observed for the purposes of an assessment as to what should be done in relation to the child's future. So equally a parent does not have a blanket immunity for whatever he does to his child; negligence in driving a car by a parent would still be actionable if the child was caused injury.

Lord Browne-Wilkinson in the *Bedfordshire* case [1995] 2 AC 633, as has been shown, accepted that in respect of some matters—failing to detect or to take action when a child was clearly not doing as well as he could be doing, a psychiatrist failing to detect and report on the child's problem—the failure could be actionable. This means I accept that each case has to be looked at on its own facts and in the light of the statutory context. But this is so in many areas of the law and it is not in itself a reason for refusing to recognise a liability in negligence.

In the present case, the allegations which I have summarised are largely directed to the way in which the powers of the local authority were *exercised*. It is arguable (and that is all we are concerned with in this case at this stage) that if some of the allegations are made out, a duty of care was owed and was broken. Others involve the exercise of a discretion which the court may consider to be not justiciable—e.g. whether it was right to arrange adoption at all, though the question of whether adoption was ever considered and if not, why not, may be a matter for investigation in a claim of negligence. I do not think it right in this case to go through each allegation in detail to assess the chances of it being justiciable. The claim is of an on-going failure of duty and must be seen as a whole. I do not think that it is the right approach to look only at each detailed allegation and to ask whether that in itself could have caused the injury. That must be done but it is appropriate also to consider whether the cumulative effect of the allegations, if true, could have caused the injury. Nor do I accept that because the court should be slow to hold that a child can sue its parents for negligent decisions in its upbringing that the same should apply necessarily to all acts of a local authority. The latter has to take decisions which parents never or rarely have to take (e.g. as to adoption or as to an appropriate foster parent or institution). In any case, in respect of some matters, parents do have an actionable duty of care.

On the basis that the *Bedfordshire* case does not conclude the present case in my view it is arguable that at least in respect of some matters alleged both individually and cumulatively a duty of care was owed and was broken.

NOTES

1. *X* v *Bedfordshire* was about the discretion whether or not to use powers: this case is about what happens when that decision has been made (here the decision to take into care) and the powers are exercised. At some stage the decisions being made become 'operational' rather than 'policy' matters, but that is a gradual process and there can be no sharp distinction between the two concepts. Nevertheless, they can provide useful guidance as to what is justiciable and what is not. Even after that stage it must be 'fair and reasonable' to impose a duty. See also *S* v *Gloucestershire CC* [2000] 3 All ER 346.

2. In *Stovin* v *Wise* (below) the policy/operational distinction was criticized by Lord Hoffmann, but does its use as appropriate guidance by Lord Slynn in *Barrett* suggest its rehabilitation? *Street on Torts* (11th edn) suggests a similar distinction between *decision-making* cases (the exercise of statutory discretion) and *implementation* cases (the manner in which the discretion is carried out).

3. The Court of Appeal had also decided that it would not be fair and reasonable to impose a duty and that too was reversed by the House of Lords, partly on the grounds (per Lord Hutton) that the 'defensive care' argument should not prevent reasonable standards being required. Also *X* v *Bedfordshire* was clearly distinguishable as more sensitive and difficult decisions were involved there, as well as the situation involving a complex interdisciplinary structure.

---

### Stovin v Wise
House of Lords [1996] AC 923; [1996] 3 WLR 388; [1996] 3 All ER 801

The Norfolk County Council was aware that a road junction in Wymondham was dangerous and in January 1988 they wrote to British Rail, the owner of the land, suggesting that at their expense part of a bank of earth should be removed to improve visibility. British Rail agreed to seek internal approval but nothing further was done by either party. The defendants were under no statutory obligation to exercise their powers. In December 1988 the claimant was involved in a road accident at the junction which would not have happened if the work had been done. Held: allowing the appeal, that the County Council owed no duty of care to the claimant.

LORD HOFFMANN: . . .

*Negligent conduct in the exercise of statutory powers*

Since *Mersey Docks and Harbour Board Trustees* v *Gibbs* (1866) LR 1 HL 93 it has been clear law that in the absence of express statutory authority, a public body is in principle liable for torts in the same way as a private person. But its statutory powers or duties may restrict its liability. For example, it may be authorised to do something which necessarily involves committing what would otherwise be a tort. In such a case it will not be liable: *Allen* v *Gulf Oil Refining Ltd* [1981] AC 1001. Or it may have discretionary powers which enable it to do things to achieve a statutory purpose notwithstanding that they involve a foreseeable risk of damage to others. In such a case, a bona fide exercise of the discretion will not attract liability: *X (Minors)* v *Bedfordshire County Council* [1995] 2 AC 633 and *Dorset Yacht Co. Ltd* v *Home Office* [1970] AC 1004.

In the case of positive acts, therefore, the liability of a public authority in tort is in principle the same as that of a private person but may be *restricted* by its statutory powers and duties. The argument in the present case, however, is that whereas a private person would have owed no duty of care in respect of an omission to remove the hazard at the junction, the duty of the highway authority is *enlarged* by virtue of its statutory powers. The existence of the statutory powers is said to create a 'proximity' between the highway authority and the highway user which would not otherwise exist.

*Negligent omission to use statutory powers*

Until the decision of this House in *Anns* v *Merton London Borough Council* [1978] AC 728, there was no authority for treating a statutory power as giving rise to a common law duty of care. Two cases in particular were thought to be against it. In *Sheppard* v *Glossop Corporation* [1921] 3 KB 132 the council had power to light the streets of Glossop. But their policy was to turn off the lamps at 9 p.m. The plaintiff was injured when he fell over a retaining wall in the dark after the lamps had been extinguished. He sued the council for negligence. The Court of Appeal said that the council owed him no duty of care. Atkin LJ said, at p. 150:

> [The local authority] is under no legal duty to act reasonably in deciding whether it shall exercise its statutory powers or not, or in deciding to what extent, over what particular area, or for what particular time, it shall exercise its powers. . . . The real complaint of the plaintiff is not that they caused the danger, but that, the danger being there, if they had lighted it he would have seen and avoided it.

In *East Suffolk Rivers Catchment Board* v *Kent* [1941] AC 74, 102 the facts of which are too well known to need repetition [see below], Lord Romer cited *Sheppard* v *Glossop Corporation* and stated the principle which he said it laid down, at p. 102:

> Where a statutory authority is entrusted with a mere power it cannot be made liable for any damage sustained by a member of the public by reason of a failure to exercise that power.

. . .

### Anns v Merton London Borough Council

. . . Lord Wilberforce had to deal with an argument by the council which was based upon two propositions. The first was that if the council owed no duty to inspect in the first place, it could be under no liability for having done so negligently. The second relied upon Lord Romer's principle in the *East Suffolk* case [1941] AC 74, 97: a public authority which has a mere statutory power cannot on that account owe a duty at common law to exercise the power. Lord Wilberforce did not deny the first proposition. This, if I may respectfully say so, seems to me to be right. If the public authority was under no duty to act, either by virtue of its statutory powers or on any other basis, it cannot be liable because it has acted but negligently failed to confer a benefit on the plaintiff or to protect him from loss. The position is of course different if the negligent action of the public authority has left the plaintiff in a worse position than he would have been in if the authority had not acted at all. Lord Wilberforce did however deny the council's second proposition.

. . . Upon what principles can one say of a public authority that not only did it have a duty in public law to consider the exercise of the power but that it would thereupon have been under a duty in private law to act, giving rise to a claim in compensation against public funds for its failure to do so? Or as Lord Wilberforce puts it in the *Anns* case [1978] AC 728, 754:

> The problem which this kind of action creates, is to define the circumstances in which the law should impose, over and above, or perhaps alongside, these public law powers and duties, a duty in private law towards individuals such that they may sue for damages in a civil court.

The only tool which the *Anns* case provides for defining these circumstances is the distinction between policy and operations . . .

The *East Suffolk* case [1941] AC 74 and *Sheppard* v *Glossop Corporation* [1921] 3 KB 132 were distinguished as involving questions of policy or discretion. The inspection of foundations, on the other hand, was 'heavily operational' and the power to inspect could therefore give rise to a duty of care. Lord Romer's statement of principle in *East Suffolk* was limited to cases in which the exercise of the power involved a policy decision.

### Policy and operations

Since *Anns* v *Merton London Borough Council*, there have been differing views, both in England and the Commonwealth, over whether it was right to breach the protection which the *East Suffolk* principle gave to public authorities. In *Sutherland Shire Council* v *Heyman* 157 CLR 424, 483, Brennan J thought that it was wrong: one simply could not derive a common law 'ought' from a statutory 'may.' But I think that he was the only member of the court to adhere to such uncompromising orthodoxy. What has become clear, however, is that the distinction between policy and operations is an inadequate tool with which to discover whether it is appropriate to impose a duty of care or not. In *Rowling* v *Takaro Properties Ltd* [1988] AC 473, 501 Lord Keith of Kinkel said:

[Their Lordships] incline to the opinion, expressed in the literature, that this distinction does not provide a touchstone of liability, but rather is expressive of the need to exclude altogether those cases in which the decision under attack is of such a kind that a question whether it has been made negligently is unsuitable for judicial resolution, of which notable examples are discretionary decisions on the allocation of scarce resources or the distribution of risks. . . . If this is right, classification of the relevant decision as a policy or planning decision in this sense may exclude liability; but a conclusion that it does not fall within that category does not, in their Lordships' opinion, mean that a duty of care will necessarily exist.

There are at least two reasons why the distinction is inadequate. The first is that, as Lord Wilberforce himself pointed out, the distinction is often elusive. This is particularly true of powers to provide public benefits which involve the expenditure of money. Practically every decision about the provision of such benefits, no matter how trivial it may seem, affects the budget of the public authority in either timing or amount. The *East Suffolk* case, about which Lord Wilberforce said in the *Anns* case [1978] AC 728, 757, that the activities of the board, though 'operational,' were 'well within a discretionary area, so that the plaintiff's task in contending for a duty of care was a difficult one' is a very good example. But another reason is that even if the distinction is clear cut, leaving no element of discretion in the sense that it would be irrational (in the public law meaning of that word) for the public authority not to exercise its power, it does not follow that the law should superimpose a common law duty of care. This can be seen if one looks at cases in which a public authority has been under a statutory or common law *duty*, to provide a service or other benefit for the public or a section of the public. In such cases there is no discretion but the courts have nevertheless not been willing to hold that a member of the public who has suffered loss because the service was not provided to him should necessarily have a cause of action, either for breach of statutory duty or for negligence at common law.

There are many instances of this principle being applied to statutory duties, but perhaps the most relevant example of the dissociation between public duty and a liability to pay compensation for breach of that duty was the ancient common law duty to repair the highway. The common law imposed this financial burden upon the inhabitants of the parish. But it saw no need to impose upon them the additional burden of paying compensation to users of the highway who suffered injury because the highway surveyor had failed to repair. . . .

In terms of public finance, this is a perfectly reasonable attitude. It is one thing to provide a service at the public expense. It is another to require the public to pay compensation when a failure to provide the service has resulted in loss. Apart from cases of reliance, which I shall consider later, the same loss would have been suffered if the service had not been provided in the first place. To require payment of compensation increases the burden on public funds. Before imposing such an additional burden, the courts should be satisfied that this is what Parliament intended.

Whether a statutory duty gives rise to a private cause of action is a question of construction: see *R v Deputy Governor of Parkhurst Prison, ex parte Hague* [1992] 1 AC 58. It requires an examination of the policy of the statute to decide whether it was intended to confer a right to compensation for breach. Whether it can be relied upon to support the existence of a common law duty of care is not exactly a question of construction, because the cause of action does not arise out of the statute itself. But the policy of the statute is nevertheless a crucial factor in the decision. . . .

The same is true of omission to perform a statutory duty. If such a duty does not give rise to a private right to sue for breach, it would be unusual if it nevertheless gave rise to a duty of care at common law which made the public authority liable to pay compensation for foreseeable loss caused by the duty not being performed. It will often be foreseeable that loss will result if, for example, a benefit or service is not provided. If the policy of the act is not to create a statutory liability to pay compensation, the same policy should ordinarily exclude the existence of a common law duty of care.

In the case of a mere statutory power, there is the further point that the legislature has chosen to confer a discretion rather than create a duty. Of course there may be cases in which Parliament has chosen to confer a power because the subject matter did not permit a duty to be stated with sufficient precision. It may nevertheless have contemplated that in circumstances in which it would be irrational not to exercise the power, a person who suffered loss because it had not been exercised, or not properly exercised, would be entitled to compensation. I therefore do not say that a statutory 'may' can never give rise to a common law duty of care. I prefer to leave open the question of whether the *Anns* case was wrong to create any exception to Lord Romer's statement of principle in the *East Suffolk* case and I shall go on to consider the circumstances (such as 'general reliance') in which it has been suggested that such a duty might arise. But the fact that Parliament has conferred a discretion must be some indication that the policy of the act conferring the power was not to create a right to compensation. The need to have regard to the policy of the statute therefore means that exceptions will be rare.

In summary, therefore, I think that the minimum preconditions for basing a duty of care upon the existence of a statutory power, if it can be done at all, are, first, that it would in the circumstances have been irrational not to have exercised the power, so that there was in effect a public law duty to act, and secondly, that there are exceptional grounds for holding that the policy of the statute requires compensation to be paid to persons who suffer loss because the power was not exercised.

*Particular and general reliance*

In *Sutherland Shire Council* v *Heyman* 157 CLR 424, 483, Brennan J, as I have mentioned, thought that a statutory power could never generate a common law duty of care unless the public authority had created an expectation that the power would be used and the plaintiff had suffered damage from reliance on that expectation. A common example is the lighthouse authority which, by the exercise of its power to build and maintain a lighthouse, creates in mariners an expectation that the light will warn them of danger. In such circumstances, the authority (unlike the Glossop Corporation in *Sheppard* v *Glossop Corporation* [1921] 3 KB 132) owes a duty of care which requires it not to extinguish the light without giving reasonable notice. This form of liability, based upon representation and reliance, does not depend upon the public nature of the authority's powers and causes no problems.

In the same case, however, Mason J, suggested a different basis upon which public powers might give rise to a duty of care. He said, at p. 464:

> there will be cases in which the plaintiff's reasonable reliance will arise out of a general dependence on an authority's performance of its function with due care, without the need for contributing conduct on the part of a defendant or action to his detriment on the part of a plaintiff. Reliance or dependence in this sense is in general the product of the grant (and exercise) of powers designed to prevent or minimise a risk of personal injury or disability, recognised by the legislature as being of such magnitude or complexity that individuals cannot, or may not, take adequate steps for their own protection. This situation generates on one side (the individual) a general expectation that the power will be exercised and on the other side (the authority) a realisation that there is a general reliance or dependence on its exercise of the power. . . . The control of air traffic, the safety inspection of aircraft and the fighting of a fire in a building by a fire authority . . . may well be examples of this type of function.

This ground for imposing a duty of care has been called 'general reliance.' It has little in common with the ordinary doctrine of reliance; the plaintiff does not need to have relied upon the expectation that the power would be used or even known that it existed. It appears rather to refer to general expectations in the community, which the individual plaintiff may or may not have shared. A widespread assumption that a statutory power will be exercised may affect the general pattern of economic and social behaviour. For example, insurance premiums may take into account the expectation that statutory powers of inspection or accident prevention will ordinarily prevent certain kinds of risk from materialising. Thus the doctrine of general reliance requires an inquiry into the role of a given statutory power in the behaviour of members of the general public, of which an outstanding example is the judgment of Richardson J in *Invercargill City Council* v *Hamlin* [1994] 3 NZLR 513, 526.

It appears to be essential to the doctrine of general reliance that the benefit or service provided under statutory powers should be of a uniform and routine nature, so that one can describe exactly what the public authority was supposed to do. Powers of inspection for defects clearly fall into this category. Another way of looking at the matter is to say that if a particular service is provided as a matter of routine, it would be irrational for a public authority to provide it in one case and arbitrarily withhold it in another. This was obviously the main ground upon which this House in the *Anns* case considered that the power of the local authority to inspect foundations should give rise to a duty of care.

But the fact that it would be irrational not to exercise the power is, as I have said, only one of the conditions which has to be satisfied. It is also necessary to discern a policy which confers a right to financial compensation if the power has not been exercised. Mason J thought in *Sutherland Shire Council* v *Heyman* 157 CLR 424, 464, that such a policy might be inferred if the power was intended to protect members of the public from risks against which they could not guard themselves. In the *Invercargill* case, as I have said, the New Zealand Court of Appeal [1994] 3 NZLR 513 and the Privy Council [1996] 2 WLR 367 found it in general patterns of socio-economic behaviour. I do not propose to explore further the doctrine of general reliance because, for reasons which I shall explain, I think that there are no grounds upon which the present case can be brought within it. I will only note in passing that its application may require some very careful analysis of the role which the expected exercise of the statutory power plays in community behaviour. For example, in one sense it is true that the fire brigade is there to protect people in situations in which they could not be expected to be able to protect themselves. On the other hand, they can and do protect themselves by insurance against the risk of fire. It is not obvious that there should be a right to compensation from a negligent fire authority which will ordinarily insure by right of subrogation to an insurance company. The only reason would be to provide a general deterrent against inefficiency. But there must be better ways of doing this than by compensating insurance companies out of public funds. And while premiums no doubt take into account the existence of the fire brigade and the likelihood that it will arrive swiftly upon the scene, it is not clear that they would be very different merely because no compensation was paid in the rare cases in which the fire authority negligently failed to perform its public duty.

NOTES

1. In *East Suffolk Rivers Catchment Board* v *Kent* [1941] AC 74 (referred to above) the defendants were the drainage board for the river Deben and had the power to repair the river banks. On 1 December 1936 a combination of a gale and a spring tide made a breach in the river bank for about 25 feet which caused flooding of the claimant's land. Three times the defendants tried to build a dam straight across the breach, but without success. The breach was finally repaired by an alternative method on 28 May 1937, 178 days after starting work. It should have been done in 14 days. Although the defendants only had a power to repair the bank and were under no duty to do so, the claimant claimed that the defendants were liable because they had voluntarily undertaken the work and by their negligence had taken too long to repair the damage. The House of Lords held that the defendants were not liable. They could be liable only if their negligence had added to the damage which would have occurred if they had done nothing at all.

2. In *Gorringe* v *Calderdale MBC* [2004] 2 All ER 326, [2004] UKHL15, the House of Lords again discussed the problem of liability of public bodies. The claimant collided with a bus which was obscured by a sharp crest in the road. In the past there had been a 'SLOW' warning sign painted on the road but this had disappeared when the road was re-surfaced. She sued the Council for failing to warn her of the danger, but the House dismissed her claim, relying on *Stovin* v *Wise*. One point to emerge is that there may be a distinction between cases where the public body has merely failed to provide a benefit, as in *Stovin*, and cases where a relationship (albeit created by a statutory duty) exists between the parties as in *X* v *Bedfordshire CC*. In *Gorringe* Lord Hoffmann said '. . . I find it difficult to imagine a case in which a common law duty can be founded simply upon the failure (however irrational) to provide some benefit which a public authority has power (or a public duty) to provide'.

3.  Is general reliance a potential way forward? Lord Hoffmann is clearly cautious, as is Lord Nicholls, for he pointed out that if it means only that the public can expect that the authority will act as a reasonable authority that is not enough to provide liability. However, in the event Lord Nicholls and Lord Slynn dissented on the grounds that there were sufficient special circumstances over and above the reasonableness or otherwise of the decision to bring about proximity.

# 7

# Special Duty Problems: Psychiatric Injury

The essential question to be asked in this chapter is the degree of proximity which is required when a person has suffered psychiatric damage as a result of the act of the defendant. This issue has an interesting history, for it was thought at first that a claimant could only succeed if he or she was also within the range of physical impact (*Dulieu* v *White* [1901] 2 KB 669). In other words, only the 'primary' victim could sue, that is the person who would foreseeably suffer physical damage. Liability was later extended to secondary victims, that is where the claimant was not at risk of physical injury, but saw or heard the accident which caused the shock with his or her own unaided senses (*Hambrook* v *Stokes* [1925] 1 KB 141). After *Bourhill* v *Young* [1943] AC 92, the appropriate test became foreseeability of injury by shock, but the problem is, when is shock foreseeable? It is suggested that the courts in effect created 'sub-rules' or guidelines which indicated the kind of case where proximity in the legal sense would exist. In *Alcock* v *Chief Constable of South Yorkshire* [1991] 3 WLR 1057, the House seems to have adopted a compromise position whereby the test is one of foresight but one where foresight has a coded meaning. Thus, where the claimant has suffered psychiatric damage, the test of proximity which is required to establish a duty of care is 'foresight', as determined in the light of the relevant guidelines.

## SECTION 1: THE PRIMARY VICTIM

If a person has or might have suffered physical damage, the problem that has arisen is whether a duty must be shown to have existed in relation to the psychiatric damage separate from the duty owed in relation to the physical damage: or is it sufficient that if the duty can be shown to exist in relation to actual or potential physical damage, then damages for psychiatric injury can be recovered so long as they are not too remote? In *Dulieu* v *White* [1901] 2 KB 669, the court allowed recovery for the claimant when a horse van burst into the pub where she was working, even though she suffered no actual physical injury but was in the range of potential impact. This has now been affirmed in *Page* v *Smith* (below).

---

***Page* v *Smith***
House of Lords [1996] 1 AC 155; [1995] 2 WLR 655; [1995] 2 All ER 736

The claimant was involved in a car accident negligently caused by the defendant. Although the claimant's car was damaged he was physically unhurt but the accident caused a revival of chronic fatigue syndrome which he had suffered from some years before. The Court of Appeal had held that the illness was not foreseeable independently from the potential physical injury. Held: allowing the appeal, that the defendant was liable for the psychiatric illness.

LORD LLOYD: . . . Otton J [at first instance] adopted the same line of reasoning:

> Once it is established that CFS exists and that a relapse or recrudescence can be triggered by the trauma of an accident and that nervous shock was suffered by the plaintiff who is actually involved in the accident, it becomes a foreseeable consequence. The nervous shock cases relied on by Mr Priest, in my judgment, have no relevance. The plaintiff was not a spectator of the accident who suffered shock from what he witnessed happening to another. He was directly involved and suffered the shock directly from experiencing the accident. The remoteness argument, therefore, must be rejected.

Since physical injury to the plaintiff was clearly foreseeable, although it did not in the event occur, the judge did not consider, as a separate question, whether the defendant should have foreseen injury by nervous shock.

When the case got to the Court of Appeal [1994] 4 All ER 522, the approach became more complicated. Mr Priest's argument was as follows, as summarised by Ralph Gibson LJ, at p. 540:

> If a plaintiff establishes that he has suffered some physical injury, he may advance a claim in respect of a recognised psychiatric illness which has resulted from that physical injury. If a plaintiff has suffered no physical injury, and his only injuries are a recognised form of psychiatric illness, he may succeed if the court decides that psychiatric illness was foreseeable in the case of a person of reasonable fortitude. There is no difference in this respect, it was submitted, between a bystander and a person directly involved in an event, except that the consequences are more likely to be foreseeable in the case of the latter than in the case of the former. . . .

Are there any disadvantages in taking the simple approach adopted by Otton J? It may be said that it would open the door too wide, and encourage bogus claims. As for opening the door, this is a very important consideration in claims by secondary victims. It is for this reason that the courts have, as a matter of policy, rightly insisted on a number of control mechanisms. Otherwise, a negligent defendant might find himself being made liable to all the world. Thus in the case of secondary victims, foreseeability of injury by shock is not enough. The law also requires a degree of proximity: see *Alcock's* case [1992] 1 AC 310 *per* Lord Keith of Kinkel, at p. 396, and the illuminating judgment of Stuart-Smith LJ in *McFarlane* v *EE Caledonia Ltd* [1994] 2 All ER 1, 14. This means not only proximity to the event in time and space, but also proximity of relationship between the primary victim and the secondary victim. A further control mechanism is that the secondary victim will only recover damages for nervous shock if the defendant should have foreseen injury by shock to a person of normal fortitude or 'ordinary phlegm'.

None of these mechanisms are required in the case of a primary victim. Since liability depends on foreseeability of physical injury, there could be no question of the defendant finding himself liable to all the world. Proximity of relationship cannot arise, and proximity in time and space goes without saying.

Nor in the case of a primary victim is it appropriate to ask whether he is a person of 'ordinary phlegm.' In the case of physical injury there is no such requirement. The negligent defendant, or more usually his insurer, takes his victim as he finds him. The same should apply in the case of psychiatric injury. There is no difference in principle, as Geoffrey Lane J pointed out in *Malcolm* v *Broadhurst* [1970] 3 All ER 508, between an eggshell skull and an eggshell personality. Since the number of potential claimants is limited by the nature of the case, there is no need to impose any further limit by reference to a person of ordinary phlegm. Nor can I see any justification for doing so.

As for bogus claims, it is sometimes said that if the law were such as I believe it to be, the plaintiff would be able to recover damages for a fright. This is not so. Shock by itself is not the subject of compensation, any more than fear or grief or any other human emotion occasioned by the defendant's negligent conduct. It is only when shock is followed by recognisable psychiatric illness that the defendant may be held liable.

There is another limiting factor. Before a defendant can be held liable for psychiatric injury suffered by a primary victim, he must at least have foreseen the risk of physical injury. So that if, to take the example given by my noble and learned friend, Lord Jauncey of Tullichettle, the defendant bumped his neighbour's car while parking in the street, in circumstances in which he could not reasonably foresee that the occupant would suffer any physical injury at all, or suffer injury so trivial as not to found an action in tort, there could be no question of his being held liable for the onset of hysteria. Since he could not reasonably foresee any injury, physical or psychiatric, he would owe the plaintiff no duty of care. That example is, however, very far removed from the present.

So I do not foresee any great increase in unmeritorious claims. The court will, as ever, have to be vigilant to discern genuine shock resulting in recognised psychiatric illness. But there is nothing new in that. The floodgates argument has made regular appearances in this field, ever since it first appeared in *Victorian Railways Commissioners* v *Coultas* (1888) 13 App Cas 222. I do not regard it as a serious obstacle here.

My provisional conclusion, therefore, is that Otton J's approach was correct. The test in every case ought to be whether the defendant can reasonably foresee that his conduct will expose the plaintiff to risk of personal injury. If so, then he comes under a duty of care to that plaintiff. If a working definition of 'personal injury' is needed, it can be found in section 38(1) of the Limitation Act 1980: ' "personal injuries" includes any disease and any impairment of a person's physical or mental condition . . .' There are numerous other statutory definitions to the same effect. In the case of a secondary victim, the question will usually turn on whether the foreseeable injury is psychiatric, for the reasons already explained. In the case of a primary victim the question will almost always turn on whether the foreseeable injury is physical. But it is the same test in both cases, with different applications. There is no justification for regarding physical and psychiatric injury as different 'kinds' of injury. Once it is established that the defendant is under a duty of care to avoid causing personal injury to the plaintiff, it matters not whether the injury in fact sustained is physical, psychiatric or both. The utility of a single test is most apparent in those cases such as *Schneider* v *Eisovitch* [1960] QB 430, *Malcolm* v *Broadhurst* [1970] 3 All ER 508 and *Brice* v *Brown* [1984] 1 All ER 997, where the plaintiff is both primary and secondary victim of the same accident.

Applying that test in the present case, it was enough to ask whether the defendant should have reasonably foreseen that the plaintiff might suffer physical injury as a result of the defendant's negligence, so as to bring him within the range of the defendant's duty of care. It was unnecessary to ask, as a separate question, whether the defendant should reasonably have foreseen injury by shock; and it is irrelevant that the plaintiff did not, in fact, suffer any external physical injury. . . .

In conclusion, the following propositions can be supported. 1. In cases involving nervous shock, it is essential to distinguish between the primary victim and secondary victims. 2. In claims by secondary victims the law insists on certain control mechanisms, in order as a matter of policy to limit the number of potential claimants. Thus, the defendant will not be liable unless psychiatric injury is foreseeable in a person of normal fortitude. These control mechanisms have no place where the plaintiff is the primary victim. 3. In claims by secondary victims, it may be legitimate to use hindsight in order to be able to apply the test of reasonable foreseeability at all. Hindsight, however, has no part to play where the plaintiff is the primary victim. 4. Subject to the above qualifications, the approach in all cases should be the same, namely, whether the defendant can reasonably foresee that his conduct will expose the plaintiff to the risk of personal injury, whether physical or psychiatric. If the answer is yes, then the duty of care is established, even though physical injury does not, in fact, occur. There is no justification for regarding physical and psychiatric injury as different 'kinds of damage.' 5. A defendant who is under a duty of care to the plaintiff, whether as primary or secondary victim, is not liable for damages for nervous shock unless the shock results in some recognised psychiatric illness. It is no answer that the plaintiff was predisposed to psychiatric illness. Nor is it relevant that the illness takes a rare form or is of unusual severity. The defendant must take his victim as he finds him.

NOTES

1. Lords Keith and Jauncey dissented. Lord Keith said that the defendant can only be liable if the hypothetical reasonable man in his position should have foreseen that the claimant, regarded as a man of normal fortitude, might suffer nervous shock leading to an identifiable illness. He thought that, on the facts, nervous shock was not foreseeable and the fact that the claimant might have suffered direct personal injury was irrelevant. Lord Jauncey also noted that there should be foreseeability of the kind of damage that actually occurred, not which *might* have occurred. The majority felt that there was no distinction between direct personal injury and psychiatric illness and that they are the same 'kind of damage', so that all that had to be foreseen was either one or the other. Do you agree that they are the same 'kind' of damage?

2. There is also a problem with regard to duty of care and remoteness. It might be thought that if a different level of proximity is required in relation to different interests, then where two such interests arise out of one event the requisite level of proximity should be established in relation to each interest. The House of Lords has said this is not so, but this could cause injustice as between a claimant who happens to be a foreseeable claimant in relation to some damage (which did not actually occur) and one who is not. This is the kind of thing *The Wagon Mound* was supposed to prevent. That criticism has also been voiced by Lord Goff in *White* v *Chief Constable of South Yorkshire* (below), where he pointed out that in *The Wagon Mound No. 1* a 'common sense' distinction had been made between damage by fire and other possible damage and it would equally be a matter of common sense to say that physical injury was different from psychiatric injury. Accordingly Lord Goff criticizes *Page* v *Smith* for abandoning foresight of psychiatric damage as a necessary requirement and the unifying link in all such cases.

3. The Scottish Law Commission (Report No 196, Damages for psychiatric injury, 2004) has recommended the rejection of *Page* v *Smith* saying that liability should only be allowed where psychiatric injury was itself foreseeable, but agreeing that this will often be the case where a person is at risk of physical harm. Is this a sensible solution to the problems of *Page*?

4. Rescuers can be 'primary victims' if they are, or believe themselves to be, exposed to physical danger, otherwise they will be treated as secondary victims (see *Frost*, below). An example of a primary rescuer is *Chadwick* v *British Railways Board* [1967] 2 All ER 945, where the claimant assisted at the Lewisham train crash in 1957. The circumstances were particularly difficult as two trains had collided under a bridge, which compressed the wreckage. Mr Chadwick, who was a fairly small man, was asked to crawl into the wreckage and give injections to the injured. It was held that he could recover damages for the neurosis which he developed. He was a primary victim because he 'might have been injured by a wrecked carriage collapsing on him as he worked among the injured' (see Lord Hoffman in *White* v *Chief Constable of South Yorkshire* [1998] 3 WLR 1509 at 1556).

5. A further class of primary victim is those who believe that they were in some way 'responsible' for the death or injury of another. For example, see *Dooley* v *Cammell Laird* [1951] 1 Lloyd's Rep 271 where a rope on a crane broke causing the load to plunge into the ship's hold. The crane driver felt responsible and was allowed to recover damages for psychiatric injury. However, in *Hunter* v *British Coal* [1998] 2 All ER 97 it has been held that this applies only when the claimant is present when the injury occurs. The claimant had accidentally knocked a water hydrant (which was badly sited) in a coal mine: when he was some 30 metres away the hydrant 'exploded' and some ten minutes after that he was told that his co-worker was dead. The defendants were not liable as the claimant was not present at the time of the injury and so was not a primary victim. Nor could he claim as a secondary victim as his reaction was regarded as 'abnormal'. There was some criticism by Sir John Vinelott of the distinction between primary and secondary victims.

6. The claimant in *Page* v *Smith* spent a long time in the courts. The accident occurred in July 1987 and he finally succeeded in March 1996 after ten judgments had been delivered in the case (see *Page* v *Smith (No. 2)* [1996] 1 WLR 855).

## SECTION 2: THE SECONDARY VICTIM

It is generally agreed that where the person suffers psychiatric illness as a result of witnessing injury to another, special rules of proximity apply. There has been considerable debate about what is required, but the argument is often about how the rules should be presented. The test is still one of foreseeability, but judges prefer to lay down guidelines as to when such liability will arise: in effect saying when such damage is or is not foreseeable.

As often happens in the law of negligence, the issue largely turns on what we can be expected to put up with. Seeing one's daughter run over by a car is different from seeing a stranger run over. In *Bourhill* v *Young* [1943] AC 92, Lord Parker said:

> the driver of a car or vehicle even though careless is entitled to assume that the ordinary frequenter of the streets has sufficient fortitude to endure such incidents as may from time to time be expected to occur in them . . . and is not to be considered negligent towards one who does not possess the customary phlegm.

Damages cannot be awarded for grief and sorrow (see also *Hinz* v *Berry* [1970] 1 All ER 1084), as that is something we are expected to put up with (customary phlegm). However, it may be difficult to say when only grief is foreseeable and when mental illness is foreseeable. In *Vernon* v *Bosley (No. 1)* [1997] 1 All ER 577, the claimant arrived at the scene of an accident and witnessed unsuccessful attempts to rescue his children. The court said that it was difficult to distinguish between post-traumatic stress disorder (i.e. damage arising from witnessing an accident) and pathological grief disorder (mental illness arising from grief). The legal test was merely whether the illness arose from the defendant's breach of duty, which would be limited to not causing psychiatric damage through the claimant's witnessing the event or its aftermath. If such a duty is owed, the claimant could recover (as a matter of remoteness of damage) even though the damage could also be regarded as a consequence of bereavement. Stuart-Smith LJ dissented on the grounds that the claimant had to prove that the cause of his illness was witnessing the aftermath of the accident, and this he had not done.

---

### *Alcock* v *Chief Constable of South Yorkshire*
House of Lords [1992] 1 AC 310; [1991] 3 WLR 1057; [1991] 4 All ER 907

Shortly before the start of a football match between Liverpool and Nottingham Forest at the Hillsborough Stadium in Sheffield, the police negligently allowed a large number of spectators to have access to the stadium which was already full. In the resulting crush 95 spectators were killed and more than 400 were injured. The match was due to be televised and the disaster was shown live on television. The claimants all claimed they suffered psychiatric damage and fell into various groups. Some were present at the match (but not in the vicinity of the disaster), some saw the events on television and some heard about them on the radio. The relationship between the claimants and the victims also varied, some being relatives of varying degrees and others being friends. Held: dismissing the appeal, that the defendant was not liable to any of the claimants.

LORD ACKNER: In *Bourhill* v *Young* [1943] AC 92, 103, Lord Macmillan said:

> in the case of mental shock there are elements of greater subtlety than in the case of an ordinary physical injury and these elements may give rise to debate as to the precise scope of the legal liability.

It is now generally accepted that an analysis of the reported cases of nervous shock establishes that it is a type of claim in a category of its own. Shock is no longer a variant of physical injury but a separate kind of damage. Whatever may be the pattern of the future development of the law in relation to this cause of action, the following propositions illustrate that the application simpliciter of the reasonable foreseeability test is, today, far from being operative.

(1)   Even though the risk of psychiatric illness is reasonably foreseeable, the law gives no damages if the psychiatric injury was not induced by shock. Psychiatric illnesses caused in other ways, such as from the experience of having to cope with the deprivation consequent upon the death of a loved one, attracts no damages. Brennan J in *Jaensch* v *Coffey*, 155 CLR 549, 569, gave as examples, the spouse who has been worn down by caring for a tortiously injured husband or wife and who suffers psychiatric illness as a result, but who, nevertheless, goes without compensation; a parent made distraught by the wayward conduct of a brain-damaged child and who suffers psychiatric illness as a result also has no claim against the tortfeasor liable to the child.

(2)   Even where the nervous shock and the subsequent psychiatric illness caused by it could both have been reasonably foreseen, it has been generally accepted that damages for merely being informed of, or reading, or hearing about the accident are not recoverable. In *Bourhill* v *Young* [1943] AC 92, 103, Lord Macmillan only recognised the action lying where the injury by shock was sustained 'through the medium of the eye or the ear without direct contact.' Certainly Brennan J in his judgment in *Jaensch* v *Coffey*, 155 CLR 549, 567, recognised:

> A psychiatric illness induced by mere knowledge of a distressing fact is not compensable; perception by the plaintiff of the distressing phenomenon is essential.

That seems also to have been the view of Banks LJ in *Hambrook* v *Stokes Brothers* [1925] 1 KB 141, 152 . . .

(3)   Mere mental suffering, although reasonably foreseeable, if unaccompanied by physical injury, is not a basis for a claim for damages. To fill this gap in the law a very limited category of relatives are given a statutory right by the Administration of Justice Act 1982, section 3 inserting a new section 1A into the Fatal Accidents Act 1976, to bring an action claiming damages for bereavement.

(4)   As yet there is no authority establishing that there is liability on the part of the injured person, his or her estate, for mere psychiatric injury which was sustained by another by reason of shock, as a result of a self-inflicted death, injury or peril of the negligent person, in circumstances where the risk of such psychiatric injury was reasonably foreseeable. On the basis that there must be a limit at some reasonable point to the extent of the duty of care owed to third parties which rests upon everyone in all his actions, Lord Robertson, the Lord Ordinary, in his judgment in the *Bourhill* case, 1941 SC 395, 399, did not view with favour the suggestion that a negligent window-cleaner who loses his grip and falls from a height, impaling himself on spiked railings, would be liable for the shock-induced psychiatric illness occasioned to a pregnant woman looking out of the window of a house situated on the opposite side of the street.

(5)   'Shock', in the context of this cause of action, involves the sudden appreciation by sight or sound of a horrifying event, which violently agitates the mind. It has yet to include psychiatric illness caused by the accumulation over a period of time of more gradual assaults on the nervous system.

I do not find it surprising that in this particular area of the tort of negligence, the reasonable foreseeability test is not given a free rein. As Lord Reid said in *McKew* v *Holland & Hannen & Cubitts (Scotland) Ltd* [1969] 3 All ER 1621, 1623:

> A defender is not liable for a consequence of a kind which is not foreseeable. But it does not follow that he is liable for every consequence which a reasonable man could foresee.

Deane J pertinently observed in *Jaensch* v *Coffey*, 155 CLR 549, 583:

Reasonable foreseeability on its own indicates no more than that such a duty of care will exist if, and to the extent that, it is not precluded or modified by some applicable overriding requirement or limitation. It is to do little more than to state a truism to say that the essential function of such requirements or limitations is to confine the existence of a duty to take reasonable care to avoid reasonably foreseeable injury to the circumstances or classes of case in which it is the policy of the law to admit it. Such overriding requirements or limitations shape the frontiers of the common law of negligence.

Although it is a vital step towards the establishment of liability, the satisfaction of the test of reasonable foreseeability does not, in my judgment, ipso facto satisfy Lord Atkin's well known neighbourhood principle enunciated in *Donoghue* v *Stevenson* [1932] AC 562, 580. For him to have been reasonably in contemplation by a defendant he must be:

so closely and directly affected by my act that I ought reasonably to have them in contempla- tion as being so affected when I am directing my mind to the acts or omissions which are called in question.

The requirement contained in the words 'so closely and directly affected . . . that' constitutes a control upon the test of reasonable foreseeability of injury. Lord Atkin was at pains to stress, at pp. 580–582, that the formulation of a duty of care, merely in the general terms of reasonable foreseeability, would be too wide unless it were 'limited by the notion of proximity' which was embodied in the restriction of the duty of care to one's 'neighbour.'

### The three elements

Because 'shock' in its nature is capable of affecting such a wide range of persons, Lord Wilberforce in *McLoughlin* v *O'Brian* [1983] 1 AC 410, 422, concluded that there was a real need for the law to place some limitation upon the extent of admissible claims and in this context he considered that there were three elements inherent in any claim. It is common ground that such elements do exist and are required to be considered in connection with all these claims. The fundamental difference in approach is that on behalf of the plaintiffs it is contended that the consideration of these three elements is merely part of the process of deciding whether, as a matter of fact, the reasonable foreseeability test has been satisfied. On behalf of the defendant it is contended that these elements operate as a control of limitation on the mere application of the reasonable foreseeability test. They introduce the requirement of 'proximity' as conditioning the duty of care.

The three elements are (1) the class of persons whose claims should be recognised; (2) the proximity of such persons to the accident—in time and space; (3) the means by which the shock has been caused.

I will deal with those three elements seriatim.

### (1) The class of persons whose claim should be recognised

When dealing with the possible range of the class of persons who might sue, Lord Wilberforce in *McLoughlin* v *O'Brian* [1983] 1 AC 410 contrasted the closest of family ties—parent and child and husband and wife—with that of the ordinary bystander. He said that while existing law recognised the claims of the first, it denied that of the second, either on the basis that such persons must be assumed to be possessed with fortitude sufficient to enable them to endure the calamities of modern life, or that defendants cannot be expected to compensate the world at large. He considered that these positions were justified, that other cases involving less close relationships must be very carefully considered, adding, at p. 422:

The closer the tie (not merely in relationship, but in care) the greater the claim for con- sideration. The claim, in any case, has to be judged in the light of the other factors, such as proximity to the scene in time and place, and the nature of the accident.

I respectfully share the difficulty expressed by Atkin LJ in *Hambrook* v *Stokes Brothers* [1925] 1 KB 141, 158–159—how do you explain why the duty is confined to the case of parent or guardian and child and does not extend to other relations of life also involving intimate associations; and why does it not eventually extend to bystanders? As regards the latter category, while it may be very difficult to envisage a case of a stranger, who is not actively and foreseeably involved in a disaster or its aftermath, other than in the role of rescuer, suffering shock-induced psychiatric injury by the mere observation of apprehended or actual injury of a third person in circumstances that could be considered reasonably foreseeable, I see no reason in principle why he should not, if in the circumstances, a reasonably strong-nerved person would have been so shocked. In the course of argument your Lordships were given, by way of an example, that of a petrol tanker careering out of control into a school in session and bursting into flames. I would not be prepared to rule out a potential claim by a passer-by so shocked by the scene as to suffer psychiatric illness.

As regards claims by those in the close family relationships referred to by Lord Wilberforce, the justification for admitting such claims is the presumption, which I would accept as being rebuttable, that the love and affection normally associated with persons in those relationships is such that a defendant ought reasonably to contemplate that they may be so closely and directly affected by his conduct as to suffer shock resulting in psychiatric illness. While as a generalisation more remote relatives and, a fortiori, friends, can reasonably be expected not to suffer illness from the shock, there can well be relatives and friends whose relationship is so close and intimate that their love and affection for the victim is comparable to that of the normal parent, spouse or child of the victim and should for the purpose of this cause of action be so treated. . . .

### (2) The proximity of the plaintiff to the accident

It is accepted that the proximity to the accident must be close both in time and space. Direct and immediate sight or hearing of the accident is not required. It is reasonably foreseeable that injury by shock can be caused to a plaintiff, not only through the sight or hearing of the event, but of its immediate aftermath.

Only two of the plaintiffs before us were at the ground. However, it is clear from *McLoughlin* v *O'Brian* [1963] 1 AC 410 that there may be liability where subsequent identification can be regarded as part of the 'immediate aftermath' of the accident. Mr Alcock identified his brother-in-law in a bad condition in the mortuary at about midnight, that is some eight hours after the accident. This was the earliest of the identification cases. Even if this identification could be described as part of the 'aftermath,' it could not in my judgment be described as part of the *immediate* aftermath. *McLoughlin's* case was described by Lord Wilberforce as being upon the margin of what the process of logical progression from case to case would allow. Mrs McLoughlin had arrived at the hospital within an hour or so after the accident. Accordingly in the post-accident identification cases before your Lordships there was not sufficient proximity in time and space to the accident.

### (3) The means by which the shock is caused

Lord Wilberforce concluded that the shock must come through sight or hearing of the event or its immediate aftermath but specifically left for later consideration whether some equivalent of sight or hearing, e.g. through simultaneous television, would suffice. . . . Of course it is common ground that it was clearly foreseeable by the defendant that the scenes at Hillsborough would be broadcast live and that amongst those who would be watching would be parents and spouses and other relatives and friends of those in the pens behind the goal at the Leppings Lane end. However he would also know of the code of ethics which the television authorities televising this event could be expected to follow, namely that they would not show pictures of suffering by recognisable individuals. Had they done so, Mr Hytner accepted that this would have been a 'novus actus' breaking the chain of causation between the defendant's alleged breach of duty and the psychiatric illness. As the defendant was reasonably entitled to expect to be the case, there were no such pictures. Although the television pictures certainly gave rise to feelings of the deepest anxiety and distress, in the circumstances of this case the simultaneous television broadcasts of what occurred cannot be equated with the 'sight or hearing of the event or its immediate aftermath.' Accordingly shocks sustained by reason of these broadcasts cannot found a claim. I agree, however, with Nolan LJ that simultaneous broadcasts of a disaster cannot in all cases by ruled out as providing the equivalent of the actual sight or hearing of the event or its immediate aftermath. Nolan LJ gave . . . an example of a situation where it was reasonable to anticipate that the television cameras, whilst filming and transmitting pictures of a special event of children travelling in a balloon, in which there was media interest, particularly amongst the parents, showed the balloon suddenly bursting into flames. Many other such situations could be imagined where the impact of the simultaneous television pictures would be as great, if not greater, than the actual sight of the accident.

*Conclusion*

Only one of the plaintiffs, who succeeded before Hidden J, namely Brian Harrison, was at the ground. His relatives who died were his two brothers. The quality of brotherly love is well known to differ widely—from Cain and Abel to David and Jonathan. I assume that Mr Harrison's relationship with his brothers was not an abnormal one. His claim was not presented upon the basis that there was such a close and intimate relationship between them, as gave rise to that very special bond of affection which would make his shock-induced psychiatric illness reasonably foreseeable by the defendant. Accordingly, the judge did not carry out the requisite close scrutiny of their relationship. Thus there was no evidence to establish the necessary proximity which would make his claim reasonably foreseeable and, subject to the other factors, to which I have referred, a valid one. The other plaintiff who was present at the ground, Robert Alcock, lost a brother-in-law. He was not, in my judgment, reasonably foreseeable as a potential sufferer from shock-induced psychiatric illness, in default of very special facts and none was established. Accordingly their claims must fail, as must those of the other plaintiffs who only learned of the disaster by watching simultaneous television. . . .

NOTES
1. In *Alcock*, Lord Ackner says that 'shock is no longer a variant of physical injury but a separate kind of damage', whereas in *Page* v *Smith* Lord Lloyd said that there is 'no justification for regarding physical and psychiatric injury as different kinds of injury'. However, in *White* (below) Lord Steyn said that while there may be no qualitative differences between physical and psychiatric harm, nevertheless they are treated differently by the law on policy grounds as the contours of tort law are profoundly affected by distinctions between different kinds of damage. This is clearly right.
2. The 'nervous shock' cases have become even more confused since *Page* v *Smith* and seem to call into question the distinction between duty and remoteness of damage since the case seems to assume that if a duty is owed to the claimant in relation to physical damage, then psychiatric damage can be recovered as a matter of remoteness of damage, even though the claimant would not have been able to recover because of proximity rules without the foreseeable physical loss. It is suggested that psychiatric damage is different and that the distinction between primary and secondary victims is unwarranted.
3. One strange consequence of *Page* v *Smith* is that psychiatric injury following physical injury will rarely be too remote. In *Simmons* v *British Steel* [2004] ICR 585, [2004] UKHL 20, the pursuer fell and banged his head. Apparently he developed a skin disease (psoriasis) and depression, not directly as a result of his injuries but because of his anger and his employer's failure to apologise and their lack of support for him. The employer was held liable for all the consequences of the injury. Lord Rodger said 'the defenders are liable in damages for both types of injury and, in particular, for the exacerbation of the pursuer's psoriasis and for the depressive illness which followed—*even if those developments were not reasonably foreseeable*' (italics added). This is very odd and apparently flows from the fact that he was a primary victim within *Page* v *Smith* and the defendants must take their victims as they find them both as regards physical and psychiatric consequences (see *Robinson* v *Post Office* above).
4. People who are not related to the victim of an accident may be able to sue, but there must be some close involvement with the event. Mere bystanders probably could not sue, as they will be assumed to have sufficient fortitude to overcome distress at witnessing an accident (*McFarlane* v *E E Caledonia Ltd* [1994] 2 All ER 1—witness of the Piper Alpha oil rig disaster). As to rescuers, they will be primary victims if they are, or believe they are, in danger of physical

injury (see *Chadwick* v *British Railways Board*, above). Otherwise they will be treated as secondary victims and dealt with under the *Alcock* rules (see *White*, below).

5. Contrary to the British rule the High Court of Australia has held that 'sudden shock' is not a necessary requirement of liability, but that there could be liability for psychiatric damage arising from a protracted state of affairs. However, there may be problems with showing such damage to be foreseeable, and with the notion of 'usual fortitude'. See *Tame* v *New South Wales* (2002) 76 ALJR 1348. This case also held that there is no action in negligence against the bearer of bad news for the way in which the news is conveyed.

6. It has been held that if a person carelessly injures himself or herself, that person owes no duty even to close relatives to prevent their psychiatric damage. In *Greatorex* v *Greatorex* [2000] 4 All ER 769, the defendant carelessly caused a road accident in which he was severely injured. His father, as a fire fighter, attended the scene and subsequently suffered post-traumatic stress disorder. It was held that the son owed no duty to the father, as to do so would 'curtail the right to self determination and liberty of the individual' and would open up the possibility of undesirable litigation within the family. Does this ignore the prevalence of liability insurance?

## *White* v *Chief Constable of South Yorkshire*
House of Lords [1999] 2 AC 455 [1998] 3 WLR 1509; [1999] 1 All ER 1

[Note: this case is also known as *Frost* v *Chief Constable of South Yorkshire*]

This case also arose out of the Hillsborough football disaster. The claimants on appeal were police officers who had been present at the ground and who had assisted the victims. The Court of Appeal had held that a duty was owed to them as employees of the defendant. Held: allowing the appeal, that the defendant was not liable.

LORD STEYN: . . . My impression is that there are at least four distinctive features of claims for psychiatric harm which in combination may account for the differential treatment. Firstly, there is the complexity of drawing the line between acute grief and psychiatric harm: see Steve Hedley, 'Nervous Shock: Wider Still and Wider?' [1997] CLJ 254. The symptoms may be the same. But there is greater diagnostic uncertainty in psychiatric injury cases than in physical injury cases. The classification of emotional injury is often controversial. In order to establish psychiatric harm expert evidence is required. That involves the calling of consultant psychiatrists on both sides. It is a costly and time consuming exercise. If claims for psychiatric harm were to be treated as generally on a par with physical injury it would have implications for the administration of justice. On its own this factor may not be entitled to great weight and may not outweigh the considerations of justice supporting genuine claims in respect of pure psychiatric injury. Secondly, there is the effect of the expansion of the availability of compensation on potential claimants who have witnessed gruesome events. I do not have in mind fraudulent or bogus claims. In general it ought to be possible for the administration of justice to expose such claims. But I do have in mind the *unconscious* effect of the prospect of compensation on potential claimants. Where there is generally no prospect of recovery, such as in the case of injuries sustained in sport, psychiatric harm appears not to obtrude often. On the other hand, in the case of industrial accidents, where there is often a prospect of recovery of compensation, psychiatric harm is repeatedly encountered and often endures until the process of claiming compensation comes to an end: see *James* v *Woodall Duckham Construction Co. Ltd* [1969] 1 WLR 903. The litigation is sometimes an unconscious disincentive to rehabilitation. It is true that this factor is already present in cases of physical injuries with concomitant mental suffering. But it may play a larger role in cases of pure psychiatric harm, particularly if the categories of potential recovery are enlarged. For my part this factor cannot be dismissed.

The third factor is important. The abolition or a relaxation of the special rules governing the recovery of damages for psychiatric harm would greatly increase the class of persons who can recover damages in tort. It is true that compensation is routinely awarded for psychiatric harm where the plaintiff has suffered some physical harm. It is also well established that psychiatric harm resulting from the apprehension of physical harm is enough: *Page* v *Smith* [1996] AC 155. These two principles are not surprising. Inbuilt in such situations are restrictions on the classes of plaintiff who can sue; the requirement of the infliction of some physical injury or apprehension of it introduces an element of immediacy which restricts the category of potential plaintiffs. But in cases of pure psychiatric harm there is potentially a wide class of plaintiffs involved. Fourthly, the imposition of liability for pure psychiatric harm in a wide range of situations may result in a burden of liability on defendants which may be disproportionate to tortious conduct involving perhaps momentary lapses of concentration, e.g. in a motor car accident.

. . .

### The employment argument

. . . it became obvious that there were two separate themes to the argument. The first rested on the duty of an employer to care for the safety of his employees and to take reasonable steps to safeguard them from harm. When analysed this argument breaks down. It is a non sequitur to say that because an employer is under a duty to an employee not to cause him physical injury, the employer should as a necessary consequence of that duty (of which there is no breach) be under a duty not to cause the employee psychiatric injury: see Chris Hilson, 'Nervous Shock and the Categorisation of Victims' (1998) 6 Tort L Rev 37, 42. The rules to be applied when an employee brings an action against his employer for harm suffered at his workplace are the rules of tort. One is therefore thrown back to the ordinary rules of the law of tort which contain restrictions on the recovery of compensation for psychiatric harm. This way of putting the case does not therefore advance the case of the police officers. . . .

The second theme is on analysis an argument as to where the justice lay on this occasion. One is considering the claims of police officers who sustained serious psychiatric harm in the course of performing and assisting their duties in harrowing circumstances. That is a weighty moral argument: the police perform their duties for the benefit of us all. The difficulty is, however, twofold. First, the pragmatic rules governing the recovery of damages for pure psychiatric harm do not at present include police officers who sustain such injuries while on duty. If such a category were to be created by judicial decision, the new principle would be available in many different situations, e.g. doctors and hospital workers who are exposed to the sight of grievous injuries and suffering. Secondly, it is common ground that police officers who are traumatised by something they encounter in their work have the benefit of statutory schemes which permit them to retire on pension. In this sense they are already better off than bereaved relatives who were not allowed to recover in the *Alcock* case. The claim of the police officers on our sympathy, and the justice of the case, is great but not as great as that of others to whom the law denies redress.

### The rescue argument

The majority in the Court of Appeal [1998] QB 254 held that three of the police officers could be classed as rescuers because they actively gave assistance in the aftermath of the tragedy: the majority used the concept of rescuer in an undefined but very wide sense: see Rose LJ, at p. 264; Henry LJ expressly agreed with this passage. This reasoning was supported by counsel for the appellant on the appeal.

The law has long recognised the moral imperative of encouraging citizens to rescue persons in peril. Those who altruistically expose themselves to danger in an emergency to save others are favoured by the law. A rescue attempt to save someone from danger will be regarded as foresee-able. A duty of care to a rescuer may arise even if the defendant owed no duty to the primary victim, for example, because the latter was a trespasser. If a rescuer is injured in a rescue attempt, a plea of volenti non fit injuria will not avail a wrongdoer. A plea of contributory negligence will usually receive short shrift. A rescuer's act in endangering himself will not be treated as a novus actus interveniens. The meaning given to the concept of a rescuer in these situations is of no assistance in solving the concrete case before the House. Here the question is: who may recover in respect of pure psychiatric harm sustained as a rescuer?

Counsel for the appellant is invoking the concept of a rescuer as an exception to the limitations recognised by the House of Lords in the *Alcock* case [1992] 1 AC 310 and *Page* v *Smith* [1996] AC 155. The restrictive rules, and the underlying policy considerations, of the decisions of the House are germane. The specific difficulty counsel faces is that it is common ground that none of the four police officers were at any time exposed to personal danger and none thought that they were so exposed. Counsel submitted that this is not a requirement. He sought comfort in the general observations in the *Alcock* case of Lord Oliver about the category of 'participants:' see p. 407**e**. None of the other Law Lords in the *Alcock* case discussed this category. Moreover, the issue of rescuers' entitlement to recover for psychiatric harm was not before the House on that occasion and Lord Oliver was not considering the competing arguments presently before the House. The explanation of Lord Oliver's observations has been the subject of much debate. It was also vigorously contested at the bar. In my view counsel for the appellant has tried to extract too much from general observations not directed to the issue now before the House: see also the careful analysis of the Lord President in *Robertson* v *Forth Road Bridge Joint Board*, 1995 SCLR 466, 473. Counsel was only able to cite one English decision in support of his argument namely the first instance judgment in *Chadwick* v *British Railways Board* [1967] 1 WLR 912. Mr Chadwick had entered a wrecked railway carriage to help and work among the injured. There was clearly a risk that the carriage might collapse. Waller J said, at p. 918:

> although there was clearly an element of personal danger in what Mr Chadwick was doing, I think I must deal with this case on the basis that it was the horror of the whole experience which caused his reaction.

On the judge's findings the rescuer had passed the threshold of being in personal danger but his psychiatric injury was caused by 'the full horror of his experience' when he was presumably not always in personal danger. This decision has been cited with approval: see *McLoughlin* v *O'Brian* [1983] 1 AC 410, *per* Lord Wilberforce, at p. 419, *per* Lord Edmund-Davies, at p. 424, and *per* Lord Bridge of Harwich, at pp. 437–38; and in the *Alcock* case [1992] 1 AC 310, *per* Lord Oliver, at p. 408. I too would accept that the *Chadwick* case was correctly decided. But it is not authority for the proposition that a person who never exposed himself to any personal danger and never thought that he was in personal danger can recover pure psychiatric injury as a rescuer. In order to recover compensation for pure psychiatric harm as rescuer it is not necessary to establish that his psychiatric condition was *caused* by the perception of personal danger. And Waller J rightly so held. But in order to contain the concept of rescuer in reasonable bounds for the purposes of the recovery of compensation for pure psychiatric harm the plaintiff must at least satisfy the threshold requirement that he objectively exposed himself to danger or reasonably believed that he was doing so. Without such limitation one would have the unedifying spectacle that, while bereaved relatives are not allowed to recover as in the *Alock* case, ghoulishly curious spectators, who assisted in some peripheral way in the aftermath of a disaster, might recover. For my part the limitation of actual or apprehended dangers is what proximity in this special situation means. In my judgment it would be an unwarranted extension of the law to uphold the claims of the police officers. I would dismiss the argument under this heading.

*Thus far and no further*

My Lords, the law on the recovery of compensation for pure psychiatric harm is a patchwork quilt of distinctions which are difficult to justify. There are two theoretical solutions. The first is to wipe out recovery in tort for pure psychiatric injury. The case for such a course has been argued by Professor Stapleton. But that would be contrary to precedent and, in any event, highly controversial. Only Parliament could take such a step. The second solution is to abolish all the special limiting rules applicable to psychiatric harm. That appears to be the course advocated by *Mullany and Handford, Tort Liability for Psychiatric Damage*. They would allow claims for pure psychiatric damage by mere bystanders: see (1997) 113 LQR 410, 415. Precedent rules out this course and, in any event, there are cogent policy considerations against such a bold innovation. In my view the only sensible general strategy for the courts is to say thus far and no further. The only prudent course is to treat the pragmatic categories as reflected in authoritative decisions such as the *Alcock* case [1992]

1 AC 310 and *Page* v *Smith* [1996] AC 155 as settled for the time being but by and large to leave any expansion or development in this corner of the law to Parliament. In reality there are no refined analytical tools which will enable the courts to draw lines by way of compromise solution in a way which is coherent and morally defensible. It must be left to Parliament to undertake the task of radical law reform.

NOTES

1. Should police officers and other professional rescuers be treated differently from other members of the public because they are more used to witnessing harrowing scenes? In *White*, Lord Hoffman rejected any automatic rule (see *Ogwo* v *Taylor* [1988] AC 431) but said that 'it is legitimate to take into account the fact that in the nature of things many [rescuers] will be from occupations in which they are trained and required to run such risks and which provide for appropriate benefits if they should suffer such injuries'. How would this work? What would be the effect, say, of generous early retirement benefits on medical grounds?

2. It is agreed that an ordinary person might suffer psychiatric illness as the result of injury to close relatives, but what degree of fortitude is expected of a person who sees his or her property destroyed? In *Attia* v *British Gas* [1988] QB 304, the claimant returned home to find her house on fire, and claimed that she suffered nervous shock as a result. The Court of Appeal held that such a claim was not automatically excluded and should proceed to trial to determine whether it was foreseeable that a reasonable householder, exposed to the experience undergone by the claimant, might suffer psychiatric illness, as opposed to grief and sorrow at the loss of his or her home. Presumably after *Page* v *Smith* (above) the claimant would be regarded as a primary victim and the issue of psychiatric damage would be one of remoteness of damage. It is suggested, however, that it should be regarded as a problem of duty, and that sufficient proximity should be established in relation to each of the claimant's interests of property and psychiatric damage.

3. The 'egg shell skull' rule applies to cases of nervous shock, but it still needs to be proved that a person of reasonable fortitude who possesses the 'customary phlegm' would have suffered *some* psychiatric damage, for the duty of care needs to be established. The egg shell skull rule relates only to remoteness, and brings in damage which is greater than would normally have been suffered. In *Brice* v *Brown* [1984] 1 All ER 997, Mrs Brice was in a taxi which was in collision with a bus, and while she suffered only slight injury, her daughter was quite seriously hurt. The claimant became mentally ill. It was held that an ordinary person might have suffered psychiatric damage and therefore a duty was owed, and the fact that, due to a personality disorder, her illness was much more severe than might have been expected did not render the damage too remote. She would now be regarded as a primary victim, but the remoteness issue remains.

4. See further Teff, 'Liability for psychiatric illness after Hillsborough' (1992) OJLS 440; Murphy, 'Negligently inflicted psychiatric harm: a re-appraisal' (1996) 15 LS 415; Mullany and Handford, *Tort Liability for Psychiatric Damage* (1993).

# 8

## Special Duty Problems: Statements, Services and Economic Loss

This chapter deals with negligent statements or services which cause economic loss. There are therefore two peculiarities in this area: the first is due to the fact that liability for statements has always been restricted, and the second is that economic loss by itself is rarely protected.

The harmful effects of a statement can carry further than the effects of an act, and it is probably easier to make a careless statement than commit a negligent act. This subject is therefore one where fairly stringent limitations have been placed on the notion of proximity, and it is said that there must be 'a special relationship' between the parties before a duty of care can arise. Indeed, until 1963 there was no duty at all in this area, but after *Hedley Byrne* v *Heller* in that year, the range of liability steadily expanded, although the ever-increasing complexity and inter-relation of communication means that new problems are always presenting themselves—the most recent being the question of the range of potential liability of accountants. This area of law is developing rapidly. The traditional view of *Hedley Byrne* liability is that it depends upon a voluntary assumption of responsibility by the defendant when giving advice or exercising skills, and the claimant acts to his or her detriment when relying on that advice or skill. However, as will be seen in section 3, that may now extend to cases where the advice is not given to the claimant but rather to a third party who acts to the detriment of the claimant (*Spring* v *Guardian Assurance*, below). Also, there may be cases where reliance is not necessary at all because the defendant has assumed a responsibility which is analogous to a fiduciary obligation (*White* v *Jones*, below). One point to note is that if a defendant is liable for a negligent statement, the claimant may recover losses, even though these may be purely economic losses. The extent to which a person who suffers pure economic loss as the result of an act may recover is discussed in the next chapter. This chapter does not deal with other wrongs which may result from a statement, such as the tort of deceit or breach of a fiduciary obligation.

The particular issues which need to be addressed are:

(a) when is a person under a duty to be careful in making a statement?;
(b) to whom is that duty owed?;
(c) when can there be liability to a third party, i.e. to a person who is not a recipient of the information but is a person who suffers damage because of the act of a person who is?; and
(d) to what extent can a person absolve himself or herself of responsibility?

## SECTION 1: BY WHOM A DUTY IS OWED

It would be too onerous a burden to hold a person responsible whenever he or she carelessly makes a statement which turns out to be wrong, and someone else has suffered loss as a result, for otherwise a person could be liable for even a casual statement made at a party. The courts have established that special rules of proximity apply in this area, so that a 'special relationship' must be established between the parties, and to a large extent this depends on the defendant knowing that the claimant is justifiably relying upon him or her for the defendant's special skill or expertise or knowledge.

### *Hedley Byrne & Co. Ltd* v *Heller and Partners Ltd*
House of Lords [1964] AC 465; [1963] 3 WLR 100; [1963] 2 All ER 575

The claimants, Hedley Byrne & Co., were advertising agents who intended to engage in an advertising programme for Easipower Ltd which would cost about £100,000. They asked their own bankers, National Provincial Bank Ltd, to obtain a reference about Easipower, and National Provincial wrote to the defendants, Heller and Partners, who were Easipower's bankers. They replied in a letter which said that it was 'For your private use and without responsibility on the part of the bank or its officials' and went on to say that Easipower was a 'respectably constituted company, considered good for its ordinary business engagements. Your figures are larger than we are accustomed to see.' Easipower went into liquidation, and the claimants lost some £17,000. Held: dismissing the appeal, that there could be a duty not to make a statement carelessly which causes only economic loss, but that in the circumstances the disclaimer prevented a duty arising and the defendants were not liable.

LORD REID: A reasonable man, knowing that he was being trusted or that his skill and judgment were being relied on, would, I think, have three courses open to him. He could keep silent or decline to give the information or advice sought: or he could give an answer with a clear qualification that he accepted no responsibility for it or that it was given without that reflection or inquiry which a careful answer would require: or he could simply answer without any such qualification. If he chooses to adopt the last course he must, I think, be held to have accepted some responsibility for his answer being given carefully, or to have accepted a relationship with the inquirer which requires him to exercise such care as the circumstances require.

LORD MORRIS: My Lords, I consider that it follows and that it should now be regarded as settled that if someone possessed of a special skill undertakes, quite irrespective of contract, to apply that skill for the assistance of another person who relies upon such skill, a duty of care will arise. The fact that the service is to be given by means of or by the instrumentality of words can make no difference. Furthermore, if in a sphere in which a person is so placed that others could reasonably rely upon his judgment or his skill or upon his ability to make careful inquiry, a person takes it upon himself to give information or advice to, or allows his information or advice to be passed on to, another person who, as he knows or should know, will place reliance upon it, then a duty of care will arise.

LORD DEVLIN: I think, therefore, that there is ample authority to justify your Lordships in saying now that the categories of special relationships which may give rise to a duty to take care in word as well as in deed are not limited to contractual relationships or to relationships of fiduciary duty, but include also relationships which in the words of Lord Shaw in *Nocton* v *Lord Ashburton* [1914] AC 932, 972 are 'equivalent to contract,' that is, where there is an assumption of responsibility in circumstances in which, but for the absence of consideration, there would be a contract. Where there is an express undertaking, an express warranty as distinct from mere representation, there can be little difficulty. The difficulty arises in discerning those cases in which the undertaking is to be implied. In this respect the absence of consideration is not irrelevant. Payment for information or advice is very good evidence that it is being relied upon and that the informer or adviser knows that it is. Where there is no consideration, it will be necessary to exercise greater care in distinguishing between social and professional relationships and between those which are of a contractual character and those which are not. It may often be material to consider whether the adviser is acting purely out of good nature or whether he is getting his reward in some indirect form. The service that a bank performs in giving a reference is not done simply out of a desire to assist commerce. It would discourage the customers of the bank if their deals fell through because the bank had refused to testify to their credit when it was good.

I shall therefore content myself with the proposition that wherever there is a relationship equivalent to contract, there is a duty of care. Such a relationship may be either general or particular. Examples of a general relationship are those of solicitor and client and of banker and customer. For the former *Nocton* v *Lord Ashburton* has long stood as the authority and for the latter there is the decision of Salmon J in *Woods* v *Martins Bank Ltd*, which I respectfully approve. There may well be others yet to be established. Where there is a general relationship of this sort, it is unnecessary to do more than prove its existence and the duty follows. Where, as in the present case, what is relied on is a particular relationship created ad hoc, it will be necessary to examine the particular facts to see whether there is an express or implied undertaking of responsibility.

I regard this proposition as an application of the general conception of proximity. Cases may arise in the future in which a new and wider proposition, quite independent of any notion of contract, will be needed. There may, for example, be cases in which a statement is not supplied for the use of any particular person, any more than in *Donoghue* v *Stevenson* [1932] AC 562, the ginger beer was supplied for consumption by any particular person; and it will then be necessary to return to the general conception of proximity and to see whether there can be evolved from it, as was done in *Donoghue* v *Stevenson*, a specific proposition to fit the case. . . .

LORD PEARCE: The law of negligence has been deliberately limited in its range by the courts' insistence that there can be no actionable negligence in vacuo without the existence of some duty to the plaintiff. For it would be impracticable to grant relief to everybody who suffers damage through the carelessness of another.

The reason for some divergence between the law of negligence in word and that of negligence in act is clear. Negligence in word creates problems different from those of negligence in act. Words are more volatile than deeds. They travel fast and far afield. They are used without being expended and take effect in combination with innumerable facts and other words. Yet they are dangerous and can cause vast financial damage. How far they are relied on unchecked (by analogy with there being no probability of intermediate inspection—see *Grant* v *Australian Knitting Mills Ltd*, [1936] AC 85) must in many cases be a matter of doubt and difficulty. If the mere hearing or reading of words were held to create proximity, there might be no limit to the persons to whom the speaker or writer could be liable. Damage by negligent acts to persons or property on the other hand is more visible and obvious; its limits are more easily defined, and it is with this damage that the earlier cases were more concerned. It was not until 1789 that *Pasley* v *Freeman*, 100 ER 450, recognised and laid down a duty of honesty in words to the world at large—thus creating a remedy designed to protect the economic as opposed to the physical interests of the community. Any attempts to extend this remedy by imposing a duty of care as well as a duty of honesty in representations by word were curbed by *Derry* v *Peek* (1889) 14 App Cas 337.

. . . There is also, in my opinion, a duty of care created by special relationships which, though not fiduciary, give rise to an assumption that care as well as honesty is demanded.

Was there such a special relationship in the present case as to impose on the defendants a duty of care to the plaintiffs as the undisclosed principals for whom the National Provincial Bank was making the inquiry? The answer to that question depends on the circumstances of the transaction. If, for instance, they disclosed a casual social approach to the inquiry no such special relationship or duty of care would be assumed ... To import such a duty the representation must normally, I think, concern a business or professional transaction whose nature makes clear the gravity of the inquiry and the importance and influence attached to the answer. It is conceded that Salmon J rightly found a duty of care in *Woods* v *Martins Bank Ltd* but the facts in that case were wholly different from those in the present case. A most important circumstance is the form of the inquiry and of the answer. Both were here plainly stated to be without liability. Mr Gardiner argues that those words are not sufficiently precise to exclude liability for negligence. Nothing, however, except negligence could, in the facts of this case, create a liability (apart from fraud, to which they cannot have been intended to refer and against which the words would be no protection, since they would be part of the fraud). I do not, therefore, accept that even if the parties were already in contractual or other special relationship the words would give no immunity to a negligent answer. But in any event they clearly prevent a special relationship from arising. They are part of the material from which one deduces whether a duty of care and a liability for negligence was assumed. If both parties say expressly (in a case where neither is deliberately taking advantage of the other) that there shall be no liability, I do not find it possible to say that a liability was assumed.

NOTES

1. For a further discussion of the elements of *Hedley Byrne* liability see also *Spring* v *Guardian Assurance* and *White* v *Jones* (below, section 3).

2. In *Caparo* v *Dickman* (below) Lord Oliver said that 'voluntary assumption of responsibility' is a convenient phrase but not intended to be a test for the existence of the duty, for it means no more than that the act of the defendant was voluntary and the law attributes to it an assumption of responsibility. However, in *Spring* v *Guardian Assurance* (below), Lord Goff speaks of an assumption or undertaking of responsibility coupled with reliance by the claimant. The issue could be important in determining whether (apart from the Unfair Contract Terms Act 1977) a disclaimer will always be effective. Note also that it was said in *Mutual Life Citizens Assurance Co.* v *Evatt* [1971] AC 793 that a duty will also be owed if the defendant has a financial interest in the transaction about which the advice was sought.

3. In *Mutual Life Citizens Assurance Co.* v *Evatt* [1971] AC 793, the Privy Council held that a defendant could not be liable if he was not in the business of giving advice (the claimant had asked MLC about the wisdom of investing in a company called HG Palmer Ltd because both were subsidiaries of the same holding company). This case was doubted in *Esso* v *Mardon* [1976] 1 QB 801 and ignored (or referred to as not binding) in *Spring* v *Guardian Assurance* [1995] 2 AC 296. There was a strong dissent by Lords Reid and Morris, the first ever dissent in the Privy Council.

4. An example of it being unreasonable to rely on advice is *Kleine* v *Canadian Propane* (1967) 64 DLR 2d 338, where there was a smell of gas which was attributed to low fuel in the tank. A delivery was made and a drop in pressure was discovered, but the tanker driver thought this might be due to an unlit pilot light. The pilot was lit and an explosion occurred one and a half hours later. It was held that it would have been unreasonable for the householder to rely on the advice of the tanker driver.

5. Can silence ever be a breach of duty? According to Slade LJ in *Banque Keyser SA* v *Skandia (UK) Insurance* [1989] 3 WLR 25, at p. 101 it can. He says 'Can a mere failure to speak ever give rise to liability in negligence under *Hedley Byrne* principles? In our view it can, subject to the all important proviso that there has been on the facts a voluntary assumption of responsibility in the relevant sense and reliance on that assumption.' He cites *Al-Kandari* v *Brown* [1988] QB 665 as a possible example, and gives the hypothetical example of a father employing an estate agent to advise his son about the proposed purchase of a house, and the agent negligently fails to tell the son that a motorway is to be built nearby. The son could sue. 'To draw a distinction on those particular facts between misinformation and a failure to inform would be to perpetuate the sort of nonsense in the law which Lord Devlin condemned in *Hedley Byrne* v *Heller*.' The point was not discussed on appeal ([1990] 2 All ER 947), where Lord Templeman merely said 'that there was no negligent misstatement and the silence of [A] did

not amount to an assertion that [B] was trustworthy and the banks did not rely on the silence of [A]'. See also *Henderson* v *Merrett Syndicates* (below).

---

## Henderson v Merrett Syndicates

House of Lords [1995] 2 AC 145; [1994] 3 WLR 761; [1994] 3 All ER 506; [1994] 2 Lloyd's Rep 468

The case concerned Lloyd's underwriters and the main issue was whether there could be concurrent liability in contract and tort which is dealt with in Chapter 12. The extract below deals only with the discussion of the *Hedley Byrne* principle.

LORD GOFF: . . . From these statements, and from their application in *Hedley Byrne*, we can derive some understanding of the breadth of the principle underlying the case. We can see that it rests upon a relationship between the parties, which may be general or specific to the particular transaction, and which may or may not be contractual in nature. All of their Lordships spoke in terms of one party having assumed or undertaken a responsibility towards the other. On this point, Lord Devlin spoke in particularly clear terms in both passages from his speech which I have quoted above. Further, Lord Morris spoke of that party being possessed of a 'special skill' which he undertakes to 'apply for the assistance of another who relies upon such skill.' But the facts of *Hedley Byrne* itself, which was concerned with the liability of a banker to the recipient for negligence in the provision of a reference gratuitously supplied, show that the concept of a 'special skill' must be understood broadly, certainly broadly enough to include special knowledge. Again, though *Hedley Byrne* was concerned with the provision of information and advice, the example given by Lord Devlin of the relationship between solicitor and client, and his and Lord Morris's statements of principle, show that the principle extends beyond the provision of information and advice to include the performance of other services. It follows, of course, that although, in the case of the provision of information and advice, reliance upon it by the other party will be necessary to establish a cause of action (because otherwise the negligence will have no causative effect), nevertheless there may be other circumstances in which there will be the necessary reliance to give rise to the application of the principle. In particular, as cases concerned with solicitor and client demonstrate, where the plaintiff entrusts the defendant with the conduct of his affairs, in general or in particular, he may be held to have relied on the defendant to exercise due skill and care in such conduct.

In subsequent cases concerned with liability under the *Hedley Byrne* principle in respect of negligent misstatements, the question has frequently arisen whether the plaintiff falls within the category of persons, to whom the maker of the statement owes a duty of care. In seeking to contain that category of persons within reasonable bounds, there has been some tendency on the part of the courts to criticise the concept of 'assumption of responsibility' as being 'unlikely to be a helpful or realistic test in most cases' (see *Smith* v *Eric S. Bush* [1990] 1 AC 831, 864–865, *per* Lord Griffiths; and see also *Caparo Industries plc* v *Dickman* [1990] 2 AC 605, 628, *per* Lord Roskill). However, at least in cases such as the present, in which the same problem does not arise, there seems to be no reason why recourse should not be had to the concept, which appears after all to have been adopted, in one form or another, by all of their Lordships in *Hedley Byrne* [1964] AC 465 (see, e.g., Lord Reid, at pp. 483, 486 and 487. Lord Morris (with whom Lord Hodson agreed), at p. 494; Lord Devlin, at pp. 529 and 531; and Lord Pearce at p. 538). Furthermore, especially in a context concerned with a liability which may arise under a contract or in a situation 'equivalent to contract,' it must be expected that an objective test will be applied when asking the question whether, in a particular case, responsibility should be held to have been assumed by the defendant to the plaintiff: see *Caparo Industries plc* v *Dickman* [1990] 2 AC 605, 637, *per* Lord Oliver of Aylmerton. In addition, the concept provides its own explanation why there is no problem in cases of this kind about liability for pure economic loss; for if a person assumes responsibility to another in respect of certain services, there is no reason why he should not be liable in damages for that other in respect of economic loss which flows from the negligent performance of those services. It follows that, once the case is identified as falling within the *Hedley Byrne* principle, there should be no need to embark upon any further enquiry whether it is 'fair, just and reasonable' to impose liability for economic loss—a point which is, I consider, of some importance in the present case. The concept indicates too that in some circumstances, for example where the undertaking to furnish the relevant service is given on an informal occasion, there may be no assumption of responsibility; and likewise that an assumption of responsibility may be negatived by an appropriate disclaimer. I wish to add in parenthesis that, as Oliver J recognised in *Midland Bank Trust Co. Ltd* v *Hett, Stubbs & Kemp* [1979] Ch 384, 416F–G, (a case concerned with concurrent liability of solicitors in tort and contract, to which I will have to refer in a moment) an assumption of responsibility by, for example, a professional man may give rise to liability in respect of negligent omissions as much as negligent acts of commission, as for example when a solicitor assumes responsibility for business on behalf of his client and omits to take a certain step, such as the service of a document, which falls within the responsibility so assumed by him.

NOTE

Lord Goff concentrates more on the 'undertaking of responsibility' and less on reliance. This leads him to suggest that the principle applies equally to the provision of services and can include omissions. The test of whether responsibility has been undertaken is objective and is then imposed by law although a disclaimer may be effective. Apart from the Unfair Contract Terms Act 1977, will it always be so, or will it merely be part of the test of reasonable reliance? Can this principle explain cases such as *Spring* v *Guardian Assurance* and *White* v *Jones* (below)? In the former there was no reliance by the claimant on any statement made by the defendant, although he did rely on his doing his job properly. In the latter case there was no reliance at all. The issue of 'mutuality' (that is reliance by the claimant upon the defendant) did not arise in *Henderson*, and therefore it might be asked whether (as Lord Goff says) there is one broad *Hedley Byrne* principle, or two separate principles, one relating to reliance and the other (as in *White* v *Jones*) to a 'quasi-fiduciary' obligation to protect the interests of someone who would obviously be affected by failing to perform a duty owed to another.

## SECTION 2: TO WHOM THE DUTY IS OWED

Information can spread far beyond the person to whom it is given, and this section is addressed to the problem of the range of potential claimants. In basic negligence the question is answered by the foreseeable claimant rule, but such an answer would not be appropriate in the area where more stringent proximity is required. Thus, the question is: Who can be within a 'special relationship' with the defendant even though the information is not strictly addressed to them?

### Smith v Eric S. Bush
House of Lords [1990] 1 AC 831; [1989] 2 WLR 790; [1989] 2 All ER 514

Mrs Smith wanted to buy a house in Norwich and approached the Abbey National Building Society for a mortgage, and they asked the defendants, Eric Bush, to do a valuation. The valuation was negligently carried out, in that, while the surveyor noticed that the chimney breasts had been removed downstairs, he did not check whether the brickwork above had also been removed or was properly supported. It was not, and the chimney later fell into the main bedroom. The contract for the valuation was between the Abbey National and the defendants, although the claimant was obliged to reimburse the Abbey National for the fee. The purpose of the valuation was to protect the security of the building society and was not strictly to advise the claimant on the value of the house, although it was foreseeable that she would rely on it. Held: dismissing the appeal, that the surveyors owed the claimant a duty. Note: the case also deals with the effect of the Unfair Contract

Terms Act 1977 on the disclaimer in the contract between the surveyor and the building society. This is dealt with below in section 3.

LORD TEMPLEMAN: The common law imposes on a person who contracts to carry out an operation an obligation to exercise reasonable skill and care. A plumber who mends a burst pipe is liable for his incompetence or negligence whether or not he has been expressly required to be careful. The law implies a term in the contract which requires the plumber to exercise reasonable skill and care in his calling. The common law also imposes on a person who carries out an operation an obligation to exercise reasonable skill and care where there is no contract. Where the relationship between the operator and a person who suffers injury or damage is sufficiently proximate and where the operator should have foreseen that carelessness on his part might cause harm to the injured person, the operator is liable in the tort of negligence. . . .

These two appeals are based on allegations of negligence in circumstances which are akin to contract. . . . Mrs Smith paid £36.89 to the Abbey National for a report and valuation and the Abbey National paid the appellants for the report and valuation. . . . the valuer knew or ought to have known that the purchaser would only contract to purchase the house if the valuation was satisfactory and that the purchaser might suffer injury or damage or both if the valuer did not exercise reasonable skill and care. In these circumstances I would expect the law to impose on the valuer a duty owed to the puchaser to exercise reasonable skill and care in carrying out the valuation.

A valuer who values property as a security for a mortgage is liable either in contract or in tort to the mortgagee for any failure on the part of the valuer to exercise reasonable skill and care in the valuation. The valuer is liable in contract if he receives instructions from and is paid by the mortgagee. The valuer is liable in tort if he receives instruction from and is paid by the mortgagor but knows that the valuation is for the purpose of a mortgage and will be relied upon by the mortgagee. . . .

In *Candler* v *Crane, Christmas & Co.* [1951] 2 KB 164, the accountants of a company showed their draft accounts to and discussed them with an investor who, in reliance on the accounts, subscribed for shares in the company. Denning LJ, whose dissenting judgment was subsequently approved in the *Hedley Byrne* case [1964] AC 465, found that the accountants owed a duty to the investor to exercise reasonable skill and care in preparing the draft accounts. Denning LJ said, at p. 176:

> If the matter were free from authority, I should have said that they clearly did owe a duty of care to him. They were professional accountants who prepared and put before him these accounts, knowing that he was going to be guided by them in making an investment in the company. On the faith of those accounts he did make the investment, whereas if the accounts had been carefully prepared, he would not have made the investment at all. The result is that he has lost his money.

Denning LJ, at pp. 178–179 rejected the argument that:

> a duty to take care only arose where the result of a failure to take care will cause physical damage to person or property. . . . I can understand that in some cases of financial loss there may not be a sufficiently proximate relationship to give rise to a duty of care; but, if once the duty exists, I cannot think that liability depends on the nature of the damage.

The duty of professional men 'is not merely a duty to use care in their reports. They have also a duty to use care in their work which results in their reports,' p. 179. The duty of an accountant is owed:

> to any third person to whom they themselves show the accounts, or to whom they know their employer is going to show the accounts, so as to induce him to invest money or take some other action on them. But I do not think the duty can be extended still further so as to include strangers of whom they have heard nothing and to whom their employer, without their knowledge may choose to show their accounts. . . . The test of proximity in these cases is: did the accountants know that the accounts were required for submission to the plaintiff and use by him?: pp. 180–181.

Subject to the effect of any disclaimer of liability, these considerations appear to apply to the valuers in the present appeals.

. . . I agree that by obtaining and disclosing a valuation, a mortgagee does not assume responsibility to the purchaser for that valuation. But in my opinion the valuer assumes responsibility to both mortgagee and purchaser by agreeing to carry out a valuation for mortgage purposes knowing that the valuation fee has been paid by the purchaser and knowing that the valuation will probably be relied upon by the purchaser in order to decide whether or not to enter into a contract to purchase the house. The valuer can escape the responsibility to exercise reasonable skill and care by an express exclusion clause, provided the exclusion clause does not fall foul of the Unfair Contract Terms Act 1977. . . .

. . . The contractual duty of a valuer to value a house for the Abbey National did not prevent the valuer coming under a tortious duty to Mrs Smith who was furnished with a report of the valuer and relied on the report.

In general I am of the opinion that in the absence of a disclaimer of liability the valuer who values a house for the purpose of a mortgage, knowing that the mortgagee will rely and the mortgagor will probably rely on the valuation, knowing that the purchaser mortgagor has in effect paid for the valuation, is under a duty to exercise reasonable skill and care and that duty is owed to both parties to the mortgage for which the valuation is made. Indeed, in both the appeals now under consideration the existence of such a dual duty is tacitly accepted and acknowledged because notices excluding liability for breach of the duty owed to the purchaser were drafted by the mortgagee and imposed on the purchaser. In these circumstances it is necessary to consider the second question which arises in these appeals, namely, whether the disclaimers of liability are notices which fall within the Unfair Contract Terms Act 1977.

NOTE

For other examples of liability on similar facts, see *Yianni v Evans* [1982] 2 QB 438 and *Merrett v Baff* [2001] 3 WLR 1.

■ QUESTION

What did the valuer know about the use to which his valuation would be put? Is a valuation for the purposes of the building society's security any different from a valuation for a purchaser? Was it relevant that the claimant in the end paid for the valuation?

### *Caparo* v *Dickman*

House of Lords [1990] 2 AC 605; [1990] 2 WLR 358; [1990] 1 All ER 568

The claimants were shareholders in Fidelity plc and after the accounts for 1984 (which were audited by the defendants) were published they purchased further shares, ultimately making a take-over bid which was successful. They alleged that they had relied on the accounts for 1984 which should have shown a loss of £465,000 rather than a profit of £1.3 million. Held: allowing the appeal, that the defendant auditors owed no duty to the claimants.

LORD BRIDGE: The salient feature of all these cases is that the defendant giving advice or information was fully aware of the nature of the transaction which the plaintiff had in contemplation, knew that the advice or information would be communicated to him directly or indirectly and knew that it was very likely that the plaintiff would rely on that advice or information in deciding whether or not to engage in the transaction in contemplation. In these circumstances the defendant could clearly be expected, subject always to the effect of any disclaimer of responsibility, specifically to anticipate that the plaintiff would rely on the advice or information given by the defendant for the very purpose for which he did in the event rely on it. So also the plaintiff, subject again to the effect of any disclaimer, would in that situation reasonably suppose that he was entitled to rely on the advice or information communicated to him for the very purpose for which he required it. The situation is entirely different where a statement is put into more or less general circulation and may foreseeably be relied on by strangers to the maker of the statement for any one of a variety of different purposes which the maker of the statement has no specific reason to anticipate. To hold the maker of the statement to be under a duty of care in respect of the accuracy of the statement to all and sundry for any purpose for which they may choose to rely on it is not only to subject him, in the classic words of Cardozo CJ to 'liability in an indeterminate amount for an indeterminate time to an indeterminate class:' see *Ultramares Corporation* v *Touche* (1931) 174 NE 441, 444; it is also to confer on the world at large a quite unwarranted entitlement to appropriate for their own purposes the benefit of the expert knowledge or professional expertise attributed to the maker of the statement. Hence, looking only at the circumstances of these decided cases where a duty of care in respect of negligent statements has been held to exist, I should expect to find that the 'limit or control mechanism . . . imposed upon the liability of a wrongdoer towards those who have suffered economic damage in consequence of his negligence' rested in the necessity to prove, in this category of the tort of negligence, as an essential ingredient of the 'proximity' between the plaintiff and the defendant, that the defendant knew that his statement would be communicated to the plaintiff, either as an individual or as a member of an identifiable class, specifically in connection with a particular transaction or transactions of a particular kind (e.g. in a prospectus inviting investment) and that the plaintiff would be very likely to rely on it for the purpose of deciding whether or not to enter upon that transaction or upon a transaction of that kind. . . .

Some of the speeches in the *Hedley Byrne* case derive a duty of care in relation to negligent statements from a voluntary assumption of responsibility on the part of the maker of the statements. In his speech in *Smith* v *Eric S. Bush* [1990] 1 AC 831, 862, Lord Griffiths emphatically rejected the view that this was the true ground of liability and concluded that:

> The phrase 'assumption of responsibility' can only have any real meaning if it is understood as referring to the circumstances in which the law will deem the maker of the statement to have assumed responsibility to the person who acts upon the advice.

I do not think that in the context of the present appeal anything turns upon the difference between these two approaches.

These considerations amply justify the conclusion that auditors of a public company's accounts owe no duty of care to members of the public at large who rely upon the accounts in deciding to buy shares in the company. If a duty of care were owed so widely, it is difficult to see any reason why it should not equally extend to all who rely on the accounts in relation to other dealings with a company as lenders or merchants extending credit to the company. A claim that such a duty was owed by auditors to a bank lending to a company was emphatically and convincingly rejected by Millett J in *Al Saudi Banque* v *Clarke Pixley* [1990] Ch 313. The only support for an unlimited duty of care owed by auditors for the accuracy of their accounts to all who may foreseeably rely upon them is to be found in some jurisdictions in the United States of America where there are striking differences in the law in different states. In this jurisdiction I have no doubt that the creation of such an unlimited duty would be a legislative step which it would be for Parliament, not the courts, to take. . . .

No doubt these provisions [of the Companies Act 1985] establish a relationship between the auditors and the shareholders of a company on which the shareholder is entitled to rely for the protection of his interest. But the crucial question concerns the extent of the shareholder's interest which the auditor has a duty to protect. The shareholders of a company have a collective interest in the company's proper management and in so far as a negligent failure of the auditor to report accurately on the state of the company's finances deprives the shareholders of the opportunity to exercise their powers in general meeting to call the directors to book and to ensure that errors in management are corrected, the shareholders ought to be entitled to a remedy. But in practice no problem arises in this regard since the interest of the shareholders in the proper management of the company's affairs is indistinguishable from the interest of the company itself and any loss suffered by the shareholders, e.g. by the negligent failure of the auditor to discover and expose a misappropriation of funds by a director of the company, will be recouped by a claim against the auditors in the name of the company, not by individual shareholders.

I find it difficult to visualise a situation arising in the real world in which the individual shareholder could claim to have sustained a loss in respect of his existing shareholding referable to the negligence of the auditor which could not be recouped by the company. But on this part of the case your Lordships were much pressed with the argument that such a loss might occur by a negligent undervaluation of the company's assets in the auditor's report relied on by the individual share-holder in deciding to sell his shares at an undervalue. The argument then runs thus. The shareholder, qua shareholder, is entitled to rely on the auditor's report as the basis of his investment decision to sell his existing shareholding. If he sells at an undervalue he is entitled to recover the loss from the auditor. There can be no distinction in law between the shareholder's investment decision to sell the shares he has or to buy additional shares. It follows, therefore, that the scope of the duty of care owed to him by the auditor extends to cover any loss sustained consequent on the purchase of additional shares in reliance on the auditor's negligent report.

I believe this argument to be fallacious. Assuming without deciding that a claim by a shareholder to recover a loss suffered by selling his shares at an undervalue attributable to an undervaluation of the company's assets in the auditor's report could be sustained at all, it would not be by reason of any reliance by the shareholder on the auditor's report in deciding to sell; the loss would be referable to the depreciatory effect of the report on the market value of the shares before ever the decision of the shareholder to sell was taken. A claim to recoup a loss alleged to flow from the purchase of overvalued shares, on the other hand, can only be sustained on the basis of the purchaser's reliance on the report. The specious equation of 'investment decisions' to sell or to buy as giving rise to parallel claims thus appears to me to be untenable. Moreover, the loss in the case of the sale would be of a loss of part of the value of the shareholder's existing holding, which, assuming a duty of care owed to individual shareholders, it might sensibly lie within the scope of the auditor's duty to protect. A loss, on the other hand, resulting from the purchase of additional shares would result from a wholly independent transaction having no connection with the existing shareholding.

I believe it is this last distinction which is of critical importance and which demonstrates the unsoundness of the conclusion reached by the majority of the Court of Appeal. It is never sufficient to ask simply whether A owes B a duty of care. It is always necessary to determine the scope of the duty by reference to the kind of damage from which A must take care to save B harmless. 'The question is always whether the defendant was under a duty to avoid or prevent that damage, but the actual nature of the damage suffered is relevant to the existence and extent of any duty to avoid or prevent it:' see *Sutherland Shire Council* v *Heyman*, 60 ALR 1, 48, *per* Brennan J. Assuming for the purpose of the argument that the relationship between the auditor of a company and individual shareholders is of sufficient proximity to give rise to a duty of care, I do not understand how the scope of that duty can possibly extend beyond the protection of any individual shareholder from losses in the value of the shares which he holds. As a purchaser of additional shares in reliance on the auditor's report, he stands in no different position from any other investing member of the public to whom the auditor owes no duty. . . .

LORD OLIVER: . . . What can be deduced from the *Hedley Byrne* case, therefore, is that the necessary relationship between the maker of a statement or giver of advice ('the adviser') and the recipient who acts in reliance upon it ('the advisee') may typically be held to exist where (1) the advice is required for a purpose, whether particularly specified or generally described, which is made known, either actually or inferentially, to the adviser at the time when the advice is given; (2) the adviser knows, either actually or inferentially, that his advice will be communicated to the advisee, either specifically or as a member of an ascertainable class, in order that it should be used by the advisee for that purpose; (3) it is known either actually or inferentially, that the advice so communicated is likely to be acted upon by the advisee for that purpose without independent inquiry, and (4) it is so acted upon by the advisee to his detriment. That is not, of course, to suggest that these conditions are either conclusive or exclusive, but merely that the actual decision in the case does not warrant any broader propositions. . . .

In seeking to ascertain whether there should be imposed on the adviser a duty to avoid the occurrence of the kind of damage which the advisee claims to have suffered it is not, I think, sufficient to ask simply whether there existed a 'closeness' between them in the sense that the advisee had a legal entitlement to receive the information upon the basis of which he has acted or in the sense that the information was intended to serve his interest or to protect him. One must, I think, go further and ask, in what capacity was his interest to be served and from what was he intended to be protected? A company's annual accounts are capable of being utilised for a number of purposes and if one thinks about it it is entirely foreseeable that they may be so employed. But many of such purposes have absolutely no connection with the recipient's status or capacity, whether as a shareholder, voting or non-voting, or as a debenture-holder. Before it can be concluded that the duty is imposed to protect the recipient against harm which he suffers by reason of the particular use that he chooses to make of the information which he receives, one must, I think, first ascertain the purpose for which the information is required to be given. Indeed the paradigmatic *Donoghue* v *Stevenson* case of a manufactured article requires, as an essential ingredient of liability, that the article has been used by the consumer in the manner in which it was intended to be used: see *Grant* v *Australian Knitting Mills Ltd* [1936] AC 85, 104 and *Junior Books Ltd* v *Veitchi Co. Ltd* [1983] 1 AC 520, 549, 552. I entirely follow that if the conclusion is reached that the very purpose of providing the information is to serve as the basis for making investment decisions or giving investment advice, it is not difficult then to conclude also that the duty imposed upon the adviser extends to protecting the recipient against loss occasioned by an unfortunate investment decision which is based on carelessly inaccurate information. . . . I do not believe and I see no grounds for believing that, in enacting the statutory provisions [of the Companies Act 1985], Parliament had in mind the provision of information for the assistance of purchasers of shares or debentures in the market, whether they be already the holders of shares or other securities or persons having no previous proprietary interest in the company. It is unnecessary to decide the point on this appeal, but I can see more force in the contention that one purpose of providing the statutory information might be to enable the recipient to exercise whatever rights he has in relation to his proprietary interest by virtue of which he receives it, by way, for instance, of disposing of that interest. I can, however, see no ground for supposing that the legislature was intending to foster a market for the existing holders of shares or debentures by providing information for the purpose of enabling them to acquire such securities from other holders who might be minded to sell.

For my part, I think that the position as regards the auditor's statutory duty was correctly summarised by O'Connor LJ, in his dissenting judgment when he said, at p. 714:

> The statutory duty owed by auditors to shareholders is, I think, a duty owed to them as a body. I appreciate that it is difficult to see how the over-statement of the accounts can cause damage to the shareholders as a body; it will be the underlying reasons for the over-statement which cause damage, for example fraudulent abstraction of assets by directors or servants, but such loss is recoverable by the company. I am anxious to limit the present case to deciding whether the statutory duty operates to protect the individual shareholders as a potential buyer of further shares. If I am wrong in thinking that under the statute no duty is owed to shareholders as individuals, then I think the duty must be confined to transactions in which the shareholder can only participate because he is a shareholder. The Companies Act 1985 imposes a duty to shareholders as a class and the duty should not extend to an individual save as a member of the class in respect of some class activity. Buying shares in a company is not such an activity.

In my judgment, accordingly, the purpose for which the auditors' certificate is made and published is that of providing those entitled to receive the report with information to enable them to exercise in conjunction those powers which their respective proprietary interests confer upon them and not for the purposes of individual speculation with a view to profit. The same considerations as limit the existence of a duty of care also, in my judgment, limit the scope of the duty and I agree with O'Connor LJ that the duty of care is one owed to the shareholders as a body and not to individual shareholders.

To widen the scope of the duty to include loss caused to an individual by reliance upon the accounts for a purpose for which they were not supplied and were not intended would be to extend it beyond the limits which are so far deducible from the decisions of this House. It is not, as I think, an extension which either logic requires or policy dictates and I, for my part, am not prepared to follow the majority of the Court of Appeal in making it. In relation to the purchase of shares of other shareholders in a company, whether in the open market or as a result of an offer made to all or a majority of the existing shareholders, I can see no sensible distinction, so far as a duty of care is concerned, between a potential purchaser who is, vis-à-vis the company, a total outsider and one who is already the holder of one or more shares. . . .

NOTES

1. There were two grounds for this decision: first that there was not sufficient proximity between the claimants and the defendants, and secondly that the accounts were produced for the purpose of informing the members of the company in order to assist the members (i.e. the shareholders) in directing the company, and not for the purpose of advising the shareholders as to further speculation. A similar rule has been adopted in Canada (see *Hercules Managements* v *Ernst Young* [1997] 2 SCR 165). Is this a realistic distinction? If a shareholder receives accounts which show the company to be in a poor state, does the shareholder think first of attending the AGM to try to influence the direction of the company or of selling his or her own shares?

2. In *Smith* v *Eric Bush* (above) the survey was directed to the building society to advise them whether the house was good security for the loan. Was this the same purpose as advising the purchaser as to the value of the house? If the functions are different, how can *Smith* v *Bush* be explained? In *Morgan Crucible* v *Hill Samuel* [1991] Ch 295, the Court of Appeal pointed out that at first instance the judge had distinguished *Smith* v *Bush* on the ground of 'the different economic relationships between the parties and the nature of the markets' but went on to say that 'we would not think it right by reference to economic considerations to dismiss as unarguable an otherwise arguable case'. Does this mean that the fact that Mrs Smith paid for the survey and was a 'consumer' is not the distinguishing feature?

3. Subsequent cases have analysed and applied *Caparo* v *Dickman*. Thus in *Al-Nakib Investments* v *Longcroft* [1990] 3 All ER 321, a company issued a prospectus to existing shareholders in relation to a rights issue. The claimants both subscribed to the rights issue and also bought shares in the market. It was held that a duty was owed in relation to the subscription to the rights issue but not in relation to the shares the claimants had bought in the open market, on the ground that the purpose of the prospectus was limited to inviting existing shareholders to subscribe to the rights issue. Again, in *McNaughton Papers Group* v *Hicks Anderson* [1991] 2 QB 113, the claimants were negotiating to take over a company called MK. Draft accounts were hurriedly drawn up by the defendants and given to MK, and these were used in the negotiations. The defendants were not liable, one ground being that the accounts had been supplied to MK and not to the claimants. In addition, the accounts were only draft accounts and the defendants could not have expected reliance on them by the claimants.

4. In *Galoo* v *Bright Grahame Murray* [1995] 1 All ER 16, the defendants audited the accounts of a company called Gamine which was purchased by Hillsdown Holdings. The auditors failed to detect that Gamine was insolvent. The terms of the agreement to sell Gamine were that the price would be 5.2 times the net profits for 1986. The defendants knew that this was how the price was to be fixed and were to deliver a set of the audited completion accounts direct to Hillsdown Holdings. Accordingly, it was held that as there was sufficient proximity on the special facts, the claim would not be struck out.

5. A potential ground of liability has been exposed in *Morgan Crucible* v *Hill Samuel* [1991] Ch 295. The claimant was engaged in a hostile take-over bid for a company called First Castle Electronics (FCE). The defendants were the directors of FCE and their financial advisers and publicly issued a number of statements. It was said that *if* the object of these statements was to encourage the claimants to increase their bid, a duty of care could be owed to them. It has been said that the intention of the defendants to influence the claimants is significant and this intention must be objectively determined. Thus, in *Possfund Custodian Trustee* v *Diamond* [1996] 2 All ER 774 it was argued that a prospectus issued in pursuance of a flotation on the unlisted securities market may be directed not only to the recipients of the prospectus but may also be designed 'to inform and encourage after-market purchasers'. Accordingly an

action by a subsequent purchaser of shares based on negligent misrepresentations in the prospectus was not struck out.

6. In *The Law Society* v *KPMG* [2000] 4 All ER 540, a firm of solicitors engaged the defendant accountants to prepare a report to be submitted to the Law Society to the effect that the solicitors had complied with the accounts rules of the Society. The accountants failed to detect that the solicitors had engaged in fraud and the Law Society successfully sued for the amount they had to pay to the defrauded clients of the firm. Although the contract was with the solicitors, the accountants knew that the purpose was to alert the Society to the need to exercise its powers of intervention, and it was foreseeable that if the Society was not alerted so as to take preventative measures a loss would fall on its compensation fund. Accordingly the requirements of *Caparo* were complied with.

7. Note that in most of these cases the issue is the liability of the *auditor* for a negligent audit of the accounts which have been drawn up by someone else, i.e. the question is, have the defendants negligently failed to detect *other people's* fraud or mistakes? In *Barings* v *Coopers and Lybrand* [1997] 1 BCLC 427 Leggatt LJ said, 'the primary responsibility for safeguarding a company's assets and preventing errors and defalcations rests with the directors. But material irregularities, and *a fortiori* fraud, will normally be brought to light by sound audit procedures, one of which is the practice of pointing out weaknesses in internal controls. An auditor's task is so to conduct the audit as to make it probable that material misstatements in financial documents will be detected.'

8. Clause 759 of the Company Law Reform Bill 2006 proposes that a court may in its discretion, having regard to all the circumstances of the case, relieve an auditor from liability for negligence, either wholly or in part, if he acted honestly and reasonably. How might this discretion be exercised?

■ QUESTION

If a house surveyor realizes that his or her report will be relied on by purchasers of a house (even though they are not his or her clients), the surveyor may be liable if the report is negligently prepared. Yet even if an auditor realizes that accounts he or she has audited may be relied on by the purchasers of the company, the auditor will not be liable. Can you explain this?

## SECTION 3: LIABILITY TO THIRD PARTIES

This section deals with the situation where A makes a statement to B but damage is caused to C (usually by B acting on A's statement). One problem is, can there be liability to C when no statement was ever made directly to C? In which case, how should 'proximity' be defined? Also *Hedley Byrne* is said largely to depend on 'reliance'. It is true that in this situation C relies on A making a non-negligent statement to B, but he does not *act* in reliance on the statement. Despite these conceptual problems liability has in fact been extended into this area and this makes it difficult to establish the true basis of *Hedley Byrne* liability. Furthermore, *White* v *Jones* below suggests that there may be cases, analogous to fiduciary duties, where reliance is not necessary at all.

### *Spring* v *Guardian Assurance*
House of Lords [1995] 2 AC 296; [1994] 3 WLR 354; [1994] 3 All ER 129

Mr Spring was employed by a company which among other things sold Guardian Assurance policies. The company was taken over by Guardian Assurance and subsequently Mr Spring was dismissed. He tried to set up a new business selling Scottish Amicable policies but it refused to appoint him as one of its representatives. The reason was that Guardian Assurance had negligently given a highly unfavourable reference to Scottish Amicable about Mr Spring. The regulatory body (Lautro) required that all persons appointed as representatives for insurance companies must provide a reference and previous employers are obliged to provide one. Held: allowing the appeal that the defendants were liable.

LORD GOFF: . . . The wide scope of the principle recognised in *Hedley Byrne* is reflected in the broad statements of principle which I have quoted. All the members of the Appellate Committee in this case spoke in terms of the principle resting upon an assumption or undertaking of responsibility by the defendant towards the plaintiff, coupled with reliance by the plaintiff on the exercise by the defendant of due care and skill. Lord Devlin, in particular, stressed that the principle rested upon an assumption of responsibility when he said, at p. 531, that 'the essence of the matter in the present case and in others of the same type is the acceptance of responsibility.' For the purpose of the case now before your Lordships it is, I consider, legitimate to proceed on the same basis. Furthermore, although *Hedley Byrne* itself was concerned with the provision of information and advice, it is clear that the principle in the case is not so limited and extends to include the performance of other services, as for example the professional services rendered by a solicitor to his client (see in particular, Lord Devlin, at pp. 529–530). Accordingly where the plaintiff entrusts the defendant with the conduct of his affairs, in general or in particular, the defendant may be held to have assumed responsibility to the plaintiff, and the plaintiff to have relied on the defendant to exercise due skill and care, in respect of such conduct.

For present purposes, I wish also to refer to the nature of the 'special skill' to which Lord Morris referred in his statement of principle. It is, I consider, clear from the facts of *Hedley Byrne* itself that the expression 'special skill' is to be understood in a broad sense, certainly broad enough to embrace special knowledge. Furthermore Lord Morris himself, when speaking of the provision of a statement in the form of information or advice, referred to the defendant's judgment or skill or ability to make careful inquiry, from which it appears that the principle may apply in a case in which the defendant has access to information and fails to exercise due care (and skill, to the extent that this is relevant) in drawing on that source of information for the purposes of communicating it to another.

The fact that the inquiry in *Hedley Byrne* itself was directed, in a case concerned with liability in respect of a negligent misstatement (in fact a reference), to whether the maker of the statement was liable to a recipient of it who had acted in reliance upon it, may have given the impression that this is the only way in which liability can arise under the principle in respect of a misstatement. But, having regard to the breadth of the principle as stated in *Hedley Byrne* itself, I cannot see why this should be so. Take the case of the relationship between a solicitor and his client, treated implicitly by Lord Morris and expressly by Lord Devlin as an example of a relationship to which the principle may apply. I can see no reason why a solicitor should not be under a duty to his client to exercise due care and skill when making statements to third parties, so that if he fails in that duty and his client suffers damage in consequence, he may be liable to his client in damages. The question whether a person who gives a reference to a third party may, if the reference is negligently prepared be liable in damages not to the recipient but to the subject of the reference, did not arise in *Hedley Byrne* and so was not addressed in that case. That is the central question with which we are concerned in the present case; and I propose first to consider it in the context of an ordinary relationship between employer and employee, and then to turn to apply the relevant principles to the more complex relationships which existed in the present case.

Prima facie (i.e., subject to the point on defamation, which I will have to consider later), it is my opinion that an employer who provides a reference in respect of one of his employees to a prospective future employer will ordinarily owe a duty of care to his employee in respect of the preparation of the reference. The employer is possessed of special knowledge, derived from his experience of the employee's character, skill and diligence in the performance of his duties while working for the employer. Moreover, when the employer provides a reference to a third party in respect of his employee, he does so not only for the assistance of the third party, but also, for what it is worth, for the assistance of the employee. Indeed, nowadays it must often be very difficult for an employee to obtain fresh employment without the benefit of a reference from his present or a previous employer. It is for this reason that, in ordinary life, it may be the employee, rather than a prospective future employer, who asks the employer to provide the reference; and even where the approach comes from the prospective future employer, it will (apart from special circumstances) be made with either the express or the tacit authority of the employee. The provision of such references is a service regularly provided by employers to their employees; indeed, references are part of the currency of the modern employment market. Furthermore, when such a reference is provided by an employer, it is plain that the employee relies upon him to exercise due skill and care in the preparation of the reference before making it available to the third party. In these circumstances, it seems to me that all the elements requisite for the application of the *Hedley Byrne* [1964] AC 465 principle are present. I need only add that, in the context under consideration, there is no question of the circumstances in which the reference is provided being, for example, so informal as to negative an assumption of responsibility by the employer. . . .

I wish however to add that, in considering the duty of care owed by the employer to the employee, although it can and should be expressed in broad terms, nevertheless the central requirement is that reasonable care and skill should be exercised by the employer in ensuring the accuracy of any facts which either (1) are communicated to the recipient of the reference from which he may form an adverse opinion of the employee, or (2) are the basis of an adverse opinion expressed by the employer himself about the employee. I wish further to add that it does not necessarily follow that, because the employer owes such a duty of care to his employee, he also owes a duty of care to the recipient of the reference. The relationship of the employer with the recipient is by no means the same as that with his employee; and whether, in a case such as this, there should be held (as was prima facie held to be so on the facts of the *Hedley Byrne* case itself) a duty of care owed by the maker of the reference to the recipient is a point on which I do not propose to express an opinion, and which may depend on the facts of the particular case before the court.

[*Note*: it had been argued that the appropriate tort for a misleading reference was the tort of defamation, and that there would have been no liability in defamation because the reference would have attracted qualified privilege which meant there could be no liability unless the writer was in law malicious. The Court of Appeal had agreed that if there was no liability in defamation there should not be in negligence, for otherwise the defence of qualified privilege would be subverted. This issue is dealt with by Lord Slynn.]

LORD SLYNN: . . . It seems to me that on the basis of these authorities two questions therefore arise. The first is whether the nature of the tort of defamation and the tort of injurious falsehood is such that it would be wrong to recognise the possibility of a duty of care in negligence for a false statement. The second question is whether, independently of the existence of the other two torts, and taking the tests adopted by Lord Bridge of Harwich in *Caparo Industries Plc* v *Dickman* [1990] 2 AC 605, a duty of care can in any event arise in relation to the giving of a reference. If the answer to the first is 'No,' and to the second 'Yes' then it remains to consider whether in all the circumstances such a duty of care was owed in this case by an employer to an ex-employee.

As to the first question the starting-point in my view is that the suggested claim in negligence and the torts of defamation and injurious and malicious falsehood do not cover the same ground, as Mr Tony Weir shows in his note in [1993] CLJ 376. They are separate torts, defamation not requiring a proof by the plaintiff that the statement was untrue (though justification may be a defence) or that he suffered economic damage, but being subject to defences quite different from those in negligence, such as the defence of qualified privilege which makes it necessary to prove malice. Malicious falsehood requires proof that the statement is false, that harm has resulted and that there was express malice. Neither of these involves the concept of a duty of care. The essence of a claim in defamation is that a person's reputation has been damaged; it may or not involve the loss of a job or economic loss. A claim that a reference has been given negligently is essentially based on the fact, not so much that reputation has been damaged, as that a job, or an opportunity, has been lost. A statement carelessly made may not be defamatory—a statement that a labourer is 'lame,' a secretary 'very arthritic' when neither statement is true, though they were true of some other employee mistakenly confused with the person named.

I do not consider that the existence of either of these two heads of claim, defamation and injurious falsehood, a priori prevents the recognition of a duty of care where, but for the existence of the other two torts, it would be fair, just and reasonable to recognise it in a situation where the giver of a reference has said or written what is untrue and where he has acted unreasonably and carelessly in what he has said.

The policy reasons underlying the requirement that the defence of qualified privilege is only dislodged if express malice is established do not necessarily apply in regard to a claim in negligence. There may be other policy reasons in particular situations which should prevail. Thus, in relation to a reference given by an employer in respect of a former employee or a departing employee (and assuming no contractual obligation to take care in giving a reference) it is relevant to consider the changes which have taken place in the employer-employee relationship, with far greater duties imposed on the employer than in the past, whether by statute or by judicial decision, to care for the physical, financial and even psychological welfare of the employee.

As to the second question it is a relevant circumstance that in many cases an employee will stand no chance of getting another job, let alone a better job, unless he is given a reference. There is at least a moral obligation on the employer to give it. This is not necessarily true when the claim is laid in defamation even if on an occasion of qualified privilege. In the case of an employee or ex-employee the damage is clearly foreseeable if a careless reference is given; there is as obvious a proximity of relationship in this context as can be imagined. The sole question therefore, in my view, is whether balancing all the factors (per Lord Bridge of Harwich in *Caparo Industries Plc v Dickman* [1990] 2 AC 605, 618):

> the situation should be one in which the court considers it fair, just and reasonable that the law should impose a duty of a given scope upon the one party for the benefit of the other.

*Hedley Byrne & Co. Ltd v Heller & Partners Ltd* [1964] AC 465 does not decide the present case, but I find it unacceptable that the person to whom a reference is given about an employee X should be able to sue for negligence if he relies on the statement (and, for example, employs X who proves to be inadequate for the job) as it appears to be assumed that he can; but that X who is refused employment because the recipient relies on a reference negligently given should have no recourse unless he can prove express malice as defined by Lord Diplock in *Horrocks v Lowe* [1975] AC 135, 149–151. . . .

I do not accept the in terrorem arguments that to allow a claim in negligence will constitute a restriction on freedom of speech or that in the employment sphere employers will refuse to give references or will only give such bland or adulatory ones as is forecast. They should be and are capable of being sufficiently robust as to express frank and honest views after taking reasonable care both as to the factual content and as to the opinion expressed. They will not shrink from the duty of taking reasonable care when they realise the importance of the reference both to the recipient (to whom it is assumed that a duty of care exists) and to the employee (to whom it is contended on existing authority there is no such duty). They are not being asked to warrant absolutely the accuracy of the facts or the incontrovertible validity of the opinions expressed but to take reasonable care in compiling or giving the reference and in verifying the information on which it is based. The courts can be trusted to set a standard which is not higher than the law of negligence demands. Even if it is right that the number of references given will be reduced, the quality and value will be greater and it is by no means certain that to have more references is more in the public interest than to have more careful references.

Those giving such references can make it clear what are the parameters within which the reference is given such as stating their limited acquaintance with the individual either as to time or as to situation. This issue does not arise in the present case but it may be that employers can make it clear to the subject of the reference that they will only give one if he accepts that there will be a disclaimer of liability to him and to the recipient of the reference.

NOTES

1. Lord Goff bases *Hedley Byrne* liability on voluntary assumption of responsibility and reliance, but does not link the two. *Hedley Byrne* was a case where the claimant was both the person to whom the statement was made as a result of the assumption of responsibility, and the person who acted on it to his detriment. However, Lord Goff says that *Hedley Byrne* can extend to cases where there is (a) an assumption of responsibility by the defendant to the claimant, and (b) the claimant 'relies' on the defendant not being negligent. This is so even if the statement is made to someone else who then acts to the detriment of the claimant. In what sense did the claimant 'rely' on the defendant? Presumably, he had no choice but to use the defendant as a referee but no doubt was entitled to expect him to act without negligence. For a different explanation of this type of liability see *White* v *Jones* (below).

2. The 'defamation' issue has been very controversial. It was argued that as the defendant would not have been liable in defamation because of the defence of qualified privilege, that defence should not be subverted by allowing the claimant to sue in negligence. Lord Slynn says there is no conflict between the two torts because defamation is about reputation and negligence, in this case, is about employability and the two may not coincide (e.g. his example of a statement that a secretary has arthritis).

3. Should, or will, referees now refuse to give a reference, or at least give one so bland as to be of little use?

4. It may be that a duty of care arises only when there is an existing relationship. In *Kapfunde* v *Abbey National* [1998] IRLR 583, a doctor retained by the defendants was not liable to a job applicant who was refused employment on the doctor's advice. It was said that *White* v *Jones* (below) was not helpful as that had not radically extended the law. Does this mean that a referee other than the current employer would not be liable?

5. If A negligently gives an unjustifiably excellent reference to B about C and B employs C, can B sue A for any damage done by C to B's business? Lord Slynn assumes A could, but Lord Goff leaves the matter open. For an example, see *T* v *Surrey County Council* [1994] 4 All ER 577.

---

### *White* v *Jones*
House of Lords [1995] 2 AC 207; [1995] 2 WLR 187; [1995] 1 All ER 691

In 1986 the testator cut his daughters out of his will, but he later relented and in July he instructed the defendant solicitors to draw up a new will giving the daughters £9,000 each. The new will had not been drawn up by 14 September when the testator died. The daughters sued the solicitors. Held: dismissing the appeal, that the defendants were liable.

LORD BROWNE-WILKINSON: My Lords, I have read the speech of my noble and learned friend, Lord Goff of Chieveley, and agree with him that this appeal should be dismissed. In particular, I agree that your Lordships should hold that the defendant solicitors were under a duty of care to the plaintiffs arising from an extension of the principle of assumption of responsibility explored in *Hedley Byrne and Co. Ltd* v *Heller & Partners Ltd* [1964] AC 465. In my view, although the present case is not directly covered by the decided cases, it is legitimate to extend the law to the limited extent proposed using the incremental approach by way of analogy advocated in *Caparo Industries Plc* v *Dickman* [1990] 2 AC 605. To explain my reasons requires me to attempt an analysis of what is meant by 'assumption of responsibility' in the law of negligence. To avoid misunderstanding I must emphasise that I am considering only whether some duty of care exists, not with the extent of that duty which will vary according to the circumstances.

Far from that concept having been invented by your Lordships' House in *Hedley Byrne*, its genesis is to be found in *Nocton* v *Lord Ashburton* [1914] AC 932. It is impossible to analyse what is meant by 'assumption of responsibility' or 'the *Hedley Byrne* principle' without first having regard to *Nocton's* case. . . .

In my judgment, there are three points relevant to the present case which should be gathered from *Nocton's* case. First, there can be special relationships between the parties which give rise to the law treating the defendant as having assumed a duty to be careful in circumstances where, apart from such relationship, no duty of care would exist. Second, a fiduciary relationship is one of those special relationships. Third, a fiduciary relationship is not the only such special relationship: other relationships may be held to give rise to the same duty.

The second of those propositions merits further consideration, since if we can understand the nature of one 'special relationship' it may cast light on when, by analogy, it is appropriate for the law to treat other relationships as being 'special.' The paradigm of the circumstances in which equity will find a fiduciary relationship is where one party, A, has assumed to act in relation to the property or affairs of another, B. A, having assumed responsibility, pro tanto, for B's affairs, is taken to have assumed certain duties in relation to the conduct of those affairs, including normally a duty of care. Thus, a trustee assumes responsibility for the management of the property of the beneficiary, a company director for the affairs of the company and an agent for those of his principal. By so assuming to act in B's affairs, A comes under fiduciary duties to B. Although the extent of those fiduciary duties (including duties of care) will vary from case to case some duties (including a duty of care) arise in each case. The importance of these considerations for present purposes is that the special relationship (i.e. a fiduciary relationship) giving rise to the assumption of responsibility held to exist in *Nocton's* case does not depend on any mutual dealing between A and B, let alone on any relationship akin to contract. Although such factors may be present, equity imposes the obligation because A has assumed to act in B's affairs. Thus, a trustee is under a duty of care to his beneficiary whether or not he has had any dealing with him: indeed he may be as yet unborn or unascertained and therefore any direct dealing would be impossible.

Moreover, this lack of mutuality in the typical fiduciary relationship indicates that it is not a necessary feature of all such special relationships that B must in fact rely on A's actions. If B is unaware of the fact that A has assumed to act in B's affairs (e.g. in the case of B being an unascertained beneficiary) B cannot possibly have relied on A. What is important is not that A knows that B is consciously relying on A, but A knows that B's economic well being is dependent upon A's careful conduct of B's affairs. Thus, in my judgment *Nocton* demonstrates that there is at least one special relationship giving rise to the imposition of a duty of care that is dependent neither upon mutuality of dealing nor upon actual reliance by the plaintiff on the defendant's actions.

I turn then to consider the *Hedley Byrne* case [1964] AC 465. In that case this House had to consider the circumstances in which there could be liability for negligent misstatement in the absence of either a contract or a fiduciary relationship between the parties. The first, and for present purposes perhaps the most important, point is that there is nothing in the *Hedley Byrne* case to cast doubt on the decision in *Nocton's* case. On the contrary, each of their Lordships treated *Nocton's* case as their starting point and asked the question 'in the absence of any contractual or fiduciary duty, what circumstances give rise to a special relationship between the plaintiff and the defendant sufficient to justify the imposition of the duty of care in the making of statements?' The House was seeking to define a further special relationship in addition to, not in substitution for, fiduciary relationships: see *per* Lord Reid, at p. 486; *per* Lord Morris of Borth-y-Gest, at p. 502; *per* Lord Hodson, at p. 511; *per* Lord Devlin, at p. 523; *per* Lord Pearce, at p. 539.

Second, since this House was concerned with cases of negligent misstatement or advice, it was inevitable that any test laid down required both that the plaintiff should rely on the statement or advice and that the defendant could reasonably foresee that he would do so. In the case of claims based on negligent statements (as opposed to negligent actions) the plaintiff will have no cause of action at all unless he can show damage and he can only have suffered damage if he has relied on the negligent statement. Nor will a defendant be shown to have satisfied the requirement that he should foresee damage to the plaintiff unless he foresees such reliance by the plaintiff as to give rise to the damage. Therefore although reliance by the plaintiff is an essential ingredient in a case based on negligent misstatement or advice, it does not follow that in all cases based on negligent action or inaction by the defendant it is necessary in order to demonstrate a special relationship that the plaintiff has in fact relied on the defendant or the defendant has foreseen such reliance. If in such a case careless conduct can be foreseen as likely to cause and does in fact cause damage to the plaintiff that should be sufficient to found liability.

Third, it is clear that the basis on which (apart from the disclaimer) the majority would have held the bank liable for negligently giving the reference was that, were it not for the disclaimer, the bank would have assumed responsibility for such reference. Although there are passages in the speeches which may point the other way, the reasoning of the majority in my judgment points clearly to the fact that the crucial element was that, by choosing to answer the enquiry, the bank had assumed to act, and thereby created the special relationship on which the necessary duty of care was founded. Thus Lord Reid, at p. 486, pointed out that a reasonable man knowing that he was being trusted, had three possible courses open to him: to refuse to answer, to answer but with a disclaimer of responsibility, or simply to answer without such disclaimer. . . .

Just as in the case of fiduciary duties, the assumption of responsibility referred to is the defendants' assumption of responsibility for the task not the assumption of legal liability. Even in cases of ad hoc relationships, it is the undertaking to answer the question posed which creates the relationship. If the responsibility for the task is assumed by the defendant he thereby creates a special relationship between himself and the plaintiff in relation to which the law (not the defendant) attaches a duty to carry out carefully the task so assumed. If this be the right view, it does much to allay the doubts about the utility of the concept of assumption of responsibility voiced by Lord Griffiths in *Smith* v *Eric S. Bush* [1990] 1 AC 831, 862 and by Lord Roskill in *Caparo Industries Plc* v *Dickman* [1992] AC 605, 628: see also Barker in 'Unreliable Assumptions in the Modern Law of Negligence' (1993) 109 LQR 461. As I read those judicial criticisms they proceed on the footing that the phrase 'assumption of responsibility' refers to the defendant having assumed legal responsibility. I doubt whether the same criticisms would have been directed at the phrase if the words had been understood, as I think they should be, as referring to a conscious assumption of responsibility for the task rather than a conscious assumption of legal liability to the plaintiff for its careful performance. Certainly, the decision in both cases is consistent with the view I take. . . .

Let me now seek to bring together these various strands so far as is necessary for the purposes of this case: I am not purporting to give any comprehensive statement of this aspect of the law. The law of England does not impose any general duty of care to avoid negligent misstatements or to avoid causing pure economic loss even if economic damage to the plaintiff was foreseeable. However, such a duty of care will arise if there is a special relationship between the parties. Although the categories of cases in which such special relationship can be held to exist are not closed, as yet only two categories have been identified, viz. (1) where there is a fiduciary relationship and (2) where the defendant has voluntarily answered a question or tenders skilled advice or services in circumstances where he knows or ought to know that an identified plaintiff will rely on his answers or advice. In both these categories the special relationship is created by the defendant voluntarily assuming to act in the matter by involving himself in the plaintiff's affairs or by choosing to speak. If he does so assume to act or speak he is said to have assumed responsibility for carrying through the matter he has entered upon. In the words of Lord Reid in *Hedley Byrne* [1964] AC 465, 486 he has 'accepted a relationship . . . which requires him to exercise such care as the circumstances require,' i.e. although the extent of the duty will vary from category to category, *some* duty of care arises from the special relationship. Such relationship can arise even though the defendant has acted in the plaintiff's affairs pursuant to a contract with a third party. . . .

The solicitor who accepts instructions to draw a will knows that the future economic welfare of the intended beneficiary is dependent upon his careful execution of the task. It is true that the intended beneficiary (being ignorant of the instructions) may not rely on the particular solicitor's actions. But, as I have sought to demonstrate, in the case of a duty of care flowing from a fiduciary relationship liability is not dependent upon actual reliance by the plaintiff on the defendant's actions but on the fact that, as the fiduciary is well aware, the plaintiff's economic well-being is dependent upon the proper discharge by the fiduciary of his duty. Second, the solicitor by accepting the instructions has entered upon, and therefore assumed responsibility for, the task of procuring the execution of a skilfully drawn will knowing that the beneficiary is wholly dependent upon his carefully carrying out his function. That assumption of responsibility for the task is a feature of both the two categories of special relationship so far identified in the authorities. It is not to the point that the solicitor only entered on the task pursuant to a contract with the third party (i.e. the testator). There are therefore present many of the features which in the other categories of special relationship have been treated as sufficient to create a special relationship to which the law attaches a duty of care. In my judgment the analogy is close.

NOTES
1. See Chapter 10 for the contractual aspects of this case. It was argued that there was a contract between the testator and the solicitor which was intended to benefit the daughters and that they ought to be able to sue directly in contract. The invitation to evade the doctrine of privity was declined but see now the Contracts (Rights of Third Parties) Act 1999.
2. Lord Browne-Wilkinson admits that this case did not fit in with traditional views of the nature of *Hedley Byrne* liability. As *Spring* v *Guardian Assurance* (above) showed there is a problem in these third party cases with 'reliance'. His Lordship has neatly avoided this problem by suggesting that there may be cases where reliance is not necessary, and this can be done by analogy with fiduciary duties where that element of 'mutuality' is not required. This was not a case of an actual fiduciary obligation, but was close enough to it. Accordingly, if the views of Lord Browne-Wilkinson are adopted there is now a new category of *Hedley Byrne* liability which has not yet been fully defined, but which places an obligation upon a person who voluntarily undertakes a task knowing that another will be directly affected if he or she fails to exercise proper skill and there is no other way the loss can be avoided.
3. The principle in *White* v *Jones* also extends to financial advisers. In *Gorham* v *BT* [2000] 4 All ER 867 Standard Life sold Mr Gorham a personal pension but failed to advise him that he and his dependants would be better off joining the BT occupational pension scheme. After his death his wife successfully claimed against Standard Life for the benefits she would have received had her husband been properly advised.
4. *Contributory negligence*. One issue that arose but was not decided in *Gorham* v *BT* (*above*) was whether the wife's claim could be affected by the husband's contributory negligence. The Law Reform (Contributory Negligence) Act 1945 could not apply as that refers to damage due partly to the *claimant's* fault, and in this situation it is not the claimant (the wife) who is at fault. However, Sir Murray Stuart thought that *White* v *Jones* should be adapted to take account of the fault of the person who relied on the advice. The other two judges expressly left the point open.
5. For a discussion of *White* v *Jones* and other cases, see McBride and Hughes, '*Hedley Byrne* in the House of Lords' (1996) 15 LS 376.

## SECTION 4: THE EFFECT OF A CLAUSE DISCLAIMING RESPONSIBILITY

In theory a clause which disclaims responsibility is not one which excludes an existing duty, but rather one which prevents that duty arising in the first place, since, according to *Hedley Byrne*, liability is based on a voluntary assumption of responsibility. However, the position has changed considerably since 1963, and it may be that a different view of the nature of the disclaimer clause should now be taken. In *Mutual Life Citizens Assurance Co.* v *Evatt* (1970) 122 CLR 556, Barwick CJ in the High Court of Australia took the view that liability was imposed and not voluntarily undertaken and that the disclaimer clause was merely one of the factors which was relevant to determine whether a duty of care had come about. This seems a sensible solution and one which accords with the view of Lord Griffiths, who said in *Smith* v *Eric Bush* (below) that assumption of responsibility 'can only have any real meaning if it is understood as referring to the circumstances in which the law will deem the maker of the statement to have assumed responsibility to the person who acts on the advice'.

Another issue is the degree of notice of a disclaimer which is necessary for it to be effective. Thus 'E. & O. E.' is commonly printed on commercial documents, but how many lay people know what it means? The matter was touched on briefly by Lord Reid in *Hedley Byrne*, where he pointed out that denying a voluntary assumption of responsibility was different from excluding a contractual obligation. However, the issue has never been resolved.

Another issue is whether a disclaimer is caught by the Unfair Contract Terms Act 1977, and this is dealt with by *Smith* v *Bush* (below).

---

### *Smith* v *Eric S. Bush*
House of Lords [1990] AC 831; [1989] 2 WLR 790; [1989] 2 All ER 514

For the facts and decision, see section 2 above. These extracts deal only with the application of the Unfair Contract Terms Act 1977. The argument for the surveyor was that liability is based on a voluntary assumption of responsibility, and as the disclaimer prevented that assumption of responsibility being made, there was therefore no liability in the first place to be excluded and the Act only applied to existing liability which was thereafter disclaimed. Held: dismissing the appeal, that the 1977 Act did apply and the exclusion clause was unreasonable.

LORD GRIFFITHS: At common law, whether the duty to exercise reasonable care and skill is founded in contract or tort, a party is as a general rule free, by the use of appropriate wording, to exclude liability for negligence in discharge of the duty. The disclaimer of liability in the present case is prominent and clearly worded and on the authority of *Hedley Byrne & Co. Ltd* v *Heller & Partners Ltd* [1964] AC 465, in so far as the common law is concerned effective to exclude the surveyors' liability for negligence. The question then is whether the Unfair Contract Terms Act 1977 bites upon such a disclaimer. In my view it does.

The Court of Appeal, however, accepted an argument based upon the definition of negligence contained in section 1(1) of the Act of 1977 which provides:

For the purposes of this part of this Act, 'negligence' means the breach—(a) of any obligation, arising from the express or implied terms of a contract, to take reasonable care or exercise reasonable skill in the performance of the contract; (b) of any common law duty to take reasonable care or exercise reasonable skill (but not any stricter duty); (c) of the common duty of care imposed by the Occupiers' Liability Act 1957 or the Occupiers' Liability Act (Northern Ireland) 1957.

They held that, as the disclaimer of liability would at common law have prevented any duty to take reasonable care arising between the parties, the Act had no application. In my view this construction fails to give due weight to the provisions of two further sections of the Act. Section 11(3) provides:

In relation to a notice (not being a notice having contractual effect), the requirement of reasonableness under this Act is that it should be fair and reasonable to allow reliance on it, having regard to all the circumstances obtaining when the liability arose or (but for the notice) would have arisen.

And section 13(1):

To the extent that this Part of this Act prevents the exclusion or restriction of any liability it also prevents—(a) making the liability or its enforcement subject to restrictive or onerous conditions; (b) excluding or restricting any right or remedy in respect of the liability, or subjecting a person to any prejudice in consequence of his pursuing any such right or remedy; (c) excluding or restricting rules of evidence or procedure; and (to that extent) sections 2 and 5 to 7 also prevent excluding or restricting liability by reference to terms and notices which exclude or restrict the relevant obligation or duty.

I read these provisions as introducing a 'but for' test in relation to the notice excluding liability. They indicate that the existence of the common law duty to take reasonable care, referred to in section 1(1)(*b*), is to be judged by considering whether it would exist 'but for' the notice excluding liability. The result of taking the notice into account when assessing the existence of a duty of care would result in removing all liability for negligent mis-statements from the protection of the Act. It is permissible to have regard to the second report of the Law Commission on Exemption Clauses (1975) (Law Com. No. 69) which is the genesis of the Unfair Contract Terms Act 1977 as an aid to the construction of the Act. Paragraph 127 of that report reads:

Our recommendations in this part of the report are intended to apply to exclusions of liability for negligence where the liability is incurred in the course of a person's business. We consider that they should apply even in cases where the person seeking to rely on the exemption clause was under no legal obligation (such as a contractual obligation) to carry out the activity. This means that, for example, conditions attached to a licence to enter on to land, and disclaimers of liability made where information or advice is given, should be subject to control. . . .

I have no reason to think that Parliament did not intend to follow this advice and the wording of the Act is, in my opinion, apt to give effect to that intention. This view of the construction of the Act is also supported by the judgment of Slade LJ in *Phillips Products Ltd* v *Hyland (Note)* [1987] 1 WLR 659, when he rejected a similar argument in relation to the construction of a contractual term excluding negligence.

# 9

# Special Duty Problems: Acts and Economic Loss

While the recovery of economic loss caused by statements is covered by the concept of 'special relationship' spelt out in *Hedley Byrne* v *Heller*, it is rather more difficult to say when, if at all, a claimant can recover for pure economic loss caused by an act. A simple example of an economic loss case is the Canadian case of *Star Village Tavern* v *Nield* (1976) 71 DLR 3d 439, where the defendant collided with a bridge across the Red River near Selkirk in Manitoba, causing it to be closed for one month for repairs. The claimant owned a pub on the far side of the bridge from Selkirk, which meant that customers from there had to travel 15 miles rather than less than two miles. The claimant sued for the decrease in his profits, but failed because he had suffered only economic loss.

The basic rule is that a person may sue for economic loss which is consequent on physical loss which that person has suffered, but may not sue if he or she has only suffered economic loss by itself. To this rule there may be exceptions where there is sufficient proximity between the parties, and one element in this may be reliance by the one on the other. However, despite the large number of cases on this subject at a very high level, no case spells out what degree of proximity would be necessary, and so far no claimant has succeeded in claiming pure economic loss, except possibly in one case which has been explained away and subsequently ignored (*Junior Books* v *Veitchi* [1982] 3 All ER 201).

Although in the past this issue was sometimes regarded as one of remoteness of damage, it is now always regarded as a duty issue. A number of cases on this subject also involve the effect of contractual terms on the standard of care, but this problem is dealt with elsewhere.

For discussion of this difficult topic see MacGrath, 'The recovery of economic loss in negligence—an emerging dichotomy' (1985) OJLS 350; Cane, *Tort Law and Economic Interests* (1996); Atiyah, 'Negligence and economic loss' (1967) 83 LQR 248; and Witting, 'Distinguishing between property damage and pure economic loss in negligence' (2001) 21 LS 481.

---

### Cattle v Stockton Waterworks
Court of Queen's Bench (1875) LR 10 QBD 453; 44 LJQB 139; 133 LT 475

The claimant was a contractor who was employed, for a fixed sum, to dig a tunnel under a road, through ground that belonged to one Knight. Unfortunately a water main belonging to the defendants was defective and caused flooding of the works, and this meant that the claimant lost money on his contract. Held: the defendants were not liable.

BLACKBURN J: In the present case the objection is technical and against the merits, and we should be glad to avoid giving it effect. But if we did so, we should establish an authority for saying that, in such a case as that of *Fletcher* v *Rylands* (1866) LR 1 Ex 265 the defendant would be liable, not only to an action by the owner of the drowned mine, and by such of his workmen as had their tools or clothes destroyed, but also to an action by every workman and person employed in the mine, who in consequence of its stoppage made less wages than he would otherwise have done. And many similar cases to which this would apply might be suggested. It may be said that it is just that all such persons should have compensation for such a loss, and that, if the law does not give them redress, it is imperfect. Perhaps it may be so. But, as was pointed out by Coleridge J, in *Lumley* v *Gye* (1853) 2 E & B 216, at p. 252, Courts of Justice should not 'allow themselves, in the pursuit of perfectly complete remedies for all wrongful acts, to transgress the bounds, which our law, in a wise consciousness as I conceive of its limited powers, has imposed on itself, of redressing only the proximate and direct consequence of wrongful acts.' In this we quite agree. No authority in favour of the plaintiff's right to sue was cited, and, as far as our knowledge goes, there was none that could have been cited. . . .

In the present case there is no pretence for saying that the defendants were malicious or had any intention to injure anyone. They were, at most, guilty of a neglect of duty, which occasioned injury to the property of Knight, but which did not injure any property of the plaintiff. The plaintiff's claim is to recover the damage which he has sustained by his contract with Knight becoming less profitable, or, it may be, a losing contract, in consequence of this injury to Knight's property. We think this does not give him any right of action.

NOTE
This case encapsulates the problems which the courts have experienced with economic loss. The objection may be technical and against the merits, but it has always succeeded, partly because of the floodgates argument and partly because of the realization that foreseeability is not by itself a sufficient limitation on the range of potential claimants. If Mr Cattle could sue, could his workers who were temporarily laid off also claim? What about the local shopkeepers and pub owners who would have taken less money while the workers were laid off?

---

### *Spartan Steel* v *Martin & Co.*
Court of Appeal [1973] QB 27; [1972] 3 All ER 557; [1972] 3 WLR 502

The defendants negligently cut a power cable supplying electricity to the claimants, who manufactured steel alloys. At the time of the power cut there was a 'melt' in progress, and in order to stop the steel solidifying the claimants had to add oxygen to it and run it off. This reduced its value by £368. Also, they would have made a profit of £400 on that melt had it been completed. They also claimed £1,767 for the profit they would have made on melts they could have processed during the time when the power was cut off. Held: allowing the appeal, that the claimants could only recover for the physical damage to the melt in progress (£368), plus loss of profit on that melt (£400), but not for the profits they would have made (£1,767) while the power was off.

LORD DENNING MR: At bottom I think the question of recovering economic loss is one of policy. Whenever the courts draw a line to mark out the bounds of *duty*, they do it as matter of policy so as to limit the responsibility of the defendant. Whenever the courts set bounds to the *damages* recoverable—saying that they are, or are not, too remote—they do it as matter of policy so as to limit the liability of the defendant.

The more I think about these cases, the more difficult I find it to put each into its proper pigeon-hole. Sometimes I say: 'There was no duty.' In others I say: 'The damage was too remote.' So much so that I think the time has come to discard those tests which have proved so elusive. It seems to me better to consider the particular relationship in hand, and see whether or not, as a matter of policy, economic loss should be recoverable, or not. Thus in *Weller & Co.* v *Foot and Mouth Disease Research Institute* [1966] 1 QB 569 it was plain that the loss suffered by the auctioneers was not recoverable, no matter whether it is put on the ground that there was no duty or that the damage was too remote. Again in *Electrochrome Ltd* v *Welsh Plastics Ltd* [1968] 2 All ER 205, it is plain that the economic loss suffered by the plaintiffs' factory (due to the damage to the fire hydrant) was not recoverable, whether because there was no duty or that it was too remote.

So I turn to the relationship in the present case. It is of common occurrence. . . .

The first consideration is the position of the statutory undertakers. If the board do not keep up the voltage or pressure of electricity, gas or water—or, likewise, if they shut it off for repairs—and thereby cause economic loss to their consumers, they are not liable in damages, not even if the cause of it is due to their own negligence. The only remedy (which is hardly ever pursued) is to prosecute the board before the magistrates. . . .

The second consideration is the nature of the hazard, namely, the cutting of the supply of electricity. This is a hazard which we all run. It may be due to a short circuit, to a flash of lightning, to a tree falling on the wires, to an accidental cutting of the cable, or even to the negligence of someone or other. And when it does happen, it affects a multitude of persons: not as a rule by way of physical damage to them or their property, but by putting them to inconvenience, and sometimes to economic loss. The supply is usually restored in a few hours, so the economic loss is not very large. Such a hazard is regarded by most people as a thing they must put up with—without seeking compensation from anyone. Some there are who instal a stand-by system. Others seek refuge by taking out an insurance policy against breakdown in the supply. But most people are content to take the risk on themselves. When the supply is cut off, they do not go running round to their solicitor. They do not try to find out whether it was anyone's fault. They just put up with it. They try to make up the economic loss by doing more work next day. This is a healthy attitude which the law should encourage.

The third consideration is this: if claims for economic loss were permitted for this particular hazard, there would be no end of claims. Some might be genuine, but many might be inflated, or even false. A machine might not have been in use anyway, but it would be easy to put it down to the cut in supply. It would be well-nigh impossible to check the claims. If there was economic loss on one day, did the claimant do his best to mitigate it by working harder next day? And so forth. Rather than expose claimants to such temptation and defendants to such hard labour—on comparatively small claims—it is better to disallow economic loss altogether, at any rate when it stands alone, independent of any physical damage.

The fourth consideration is that, in such a hazard as this, the risk of economic loss should be suffered by the whole community who suffer the losses—usually many but comparatively small losses—rather than on the one pair of shoulders, that is, on the contractor on whom the total of them, all added together, might be very heavy.

The fifth consideration is that the law provides for deserving cases. If the defendant is guilty of negligence which cuts off the electricity supply and causes actual physical damage to person or property, that physical damage can be recovered. . . .

These considerations lead me to the conclusion that the plaintiffs should recover for the physical damage to the one melt (£368), and the loss of profit on that melt consequent thereon (£400): but not for the loss of profit on the four melts (£1,767), because that was economic loss independent of the physical damage. I would, therefore, allow the appeal and reduce the damages to £768.

NOTES

1. The point made in the above case can be illustrated by contrasting two cases. The first is *British Celanese* v *Hunt Capacitors* [1969] 2 All ER 1253, where strips of metal foil escaped from the defendant's premises and struck an electricity sub-station, causing a power cut. The claimants made synthetic yarn, and material in their machines solidified. They were able to recover damages for their physical loss, together with consequent economic loss. On the other hand, in *Electrochrome* v *Welsh Plastics* [1968] 2 All ER 205, the defendants struck a fire hydrant which caused the water supply to the claimants' factory to be cut off for some hours. (The hydrant did not belong to the claimants.) The claimants were engaged in electroplating

hardware, and the factory was closed for a day as the process depended on the supply of water. However, as they suffered no physical damage they were unable to sue.

2. This decision has been rejected in similar circumstances in New Zealand. In *New Zealand Forest Products* v *A-G* [1986] 1 NZLR 14, an electricity cable which supplied only the claimants (as did the cable in *Spartan Steel*) was cut by the negligence of the defendants, causing pumps to stop and the claimants' mill came to a standstill. The claimants were able to recover all their loss of profit even though no physical damage had been caused. The *Caltex Oil* principle (below) was applied, and it seems to have been significant that the defendants knew that the cable supplied only the claimants. However, this factor was not regarded as decisive in *Mainguard Packaging* v *Hilton Haulage* [1990] 1 NZLR 360, where liability was imposed because the defendants should have realized the damage to the relevant cable would cut off the claimants among others.

---

### The Mineral Transporter: Candlewood Navigation  v  Mitsui OSK Lines
Privy Council [1986] AC 1; [1985] 3 WLR 381; [1985] 2 All ER 935

*The Ibaraki Maru* and *The Mineral Transporter* collided off Port Kembla in New South Wales due to the fault of *The Mineral Transporter*. Mitsui Lines (the claimants) owned *The Ibaraki Maru* but had let it under a bareboat charter, or charter by demise (i.e. like a lease) to Matsuoka Steamship Co. Matsuoka then let the ship under a time charter back to the claimants, Mitsui Lines. Under the various charters Matsuoka were responsible for the cost of repairs, and the claimants remained liable to pay for the hire of the ship, although at a reduced rate. Matsuoka could sue for the physical damage to the ship, as they had a property interest in it under the bareboat charter. The question was whether the claimants, as time charterers, could sue for the hire payments they had to pay while the ship was idle. (Note: the fact that the claimants were also owners of the ship was irrelevant because they were suing for losses incurred as time charterers and the time charter gave them no property rights in the ship.) Held: allowing the appeal, that the defendants were not liable for the economic loss.

NOTE
In the *Caltex* case, referred to below (*Caltex Oil* v *The Dredge Willemstad*, (197) 136 CLR 529) AOR Ltd owned a pipeline across Botany Bay which led from the Caltex Oil terminal to the AOR refinery. The dredge *Willemstad* negligently broke the pipeline. Caltex claimed the extra expense caused by having to transport oil round the bay. The High Court of Australia held the defendants liable even though the claimants had only suffered economic loss. Mason J said that a defendant will be liable for economic loss if he can reasonably foresee that a specific individual, as distinct from a general class of persons, will suffer financial loss. Gibbs J said that there would be liability where the defendant has knowledge or means of knowledge that the claimant individually and not as a member of an unascertained class might suffer loss.

LORD FRASER: Their Lordships have carefully considered these reasons for the decision in the *Caltex* case, 136 CLR 529. With regard to the reasons given by Gibbs and Mason JJ, their Lordships have difficulty in seeing how to distinguish between a plaintiff as an individual and a plaintiff as a member of an unascertained class. The test can hardly be whether the plaintiff is known by name to the wrongdoer. Nor does it seem logical for the test to depend upon the plaintiff being a single individual. Further, why should there be a distinction for this purpose between a case where the wrongdoer knows (or has the means of knowing) that the persons likely to be affected by his negligence consist of a definite number of persons whom he can identify either by name or in some other way (for example as being the owners of particular factories or hotels) and who may therefore be regarded as an ascertained class, and a case where the wrongdoer knows only that there are several persons, the exact number being to him unknown, and some or all of whom he could not identify by name or otherwise, and who may therefore be regarded as an unascertained class? Moreover much of the argument in favour of an ascertained class seems to depend upon the view that the class would normally consist of only a few individuals. But would it be different if the class, though ascertained, was large? Suppose for instance that the class consisted of all the pupils in a particular school. If it was a kindergarten school with only six pupils they might be regarded as constituting an ascertained class, even if their names were unknown to the wrongdoer. If the school was a large one with over a thousand pupils it might be suggested that they were not an ascertained class. But it is not easy to see a distinction in principle merely because the number of possible claimants is larger in one case than in the other. Apart from cases of negligent misstatement, with which their Lordships are not here concerned, they do not consider that it is practicable by reference to an ascertained class to find a satisfactory control mechanism which could be applied in such a way as to give reasonable certainty in its results. . . .

In these circumstances their Lordships have concluded that they are entitled, and indeed bound, to reach their own decision without the assistance of any single ratio decidendi to be found in the *Caltex* case. . . .

Their Lordships consider that some limit or control mechanism has to be imposed upon the liability of a wrongdoer towards those who have suffered economic damage in consequence of his negligence. The need for such a limit has been repeatedly asserted in the cases, from *Cattle's* case, LR 10 QB 453, to *Caltex*, 136 CLR 529, and their Lordships are not aware that a view to the contrary has ever been judicially expressed. . . .

Almost any rule will have some exceptions, and the decision in the *Caltex* case may perhaps be regarded as one of the 'exceptional cases' referred to by Gibbs J in the passage already quoted from his judgment. . . . Certainly the decision in *Caltex* does not appear to have been based upon a rejection of the general rule stated in *Cattle's* case. For these reasons their Lordships are of the opinion that Yeldham J erred in holding that the time charterer was entitled to recover damages from the defendant in this case.

NOTE

A similar conclusion was reached in *The Aliakmon, Leigh and Sillavan Ltd* v *Aliakmon Shipping* [1986] AC 785, which is one in a long series of cases dealing with the problem where goods are damaged which do not belong to the claimant, but for which he has to bear the risk of damage. In that case the claimants were buyers of steel coil which was damaged on its voyage in the Aliakmon. The effect of the contractual arrangements was such that the sellers reserved title to the steel, whereas it was at the claimants' risk. Thus, the sellers owned the steel, but the buyers had to take the risk of its being damaged. The House of Lords held that the buyers could not sue for the loss, since it was purely economic loss. Lord Brandon said that:

. . . there is a long line of authority for the principle that, in order to enable a person to claim in negligence for loss caused to him by reason of loss of or damage to property, he must have had either the legal ownership of or a possessory title to the property concerned at the time when the loss or damage occurred, and it is not enough for him to have only had contractual rights in relation to such property which have been adversely affected by the loss or damage to it.

The result is that the sellers could sue, but would not bother to do so because they have received full price from the buyers. The buyers have paid the full price for damaged steel, but are unable to recover from the person who damaged it. However, as the House of Lords pointed out, the buyers could have so ordered their contractual arrangements so as to avoid this result, and the best solution to the problem probably lies in contract rather than tort. The case is further discussed in the next chapter.

---

*Murphy* v *Brentwood District Council*
House of Lords [1991] AC 398; [1990] 3 WLR 414; [1990] 2 All ER 908

In 1970, the claimant purchased a house which was constructed on a concrete raft foundation over an in-filled site. From 1981 cracks began appearing in the internal walls of the house and it was found that the concrete raft had subsided. In an action against the local authority for negligently approving the design of the concrete raft (for which see Chapter 12 below), the question was whether the claimant had suffered only economic loss. The House of Lords held that he had, as the house had only damaged itself and was therefore merely a defective house which was a bad bargain. Lord Oliver made the following comments about the nature of the economic loss problem and the circumstances in which such loss might be recoverable.

LORD OLIVER: It does not, of course, at all follow as a matter of necessity from the mere fact that the only damage suffered by a plaintiff in an action for the tort of negligence is pecuniary or 'economic' that this claim is bound to fail. It is true that, in an uninterrupted line of cases since 1875, it has consistently been held that a third party cannot successfully sue in tort for the interference with his economic expectations or advantage resulting from injury to the person or property of another person with whom he has or is likely to have a contractual relationship: see *Cattle* v *Stockton Waterworks Co.* (1875) LR 10 QB 453; *Simpson & Co.* v *Thomson* (1877) 3 App Cas 279; *Société Anonyme de Remorquage à Hélice* v *Bennetts* [1911] 1 KB 243. That principle was applied more recently by Widgery J in *Weller & Co.* v *Foot and Mouth Disease Research Institute* [1966] QB 569 and received its most recent reiteration in the decision of this House in *Leigh and Sillavan Ltd* v *Aliakmon Shipping Co. Ltd* [1986] AC 785. But it is far from clear from these decisions that the reason for the plaintiff's failure was simply that the only loss sustained was 'economic.' Rather they seem to have been based either upon the remoteness of the damage as a matter of direct causation or, more probably, upon the 'floodgates' argument of the impossibility of containing liability within any acceptable bounds if the law were to permit such claims to succeed. The decision of this House in *Morrison Steamship Co. Ltd* v *Greystoke Castle (Cargo Owners)* [1947] AC 265 demonstrates that the mere fact that the primary damage suffered by a plaintiff is pecuniary is no necessary bar to an action in negligence given the proper circumstances—In that case, what was said to be the 'joint venture' interest of shipowners and the owners of cargo carried on board—and if the matter remained in doubt that doubt was conclusively resolved by the decision of this House in *Hedley Byrne & Co. Ltd* v *Heller & Partners Ltd* [1964] AC 465 where Lord Devlin, at p. 517, convincingly demonstrated the illogicality of a distinction between financial loss caused directly and financial loss resulting from physical injury to personal property.

The critical question, as was pointed out in the analysis of Brennan J in his judgment in *Council of the Shire of Sutherland* v *Heyman* (1985) 157 CLR 424, Is not the nature of the damage In itself, whether physical or pecuniary, but whether the scope of the duty of care in the circumstances of the case is such as to embrace damage of the kind which the plaintiff claims to have sustained: see *Caparo Industries Plc* v *Dickman* [1990] 2 WLR 358. The essential question which has to be asked in every case, given that damage which is the essential ingredient of the action has occurred, is whether the relationship between the plaintiff and the defendant is such—or, to use the favoured expression, whether it is of sufficient 'proximity'—that it imposes upon the latter a duty to take care to avoid or prevent that loss which has in fact been sustained. That the requisite degree of proximity may be established in circumstances in which the plaintiff's injury results from his reliance upon a statement or advice upon which he was entitled to rely and upon which it was contemplated that he would be likely to rely is clear from *Hedley Byrne* and subsequent cases, but *Anns* [1978] AC 728 was not such a case and neither is the instant case. It is not, however, necessarily to be assumed that the reliance cases form the only possible category of cases in which a duty to take reasonable care to avoid or prevent pecuniary loss can arise. *Morrison Steamship Co. Ltd* v *Greystoke Castle (Cargo Owners)*, for instance, clearly was not a reliance case. Nor indeed was *Ross* v *Caunters* [1980] Ch 297 so far as the disappointed beneficiary was concerned. Another example may be *Ministry of Housing and Local Government* v *Sharp* [1980] 2 QB 223, although this may, on analysis, properly be categorised as a reliance case.

Nor is it self-evident logically where the line is to be drawn. Where, for instance, the defendant's careless conduct results in the interruption of the electricity supply to business premises adjoining the highway, it is not easy to discern the logic in holding that a sufficient relationship of proximity exists between him and a factory owner who has suffered loss because material in the course of manufacture is rendered useless but that none exists between him and the owner of, for instance, an adjoining restaurant who suffers the loss of profit on the meals which he is unable to prepare and sell. In both cases the real loss is pecuniary. The solution to such borderline cases has so far been achieved pragmatically (see *Spartan Steel & Alloys Ltd* v *Martin & Co. (Contractors) Ltd* [1973] QB 27) not by the application of logic but by the perceived necessity as a matter of policy to place some limits—perhaps arbitrary limits—to what would otherwise be an endless, cumulative causative chain bounded only by theoretical foreseeability.

I frankly doubt whether, in searching for such limits, the categorisation of the damage as 'material', 'physical', 'pecuniary' or 'economic' provides a particularly useful contribution. Where it does, I think, serve a useful purpose is in identifying those cases in which it is necessary to search for and find something more than the mere reasonable foreseeability of damage which has occurred as providing the degree of 'proximity' necessary to support the action. In his classical exposition in *Donoghue* v *Stevenson* [1932] AC 562, 580–581, Lord Atkin was expressing himself in the context of the infliction of direct physical injury resulting from a carelessly created latent defect in a manufactured product. In his analysis of the duty in those circumstances he clearly equated 'proximity' with the reasonable foresight of damage. In the straightforward case of the direct infliction of physical injury by the act of the plaintiff there is, indeed, no need to look beyond the foreseeability by the defendant of the result in order to establish that he is in a 'proximate' relationship with the plaintiff. But, as was pointed out by Lord Diplock in *Dorset Yacht Co. Ltd* v *Home Office* [1970] AC 1004, 1060, Lord Atkin's test, though a useful guide to characteristics which will be found to exist in conduct and relationships giving rise to a legal duty of care, is manifestly false if misused as a universal; and Lord Reid, in the course of his speech in the same case, recognised that the statement of principle enshrined in that test necessarily required qualification in cases where the only loss caused by the defendant's conduct was economic. The infliction of physical injury to the person or property of another universally requires to be justified. The causing of economic loss does not. If it is to be categorised as wrongful it is necessary to find some factor beyond the mere occurrence of the loss and the fact that its occurrence could be foreseen. Thus the categorisation of damage as economic serves at least the useful purpose of indicating that something more is required. . . .

NOTES

1. For an explanation as to why the loss in *Murphy* v *Brentwood District Council* was regarded as economic loss see the discussion of that case in Chapter 13 (liability for defective structures).

2. In *Murphy* v *Brentwood DC*, Lord Oliver suggests that 'economic' loss may be recoverable where there is sufficient proximity, but does not say what criteria will be used to bring about that necessary degree of proximity. In the search for an appropriate test to allow the recovery of economic loss in restricted circumstances, a number of factors have been discussed, but none has yet won the day. These include close proximity, as in *Caltex Oil*, reliance, as in *Junior Books* and *Muirhead Tank*, and voluntary assumption of responsibility, as in *Hedley Byrne*. The *Caltex Oil* test has been rejected in this country and the idea that *Hedley Byrne* liability is based on a voluntary assumption of responsibility was denied in *Smith* v *Eric Bush*. As to reliance, it was said by Dillon LJ in *Simaan* v *Pilkington Ltd* [1988] 1 QB 758, at p. 784, 'Indeed I find it difficult to see that future citation from the *Junior Books* case can ever serve any useful purpose', and yet in *Murphy* v *Brentwood DC* Lord Bridge said, citing *Junior Books*, that 'there may be situations where, even in the absence of contract, there is a special relationship of proximity . . . which is sufficiently akin to contract to introduce the element of reliance so that the scope of the duty of care owed . . . is wide enough to embrace purely economic loss'. It seems, therefore, that reliance may be the way forward, but it is too early to say in what circumstances reliance will give rise to the duty to avoid economic loss. However, see Stapleton, 'Duty of Care and Economic Loss: A Wider Agenda' (1991) 107 LQR 249, where it is argued that reliance is not the answer but that the courts should adopt a policy-based approach whereby claimants must establish their worthiness to be protected by satisfying various conditions, including the absence of indeterminate liability, the inadequacy of alternative means of protection, that the area is not one more appropriate to Parliamentary

action and that a duty would not allow a circumvention of a positive arrangement regarding the allocation of the risk which had been accepted by the claimant.

3. The contractual problems which often arise in economic loss cases, such as *Simaan*, are dealt with in the next chapter.

---

### Canadian National Railway v Norsk Pacific Steamship Co.

Supreme Court of Canada [1992] 1 SCR 1021; (1992) 91 DLR 4th 289

The New Westminster Railway Bridge spans the Fraser river in British Columbia. It is owned by the Canadian Government through Public Works Canada (PWC) and is used by four different railway companies including the claimants. On 28 November 1987 the barge Crown Forest No. 4 collided with the bridge and damaged it. As a result the claimants had to re-route their trains for several weeks and sued for that additional cost. Held: the economic loss was recoverable as there was sufficient proximity between the claimants and defendants.

McLACHLIN J:

*2. Implications of the comparative review*

The foregoing comparative review suggests that in some cases damages for economic loss should be available where the plaintiff has neither suffered physical damage nor relied in the sense of *Hedley Byrne*. Civil law jurisdictions, far from precluding such recovery, require it where it is direct and certain. The common law jurisdictions started from a narrow rule excluding most pure economic loss, but found themselves in a situation where judges on a case-by-case basis persisted in awarding damages for economic loss outside the categories. Even in the United States, where fear of the floodgates of unlimited liability has held the strongest sway, courts have been forced to make exceptions in the interests of justice. The fact is that situations arise, other than those falling within the old exclusionary rule, where it is manifestly fair and just that recovery of economic loss be permitted. Faced with these situations, courts will strain to allow recovery, provided they are satisfied that the case will not open the door to a plethora of undeserving claims. They will refuse to accept injustice merely for the sake of the doctrinal tidiness which is the motivating spirit of *Murphy v Brentwood District Council*. This is in the best tradition of the law of negligence, the history of which exhibits a sturdy refusal to be confined by arbitrary forms and rules where justice indicates otherwise. It is the tradition to which this Court has adhered in suggesting in *Kamloops v Nielsen* [1984] 2 SCR 2 that the search should not be for a universal rule but for the elaboration of categories where recovery of economic loss is justifiable on a case-by-case basis.

If a comparative review suggests that economic loss should be recoverable in circumstances not covered by the traditional exclusionary rule, it also suggests that the need for some limit on such recovery is universally recognized. To permit all economic loss related to a negligent act to be recovered would be to subject potential defendants to liability which is not only unfair, but which may cripple their ability to do business.

The search then must be for a legal formulation which will permit recovery of economic loss in appropriate cases, while excluding frivolous and remote claims. The comparative jurisprudence indicates that this may be accomplished in different ways. In the civil law, a direct connection test appears to provide appropriate limits. At common law, two approaches present themselves: the 'exhaustive rule' solution typified by *Murphy* and the incremental approach adopted in *Kamloops*. I turn next to a consideration of which of these two approaches should prevail.

*3. The approach which should be adopted to recovery of pure economic loss*

*(a) Doctrinal consideration*

*Murphy* makes an important point. It is not enough that a rule of law be defensible on moral and economic terms. It should, in addition, provide a logical basis upon which individuals can predicate their conduct and courts can decide future cases. The history of the problem in different jurisdictions demonstrates a clear need to allow recovery of economic loss for negligence in some cases where the criteria of physical damage and reliance do not apply. On the other hand, a fair and functional legal system cannot accept that all economic loss related to negligence should be recoverable. Judges seem able to pick out deserving cases when they see them. The difficulty lies in formulating a rule which explains why judges allow recovery of economic loss in some cases and not in others. . . .

The matter may be put thus: before the law will impose liability there must be a connection between the defendant's conduct and plaintiff's loss which makes it just for the defendant to indemnify the plaintiff. In contract, the contractual relationship provides this link. In trust, it is the fiduciary obligation which establishes the necessary connection. In tort, the equivalent notion is proximity. Proximity may consist of various forms of closeness—physical, circumstantial, causal or assumed—which serve to identify the categories of cases in which liability lies.

Viewed thus, the concept of proximity may be seen as an umbrella, covering a number of disparate circumstances in which the relationship between the parties is so close that it is just and reasonable to permit recovery in tort. The complexity and diversity of the circumstances in which tort liability may arise defy identification of a single criterion capable of serving as the universal hallmark of liability. The meaning of 'proximity' is to be found rather in viewing the circumstances in which it has been found to exist and determining whether the case at issue is similar enough to justify a similar finding.

In summary, it is my view that the authorities suggest that pure economic loss is *prima facie* recoverable where, in addition to negligence and foreseeable loss, there is sufficient proximity between the negligent act and the loss. Proximity is the controlling concept which avoids the spectre of unlimited liability. Proximity may be established by a variety of factors, depending on the nature of the case. To date, sufficient proximity has been found in the case of negligent misstatements where there is an undertaking and correlative reliance (*Hedley Byrne*); where there is a duty to warn (*Rivtow*); and where a statute imposes a responsibility on a municipality towards the owners and occupiers of land (*Kamloops*). But the categories are not closed. As more cases are decided, we can expect further definition on what factors give rise to liability for pure economic loss in particular categories of cases. In determining whether liability should be extended to a new situation, courts will have regard to the factors traditionally relevant to proximity such as the relationship between the parties, physical propinquity, assumed or imposed obligations and close causal connection. And they will insist on sufficient special factors to avoid the imposition of indeterminate and unreasonable liability. The result will be a principled, yet flexible, approach to tort liability for pure economic loss. It will allow recovery where recovery is justified, while excluding indeterminate and inappropriate liability, and it will permit the coherent development of the law in accordance with the approach initiated in England by *Hedley Byrne* and followed in Canada in *Rivtow, Kamloops* and *Hofstrand*.

I add the following observations on proximity. The absolute exclusionary rule adopted in *Stockton* and affirmed in *Murphy* (subject to *Hedley Byrne*) can itself be seen as an indicator of proximity. Where there is physical injury or damage, one posits proximity on the ground that if one is close enough to someone or something to do physical damage to it, one is close enough to be held legally responsible for the consequences. Physical injury has the advantage of being a clear and simple indicator of proximity. The problem arises when it is taken as the *only* indicator of proximity. As the cases amply demonstrate, the necessary proximity to found legal liability fairly in tort may well arise in circumstances where there is no physical damage.

Viewed in this way, proximity may be seen as paralleling the requirement in civil law that damages be direct and certain. Proximity, like the requirement of directness, posits a close link between the negligent act and the resultant loss. Distant losses which arise from collateral relationships do not qualify for recovery.

In many of the cases discussed above, the judiciary has focused upon the relationship between the tortfeasor and the plaintiff as an indication of proximity, a focus closely related to the foreseeability analysis inherent to all negligence actions. In the classic case of *Hedley Byrne*, the reliance analysis focused upon the connection between the party who made the negligent misstatement and the injured party, i.e., is that plaintiff a party that the tortfeasor ought reasonably to have foreseen would rely on his or her statement? The judgments below focused on the relationship between the tortfeasor Norsk and the plaintiff CN both within and outside their discussion of proximity. A more comprehensive, and I submit objective, consideration of proximity requires that the court review all of the factors connecting the negligent act with the loss; this includes not only the relationship between the parties but all forms of proximity—physical, circumstantial, causal or assumed indicators of closeness. While it is impossible to define comprehensively what will satisfy the requirements of proximity or directness, precision may be found as types of relationships or situations are defined in which the necessary closeness between negligence and loss exists.

While proximity is critical to establishing the right to recover pure economic loss in tort, it does not always indicate liability. It is a necessary but not necessarily sufficient condition of liability. Recognizing that proximity is itself concerned with policy, the approach adopted in *Kamloops* (paralleled by the second branch of *Anns*) requires the Court to consider the purposes served by permitting recovery as well as whether there are any residual policy considerations which call for a limitation on liability. This permits courts to reject liability for pure economic loss where indicated by policy reasons not taken into account in the proximity analysis.

I conclude that, from a doctrinal point of view, this Court should continue on the course charted in *Kamloops* rather than reverting to the narrow exclusionary rule as the House of Lords did in *Murphy*.

### 4. Application to this case

The plaintiff CN suffered economic loss as a result of being deprived of its contractual right to use the bridge damaged by the defendants' negligence. Applying the *Kamloops* approach, its right to recover depends on: (1) whether it can establish sufficient proximity or 'closeness', and (2) whether extension of recovery to this type of loss is desirable from a practical point of view.

The first question is whether the evidence in this case establishes the proximity necessary to found liability. The case does not fall within any of the categories where proximity and liability have been hitherto found to exist. So we must consider the matter afresh . . .

In addition to focusing upon the relationship between the appellant Norsk and CN —a significant indicator of proximity in and of itself—the trial judge based his conclusion that there was sufficient proximity on a number of factors related to CN's connection with the property damaged, the bridge, including the fact that CN's property was in close proximity to the bridge, that CN's property could not be enjoyed without the link of the bridge, which was an integral part of its railway system and that CN supplied materials, inspection and consulting services for the bridge, was its preponderant user, and was recognized in the periodic negotiations surrounding the closing of the bridge.

MacGuigan JA summarized the trial judge's findings on proximity as follows, at p. 167:

> In effect, the Trial Judge found that the CNR was so closely assimilated to the position of PWC that it was very much within the reasonable ambit of risk of the appellants at the time of the accident. That, it seems to me, is sufficient proximity: in Deane J's language, it is both physical and circumstantial closeness.

Such a characterization brings the situation into the 'joint' or 'common venture' category under which recovery for purely economic loss has heretofore been recognized in maritime law cases from the United Kingdom (*The Greystoke Castle*, [1947] AC 265) and the United States (*Amoco Transport*, 768 F2d 659 (1985)). The reasoning, as I apprehend it, is that where the plaintiff's operations are so closely allied to the operations of the party suffering physical damage and to its property (which—as damaged—causes the plaintiff's loss) that it can be considered a joint venturer with the owner of the property, the plaintiff can recover its economic loss even though the plaintiff has suffered no physical damage to its own property. To deny recovery in such circumstances would be to deny it to a person who for practical purposes is in the same position as if he or she owned the property physically damaged.

The second question is whether extension of recovery to this type of loss is desirable from a practical point of view. Recovery serves the purpose of permitting a plaintiff whose position for practical purposes, vis-à-vis the tortfeasor, is indistinguishable from that of the owner of the damaged property, to recover what the actual owner could have recovered. This is fair and avoids an anomalous result. Nor does the recovery of economic loss in this case open the floodgates to unlimited liability. The category is a limited one. It has been applied in England and the United States without apparent difficulty. It does not embrace casual users of the property or those secondarily and incidentally affected by the damage done to the property. Potential tortfeasors can gauge in advance the scope of their liability. Businesses are not precluded from self-insurance or from contracting for indemnity, nor are they 'penalized' for not so doing. Finally, frivolous claims are not encouraged.

I conclude that here, as in *Kamloops*, the necessary duty and proximity are established, that valid purposes are served by permitting recovery, and that recovery will not open the floodgates to unlimited liability. In such circumstances, recovery should be permitted.

NOTES

1. The above represents the view of the majority in the Supreme Court of Canada. Stevenson J decided the case in favour of the claimants on the basis of the *Caltex Oil* principles and La Forest J dissented on the ground that economic loss should not be recoverable where it arises out of damage to the property of a third party with whom the claimant has a contractual arrangement.

2. In *Bow Valley Husky (Bermuda) Ltd* v *Saint John Shipbuilding* [1997] 3 SCR 1210 Mclachlin J. in the Supreme Court of Canada said that *Norsk* stood for the proposition that 'relational' economic loss is only recoverable in special situations and these are (1) cases where the claimant has a possessory or proprietary interest in the damaged property, (2) general average cases and (3) where the relationship between the claimant and the property owner constitutes a joint venture. These categories are not closed but here the court rejected a proposed extension because of the problems of indeterminate liability.

# 10

## Special Duty Problems:
## Contract and Duty of Care

There are two classes of problem concerning the relationship of contract and tort. The first is whether there can be a duty in tort when there is a contract between the same parties, and the second is whether a contract between A and B can affect a duty owed by C to A.

The first issue has been a matter of debate for many years but now appears to have been settled by *Henderson* v *Merrett Syndicates* (below). There will not be many cases where it will be beneficial to sue in tort rather than contract, but there are some. These include extended limitation periods, less restricted remoteness rules, more liberal rules on suing out of the jurisdiction and different rules on contribution.

The second problem to be dealt with in this chapter occurs where a duty is owed by the defendant to the claimant, but the content of that duty is also the subject of a contractual relationship with a third party. Thus, where there is a contract between A and B and between B and C it may be that because of the connection, C owes a duty in tort to A. The question is whether any term in the contract between A and B or between B and C can affect the duty owed by C to A.

The issue is essentially one of privity of contract and to some extent the problem is solved by the Contracts (Rights of Third Parties) Act 1999 (below) but this extends an exemption clause to a third party only when he is specifically mentioned in the main contract. Now that such clauses are effective they may become more common.

An example of the problem could occur if a company (A) engages a builder (B) to build an extension to its factory, and the builder engages an electrician (C) to do the electrical work. Both the main contract between the owner and the builder, and the subcontract between the builder and the electrician contain exemption clauses excluding liability for damage caused to the main building by any work on the extension but the exemption clause in the main contract is not specifically extended to the subcontractor. Thus C (the electrician) has a contract with B (the builder) in relation to the same issue in relation to which he owes a duty in tort to the building owner (A). Presumably, under such an arrangement both the builder and the electrician have tendered at a lower price because they will not be bearing the risk of damage. If the electrician causes damage to the factory, would it be right in such circumstances to make him owe a higher duty in tort to A than he owes under his contract with B, or for A to have greater rights in tort against C than he has under his contract with B? The problem will only matter where for some reason the owner is unable to enforce his contractual rights against the builder, either because the builder is bankrupt or because there is an exclusion clause in the contract between them.

For a proposed solution to the problems discussed in this chapter see Adams and Brownsword, 'Privity and the concept of a network contract' (1990) 10 LS 12.

## SECTION 1: CONCURRENT LIABILITY

### *Henderson* v *Merrett Syndicates*
House of Lords [1995] 2 AC 145; [1994] 3 WLR 761; [1994] 3 All ER 506; [1994] 2 Lloyd's Rep 468

The claimants were Lloyd's underwriters (names) who were suing defendants for the negligent management of syndicates to which they belonged. Sometimes the names' agents themselves managed the syndicate which made the names 'direct names'. In other cases the names' agent placed the name in a syndicate managed by a different agent by way of a subagency agreement. These were 'indirect names'. The names wished to take advantage of more liberal limitation periods in tort and thus the question arose whether there could be liability in tort at the same time as there were contractual relationships in place between the parties. Held: dismissing the appeal, that the defendants were liable in tort to both the direct and indirect names.

LORD GOFF:

*The impact of the contractual context*

The judgment of Oliver J in the *Midland Bank Trust Co.* case [1979] Ch 384 provided the first analysis in depth of the question of concurrent liability in tort and contract. Following upon *Esso Petroleum Co. Ltd* v *Mardon* [1976] QB 801, it also broke the mould, in the sense that it undermined the view which was becoming settled that, where there is an alternative liability in tort, the claimant must pursue his remedy in contract alone. The development of the case law in other common law countries is very striking. In the same year as the *Midland Bank Trust Co.* case, the Irish Supreme Court held that solicitors owed to their clients concurrent duties in contract and tort: see *Finley* v *Murtagh* [1979] IR 249. Next, in *Central Trust Co.* v *Rafuse* (1986) 31 DLR (4th) 481, Le Dain J, delivering the judgment of the Supreme Court of Canada, conducted a comprehensive and most impressive survey of the relevant English and Canadian authorities on the liability of solicitors to their clients for negligence, in contract and in tort, in the course of which he paid a generous tribute to the analysis of Oliver J in the *Midland Bank Trust Co.* case. His conclusions are set out in a series of propositions at pp. 521–522; but his general conclusion was to the same effect as that reached by Oliver J. He said, at p. 522:

> A concurrent or alternative liability in tort will not be admitted if its effect would be to permit the plaintiff to circumvent or escape a contractual exclusion or limitation of liability for the act or omission that would constitute the tort. Subject to this qualification, where concurrent liability in tort and contract exists the plaintiff has the right to assert the cause of action that appears to be the most advantageous to him in respect of any particular legal consequences.

I respectfully agree. . . .

So far as *Hedley Byrne* itself is concerned, Mr Kaye ['Liability of Solicitors in Tort' (1984) 100 LQR 680] reads the speeches as restricting the principle of assumption of responsibility there established to cases where there is no contract; indeed, on this he tolerates no dissent, stating (at p. 706) that 'unless one reads [*Hedley Byrne*] with deliberate intent to find obscure or ambiguous passages' it will not bear the interpretation favoured by Oliver J. I must confess however that, having studied yet again the speeches in *Hedley Byrne* [1964] AC 465 in the light of Mr Kaye's critique, I remain of the opinion that Oliver J's reading of them is justified. It is, I suspect, a matter of the angle of vision with which they are read. For here, I consider, Oliver J was influenced not only by what he read in the speeches themselves, notably the passage from Lord Devlin's speech at pp. 528–529 (quoted above), but also by the internal logic reflected in that passage, which led inexorably to the conclusion which he drew. Mr Kaye's approach involves regarding the law of tort as supplementary to the law of contract, i.e. as providing for a tortious liability in cases where there is no contract. Yet the law of tort is the general law, out of which the parties can, if they wish, contract; and, as Oliver J demonstrated, the same assumption of responsibility may, and frequently does, occur in a contractual context. Approached as a matter of principle, therefore, it is right to attribute to that assumption of responsibility, together with its concomitant reliance, a tortious liability, and then to inquire whether or not that liability is excluded by the contract because the latter is inconsistent with it. This is the reasoning which Oliver J, as I understand it, found implicit, where not explicit, in the speeches in *Hedley Byrne*. With his conclusion I respectfully agree. But even if I am wrong in this, I am of the opinion that this House should now, if necessary, develop the principle of assumption of responsibility as stated in *Hedley Byrne* to its logical conclusion so as to make it clear that a tortious duty of care may arise not only in cases where the relevant services are rendered gratuitously, but also where they are rendered under a contract. This indeed is the view expressed by my noble and learned friend, Lord Keith of Kinkel, in *Murphy* v *Brentwood District Council* [1991] 1 AC 398, 466, in a speech with which all the other members of the Appellate Committee agreed.

An alternative approach, which also avoids the concurrence of tortious and contractual remedies, is to be found in the judgment of Deane J, in *Hawkins* v *Clayton*, 164 CLR 539, 582–586, in which he concluded, at p. 585:

> On balance, however, it seems to me to be preferable to accept that there is neither justification nor need for the implication of a contractual term which, in the absence of actual intention of the parties, imposes upon a solicitor a contractual duty (with consequential liability in damages for its breach) which is coextensive in content and concurrent in operation with a duty (with consequential liability in damages for its breach) which already exists under the common law of negligence.

It is however my understanding that by the law in this country contracts for services do contain an implied promise to exercise reasonable care (and skill) in the performance of the relevant services; indeed, as Mr Tony Weir has pointed out (XI *Int. Encycl. Comp. L.*, ch. 12, para. 67), in the 19th century the field of concurrent liabilities was expanded 'since it was impossible for the judges to deny that contracts contained an implied promise to take reasonable care, at the least not to injure the other party.' My own belief is that, in the present context, the common law is not antipathetic to concurrent liability, and that there is no sound basis for a rule which automatically restricts the claimant to either a tortious or a contractual remedy. The result may be untidy; but, given that the tortious duty is imposed by the general law, and the contractual duty is attributable to the will of the parties, I do not find it objectionable that the claimant may be entitled to take advantage of the remedy which is most advantageous to him, subject only to ascertaining whether the tortious duty is so inconsistent with the applicable contract that, in accordance with ordinary principle, the parties must be taken to have agreed that the tortious remedy is to be limited or excluded.

In the circumstances of the present case, I have not regarded it as necessary or appropriate to embark upon yet another detailed analysis of the case law, choosing rather to concentrate on those authorities which appear to me to be here most important. I have been most anxious not to overburden an inevitably lengthy opinion with a discussion of an issue which is only one (though an important one) of those which fall for decision; and, in the context of the relationship of solicitor and client, the task of surveying the authorities has already been admirably performed by both Oliver J and Le Dain J. But, for the present purposes more important, in the present case liability can, and in my opinion should, be founded squarely on the principle established in *Hedley Byrne* itself, from which it follows that an assumption of responsibility coupled with the concomitant reliance may give rise to a tortious duty of care irrespective of whether there is a contractual relationship between the parties, and in consequence, unless his contract precludes him from doing so, the plaintiff, who has available to him concurrent remedies in contract and tort, may choose that remedy which appears to him to be the most advantageous.

NOTES

1. This case decides that there is no reason in principle why there should not be concurrent liability in contract and tort. Usually, the substantive liability derived from an implied term will be the same as the tort duty, but this need not be so. As was said in *Holt* v *Payne Shillington* The Times, 22 December 1995, the duties may be concurrent but need not be coextensive: 'The difference in scope between the two would reflect the more limited factual basis which gave rise to the contract and the absence of any term in the contract which precluded or restricted the duty of care in tort.'

2. For a discussion of *Henderson*, see Whittaker, 'The application of the broad principle of *Hedley Byrne* as between parties to a contract' (1997) 17 LS 169, who argues that the principle should not be adopted (at least in cases where there is a contract) because it would subvert the doctrine of consideration and other contractual rules.

## SECTION 2: LIABILITY TO THIRD PARTIES

### CONTRACTS (RIGHTS OF THIRD PARTIES) ACT 1999

**1. Right of third party to enforce contractual term**

(1) Subject to the provisions of this Act, a person who is not a party to a contract (a 'third party') may in his own right enforce a term of the contract if—

(a) the contract expressly provides that he may, or

(b) subject to subsection (2), the term purports to confer a benefit on him.

(2) Subsection (1)(b) does not apply if on a proper construction of the contract it appears that the parties did not intend the term to be enforceable by the third party.

(3) The third party must be expressly identified in the contract by name, as a member of a class or as answering a particular description but need not be in existence when the contract is entered into.

(4) This section does not confer a right on a third party to enforce a term of a contract otherwise than subject to and in accordance with any other relevant terms of the contract.

(5) For the purpose of exercising his right to enforce a term of the contract, there shall be available to the third party any remedy that would have been available to him in an action for breach of contract if he had been a party to the contract (and the rules relating to damages, injunctions, specific performance and other relief shall apply accordingly).

(6) Where a term of a contract excludes or limits liability in relation to any matter references in this Act to the third party enforcing the term shall be construed as references to his availing himself of the exclusion or limitation.

(7) In this Act, in relation to a term of a contract which is enforceable by a third party—

'the promisor' means the party to the contract against whom the term is enforceable by the third party, and
'the promisee' means the party to the contract by whom the term is enforceable against the promisor.

NOTES

1. The main effect of this section in tort will be to allow C to take advantage of an exemption clause contained in a contract between A and B, but only if he is specifically mentioned in the main contract, either as an individual or as a member of a class answering a particular description. Section 1(3) points out that the third party need not actually be in existence or identifiable at the time of the contract, so that, for example, a main contract may exempt all subcontractors even though they have not been appointed at the time of the contract.

2. The mere existence of a chain of contracts will not necessarily render the Act applicable, since the context may be such, especially in a chain of building contracts, that it was never

intended to confer benefits up and down the chain and so s. 1(2) would prevent the Act applying. See, for example, *Simaan* v *Pilkington Glass* (below), which would probably be decided the same way after the Act.

3. For the background to the Act, see the Law Commission Report No. 242 on Privity of Contract and Macdonald, *Exemption Clauses and Unfair Terms* (1999), ch. 5.

## The Aliakmon: Leigh and Sillavan Ltd v Aliakmon Ltd

The claimants bought coils of steel from Japanese sellers which were shipped aboard *The Aliakmon*, owned by the defendants. During the voyage the steel was damaged due to poor ventilation and storage. There was a contract of carriage between the defendant shipowners and the sellers, and a contract of sale between the sellers and the claimant buyers. For various reasons the contractual arrangements meant that the sellers retained title to the steel, whereas the risk of its being damaged was upon the buyers. In the event it was held by both the Court of Appeal and the House of Lords that, as the buyers did not own the steel at the time of its damage, they had suffered only pure economic loss and could not sue. One complication was that the contract between the defendant shipowners and the sellers was subject to the terms of the bill of lading, and this incorporated internationally agreed terms which limited the liability of the shipowner (the Hague rules). Hence, one issue was, assuming the shipowners could be liable to the buyers (which they were not), would their liability be subject to the Hague rules contained in the contract between the shipowners and the sellers? Held: that both the Court of Appeal and the House of Lords doubted that the duty in tort could be limited in this way, and this was one factor in deciding against the buyers.

## Court of Appeal

[1985] 1 QB 350; [1985] 2 All ER 44; [1985] 2 WLR 289

SIR JOHN DONALDSON MR: Mr Sumption's second and third considerations can be taken together. They are:

> The existence of a duty of care owed to others than the owners of cargo would impose on a shipowner most of the liabilities which he will generally assume by contract by virtue of the Hague Rules without the protection which those Rules afford and which it is recognised as a matter of international and domestic public policy that he should have.

And:

> if it be accepted that a shipowner is liable to others than the owners of the goods at the relevant time, then he is potentially exposed to liability to anyone who may suffer loss because the nature of his contractual arrangements prevent him from recovering from anyone other than the shipowner, e.g., the purchaser (whenever the purchase occurs) of goods suffering from a latent defect acquired on board ship, or of goods sold 'as is where is.'

Mr Sumption might, perhaps, have added that without some limitation the shipowner would also be liable to cargo underwriters, although Mr Clarke, who has appeared for the plaintiff buyers, did not seek to contend that the shipowner's liability was as extensive as this.

I find these considerations wholly compelling. The relationship between buyer and seller on the one hand and cargo-owner and shipowner on the other are quite distinct. In each case the parties seek to establish an economic balance, but there is no reason why it should be the same balance. The buyer may well be able to obtain the goods more cheaply if he undertakes not to hold the seller liable if the goods are lost or damaged after shipment and before they are delivered to him and to pay the price in any event. The shipowner may well charge a lower freight if, in return, he is to enjoy the protection of exceptions and limitations upon his liability. Indeed he may be unwilling to accept the goods for carriage at all, if to do so will involve him in assuming any more extended duty of care or more extended liability for breach of that duty.

In the instant case the buyers claim the right to impose upon the shipowners a higher duty of care than the shipowners owed to the seller under the bill of lading contract or, as the case may be, the charter and to do so without the shipowners' leave or licence, by means of a contract with the sellers.

I have, of course, considered whether any duty of care owed in tort to the buyer could in some way be equated to the contractual duty of care owed to the shipper, but I do not see how this could be done. The commonest form of contract of carriage by sea is one on the terms of the Hague Rules. But this is an intricate blend of responsibilities and liabilities (Article III), rights and immunities (Article IV), limitations in the amount of damages recoverable (Article IV, r. 5), time bars (Article III, r. 6), evidential provisions (Article III, rr. 4 and 6), indemnities (Article III, r. 5 and Article IV, r. 6) and liberties (Article IV, rr. 4 and 6). I am quite unable to see how these can be synthesised into a standard of care.

### House of Lords
[1986] AC 785; [1986] 2 WLR 902; [1986] 2 All ER 145

LORD BRANDON: As I said earlier, Mr Clarke submitted that your Lordships should hold that a duty of care did exist in the present case, but that it was subject to the terms of the bill of lading. With regard to this suggestion Sir John Donaldson MR said in the present case [1985] QB 350, 368: [His Lordship quoted from the extract above.]

I find myself suffering from the same inability to understand how the necessary synthesis could be made as the Master of the Rolls . . .

*Ground (5): the judgment of Robert Goff LJ*

My Lords, after a full examination of numerous authorities relating to the law of negligence Robert Goff LJ (now Lord Goff of Chieveley) said [1985] QB 350, 399:

> In my judgment, there is no good reason in principle or in policy, why the c. and f. buyer should not have . . . a direct cause of action. The factors which I have already listed point strongly towards liability. I am particularly influenced by the fact that the loss in question is of a character which will ordinarily fall on the goods owner who will have a good claim against the shipowner, but in a case such as the present the loss may, in practical terms, fall on the buyer. It seems to me that the policy reasons pointing towards a direct right of action by the buyer against the shipowner in a case of this kind outweigh the policy reasons which generally preclude recovery for purely economic loss. There is here no question of any wide or indeterminate liability being imposed on wrongdoers; on the contrary, the shipowner is simply held liable to the buyer in damages for loss for which he would ordinarily be liable to the goods owner. There is a recognisable principle underlying the imposition of liability, which can be called the principle of transferred loss. Further, that principle can be formulated. For the purposes of the present case, I would formulate it in the following deliberately narrow terms, while recognising that it may require modification in the light of experience. Where A owes a duty of care in tort not to cause physical damage to B's property, and commits a breach of that duty in circumstances in which the loss of or physical damage to the property will ordinarily fall on B but (as is reasonably foreseeable by A) such loss or damage, by reason of a contractual relationship between B and C, falls upon C, then C will be entitled, subject to the terms of any contract restricting A's liability to B, to bring an action in tort against A in respect of such loss or damage to the extent that it falls on him, C. To that proposition there must be exceptions. In particular, there must, for the reasons I have given, be an exception in the case of contracts of insurance. I have also attempted so to draw the principle as to exclude the case of the time charterer who remains liable for hire for the chartered ship while under repair following collision damage, though this could if necessary be treated as another exception having regard to the present state of the authorities.

With the greatest possible respect to Lord Goff the principle of transferred loss which he there enunciated, however useful in dealing with special factual situations it may be in theory, is not only not supported by authority, but is on the contrary inconsistent with it. Even if it were necessary to introduce such a principle in order to fill a genuine lacuna in the law, I should myself, perhaps because I am more faint-hearted than Lord Goff, be reluctant to do so. As I have tried to show earlier, however, there is in truth no such lacuna in the law which requires to be filled. Neither Sir John Donaldson MR nor Oliver LJ (now Lord Oliver of Aylmerton) was prepared to accept the introduction of such a principle and I find myself entirely in agreement with their unwillingness to do so.

NOTE

The problem here is essentially one of privity of contract. Under normal circumstances in international trade, the bill of lading would have been transferred from the seller to the buyer, putting the buyer into a contractual relationship with the shipowner by virtue of what is now the Carriage of Goods by Sea Act 1992. Thus, the problem arose only because things did not work out as planned, and this would occur only rarely. However, the point of the judgments is that, as the shipowner should not be under any greater obligation to the buyer in tort than he is to the seller under the contract, and as the terms of the contract cannot be easily translated into a duty of care, therefore no duty at all should be owed to the buyer.

---

### White v Jones
House of Lords [1995] 2 AC 207; [1995] 2 WLR 187; [1995] 1 All ER 691

In 1986 the testator cut his daughters out of his will, but he later relented and in July he instructed the defendant solicitors to draw up a new will giving the daughters £9,000 each. The new will had not been drawn up by 14 September when the testator died. The daughters sued the solicitors. It was held that the solicitors were liable on the *Hedley Byrne* principle (see Chapter 10), but the extracts below deal with contractual issues which arose. The particular difficulty arises where A makes a contract with B and B's breach of contract causes loss to C but not to A. In pure contract A could sue but has suffered no loss, whereas C has suffered loss but cannot sue because of lack of privity with B.

LORD GOFF: . . .

*Transferred loss in English law*

I can deal with this topic briefly. The problem of transferred loss has arisen in particular in maritime law, when a buyer of goods seeks to enforce against a shipowner a remedy in tort in respect of loss of or damage to goods at his risk when neither the rights under the contract nor the property in the goods has passed to him (see *Leigh and Sillavan Ltd* v *Aliakmon Shipping Co. Ltd* [1985] QB 350, 399, *per* Robert Goff LJ and [1986] AC 785, 820, *per* Lord Brandon of Oakbrook). In cases such as these (with all respect to the view expressed by Lord Brandon [1986] AC 785, 819) there was a serious lacuna in the law, as was revealed when all relevant interests in the city of London called for reform to make a remedy available to the buyers who under the existing law were without a direct remedy against the shipowners. The problem was solved, as a matter of urgency, by the Carriage of Goods by Sea Act 1992, I myself having the honour of introducing the Bill into your Lordships' House (acting in its legislative capacity) on behalf of the Law Commission. The solution adopted by the Act was to extend the rights of suit available under section 1 of the Bills of Lading Act 1855 (there restricted to cases where the property in the goods had passed upon or by reason of the consignment or endorsement of the relevant bill of lading) to all holders of bills of lading (and indeed other documents): see section 9(1) of the Act of 1992. Here is a sweeping statutory reform, powered by the needs of commerce, which has the effect of enlarging the circumstances in which contractual rights may be transferred by virtue of the transfer of certain documents. For present purposes, however, an important consequence is the solution in this context of a problem of transferred loss, the lacuna being filled by statute rather than by the common law. Moreover this result has been achieved, as in German law, by vesting in the plaintiff, who has suffered the relevant loss, the contractual rights of the person who has stipulated for the carrier's obligation but has suffered no loss.

I turn next to English law in relation to cases such as the present. Here there is a lacuna in the law, in the sense that practical justice requires that the disappointed beneficiary should have a remedy against the testator's solicitor in circumstances in which neither the testator nor his estate has in law suffered a loss. Professor Lorenz (*Essays in Memory of Professor F. H. Lawson*, p. 90) has said that 'this is a situation which comes very close to the cases of "transferred loss," the only difference being that the damage due to the solicitor's negligence could never have been caused to the testator or to his executor.' In the case of the testator, he suffers no loss because (in contrast to a gift by an inter vivos settlor) a gift under a will cannot take effect until after the testator's death, and it follows that there can be no depletion of the testator's assets in his lifetime if the relevant asset is, through the solicitors' negligence, directed to a person other than the intended beneficiary. The situation is therefore not one in which events have subsequently occurred which have resulted in the loss falling on another. It is one in which the relevant loss could never fall on the testator to whom the solicitor owed a duty, but only on another; and the loss which is suffered by that other, i.e. an expectation loss, is of a character which in any event could never have been suffered by the testator. Strictly speaking, therefore, this is not a case of transferred loss.

Even so, the analogy is very close. In practical terms, part or all of the testator's estate has been lost because it has been dispatched to a destination unintended by the testator. Moreover, had a gift been similarly misdirected during the testator's lifetime, he would either have been able to recover it from the recipient or, if not, he could have recovered the full amount from the negligent solicitor as damages. In a case such as the present, no such remedies are available to the testator or his estate. The will cannot normally be rectified: the testator has of course no remedy: and his estate has suffered no loss, because it has been distributed under the terms of a valid will. In these circumstances, there can be no injustice if the intended beneficiary has a remedy against the solicitor for the full amount which he should have received under the will, this being no greater than the damage for which the solicitor could have been liable to the donor if the loss had occurred in his lifetime.

NOTE

This case would not be affected by the Contracts (Rights of Third Parties) Act 1999, because that Act only allows a third party to sue on a term which 'purports to confer a benefit on him'. The Law Commission (Report No. 242) argued that where a testator asks a solicitor to draft a will, the promise by the solicitor to exercise due care is not intended to confer a benefit on the legatee, but rather is to enable the testator to do so.

■ QUESTIONS

1. Considering the point in *The Aliakmon*, what would have happened *White* v *Jones* if either the solicitor had excluded liability for any delay or the testator had agreed that the matter could wait until the clerk returned from his holidays? (See the speech of Lord Goff in Chapter 8.)

2. If a contract between A and B is ineffective to give C any contractual rights, why should the terms of that contract affect the duty of care?

---

*Simaan Contracting Co.* v *Pilkington Glass*
Court of Appeal [1988] QB 758; [1988] 1 All ER 791; [1988] 2 WLR 761

Simaan had a contract with Sheikh Al-Oteiba to build a building in Abu Dhabi. The erection of some curtain walling was subcontracted to a company called Feal. Feal contracted with Pilkington for the supply of certain coloured glass. The glass was defective, in that it was the wrong colour, and the Sheikh withheld money from

Simaan, the main contractor. Simaan sued Pilkington in tort for negligently causing the withholding of the money. Held: that this was pure economic loss and not
recoverable. The extracts below deal with the possible effects of the contractual
arrangements on any duty of care.

BINGHAM LJ: . . . I do not think it just and reasonable to impose on the defendants a duty of
care towards the plaintiffs of the scope contended for. (a) Just as equity remedied the inadequacies
of the common law, so has the law of torts filled gaps left by other causes of action where the
interests of justice so required. I see no such gap here, because there is no reason why claims
beginning with the Sheikh should not be pursued down the contractual chain, subject to any short-
cut which may be agreed upon, ending up with a contractual claim against the defendants. That is
the usual procedure. It must be what the parties contemplated when they made their contracts. I
see no reason for departing from it. (b) Although the defendants did not sell subject to exempting
conditions, I fully share the difficulty which others have envisaged where there were such conditions.
Even as it is, the defendants' sale may well have been subject to terms and conditions imported by
the Sale of Goods Act 1979. Some of those are beneficial to the seller. If such terms are to circum-
scribe a duty which would be otherwise owed to a party not a party to the contract and unaware of
its terms, then that could be unfair to him. But if the duty is unaffected by the conditions on which
the seller supplied the goods, it is in my view unfair to him and makes a mockery of contractual
negotiation.

DILLON LJ: It might at first glance seem reasonable that, if the plaintiffs have a right of action in
contract against Feal and Feal has in respect of the same general factual matters a claim in contract—albeit a different contract—against the defendants, the plaintiffs should be allowed a direct
claim against the defendants. But in truth to allow the plaintiffs a direct claim against the defendants
where there is no contract between them would give rise to formidable difficulties.
    If the plaintiffs have a direct claim against the defendants so equally or a fortiori has the Sheikh.
Feal has its claim in contract also. All three claims should be raised in separate proceedings, whether
by way of arbitration or litigation, and possibly in separate jurisdictions. The difficulties of awarding
damages to any one claimant would be formidable, in view of the differing amounts of retentions by
the Sheikh against the plaintiffs and by the plaintiffs against Feal and other possibilities of set off, and
in view, even more, of the fact that none of the parties has yet actually incurred the major cost of
replacing the defendants' (assumedly) defective glass panels with new panels of the correct colour. It
would not be practicable, in my view, for the court to award damages against the defendants in a
global sum for all possible claimants and for the court subsequently to apportion that fund between
all claimants and administer it accordingly.
    Moreover, if in principle it were to be established in this case that a main contractor or an owner
has a direct claim in tort against the nominated supplier to a sub-contractor for economic loss
occasioned by defects in the quality of the goods supplied, the formidable question would arise, in
future cases if not in this case, as to how far exempting clauses in the contract between the
nominated supplier and the sub-contractor were to be imported into the supposed duty in tort owed
by the supplier to those higher up the chain. Such difficulties were dismissed by Lord Brandon in
*Leigh and Sillavan Ltd* v *Aliakmon Shipping Co. Ltd* [1986] 785, 817–819, and provided, as I read
his speech, part of his reasoning for maintaining the established principle which I have set out at the
beginning of his judgment.
    If, by contrast, the court does not extend—and in my judgment it would be an extension—the
principle of the *Hedley Byrne* case [1964] AC 465 to cover a direct claim by the plaintiffs against the
defendants, no party will be left without a remedy, by English law at any rate, which is the only
system of law we have been asked to consider. There will be the 'normal chain of liability,' as Lord
Pearce called it in *Young & Marten Ltd* v *McManus Childs Ltd* [1969] 1 AC 454, 470, in that the Sheikh
can sue the plaintiffs on the main building contract, the plaintiffs can sue Feal on the sub-contract
and Feal can sue the defendants. Each liability would be determined in the light of such exemptions
as applied contractually at that stage. There is thus no warrant for extending the law of negligence to
impose direct liability on the defendants in favour of the plaintiffs.

NOTE

A somewhat similar situation arose in *Greater Nottingham Co-operative Society* v *Cementation Piling and Foundations Ltd* [1989] QB 71, but it was resolved by rather different means. There, a contract was entered into between the claimants, Nottingham Co-op, and main contractors, Shepherd Constructions, who in turn subcontracted piling work to the defendants, Cementation. The piling work was negligently done, but what made this case different was that there was a direct collateral contract between the claimants and the subcontractors. Thus, this was in effect a two-party and not a three-party case, and hence the relationship between the claimants and the subcontractors was governed by the collateral contract, and tort duties were irrelevant. Mann LJ said 'I ask myself whether it is just and reasonable to impose a duty in tort where the parties are united by a contract which is notably silent upon the liability which it is sought to enforce by tort. In my judgment it is not', and he cited Cumming-Bruce LJ who said, in *William Hill* v *Bernard Sunley & Sons* (1982) 22 BLR 1, that 'the plaintiffs [claimants] are not entitled to claim a remedy in tort which is wider than the obligations assumed by the defendants under their contract'.

---

### Norwich City Council v Harvey
Court of Appeal [1989] 1 WLR 828; [1989] 1 All ER 1180

Norwich City Council, the claimants, entered into a contract with Bush Builders (Norwich) Ltd to build an extension to the swimming pool at St Augustines. They in turn entered into a subcontract with Briggs Amasco, the second defendant, for some roofing work. One of their employees, the first defendant, while using a blow torch, set fire to the building, damaging both the new and the existing structures. Clause 20[C] of the main contract stated that the existing structures 'shall be at the sole risk of the employer [i.e. Norwich Council] as regards loss or damage by fire and the employer shall maintain adequate insurance against those risks.' The subcontract incorporated the terms of the main contract. The claimants sued both the subcontractors and their employee. Held: dismissing the appeal, that the defendants were not liable.

MAY LJ: I trust I do no injustice to the plaintiff's argument in this appeal if I put it shortly in this way. There is no dispute between the employer and the main contractor that the former accepted the risk of fire damage: see *James Archdale & Co. Ltd* v *Comservices Ltd* [1954] 1 WLR 459 and *Scottish Special Housing Association* v *Wimpey Construction UK Ltd* [1986] 1 WLR 995. However clause 20[C] does not give rise to any obligation on the employer to indemnify the subcontractor. That clause is primarily concerned to see that the works were completed. It was intended to operate only for the mutual benefit of the employer and the main contractor. If the judge and the subcontractor are right, the latter obtains protection which the rules of privity do not provide. Undoubtedly the sub-contractor owed duties of care in respect of damage by fire to other persons and in respect of other property (for instance the lawful visitor, employees of the employer, or other buildings outside the site); in those circumstances it is impracticable juridically to draw a sensible line between the plaintiff on the one hand and others on the other to whom a duty of care was owed. The employer had no effective control over the terms upon which the relevant subcontract was let and no direct contractual control over either the subcontractor or any employee of its.

In addition, the plaintiff pointed to the position of the first defendant, the subcontractor's employee. Ex hypothesi he was careless and even if his employer be held to have owed no duty to the building employer, on what grounds can it be said that the employee himself owed no such duty? In my opinion, however, this particular point does not take the matter very much further. If in principle the subcontractor owed no specific duty to the building owner in respect of damage by fire, then neither in my opinion can any of its employees have done so.

In reply the defendants contend that the judge was right to hold that in all the circumstances there was no duty of care on the subcontractor in this case. Alternatively they submit that the employer's insurers have no right of subrogation to entitle them to maintain this litigation against the subcontractor. . . .

In my opinion the present state of the law on the question whether or not a duty of care exists is that, save where there is already good authority that in the circumstances there is such a duty, it will only exist in novel situations where not only is there foreseeability of harm, but also such a close and direct relation between the parties concerned, not confined to mere physical proximity, to the extent contemplated by Lord Atkin in his speech in *Donoghue* v *Stevenson* [1932] AC 562. Further, a court should also have regard to what it considers just and reasonable in all the circumstances and facts of the case.

In the instant case it is clear that as between the plaintiff and the main contractor the former accepted the risk of damage by fire to its premises arising out of and in the course of the building works. Further, although there was no privity between the plaintiff and the subcontractor, it is equally clear from the documents passing between the main contractor and the subcontractor to which I have already referred that the subcontractor contracted on a like basis . . . Approaching the question on the basis of what is just and reasonable I do not think that the mere fact that there is no strict privity between the employer and the subcontractor should prevent the latter from relying upon the clear basis upon which all the parties contracted in relation to damage to the employer's building caused by fire, even when due to the negligence of the contractors or subcontractors.

NOTES

1. This is therefore a clear case where an exemption clause in a contract between A and B was effective to prevent a duty being owed by C, but it is important to note that it was clear to all parties that by virtue of the contractual arrangements the risk of fire was on the claimants. A much more difficult case would be where there is no exemption clause in the contract between A and B, but there is in the contract between B and C. Could C be liable to A? On the one hand it could be argued that A has not voluntarily taken the risk upon himself and therefore should be able to sue. On the other hand C could argue that he should not be under any greater duty to A in tort than he is to B in contract. See generally Beyleveld and Brownsword, 'Privity, Transitivity and Rationality' (1991) 54 MLR 48, which argues that in a three-party case A should be able to sue C and C could rely on exemption clauses in the contract between A and B or between B and C.

2. Another example is *Southern Water Authority* v *Carey* [1985] 2 All ER 1077, where the predecessors of Southern Water entered into a main contract for the construction of a sewage works with Mather & Platt, who entered into subcontracts with Simon Hartley Ltd and Vokes Ltd. The main contract contained a clause limiting liability. The sewage works proved to be defective. Judge Smout held that, even though the main contract stated that the contractors were deemed to have contracted on their own behalf and on behalf of the subcontractors, the subcontractors could not take the benefit of this in contract due to the rules of privity. Nevertheless, he held that the subcontractors were not liable to the claimants. He said:

   We must look to see the nature of such limitation clause to consider whether or not it is relevant in defining the scope of the duty in tort. The contractual setting may not necesarily be overriding, but it is relevant in the consideration of the scope of the duty in tort for it indicates the extent of the liability which the plaintiff's predecessor wished to impose. To put it more crudely . . . the contractual setting defines the area of risk which the plaintiff's predecessor chose to accept and for which it may or may not have sought commercial insurance.

3. The impact of insurance provisions was considered by the House of Lords in *BT* v *Thomson* [1999] 2 All ER 241. BT engaged a contractor to undertake work on a switching station. The contract between them required BT to insure against damage and stated that 'nominated' subcontractors were to be regarded as insured parties. The contractors appointed the defendants, not as nominated subcontractors but as 'domestic' subcontractors. The result was that while BT were insured against damage, the insurers would have a right of subrogation against domestic contractors but not against nominated subcontractors. When

the defendants caused a fire it was held that BT's insurers could sue, because even though it was agreed that BT should cover the loss, the distinction between the two types of subcontractor meant that a lower premium would be set because of the insurers' ability to claim against domestic subcontractors. This therefore strengthened the argument for a duty to be owed by the domestic subcontractor to BT rather than weakening it. Thus, what mattered was not the fact that the loss had been allocated to BT by the contract, but rather the way the premium to cover that loss would be calculated. This suggests that there is a difference between a contract which excludes a main contractor's liability (*Norwich City Council*) and one which requires the employer to insure (*Thomson*).

■ QUESTION

Should it matter whether the subcontractor knew of the exemption clause in the main contract? What if it did not know and quoted a higher price than otherwise in order to pay the premiums to cover the risk which came about? Which insurance company should pay?

# 11

# Special Duty Problems: Defective Structures

The question of liability for negligently constructed buildings has always caused problems. At one time it was said that the tort of negligence did not apply to a builder of defective premises, but it is now clear that it does, at least where a defect causes physical injury (see *Murphy v Brentwood District Council* [1991] 1 AC 398). There is also statutory liability in the Defective Premises Act 1972 (below), but by far the most difficult question has been the liability of builders and others where the defect is one of quality which affects only the building itself, on which see *Murphy v Brentwood DC*, below. Other issues relate to whether the damage is economic or physical loss, and whether there can be liability where one part of a building damages another part (because there can be liability only if the defective part damages 'other' property).

---

**DEFECTIVE PREMISES ACT 1972**

**1. Duty to build dwellings properly**

(1) A person taking on work for or in connection with the provision of a dwelling (whether the dwelling is provided by the erection or by the conversion or enlargement of a building) owes a duty—

(a) if the dwelling is provided to the order of any person, to that person; and

(b) without prejudice to paragraph (a) above, to every person who acquires an interest (whether legal or equitable) in the dwelling;

to see that the work which he takes on is done in a workmanlike or, as the case may be, professional manner, with proper materials and so that as regards that work the dwelling will be fit for habitation when completed.

(2) A person who takes on any such work for another on terms that he is to do it in accordance with instructions given by or on behalf of that other shall, to the extent to which he does it properly in accordance with those instructions, be treated for the purposes of this section as discharging the duty imposed on him by subsection (1) above except where he owes a duty to that other to warn him of any defects in the instructions and fails to discharge that duty.

(3) A person shall not be treated for the purposes of subsection (2) above as having given instructions for the doing of work merely because he has agreed to the work being done in a specified manner, with specified materials or to a specified design.

(4) A person who—

(a) in the course of a business which consists of or includes providing or arranging for the provision of dwellings or installations in dwellings; or

(b) in the exercise of a power of making such provision or arrangements conferred by or by virtue of any enactment;

arranges for another to take on work for or in connection with the provision of a dwelling shall be treated for the purposes of this section as included among the persons who have taken on the work.

(5) Any cause of action in respect of a breach of the duty imposed by this section shall be deemed, for the purposes of the Limitation Act 1939, the Law Reform (Limitation of Actions, &c.) Act 1954 and the Limitation Act 1963, to have accrued at the time when the dwelling was completed, but if after that time a person who has done work for or in connection with the provision of the dwelling does further work to rectify the work he has already done, any such cause of action in respect of that further work shall be deemed for those purposes to have accrued at the time when the further work was finished.

### 2. Cases excluded from the remedy under section 1

(1) Where—

(a) in connection with the provision of a dwelling or its first sale or letting for habitation any rights in respect of defects in the state of the dwelling are conferred by an approved scheme to which this section applies on a person having or acquiring an interest in the dwelling; and

(b) it is stated in a document of a type approved for the purposes of this section that the requirements as to design or construction imposed by or under the scheme have, or appear to have, been substantially complied with in relation to the dwelling;

no action shall be brought by any person having or acquiring an interest in the dwelling for breach of the duty imposed by section 1 above in relation to the dwelling.

(2) A scheme to which this section applies—

(a) may consist of any number of documents and any number of agreements or other transactions between any number of persons; but

(b) must confer, by virtue of agreements entered into with persons having or acquiring an interest in the dwellings to which the scheme applies, rights on such persons in respect of defects in the state of the dwellings.

(3) In this section 'approved' means approved by the Secretary of State, and the power of the Secretary of State to approve a scheme or document for the purposes of this section shall be exercisable by order, except that any requirements as to construction or design imposed under a scheme to which this section applies may be approved by him without making any order or, if he thinks fit, by order.

(4)–(6) . . .

(7) Where an interest in a dwelling is compulsorily acquired—

(a) no action shall be brought by the acquiring authority for breach of the duty imposed by section 1 above in respect of the dwelling; and

(b) if any work for or in connection with the provision of the dwelling was done otherwise than in the course of a business by the person in occupation of the dwelling at the time of the compulsory acquisition, the acquiring authority and not that person shall be treated as the person who took on the work and accordingly as owing that duty.

### 3. Duty of care with respect to work done on premises not abated by disposal of premises

(1) Where work of construction, repair, maintenance or demolition or any other work is done on or in relation to premises, any duty of care owed, because of the doing of the work, to persons who might reasonably be expected to be affected by defects in the state of the premises created by the doing of the work shall not be abated by the subsequent disposal of the premises by the person who owed the duty.

(2) This section does not apply—

(a) in the case of premises which are let, where the relevant tenancy of the premises commenced, or the relevant tenancy agreement of the premises was entered into, before the commencement of this Act;

(b) in the case of premises disposed of in any other way, when the disposal of the premises was completed, or a contract for their disposal was entered into, before the commencement of this Act; or

(c) in either case, where the relevant transaction disposing of the premises is entered into in pursuance of an enforceable option by which the consideration for the disposal was fixed before the commencement of this Act.

### 5. Application to Crown

This Act shall bind the Crown, but as regards the Crown's liability in tort shall not bind the Crown further than the Crown is made liable in tort by the Crown Proceedings Act 1947.

### 6. Supplemental

(1) In this Act—

'disposal', in relation to premises, includes a letting, and an assignment or surrender of a tenancy, of the premises and the creation by contract of any other right to occupy the premises, and 'dispose' shall be construed accordingly;

'personal injury' includes any disease and any impairment of a person's physical or mental condition;

'tenancy' means—

(a) a tenancy created either immediately or derivatively out of the freehold, whether by a lease or underlease, by an agreement for a lease or underlease or by a tenancy agreement, but not including a mortgage term or any interest arising in favour of a mortgagor by his attorning tenant to his mortgagee; or

(b) a tenancy at will or a tenancy on sufferance; or

(c) a tenancy, whether or not constituting a tenancy at common law, created by or in pursuance of any enactment;

and cognate expressions shall be construed accordingly.

(2) Any duty imposed by or enforceable by virtue of any provision of this Act is in addition to any duty a person may owe apart from that provision.

(3) Any term of an agreement which purports to exclude or restrict, or has the effect of excluding or restricting, the operation of any of the provisions of this Act, or any liability arising by virtue of any such provision, shall be void.

NOTES

1. It appears that the NHBC Vendor-Purchaser Insurance Scheme is no longer an approved scheme under s. 2: see Wallace, '*Anns* beyond repair' (1991) 107 LQR 230.

2. In *Andrews* v *Schooling* [1991] 3 All ER 723 the defendants converted two houses into flats and granted a long lease of a ground floor flat to the claimant. While converting the property the defendants did no work to the cellar, and because they had failed to put in a damp proofing system, damp came up to the claimant's flat from the cellar. The claimant sought damages but the defendants claimed that s. 1 of the 1972 Act did not apply to omissions. The Court of Appeal held that the Act applied both to a failure to carry out necessary work and to carrying out work badly.

---

## BUILDING ACT 1984

### 38. Civil Liability

(1) Subject to this section—

(a) breach of a duty imposed by building regulations, so far as it causes damage, is actionable, except in so far as the regulations provide otherwise, and

(b) as regards such a duty, building regulations may provide for a prescribed defence to be available in an action for breach of that duty brought by virtue of this subsection.

(2) Subsection (1) above, and any defence provided for in regulations made by virtue of it, do not apply in the case of a breach of such a duty in connection with a building erected before the date on which that subsection comes into force unless the regulations imposing the duty apply to

or in connection with the building by virtue of section 2(2) above or paragraph 8 of Schedule 1 to this Act.

(3) This section does not affect the extent (if any) to which breach of—

(a) a duty imposed by or arising in connection with this Part of this Act or any other enactment relating to building regulations, or

(b) a duty imposed by building regulations in a case to which subsection (1) above does not apply,

is actionable, or prejudice a right of action that exists apart from the enactments relating to building regulations.

(4) In this section, 'damage' includes the death of, or injury to, any person (including any disease and any impairment of a person's physical or mental condition).

NOTE

This section is not yet in force.

---

### *Murphy* v *Brentwood District Council*

House of Lords [1991] 1 AC 398; [1990] 3 WLR 414; [1990] 2 All ER 908

In 1970, the claimant purchased 38 Vineway, Brentwood. The house had been built by ABC Homes and was constructed on a concrete raft foundation over an in-filled site. The design of the raft was submitted to the defendant council for approval under the Public Health Act 1936, and, after seeking the advice of consulting engineers, the design was approved. From 1981 cracks began appearing in the internal walls of the house and it was found that the concrete raft had subsided. This also caused breakage of soil and gas pipes. The claimant eventually sold the house for £35,000 less than its value in good condition and sued the council as being responsible for the negligent approval of the design by the consulting engineers. Held: allowing the appeal and overruling *Anns* v *London Borough of Merton*, that the council was not liable.

LORD BRIDGE: If a manufacturer negligently puts into circulation a chattel containing a latent defect which renders it dangerous to persons or property, the manufacturer, on the well known principles established by *Donoghue* v *Stevenson* [1932] AC 562, will be liable in tort for injury to persons or damage to property which the chattel causes. But if a manufacturer produces and sells a chattel which is merely defective in quality, even to the extent that it is valueless for the purpose for which it is intended, the manufacturer's liability at common law arises only under and by reference to the terms of any contract to which he is a party in relation to the chattel; the common law does not impose on him any liability in tort to persons to whom he owes no duty in contract but who, having acquired the chattel, suffer economic loss because the chattel is defective in quality. If a dangerous defect in a chattel is discovered before it causes any personal injury or damage to property, because the danger is now known and the chattel cannot safely be used unless the defect is repaired, the defect becomes merely a defect in quality. The chattel is either capable of repair at economic cost or it is worthless and must be scrapped. In either case the loss sustained by the owner or hirer of the chattel is purely economic. It is recoverable against any party who owes the loser a relevant contractual duty. But it is not recoverable in tort in the absence of a special relationship of proximity imposing on the tortfeasor a duty of care to safeguard the plaintiff from economic loss. There is no such special relationship between the manufacturer of a chattel and a remote owner or hirer.

I believe that these principles are equally applicable to buildings. If a builder erects a structure containing a latent defect which renders it dangerous to persons or property, he will be liable in tort for injury to persons or damage to property resulting from that dangerous defect. But if the defect becomes apparent before any injury or damage has been caused, the loss sustained by the building owner is purely economic. If the defect can be repaired at economic cost, that is the measure of the loss. If the building cannot be repaired, it may have to be abandoned as unfit for occupation and therefore valueless. These economic losses are recoverable if they flow from breach of a relevant contractual duty, but, here again, in the absence of a special relationship of proximity they are not recoverable in tort. The only qualification I would make to this is that, if a building stands so close to the boundary of the building owner's land that after discovery of the dangerous defect it remains a potential source of injury to persons or property on neighbouring land or on the highway, the building owner ought, in principle, to be entitled to recover in tort from the negligent builder the cost of obviating the danger, whether by repair or by demolition, so far as that cost is necessarily incurred in order to protect himself from potential liability to third parties.

The fallacy which, in my opinion, vitiates the judgments of Lord Denning MR and Sachs LJ in *Dutton* [1972] 1 QB 373 is that they brush these distinctions aside as of no consequence . . . Stamp LJ on the other hand, fully understood and appreciated them and his statement of the applicable principles as between the building owner and the builder . . . seems to me unexceptionable. He rested his decision in favour of the plaintiff against the local authority on a wholly distinct principle which will require separate examination.

### The complex structure theory

In my speech in *D. & F. Estates* [1989] AC 177, 206G–207H I mooted the possibility that in complex structures or complex chattels one part of a structure or chattel might, when it caused damage to another part of the same structure or chattel, be regarded in the law of tort as having caused damage to 'other property' for the purpose of the application of *Domoghue* v *Stevenson* principles. I expressed no opinion as to the validity of this theory, but put it forward for consideration as a possible ground on which the facts considered in *Anns* [1978] AC 728 might be distinguishable from the facts which had to be considered in *D. & F. Estates* itself. I shall call this for convenience 'the complex structure theory' and it is, so far as I can see, only if and to the extent that this theory can be affirmed and applied that there can be any escape from the conclusions I have indicated above under the rubric 'Dangerous defects and defects of quality.'

. . . The reality is that the structural elements in any building form a single indivisible unit of which the different parts are essentially interdependent. To the extent that there is any defect in one part of the structure it must to a greater or lesser degree necessarily affect all other parts of the structure. Therefore any defect in the structure is a defect in the quality of the whole and it is quite artificial, in order to impose a legal liability which the law would not otherwise impose, to treat a defect in an integral structure, so far as it weakens the structure, as a dangerous defect liable to cause damage to 'other property.'

A critical distinction must be drawn here between some part of a complex structure which is said to be a 'danger' only because it does not perform its proper function in sustaining the other parts and some distinct item incorporated in the structure which positively malfunctions so as to inflict positive damage on the structure in which it is incorporated. Thus, if a defective central heating boiler explodes and damages a house or a defective electrical installation malfunctions and sets the house on fire, I see no reason to doubt that the owner of the house, if he can prove that the damage was due to the negligence of the boiler manufacturer in the one case or the electrical contractor in the other, can recover damages in tort on *Donoghue* v *Stevenson* [1932] AC 562 principles. But the position in law is entirely different where, by reason of the inadequacy of the foundations of the building to support the weight of the superstructure, differential settlement and consequent cracking occurs. Here, once the first cracks appear, the structure as a whole is seen to be defective and the nature of the defect is known. Even if, contrary to my view, the initial damage could be regarded as damage to other property caused by a latent defect, once the defect is known the situation of the building owner is analogous to that of the car owner who discovers that the car has faulty brakes. He may have a house which, until repairs are effected, is unfit for habitation, but, subject to the reservation I have expressed with respect to ruinous buildings at or near the boundary of the owner's property, the building no longer represents a source of danger and as it deteriorates will only damage itself.

For these reasons the complex structure theory offers no escape from the conclusion that damage to a house itself which is attributable to a defect in the structure of the house is not recoverable in tort on *Donoghue* v *Stevenson* principles, but represents purely economic loss which is only recoverable in contract or in tort by reason of some special relationship of proximity which imposes on the tortfeasor a duty of care to protect against economic loss.

### The relative positions of the builder and the local authority

I have so far been considering the potential liability of a builder for negligent defects in the structure of a building to persons to whom he owes no contractual duty. Since the relevant statutory function of the local authority is directed to no other purpose than securing compliance with building byelaws or regulations by the builder, I agree with the view expressed in *Anns* [1978] AC 728 and by the majority of the Court of Appeal in *Dutton* [1972] 1 QB 373 that a negligent performance of that function can attract no greater liability than attaches to the negligence of the builder whose fault was the primary tort giving rise to any relevant damage. I am content for present purposes to assume, though I am by no means satisfied that the assumption is correct, that where the local authority, as in this case or in *Dutton*, have in fact approved the defective plans or inspected the defective foundations and negligently failed to discover the defect, their potential liability in tort is coextensive with that of the builder.

Only Stamp LJ in *Dutton* was prepared to hold that the law imposed on the local authority a duty of care going beyond that imposed on the builder and extending to protection of the building owner from purely economic loss. I must return later to consider the question of liability for economic loss more generally, but here I need only say that I cannot find in *Hedley Byrne & Co. Ltd* v *Heller & Partners Ltd* [1964] AC 465 or *Dorset Yacht Co. Ltd* v *Home Office* [1970] AC 1004 any principle applicable to the circumstances of *Dutton* or the present case that provides support for the conclusion which Stamp LJ sought to derive from those authorities.

### Imminent danger to health or safety

A necessary element in the building owner's cause of action against the negligent local authority, which does not appear to have been contemplated in *Dutton* but which, it is said in *Anns*, must be present before the cause of action accrues, is that the state of the building is such that there is present or imminent danger to the health or safety of persons occupying it. Correspondingly the damages recoverable are said to include the amount of expenditure necessary to restore the building to a condition in which it is no longer such a danger, but presumably not any further expenditure incurred in any merely qualitative restoration. I find these features of the *Anns* doctrine very difficult to understand. The theoretical difficulty of reconciling this aspect of the doctrine with previously accepted legal principle was pointed out by Lord Oliver of Aylmerton in *D. & F. Estates* [1989] AC 177, 212D–213D. But apart from this there are, as it appears to me, two insuperable difficulties arising from the requirement of imminent danger to health or safety as an ingredient of the cause of action which lead to quite irrational and capricious consequences in the application of the *Anns* doctrine. The first difficulty will arise where the relevant defect in the building, when it is first discovered, is not a present or imminent danger to health or safety. What is the owner to do if he is advised that the building will gradually deteriorate, if not repaired, and will in due course become a danger to health and safety, but that the longer he waits to effect repairs the greater the cost will be? Must he spend £1,000 now on the necessary repairs with no redress against the local authority? Or is he entitled to wait until the building has so far deteriorated that he has a cause of action and then to recover from the local authority the £5,000 which the necessary repairs are now going to cost? I can find no answer to this conundrum. A second difficulty will arise where the latent defect is not discovered until it causes the sudden and total collapse of the building, which occurs when the building is temporarily unoccupied and causes no damage to property except to the building itself. The building is now no longer capable of occupation and hence cannot be a danger to health or safety. It seems a very strange result that the building owner should be without remedy in this situation if he would have been able to recover from the local authority the full cost of repairing the building if only the defect had been discovered before the building fell down.

*Liability for economic loss*

All these considerations lead inevitably to the conclusion that a building owner can only recover the cost of repairing a defective building on the ground of the authority's negligence in performing its statutory function of approving plans or inspecting buildings in the course of construction if the scope of the authority's duty of care is wide enough to embrace purely economic loss. The House has already held in *D. & F. Estates* that a builder, in the absence of any contractual duty or of a special relationship of proximity introducing the *Hedley Byrne* principle of reliance, owes no duty of care in tort in respect of the quality of his work. As I pointed out in *D. & F. Estates*, to hold that the builder owed such a duty of care to any person acquiring an interest in the product of the builder's work would be to impose upon him the obligations of an indefinitely transmissible warranty of quality.

By section 1 of the Defective Premises Act 1972 Parliament has in fact imposed on builders and others undertaking work in the provision of dwellings the obligations of a transmissible warranty of the quality of their work and of the fitness for habitation of the completed dwelling. But besides being limited to dwellings, liability under the Act is subject to a limitation period of six years from the completion of the work and to the exclusion provided for by section 2. It would be remarkable to find that similar obligations in the nature of a transmissible warranty of quality, applicable to buildings of every kind and subject to no such limitations or exclusions as are imposed by the Act of 1972, could be derived from the builder's common law duty of care or from the duty imposed by building byelaws or regulations. In *Anns* Lord Wilberforce expressed the opinion that a builder could be held liable for a breach of statutory duty in respect of buildings which do not comply with the byelaws. But he cannot, I think, have meant that the statutory obligation to build in conformity with the byelaws by itself gives rise to obligations in the nature of transmissible warranties of quality. If he did mean that, I must respectfully disagree. I find it impossible to suppose that anything less than clear express language such as is used in section 1 of the Act of 1972 would suffice to impose such a statutory obligation.

As I have already said, since the function of a local authority in approving plans or inspecting buildings in course of construction is directed to ensuring that the builder complies with building byelaws or regulations, I cannot see how, in principle, the scope of the liability of the authority for a negligent failure to ensure compliance can exceed that of the liability of the builder for his negligent failure to comply.

There may, of course, be situations where, even in the absence of contract, there is a special relationship of proximity between builder and building owner which is sufficiently akin to contract to introduce the element of reliance so that the scope of the duty of care owed by the builder to the owner is wide enough to embrace purely economic loss. The decision in *Junior Books Ltd* v *Veitchi Co. Ltd* [1983] 1 AC 520 can, I believe, only be understood on this basis.

NOTES

1. *Murphy* was applied in *Department of Environment* v *T. Bates Ltd* [1990] 3 WLR 457, where the defendants had built a two-storey building with a flat roof and an 11-storey office block. The claimants were sub-lessees of the buildings and discovered that some of the concrete in the buildings was soft, and they sued the builder for the cost of the remedial work and the cost of alternative accommodation while the work was carried out. The House of Lords held that there was no liability, since the buildings were not unsafe but rather suffered a defect of quality in that they could not be loaded to their designed capacity unless repaired. The loss resulted from the quality of the building itself and was therefore pure economic loss and irrecoverable.

2. An example of the line between liability and non-liability is *Nitrigin Eireann Teoranta* v *Inco Alloys* [1992] 1 All ER 854, where the claimants operated a chemical factory. In 1983 they discovered a crack in a steel pipe supplied by the defendants. The pipe was repaired but it was held that no cause of action arose as the pipe had merely damaged itself and the loss was economic loss. However, in 1984 the pipe burst, and this caused damage to surrounding parts of the factory. This did give rise to a cause of action as 'other' property was damaged.

3. In *Junior Books* v *Veitchi* [1983] 1 AC 520, mentioned by Lord Bridge, Ogilvie Builders Ltd (the main contractors) built a factory for Junior Books Ltd. The architects of Junior Books nominated Veitchi Co. Ltd to lay a floor, and they as subcontractors entered into a contract with the main contractors (Ogilvie). The floor turned out to be inadequate for the required purpose and Junior Books successfully sued for the cost of its replacement. This case has often been doubted (and never followed) but has not been overruled. It is now explained on the basis that the relationship between Junior Books and the subcontractors (Veitchi) was so close as to be as good as a contract, so that a duty based on reliance came about.

4. *Murphy* has been rejected in most Commonwealth countries. In *Bryan* v *Maloney* (1994) 128 ALR 163, the High Court of Australia held that there was sufficient proximity between a builder and subsequent purchasers because the house was a permanent structure intended to be used indefinitely (liability for subsidence caused by inadequate foundations). In *Invercargill City Council* v *Hamlin* [1996] 1 All ER 756 the Privy Council accepted that the law in New Zealand was different, saying that policy conditions were such as to lead to liability, although this did not cast doubt on the correctness of *Murphy* in England and Wales. The New Zealand Court of Appeal, [1994] 3 NZLR 519, had said that house buyers rely on building inspectors to ensure compliance by builders with building regulations. Accordingly, the Council was liable for negligent inspection of foundations when subsidence later occurred. In Canada the Supreme Court held in *Winnipeg Condominium Corporation* v *Bird Construction* (1995) 121 DLR 193, that a builder or architect could be liable where negligence caused the building to be dangerous. Liability was limited to the cost of making the building safe.

5. In England it was suggested in *The Orjula* [1995] 2 Lloyd's Rep 395 at 403 that where dangerous property was put into circulation, the person who was obliged to make it safe could sue even though no damage to other property had yet occurred. It was said that this principle has survived *Murphy*. The case concerned contaminated containers but presumably it would also apply to premises that are dangerous rather than merely of poor quality.

6. The rejection of *Murphy* has led to a loosening of the bonds of the common law. In *Invercargill City Council* (above) Cooke P said, 'While the disharmony may be regrettable, it is inevitable now that the Commonwealth jurisdictions have gone on their own paths without taking English decisions as the invariable starting point. The ideal of a uniform Common-law has proved as unattainable as any ideal of a uniform law. It could not survive the independence of the United States; constitutional evolution in the Commonwealth has done the rest. What of course is both desirable and feasible . . . is to take account and learn from decisions in other jurisdictions.'

7. For a full discussion of the effect of *Murphy* v *Brentwood DC* on the liability of builders and others, see Wallace, '*Anns* beyond repair' (1991) 107 LQR 230 and Stychin, 'Dangerous liaisons: new developments in the law of defective premises' (1996) 16 LS 387.

# 12

## Special Duty Problems: Unborn Children, Wrongful Life and Wrongful Birth

The problem of whether a duty was owed to a foetus which suffered damage before birth was brought to the fore by the Thalidomide tragedy in the 1960s, when the initial settlement with the manufacturers (Distillers) involved a payment of only 40 per cent of the damages because of the uncertainty of liability (see *S* v *Distillers Co. Ltd* [1969] 3 All ER 1412). Due to public pressure the settlement was later substantially increased, but that did not solve the legal problem, although other common law jurisdictions had found in favour of liability to unborn children—see, for example, *Watt* v *Rama* [1972] VR 353 and *Duval* v *Seguin* (1972) 26 DLR 3d 418. In 1991, the English courts finally followed suit, and held in *B* v *Islington Health Authority* [1992] 3 All ER 833, that injury to an unborn child could give rise to an action at common law. However, this only applies to births before 22 July 1976, because under the Congenital Disabilities (Civil Liability) Act 1976, s. 4(5), all births after that date are covered by that Act, which supplants the common law and which may be narrower in effect. (In 1974 the Law Commission had recommended legislation to establish liability (see Report No. 60, *Injuries to Unborn Children*) and this became the Congenital Disabilities (Civil Liability) Act 1976.)

---

### SECTION 1: INJURIES TO UNBORN CHILDREN

---

**CONGENITAL DISABILITIES (CIVIL LIABILITY) ACT 1976**

**1. Civil liability to child born disabled**

(1)  If a child is born disabled as the result of such an occurrence before its birth as is mentioned in subsection (2) below, and a person (other than the child's own mother) is under this section answerable to the child in respect of the occurrence, the child's disabilities are to be regarded as damage resulting from the wrongful act of that person and actionable accordingly at the suit of the child.

(2)  An occurrence to which this section applies is one which—

(a) affected either parent of the child in his or her ability to have a normal, healthy child; or

(b) affected the mother during her pregnancy, or affected her or the child in the course of its birth, so that the child is born with disabilities which would not otherwise have been present.

(3) Subject to the following subsections, a person (here referred to as 'the defendant') is answerable to the child if he was liable in tort to the parent or would, if sued in due time, have been so; and it is no answer that there could not have been such liability because the parent

suffered no actionable injury, if there was a breach of legal duty which, accompanied by injury, would have given rise to the liability.

(4) In the case of an occurrence preceding the time of conception, the defendant is not answerable to the child if at that time either or both of the parents knew the risk of their child being born disabled (that is to say, the particular risk created by the occurrence); but should it be the child's father who is the defendant, this subsection does not apply if he knew of the risk and the mother did not.

(5) The defendant is not answerable to the child, for anything he did or omitted to do when responsible in a professional capacity for treating or advising the parent, if he took reasonable care having due regard to then received professional opinion applicable to the particular class of case; but this does not mean that he is answerable only because he departed from received opinion.

(6) Liability to the child under this section may be treated as having been excluded or limited by contract made with the parent affected, to the same extent and subject to the same restrictions as liability in the parent's own case; and a contract term which could have been set up by the defendant in an action by the parent, so as to exclude or limit his liability to him or her, operates in the defendant's favour to the same, but no greater, extent in an action under this section by the child.

(7) If in the child's action under this section it is shown that the parent affected shared the responsibility for the child being born disabled, the damages are to be reduced to such extent as the court thinks just and equitable having regard to the extent of the parent's responsibility.

### 1A. Extension of section 1 to cover infertility treatments

(1) In any case where—
  (a) a child carried by a woman as the result of the placing in her of an embryo or of sperm and eggs or her artificial insemination is born disabled,
  (b) the disability results from an act or omission in the course of the selection, or the keeping or use outside the body, of the embryo carried by her or of the gametes used to bring about the creation of the embryo, and
  (c) a person is under this section answerable to the child in respect of the act or omission,
the child's disabilities are to be regarded as damage resulting from the wrongful act of that person and actionable accordingly at the suit of the child.

(2) Subject to subsection (3) below and the applied provisions of section 1 of this Act, a person (here referred to as 'the defendant') is answerable to the child if he was liable in tort to one or both of the parents (here referred to as 'the parent or parents concerned') or would, if sued in due time, have been so; and it is no answer that there could not have been such liability because the parent or parents concerned suffered no actionable injury, if there was a breach of legal duty which, accompanied by injury, would have given rise to the liability.

(3) The defendant is not under this section answerable to the child if at the time the embryo, or the sperm and eggs, are placed in the woman or the time of her insemination (as the case may be) either or both of the parents knew the risk of the child being born disabled (that is to say, the particular risk created by the act or omission).

(4) Subsections (5) to (7) of section 1 of this Act apply for the purposes of this section as they apply for the purposes of that but as if references to the parent or the parent affected were references to the parent or parents concerned.

### 2. Liability of woman driving when pregnant

A woman driving a motor vehicle when she knows (or ought reasonably to know) herself to be pregnant is to be regarded as being under the same duty to take care for the safety of her unborn child as the law imposes on her with respect to the safety of other people; and if in consequence of her breach of that duty her child is born with disabilities which would not otherwise have been present, those disabilities are to be regarded as damage resulting from her wrongful act and actionable accordingly at the suit of the child.

### 3. Disabled birth due to radiation

(1) Section 1 of this Act does not affect the operation of the Nuclear Installations Act 1965 as to liability for, and compensation in respect of, injury or damage caused by occurrences involving nuclear matter or the emission of ionising radiations.

(2) For the avoidance of doubt anything which—

(a) affects a man in his ability to have a normal, healthy child; or

(b) affect a woman in that ability, or so affects her when she is pregnant that her child is born with disabilities which would not otherwise have been present,

is an injury for the purposes of that Act.

(3) If a child is born disabled as the result of an injury to either of its parents caused in breach of a duty imposed by any of sections 7 to 11 of that Act (nuclear site licensees and others to secure that nuclear incidents do not cause injury to persons, etc.), the child's disabilities are to be regarded under the subsequent provisions of that Act (compensation and other matters) as injuries caused on the same occasion, and by the same breach of duty, as was the injury to the parent.

(4) As respects compensation to the child, section 13(6) of that Act (contributory fault of person injured by radiation) is to be applied as if the reference there to fault were to the fault of the parent.

(5) Compensation is not payable in the child's case if the injury to the parent preceded the time of the child's conception and at that time either or both of the parents knew the risk of their child being born disabled (that is to say, the particular risk created by the injury).

### 4. Interpretation and other supplementary provisions

(1) References in this Act to a child being born disabled or with disabilities are to its being born with any deformity, disease or abnormality, including predisposition (whether or not susceptible of immediate prognosis) to physical or mental defect in the future.

(2) In this Act—

(a) 'born' means born alive (the moment of a child's birth being when it first has a life separate from its mother), and 'birth' has a corresponding meaning; and

(b) 'motor vehicle' means a mechanically propelled vehicle intended or adapted for use on roads,

and references to embryos shall be construed in accordance with section 1 of the Human Fertilisation and Embryology Act 1990.

(3) Liability to a child under section 1, 1A or 2 of this Act is to be regarded—

(a) as respects all its incidents and any matters arising or to arise out of it; and

(b) subject to any contrary context or intention, for the purpose of construing references in enactments and documents to personal or bodily injuries and cognate matters,

as liability for personal injuries sustained by the child immediately after its birth.

(4) No damage shall be recoverable under any of those sections in respect of any loss of expectation of life, nor shall any such loss be taken into account in the compensation payable in respect of a child under the Nuclear Installations Act 1965 as extended by section 3, unless (in either case) the child lives for at least 48 hours.

(5) This Act applies in respect of births after (but not before) its passing, and in respect of any such birth it replaces any law in force before its passing, whereby a person could be liable to a child in respect of disabilities with which it might be born; but in section 1(3) of this Act the expression 'liable in tort' does not include any reference to liability by virtue of this Act, or to liability by virtue of any such law.

NOTES

1. For commentaries on the Act, see Pace, 'Civil Liability for Pre-Natal Injuries' (1977) 40 MLR 141, and Cave, 'Injuries to Unborn Children' (1977) 51 ALJ 704.

2. The issue of antenatal injury was discussed by the Pearson Commission (Cmnd 7054), who suggested the following changes to the 1976 Act:

(a) The law of tort should continue to apply in the case of a child born alive and suffering from the effects of antenatal injury (such liability is excluded by s. 4(5)).

(b) A child should not have a right of action against either parent for antenatal injury, except where the claim arises out of an activity where insurance is compulsory.

(c) Section 1(7) of the Act should be repealed—i.e. the contributory negligence of the parent should not be visited on the child.

## SECTION 2: WRONGFUL LIFE

An action for wrongful *life* means an action whereby a child claims that he or she would not have been born at all but for the defendant's negligence. On the other hand, an action for wrongful *birth* is one by the parents claiming *their* losses arising from having to bring up a child which they claim would not have been born. The courts have rejected wrongful life cases, but have accepted wrongful birth ones.

### McKay v Essex Health Authority
Court of Appeal [1982] QB 1166; [1982] 2 All ER 771; [1982] 2 WLR 890

The claimant, Mary McKay, was born in 1975. The defendants were the mother's doctor and the Health Authority. In April 1975 the mother saw her doctor and told him that she was pregnant and that she had been in contact with rubella (German measles), which can cause a child to be born disabled. The doctor took a blood sample and the mother was subsequently told (wrongly) that her unborn child had not been infected with rubella. The mother alleged that if she had been told that the child had been infected she would have had an abortion. The claimant was born in August 1975 and was partly blind and deaf. Held: allowing the appeal, that the defendants were not liable at common law, as in essence the claimant's claim was that the defendants had negligently allowed her to be born alive and this could not be actionable. It was also noted that the terms of the 1976 Act would prevent any such cases in the future. Note: it is important to bear in mind that the claimant's disabilities were caused by the rubella and not by the defendants. The claim discussed here was not for the disabilities the claimant suffered, but only for failing to give the mother the chance to have an abortion.

ACKNER LJ: . . . The Congenital Disabilities (Civil Liability) Act 1976 received the Royal Assent on July 22, 1976. Section 1, which deals with civil liability to a child born disabled, was in the terms of clause 1 of a draft annexed to the Law Commission Report on Injuries to Unborn Children (1974) (Law Com. No. 60) (Cmnd. 5709). . . . Subsection (2)(b) is so worded as to import the assumption that, but for the occurrence giving rise to a disabled birth, the child would have been born normal and healthy—not that it would not have been born at all. Thus, the object of the Law Commission that the child should have no right of action for 'wrongful life' is achieved. In paragraph 89 of the Report the Law Commission stated that they were clear in their opinion that no cause of action should lie:

> Such a cause of action, if it existed, would place an almost intolerable burden on medical advisers in their socially and morally exacting role. The danger that doctors would be under subconscious pressures to advise abortions in doubtful cases through fear of an action for damages is, we think, a real one.

This view was adopted by the Royal Commission on Civil Liability and Compensation for Personal Injury (1978) (Cmnd. 7054–1), paragraph 1485.

(4) Section 4(5) of the Act provides: 'This Act applies in respect of births after (but not before) its passing, and in respect of any such birth it replaces any law in force before its passing, whereby a person could be liable to a child in respect of disabilities with which it might be born; . . .'

Thus, there can be no question of such a cause of action arising in respect of births after July 22, 1976. This case therefore raises no point of general public importance. It can, for all practical purposes, be considered as a 'one-off' case.

NOTE

For a discussion of wrongful life cases, see Teff, 'Wrongful life in England and the United States' (1985) 34 ICLQ 423.

## SECTION 3: WRONGFUL BIRTH

This section deals with cases where the *parents* are claiming that, but for the negligence of the defendant, they would not have had the child in question. The most obvious example of such a case is where a sterilization operation is ineffective and a child is born unexpectedly.

### Thake v Maurice
Court of Appeal [1986] QB 644; [1986] 1 All ER 497; [1986] 2 WLR 337

Mr and Mrs Thake had five children and, accordingly, Mr Thake had a vasectomy which was done by the defendant. Some three years later Mrs Thake began to miss her periods, but, believing her husband to be sterile, thought that she could not be pregnant. When she finally went to the doctor she discovered that she was five months pregnant. Mr Thake's vasectomy had reversed itself naturally, and the claimants sued on the basis that the defendant had failed to warn them of the small chance that this might occur. If Mrs Thake had been aware of the possibility she would have realised she was pregnant sooner and would have been in time to have an abortion. Held: dismissing the appeal, that the defendant was liable.

KERR LJ: The plaintiffs' claim was pleaded both in contract and in tort, i.e., what was for convenience referred to as 'contractual negligence' as well as negligence simpliciter resulting from the duty of care owed by a surgeon to his patient. For present purposes I do not think that it is necessary to distinguish between them. On both aspects the issue turned on the defendant's failure—found by the judge—to give his usual warning of the slight risk that 'late recanalisation' might lead to defeat by nature of a vasectomy operation performed properly, and even after two successful sperm tests. The only issue raised explicitly by the pleadings in this connection was whether or not this warning had been given. . . .

*Foreseeability and causation*

The plaintiffs' case was not that Mr Thake would not have had the operation if they had been warned of a risk that it might not render him permanently sterile; they said that he would still have had the operation, but that Mrs Thake would then have been alert to the risk that she might again become pregnant and would then have had an abortion at an early stage. In the circumstances, however, it never occurred to her that she might be pregnant when she missed a number of her periods, attributing this to her age and the 'change of life.' In the result, as explained by the judge, she was astonished and very upset on being told that she was five months pregnant and that it was too late for an abortion.

On behalf of the defendant it was not suggested that Mrs Thake should have realised earlier that she was pregnant, nor that she could possibly have had an abortion when she became aware of the position. Two points were taken. First, so far as the claim in contract was concerned, it was submitted that it could not have been in the reasonable contemplation of the defendant that a failure to give his usual warning might have the result that Mrs Thake would not appreciate, at a sufficiently early stage to enable her to have an abortion if she wished, that she had again become pregnant. In this connection the defendant relied on the principles laid down by the House of Lords in *C. Czarnikow Ltd* v *Koufos* [1969] 1 AC 350. In so far as the claim lay in tort, it was accepted on his behalf that this consequence was reasonably foreseeable as liable to happen and not too remote: see the remarks of Lord Reid, at pp. 385 and 386. Having held that the plaintiffs succeeded in contract, the judge only dealt with this aspect on this basis, but we permitted the plaintiffs to amend their respondents' notice, without opposition on behalf of the defendant, to contend that the judge's decision on this aspect should be upheld in tort in any event. Accordingly, this particular issue became largely academic on the appeal, but I respectfully agree with the judge when he concluded that the risk of Mrs Thake failing to appreciate at an early stage that she had once again become pregnant must have been in the reasonable contemplation of the defendant. Indeed, in his evidence he virtually conceded this himself.

The second point taken on behalf of the defendant was that the plaintiffs had not proved on a balance of probability that Mrs Thake would have been able to have a lawful abortion even if she had become aware of her renewed pregnancy as soon as this occurred. The plaintiffs accepted that the test was not whether she could have secured an abortion, but whether she could have secured one which would have been lawful under section 1 of the Abortion Act 1967. The judge dealt with this issue on the same page; again I agree, and again this was virtually frankly conceded by the defendant himself. Having regard to Mrs Thake's age, her family, financial and housing situation, and also bearing in mind that her general practitioner had already put her on the National Health Service list for sterilisation, I do not see how one can realistically reach any different conclusion on the probabilities. That disposes of the appeal.

NOTES

1. In another case the claimant succeeded in a similar situation, even though she could have had an abortion. In *Emeh* v *Kensington Area Health Authority* [1985] QB 1012, the claimant underwent a sterilization operation, but she later discovered that she was 20 weeks pregnant. It was held that her failure to have an abortion 'was not so unreasonable as to eclipse the defendant's wrongdoing'. Would this be so if she was only eight weeks pregnant?

2. Who can sue? In *Goodwill* v *Pregnancy Advisory Service* [1996] 2 All ER 161, Mr M had a vasectomy in 1985 which later reversed itself. In 1988 he began sexual relations with the claimant who became pregnant in 1989. It was argued on the basis of *White* v *Jones* [1995] 2 AC 107 (see Chapter 8) that just as there the solicitor was engaged to confer a benefit on the intended beneficiaries of the will, so here the doctor was engaged to confer a benefit (non-pregnancy) on future sexual partners of M. (The case was based on the doctor's failure to warn M of the possibility of reversal.) The claim was rejected on the grounds that no duty could be owed to all future potential partners of M.

   Would a duty be owed to the current wife or partner of M in 1985? (See *Thake* v *Maurice* (above).) Would the doctor need to know that M was married or had a regular partner? What if M told the doctor that the reason M wanted the vasectomy was because he was promiscuous and had a number of partners?

3. In *McFarlane* v *Tayside Health Board* [1999] 4 All ER 961, it was held that while a claimant in a wrongful birth case could claim for pain and suffering during the pregnancy and in giving birth, the parents could not claim for the cost of bringing up the child as that was 'economic' loss. The reason was that while it was the hospital's duty to prevent discomfort to the mother, it was not their duty to prevent economic loss for which special levels of proximity are required and the doctor does not assume responsibility for those costs. Also it would not be fair and reasonable to impose that liability. Lord Steyn added the view that recovery would be contrary to ideas of 'distributive justice', that is 'the just distribution of burdens and losses

among members of a society', and that the public would not favour such a claim when other claims, perhaps more deserving, were denied. The *McFarlane* principle was accepted by the House of Lords in *Rees* v *Darlington Memorial Hospital NHS Trust* [2003] 4 All ER 987, where Lord Bingham said that the reasons of legal policy were 'an unwillingness to regard a child (even if unwanted) as a financial liability and nothing else, a recognition that the rewards which parenthood (even if involuntary) may or may not bring cannot be quantified and a sense that to award potentially very large sums of damages against a National Health service always in need of funds to meet pressing demands would rightly offend the community's sense of how public resources should be allocated'. However, the House added that a modest award (over and above pain and suffering) should be made to recognize that the parent has suffered a legal wrong. (In this case the award was £15,000.) By a narrow majority the High Court of Australia has not followed *McFarlane*: see *Cattanach* v *Melchior* (2002) 199 ALR 131. On this subject generally see Hoyano, 'Misconceptions about Wrongful Conception' (2002) 65 MLR 883.

4. In *Parkinson* v *St James Hospital* [2001] 3 All ER 97 it was said that where a *disabled* child was born damages would be awarded to cover the additional costs arising from the disability but not the full maintenance of the child. Where the *mother* is disabled and she has a healthy child, the House of Lords held in *Rees* (above) by a 4–3 majority that she cannot claim damages for the extra costs of bringing up the child which are attributable to her disability.

# 13

# Defences to Negligence

The principle of contributory negligence is that the damages awarded to a claimant who has himself been at fault should be reduced to the extent that his fault contributed to the accident or the damage. It might seem logical that if a defendant is to be held responsible for his fault, then so should a claimant for his, but it should be borne in mind that in practice the effect of a finding of contributory negligence on the part of the claimant is entirely different from a finding of fault on the part of the defendant. The reason is that, at least in personal injury cases, a defendant will usually be insured, or may be able to distribute his loss in some other way. Thus, a defendant who is made liable will not often bear the burden himself. But where a *claimant* is held to be contributorily negligent and his damages are reduced, he will almost always bear the burden himself. Why should we deliberately under-compensate people in this way? It is doubtful whether the doctrine has any deterrent effect: for example, it is highly unlikely that in the past the fact that a person who was not wearing a seat belt would be held contributorily negligent had any effect on the numbers of people who wore seat belts. (Television advertising was not very successful either, and it was not until the criminal law was used that wearing seat belts became common.) See generally on the problems associated with contributory negligence, Cane, *Atiyah's Accidents, Compensation and the Law* 6th edn, pp. 44–50.

The cases below show that the rules for establishing contributory negligence on the part of the claimant are not the same as the rules for establishing liability for negligence on the part of the defendant. There is, for example, no room for the concept of duty of care, and the question is rather simply whether the claimant has taken proper care for his or her own safety. One of the most difficult problems relates to causation, i.e. was the act of the claimant merely the background against which the negligence of the defendant operated, or did it causally contribute to the accident?

---

### LAW REFORM (CONTRIBUTORY NEGLIGENCE) ACT 1945

**1. Apportionment of liability in case of contributory negligence**

Where any person suffers damage as the result partly of his own fault and partly of the fault of any other person or persons, a claim in respect of that damage shall not be defeated by reason of the fault of the person suffering the damage, but the damages recoverable in respect thereof shall be reduced to such extent as the court thinks just and equitable having regard to the claimant's share in the responsibility for the damage. . . .)

#### 4. Interpretation

The following expressions have the meanings hereby respectively assigned to them, that is to say—

'court' means, in relation to any claim, the court or arbitrator by or before whom the claim falls to be determined;

'damage' includes loss of life and personal injury;

. . .

'fault' means negligence, breach of statutory duty or other act or omission which gives rise to a liability in tort or would apart from this Act, give rise to the defence of contributory negligence.

NOTES

1. It may not be possible under this Act to say that a person has been 100 per cent contributorily negligent. In *Pitts* v *Hunt* [1991] 1 QB 24, Balcombe LJ referred to such a view as logically unsupportable, and Beldam LJ said:

   > Section 1 begins with the premise that the person 'suffers damage as the result partly of his own fault and partly of the fault of any other person or persons . . .' Thus before the section comes into operation, the court must be satisfied that there is fault on the part of both parties which has caused damage. It is then expressly provided that the claim 'shall not be defeated by reason of the fault of the person suffering the damage . . .' To hold that he is himself entirely responsible for the damage effectively defeats his claim. It is then provided that 'the damages recoverable in respect thereof—that is, the damage suffered partly as a result of his own fault and partly the fault of any other person—'shall be reduced . . .' It therefore presupposes that the person suffering the damage will recover some damages.

   However, in *Reeves* v *Commissioner of Police* [1998] 2 All ER 381 Morritt LJ (dissenting) doubted this proposition preferring the case of *Jayes* v *IMI (Kynoch)* [1985] ICR 155 where the Court of Appeal had applied 100 per cent contributory negligence. The House of Lords in *Reeves* ([1999] 3 All ER 897) did not discuss this issue, but by implication Lord Hoffman seems to have accepted a 100 per cent deduction as a theoretical possibility.

2. There is considerable debate about whether contributory negligence may be pleaded in intentional torts. In *Quinn* v *Leathem* [1901] AC 495 Lord Lindley said that 'the intention to injure the plaintiff [claimant] negatives all excuses'. It has been decided in *Standard Chartered Bank* v *PNSC* [2003] 1 All ER 173 that contributory negligence is no defence to deceit, nor is it a defence to conversion or intentional trespass to goods (Torts Act 1997, s. 11) except for conversion of a cheque (Banking Act 1979, s. 47). On the confused situation in relation to trespass to the person, UK and Commonwealth courts have differed, for which see Chapter 22.

3. Contributory negligence can be pleaded even where the responsibility of the claimant for his or her own damage was the very thing which it was the duty of the defendant to prevent. In *Reeves* v *Commissioner of Police* [1999] 3 All ER 897 the claimant committed suicide when it was the duty of the police to prevent that happening. The House of Lords held that in exceptional circumstances contributory negligence can apply where a claimant intends to injure himself and a deduction of 50 per cent was made. *Volenti* was not applicable, because that would have negatived the duty of the police to prevent the suicide.

---

#### *Jones* v *Livox Quarries Ltd*
Court of Appeal [1952] 2 QB 608; [1952] 1 TLR 1377

The claimant worked in a quarry and was riding on the back of a 'traxcavator', 'very much in the position in which a footman stood at the back of an eighteenth century carriage'. The traxcavator, which had a speed of two mph, rounded an obstruction and stopped to change gear, when it was run into from behind by a dumper truck and the claimant was injured. Held: dismissing the appeal, that the claimant was contributorily negligent.

DENNING LJ: . . . Although contributory negligence does not depend on a duty of care, it does depend on foreseeability. Just as actionable negligence requires the foreseeability of harm to others, so contributory negligence requires the foreseeability of harm to oneself. A person is guilty of contributory negligence if he ought reasonably to have foreseen that, if he did not act as a reasonable, prudent man, he might be hurt himself; and in his reckonings he must take into account the possibility of others being careless.

Once negligence is proved, then no matter whether it is actionable negligence or contributory negligence, the person who is guilty of it must bear his proper share of responsibility for the consequences. The consequences do not depend on foreseeability, but on causation. The question in every case is: What faults were there which caused the damage? Was his fault one of them? The necessity of causation is shown by the word 'result' in section 1 (1) of the Act of 1945, and it was accepted by this court in *Davies v Swan Motor Co. (Swansea) Ltd.*

There is no clear guidance to be found in the books about causation. All that can be said is that causes are different from the circumstances in which, or on which, they operate. The line between the two depends on the facts of each case. It is a matter of common sense more than anything else. In the present case, as the argument of Mr Arthian Davies proceeded, it seemed to me that he sought to make foreseeability the decisive test of causation. He relied on the trial judge's statement that a man who rode on the towbar of the traxcavator 'ran the risk of being thrown off and no other risk.' That is, I think, equivalent to saying that such a man could reasonably foresee that he might be thrown off the traxcavator, but not that he might be crushed between it and another vehicle.

In my opinion, however, foreseeability is not the decisive test of causation. It is often a relevant factor, but it is not decisive. Even though the plaintiff did not foresee the possibility of being crushed, nevertheless in the ordinary plain common sense of this business the injury suffered by the plaintiff was due in part to the fact that he chose to ride on the towbar to lunch instead of walking down on his feet. If he had been thrown off in the collision, Mr Arthian Davies admits that his injury would be partly due to his own negligence in riding on the towbar; but he says that, because he was crushed, and not thrown off, his injury is in no way due to it. That is too fine a distinction for me. I cannot believe that that purely fortuitous circumstance can make all the difference to the case. As Scrutton LJ said in *In re Polemis and Another and Furness, Withy & Co. Ltd* [1921] 3 KB 560, 577 'Once the act is negligent, the fact that its exact operation was not foreseen is immaterial.'

In order to illustrate this question of causation, I may say that if the plaintiff, whilst he was riding on the towbar, had been hit in the eye by a shot from a negligent sportsman, I should have thought that the plaintiff's negligence would in no way be a cause of his injury. It would only be the circumstance in which the cause operated. It would only be part of the history. But I cannot say that in the present case. The man's negligence here was so much mixed up with his injury that it cannot be dismissed as mere history. His dangerous position on the vehicle was one of the causes of his damage just as it was in *Davies v Swan Motor Co. (Swansea) Ltd.*

The present case is a good illustration of the practical effect of the Act of 1945. In the course of the argument my Lord suggested that before the Act of 1945 he would have regarded this case as one where the plaintiff should recover in full. That would be because the negligence of the dumper driver would then have been regarded as the predominant cause. Now, since the Act, we have regard to all the causes, and one of them undoubtedly was the plaintiff's negligence in riding on the towbar of the traxcavator. His share in the responsibility was not great—the trial judge assessed it at one-fifth—but, nevertheless, it was his share, and he must bear it himself. . . .

NOTE

Another case on the causation problem is *Stapley v Gypsum Mines Ltd* [1953] AC 663, where the claimant, Seagull Gladys Stapley, was the widow of John Stapley who worked in a gypsum mine. He and another miner, Dale, had been told to take down a dangerous part of the roof in a stope where they were working. They tried to do so, but after about half an hour they gave up and decided to carry on with their normal work. Later the roof fell and killed Stapley. The House of

Lords held that the employers were vicariously liable for the negligence of Dale, and that Stapley was 80 per cent contributorily negligent. Dale was negligent in that, if he had not agreed with Stapley to cease trying to bring the roof down, Stapley would not have stood out against him and so would not have started to work under the dangerous roof. Lord Reid said:

> One may find that as a matter of history several people have been at fault and that if any one of them had acted properly the accident would not have happened, but that does not mean that the accident must be regarded as having been caused by the faults of all of them. One must discriminate between those faults which must be discarded as being too remote and those which must not.

He went on to say that the question is whether Dale's fault was 'so much mixed up with the state of things brought about by Stapley that in the ordinary plain commonsense of this business it must be regarded as having contributed to the accident'.

■ QUESTIONS

1. A leaves his car parked near a sharp bend in a 30 mph area where the view is obstructed. B, driving at 45 mph, crashes into it. Had B been driving at 30 mph he could have stopped in time. Is A contributorily negligent, i.e. is the fact that the car is badly parked merely the background against which the negligence of B operates, or did it contribute to the accident? See the comments about *Davies v Mann* (1842) 152 ER 588 in *Davies v Swan Motor Co.* [1949] 2 KB 291.

2. What degree of carelessness by others is foreseeable? Note the comment of Lord Uthwatt in *LPTB v Upson* [1949] AC 155, at p. 173 that 'a driver is not of course bound to anticipate folly in all its forms but he is not, in my opinion, entitled to put out of consideration the teachings of experience as to the form these follies commonly take'.

---

### *Froom v Butcher*
Court of Appeal [1976] QB 286; [1975] 3 WLR 379; [1975] 3 All ER 520

The claimant was involved in a collision due to the defendant's negligence. He was not wearing a seat belt. He suffered injuries to his head and chest which would not have occurred had he been wearing a belt. He also suffered injury to his finger, which would have happened anyway. Held: allowing the appeal, that the claimant was contributorily negligent.

> LORD DENNING MR: . . .
>
> *The cause of the damage*
>
> In the seat belt cases, the injured plaintiff is in no way to blame for the accident itself. Sometimes he is an innocent passenger sitting beside a negligent driver who goes off the road. At other times he is an innocent driver of one car which is run into by the bad driving of another car which pulls out on to its wrong side of the road. It may well be asked: why should the injured plaintiff have his damages reduced? The accident was solely caused by the negligent driving of the defendant. Sometimes outrageously bad driving. It should not lie in his mouth to say: 'You ought to have been wearing a seat belt.' That point of view was strongly expressed in *Smith v Blackburn (Note)* [1974] RTR 533, 536 by O'Connor J: '. . . the idea that the insurers of a grossly negligent driver should be relieved in any degree from paying what is proper compensation for injuries is an idea that offends ordinary decency. Until I am forced to do so by higher authority I will not so rule.' I do not think that is the correct approach. The question is not what was the cause of the accident. It is rather what was the cause of the damage. In most accidents on the road the bad driving, which causes the accident, also

causes the ensuing damage. But in seat belt cases the cause of the accident is one thing. The cause of the damage is another. The *accident* is caused by the bad driving. The *damage* is caused in part by the bad driving of the defendant, and in part by the failure of the plaintiff to wear a seat belt. If the plaintiff was to blame in not wearing a seat belt, the damage is in part the result of his own fault. He must bear some share in the responsibility for the damage: and his damages fall to be reduced to such extent as the court thinks just and equitable. . . .

*The share of responsibility*

Whenever there is an accident, the negligent driver must bear by far the greater share of responsibility. It was his negligence which caused the accident. It also was a prime cause of the whole of the damage. But in so far as the damage might have been avoided or lessened by wearing a seat belt, the injured person must bear some share. But how much should this be? Is it proper to inquire whether the driver was grossly negligent or only slightly negligent? or whether the failure to wear a seat belt was entirely inexcusable or almost forgivable? If such an inquiry could easily be undertaken, it might be as well to do it. In *Davies v Swan Motor Co. (Swansea) Ltd* [1949] 2 KB 291, 326, the court said that consideration should be given not only to the causative potency of a particular factor, but also its blameworthiness. But we live in a practical world. In most of these cases the liability of the driver is admitted, the failure to wear a seat belt is admitted, the only question is: what damages should be payable? This question should not be prolonged by an expensive inquiry into the degree of blameworthiness on either side, which would be hotly disputed. Suffice it to assess a share of responsibility which will be just and equitable in the great majority of cases.

Sometimes the evidence will show that the failure made no difference. The damage would have been the same, even if a seat belt had been worn. In such case the damages should not be reduced at all. At other times the evidence will show that the failure made all the difference. The damage would have been prevented altogether if a seat belt had been worn. In such cases I would suggest that the damages should be reduced by 25 per cent. But often enough the evidence will only show that the failure made a considerable difference. Some injuries to the head, for instance, would have been a good deal less severe if a seat belt had been worn, but there would still have been some injury to the head. In such case I would suggest that the damages attributable to the failure to wear a seat belt should be reduced by 15 per cent.

NOTE

The important point here is that the negligence of the claimant in no way contributed to the accident happening, but rather only to the extent of the damage. If we assume that a driver is 100 per cent responsible for the accident occurring, and the claimant is 100 per cent responsible for the extent of the damage, how can these different factors be balanced? To what extent has each contributed to the damage?

■ QUESTION

Who gains and who loses from the rule that failure to wear a seat belt amounts to contributory negligence? What makes people wear seat belts? Is the contributory negligence rule a factor in making people wear seat belts? If not, what is its function?

---

### *Owens v Brimmell*
Queen's Bench Division [1977] QB 859; [1977] 2 WLR 943; [1976] 3 All ER 765

The claimant and defendant went out drinking together in Cardiff, and each consumed eight or nine pints of beer. On the way home at about 2 a.m. the defendant negligently drove into a lamp post. Held: the claimant was 20 per cent contributorily negligent in getting in the car with a driver whom he knew to be drunk.

WATKINS J: The other allegation of contributory negligence gives rise to very different considerations, although it is based upon the same fundamental principle as explained by Lord Denning MR in *Froom's* case. He said, at p. 291: 'Contributory negligence is a man's carelessness in looking after his own safety. He is guilty of contributory negligence if he ought reasonably to have foreseen that, if he did not act as a reasonable prudent man, he might be hurt himself: . . .

But, is a man who voluntarily allows himself to be carried as a passenger in a motor car, driven by someone whom he knows has consumed a substantial quantity of alcohol which, as he must have been aware, reduced his capacity to drive properly, guilty of contributory negligence if the driver does drive negligently and the passenger is thereby injured? . . .

In the American Law Institution Restatement of the Law of Torts [*Restatement, Second, Torts*], section 466, it is stated that a plaintiff's contributory negligence may consist in an intentional and unreasonable exposure of himself to danger created by the defendant's negligence, of which danger the plaintiff knows or has reason to know. In subsection (e) it is stated, in illustration of this rule, that if a plaintiff rides a car knowing that the driver is drunk or that the car has insufficient brakes or headlights, he is ordinarily guilty of contributory negligence unless there are special circumstances which may make such conduct reasonable.

In Australia it seems to be accepted that contributory negligence can successfully be established upon this basis: see *Insurance Commissioner* v *Joyce*, 77 CLR 39. In that case Latham CJ expressed himself, at p. 47, of the opinion that he found himself in this dilemma:

> If . . . the plaintiff was sober enough to know and understand the danger of driving with [the defendant] in a drunken condition, he was guilty of contributory negligence. . . . But if he was not sober enough to know and understand such a danger . . . if he drank himself into a condition of stupidity or worse, he thereby disabled himself from avoiding the consequences of negligent driving by [the defendant], and his action fails on the ground of contributory negligence.

Thus, it appears to me that there is widespread and weighty authority for the proposition that a passenger may be guilty of contributory negligence if he rides with the driver of a car whom he knows has consumed alcohol in such quantity as is likely to impair to a dangerous degree that driver's capacity to drive properly and safely. So, also, may a passenger be guilty of contributory negligence if he, knowing that he is going to be driven in a car by his companion later, accompanies him upon a bout of drinking which has the effect, eventually, of robbing the passenger of clear thought and perception and diminishes the driver's capacity to drive properly and carefully. Whether this principle can be relied upon successfully is a question of fact and degree to be determined in the circumstances out of which the issue is said to arise.

In the instant case the plaintiff and the defendant drank a fairly considerable amount of beer, much of it within a relatively short period before the beginning of the fateful journey. They were both reasonably intelligent young men and the plaintiff, in particular, must have appreciated at some part of the evening, in my view, that to continue the bout of drinking would be to expose himself to the risk of being driven later by someone who would be so much under the influence of drink as to be incapable of driving safely. I think it more than likely, however, that the two of them were bent on a kind of what is known as a pub crawl and gave little, if any, thought to the possible consequences of it, or were recklessly indifferent to them.

I think this is a clear case on the facts of contributory negligence, either upon the basis that the minds of the plaintiff and the defendant, behaving recklessly, were equally befuddled by drink so as to rid them of clear thought and perception, or, as seems less likely, the plaintiff remained able to, and should have if he actually did not, foresee the risk of being hurt by riding with the defendant as passenger. In such a case as this the degree of blameworthiness is not, in my opinion, equal. The driver, who alone controls the car and has it in him, therefore, to do, whilst in drink, great damage, must bear by far the greater responsibility. I, therefore, adjudge the plaintiff's fault to be of the degree of 20 per cent. . . .

NOTES

1. The idea that a person may be contributorily negligent either in getting into a car knowing the driver is drunk or in going out with the defendant knowing that he or she will be driven back by the defendant later when he is drunk, does not solve one problem: what if a person meets a driver when both he and the driver are drunk, and then he is unable to appreciate what he ought to do for his own safety? An extreme form of this occurred in New Zealand in *Dixon* v *King* [1975] 2 NZLR 357, where the claimant was so drunk that he was unconscious, and he was loaded into the defendant's van. The court logically held that the defence of consent could not apply, and, although it was not raised, contributory negligence could not apply either. Thus, a claimant who accepts a lift, not having made previous arrangements, is better off if he is very drunk rather than slightly drunk, because his judgment is impaired and he is unable to appreciate the risk he runs or what he ought to do about it.

2. The defence of consent has been raised in this context, but it is clear from *Pitts* v *Hunt* [1991] 1 QB 24 that the Road Traffic Act 1988, s. 149(3) prevents that defence operating in relation to motor vehicles where compulsory insurance is required: see section 3 below. However, it can apply in other situations: see *Morris* v *Murray* [1991] 2 QB 6, where the claimant was a passenger on a plane the pilot of which was drunk.

---

### Jones v Boyce

Nisi Prius (1816) 1 Stark 492; 171 ER 540

The claimant was a passenger on the defendant's coach. A defective coupling rein broke while the coach was going downhill. The driver forced the coach into the side of the road and it was stopped by a post. However, the claimant, fearing a crash, had thrown himself from the coach and broke a leg. Had he stayed where he was he would have been safe. Held: the claimant was not contributorily negligent.

LORD ELLENBOROUGH: This case presents two questions for your consideration; first, whether the proprietor of the coach was guilty of any default in omitting to provide the safe and proper means of conveyance, and if you should be of that opinion, the second question for your consideration will be, whether that default was conducive to the injury which the plaintiff has sustained; for if it was not so far conducive as to create such a reasonable degree of alarm and apprehension in the mind of the plaintiff, as rendered it necessary for him to jump down from the coach in order to avoid immediate danger, the action is not maintainable. To enable the plaintiff to sustain the action, it is not necessary that he should have been thrown off the coach; it is sufficient if he was placed by the misconduct of the defendant in such a situation as obliged him to adopt the alternative of a dangerous leap, or to remain at certain peril; if that position was occasioned by the default of the defendant, the action may be supported. On the other hand, if the plaintiff's act resulted from a rash apprehension of danger, which did not exist, and the injury which he sustained is to be attributed to rashness and imprudence, he is not entitled to recover. The question is, whether he was placed in such a situation as to render what he did a prudent precaution, for the purpose of self-preservation. . . . Therefore it is for your consideration, whether the plaintiff's act was the measure of an unreasonably alarmed mind, or such as a reasonable and prudent mind would have adopted. If I place a man in such a situation that he must adopt a perilous alternative, I am responsible for the consequences; if, therefore, you should be of opinion, that the reins were defective, did this circumstance create a necessity for what he did, and did he use proper caution and prudence in extricating himself from the apparently impending peril. If you are of that opinion, then, since the original fault was in the proprietor, he is liable to the plaintiff for the injury which his misconduct has occasioned. This is the first case of the kind which I recollect to have occurred. A coach proprietor certainly is not to be responsible for the rashness and imprudence of a passenger; it must appear that there existed a reasonable cause for alarm.

NOTE

A modern example of this principle is *Holomis* v *Dubuc* (1975) 56 DLR 3d 351. The defendant landed a seaplane in which the claimant was travelling on a remote lake in British Columbia, and the plane hit a submerged object. Water began to pour into the passenger compartment and the claimant leaped out and was drowned. Had he remained in the plane he would have been safe, as the plane was successfully beached. However, the claimant was held to be 50 per cent responsible for his own death, not for jumping out, but for jumping out without a life jacket. Is it contributorily negligent to panic?

### *Fitzgerald* v *Lane and Patel*

House of Lords [1989] AC 328; [1988] 2 All ER 961; [1988] 3 WLR 365

The claimant was a pedestrain who carelessly stepped into the road and was hit by a car driven by the first defendant. This propelled him further into the road and he was struck again by a car driven by the second defendant. The trial judge determined that all three were equally to blame, and gave judgment for the claimant for two-thirds of his damages. The Court of Appeal held that the trial judge's finding meant that the claimant should have judgment for only 50 per cent of his damages. Held: dismissing the appeal, that the claimant should receive 50 per cent of his damages.

LORD ACKNER:

*The correct approach to the determination of contributory negligence, apportionment and contribution*

It is axiomatic that whether the plaintiff is suing one or more defendants, for damages for personal injuries, the first question which the judge has to determine is whether the plaintiff has established liability against one or other or all the defendants, i.e. that they, or one or more of them, were negligent (or in breach of statutory duty) and that the negligence (or breach of statutory duty) caused or materially contributed to his injuries. The next step, of course, once liability has been established, is to assess what is the total of the damage that the plaintiff has sustained as a result of the established negligence. It is only after these two decisions have been made that the next question arises, namely, whether the defendant or defendants have established (for the onus is upon them) that the plaintiff, by his own negligence, contributed to the damage which he suffered. If, and only if, contributory negligence is established does the court then have to decide, pursuant to section 1 of the Law Reform (Contributory Negligence) Act 1945, to what extent it is just and equitable to reduce the damages which would otherwise be recoverable by the plaintiff, having regard to his 'share in the responsibility for the damage.'

All the decisions referred to above are made in the main action. Apportionment of liability in a case of contributory negligence between plaintiff and defendants must be kept separate from apportionment of *contribution between the defendants inter se*. Although the defendants are each liable to the plaintiff for the whole amount for which he has obtained judgment, the proportions in which, as between themselves, the defendants must meet the plaintiff's claim, do not have any direct relationship to the extent to which the total damages have been reduced by the contributory negligence, although the facts of any given case may justify the proportions being the same.

Once the questions referred to above in the main action have been determined in favour of the plaintiff to the extent that he has obtained a judgment against two or more defendants, then and only then should the court focus its attention on the claims which may be made between those defendants for contribution pursuant to the Civil Liability (Contribution) Act 1978, re-enacting and extending the court's powers under section 6 of the Law Reform (Married Women and Tortfeasors) Act 1935. In the contribution proceedings, whether or not they are heard during the trial of the main action or by separate proceedings, the court is concerned to discover what contribution is just and equitable, having regard to the responsibility between the tortfeasors inter se, for the damage which the plaintiff has been adjudged entitled to recover. That damage may, of course, have been subject to a reduction as a result of the decision in the main action that the plaintiff, by his own negligence, contributed to the damage which he sustained.

Thus, where the plaintiff successfully sues more than one defendant for damages for personal injuries, and there is a claim between co-defendants for contribution, there are two distinct and different stages in the decision-making process—the one in the main action and the other in the contribution proceedings.

*The trial judge's error*

Mr Stewart accepts that the judge telescoped or elided the two separate stages referred to above into one when he said: 'I find that it is impossible to say that one of the parties is more or less to blame than the other and hold that the responsibility should be borne equally by all three.' The judge, in my judgment, misdirected himself by thinking in tripartite terms, instead of pursuing separately the two stages—phase 1: was the plaintiff guilty of contributory negligence and, if so, to what extent should the recoverable damages be reduced, issues which concerned the plaintiff on the one hand and the defendants jointly on the other hand; and phase 2: the amount of the contribution recoverable between the two defendants having regard to the extent of their responsibility for the damage recovered by the plaintiff—an issue which affected only the defendants inter se and in no way involved the plaintiff.

NOTE

This case makes clear that one should first assess the degree of responsibility of the claimant for his or her own loss in relation to the totality of the actions of the defendants, and only at a later stage should one assess the responsibility of the defendants as between themselves. This solves one version of the 'relativities' problem, in that a claimant is no better off being injured by two defendants than by one. However, other problems remain. The difficulty arises from the fact that the claimant's responsibility is assessed relative to that of the defendant, so that a claimant is better off if he is injured by a grossly negligent defendant. For example, a claimant acts carelessly: this carelessness will have a lower relative value in relation to a very negligent defendant than in relation to a slightly negligent defendant. Thus, the *same* conduct by the claimant will be assessed at, say, 50 per cent in relation to a slightly negligent defendant, but at only 25 per cent in relation to a very negligent defendant. Can this problem be solved? See further Cane, *Atiyah's Accidents, Compensation and the Law*, 6th edn, p. 48.

## SECTION 2: CONSENT

Consent or, as it is sometimes referred to, *volenti non fit injuria* provides a complete defence to an action, and, if successful, the claimant gets nothing. The defence is based on the view that a person cannot sue if he *consents* to the risk of damage. It is not enough merely to *know* of the risk, but no doubt where the risk is extremely obvious the claimant will be taken to have consented. This presumption should be used sparingly. An example where it was perhaps justified was *O'Reilly v National Rail and Tramway Appliances* [1966] 1 All ER 499, where the claimant and others were sorting scrap when they found a live ammunition shell nine inches long and one inch in diameter. After it had been rolled about, someone said to the claimant, who was holding a sledgehammer, 'Hit it: what are you scared of?', and the claimant did so, suffering severe injuries.

The defence of consent is fairly rare, especially in cases involving employees, but sometimes a similar device is used: that is that there was no breach of duty, either because there was no breach to that particular claimant (for example as between competitors in a sport) or because the claimant would have been injured even if the duty had been fulfilled. The relationship between duty, breach of duty and consent is illustrated by *McGinlay* v *British Railways Board* (below).

For a general discussion of this defence, where it is argued that the defence should not apply in the absence of an agreement to absolve the defendant, see Jaffey, 'Volenti non fit injuria' [1985] CLJ 87.

### *Morris* v *Murray*
Court of Appeal [1991] 2 QB 6; [1991] 2 WLR 195; [1990] 3 All ER 801

The claimant and the defendant spent the afternoon drinking, during which time the defendant consumed the equivalent of 17 whiskies, the alcohol concentration in his blood being more than three times that permitted for a car driver. The defendant then suggested that they go for a flight in his light aircraft for which he held a pilot's licence. The defendant took off down wind rather than up wind as he should have done, and the plane climbed to 300 feet, stalled and dived into the ground. The pilot was killed and the claimant passenger injured. Held: allowing the appeal, that the defendant was not liable as the claimant had consented to the risk.

FOX LJ: *Nettleship* v *Weston* [1971] 2 QB 691 was a case of a driving instructor injured by the negligent driving of the pupil. It is not, as a decision, of much relevance to the present case since, before giving the lesson, the instructor had asked for and obtained an assurance that there was in existence a policy of insurance. He was in fact shown a comprehensive policy which covered a passenger. That was unhopeful ground for a volens plea. There are, however, observations of Lord Denning MR and Salmon LJ to which I should refer. Lord Denning said, at p. 701:

> Knowledge of the risk of injury is not enough. . . . Nothing will suffice short of an agreement to waive any claim for negligence. The plaintiff must agree, expressly or impliedly, to waive any claim for any injury that may befall him due to the lack of reasonable care by the defendant: or, more accurately, due to the failure by the defendant to measure up to the standard of care which the law requires of him.

Salmon LJ, at p. 704, adopted, in a dissenting judgment, a different approach. He said that if, to the knowledge of the passenger, the driver was so drunk as to be incapable of driving safely, a passenger having accepted a lift could not expect the driver to drive other than dangerously. The duty of care, he said, sprang from relationship. The relationship which the passenger has created in accepting a lift in such circumstances cannot entitle him to expect the driver to discharge a duty of care which the passenger knows that he is incapable of discharging. The result is that no duty is owed by the driver to the passenger to drive safely. The difficulty about this analysis is that it may tend to equate 'sciens' with 'volens' which is not the law. However, there must be cases where the facts are so strong that 'volens' is the only sensible conclusion. Salmon LJ said that, alternatively, if there is a duty owed to the passenger to drive safely, the passenger by accepting the lift clearly assumed the risk of the driver failing to discharge that duty.

I doubt whether the gap between Lord Denning MR's approach and that of Salmon LJ is a very wide one. On the one hand, you may have an implicit waiver of any claims by reason of an exhibited notice as to the assumption of risk: see *Bennett* v *Tugwell* [1971] QB 267, which was decided before the Road Traffic Act 1972. On the other hand, if it is evident to the passenger from the first that the driver is so drunk that he is incapable of driving safely, the passenger must have accepted the obvious risk of injury. You may say that he is volens or that he has impliedly waived the right to claim or that the driver is impliedly discharged from the normal duty of care. In general, I think that the volenti doctrine can apply to the tort of negligence, though it must depend upon the extent of the risk, the passenger's knowledge of it and what can be inferred as to his acceptance of it. The passenger cannot be volens (in the absence of some form of express disclaimer) in respect of acts of negligence which he had no reason to anticipate and he must be free from compulsion. Lord Pearce in *Imperial Chemical Industries Ltd* v *Shatwell* [1965] AC 656, 687–688, said:

> as concerns common law negligence, the defence of volenti non fit injuria is clearly applicable if there was a genuine full agreement, free from any kind of pressure, to assume the risk of loss. In *Williams* v *Port of Liverpool Stevedoring Co. Ltd* [1956] 1 WLR 551 Lynskey J rejected the defence where one stevedore was injured by the deliberate negligence of the whole gang (to which the plaintiff gave 'tacit consent') in adopting a dangerous system of unloading. There was an overall duty on the master to provide a safe system of work, and it is difficult for one man to stand out against his gang. In such circumstances one may not have that deliberate free assumption of risk which is essential to the plea and which makes it as a rule unsuitable in master and servant cases owing to the possible existence of indefinable social and economic pressure. If the plaintiff had been shown to be a moving spirit in the decision to unload in the wrong manner it would be different. But these matters are questions of fact and degree.

> . . . I think that in embarking upon the flight the plaintiff had implicitly waived his rights in the event of injury consequent on Mr Murray's failure to fly with reasonable care. . . .

> Considerations of policy do not lead me to any different conclusion. Volenti as a defence has, perhaps, been in retreat during this century—certainly in relation to master and servant cases. It might be said that the merits could be adequately dealt with by the application of the contributory negligence rules. The judge held that the plaintiff was only 20 per cent to blame (which seems to me to be too low) but if that were increased to 50 per cent so that the plaintiff's damages were reduced by half, both sides would be substantially penalised for their conduct. It seems to me, however, that the wild irresponsibility of the venture is such that the law should not intervene to award damages and should leave the loss where it falls. Flying is intrinsically dangerous and flying with a drunken pilot is great folly. . . .

NOTES

1. One issue that arose was whether the claimant was so drunk that he could not appreciate and therefore consent to the risk he was running. It was held that in fact he was capable of understanding the risks. See further *Dixon* v *King* [1975] 2 NZLR 357 and *Kirkham* v *Chief Constable of Manchester* [1990] 2 QB 283, in both of which the claimants were unable to appreciate the risk and therefore did not consent.

2. This case does not apply to drunk drivers of motor vehicles, as by the Road Traffic Act 1988, s. 149(3), *volenti* cannot be pleaded by a person driving a motor vehicle in circumstances where compulsory insurance applies: see section 3 below.

■ QUESTION

Do you agree with Fox LJ that contributory negligence is not the appropriate principle to apply? Does this mean that the greater the fault of the defendant the less he has to pay?

---

### *McGinlay (or Titchener)* v *British Railways Board*
House of Lords [1983] 1 WLR 1427; [1983] 3 All ER 770

The pursuer and her friend, John Grimes, were struck by a train near Shettleston in Glasgow. There was a fence alongside the railway consisting of old sleepers, but this was in disrepair, and the pursuer and her friend had climbed up the embankment, through the broken fence and on to the railway line in order to get to a disused brickworks which was popular with courting couples. The pursuer was injured and her friend killed. The defendants knew that the fence was in disrepair and that people often crossed the line at that point. The House of Lords held: dismissing the appeal, (1) that the defendants had discharged their duty to the pursuer since the fence, although in disrepair, was a sufficient warning to the claimant to keep off the railway, (2) alternatively, that there was no breach of duty because the pursuer would have crossed the line even if the fence had been in good repair, and (3) alternatively, that the pursuer consented to the risk of injury within the terms of s. 2(3) of the Occupiers' Liability (Scotland) Act 1960 which absolves a defendant from liability to a person 'in respect of risks which that person has willingly accepted as his'.

LORD FRASER: . . . The existence and extent of a duty to fence will depend on the circumstances of the case including the age and intelligence of the particular person entering upon the premises; the duty will tend to be higher in a question with a very young or a very old person than in the question with a normally active and intelligent adult or adolescent. The nature of the locus and the obviousness or otherwise of the railway may also be relevant. In the circumstances of this case, and in a question with this appellant, I have reached the opinion that the Lord Ordinary was well entitled to hold, as he did, that the respondents owed no duty to her to do more than they in fact did to maintain the fence along the line. I reach that view primarily because the appellant admitted that she was fully aware that the line existed, that there was danger in walking across it or along it, that she ought to have kept a look out for trains, and that she had done so when crossing the line on previous occasions.

If I am right so far, that would be enough to dispose of this appeal in favour of the respondents. But the Lord Ordinary and the Division based their decisions also on other grounds and I ought briefly to consider those additional grounds. In the first place the Lord Ordinary held that, even if the respondents were at fault in failing to maintain the fence and to repair the gaps in it, the appellant had failed to prove, as a matter of probability, that if the respondents had performed their duty in those respects, the accident would have been prevented. The Lord Ordinary expressed himself strongly on this point and concluded that the appellant and her companion would not have been stopped by anything short of an impenetrable barrier. No doubt he reached that conclusion mainly because of the appellant's evidence in cross-examination, that the respondents should have put up an impenetrable barrier which would have been 'impossible to get through.' That extreme view is clearly untenable; even in the *M'Glone* case, 1966 SC(HL) 1, where the danger (from a transformer) was at least as great as the danger in this case and where the injured intruder was a boy aged only 12, Lord Reid, at p. 11, described the suggestion that the defenders owed him a duty to surround the transformer with an impenetrable and unclimbable fence as 'quite unreasonable.' But the appellant also said that even an ordinary post and wire fence would have been enough to prevent her from crossing the line because she could not have climbed over it. This was at least partly because she was wearing platform shoes. . . . Having regard to the fact that the appellant, helped perhaps by her boyfriend, was apparently able to climb up the embankment and walk across the line, platform shoes and all, I consider that the Lord Ordinary was fully entitled to conclude that she had failed to satisfy him that a post and wire fence would have deterred her. It follows that the respondents' failure to maintain the fence in a reasonable condition, even assuming that it was their duty to have done so, did not cause the accident. The respondents aver that post and wire fencing was the type of fencing mainly relied on by them near the locus and that it was subject to frequent vandalism, but these matters were not explored in evidence.

Secondly the Lord Ordinary held that the respondents had established a defence under section 2(3) of the Act of 1960 by proving that the appellant had willingly accepted the risks of walking across the line. As Lord Reid said in the *M'Glone* case, 1966 SC(HL) 1, 13, subsection (3), merely puts in words the principle volenti non fit injuria. That principle is perhaps less often relied upon in industrial accident cases at the present time than formerly, but so far as cases under the Act of 1960 are concerned, the principle is expressly stated in subsection (3) and there is no room for an argument that it is out of date or discredited. If the Lord Ordinary was entitled to sustain this defence, the result would be that, whether the respondents would otherwise have been in breach of their duty to the appellant or not, the appellant had exempted them from any obligation towards her: see *Salmond & Heuston on Torts*, 18th ed. (1981), p. 467. On this matter I am of opinion, in agreement with Lord Hunter, that the Lord Ordinary was well founded in sustaining this defence. The reasons for doing so are in the main the same as the reasons for holding that the respondents were not in breach of their duty. The appellant admitted that she was fully aware that this was a line along which trains ran, and that it would be dangerous to cross the line because of the presence of the trains. She said in cross-examination 'it was just a chance I took,' and the Lord Ordinary evidently accepted that she understood what she was saying. She was in a different position from the boy in the *M'Glone* case, 1966 SC(HL) 1, who did not have a proper appreciation of the danger from live wires: see Lord Reid at p. 13 and Lord Pearce at p. 18. As I have said already the appellant did not suggest that the train which injured her had been operated in an improper or unusual way. The importance of that is that the chance which she took was no doubt limited to the danger from the train operated properly, in the 'ordinary and accustomed way': see *Slater* v *Clay Cross Co. Ltd* [1956] 2 QB 264, 271, *per* Denning LJ. Had there been evidence to show that the train which injured the appellant was driven negligently, like the train in *Slater's* case, the risk which materialised would not have been within the risks that the appellant had accepted. But there is nothing of that kind here. In my opinion therefore the defence under section 2(3) is established.

In these circumstances no question of apportioning the blame on the ground of contributory negligence arises.

NOTES

1. The Scottish Court of Session has used *Titchener* to justify rejecting a claim by the widow of a smoker against the manufacturer of the cigarettes. In *McTear* v *Imperial Tobacco* [2005] ScotCS CSOH 69 Lord Nimmo Smith said that if someone exposed themselves to a risk of harm in the knowledge that they were taking a chance, then there was no breach of the duty of care. He also referred to *Tomlinson* v *Congleton BC* (see Chapter 18) saying that there is no duty to save people from themselves.

2. Rescuers might be thought to consent to the risks that their rescue involves, but this has never been a defence for the defendant who created the initial risk. In *Baker* v *Hopkins* [1959] 1 WLR 966 the defendant had adopted a dangerous system of working, in cleaning a well by lowering a petrol engine which emitted poisonous fumes. Two of his workers were overcome by fumes, and the claimant, a doctor, volunteered to go down the well, knowing of the existence of fumes. He too was overcome, but he could not be pulled out of the well because the rope which was tied to his waist became caught. The defendants were liable and unable to rely on consent. Morris LJ said:

> If C, activated by an impulsive desire to save life, acts bravely and promptly and subjugates any timorous over-concern for his own well being or comfort, I cannot think it would be either rational or seemly to say that he freely and voluntarily agreed to incur the risks of the situation which had been created by A's negligence.

■ QUESTION

Is a person justified in exposing himself or herself to danger to recover a dead body, or a live dog?

## SECTION 3: EXCLUSION CLAUSES AND NOTICES

Tortious liability can be excluded by the term of a contract, but this is subject to the effect of the Unfair Contract Terms Act 1977 (below). For the effect of exclusion notices on occupiers' liability, see Chapter 18 below; and for the effect of the 1977 Act on a disclaimer of liability for a negligent statement, see Chapter 8.

## UNFAIR CONTRACT TERMS ACT 1977

### PART I

**1. Scope of Part I**

(1) For the purposes of this Part of this Act, 'negligence' means the breach—

(a) of any obligation, arising from the express or implied terms of a contract, to take reasonable care or exercise reasonable skill in the performance of the contract;

(b) of any common law duty to take reasonable care or exercise reasonable skill (but not any stricter duty);

(c) of the common duty of care imposed by the Occupiers' Liability Act 1957 or the Occupiers' Liability Act (Northern Ireland) 1957.

. . .

(3) In the case of both contract and tort, sections 2 to 7 apply . . . only to business liability, that is liability for breach of obligations or duties arising—

(a) from things done or to be done by a person in the course of a business (whether his own business or another's); or

(b) from the occupation of premises used for business purposes of the occupier;

and references to liability are to be read accordingly, but liability of an occupier of premises for breach of an obligation or duty towards a person obtaining access to the premises for recreational or educational purposes, being liability for loss or damage suffered by reason of the dangerous state of the premises, is not a business liability of the occupier unless granting that person such access for the purposes concerned falls within the business purposes of the occupier.

(4) In relation to any breach of duty or obligation, it is immaterial for any purpose of this Part of this Act whether the breach was inadvertent or intentional, or whether liability for it arises directly or vicariously.

*Avoidance of liability for negligence, breach of contract, etc.*

**2. Negligence liability**

(1) A person cannot by reference to any contract term or to a notice given to persons generally or to particular persons exclude or restrict his liability for death or personal injury resulting from negligence.

(2) In the case of other loss or damage, a person cannot so exclude or restrict his liability for negligence except in so far as the term or notice satisfies the requirement of reasonableness.

(3) Where a contract term or notice purports to exclude or restrict liability for negligence a person's agreement to or awareness of it is not of itself to be taken as indicating his voluntary acceptance of any risk.

*Liability arising from sale or supply of goods*

**5. 'Guarantee' of consumer goods**

(1) In the case of goods of a type ordinarily supplied for private use or consumption, where loss or damage—

(a) arises from the goods proving defective while in consumer use; and

(b) results from the negligence of a person concerned in the manufacture or distribution of the goods,

liability for the loss or damage cannot be excluded or restricted by reference to any contract term or notice contained in or operating by reference to a guarantee of the goods.

(2) For these purposes—

(a) goods are to be regarded as 'in consumer use' when a person is using them, or has them in his possession for use, otherwise than exclusively for the purposes of a business; and

(b) anything in writing is a guarantee if it contains or purports to contain some promise or assurance (however worded or presented) that defects will be made good by complete or partial replacement, or by repair, monetary compensation or otherwise.

(3) This section does not apply as between the parties to a contract under or in pursuance of which possession or ownership of the goods passed.

*Explanatory provisions*

### 11. The 'reasonableness' test

(1) In relation to a contract term, the requirement of reasonableness for the purposes of this Part of this Act, . . . is that the term shall have been a fair and reasonable one to be included having regard to the circumstances which were, or ought reasonably to have been, known to or in the contemplation of the parties when the contract was made.

. . .

(3) In relation to a notice (not being a notice having contractual effect), the requirement of reasonableness under this Act is that it should be fair and reasonable to allow reliance on it, having regard to all the circumstances obtaining when the liability arose or (but for the notice) would have arisen.

(4) Where by reference to a contract term or notice a person seeks to restrict liability to a specified sum of money, and the question arises (under this or any other Act) whether the term or notice satisfies the requirement of reasonableness, regard shall be had in particular (but without prejudice to subsection (2) above in the case of contract terms) to—

(a) the resources which he could expect to be available to him for the purpose of meeting the liability should it arise; and

(b) how far it was open to him to cover himself by insurance.

(5) It is for those claiming that a contract term or notice satisfies the requirement of reasonableness to show that it does.

### 13. Varieties of exemption clause

(1) To the extent that this Part of this Act prevents the exclusion or restriction of any liability it also prevents—

(a) making the liability or its enforcement subject to restrictive or onerous conditions;

(b) excluding or restricting any right or remedy in respect of the liability, or subjecting a person to any prejudice in consequence of his pursuing any such right or remedy;

(c) excluding or restricting rules of evidence or procedure;

and (to that extent) sections 2 and 5 to 7 also prevent excluding or restricting liability by reference to terms and notices which exclude or restrict the relevant obligation or duty.

(2) But an agreement in writing to submit present or future differences to arbitration is not to be treated under this Part of this Act as excluding or restricting any liability.

### 14. Interpretation of Part I

In this Part of this Act—

'business' includes a profession and the activities of any government department or local or public authority;

'goods' has the same meaning as in the Sale of Goods Act 1979;

. . .

'negligence' has the meaning given by section 1(1);

'notice' includes an announcement, whether or not in writing, and any other communication or pretended communication; and

'personal injury' includes any disease and any impairment of physical or mental condition.

## ROAD TRAFFIC ACT 1988

### 149. Avoidance of certain agreements as to liability towards passengers

(1)  This section applies where a person uses a motor vehicle in circumstances such that under section 143 of this Act there is required to be in force in relation to his use of it such a policy of insurance or such a security in respect of third-party risks as complies with the requirements of this Part of this Act.

(2)  If any other person is carried in or upon the vehicle while the user is so using it, any antecedent agreement or understanding between them (whether intended to be legally binding or not) shall be of no effect so far as it purports or might be held—

   (a) to negative or restrict any such liability of the user in respect of persons carried in or upon the vehicle as is required by section 145 of this Act to be covered by a policy of insurance, or

   (b) to impose any conditions with respect to the enforcement of any such liability of the user.

(3)  The fact that a person so carried has willingly accepted as his the risk of negligence on the part of the user shall not be treated as negativing any such liability of the user.

(4)  For the purposes of this section—

   (a) references to a person being carried in or upon a vehicle include references to a person entering or getting on to, or alighting from, the vehicle, and

   (b) the reference to an antecedent agreement is to one made at any time before the liability arose.

NOTES

1. This important provision prevents a driver excluding liability where insurance is compulsory. One problem was that drivers put exclusion notices in their cars, believing that this excluded only their personal liability and not that of the insurance company, but of course if the liability of the owner is excluded so is that of the insurance company.

2. In *Pitts v Hunt* [1991] 1 QB 24, it was made clear that this statute applies to all cases of consent, including that of a passenger who gets into a car driven by a drunk driver. Beldam LJ said that 'it is no longer open to the driver of a motor vehicle to say that the fact of his passenger travelling in circumstances in which for one reason or another it could be said that he had willingly accepted a risk of negligence on the driver's part, relieves him of liability for such negligence'. However, it should be noted that s. 149(3) does not prevent the operation of the defence of participation in an unlawful act (below).

## SECTION 4: PARTICIPATING IN AN UNLAWFUL ACT

This defence, sometimes referred to as *ex turpi causa non oritur actio*, is ill-defined, at least in relation to tort. The difficulty is to distinguish between those unlawful acts which do and those which do not preclude recovery by the victim, but different tests have been suggested. These are discussed in *Pitts v Hunt* but no clear view has yet emerged.

### *Pitts* v *Hunt*

Court of Appeal [1991] QB 24; [1990] 3 WLR 542; [1990] 3 All ER 344

The claimant, Andrew Pitts, was a pillion passenger on a motorbike driven by the defendant, Mark Hunt. The defendant was 16, did not have a driving licence and was not insured. Both parties went to a disco where they were drinking, and on the way home the bike was driven at about 50 mph and was weaving from side to side of the road when it collided with a car. The trial judge found that the defendant was unfit to drive through drink and was deliberately trying to frighten others on the road. He also found that the claimant aided and abetted the defendant and 'was fully in agreement with and was encouraging the way in which the [defendant] was manipulating the controls'. Held: dismissing the appeal, that the defendant was not liable as the damage to the claimant arose from a joint unlawful act.

DILLON LJ: Mr Peppitt for the plaintiff founds on certain recent authorities in this country which he relied on as establishing a 'conscience test' to be applied in cases of illegality. The starting point is the judgment of Hutchison J in *Thackwell* v *Barclays Bank plc* [1986] 1 All ER 676. In that case the plaintiff claimed damages from the bank for having paid a cheque drawn in favour of the plaintiff to a third party in reliance on a forgery of the plaintiff's signature on an endorsement of the cheque. The claim was rejected on the ground that the cheque represented the proceeds of a fraud on a fourth party, to which the plaintiff, the drawer of the cheque, and the forger of the endorsement were all parties. Hutchison J, at p. 689, treated the case as one in which public policy would prevent the plaintiff suing:

> just as it would prevent a burglar from whom the stolen goods were snatched by a third party just as the burglar left the victim's house from maintaining an action in conversion against the third party.

The judge in reaching that conclusion seems to have accepted a submission from counsel for the defendants that there were two distinct but related lines of authority running through the cases on illegality, the second of which laid down the 'conscience test.' That test was put as follows, at p. 687:

> That test, [counsel] suggested, involved the court looking at the quality of the illegality relied on by the defendant and all the surrounding circumstances, without fine distinctions, and seeking to answer two questions: first, whether there had been illegality of which the court should take notice and, second, whether in all the circumstances it would be an affront to the public conscience if by affording him the relief sought the court was seen to be indirectly assisting or encouraging the plaintiff in his criminal act.

. . . I find a test that depends on what would or would not be an affront to the public conscience very difficult to apply, since the public conscience may well be affected by factors of an emotional nature, e.g., that these boys by their reckless and criminal behaviour happened to do no harm to anyone but themselves. Moreover if the public conscience happened to think that the plaintiff should be compensated for his injuries it might equally think that the deceased driver of the motor cycle, had he survived and merely been injured, ought to be compensated, and that leads into the much-debated question whether there ought to be a universal scheme for compensation for the victims of accidents without regard to fault.

Beyond that, appeal to the public conscience would be likely to lead to a graph of illegalities according to moral turpitude, and I am impressed by the comments of Mason J in *Jackson* v *Harrison*, 138 CLR 438, 455:

> there arises the difficulty, which I regard as insoluble, of formulating a criterion which would separate cases of serious illegality from those which are not serious. Past distinctions drawn between felonies and misdemeanours, malum in se and malum prohibitum, offences punishable by imprisonment and those which are not, non-statutory and statutory offences offer no acceptable discrimen.

Bingham LJ's dichotomy in *Saunders* v *Edwards* [1987] 1 WLR 1116 between cases where the plaintiff's action in truth arises directly ex turpi causa and cases where the plaintiff has suffered a genuine wrong to which allegedly unlawful conduct is incidental avoids this difficulty, in that it does not involve grading illegalities according to moral turpitude . . .

I find it, at this stage, both necessary and helpful to examine the principal Australian cases.

In *Smith* v *Jenkins*, 44 ALJR 78 a group of four youths all about 16 years of age, who had been drinking, robbed a man, stole his car keys, and then, having found out where his car was, stole the car and drove it off on a joyride. The plaintiff was the first driver, but after a couple of changes of driver he was merely a passenger; a relatively few miles from the scene of the theft the car left the road at 80 or 90 mph and hit a tree. The plaintiff was seriously injured and sued the youth who had been the driver at the time of the accident; it was held that he could not recover anything.

In *Bondarenko* v *Sommers* (1968) 69 SR (NSW) 269, a decision of the Court of Appeal of New South Wales, a group of youths stole a car and proceeded to race the stolen car against a car one of them owned along a rough and fairly narrow road containing potholes and ruts. The result of such reckless driving was that the stolen car turned over. One of the youths who was a passenger in the stolen car at the time of that accident claimed damages for his injuries, but was held not entitled to recover.

Then in *Jackson* v *Harrison*, 138 CLR 438 a passenger was injured through the neglient driving of a motor car by a driver who was at the time of the accident and to the passenger's knowledge disqualified from driving. It was held by the majority of the High Court, Barwick CJ dissenting, that the passenger was not thereby disabled from recovering damages from the driver. The view of the majority, Mason, Jacobs and Aickin JJ, was that the illegality did not bear on the standard of care reasonably to be expected of the driver . . .

Barwick CJ held in *Smith* v *Jenkins*, 44 ALJR 78, 78–79, that the failure of the plaintiff to recover damages was to be attributable to a refusal of the law to erect a duty of care as between persons jointly participating in the performance of an illegal act, rather than to a refusal of the courts, upon grounds of public policy, to lend their assistance to the recovery of damages for breach, in those circumstances, of a duty of care owed by the one to the other because of the criminally illegal nature of the act out of which the harm arose. The other members of the High Court seem to have taken the same view. Owen J commented, at p. 89, that:

> It would . . . be an odd state of affairs if in a case such as that put by Lord Asquith in *National Coal Board* v *England* [1954] AC 403, at p. 429, a court was called upon to consider and decide the standard of care to be expected, in particular circumstances, of a prudent safebreaker or whether in the case suggested by Scrutton LJ in *Hillen* v *ICI (Alkali) Ltd* [1934] 1 KB 455, at p. 467, the smuggler who had not warned his confederates of a defect in the rope which they were using in the course of hiding smuggled goods had acted with the degree of care to be expected in the circumstances, of a reasonably careful smuggler.

The court considered that the doctrine of volenti did not provide a satisfactory solution of the problem.

On the facts of *Progress and Properties Ltd* v *Craft*, 135 CLR 651 it became clear that merely to say that if the parties were engaging in a joint illegal act neither would owe any duty of care to the other was to put the proposition too widely. The distillation of the law by the High Court of Australia rests therefore now on the judgment of Jacobs J, with which the other members of the majority of the court concurred, in *Progress and Properties Ltd* v *Craft* and in the judgments of Mason and Jacobs JJ, with whom Aickin J concurred, in *Jackson* v *Harrison*, 138 CLR 438. For relief to be denied on the ground of the illegality, the circumstances of the joint illegal venture in the course of which the accident which caused the plaintiff's injuries occurred must be such as to negate, as between the two of them, any ordinary standard of care. Thus Mason J said in *Jackson* v *Harrison*, at p. 456:

> A plaintiff will fail when the joint illegal enterprise in which he and the defendant are engaged is such that the court cannot determine the particular standard of care to be observed.

and Jacobs J said in *Progress and Properties Ltd* v *Craft*, 135 CLR 651, 668:

> Where there is a joint illegal activity the actual act of which the plaintiff in a civil action may be complaining as done without care may itself be a criminal act of a kind in respect of which a court is not prepared to hear evidence for the purpose of establishing the standard of care which was reasonable in the circumstances.

This formulation would clearly cover the instances given in the authorities of the careless smuggler or safebreaker, or the reckless driving, to escape capture, of the getaway car after a robbery, as in the English case of *Ashton* v *Turner* [1981] QB 137. It was regarded in *Jackson* v

*Harrison* as also covering the factual situations in *Bondarenko* v *Sommers*, 69 SR (NSW) 269 where there was, in the words of Mason J in *Jackson* v *Harrison*, an agreement to drive the stolen car recklessly for the purpose of racing on the highway, and the factual situation in *Smith* v *Jenkins*, 44 ALJR 78. In reference to *Smith* v *Jenkins*, Jacobs J said in *Jackson* v *Harrison*, 138 CLR 438, 460:

> It was a jaunt, an escapade, a joyride even though of a most serious kind from the beginning to the end. How could a standard of care be determined for such a course of criminal activity?

I feel unable to draw any valid distinction between the reckless riding of the motor cycle in the present case by the deceased boy Hunt and the plaintiff under the influence of drink, and the reckless driving of the cars, albeit stolen, in *Smith* v *Jenkins* and *Bondarenko* v *Sommers*. The words of Barwick CJ in *Smith* v *Jenkins*, 44 ALJR 78:

> The driving of the car by the appellant, the manner of which is the basis of the respondent's complaint, was in the circumstances as much a use of the car by the respondent as it was a use by the appellant. That use was their joint enterprise of the moment

apply with equal force to the riding of the motor cycle in the present case. This is a case in which, in Bingham LJ's words in *Saunders* v *Edwards* [1987] 1 WLR 1116, 1134, the plaintiff's action in truth arises directly ex turpi causa.

## NOTES

1. The public conscience test (doubted by Dillon LJ) was used by Beldam LJ in *Pitts* v *Hunt*, on the ground that the claimant was jointly engaged in an activity which, if it had caused the death of a person other than the defendant driver, would have amounted to manslaughter. It has also been accepted in New Zealand in *Brown* v *Dunsmuir* [1994] 3 NZLR 485. However, in *Tinsley* v *Milligan* [1993] 3 All ER 65 the House of Lords rejected the test, at least in so far as it might apply in contract and in *Hewison* v *Meridian Shipping Services* [2003] ICR 766 Ward LJ said that the public conscience test was a false guide.

2. In *Vellino* v *Chief Constable of Greater Manchester* [2002] 1 WLR 218 at 236 Sir Murray Stuart-Smith summarized the doctrine as:

> (1) The operation of the principle arises where the claimant's claim is founded upon his own criminal or immoral act. The facts which give rise to the claim must be inextricably linked with the criminal activity. It is not sufficient if the criminal activity merely gives occasion for tortious conduct of the defendant.
>
> (2) The principle is one of public policy; it is not for the benefit of the defendant. Since if the principle applies, the cause of action does not arise, the defendant's conduct is irrelevant. There is no question of proportionality between the conduct of the claimant and defendant.
>
> (3) In the case of criminal conduct this has to be sufficiently serious to merit the application of the principle. Generally speaking a crime punishable with imprisonment could be expected to qualify. If the offence is criminal but relatively trivial, it is in any event difficult to see how it could be integral to the claim.

In this case the police were not liable when the claimant injured himself in escaping from police custody on the ground that there was no duty owed. Sedley LJ dissented noting that the authorities on illegality are not reconcilable. For a full discussion see the Law Commission consultation paper no. 160 'The illegality defence in tort' (2001).

3. In *Gala* v *Preston* (1991) 172 CLR 243 the High Court of Australia adopted the 'proximity' approach to cases involving illegality. In that case four men had stolen a car to travel north and over four hours later the claimant passenger (one of the four) was injured due to the defendant's careless driving. The majority held that since 'proximity' was the test of whether a duty of care was owed and as this involved policy issues, a relevant factor would be the inappropriateness of trying to define the content of a duty of care where the parties were involved in joint criminal activity. In other words the relationship between the parties determines whether a duty is owed, and one thief does not owe another a duty of care. The majority said that 'to conclude that he should have observed the ordinary standard of care to

be expected of a competent driver would be to disregard the actual relationship between the parties.' However, the High Court has now indicated that *Gala* v *Preston* may need to be reconsidered. In *Joslyn* v *Berryman* (2003) 77 AJLR 1233 the claimant was injured in a car accident while the defendant was driving. Both parties had been drinking heavily the previous night and the Court said that the claimant was contributorily negligent in that a reasonable person would have realized the risk even if the actual claimant did not. On the subject of the 'proximity' test McHugh J said that 'now that this Court has rejected the doctrine of proximity, it may be that it would no longer follow the reasoning of *Cook* and *Gala*. Moreover, the notion of a standard of care that fluctuates with the sobriety of the driver is one that tribunals of fact must have difficulty in applying'. Nevertheless he said that as the authorities in Australia stand the 'no duty' argument is still open to defendants. The difficulties of the 'variable standard' have been referred to in this country to reject the proximity basis of defences to negligence.

4. The Supreme Court of Canada has rejected the 'proximity' view, saying that 'the legality or morality of the claimant's conduct is an extrinsic consideration' to the question whether a duty arises on the basis of foreseeable harm. In *Hall* v *Hebert* (1993) 101 DLR 4th 129 the court preferred to see *ex turpi causa* as a proper defence rather than as an element in the duty of care equation, and also criticized the proximity view on the ground that it was an 'all or nothing' approach. The majority preferred the view that 'there is a need in the law of tort for a principle which permits judges to deny recovery to a plaintiff [claimant] on the ground that to do so would undermine the integrity of the justice system. The power is a limited one. Its use is justified where allowing the plaintiff's claim would introduce inconsistency into the fabric of the law either by permitting the plaintiff to profit from an illegal or wrongful act, or to evade a penalty prescribed by criminal law. Its use is not justified where the plaintiff's claim is merely for compensation for personal injuries sustained as a consequence of the negligence of the defendant'.

5. Most cases of *ex turpi causa* will also be cases of consent, but in one area there is an important difference. The Road Traffic Act 1988, s. 149(3), prevents the defence of consent applying where the defendant has negligently driven a motor vehicle when insurance is compulsory (see section 3). That section does not, however, prevent the *ex turpi causa* doctrine applying (*Pitts* v *Hunt*), and care will need to be taken that the *ex turpi causa* doctrine is not used as a way of avoiding s. 149(3). In this situation, what extra factors need to be shown, over and above consent, for the *ex turpi causa* doctrine to apply?

6. A trespasser who is engaged in criminal activities is not barred from making a claim for personal injuries against the occupier because to do so would be to make him an outlaw. It is one thing to deny him any fruits of his illegal conduct but another to deprive him of compensation for injury. See *Revill* v *Newbery* [1996] 1 All ER 291, where the claimant who was attempting to break into the defendant's allotment shed was shot. The defendant was liable. However, if the unlawful act is a necessary element in pleading the cause of action the defence will apply. In *Clunis* v *Camden and Islington Health Authority* [1998] 3 All ER 180, the claimant, who was mentally ill, was convicted of manslaughter and sued the health authority on the ground that they should have predicted and prevented his criminal act. He lost, as public policy requires that a court will not assist a litigant who relies on his own criminal or immoral act.

# 14

## Damages for Death and Personal Injuries

The law relating to damages for personal injuries is a large and complicated subject, and only a few of the topics can be dealt with here, and even then only in outline. The object of this chapter is to give some idea of what damages are awarded for and how they are calculated, but the subject is highly unscientific and can really only be understood by experience.

SECTION 1: **TYPES OF ACTION FOR DAMAGES**

Where a live claimant sues, the award will usually be for a lump sum to compensate for such matters as loss of future income, loss of amenity and pain and suffering. This once and for all payment has the advantage of finality and is preferred by claimants, but there may be occasions where it is inappropriate. Accordingly the court can now order that the damages should be paid by way of periodic payments, and in cases where the prognosis is uncertain there can be an interim payment. Furthermore, a claimant may prefer to negotiate a structured settlement which essentially is a lump sum commuted to an annuity. This has considerable tax advantages.

Where a person dies as the result of a tort there are two methods of claiming damages and their relationship can be complicated. First, there is an action by the deceased through his estate under the Law Reform (Miscellaneous Provisions) Act 1934. Secondly, there can be an action by the dependants of the deceased. This is independent of the action by the estate, for the dependants sue for their own loss, although their right to sue is conditional upon the deceased having had a right of action. There can be an action both by the estate and by the dependants for their separate losses, but it should be remembered that any damages received by the estate will be distributed according to the deceased's will (or on the deceased's intestacy), and the money may not have been left to the dependants.

---

**DAMAGES ACT 1996**

**2. Periodical payments**

(1) A court awarding damages for future pecuniary loss in respect of personal injury—
   (a) may order that the damages are wholly or partly to take the form of periodical payments, and
   (b) shall consider whether to make that order.

(2) A court awarding other damages in respect of personal injury may, if the parties consent, order that the damages are wholly or partly to take the form of periodical payments.

(3) A court may not make an order for periodical payments unless satisfied that the continuity of payment under the order is reasonably secure.

NOTES

1. This section was amended by the Courts Act 2003 and allows for a periodic payment order in relation to future income loss without the consent of the parties. An order is 'reasonably secure' if (a) there is a Financial Services Compensation Scheme set up under the Financial Services and Markets Act 2000, s. 213 or (b) a Minister has provided a guarantee in relation to a designated body under the Damages Act 1996, s. 6 or (c) the defendant is a government or health service body. The Damages (Variation of Periodical Payments) Order 2004 allows for a variable order to be made.

2. A periodic payment includes a structured settlement which is an arrangement whereby a claimant purchases an annuity from an insurance company with the damages he has been awarded or is entitled to. It works in the same way as any insurance policy whereby the insurer agrees to make a regular payment to the insured. If the policy is to last for the life of the claimant, the insurance company will make the usual actuarial assessments of his life expectancy. The advantage of a structured settlement is the tax benefit, but in negotiations with the insurance company as to the amount of the annuity some of this benefit may well accrue to them rather than to the claimant. See generally Law Commission Report No. 224, 'Structured settlements and interim and provisional damages'.

## SENIOR COURTS ACT 1981
## (formerly Supreme Court Act 1981)

### 32A. Orders for provisional damages for personal injuries

(1) This section applies to an action for damages for personal injuries in which there is proved or admitted to be a chance that at some definite or indefinite time in the future the injured person will, as a result of the act or omission which gave rise to the cause of action, develop some serious disease or suffer some serious deterioration in his physical or mental condition.

(2) Subject to subsection (4) below, as regards any action for damages to which this section applies in which a judgement is given in the High Court, provision may be made by rules of court for enabling the court, in such circumstances as may be prescribed, to award the injured person—

(a) damages assessed on the assumption that the injured person will not develop the disease or suffer the deterioration in his condition; and

(b) further damages at a future date if he develops the disease or suffers the deterioration.

(3) [omitted]

(4) Nothing in this section shall be construed—

(a) as affecting the exercise of any power relating to costs, including any power to make rules of court relating to costs; or

(b) as prejudicing any duty of the court under any enactment or rule of law to reduce or limit the total damages which would have been recoverable apart from any such duty.

NOTE

This provision is intended for the cases where liability is clear but the medical prognosis is not. In that situation the claimant may apply for the loss known at the time of the trial and return to court for a further award if his condition deteriorates as a result of the tort. By the Civil Procedure Rules (CPR) 1998, r. 25.7, the section only applies if: (a) the defendant has admitted liability; or (b) the claimant has obtained judgment for damages to be assessed; or (c) if the action proceeded to trial the claimant would obtain substantial damages. Furthermore, the defendant must either: (a) be insured; or (b) be a public authority. Note also that where a claimant has been awarded provisional damages and he subsequently dies within three years of the original cause of action arising, then the dependants may still claim under the Fatal Accidents Act 1976. (See the Damages Act 1996.)

## LAW REFORM (MISCELLANEOUS PROVISIONS) ACT 1934

### 1. Effect of death on certain causes of action

(1) Subject to the provisions of this section, on the death of any person after the commencement of this Act all causes of action subsisting against or vested in him shall survive against, or, as the case may be, for the benefit of, his estate. Provided that this subsection shall not apply to causes of action for defamation . . .

(1A) The right of a person to claim under section 1A of the Fatal Accidents Act 1976 (bereavement) shall not survive for the benefit of his estate on his death.

(2) Where a cause of action survives as aforesaid for the benefit of the estate of a deceased person, the damages recoverable for the benefit of the estate of that person—

    (a) shall not include:

        (i) any exemplary damages;

        (ii) any damages for loss of income in respect of any period after that person's death.

    (b) [repealed]

    (c) Where the death of that person has been caused by the act or omission which gives rise to the cause of action, shall be calculated without reference to any loss or gain to his estate consequent on his death, except that a sum in respect of funeral expenses may be included.

(3) [repealed]

(4) Where damage has been suffered by reason of any act or omission in respect of which a cause of action would have subsisted against any person if that person had not died before or at the same time as the damage was suffered, there shall be deemed, for the purposes of this Act, to have been subsisting against him before his death such cause of action in respect of that act or omission as would have subsisted if he had died after the damage was suffered.

(5) The rights conferred by this Act for the benefit of the estates of deceased persons shall be in addition to and not in derogation of any rights conferred on the dependants of deceased persons by the Fatal Accidents Act 1976, and so much of this Act as relates to causes of action against the estates of deceased persons shall apply in relation to causes of action under the said Act as it applies in relation to other causes of action not expressly excepted from the operation of subsection (1) of this section.

(6) In the event of the insolvency of an estate against which proceedings are maintainable by virtue of this section, any liability in respect of the cause of action in respect of which the proceedings are maintainable shall be deemed to be a debt provable in the administration of the estate, notwithstanding that it is a demand in the nature of unliquidated damages arising otherwise than by a contract, promise or breach of trust.

NOTE

The question of 'lost years' has caused considerable difficulty. This refers to the years the claimant would have lived but for the act of the defendant. If the estate is suing under the 1934 Act, damages for those lost years are not recoverable, but rather the dependants will have an action under the Fatal Accidents Act 1976 for the years they would have been supported by the deceased had he remained alive. Note that if a victim sues while he is alive he is able to recover for the lost years, because in those circumstances the dependants will not have an action and the damages for the lost years will be needed to support them after the claimant's death.

## FATAL ACCIDENTS ACT 1976

### 1. Right of action for wrongful act causing death

(1) If death is caused by any wrongful act, neglect or default which is such as would (if death had not ensued) have entitled the person injured to maintain an action and recover damages in respect thereof, the person who would have been liable if death had not ensued shall be liable to an action for damages, notwithstanding the death of the person injured.

(2) Subject to section 1A(2) below, every such action shall be for the benefit of the dependants of the person ('the deceased') whose death has been so caused.

(3) In this Act 'dependant' means—

(a) the wife or husband or former wife or husband of the deceased;

(aa) the civil partner or former civil partner of the deceased;

(b) any person who—

(i) was living with the deceased in the same household immediately before the date of the death; and

(ii) had been living with the deceased in the same household for at least two years before that date; and

(iii) was living during the whole of that period as the husband or wife or civil partner of the deceased;

(c) any parent or other ascendant of the deceased;

(d) any person who was treated by the deceased as his parent;

(e) any child or other descendant of the deceased;

(f) any person (not being a child of the deceased) who, in the case of any marriage to which the deceased was at any time a party, was treated by the deceased as a child of the family in relation to that marriage;

(fa) any person (not being a child of the deceased) who, in the case of any civil partnership in which the deceased was at any time a civil partner, was treated by the deceased as a child of the family in relation to that civil partnership;

(g) any person who is, or is the issue of, a brother, sister, uncle or aunt of the deceased.

(4) The reference to the former wife or husband of the deceased in subsection (3)(a) above includes a reference to a person whose marriage to the deceased has been annulled or declared void as well as a person whose marriage to the deceased has been dissolved.

(4A) The reference to the former civil partner of the deceased in subsection (3)(aa) above includes a reference to a person whose civil partnership with the deceased has been annulled as well as a person whose civil partnership with the deceased has been dissolved.

(5) In deducing any relationship for the purposes of subsection (3) above—

(a) any relationship by marriage or civil partnership shall be treated as a relationship by consanguinity, any relationship of the half blood as a relationship of the whole blood, and the stepchild of any person as his child, and

(b) an illegitimate person shall be treated as the legitimate child of his mother and reputed father.

(6) Any reference in this Act to injury includes any disease and any impairment of a person's physical or mental condition.

### 1A. Bereavement

(1) An action under this Act may consist of or include a claim for damages for bereavement.

(2) A claim for damages for bereavement shall only be for the benefit—

(a) of the wife or husband or civil partner of the deceased; and

(b) where the deceased was a minor who was never married or a civil partner—

(i) of his parents, if he was legitimate; and

(ii) of his mother, if he was illegitimate.

(3) Subject to subsection (5) below, the sum to be awarded as damages under this section shall be £10,000.

(4) Where there is a claim for damages under this section for the benefit of both the parents of the deceased, the sum awarded shall be divided equally between them (subject to any deduction falling to be made in respect of costs not recovered from the defendant).

(5) The Lord Chancellor may by order made by statutory instrument, subject to annulment in pursuance of a resolution of either House of Parliament, amend this section by varying the sum for the time being specified in subsection (3) above.

### 2. Persons entitled to bring the action

(1) The action shall be brought by and in the name of the executor or administrator of the deceased.

(2) If—

    (a) there is no executor or administrator of the deceased, or

    (b) no action is brought within six months after the death by and in the name of an executor or administrator of the deceased,

the action may be brought by and in the name of all or any of the persons for whose benefit an executor or administrator could have brought it.

(3) Not more than one action shall lie for and in respect of the same subject matter of complaint.

(4) The plaintiff in the action shall be required to deliver to the defendant or his solicitor full particulars of the persons for whom and on whose behalf the action is brought and of the nature of the claim in respect of which damages are sought to be recovered.

### 3. Assessment of damages

(1) In the action such damages, other than damages for bereavement, may be awarded as are proportioned to the injury resulting from the death to the dependants respectively.

(2) After deducting the costs not recovered from the defendant any amount recovered otherwise than as damages for bereavement shall be divided among the dependants in such shares as may be directed.

(3) In an action under this Act where there fall to be assessed damages payable to a widow in respect of the death of her husband there shall not be taken account the re-marriage of the widow or her prospects of re-marriage.

(4) In an action under this Act where there fall to be assessed damages payable to a person who is a dependant by virtue of section 1(3)(b) above in respect of the death of the person with whom the dependant was living as husband or wife or civil partner there shall be taken into account (together with any other matter that appears to the court to be relevant to the action) the fact that the dependant had no enforceable right to financial support by the deceased as a result of their living together.

(5) If the dependants have incurred funeral expenses in respect of the deceased, damages may be awarded in respect of those expenses.

(6) Money paid into court in satisfaction of a cause of action under this Act may be in one sum without specifying any person's share.

### 4. Assessment of damages: disregard of benefits

In assessing damages in respect of a person's death in an action under this Act, benefits which have accrued or will or may accrue to any person from his estate or otherwise as a result of his death shall be disregarded.

### 5. Contributory negligence

Where any person dies as the result partly of his own fault and partly of the fault of any other person or persons, and accordingly if an action were brought for the benefit of the estate under the Law Reform (Miscellaneous Provisions) Act 1934 the damages recoverable would be reduced under section 1(1) of the Law Reform (Contributory Negligence) Act 1945, any damages recoverable in an action under this Act shall be reduced to a proportionate extent.

NOTES

1. The Law Commission has proposed a number of reforms of the Fatal Accidents Act ('Claims for Wrongful Death', Report No. 263). It recommends that the present structure should remain, but with the following amendments:

   (a) *Who can claim?* The fixed list in s. 1 would remain but with the addition of a general clause to cover anyone who 'was being wholly or partly maintained by the deceased immediately before the death or who would, but for the death, have been so maintained at a time beginning after the death'.

   (b) *Prospects of re-marriage*—see note 2 below.

   (c) *Collateral benefits*. A new section would specify that in addition to benefits accruing from the estate, insurance money, pensions and gifts should also not be deducted.

   (d) *Bereavement*—see note 3 below.

2. *Prospects of remarriage*. Section 3(3) states that the chances of a widow remarrying are not to be taken into account in assessing damages. This rule was introduced because it was felt to be disparaging for a woman's looks and character to be assessed by judges with a view to her eligibility in the marriage market. Nevertheless, the rule does have some absurd consequences: in *Thompson* v *Price* [1973] 2 All ER 846 the widow had already remarried before the trial, and this fact was ignored in assessing damages. Thus she received damages for the support she would have received from the deceased, even though her new husband was now legally obliged to support her. Further oddities are that the widow's chances of remarriage *can* be taken into account when assessing the children's damages, and that, where the deceased is the wife, the husband's chances of marrying again can be taken into account.

   The Law Commission has recommended (Report No. 263) that prospects of remarriage should be taken into account only where at the time of the trial the dependant has actually remarried, or is engaged to marry or has entered into financially supportive cohabitation. Equally, prospects of divorce or separation should not be taken into account unless at the time of the death the parties were not living in the same household, or one of the parties was petitioning for divorce, separation or nullity.

   A related problem is whether a widow's prospects of earning should be taken into account. Should a widow of 25 who has no children be provided with the equivalent of income for the rest of her life, even though she is able to earn for herself? In fact such issues are ignored (see *Howitt* v *Heads* below).

3. *Bereavement*. The statute now provides for a fixed sum of £10,000 for bereavement. One function of this is to provide damages where no other loss is apparent. Thus, in the case of the death of a young child this will be the only loss. There has been much criticism by parents in such cases that this grossly undervalues a life, but the fact remains that the purpose of damages here is to compensate for a pecuniary loss, and such parents have in fact suffered no monetary loss. (The hard hearted would point out that, economically speaking, the parents have made a gain by the loss of their child, in that they will no longer be put to the expense of its upbringing.)

   The Law Commission states that the function of bereavement damages is 'to compensate, in so far as a standardised award of money can, grief, sorrow and the loss of non-pecuniary benefits of the deceased's care, guidance and society'. It suggests that the standard award should be £10,000, index-linked. Those entitled to the payment would be a spouse, a parent, a child, a brother or sister, a person engaged to be married and cohabitants (including persons of the same sex) for at least two years. Where more than one person would be entitled the maximum payable by the defendant would be £30,000, index-linked. If there were more than three claimants they would share pro rata.

## SECTION 2: CALCULATION OF LOSS OF EARNINGS

This is the most difficult part of the subject, for the principles involved are wholly unscientific, and assessments are made on the basis of assumptions which need to be explained. The problem is to calculate a future income stream as a lump sum, and the situation is the same in the case of both fatal accident cases and claims by living claimants.

The objective of an award of damages is to provide the equivalent of the income which would have been received by the claimant (whether the victim himself or the dependants of a deceased victim) for the period during which he is unable to earn due to the tort committed by the defendant. There are three steps in the calculation:

(1) Work out the period for which the earnings have been lost, or, in a fatal accident case, the period during which the dependants would have been supported by the deceased.

(2) Second, work out the amount of loss, or the dependency, in weekly, monthly or annual terms.

(3) Work out the present capital value of that future loss.

It is the third step which produces the problems: obviously you do not simply multiply the amount of the loss by the number of years for which it will occur, because when you give the claimant a lump sum he or she will be able to earn interest on that money, and that must be taken into account. Thus, if a person has lost £10,000 per year for ten years, the person would be overcompensated if awarded £100,000, for he or she would be able to earn, say, £6,000 per year interest on this sum. What is needed is to work out a capital sum from which the person can, after investing it, withdraw £10,000 per year, and which will be exhausted at the end of the period of loss. What this sum will be will depend to a great extent on the assumed rate of interest gained on the capital sum, the 'discount rate', and this is now set at 2.5 per cent as this is approximately what might be gained on top of inflation.

In practice, the judges talk about a 'multiplier'. This is the figure which, when multiplied by the amount of annual loss, will produce a capital sum from which the amount of the loss may be drawn (net of tax) for the period of loss. For example, in the first case, *Howitt* v *Heads*, the loss was £936 per year for 40 years, and the judge awarded a capital sum of £16,848, that is 18 times the annual loss. The figure 18 was chosen because if the capital sum (18 × 936) is invested at about 5 per cent, then £936 could be drawn out of the fund each year for 40 years. Another way to explain the multiplier is to say that if A gives B £18 he should be able to draw out £1 per year for 40 years, assuming that it is invested at about 5 per cent net of tax.

The actual multiplier selected will also be affected by other uncertainties about the future: for example, a slight reduction will be made for what are called 'the vicissitudes of life', that is the chance that the claimant will not survive for the period of the loss or that some other injury will occur to the claimant. In the past calculating these chances was often a matter of intuition and guesswork but now, by virtue of the Civil Evidence Act 1995, s. 10, actuarial tables prepared by the government actuary (the so-called 'Ogden tables') may be used in assessing the chance of future risks materializing.

The first case, *Howitt* v *Heads*, is given as a simple example of the application of the Fatal Accidents Act and of the calculation of the multiplier.

---

### *Howitt* v *Heads*
Queen's Bench Division [1973] 1 QB 64; [1972] 2 WLR 183; [1972] 1 All ER 491

The claimant was a widow aged 21 who had a young son, and she was suing under the Fatal Accidents Act for the loss of her husband. The dependency was calculated at £936 per year for a period of 40 years. Held: neither prospects of remarriage nor of the claimant being able to earn should be taken into account, and a multiplier of 18 should be applied, giving damages of £16,848.

CUMMING-BRUCE J: On the basis of that dependency [of £18 per week] I approach the next problem, which is the problem of the capital sum which fairly represents the injury to the wife occurring from the death. I have to do it with rather less guidance from authority than has for many years been possible in fatal accident cases, as a consequence of the new situation flowing from the effect of section 4(1) of the Law Reform (Miscellaneous Provisions) Act 1971. Here is a young lady now, I think, 21, with one child. Her prospects of remarriage are not to be taken into account. The situation as I see it is this: on the wife's evidence it is likely, being evidently a lady of ability, that when it is convenient for her to make suitable arrangements for their son, she probably will at some stage—perhaps when the boy starts going to school—resume employment, not only to have the advantage of the money, but also because obviously it is likely to make life more interesting for her. And so, peering into the future, I envisage a situation in which it is likely that after a period of years, probably not very far ahead, she will resume employment and make a good deal of money every week as a result. That, of course, is upon the contingency that she does not remarry with all the implications that that might have—implications which I have to leave out of account.

What is the correct approach in a Fatal Accidents Act case to the situation of a widow who has an earning capacity which she will probably use after a fairly short period of years? As far as I know there is no explicit authority in English cases, though there is a good deal of authority to the effect that a wife's private means are not to be taken into account. There is a useful discussion in the well known textbook of *Kemp and Kemp, The Quantum of Damages*, 2nd ed., vol. 2 (1962), p. 272, upon the relevance or otherwise of a widow's capacity to support herself, and there have been two cases in Australia, which were approved in the High Court of Australia, dealing with the matter: see *Carroll* v *Purcell* (1927) 35 ALJR 384. And in *Goodger* v *Knapman* [1924] SASR 347 (and I rely on the citation from that case given in the textbook to which I have referred) Murray CJ said, at p. 358:

'Mr Thomson asked me to make a further reduction by reason of the widow being relieved from the heavier part of her domestic duties, and thereby set free to go out and earn something on her own account. I do not accede to the suggestion, as I am unable to see how liberty to work can reasonably be brought within the description of a pecuniary advantage she has derived from the death of her husband. Any money she might earn would be the result of her labour, not of his death.' The same decision was made by Wolff J in Western Australia in *Usher* v *Williams* (1955) 60 WALR 69, 80: 'The argument for the diminution of the claim by some allowance of the widow's earning potential proceeds on the theory that the husband's death has released a flood of earning capacity. . . . In my opinion the plaintiff's ability to earn is not a gain resulting from the death of her husband within the principle established by *Davies* v *Powell Duffryn Collieries Ltd* [1942] AC 601. The widow's ability to work was always there and she could perhaps, as many women do—particularly in profes-sions—have preferred to work after marriage. The same argument that is put forward for the defendants could be applied to any woman who goes out to work through necessity to support herself and her children following her husband's death; and if it can be applied to the widow there is no reason why it should not be used to diminish or extinguish the children's claims in a case where, by her efforts, she is able to support them as well as her husband did in his lifetime. . . . I therefore hold that the widow's earning capacity is not to be taken into account in diminution of damages.'

I agree with the principle enunciated in those cases and I follow them. I therefore make no deduction in respect of the widow's capacity to earn, even though I am satisfied as a matter of probability that she will fairly soon be obtaining a significant degree of financial independence. . . .

The exercise upon which I embark, in seeking to capitalise her loss therefore, has two elements of some artificiality, but by statute I consider that I am bound to postulate one artificiality and on principle, having regard to the approach of the court to the widow's own capacity to earn, I think it is my duty to introduce the second artificiality. Having regard to the age and good health of the husband, subject to what is commonly described as the changes and chances of life, he had a prospect of remunerative employment of not less than 40 years, and having regard to the lady's health and youth, her expectation of life is at least as good as his. And so, subject as I say to changes and chances of the unknown future, this widow has been deprived of the prospect of a settled and stable financial future afforded by her husband over a period of some 40 years.

Mr Cobb put in, as an aid to testing the effect of an award of £15,000 some tables showing what the effect would be if such a sum was invested to yield either 3 per cent or 4 per cent and I approach the case on the basis of the guidance given in the House of Lords in *Taylor* v *O'Connor* [1971] AC 115. I cite in particular a passage from the speech of Lord Pearson, which I think Mr Cobb had in mind when he caused to be prepared the tables that he put before me. Lord Pearson said, at p. 143:

> 'The fund of damages is not expected to be preserved intact. It is expected to be used up gradually over the relevant period—15 or 18 years in this case—so as to be exhausted by the end of the period.' The case with which their Lordships were dealing was a case where the deceased was 53 at the time of death and the respondent 52. 'Therefore, what the widow received annually—£3,750 in this case—is made up partly of income and partly of capital. As the fund is used up, the income becomes less and less and the amounts withdrawn from the capital of the fund become greater and greater, because the total sum to be provided in each year—£3,750—is assumed (subject to what is said below) to remain constant throughout the relevant period. It is not difficult, though somewhat laborious, to work out without expert assistance how long a given fund will last with a given rate of interest and a given sum of money to be provided in each year.'

Then he gives the first few lines of such a calculation to show the method, which was the method Mr Cobb presented to me. And when one looks at Mr Cobb's figures showing the consequences of an award of £15,000 invested at 3 per cent on the basis that the loss of dependency was £1,000, so that that is the income one is seeking to afford the widow throughout the future, it appears that on that investment of 3 per cent the fund disappears altogether in the 20th year. And at 4 per cent it disappears in the 23rd year. . . . On an £18 a week dependency the annual loss of dependency is £936. So that I seek by my award to provide the widow with capital that will afford her and her son over the foreseeable future an income of £936, and I find in the speeches of the House of Lords in *Taylor* v *O'Connor*, an indication that it is by the management of the capital fund that the widow may reasonably expect to counteract the probable fall in the value of money as a consequence of inflation. I have looked at annuity tables and I have taken them into account as providing one test of the appropriateness of the calculations, but I accept unhesitatingly the view frequently expressed that the actual evidence of such computations (and there is no evidence in this case of an actuarial character), is of limited value in assistance in a fatal accidents case.

I hope that I have thus indicated the factors that have affected my mind, and I have decided that the capital value that should be placed on the loss of dependency by this widow is the sum of £16,848. If my arithmetic is correct it will be found that can be represented as a multiplier of 18. . . .

NOTE

This case illustrates the traditional method of calculating damages and what is meant by a 'multiplier'. It also shows the relationship between the three elements in the calculation (period of loss, amount of loss and present capital value of future income) and how the total is arrived at.

### *Wells* v *Wells*
House of Lords [1999] 1 AC 345; [1998] 3 WLR 329; [1998] 3 All ER 481

This case involved the assessment of damages in three personal injury cases. The particular point at issue was the amount of 'discount' to be applied in capitalising the loss of future earnings, and thus how future inflation should be dealt with. The traditional view was to ignore inflation but to apply a rate of discount which would represent earnings on investments in times of stable currencies. This was taken to be 4–5 per cent. The alternative (adopted here) is to use the rate available for Index Linked Government Stock (ILGS) which pays approximately 2.5–3.5 per cent on top of inflation. The rate is now fixed by statutory instrument at 2.5 per cent.

LORD LLOYD: . . . The starting-point is the multiplicand, that is to say the annual loss of earnings or the annual cost of care, as the case may be. . . . The medical evidence may be that the need for care will increase or decrease as the years go by, in which case it may be necessary to take different multiplicands for different periods covered by the award. But to simplify the illustration one can take an average annual cost of care of £10,000 on a life expectancy of 20 years. If one assumes a constant value for money, then if the court were to award 20 times £10,000 it is obvious that the plaintiff would be over-compensated. For the £10,000 needed to purchase care in the twentieth year should have been earning interest for 19 years. The purpose of the discount is to eliminate this element of over-compensation. The objective is to arrive at a lump sum which by drawing down both interest and capital will provide exactly £10,000 a year for 20 years, and no more. This is known as the annuity approach. It is a simple enough matter to find the answer by reference to standard tables. The higher the assumed return on capital, net of tax, the lower the lump sum. If one assumes a net return of 5 per cent the discounted figure would be £124,600 instead of £200,000. If one assumes a net return of 3 per cent the figure would be £148,800.

The same point can be put the other way round. £200,000 invested at 5 per cent will produce £10,000 a year for 20 years. But there would still be £200,000 left at the end.

So far there is no problem. The difficulty arises because, contrary to the assumption made above, money does not retain its value. How is the court to ensure that the plaintiff receives the money he will need to purchase the care he needs as the years go by despite the impact of inflation? In the past the courts have solved this problem by assuming that the plaintiff can take care of future inflation in a rough and ready way by investing the lump sum sensibly in a mixed 'basket' of equities and gilts. But the advent of the index-linked government stock ('I.L.G.S.') (they were first issued in 1981) has provided an alternative. The return of income and capital on I.L.G.S. is fully protected against inflation. Thus the purchaser of £100 of I.L.G.S. with a maturity date of 2020 knows that his investment will then be worth £100 plus $x$ per cent of £100, where $x$ represents the percentage increase in the retail price index between the date of issue and the date of maturity (or, more accurately, eight months before the two dates). Of course if the plaintiff were to invest his £100 in equities it might then be worth much more. But it might also be worth less. The virtue of I.L.G.S. is that it provides a risk-free investment.

The first-instance judges in these appeals have broken with the past. They have each assumed for the purpose of the calculation that the plaintiffs will go into the market, and purchase the required amount of I.L.G.S. so as to provide for his or her future needs with the minimum risk of their damages being eroded by inflation. How the plaintiffs will in fact invest their damages is, of course, irrelevant. That is a question for them. It cannot affect the calculation. The question for decision therefore is whether the judges were right to assume that the plaintiffs would invest in I.L.G.S. with a low average net return of 2.5 per cent, instead of a mixed portfolio of equities and gilts. The Court of Appeal has held not. They have reverted to the traditional 4 to 5 per cent with the consequential reduction in the sums awarded.

*Conclusion*

My conclusion is that the judges in these three cases were right to assume for the purpose of their calculations that the plaintiffs would invest their damages in I.L.G.S. for the following reasons.

(1) Investment in I.L.G.S. is the most accurate way of calculating the present value of the loss which the plaintiffs will actually suffer in real terms.

(2) Although this will result in a heavier burden on these defendants, and, if the principle is applied across the board, on the insurance industry in general, I can see nothing unjust. It is true that insurance premiums may have been fixed on the basis of the 4 to 5 per cent discount rate indicated in *Cookson* v *Knowles* [1979] AC 556 and the earlier authorities. But this was only because there was then no better way of allowing for future inflation. The objective was always the same. No doubt insurance premiums will have to increase in order to take account of the new lower rate of discount. Whether this is something which the country can afford is not a subject on which your Lordships were addressed. So we are not in a position to form any view as to the wider consequences.

(3) The search for a prudent investment will always depend on the circumstances of the particular investor. Some are able to take a measure of risk, others are not. For a plaintiff who is not in a position to take risks, and who wishes to protect himself against inflation in the short term of up to 10 years, it is clearly prudent to invest in I.L.G.S. It cannot therefore be assumed that he will invest in equities and gilts. Still less is it his duty to invest in equities and gilts in order to mitigate his loss.

(4) Logically the same applies to a plaintiff investing for the long term. In any event it is desirable to have a single rate applying across the board, in order to facilitate settlements and to save the expense of expert evidence at the trial. I take this view even though it is open to the Lord Chancellor under section 1(3) of the Act of 1996 to prescribe different rates of return for different classes of case. Mr Leighton Williams conceded that it is not desirable in practice to distinguish between different classes of plaintiff when assessing the multiplier.

(5) How the plaintiff, or the majority of plaintiffs, in fact invest their money is irrelevant. The research carried out by the Law Commission suggests that the majority of plaintiffs do not in fact invest in equities and gilts but rather in a building society or a bank deposit.

(6) There was no agreement between the parties as to how much greater, if at all, the return on equities is likely to be in the short or long term. But it is at least clear that an investment in I.L.G.S. will save up to 1 per cent per annum by obviating the need for continuing investment advice.

(7) The practice of the Court of Protection when investing for the long term affords little guidance. In any event the policy may change when lump sums are calculated at a lower rate of return.

(8) The views of the Ogden Working Party, the Law Commission and the author of *Kemp & Kemp, The Quantum of Damages* in favour of an investment in I.L.G.S. are entitled to great weight.

(9) There is nothing in the previous decisions of the House which inhibits a new approach. It is therefore unnecessary to have resort to the *Practice Statement (Judicial Precedent)* [1966] 1 WLR 1234.

NOTES

1. In the event the House set the rate at 3 per cent, but this has now been superseded by a statutory instrument setting the rate at 2½ per cent. Nevertheless, the point is that rather than set a rate based on the total returns from equities (which would include sufficient return to cover inflation), the new method uses a return based on what might be gained over and above inflation. Note that the lower the rate of discount the higher will be the damages.

2. The rate of discount has been a matter of debate for many years and most commentators have recommended a change of the kind now adopted. The result will be an increase in personal injury damages and thus an increase in insurance premiums. This was felt to be necessary if we are to retain the notion of 'full compensation'. Lord Steyn discussed whether this should be so, noting that judges have in practice adopted a maximum multiplier of 18 and have made deductions for the future uncertainties of life. He noted *Atiyah's* criticism of the full compensation principle, that it is very expensive and reduces the incentive to return to work (see now Cane, *Atiyah's Accidents, Compensation and the Law*, 6th edn., p. 131).

## DAMAGES ACT 1996

### 1. Assumed rate of return on investment of damages

(1) In determining the return to be expected from the investment of a sum awarded as damages for future pecuniary loss in an action for personal injury the court shall, subject to and in accordance with rules of court made for the purposes of this section, take into account such rate of return (if any) as may from time to time be prescribed by an order made by the Lord Chancellor.

(2) Subsection (1) above shall not however prevent the court taking a different rate of return into account if any party to the proceedings shows that it is more appropriate in the case in question.

(3) An order under subsection (1) above may prescribe different rates for different classes of case.

NOTE

The discount rate to be applied under this Act has now been set at 2½ per cent by the Damages (Personal Injury) Order 2001, SI No. 2301. For a discussion of when this rate may be departed from see *Warriner* v *Warriner* [2003] 3 All ER 447, where it was said that certainty was extremely important and a different rate could only be applied where there were special features material to the rate of return and it could be shown that these were factors which had not been taken into account by the Lord Chancellor when setting the rate. A long life expectancy would not justify a different rate. (The claimant had a life expectancy of 46 years and asked for a 2 per cent rate to be applied: this was refused.)

### SECTION 3: INTANGIBLE LOSSES

Intangible losses include damages for pain and suffering and loss of amenity, and the amounts awarded tend to be conventional and are arrived at on the basis of experience. Thus *Kemp and Kemp, Quantum of Damages* lists awards under these heads, and these are used as guidelines in any given case.

'Loss of amenity' means loss by the claimant of the ability to enjoy life to the full. However, one issue over which there has been disagreement is whether damages should be awarded under this head for a person who is unable to appreciate his loss, such as someone in a coma. Are the damages for the deprivation or for the awareness of the deprivation? *West* v *Shepherd* deals with that problem.

### West v Shepherd
House of Lords [1964] AC 326; [1963] 2 WLR 1359; [1963] 2 All ER 625

The claimant, aged 41, was injured in a road accident and she suffered from 'post-traumatic spastic quadriplegia and intellectual deficit'. She may have been aware of her condition to a slight degree, but the House of Lords discussed the question of the basis of awards for loss of amenities. Held: that a person would be entitled to damages even if unaware of the loss.

LORD PEARCE: My Lords, the appellants seek to use the plaintiff's condition as the foundation for two arguments in extinction or diminution of damages claimed in respect of her injuries and pain and loss of amenities.

First it is argued that such damages are given as compensation or consolation, and therefore, when the plaintiff's condition is so bad that they cannot be used by her to compensate or console they should either be greatly reduced or should not be awarded at all. No authority is cited in favour of such a proposition nor can I see any principle of common law that supports it.

The argument contains the assumption, which in my opinion is fallacious, that the court is concerned with what happens to the damages when they have been awarded. The court has to perform the difficult and artificial task of converting into monetary damages the physical injury and deprivation and pain and to give judgment for what it considers to be a reasonable sum. It does not look beyond the judgment to the spending of the damages. If it did so, many difficult problems would arise. Similar sums awarded for similar suffering may produce wholly different results. To a poor man who is thereby enabled to achieve some cherished object such as the education of his family the sum awarded may prove to be a more than adequate consolation. To a man who already has more money than he wants, it may be no consolation at all. But these are matters with which the court is not concerned. Whether the sum awarded is spent or how it is spent is entirely a matter for the plaintiff or the plaintiff's legal representatives. If the plaintiff's personal ability to use or enjoy the damages awarded for injury and pain and loss of amenity were a condition precedent to their award, it would be impossible for the executors of an injured person to obtain such damages. Yet they did so in *Rose* v *Ford* [1937] AC 826 and *Benham* v *Gambling* [1941] ACt 157 and many other cases.

The second argument is founded on *Benham* v *Gambling* and would affect the whole basis of damages awarded for personal injury, apart, of course, from economic loss with which the argument is not concerned. Substantial damages are not awarded, it is said, for physical injury simpliciter, but only for the pain and suffering and general loss of happiness which it occasions. Therefore the deprivation of a limb can only command any substantial compensation in so far as it results in suffering or loss of happiness; and where there is little or no consciousness of deprivation there can be little or no damages. For this argument the appellants rely on *Benham* v *Gambling* and on the minority judgment of Diplock LJ in *Wise* v *Kaye* [1962] 1 QB 368.

The practice of the courts hitherto has been to treat bodily injury as a deprivation which in itself entitles a plaintiff to substantial damages according to its gravity. In *Phillips* v *London and South Western Railway Co.* 4 QBD 406 Cockburn CJ in enumerating the heads of damage which the jury must take into account and in respect of which a plaintiff is entitled to compensation, said: 'These are the bodily injury sustained; the pain undergone; the effect on the health of the sufferer, according to its degree and its probable duration as likely to be temporary or permanent; the expenses incidental to attempts to effect a cure, or to lessen the amount of injury; the pecuniary loss.' In *Rose* v *Ford* Lord Roche said: 'I regard impaired health and vitality not merely as a cause of pain and suffering but as a loss of a good thing in itself.' If a plaintiff has lost a leg, the court approaches the matter on the basis that he has suffered a serious physical deprivation no matter what his condition or temperament or state of mind may be. That deprivation may also create future economic loss which is added to the assessment. Past and prospective pain and discomfort increase the assessment. If there is loss of amenity apart from the obvious and normal loss inherent in the deprivation of the limb—if, for instance, the plaintiff's main interest in life was some sport or hobby from which he will in future be debarred, that too increases the assessment. If there is a particular consequential injury to the nervous system, that also increases the assessment. So, too, with other personal and subjective matters that fall to be decided in the light of common sense in particular cases. These considerations are not dealt with as separate items but are taken into account by the court in fixing one inclusive sum for general damages . . .

The loss of happiness of the individual plaintiffs is not, in my opinion, a practicable or correct guide to reasonable compensation in cases of personal injury to a living plaintiff. A man of fortitude is not made less happy because he loses a limb. It may alter the scope of his activities and force him to seek his happiness in other directions. The cripple by the fireside reading or talking with friends may achieve happiness as great as that which, but for the accident, he would have achieved playing golf in the fresh air of the links. To some ancient philosopher the former kind of happiness might even have seemed of a higher nature than the latter, provided that the book or the talk were such as they would approve. Some less robust persons, on the other hand, are prepared to attribute a great loss of happiness to a quite trivial event. It would be lamentable if the trial of a personal injury claim put a premium on protestations of misery and if a long face was the only safe passport to a large award. Under the present practice there is no call for a parade of personal unhappiness. A plaintiff who cheerfully admits that he is happy as ever he was, may yet receive a large award as reasonable compensation for the grave injury and loss of amenity over which he has managed to triumph.

NOTE

The Pearson Commission (para. 398) disagreed with this view, saying that non-pecuniary damages should not be recoverable for permanent unconsciousness. They took the view that damages should be paid under this head only where they can serve some useful purpose, such as providing some alternative source of satisfaction to replace one that has been lost. The High Court of Australia, in *Skelton* v *Collins* (1966) 39 AJLR 480, also, by a majority, took this view, saying that the subjective element could not be ignored, although some damages should be awarded for the objective elements.

## SECTION 4: DEDUCTION OF OTHER BENEFITS

The law of tort may not be the only source of compensation available to an injured person, and a difficult question is the extent to which benefits received from other quarters should be deducted from the damages. It is agreed that gifts to the claimant should not be deducted, nor should the proceeds of private insurance taken out by the claimant, since these are the result of the claimant's own payments and are not caused by the defendant's negligence. Also it would be odd if the defendant's liability to pay damages is reduced because of the claimant's payment of premiums. It is also agreed (*Parry* v *Cleaver* [1970] AC 1) that a pension is not deductible from damages, for a pension is different from lost wages. Also, in fatal accident cases, s. 4 of the 1976 Act makes it clear that insurance payments or pensions are not to be deducted from damages payable to the dependants.

However, two important areas of collateral benefit remain: sick pay and social security payments. *Hussain* v *New Taplow Mills* deals with the first, and statutory provisions deal with the second.

### *Hussain* v *New Taplow Paper Mills*

House of Lords [1988] AC 514; [1988] 2 WLR 266; [1988] 1 All ER 541

The claimant was injured at work and his left arm was amputated below the elbow. Under his contract of employment the claimant was entitled to receive full pay for 13 weeks and, if fully incapacitated, half pay thereafter. Held: dismissing the appeal, that the sick pay should be deducted from the damages.

LORD BRIDGE: In *Parry* v *Cleaver* [1970] AC 1, Lord Reid, discussing the general principles applicable to the assessment of damages for financial loss said, at p. 13:

> Two questions can arise. First, what did the plaintiff lose as a result of the accident? What are the sums which he would have received but for the accident but which by reason of the accident he can no longer get? And secondly, what are the sums which he did in fact receive as a result of the accident? And then the question arises whether the latter sums must be deducted from the former in assessing the damages. *British Transport Commission* v *Gourley* [1956] AC 185 did two things. With regard to the first question it made clear, if it had not been clear before, that it is a universal rule that the plaintiff cannot recover more than he has lost. And, more important, it established the principle that in this chapter of the law we must have

regard to realities rather than technicalities. The plaintiff would have had to pay tax in respect of the income which he would have received but for the accident. So what he really lost was what would have remained to him after payment of tax. . . . But *Gourley's* case had nothing whatever to do with the second question.

This dichotomy, however, must not be allowed to obscure the rule that prima facie the only recoverable loss is the net loss. Financial gains accruing to the plaintiff which he would not have received but for the event which constitutes the plaintiff's cause of action are prima facie to be taken into account in mitigation of losses which that event occasions to him. In many, perhaps most cases, both losses and gains will come into the calculation. Just as in a claim for damages for wrongful dismissal the plaintiff must, if he can, mitigate his damage by securing other employment, so also a plaintiff disabled by personal injury from continuing his pre-accident occupation mitigates his damage suffered by the loss of the whole of his earnings in that occupation by exercising some other skill, which he already possesses or acquires by training, to earn money in a new occupation which, but for the accident, he would never have pursued. One may ask either 'What is his real loss?' or 'Is the gain accruing from earnings in the new occupation deductible from the loss of earnings of the old occupation?' to arrive at the same answer. But to the prima facie rule there are two well established exceptions. First, where a plaintiff recovers under an insurance policy for which he has paid the premiums, the insurance moneys are not deductible from damages payable by the tortfeasor: *Bradburn* v *Great Western Railway Co.* (1864) LR 10 EX 1. Secondly, when the plaintiff receives money from the benevolence of third parties prompted by sympathy for his misfortune, as in the case of a beneficiary from a disaster fund, the amount received is again to be disregarded: *Redpath* v *Belfast and County Down Railways* [1967] NI 147. In both these cases there is in one sense double recovery. If the award of damages adequately compensates the plaintiff, as it should, the additional amounts received from the insurer or from third party benevolence may be regarded as a net gain to the plaintiff resulting from his injury. But in both cases the common sense of the exceptions stares one in the face. It may be summed up in the rhetorical question: 'Why should the tortfeasor derive any benefit, in the one case, from the premiums which the plaintiff has paid to insure himself against some contingency, however caused, in the other case, from the money provided by the third party with the sole intention of benefiting the injured plaintiff?'

Given the inevitable divergencies of judicial opinion as to what justice, reasonableness and public policy require, it is not surprising that courts in different common law jurisdictions should sometimes have solved similar problems in this field in different ways, nor that, in the leading case of *Parry* v *Cleaver* [1970] AC 1 itself, this House should have reversed the Court of Appeal by a majority of three to two in holding that a disability pension payable to a police officer compelled to retire from the police force by injury caused by the defendant's negligence was not to be taken into account in mitigation of his loss of earnings and loss of earning capacity up to the date of police retiring age, but only in mitigation of his loss of police retirement pension after that age. Lord Reid said, at p. 15: 'Surely the distinction between receipts which must be brought into account and those which must not must depend not on their source but on their intrinsic nature.'

He went on to consider the nature of the police disability pension and concluded, in effect, that it was the fruit of a form of insurance for which the plaintiff had in substance contributed the premiums by his pre-accident service. He contrasted it with sick pay in the following passage, at p. 16:

> Then it is said that instead of getting a pension he may get sick pay for a time during his disablement—perhaps his whole wage. That would not be deductible, so why should a pension be different? But a man's wage for a particular week is not related to the amount of work which he does during that week. Wages for the period of a man's holiday do not differ in kind from wages paid to him during the rest of the year. And neither does sick pay; it is still wages. So during the period when he receives sick pay he has lost nothing. We never reach the second question of how to treat sums of a different kind which he would never have received but for his accident.

Later he said, pp. 20–21:

> As regards police pension, his loss after reaching police retiring age would be the difference between the full pension which he would have received if he had served his full time and his

ill-health pension. It has been asked why his ill-health pension is to be brought into account at this point if not brought into account for the earlier period. The answer is that in the earlier period we are not comparing like with like. He lost wages but gained something different in kind, a pension. But with regard to the period after retirement we are comparing like with like. Both the ill-health pension and the full retirement pension are the products of the same insurance scheme; his loss in the later period is caused by his having been deprived of the opportunity to continue in insurance so as to swell the ultimate product of that insurance from an ill-health to a retirement pension. There is no question as regards that period of a loss of one kind and a gain of a different kind. . . .

Mr Andrew Collins, for the plaintiff, seeks to apply by analogy a principle said to be established by *Parry* v *Cleaver* [1970] AC 1 in support of the argument that all payments to an employee enjoying the benefit of the defendants' permanent health insurance scheme are effectively in the nature of the fruits of insurance accruing to the benefit of the employee in consideration of the contributions he has made by his work for the defendants prior to incapacity. Much emphasis was laid on the long term nature of the scheme payments to which the plaintiff has become entitled and it was submitted that they are strictly comparable to a disability pension. Both these arguments fall to the ground, as it seems to me, in the light of the concession rightly made at an early stage that the nature of payments under the scheme is unaffected by the duration of the incapacity which determines the period for which payments will continue to be made. The question whether the scheme payments are or are not deductible in assessing damages for loss of earnings must be answered in the same way whether, after the first 13 weeks of incapacity, the payments fall to be made for a few weeks or for the rest of an employee's working life. Looking at the payments made under the scheme by the defendants in the first weeks after the expiry of the period of 13 weeks of continuous incapacity, they seem to me indistinguishable in character from the sick pay which the employee receives during the first 13 weeks. They are payable under a term of the employee's contract by the defendants to the employee qua employee as a partial substitute for earnings and are the very antithesis of a pension, which is payable only after employment ceases. The fact that the defendants happen to have insured their liability to meet these contractual commitments as they arise cannot affect the issue in any way.
    . . . From the point of view of justice, reasonableness and public policy the case seems to me far removed from the principle underlying the insurance cases stemming from *Bradburn* v *Great Western Railway Co.*, LR 10 Ex 1. It positively offends my sense of justice that a plaintiff, who has certainly paid no insurance premiums as such, should receive full wages during a period of incapacity to work from two different sources, his employer and the tortfeasor. It would seem to me still more unjust and anomalous where, as here, the employer and the tortfeasor are one and the same.

NOTE

One exception to the principle in *Hussain* is the 'benevolence principle' where payments have been made to the claimant by a third party from motives of sympathy. These are not deducted as it 'would be revolting to the ordinary man's sense of justice and therefore contrary to public policy'. However it was held in *Gaca* v *Pirelli* [2004] 3 All ER 348, [2004] EWCA (Civ) 373, that where it is the *tortfeasor* who makes a voluntary payment the payment is deducted from the claimant's damages. Thus where an employer has voluntarily arranged insurance to cover his employees, payments made under this policy to an injured employee will be deducted, unless it can be shown that the employee has directly or indirectly contributed to paying the premium. (Merely being an employee will not be regarded as an indirect contribution.)

■ QUESTIONS

1. If the claimant is dismissed and becomes eligible for a disability pension rather than sick pay, should this be deducted?

2. Lord Bridge said that in *Hussain* the claimant had not paid insurance premiums as such. If an employee was given a choice of being covered by a sick pay scheme or receiving higher wages, would this alter the situation? If he is not given a choice, could the provision of cover be regarded as forgone wages?

3. If the contract of employment had stated that if the claimant recovered damages from a tortfeasor he must repay the sick pay to the employer, should the sick pay have been deducted?

## ADMINISTRATION OF JUSTICE ACT 1982

### 5. Maintenance at public expense to be taken into account in assessment of damages

In an action under the law of England and Wales or the law of Northern Ireland for damages for personal injuries (including any such action arising out of a contract) any saving to the injured person which is attributable to his maintenance wholly or partly at public expense in a hospital, nursing home or other institution shall be set off against any income lost by him as a result of his injuries.

## LAW REFORM (PERSONAL INJURIES) ACT 1948

### 2. Measure of damages

(4) In an action for damages for personal injuries (including any such action arising out of a contract), there shall be disregarded, in determining the reasonableness of any expenses, the possibility of avoiding those expenses or part of them by taking advantage of facilities available under the National Health Service Act 1977 or the National Health Service (Scotland) Act 1978, or of any corresponding facilities in Northern Ireland.

### 3. Definition of 'personal injury'

In this Act the expression 'personal injury' includes any disease and any impairment of a person's physical or mental condition, and the expression 'injured' shall be construed accordingly.

## SOCIAL SECURITY (RECOVERY OF BENEFITS) ACT 1997

*Introductory*

### 1. Cases in which this Act applies

(1) This Act applies in cases where—
  (a) a person makes a payment (whether on his own behalf or not) to or in respect of any other person in consequence of any accident, injury or disease suffered by the other, and
  (b) any listed benefits have been, or are likely to be, paid to or for the other during the relevant period in respect of the accident, injury or disease.

(2) The reference above to a payment in consequence of any accident, injury or disease is to a payment made—
  (a) by or on behalf of a person who is, or is alleged to be, liable to any extent in respect of the accident, injury or disease, or
  (b) in pursuance of a compensation scheme for motor accidents;
but does not include a payment mentioned in Part 1 of Schedule 1.

(3) Subsection (1)(a) applies to a payment made—
  (a) voluntarily, or in pursuance of a court order or an agreement, or otherwise, and
  (b) in the United Kingdom or elsewhere.

(4) In a case where this Act applies—
  (a) the 'injured person' is the person who suffered the accident, injury or disease,
  (b) the 'compensation payment' is the payment within subsection (1)(a), and

(c) 'recoverable benefit' is any listed benefit which has been or is likely to be paid as mentioned in subsection (1)(b).

### 3. 'The relevant period'

(1) In relation to a person ('the claimant') who has suffered any accident, injury or disease, 'the relevant period' has the meaning given by the following subsections.

(2) Subject to subsection (4), if it is a case of accident or injury, the relevant period is the period of five years immediately following the day on which the accident or injury in question occurred.

(3) Subject to subsection (4), if it is a case of disease, the relevant period is the period of five years beginning with the date on which the claimant first claims a listed benefit in consequence of the disease.

(4) If at any time before the end of the period referred to in subsection (2) or (3)—

(a) a person makes a compensation payment in final discharge of any claim made by or in respect of the claimant and arising out of the accident, injury or disease, or

(b) an agreement is made under which an earlier compensation payment is treated as having been made in final discharge of any such claim,

the relevant period ends at that time.

*Certificates of recoverable benefits*

### 4. Applications for certificates of recoverable benefits

(1) Before a person ('the compensator') makes a compensation payment he must apply to the Secretary of State for a certificate of recoverable benefits.

*Liability of person paying compensation*

### 6. Liability to pay Secretary of State amount of benefits

(1) A person who makes a compensation payment in any case is liable to pay to the Secretary of State an amount equal to the total amount of the recoverable benefits.

(2) The liability referred to in subsection (1) arises immediately before the compensation payment or, if there is more than one, the first of them is made.

(3) No amount becomes payable under this section before the end of the period of 14 days following the day on which the liability arises.

(4) Subject to subsection (3), an amount becomes payable under this section at the end of the period of 14 days beginning with the day on which a certificate of recoverable benefits is first issued showing that the amount of recoverable benefit to which it relates has been or is likely to have been paid before a specified date.

*Reduction of compensation payment*

### 8. Reduction of compensation payment

(1) This section applies in a case where, in relation to any head of compensation listed in column 1 of Schedule 2—

(a) any of the compensation payment is attributable to that head, and

(b) any recoverable benefit is shown against that head in column 2 of the Schedule.

(2) In such a case, any claim of a person to receive the compensation payment is to be treated for all purposes as discharged if—

(a) he is paid the amount (if any) of the compensation payment calculated in accordance with this section, and

(b) if the amount of the compensation payment so calculated is nil, he is given a statement saying so by the person who (apart from this section) would have paid the gross amount of the compensation payment.

(3) For each head of compensation listed in column 1 of the Schedule for which paragraphs (a) and (b) of subsection (1) are met, so much of the gross amount of the compensation payment as

is attributable to that head is to be reduced (to nil, if necessary) by deducting the amount of the recoverable benefit or, as the case may be, the aggregate amount of the recoverable benefits shown against it.

(4) Subsection (3) is to have effect as if a requirement to reduce a payment by deducting an amount which exceeds that payment were a requirement to reduce that payment to nil.

(5) The amount of the compensation payment calculated in accordance with this section is—

(a) the gross amount of the compensation payment, less

(b) the sum of the reductions made under subsection (3), (and, accordingly, the amount may be nil).

*Courts*

**15. Court orders**

(1) This section applies where a court makes an order for a compensation payment to be made in any case, unless the order is made with the consent of the injured person and the person by whom the payment is to be made.

(2) The court must, in the case of each head of compensation listed in column 1 of Schedule 2 to which any of the compensation payment is attributable, specify in the order the amount of the compensation payment which is attributable to that head.

**17. Benefits irrelevant to assessment of damages**

In assessing damages in respect of any accident, injury or disease, the amount of any listed benefits paid or likely to be paid is to be disregarded.

## SCHEDULE 2   CALCULATION OF COMPENSATION PAYMENT

| (1)<br>Head of compensation | (2)<br>Benefit |
|---|---|
| 1. Compensation for earnings lost during the relevant period | Disablement pension payable under section 103 of the 1992 Act |
| | Incapacity benefit |
| | Income support |
| | Invalidity pension and allowance |
| | Jobseeker's allowance |
| | Reduced earnings allowance |
| | Severe disablement allowance |
| | Sickness benefit |
| | Statutory sick pay |
| | Unemployability supplement |
| | Unemployment benefit |
| 2. Compensation for cost of care incurred during the relevant period | Attendance allowance |
| | Care component of disability living allowance |
| | Disablement pension increase payable under section 104 or 105 of the 1992 Act |
| 3. Compensation for loss of mobility during the relevant period | Mobility allowance |
| | Mobility component of disability living allowance |

NOTES
1. Exempt payments include any contractual payment paid to an employee by his employer in respect of incapacity for work, payments in pursuance of a claim under the Fatal Accidents Act 1976, or awards under the Vaccine Damage Payments Act 1979 or through the Criminal Injuries Compensation Scheme.
2. The Law Commission ('Claims for Wrongful Death', Report No. 263) recommends that this scheme should also apply to claims under the Fatal Accidents Act.

# 15

# Vicarious Liability

Vicarious liability is a system whereby an employer is liable for the torts of his employees committed in the course of employment. This is the usual case, but there may be other examples, and these will be dealt with in section 3. The principle of placing liability on the employer as well as upon the individual tort-feasor is mainly justified by the concept of loss distribution, that is that the employer will usually be better able to distribute the loss, either through insurance or through his customers. Other factors have also been put forward (see *Atiyah, Vicarious Liability in the Law of Torts*, 1967, Chapter 2): these include encouraging an employer to exercise proper control over his employees, thus supporting a policy of accident prevention; encouraging an employer to be careful in the selection of his employees; and the fact that as an employer gets the benefit of the work done by his employees he should also take the risks attached to that activity.

There are also problems as to the legal theory behind vicarious liability. It may be too simplistic to say that the employer is liable because the employee is liable, although in most cases this will be so. The problem can be illustrated by *Broom* v *Morgan* [1953] 1 QB 597, where a husband and wife were both employed by the same employer, and the husband negligently injured the wife. At that time, but no longer, a wife could not sue her husband, but nevertheless the employer was held vicariously liable for the husband's negligence, even though the husband himself could not be sued. It is probable that this case does not alter the theory of vicarious liability, but rather only means that an employer cannot take advantage of a procedural bar available to the employee.

A more difficult case would be where the employee is absolved because of insanity, as in *Buckley* v *Smith Transport* [1946] 4 DLR 721, where a Canadian court said that an employer would not be liable for the negligence of an insane employee, because an employer could not be liable if the employee was not liable, but the point was not argued. It is not clear, therefore, whether liability is imposed because the employee is liable, or because the acts and state of mind of the employee are attributed to the employer, or whether the acts are attributed to the employer, which if done by him would render him liable.

Vicarious liability is not limited to common law torts. In *Majrowski* v *Guy's and St Thomas's NHS Trust* [2005] QB 848; [2005] EWCA (Civ) 251, the Court of Appeal said that in principle 'there is no logical basis for differentiating between the legal categories of an employee's wrong. What matters is the closeness of the connection between the offending conduct of the employee with the nature and circumstances of that employment'. Thus there can be vicarious liability for breach of a statutory duty, and in that case vicarious liability was imposed for harassment of an employee by a fellow employee contrary to the Protection from Harassment Act 1997.

## SECTION 1: WHO IS AN EMPLOYEE?

The need to define an employee arises in many areas of the law, and it can mean different things for different purposes. Accordingly, while cases, for example, on the definition for the purposes of social security, are analogous and relevant, care must be taken to ensure that there are no special factors which render it inapplicable for the purposes of vicarious liability. The function of the definition here is to determine who should bear the risks created in the course of the enterprise, and a wider view may be more appropriate than in other areas of the law.

The main technical function is to distinguish employees, for whom an employer generally is vicariously liable, from independent contractors, for whom he is usually not liable. The distinction is sometimes said to be between a contract of service (employee) and a contract for services (independent contractor). Also, it should be noted that some of the older cases use the words 'master' and 'servant' instead of 'employer' and 'employee'.

---

### *Performing Right Society* v *Mitchell and Booker (Palais De Danse) Ltd*
King's Bench Division [1924] 1 KB 762; 93 LJKB 306; 131 LT 243

The defendants engaged a band called 'The Original Lyrical Five' to play at their dance hall, and the band played two songs without the permission of the claimants, the owners of the copyright. Held: the members of the band were employees of the defendants who were liable for the breach of copyright.

MCCARDIE J: The nature of the task undertaken, the freedom of action given, the magnitude of the contract amount, the manner in which it is to be paid, the powers of dismissal and the circumstances under which payment of the reward may be withheld, all these bear on the solution of the question. . . . It seems, however, reasonably clear that the final test, if there be a final test, and certainly the test to be generally applied, lies in the nature and degree of detailed control over the person alleged to be a servant. This circumstance is, of course, one only of several to be considered, but it is usually of vital importance. The point is put well in Pollock on Torts, 12th ed., pp. 79, 80.

> The relation of master and servant exists only between persons of whom the one has the order and control of the work done by the other. A master is one who not only prescribes to the workman the end of his work, but directs or at any moment may direct the means also, or, as it has been put, 'retains the power of controlling the work': see per Crompton J in *Sadler* v *Henlock*, 119 ER 209. A servant is a person subject to the command of his master as to the manner in which he shall do his work: see per Bramwell LJ in *Yewens* v *Noakes* (1880) 6 QBD 530, 532, and the master is liable for his acts, neglects and defaults, to the extent to be specified. An independent contractor is one who undertakes to produce a given result, but so that in the actual execution of the work he is not under the order or control of the person for whom he does it, and may use his own discretion in things not specified beforehand.

NOTE
The factor of control is not the only test of employment. A further factor may be the extent to which the job is integrated into the organization. In *Stevenson* v *MacDonald* [1952] 1 TLR 101, at p. 111 Denning LJ said:

It is often easy to recognise a contract of service when you see it, but difficult to say wherein the difference lies. A ship's master, a chauffeur, and a reporter on the staff of a newspaper are all employed under a contract of service; but a ship's pilot, a taxi-man and a newspaper contributor are employed under a contract for services. One feature which seems to run through the instances is that, under a contract of service, a man is employed as part of the business, and his work is done as an integral part of the business; whereas, under a contract for services, his work, although done for the business, is not integrated into it but is only accessory to it.

## *Market Investigations Ltd* v *Ministry of Social Security*
Queens Bench Division [1969] 2 QB 173; [1969] 1 WLR 1; [1968] 3 All ER 732

The question was whether a Mrs Irving was an employed person for the purposes of social security legislation. She was engaged as an interviewer by a company involved in market research and was free to work when she wanted. Held: Mrs Irving was an employee.

COOKE J: If control is not a decisive test, what then are the other considerations which are relevant? No comprehensive answer has been given to this question but assistance is to be found in a number of cases.

In *Montreal* v *Montreal Locomotive Works Ltd* [1947] 1 DLR 161, Lord Wright said, at p. 169:

In earlier cases a single test, such as the presence or absence of control, was often relied on to determine whether the case was one of master and servant, mostly in order to decide issues of tortious liability on the part of the master or superior. In the more complex conditions of modern industry, more complicated tests have to be applied. It has been suggested that a fourfold test would in some cases be more appropriate, a complex involving (1) control; (2) ownership of the tools; (3) chance of profit; (4) risk of loss. Control in itself is not always conclusive. Thus the master of a chartered vessel is generally the employee of the shipowner though the charterer can direct the employment of the vessel. Again the law often limits the employer's right to interfere with the employee's conduct, as also do trade union regulations. In many cases the question can only be settled by examining the whole of the various elements which constitute the relationship between the parties. In this way it is in some cases possible to decide the issue by raising as the crucial question whose business is it, or in other words by asking whether the party is carrying on the business, in the sense of carrying it on for himself or on his own behalf and not merely for a superior.

In *Bank voor Handel en Scheepvaart NV* v *Slatford* [1953] 1 QB 248, Denning LJ said, at p. 295:

The test of being a servant does not rest nowadays on submission to orders. It depends on whether the person is part and parcel of the organisation.

In *United States of America* v *Silk* (1946) 3312 US 704, the question was whether certain men were 'employees' within the meaning of that word in the Social Security Act 1935. The judges of the Supreme Court decided that the test to be applied was not 'power of control, whether exercised or not, over the manner of performing service to the undertaking', but whether the men were employees 'as a matter of economic reality.'

The observations of Lord Wright, of Denning LJ and of the judges of the Supreme Court suggest that the fundamental test to be applied is this: 'Is the person who has engaged himself to perform these services performing them as a person in business on his own account?' If the answer to that question is 'yes', then the contract is a contract for services. If the answer is 'no', then the contract is a contract of service. No exhaustive list has been compiled and perhaps no exhaustive list can be compiled of the considerations which are relevant in determining that question, nor can strict rules be laid down as to the relative weight which the various considerations should carry in particular cases. The most that can be said is that control will no doubt always have to be considered, although it can no longer be regarded as the sole determining factor; and that factors which may be of importance are such matters as whether the man performing the services provides his own equipment, whether he hires his own helpers, what degree of financial risk he takes, what degree of responsibility for investment and management he has, and whether and how far he has an opportunity of profiting from sound management in the performance of his task.

The application of the general test may be easier in a case where the person who engages himself to perform the services does so in the course of an already established business of his own; but this factor is not decisive, and a person who engages himself to perform services for another may well be an independent contractor even though he has not entered into the contract in the course of an existing business carried on by him.

NOTES

1. The nature of employment is changing for there are now more part-time workers, agency workers, home workers, contract workers and trainees. The traditional 'control' test may be inadequate to determine whether such persons are 'employees' for the purposes of vicarious liability. The question is what risks are properly attributable to the enterprise, and for this purpose it makes sense to ask whether or not the worker was working on his own account (the entrepreneur test)—i.e. is he taking the financial risk with the chance of loss as well as profit? Such a test may mean that 'employee' means different things for different purposes: see further Kidner, 'Vicarious liability: for whom should the employer be liable?' (1995) 15 Legal Studies 47.

2. There have been a number of cases in employment law which deal with peripheral types of employment, such as casual workers or agency workers, but it is suggested that these should not be directly relevant for vicarious liability. For example, in *O'Kelly* v *Trust House Forte* [1983] ICR 728, the applicants were casual wine waiters who worked when required, but it was held for the purposes of employment law that they were not 'employees' as there was no 'mutuality of obligation', that is that even if asked to work they were not required to do so. However, if they *did* work and one of them spilt wine on a customer, surely the hotel owner should be vicariously liable? The wine waiters could not be said to be in business on their own account but were, albeit temporarily, under the control of the hotel managers and were an essential part of the organization. Accordingly, whatever technical status they may have in employment law, policy factors suggest that the hotel should be vicariously liable for their activities while they are actually working.

3. As to 'agency' workers it had been said in *Montgomery* v *Johnson Underwood* [2001] IRLR 269 that they are neither employees of the agency, because the agency does not control the work done, nor of the 'client' company where the person actually works, because there is no contract of any kind between the worker and the client. However In *Dacas* v *Brook Street Bureau* [2004] IRLR 358 the Court of Appeal held that an agency worker *can* be the employee of the 'client' company where the worker actually works. Mummery LJ said that in a tri-angular relationship where there is a contract between the worker and the agency and between the agency and the client, there can still be an *implied* contract between the worker and the client. The crucial factor is the degree of control exercised by the client over the worker. This obviously makes sense in relation to vicarious liability. Thus in *Hawley* v *Luminar Leisure* [2006] EWCA Civ 18 the claimant was assaulted at a club by a 'door steward' who was employed by a contractor who supplied security services to the club. It was held that the club was vicariously liable even though technically the steward was not employed by them. This was because they controlled the stewards. (Note: the claimant sued the club because the contractor had gone into liquidation.)

---

### *Mersey Docks and Harbour Board* v *Coggins and Griffith Ltd*
House of Lords [1947] AC 1; [1946] 2 All ER 345; 175 LJ 270

The Harbour Board hired out a mobile crane, together with a driver, Mr Newall, to the defendant stevedores. Mr Newall was paid and liable to be dismissed by the Board, but the contract of hire stated that he was to be regarded as the employee of the stevedores. The stevedores could tell him what to do, but not how he was to operate the crane. Mr Newall negligently injured a Mr McFarlane. Held: on the question whether the Board or the stevedores were to be held vicariously liable for the negligence of Mr Newall, dismissing the appeal, that the Board was liable.

LORD PORTER: Many factors have a bearing on the result. Who is paymaster, who can dismiss, how long the alternative service lasts, what machinery is employed, have all to be kept in mind. The expressions used in any individual case must always be considered in regard to the subject matter under discussion but amongst the many tests suggested I think that the most satisfactory, by which to ascertain who is the employer at any particular time, is to ask who is entitled to tell the employee the way in which he is to do the work upon which he is engaged. If someone other than his general employer is authorized to do this he will, as a rule, be the person liable for the employee's negligence. But it is not enough that the task to be performed should be under his control, he must also control the method of performing it. It is true that in most cases no orders as to how a job should be done are given or required: the man is left to do his own work in his own way. But the ultimate question is not what specific orders, or whether any specific orders, were given but who is entitled to give the orders as to how the work should be done. Where a man driving a mechanical device, such as a crane, is sent to perform a task, it is easier to infer that the general employer continues to control the method of performance since it is his crane and the driver remains responsible to him for its safe keeping. In the present case if the appellants' contention were to prevail, the crane driver would change his employer each time he embarked on the discharge of a fresh ship. Indeed, he might change it from day to day, without any say as to who his master should be and with all the concomitant disadvantages of uncertainty as to who should be responsible for his insurance in respect of health, unemployment and accident. I cannot think that such a conclusion is to be drawn from the facts established. . . .

NOTES

1. The question in this case was not whether Mr Newall was an employee, but rather who was to be responsible. It shows that it is possible, although it was not actually so in this case, for a person to be vicariously liable, even though he would not for other purposes, such as employment law, be regarded as the employer. Such a case could occur if a labourer is hired out without any accompanying machinery. Further, the point of the case is not who pays in the end, for that might be settled by the terms of the hiring contract, but rather who the claimant should sue. Why should this depend on contracts of which he knows nothing?

2. However there *can* be 'dual' vicarious liability—in other words it is possible for two different 'employers' to be liable for the same event. In *Viasystems* v *Thermal Transfer Ltd* [2005] 4 All ER 1181, [2005] EWCA(Civ) 1151, the claimants engaged A Ltd to install air conditioning in its factory. A Ltd subcontracted the ducting work to B Ltd who then contracted with C Ltd to provide the labour. H (employed by B Ltd) and M (employed by C Ltd) were in charge of the work. S, an employee of C Ltd, negligently caused a flood and it was held that both H and M were entitled to control S even though strictly speaking he was employed by C Ltd. Accordingly both B Ltd and C Ltd (employers of H and M) were vicariously liable for the flood. Rix LJ thought the issue was not just one of control but rather 'what one is looking for is a situation where the employee in question . . . is so much part of the work, business or organization of both employers that it is just to make both employers answer for his negligence.' Where does this leave *Mersey Docks*? The court tended to think that sole vicarious liability would still rest with the Board and would not be shared with the stevedores as the use of the crane by the stevedores was temporary and the crane driver was exercising his own discretion as driver of the crane.

3. *Mersey Docks* also illustrates the difficulty with the control test: in evidence Mr Newall said 'I take no orders from anybody.' As Lord Parker pointed out, this 'sturdy reply' meant that he was a skilled man, but nevertheless the Board had the power to give him directions as to how he should carry out the work, and could dismiss him if he refused to carry them out. Does the control test make sense, for example, when applied to a surgeon? See *Cassidy* v *Ministry of Health* [1951] 2 KB 343.

■ QUESTION

Is the control test based on a circular argument? (Who is a servant? A person the employer can direct: Who can the employer direct? A servant.)

## SECTION 2: LIABILITY OF THE EMPLOYEE

It is generally assumed that even if the employer is liable the employee can also be sued. This may produce wholly inequitable results where, for example, the employer is bankrupt or an exemption clause limits his liability and the contracting party decides to sue the employee in tort. In *Lister* v *Romford Ice and Cold Storage Co.* [1957] AC 533, the House of Lords went so far as to hold that an employee may even be required to indemnify an employer if he has had to pay damages, but companies which insure employers have refused to take advantage of so unfair a rule.

This issue is now affected by the Contracts (Rights of Third Parties) Act 1999 (for which see Chapter 12). The effect of s. 1 is that where the contract between a customer and the employer contains an exemption clause which *specifically* states that it shall be extended to the employer's employees, the employees will gain the benefit of the exemption clause. However, this still leaves open the more common problem of what happens if there is no specific extension of the exemption clause. Traditionally it is assumed that the employee may be sued, but this view has been challenged by the Supreme Court of Canada in *London Drugs* (below), where the majority decided that the exemption clause could be *impliedly* extended to the employees. But La Forest J (dissenting) considered a more radical solution, that as a matter of *tort* rather than contract the employee should not be liable if there was no reliance by the customer on the potential liability of the employee.

---

### *London Drugs* v *Kuehne & Nagel International*
Supreme Court of Canada [1992] 3 SCR 299; (1993) 97 DLR 4th 261

London Drugs bought a transformer and arranged for it to be stored by Kuehne and Nagel International (KNI). The contract between London Drugs and KNI limited liability to $40 and London Drugs refused to purchase insurance through KNI but preferred to arrange their own insurance. Two employees of KNI, Dennis Brassart and Hank Vanwinkel negligently damaged the transformer causing damage worth $33,955.41. London Drugs sued KNI but obtained only $40 by virtue of the limitation clause. They then sued the two employees for the full damages. The High Court allowed the full claim but the British Columbia Court of Appeal limited it to $40. Held: dismissing the appeal, that the liability of the employees was limited to $40. (Note: the majority decided the case on the basis that the employees were impliedly entitled to take advantage of the limitation clause between the claimants and the employers. La Forest J dissented on the ground that in the circumstances the employees should not be liable in tort at all. MacLachlin J limited damages to $40 on the ground that in tort the claimants had taken the risk of further damage.)

LA FOREST J (dissenting):

*Vicarious Liability*

. . . In my opinion, the vicarious liability regime is best seen as a response to a number of policy concerns. In its traditional domain, these are primarily linked to compensation, deterrence and loss internalization. In addition, in a case like the one at bar, which involves a planned transaction or a contractual matrix, the issue of tort liability in the context of contractual relations involves a wider range of policy concerns. Alongside those respecting compensation, deterrence and loss internalization, there are important concerns regarding planning and agreed risk allocation.

The most important policy considerations lying behind the doctrine of vicarious liability are based on the perception that the employer is *better* placed to incur liability, both in terms of fairness and effectiveness, than the employee. Fleming admirably summarizes the policy concerns in the following passage from *The Law of Torts* (7th ed. 1987), at p. 340:

> Despite the frequent invocation of such tired tags as *Respondeat superior* or *Qui facit per alium, facit per se*, the modern doctrine of vicarious liability cannot parade as a deduction from legalistic premises, but should be frankly recognised as having its basis in a combination of policy considerations. Most important of these is the belief that a person who employs others to advance his own economic interest should in fairness be placed under a corresponding liability for losses incurred in the course of the enterprise; that the master is a more promising source for recompense than his servant who is apt to be a man of straw; and that the rule promotes wide distribution of tort losses, the employer being a most suitable channel for passing them on through liability insurance and higher prices. The principle gains additional support for its admonitory value in accident prevention. In the first place, deterrent pressures are most effectively brought to bear on larger units like employers who are in a strategic position to reduce accidents by efficient organisation and supervision of their staff. Secondly, the fact that employees are, as a rule, not worth suing because they are rarely financially responsible, removes from them the spectre of tort liability as a discouragement of wrongful conduct. By holding the master liable, the law furnishes an incentive to discipline servants guilty of wrongdoing, if necessary by insisting on an indemnity or contribution.

It is useful to separate out the various policy concerns identified by Fleming.

First, the vicarious liability regime allows the plaintiff to obtain compensation from someone who is financially capable of satisfying a judgment. As Lord Wilberforce noted in *Kooragang Investments Pty Ltd* v *Richardson & Wrench Ltd* [1981] 3 All ER 65 (PC), at p. 68, the manner in which the common law has dealt with the liability of employers for acts of employees (masters for servants, principals for agents) has been progressive; the tendency has been toward more liberal protection of innocent third parties; see also Fridman, at pp. 315–16. The plaintiff benefits greatly from the doctrine of vicarious liability, which allows access to the deep pocket of the company, even where the company is blameless in any ordinary sense.

Second, a person, typically a corporation, who employs others to advance its own economic interest should in fairness be placed under a corresponding liability for losses incurred in the course of the enterprise. As Lord Denning noted in *Morris* v *Ford Motor Co.* [1973] 1 QB 792 (CA) at p. 798, the courts 'would not find negligence so readily—or award sums of such increasing magnitude— except on the footing that the damages are to be borne, not by the man himself, but by an insurance company' through coverage purchased by the employer.

Third, the regime promotes a wide distribution of tort losses since the employer is a most suitable channel for passing them on through liability insurance and higher prices. In *Hamilton* v *Farmers' Ltd* [1953] 3 DLR 382 (NSSC), MacDonald J noted, at p. 393, that the principle of vicarious liability 'probably reflects a conclusion of public policy that the master should be held liable for the incidental results of the conduct of his business by means of his servants as a means of distributing the social loss arising from the conduct of his enterprises'.

Fourth, vicarious liability is also a coherent doctrine from the perspective of deterrence. KNI is in a much better situation than Vanwinkel and Brassart to adopt policies with respect to the use of cranes, the inspection of stickers and so on in order to prevent accidents of this type. Given that it will either be held liable or its customers' insurance costs will reflect its carefulness, KNI has every incentive to encourage its employees to perform well on the job and to discipline those who are guilty of wrongdoing.

It is apparent that the vicarious liability regime is not merely a mechanism by which the employer guarantees the employee's primary liability. The regime responds to wider policy concerns than simply the desire to protect the plaintiff from the consequences of the possible and indeed likely incapacity of the employee to afford sufficient compensation, although obviously that concern remains of primary importance. Vicarious liability has the broader function of transferring to the enterprise itself the risks created by the activity performed by its agents.

In my view, where the plaintiff has suffered injury to his property pursuant to contractual relations with the company, he can be considered to have chosen to deal *with a company*. Company legislation typically provides for notice and publicity of the fact that a company is under a limited liability regime; customers and creditors are thereby put on notice that in ordinary circumstances they can only look to the company for the satisfaction of their claims. In British Columbia, corporations are also required to set out their name in all contracts, invoices, negotiable instruments and orders for goods and services; see British Columbia *Company Act*, RSBC 1979, c. 59, ss. 16 and 130.

In my view, in contracting for services to be provided by a business corporation like KNI in the circumstances of the present case, London Drugs can fairly be regarded as relying upon performance by the corporation, and upon the liability of that body if the services are negligently performed. As Reiter, *supra*, suggests, at p. 290:

> The plaintiff did not rely, or cannot be regarded as having relied reasonably, upon the liability of any individual where the individual is acting in furtherance of a contract between plaintiff and a principal or employer of the individual: the individual defendant cannot reasonably be regarded as appreciating that he is being looked to (personally) to satisfy the expectations of the plaintiff.

Nor can Vanwinkel and Brassart be taken on the facts of this case to appreciate that the plaintiff is relying on *them* for compensation at all. As Reiter underlines, the intention to transfer the responsibility to the corporation or association is a most explicit risk allocation by contract in the three-party enterprise. . . .

### The Test: Reliance, Undertaking and Insurance

In my view, a requirement of specific and reasonable reliance on the defendant employees is justified in this type of case. I find it to be a necessary condition for recovery in cases of employee negligence where the law provides for the possibility of compensation through recourse to the employer and where, accordingly, the plaintiff's interest in compensation for its loss caused by the fault of another is substantially looked after. I also find it to be necessary in cases in which the defendant has no real opportunity to decline the risk.

In my view, there is no reason to limit the requirement of reasonable reliance to employee torts involving negligent misrepresentation. In the case of negligent misrepresentations, the requirement of reasonable reliance exists in part to respond to policy concerns about potentially indeterminate liability in the context of negligent words and economic loss. Here, the policy concerns are different, but a requirement of reasonable reliance is equally justified in light of my analysis of the situation of the employees in this case and the policies underlying vicarious liability. Reliance has been found to be relevant to findings of proximity by this Court in cases not involving negligent misrepresentations; see *B.D.C. Ltd* v *Hofstrand forms Ltd* [1986] 1 SCR 228.

Reliance on an ordinary employee will rarely if ever be reasonable. In most if not all situations, reliance on an employee will not be reasonable in the absence of an express or implied undertaking of responsibility by the employee to the plaintiff. Mere performance of the contract by the employee, without more, is not evidence of the existence of such an undertaking since such performance is required under the terms of the employee's contract with his employer. It may well be, as Blom argues, 'Fictions and Frictions', at p. 179, that the further one moves away from a wholly commercial type of case, the more scope there is for asserting reasonable reliance on something less than promises. This case, at any rate, is wholly commercial. With respect for those of a contrary opinion. I find any reliance by London Drugs on Vanwinkel and Brassart was certainly not reasonable in this case . . .

Subject to consideration by this Court of the arguments put forward by Fleming and others with respect to employee liability generally under the vicarious liability regime, the employee also remains liable to the plaintiff for his independent torts. The employer may also be vicariously liable for some independent torts in accordance with the general rules for establishing the employer's liability. The term 'independent tort' has been used with different meanings in different contexts. I should make clear that by independent tort in this context I mean a tort that is unrelated to the performance of the contract. It is not necessary in this case to consider the question of the definition of independent tort at length, since the tort in question was obviously not unrelated to the performance of the contract between London Drugs and KNI. Furthermore, since it is very likely that the only time a plaintiff will need to allege an independent tort is when the company is unable to satisfy a judgment, it can be expected that the issue will not arise with great frequency. . . .

It may be helpful to set out an appropriate approach to cases of this kind. The first question to be resolved is whether the tort alleged against the employee is an independent tort or a tort related to a contract between the employer and the plaintiff. In answering this question, it is legitimate to consider the scope of the contract, the nature of the employee's conduct and the nature of the plaintiff's interest. If the alleged tort is independent, the employee is liable to the plaintiff if the elements of the tort action are proved. The liability of the company to the plaintiff is determined under the ordinary rules applicable to cases of vicarious liability. If the tort is related to the contract, the next question to be resolved is whether any reliance by the plaintiff on the employee was reasonable. The question here is whether the plaintiff reasonably relied on the eventual legal responsibility of the defendants under the circumstances.

In this case, as I noted, the tort was related to the contract and any reliance by the plaintiff on Vanwinkel and Brassart was not reasonable.

■ QUESTIONS

1. Do you think the employees should have paid $33,955.41, $40 or nothing?

2. If you believe it should not be $33,955.41, would you prefer to resolve the question by extending the benefit of the exemption clause to the employees (as the majority did) or by adopting La Forest J's suggestion about vicarious liability?

NOTES

1. In England the employee could only take advantage of an exemption clause between his employer and the customer if he is specifically mentioned in the contract: see the Contracts (Rights of Third Parties) Act 1999. However the Law Commission has left open the possibility of the doctrine of 'vicarious immunity' being adopted in England. In its Report on Privity of Contract (No. 242) the Commission specifically states that the passing of the 1999 Act should not inhibit the courts from judicial development of third party rights, mentioning in particular the development of a form of vicarious immunity (see para. 5.10 of the Report).

2. The Privy Council has indicated that it may be willing to move in this direction. In *The Mahkutai* [1996] AC 650, Lord Goff considered whether the courts should follow *London Drugs* in moving to a fully-fledged exception to privity, but decided that the case before them was not a suitable vehicle for such a change.

## SECTION 3: THE COURSE OF EMPLOYMENT

An employer is liable for the torts of his employee only if the act is committed 'in the course of his employment'. This is one of the most litigated phrases in the English language, and it has many functions: for example in *Lister* v *Hesley Hall* (below) it was said that it was not necessary to refer to the use of the phrase in the Race Relations and Sex Discrimination Acts where a very wide interpretation has been adopted. Thus, it may mean something different for the purposes of vicarious liability than for other purposes, and one must bear in mind that its function is to limit the liability to those risks which can properly be seen as a function of the enterprise. The traditional test is to ask whether the act of the employee was merely an improper mode of doing what he was employed to do, but it is now clear that the overriding test is the degree of connection between the act and the employment (see *Lister* v *Hesley Hall*, below).

There are two basic issues: first, was the employee in the course of his employment as regards time and space; and, secondly, was what he was doing, or the way he was doing it, within his employment?

## A: Time and space

### Compton v McClure
Queen's Bench Division [1975] ICR 378

The first defendant, McClure, was late for work and, in an effort to 'clock in' in time, he drove onto the premises of his employer, the second defendants, too fast and negligently injured the claimant. Held: the employers were vicariously liable.

MAY J: Most of the decided cases on this issue are ones in which there was no question that the course of the employment prima facie existed, but where the issue was whether the servant or agent had gone outside the course of that employment, whether he had gone, as it is said, 'on a frolic of his own.' In the present case the question is whether the course of the employment had in fact started.

The facts of *Staton* v *National Coal Board* [1957] 1 WLR 893, were these. One of the National Coal Board's employees, having finished his week's work, was riding his bicycle across their premises in order to collect his wages from a part of those premises different from the part on which he worked. While he was doing so he knocked over and killed another employee of the National Coal Board. The question was whether the National Coal Board was liable vicariously for the negligence of the cyclist employee. It was contended on behalf of the National Coal Board that they were not liable because the course of that employee's employment had ceased when he had finished work: the fact that he was merely going to collect his wages was neither here nor there; that did not, as it were, keep the chain of the course of employment in existence. On behalf of the plaintiff it was asked, what could be more part of the course of a person's employment than collecting his wages? The employee was still on the National Coal Board's premises; he was merely going to collect his wages from a place also on those premises; it could not in those circumstances be said that the course of employment had ceased.

Finnemore J, in a long judgment in which he considered all the cases to which he had been referred, came to the conclusion that the course of employment had not ceased, that the chain had not been broken, and that accordingly the board was vicariously liable for the negligent cyclist. . . .

Mr Wolton, on the second defendants' behalf, also referred me to *Nottingham* v *Aldridge* [1971] 2 QB 739, a decision at first instance of Eveleigh J. However, I do not propose to deal with that case in any great detail because, once again, I think that its facts can equally easily be distinguished from the facts of the present case as can those in *Staton's* case. In *Nottingham* v *Aldridge* the relevant accident occurred on a Sunday/Monday night. One employee of the employers was driving another back to the town in which on the Monday both of them had to go to work in the course of their apprenticeships. The driver of the car in which the plaintiff apprentice was being driven was entitled to claim from his employers petrol and mileage allowance for the journey he was making, and he was, as I have said, taking his fellow-apprentice back to the place at which the following morning they were both to do their work. Nevertheless the accident happened hours before they were due to re-start such work and on the public highway. It was held that the accident did not happen in the course of the driver's employment. . . .

Doing the best I can on the authorities to which I have been referred, I find myself driven to the conclusion that the least artificial place at which to draw the line in the circumstances of the present case is at the boundary of the factory premises; at the gates where employees coming in find that control by the employers starts; where the 5 mph speed limit begins; where there are security officers to see that the traffic is proceeding properly; where employees at this point are clearly coming to work—providing, of course, that that is the purpose for which they cross the boundary. I see the force of Mr Wolton's contrary argument, that at this time the employee is still using the roadway for his own purposes and not for his employers' purposes, but I do not think that it is straining language to say that in fact it is for the employers' purposes that an employee is on the former's premises when he is coming to work. Thus in cases such as the present, unless the circumstances of the entry to the employers' premises are such as, for instance, to make it a frolic of the employee's own, or unless the purposes of the entry were, as Mr Wolton suggested, that he was merely coming back to collect a coat which he had left behind, then in my judgment the course of the employment prima facie begins and the conditions giving rise to vicarious liability are fulfilled when the employee comes onto his employers' premises in order to start the work that he is employed to do. For these reasons I have come to the conclusion in the present case that the second defendants must be held to be vicariously liable for the clear negligence of the first defendant and, accordingly, that there must be judgment for the plaintiff against both defendants for whatever sum I consider to be the appropriate award by way of damages.

■ QUESTION

What if McClure had been early for work by 30 minutes because he wanted to play cards before the shift started?

## B: The connection between the act and the employment

### *Lister* v *Hesley Hall*
House of Lords [2002] 1 AC 215; [2001] 2 WLR 1311; [2001] 2 All ER 769; [2001] UKHL 22

The claimants were residents at a school boarding house owned by the defendants. They employed a warden to supervise the boys but he sexually abused some of them. The claimants sued on the basis that the defendants were vicariously liable for the acts of their employee. Held, allowing the appeal, that the defendants were liable.

LORD STEYN:

*The perspective of principle*

**14** Vicarious liability is legal responsibility imposed on an employer, although he is himself free from blame, for a tort committed by his employee in the course of his employment. Fleming observed that this formula represented 'a compromise between two conflicting policies: on the one end, the social interest in furnishing an innocent tort victim with recourse against a financially responsible defendant; on the other, a hesitation to foist any undue burden on business enterprise': *The Law of Torts*, 9th ed. (1998), pp. 409–410.

**15** For nearly a century English judges have adopted Salmond's statement of the applicable test as correct. Salmond said that a wrongful act is deemed to be done by a 'servant' in the course of his employment if 'it is either (a) a wrongful act authorised by the master, or (b) a wrongful and unauthorised *mode* of doing some act authorised by the master': *Salmond, Law of Torts*, 1st ed. (1907), p. 83; and *Salmond & Heuston on the Law of Torts*, 21st ed., p. 443. Situation (a) causes no problems. The difficulty arises in respect of cases under (b). Salmond did, however, offer an explanation which has sometimes been overlooked. He said (*Salmond on Torts*, 1st ed., pp. 83–84) that 'a master . . . is liable even for acts which he has not authorised, provided they are *so connected* with acts which he has authorised, that they may rightly *be regarded* as modes—although improper modes—of doing them' (my emphasis) . . .

**16** It is not necessary to embark on a detailed examination of the development of the modern principle of vicarious liability. But it is necessary to face up to the way in which the law of vicarious liability sometimes may embrace intentional wrongdoing by an employee. If one mechanically applies *Salmond's* test, the result might at first glance be thought to be that a bank is not liable to a customer where a bank employee defrauds a customer by giving him only half the foreign exchange which he paid for, the employee pocketing the difference. A preoccupation with conceptualistic reasoning may lead to the absurd conclusion that there can only be vicarious liability if the bank carries on business in defrauding its customers. Ideas divorced from reality have never held much attraction for judges steeped in the tradition that their task is to deliver principled but practical justice. How the courts set the law on a sensible course is a matter to which I now turn.

**17** It is easy to accept the idea that where an employee acts for the benefit of his employer, or intends to do so, that is strong evidence that he was acting in the course of his employment. But until the decision of the House of Lords in *Lloyd* v *Grace, Smith & Co.* [1912] AC 716 it was thought that vicarious liability could only be established if such requirements were satisfied. This was an overly restrictive view and hardly in tune with the needs of society. In *Lloyd* v *Grace, Smith & Co.* it was laid to rest by the House of Lords. A firm of solicitors were held liable for the dishonesty of their managing clerk who persuaded a client to transfer property to him and then disposed of it for his own advantage. The decisive factor was that the client had been invited by the firm to deal with their managing clerk. This decision was a breakthrough: it finally established that vicarious liability is not necessarily defeated if the employee acted for his own benefit. On the other hand, an intense focus on the connection between the nature of the employment and the tort of the employee became necessary.

. . .

**19** The classic example of vicarious liability for intentional wrongdoing is *Morris* v *C W Martin & Sons Ltd* [1966] 1 QB 716. A woman wanted her mink stole cleaned. With her permission it was delivered to the defendants for cleaning. An employee took charge of the fur and stole it. At first instance the judge held that the defendants were not liable because the theft was not committed in the course of employment. The Court of Appeal reversed the judge's decision and held the defendants liable. It is possible to read the case narrowly simply as a bailment case, the wrong being failure to redeliver. But two of the judgments are authority for the proposition that the employee converted the fur in the course of his employment. Diplock LJ observed, at pp. 736–737:

> If the principle laid down in *Lloyd* v *Grace, Smith & Co.* [1912] AC 716 is applied to the facts of the present case, the defendants cannot in my view escape liability for the conversion of the plaintiff's fur by their servant Morrissey. They accepted the fur as bailees for reward in order

to clean it. They put Morrissey as their agent in their place to clean the fur and to take charge of it while doing so. The manner in which he conducted himself in doing that work was to convert it. What he was doing, albeit dishonestly, he was doing in the scope or course of his employment in the technical sense of that infelicitous but time-honoured phrase. The defendants as his masters are responsible for his tortious act.

Salmon LJ held, at p. 738, that 'the defendants are liable for what amounted to negligence and conversion by their servant in the course of his employment'. The deciding factor was that the employee had been given custody of the fur. *Morris's* case has consistently been regarded as high authority on the principles of vicarious liability. *Atiyah, Vicarious Liability in the Law of Torts* (1967), p. 271 described it as 'a striking and valuable extension of the law of vicarious liability'. *Palmer on Bailment*, 2nd ed. (1991), pp. 424–425 treats *Morris's* case as an authority on vicarious liability beyond bailment. He states that 'if a television repairman steals a television he is called in to repair, his employers would be liable, for the loss occurred whilst he was performing one of the class of acts in respect of which their duty lay'. And that does not involve bailment. Moreover, in *Port Swettenham Authority* v *T W Wu & Co. (M) Sdn Bhd* [1979] AC 580 the Privy Council expressly approved *Morris's* case in respect of vicarious liability as explained by Diplock and Salmon LLJ.

**20** Our law no longer struggles with the concept of vicarious liability for intentional wrongdoing. Thus the decision of the House of Lords in *Racz* v *Home Office* [1994] 2 AC 45 is authority for the proposition that the Home Office may be vicariously liable for acts of police officers which amounted to misfeasance in public office—and hence for liability in tort involving bad faith. It remains, however, to consider how vicarious liability for intentional wrongdoing fits in with Salmond's formulation. The answer is that it does not cope ideally with such cases. It must, however, be remembered that the great tort writer did not attempt to enunciate precise propositions of law on vicarious liability. At most he propounded a broad test which deems as within the course of employment 'a wrongful and unauthorised mode of doing some *act* authorised by the master'. And he emphasised the connection between the authorised *acts* and the 'improper modes' of doing them. In reality it is simply a practical test serving as a dividing line between cases where it is or is not just to impose vicarious liability. The usefulness of the *Salmond* formulation is, however, crucially dependent on focusing on the right act of the employee. This point was explored in *Rose* v *Plenty* [1976] 1 WLR 141. The Court of Appeal held that a milkman who deliberately disobeyed his employers' order not to allow children to help on his rounds did not go beyond his course of employment in allowing a child to help him. The analysis in this decision shows how the pitfalls of terminology must be avoided. Scarman LJ said, at pp. 147–148:

> The servant was, of course, employed at the time of the accident to do a whole number of operations. He was certainly not employed to give the boy a lift, and if one confines one's analysis of the facts to the incident of injury to the plaintiff, then no doubt one would say that carrying the boy on the float—giving him a lift—was not in the course of the servant's employment. But in *Ilkiw* v *Samuels* [1983] 1 WLR 991 Diplock LJ indicated that the proper approach to the nature of the servant's employment is a broad one. He says, at p. 1004: 'As each of these nouns implies'—he is referring to the nouns used to describe course of employment, sphere, scope and so forth—'the matter must be looked at broadly, not dissecting the servant's task into its component activities—such as driving, loading, sheeting and the like—by asking: what was the job on which he was engaged for his employer? and answering that question as a jury would.'
>
> Applying those words to the employment of this servant, I think it is clear from the evidence that he was employed as a roundsman to drive his float round his round and to deliver milk, to collect empties and to obtain payment. That was his job . . . He chose to disregard the prohibition and to enlist the assistance of the plaintiff. As a matter of common sense, that does seem to me to be a mode, albeit a prohibited mode, of doing the job with which he was entrusted. Why was the plaintiff being carried on the float when the accident occurred? Because it was necessary to take him from point to point so that he could assist in delivering milk, collecting empties and, on occasions obtaining payment.

If this approach to the nature of employment is adopted, it is not necessary to ask the simplistic question whether in the cases under consideration the acts of sexual abuse were modes of doing authorised acts. It becomes possible to consider the question of vicarious liability on the basis that the employer undertook to care for the boys through the services of the warden and that there is a very close connection between the torts of the warden and his employment. After all, they were committed in the time and on the premises of the employers while the warden was also busy caring for the children.

. . .

### The application of the correct test

**27** My Lords, I have been greatly assisted by the luminous and illuminating judgments of the Canadian Supreme Court in *Bazley* v *Curry* 174 DLR (4th) 45 and *Jacobi* v *Griffiths* 174 DLR (4th) 71. Wherever such problems are considered in future in the common law world these judgments will be the starting point. On the other hand, it is unnecessary to express views on the full range of policy considerations examined in those decisions.

**28** Employing the traditional methodology of English law, I am satisfied that in the case of the appeals under consideration the evidence showed that the employers entrusted the care of the children in Axeholme House to the warden. The question is whether the warden's torts were so closely connected with his employment that it would be fair and just to hold the employers vicariously liable. On the facts of the case the answer is yes. After all, the sexual abuse was inextricably interwoven with the carrying out by the warden of his duties in Axeholme House. Matters of degree arise. But the present cases clearly fall on the side of vicarious liability.

LORD HOBHOUSE:

**59** The classic *Salmond* test for vicarious liability and scope of employment has two limbs. The first covers authorised acts which are tortious. These present no relevant problem and the present cases clearly do not fall within the first limb. The defendants did not authorise Mr Grain to abuse the children in his charge. The argument of the respondent (accepted by the Court of Appeal) is that Mr Grain's acts of abuse did not come within the second limb either: abusing children cannot properly be described as a mode of caring for children. The answer to this argument is provided by the analysis which I have set out in the preceding paragraphs. Whether or not some act comes within the scope of the servant's employment depends upon an identification of what duty the servant was employed by his employer to perform. . . . If the act of the servant which gives rise to the servant's liability to the plaintiff amounted to a failure by the servant to perform that duty, the act comes within 'the scope of his employment' and the employer is vicariously liable. If, on the other hand, the servant's employment merely gave the servant the opportunity to do what he did without more, there will be no vicarious liability, hence the use by Salmond and in the Scottish and some other authorities of the word 'connection' to indicate something which is not a casual coincidence but has the requisite relationship to the employment of the tortfeasor (servant) by his employer: *Kirby* v *National Coal Board* 1958 SC 514; *Williams* v *A & W Hemphill Ltd* 1966 SC(HL) 31.

**60** My Lords, the correct approach to answering the question whether the tortious act of the servant falls within or without the scope of the servant's employment for the purposes of the principle of vicarious liability is to ask what was the duty of the servant towards the plaintiff which was broken by the servant and what was the contractual duty of the servant towards his employer. The second limb of the classic *Salmond* test is a convenient rule of thumb which provides the answer in very many cases but does not represent the fundamental criterion which is the comparison of the duties respectively owed by the servant to the plaintiff and to his employer. Similarly, I do not believe that it is appropriate to follow the lead given by the Supreme Court of Canada in *Bazley* v *Curry* 174 DLR (4th) 45. The judgments contain a useful and impressive discussion of the social and economic reasons for having a principle of vicarious liability as part of the law of tort which extends to embrace acts of child abuse. But an exposition of the policy reasons for a rule (or even a description) is not the same as defining the criteria for its application. Legal rules have to have a greater degree of clarity and definition than is provided by simply explaining the reasons for the existence of the rule and the social need for it, instructive though that may be. In English law that clarity is provided by the application of the criterion to which I have referred derived from the English authorities.

**61** It follows that the reasoning of the Court of Appeal in *Trotman* v *North Yorkshire County Council* [1999] LGR 584 and the present cases cannot be supported. On the undisputed facts, the present cases satisfy the criteria for demonstrating the vicarious liability of the defendants for the acts of Mr Grain.

NOTES

1. In *Lister* Lord Millet said that the 'connection' test avoids 'the awkward reference to improper modes of carrying out the employee's duties' and that 'what is critical is that attention should be directed to the closeness of the connection between the employee's duties and his wrongdoing and not to verbal formulae'. Nevertheless, as Lord Hobhouse pointed out, it is still necessary to discover and define what it is that the employee is employed to do, and this can be highly ambiguous, depending as it does on such factors as what he *actually* does, what the contract says he can do and the effect of prohibitions. Further, the 'wrongful mode' test will still be useful in probing the connection between what he does and what he is authorized to do, although it will no longer be necessary to construct fanciful semantic arguments to align the wrongful act with the duties under the contract.

2. In *Bazley* v *Curry* [1999] 2 SCR 53, referred to above, a worker in a children's home abused a child. The Supreme Court of Canada held the home liable and McLachlin J said that one common feature was that the employer's enterprise had created the risk that produced the tortious act and that the concept of enterprise risk underlies the dishonest employee cases. Accordingly the court said that the fundamental question is whether the wrongful act is sufficiently related to conduct authorized by the employer to justify the imposition of vicarious liability, and that such liability is generally appropriate where there is sufficient connection between the creation or enhancement of risk and the wrong that accrues therefrom. In relation to intentional torts the court said that significant linking factors would include (a) the opportunity that the enterprise afforded the employee to abuse his or her power; (b) the extent to which the wrongful act may have furthered the employer's aims; (c) the extent to which the wrongful act was related to friction, confrontation or intimacy inherent in the employer's enterprise; (d) the extent of power conferred on the employee in relation to the victim; and (e) the vulnerability of potential victims to wrongful exercise of the employee's power. See also *Jacobs* v *Griffiths* [1999] 2 SCR 570.

3. The rule that the mere opportunity to commit the tort does not by itself bring about vicarious liability is illustrated by *Heasmans* v *Clarity Cleaning Co.* [1987] ICR 949 where the defendants provided office cleaning services and employed one Bonsu as a cleaner. He cleaned the claimants' offices, and while doing so made international telephone calls costing £1,411. His duties included cleaning the telephone. It was held that the defendants were not vicariously liable on the ground (per Purchas LJ) that merely providing the opportunity to commit a tort or a crime was not sufficient to render the employer liable, but rather a closer connection must exist between the nature of the employment and the act of the employee, or (per Nourse LJ) that using a telephone is not merely an unauthorized mode of cleaning it.

4. In *General Engineering Ltd* v *Kingston Corporation* [1989] ICR 88 firemen were engaged in an industrial dispute and conducting a 'go slow'. The claimant's property caught fire and the fire brigade took 17 rather than the normal three minutes to arrive. The Privy Council held that the local authority, as employer of the firefighters, was not liable, as the strike was a repudiation of the contract of employment. Does it matter that the repudiation had not been accepted by the employer? Why was driving slowly not merely regarded as a wrongful mode of driving fast? How closely was driving slowly connected to driving fast? Should this case be reconsidered?

### ■ QUESTIONS

1. What if in *Morris* v *Martin*, referred to in *Lister*, the coat had been stolen by (a) an accounts clerk, or (b) the person on the counter?

2. What if in *Clarity Cleaning* the phone had been used by the nightwatchman who was authorized to use the telephone to make emergency calls?

---

### *Jefferson* v *Derbyshire Farmers Ltd*
Court of Appeal [1921] 2 KB 281; 90 LJKB 1361; 124 LJ 775

Charles Booth, aged 16, was told by his employer to fill some tins with petrol from a drum. He turned on the tap on the drum and then lit a cigarette and threw the match on the floor. The garage where he was working, owned by the claimant, was destroyed. Held: dismissing the appeal, that the employers were vicariously liable.

WARRINGTON LJ: There is no doubt or question that the fire was caused by the negligent act of Booth. It would have been a negligent act to smoke at all in the immediate neighbourhood of the spirit. Still more was it a negligent act to light a match while the spirit was flowing from the drum. Horridge J decided in favour of the defendants on this point on the ground that what the boy did in lighting and throwing away the match was not in the scope of his employment. In one sense it was not; he was not employed to light the match and throw it away; but that is not the way in which to approach the question. It was in the scope of his employment to fill the tin with motor spirit from the drum. That work required special precautions. The act which caused the damage was an act done while he was engaged in this dangerous operation, and it was an improper act in the circumstances. That is to say, the boy was doing the work of his employers in an improper way and without taking reasonable precautions; and in that case the employers are liable. . . .

NOTE
Even skylarking may be within the course of employment. In *Harrison* v *Michelin Tyre Co.* [1985] ICR 696, Mr Smith in the proper course of his employment was wheeling a hand truck along a passageway when he deliberately, as a matter of ordinary horseplay, turned the truck a couple of inches and pushed the edge of it under a duckboard on which the claimant was standing. The claimant fell and was injured. It was held that the employer was vicariously liable. Does this follow from the principle in *Jefferson* above? Was this a risk properly attributable to the enterprise?

---

### *Mattis* v *Pollock*
Court of Appeal [2003] 1 WLR 2158; [2003] ICR 1335; [2004] 4 All ER 85; [2003] EWCA Civ 887

The claimant was stabbed by one Cranston who was employed as a 'bouncer' at the defendant's club. On 31 July 1998 the claimant entered the club with friends. Cranston was involved in a fight with other customers, and the claimant intervened and Cranston was forced to flee. He left the club and went home but then returned to the club intent on revenge, and outside the club he stabbed the claimant. Held: the defendant was vicariously liable for the torts of the bouncer.

JUDGE LJ:
   **19** The essential principle we derive from the reasoning in *Lister* v *Hesley Hall* [2002] AC 215 and *Dubai Aluminium* v *Salaam* [2003] 2 AC 366 is that Mr Pollock's vicarious liability to Mr Mattis for Cranston's attack requires a deceptively simple question to be answered. Approaching the matter broadly, was the assault 'so closely connected' with what Mr Pollock authorised or expected of

Cranston in the performance of his employment as doorman at his nightclub, that it would be fair and just to conclude that Mr Pollock is vicariously liable for the damage Mr Mattis sustained when Crantson stabbed him.

**20** In answering this question, we have borne in mind the further clarification of several important features of the principles relating to vicarious liability, conveniently summarised by Lord Millett in *Dubai Aluminium* at paragraph 121. It is

> no answer to a claim against the employer to say that the employee was guilty of intentional wrong-doing, or that his act was not merely cautious but criminal, or that he was acting exclusively for his own benefit, or that he was acting contrary to express instructions, or that his conduct was the very negation of his employer's duty . . . vicarious liability is not necessarily defeated if the employee acted for his own benefit.

Moreover, as Lord Millett explained, vicarious liability may arise even if the act of the employee is 'an independent act in itself', and, at paragraph 128, he underlined that 'the mere fact that he was acting dishonestly or for his own benefit is seldom likely to be sufficient' to show that an employee was not acting in the course of his employment. *Lister* itself demonstrated the heresy of the proposition that an employer cannot be vicariously liable for an independent act of 'self indulgence or self gratification' by his employee.

**21** Mr Paul Rose QC, for the appellant, drew attention to the decision of the Supreme Court of Canada in *Bazley* v *Curry* [1999] 174 DLR (4th) 45. When considering a claim against an employer based on a tort deliberately committed by an employee, a number of distinct factors may be relevant. These include:

(a) The opportunity that the enterprise afforded the employee to abuse his or her power;
(b) The extent to which the wrongful act may have furthered the employer's aims (and hence be more likely to have been committed by the employee);
(c) The extent to which the wrongful act was related to friction, confrontation or intimacy inherent in the employer's enterprise;
(d) The extent of the power conferred on the employee in relation to the victim;
(e) The vulnerability of potential victims to wrongful exercise of the employee's power.

**23** While we acknowledge the value of this guidance, and in the present context, paragraph (b) and (c) in particular, the list is not, and is expressly stated not to be either complete or conclusive. . . .

**24** In reviewing some of the earlier authorities in which vicarious liability was said to arise from violent assaults committed by an employee, we do not intend to give the impression that such cases raise different issues of principle, distinct from cases where an employee's criminal behaviour takes a non-violent form. Nevertheless, this group of cases itself serves to demonstrate the fact specific nature of the enquiry. Thus, even where an employee behaves violently towards a fellow employee, while at work, that is, at his employer's premises and during working hours, the claim against the employer for vicarious liability may nevertheless fall (see *Bazley* v *Curry*). Equally, such liability may nevertheless be established for an assault committed outside the employer's premises by an individual whose duties are normally expected to be performed within the premises (*Vasey* v *Surrey Free Inns plc* [1995] PIQR 373), or indeed, when the assault takes place in the victim's own home (*Dyer* v *Munday* [1895] 1QB 742, a decision of the Court of Appeal which has perhaps attracted rather less attention than it merited). These examples underline the importance of focusing on the individual circumstances of the case under consideration.

**25** In an article entitled, 'Liability for an Employee's Assault' (F.D. Rose, 40 Modern Law Review [1977] at 420), after considering all the relevant authorities, the writer suggested:

> Courts within the British Commonwealth have demonstrated a persistent reluctance to hold that an employee's assault has been committed within the course of his employment so as to make his employer vicariously liable for the tort.

Mr F.D. Rose identified a number of different circumstances in which an employer escaped liability to the victim for an assault by his employee. These were summarised as, and Mr Browne would seek to rely on:

A quarrelsome drunk threatened with ejection from a bar (*Griggs* v *Southside Hotel Co*: see also *Deatons PTY Ltd* v *Flew* [1949] 79 CLR 370); a customer threatening to report a garageman's conduct in the performance of his duties to his employers (*Warren* v *Henlys Ltd* [1948] 2 AER 935); an aggrieved customer whom he had wrongly accused of not paying his bill (*Fontin* v *Katapodis* [1962] 108 CLR 177); a patron whom he had ejected from a dance hall in the course of his employment, and whom he wrongly suspected of assaulting him during the ejection (*Daniels* v *Whetstone Entertainments Ltd* [1962] 2 Lloyd's Rep 1); a customer who became aggressive subsequently to the employee's attempt to defraud her during a car sale (*K* v *Ritchie Motors Ltd* [1972] 34 DLR (3rd) 141); and a passenger complaining of his manner during the performance of his duties as a bus conductor (*Kepple Bus Co* v *Ahmad* [1974] 1 WLR 1082).

The writer's avowed intention was

to call for a more liberal approach in applying the traditional tests of vicarious liability and a greater readiness to hold the employer liable for assaults arising out of circumstances connected with his servant's employment, especially where the trouble arises out of the latter's conduct in the performance of his duties.

From the authorities Mr F.D. Rose drew a distinction between assaults committed by employees who were authorised to use violence in the course of their employment, and those who were not. He pointed out that the duties of some employees might involve the risk 'of an assault being committed during the discharge of his duties', adding that in such a case 'the character of the employee will be important.' We acknowledge the validity of the distinction at the time when it was drawn, and, following the decisions in *Lister* and *Dubai Aluminium*, it is clear that where an employee is expected to use violence while carrying out his duties, the likelihood of establishing that an act of violence fell within the broad scope of his employment is greater than it would be if he were not.

**30** Cranston was indeed employed by Mr Pollock to keep order and discipline at the nightclub. That is what bouncers are employed to do. Moreover, however, he was encouraged and expected to perform his duties in an aggressive and intimidatory manner, which included physical man-handling of customers. In our judgment this aspect of the evidence was not sufficiently addressed by Judge Seymour. He suggested that the evidence went no further than a single incident of inappropriate violence (on 18 July) which would not have justified immediate dismissal. Whether, taking Cranston's behaviour as a whole, it would have been appropriate to dismiss him, is a moot point. The reality was that Mr Pollock should not have been employing Cranston at all, and certainly should not have been encouraging him to perform his duties as he did. It was not perhaps anticipated that Cranston's behaviour would be counter-productive, and that by way of self-defence, and indeed revenge, his behaviour would provoke a violent response. That is because the customers with whom he tangled were supposed to be intimidated, and to go quietly. The whole point of any physical confrontation with Mr Pollock's customers in the nightclub, whether engineered by Cranston or not, was that he should win it.

NOTES

1. It may have been significant here that the bouncer was employed to intimidate customers and indeed to be violent towards them if necessary. Although his motives were personal and his reaction excessive, nevertheless the use of violence was the kind of thing his employer condoned. Also it seems that although Cranston had gone home and then returned, he was at all times still within his working hours. Would it have been different if the attack had taken place the following afternoon?

2. The approach to the problem of 'personal' acts of employees has varied, and is exemplified by the 'barmaid' cases mentioned above in *Mattis*. In *Deatons* v *Flew* (1949) 79 CLR 370, referred to above, a barmaid threw a glass of beer and then the glass at the claimant, allegedly because the claimant had struck her. Her employer was held not liable as the response was a personal and independent act of the barmaid. See also *Griggs* v *Southside Hotel* [1947] 4 DLR 49. In *Petterson* v *Royal Oak Hotel* [1948] NZLR 136 a barman refused a drink to a customer, who thereupon threw a glass at the barman. The barman picked up a piece of the broken glass and

threw it at the customer, but a piece of the glass struck a bystander in the eye. It was held that the barman's employer was vicariously liable, as he was engaged in an improper mode of keeping order. Who should pay for the torts of irascible (or provoked) barmen?

3. The traditional distinction between an improper mode of doing an authorized thing and doing something you are not employed to do at all is illustrated by the following two cases. In *Limpus* v *London General Omnibus Company* a bus driver deliberately obstructed a rival bus, despite being prohibited from doing so. (Willis J pointed out that 'He was employed not only to drive the omnibus, . . . but also to get as much money as he could for his master and to do it in rivalry with other omnibuses on the road'.)

The case can be explained by saying that driving recklessly is merely a wrongful mode of driving, i.e. an unauthorized mode of doing an authorized thing. In *Beard* v *London General Omnibus Co.* [1900] 2 QB 530, a bus conductor turned a bus round negligently and injured somebody. It was held that the employer was not liable, as driving a bus is not what a conductor is employed to do.

## SECTION 4: LIABILITY FOR INDEPENDENT CONTRACTORS

The principle whereby one person may be liable for the acts of another is not limited to the relationship of employer and employee, but outside that category the law is vague and undeveloped. As to the engagement of independent contractors, the rule is that the 'employer' may be liable if he has himself been negligent, for example in selecting the contractor, or if he has authorized the tort or if the law imposes upon him a 'non-delegable' duty of care, as in the case of inherently hazardous activities.

There is probably no liability for a mere agent, unless the degree of control is sufficient to make him both an agent and a 'servant' at the same time. However, there may be cases where a person is engaged in an activity for the mutual benefit of himself and another whereby that other is held responsible.

## A: Independent contractors

### *Salsbury* v *Woodland*
Court of Appeal [1970] 1 QB 324; [1969] 3 All ER 863; [1969] 3 WLR 29

Mr Woodland wanted a hawthorn tree cut down. The tree was 25 feet high and stood 28 feet from the road, and running across the garden diagonally was a pair of telephone wires. Mr Woodland engaged Terence Coombe to cut the tree down and he did so negligently. The tree hit the telephone wires which landed in the roadway. The claimant intended to coil up the wires, but on seeing the third defendant, Mr Waugh, approaching too fast in his Morris Cooper, he flung himself to the ground to avoid being hit by the wires (which would have whipped around on being struck by the car). The claimant had a tumour on his spine and the falling to the ground dislodged this and caused damage to the claimant. Held: allowing the appeal by Mr Woodland, that he was not liable for the negligence of his independent contractor. (Note: the driver was held partly responsible as he was driving too fast.)

WIDGERY LJ: It is trite law that an employer who employs an independent contractor is not vicariously responsible for the negligence of that contractor. He is not able to control the way in which the independent contractor does the work, and the vicarious obligation of a master for the negligence of his servant does not arise under the relationship of employer and independent contractor. I think that it is entirely accepted that those cases—and there are some—in which an employer has been held liable for injury done by the negligence of an independent contractor are in truth cases where the employer owes a direct duty to the person injured, a duty which he cannot delegate to the contractor on his behalf. The whole question here is whether the occupier is to be judged by the general rule, which would result in no liability, or whether he comes within one of the somewhat special exceptions—cases in which a direct duty to see that care is taken rests upon the employer throughout the operation.

This is clear from authority; and for convenience I take from *Salmond on Torts*, 14th ed. (1965), p. 687, this statement of principle:

> One thing can, however, be said with confidence: the mere fact that the work entrusted to the contractor is of a character which may cause damage to others unless precautions are taken is not sufficient to impose liability on the employer. There are few operations entrusted to an agent which are not capable, if due precautions are not observed, of being sources of danger and mischief to others; and if the principal was responsible for this reason alone, the distinction between servants and independent contractors would be practically eliminated from the law.

I am satisfied that that statement is supported by authority, and I adopt it for the purposes of this judgment. . . .

In truth, according to the authorities there are a number of well-determined classes of case in which this direct and primary duty upon an employer to see that care is taken exists. Two such classes are directly relevant for consideration in the present case. The first class concerns what have sometimes been described as 'extra-hazardous acts'—acts commissioned by an employer which are so hazardous in their character that the law has thought it proper to impose this direct obligation on the employer to see that care is taken. An example of such a case is *Honeywill & Stein Ltd* v *Larkin Bros (London's Commercial Photographers) Ltd* [1934] 1 KB 191. Other cases which one finds in the books are cases where the activity commissioned by the employer is the keeping of dangerous things within the rule in *Rylands* v *Fletcher* (1868) LR 3 HL 330 and where liability is not dependent on negligence at all.

I do not propose to add to the wealth of authority on this topic by attempting further to define the meaning of 'extra-hazardous acts'; but I am confident that the act commissioned in the present case cannot come within that category. The act commissioned in the present case, if done with ordinary elementary caution by skilled men, presented no hazard to anyone at all.

The second class of case, which is relevant for consideration, concerns dangers created in a highway. There are a number of cases on this branch of the law, a good example of which is *Holliday* v *National Telephone Co.* [1899] 2 QB 392. These, on analysis, will all be found to be cases where work was being done in a highway and was work of a character which would have been a nuisance unless authorised by statute. It will be found in all these cases that the statutory powers under which the employer commissioned the work were statutory powers which left upon the employer a duty to see that due care was taken in the carrying out of the work, for the protection of those who passed on the highway. In accordance with principle, an employer subject to such a direct and personal duty cannot excuse himself, if things go wrong, merely because the direct cause of the injury was the act of the independent contractor.

This again is not a case in that class. It is not a case in that class because in the instant case no question of doing work in the highway, which might amount to a nuisance if due care was not taken, arises. In my judgment, the present case is clearly outside the well defined limit of the second class to which I have referred. Mr Bax, accordingly, invited us to say that there is a third class into which the instant case precisely falls, and he suggested that the third class comprised those cases where an employer commissions work to be done *near* a highway in circumstances in which, if due care is not taken, injury to passers-by on the highway may be caused. If that be a third class of case to which the principle of liability of the employer applies, no doubt the present case would come within that description. The question is, is there such a third class?

Reliance was placed primarily on three authorities. . . .

The second case relied upon was *Tarry* v *Ashton* (1876) 1 QBD 314. That was a case where a building adjoining the highway had attached to it a heavy lamp, which was suspended over the footway and which was liable to be a source of injury to passers-by if allowed to fall into disrepair. It fell into disrepair, and injury was caused. The defendant sought to excuse himself by saying that he had employed a competent independent contractor to put the lamp into good repair and that the cause of the injury was the fault of the independent contractor. Mr Bax argued that that case illustrated the special sympathy with which the law regards passers-by on the highway. He said that it demonstrated that the law has always been inclined to give special protection to persons in that category and so supported his argument that any action adjacent to the highway might be subject to special rights. But, in my judgment, that is not so. *Tarry* v *Ashton* seems to me to be a perfectly ordinary and straightforward example of a case where the employer was under a positive and continuing duty to see that the lamp was kept in repair. That duty was imposed upon him before the contractor came and after the contractor had gone; and on the principle that such a duty cannot be delegated the responsibility of the employer in that case seems to me to be fully demonstrated. I cannot find that it produces on a side-wind, as it were, anything in support of Mr Bax's contention.

NOTES

1. An example where a person was liable on the basis of extra-hazardous activities is *Honeywill & Stein Ltd* v *Larkin* [1934] 1 KB 191, where the claimants engaged the defendants, Larkin Brothers, to take photographs of the interior of the cinema. In those days this involved igniting magnesium powder in a metal tray. The defendants did this some four feet from a curtain, which caught fire. In an action in which the question arose whether the claimants would have been liable to the cinema owners, it was held they would. Slesser LJ referred to 'acts which in their very nature involve in the eyes of the law special danger to others'. The difficulty is that the taking of the photograph would have been quite safe if it had not been done negligently. What does extra-hazardous mean? Does it mean a greater risk of damage or a risk of greater damage, or both?

2. It is sometimes said that under this head there can be no liability on the 'employer' for acts of 'collateral' negligence by the contractor—for example, if the camera tripod in *Honeywill* had been placed so as to render it likely that someone would trip over it. In *Salsbury* v *Woodland* (above) Sachs LJ said:

I derived no assistance at all from any distinction between 'collateral and casual' negligence and other negligence. Such a distinction provides too many difficulties for me to accept without question, unless it simply means that one must ascertain exactly what was the occupier's duty and then treat any act that is not part of that duty as giving rise to no liability on his part.

---

## B: Mutual benefit

### *Ormrod* v *Crosville Motor Services: Murphie, Third Party*
[1953] 1 WLR 1120; [1953] 2 All ER 5753

Mr Murphie intended to take part in the Monte Carlo rally and then go on holiday with Mr and Mrs Ormrod. The arrangement was that the Ormrods would drive Murphie's car to Monte Carlo, which would then be used for the joint holiday (Murphie was using a different car for the rally). Mr Ormrod drove off but soon ran into a Crosville bus and Mrs Ormrod was injured. Held: dismissing the appeal, that Murphie, the owner of the car, was liable for the negligent driving of Mr Ormrod.

DENNING LJ: It has often been supposed that the owner of a vehicle is only liable for the negligence of the driver if that driver is his servant acting in the course of his employment. But that is not correct. The owner is also liable if the driver is his agent, that is to say, if the driver is, with the owner's consent, driving the car on the owner's business or for the owner's purposes. In the present case the driver was, by mutual arrangement, driving the car partly for his own purposes and partly for the owner's purposes. The owner wanted the car taken to Monte Carlo, and the driver himself wanted to go with his wife to Monte Carlo, and he intended to visit friends in Normandy on the way. On this account he started two or three days earlier than he would have done if he had been going solely for the owner's purposes. Mr Scholefield Allen says that this should exempt the owner from liability for the driver's negligence, because the accident might never have happened if he had started later. He says that the owner would not have been liable for any negligence of the driver on the trip from Calais to Normandy and should not be liable for negligence on the early start. I do not think that this argument is correct. The law puts an especial responsibility on the owner of a vehicle who allows it out on to the road in charge of someone else, no matter whether it is his servant, his friend, or anyone else. If it is being used wholly or partly on the owner's business or for the owner's purposes, then the owner is liable for any negligence on the part of the driver. The owner only escapes liability when he lends it out or hires it out to a third person to be used for purposes in which the owner has no interest or concern: see *Hewitt* v *Bonvin* [1940] 1 KB 188. That is not this case. The trip to Monte Carlo must be considered as a whole, including the proposed excursion to Normandy, and, as such, it was undertaken with the owner's consent for the purposes of both of them, and the owner is liable for any negligence of the driver in the course of it. . . .

NOTES

1. At that time (but no longer) a wife could not sue her husband. Accordingly Crosville could not join Mr Ormrod as co-defendant and chose to join Mr Murphie instead. In the past this principle has mainly been used in cases where a car driver is uninsured. The existence of the Motor Insurers Bureau and changes in the rules of insurance law have meant that this principle is not often needed to provide compensation of victims of uninsured drivers, except perhaps where compulsory insurance is not required.

2. The 'agency' referred to in *Ormrod* is not a true agency as in the law of contract, but is based on the delegation of a task or duty. In *Morgans* v *Launchbury* [1972] 2 All ER 606 the House of Lords said that it was a general principle and not confined to cars, but in *Scott* v *Davis* (2000) 175 ALR 217 the High Court of Australia thought the principle anomalous being based neither on agency nor on vicarious liability and they refused to extend the principle beyond motor vehicles. (In that case the defendant had requested a pilot to take the claimants for a flight: held, he was not liable for the pilot's negligence.)

3. That the mutual benefit argument is still alive, and perhaps capable of extension, is illustrated by the strange case of *Moynihan* v *Moynihan* [1975] IR 192, where the defendant grandmother invited the claimant, aged 2, her parents and her aunt for a meal. After the meal the aunt made a pot of tea and, covering it with a brightly coloured tea cosy, placed it on the table. The claimant upset the teapot and was scalded. The court held that the grandmother was liable for the negligence of the aunt on the ground that the negligence of the aunt was not the casual negligence of a fellow guest, but rather the negligence of a person engaged in one of the duties of the grandmother's household. The grandmother's power of control was not dependent on the relationship of mother and daughter, but upon the relationship of the head of a household with a person to whom some of the duties of the head of the household had been delegated by that head. Do you agree? Was the aunt an independent contractor, or an agent in a mutually beneficial enterprise? If the former, was the teapot extra-hazardous? If the latter, would it have mattered if either the aunt or the grandmother did not intend to have any tea? Should the head of a household be liable for acts committed by others in the running of the household? Who do you think was insured in *Moynihan*?

# 16

## Breach of Statutory Duty

The idea behind the form of liability discussed in this chapter is that there may be cases where a statute renders a certain activity a crime, and the law imposes an additional civil liability towards a person harmed by the act. Some statutes state this directly: for example, the Consumer Protection Act 1987 makes it an offence to supply goods, such as flammable nightdresses, which contravene the safety regulations, and s. 41 expressly states that a person contravening the regulations will also be liable to pay compensation to a person harmed by the breach. On the other hand, the Guard Dogs Act 1975 (which makes it an offence to have a guard dog free to roam about the premises or not under the control of a handler), in s. 5 states that no civil liability will arise from a breach of the Act. Most statutes, however, make no mention of potential civil liability, but nevertheless liability may be imposed if the court believes that Parliament impliedly intended there to be a remedy. (In 1969 the Law Commission, in Report No. 21 on the Interpretation of Statutes, recommended that rather than courts trying to answer this impossible question, it should be presumed, unless stated to the contrary, that any statute which imposes a duty is intended to give rise to a civil remedy. This was never implemented.)

Not only are there difficulties about when a civil duty will be spelt out of a criminal or regulatory statute, but there are also problems about the role and function of the tort of statutory duty, and, as will be seen, different jurisdictions in the Common Law have taken different views on this. The main importance of the tort lies in its application to breaches of the factories regulations, but how useful it is outside this sphere is a matter of current debate, for the decisions are rather haphazard.

For thorough discussion of the tort outside the standard textbooks, see K. M. Stanton, *Breach of Statutory Duty in Tort* (1985) and Buckley, 'Liability in Tort for Breach of Statutory Duty' (1984) 100 LQR 204.

---

### *Phillips* v *Britannia Hygienic Laundry*
Court of Appeal [1923] 2 KB 832

The axle of a lorry owned by the defendants was defective and broke. A wheel came off and damaged the claimant's van. The Motor Cars (Use and Construction) Order 1904 stated that 'the motor car and all the fittings thereof shall be in such a condition as not to cause, or to be likely to cause, danger to any person in the motor car or on any highway'. Held: dismissing the appeal, that the regulations did not give rise to any civil liability.

ATKIN LJ: . . . This is an important question, and I have felt some doubt upon it, because it is clear that these regulations are in part designed to promote the safety of the public using highways. The question is whether they were intended to be enforced only by the special penalty attached to them in the Act. In my opinion, when an Act imposes a duty of commission or omission, the question whether a person aggrieved by a breach of the duty has a right of action depends on the intention of the Act. Was it intended to make the duty one which was owed to the party aggrieved as well as to the State, or was it a public duty only? That depends on the construction of the Act and the circumstances in which it was made and to which it relates. One question to be considered is, does the Act contain reference to a remedy for breach of it? Prima facie if it does that is the only remedy. But that is not conclusive. The intention as disclosed by its scope and wording must still be regarded, and it may still be that, though the statute creates the duty and provides a penalty, the duty is nevertheless owed to individuals. Instances of this are *Groves* v *Lord Wimborne* [1898] 2 QB 402, and *Britannic Merthyr Coal Co.* v *David* [1910] AC 74. To my mind, and in this respect I differ from McCardie J, the question is not to be solved by considering whether or not the person aggrieved can bring himself within some special class of the community or whether he is some designated individual. The duty may be of such paramount importance that it is owed to all the public. It would be strange if a less important duty, which is owed to a section of the public, may be enforced by an action, while a more important duty owed to the public at large cannot. The right of action does not depend on whether a statutory commandment or prohibition is pronounced for the benefit of the public or for the benefit of a class. It may be conferred on any one who can bring himself within the benefit of the Act, including one who cannot be otherwise specified than as a person using the highway. Therefore I think McCardie J is applying too strict a test when he says ([1923] 1 KB 547): 'The Motor Car Acts and Regulations were not enacted for the benefit of any particular class of folk. They are provisions for the benefit of the whole public, whether pedestrians or vehicle users, whether aliens or British citizens, and whether working or walking or standing upon the highway.' Kelly CB in stating the argument for the defendant in *Gorris* v *Scott* LR 9 Ex 125, refers to the obligation imposed upon railway companies by s. 47 of the Railways Clauses Consolidation Act, 1845, to erect gates across public carriage roads crossed by the railway on the level, and to keep the gates closed except when the crossing is being actually and properly used, under the penalty of 40s. for every default. It was never doubted that if a member of the public crossing the railway were injured by the railway company's breach of duty, either in not erecting a gate or in not keeping it closed, he would have a right of action. Therefore the question is whether these regulations, viewed in the circumstances in which they were made and to which they relate, were intended to impose a duty which is a public duty only or whether they were intended, in addition to the public duty, to impose a duty enforceable by an individual aggrieved. I have come to the conclusion that the duty they were intended to impose was not a duty enforceable by individuals injured, but a public duty only, the sole remedy for which is the remedy provided by way of a fine. They impose obligations of various kinds, some are concerned more with the maintenance of the highway than with the safety of passengers; and they are of varying degrees of importance; yet for breach of any regulation a fine not exceeding 10*l*. is the penalty. It is not likely that the Legislature, in empowering a department to make regulations for the use and construction of motor cars, permitted the department to impose new duties in favour of individuals and new causes of action for breach of them in addition to the obligations already well provided for and regulated by the common law of those who bring vehicles upon highways. In particular it is not likely that the Legislature intended by these means to impose on the owners of vehicles an absolute obligation to have them roadworthy in all events even in the absence of negligence. . . .

NOTES
1. This seems a surprising decision, as it may be thought that the purpose of the regulation was to protect other road users; but at the time the control of motor cars was a highly contentious and political issue, and it may be that the court felt inhibited from entering such an arena. A more important reason may have been that compulsory insurance had not yet been introduced. However, this rule is still followed. For example, in *Exel Logistics* v *Curran* [2004] EWCA Civ 1249, it was held that no statutory liability arose where one cause of an accident

was that two tyres of a Land Rover were seriously underinflated contrary to the Road Vehicles (Construction and Use) Regulations 1986.

2. An earlier case, where liability was imposed for a breach of the Factory and Workshop Act 1878 (in fact for failing to fence machinery), was *Groves* v *Lord Wimborne* [1898] 2 QB 402, where it was said that the Act was clearly passed for the protection of workmen. A. L. Smith LJ said that it was material to ask whether the Act was passed for the protection of a particular class of persons or in the interests of the public at large. This is not to say that a statute creating general public rights cannot give rise to civil liability, but only that it will be *easier* to show that the aim of the statute was to provide a right of action where a particular group is selected.

3. The existence of a criminal penalty may militate against civil liability as in *Todd* v *Adams and Chope (The Maragetha Maria)* [2002] 2 Lloyds Rep 293, where the dependants of drowned fishermen failed in their claim for liability for a breach of the rules establishing stability criteria for fishing vessels. A further factor was that the Minister had a wide power to exempt vessels from the rules. Does this undermine the factory cases?

4. In *R* v *Deputy Governor of Parkhurst, ex parte Hague* [1991] 3 WLR 341, Lord Jauncey said, in relation to breach of statutory duty, that:

> it must always be a matter for consideration whether the legislature intended that private law rights of action should be conferred upon individuals in respect of breaches of the relevant statutory provision. The fact that a particular provision was intended to protect certain individuals is not of itself sufficient to confer private law rights of action upon them. Something more is required to show that the legislature intended such conferment.

The 'more' that is required is the intention of the legislature to provide a right of action, and according to Lord Bridge in the same case that is a matter of statutory construction like any other. But how can that be when the problem arises only because the statute says nothing about the issue? On this approach see further the *Saskatchewan Wheat Pool* case, below. In *Hague* itself it was held that the Prison Rules were administrative only and gave rise to no right of action (the claimant had claimed that segregation in breach of the Prison Rules gave him an action in private law).

5. In *The Queen* v *Saskatchewan Wheat Pool* [1983] 1 SCR 205 the Supreme Court of Canada rejected the British position on breach of statutory duty, saying that 'the legislature has imposed a penalty on a strictly admonitory basis and there seems little justification to add civil liability when such liability would tend to produce liability without fault'. It was said that the tort should be subsumed within negligence, although the statutory formulation of the duty may afford a specific and useful standard of reasonable conduct. For a discussion of the basis of the tort see Matthews (1984) 4 Oxf JLS 429 and Buckley 100 LQR 204.

---

### *Lonrho* v *Shell Petroleum (No. 2)*
House of Lords [1982] AC 173; [1981] 3 WLR 33; [1981] 2 All ER 456

After the unilateral declaration of independence by the government of Southern Rhodesia, Parliament passed the Southern Rhodesia (Petroleum) Order 1965, which prohibited the supply of oil to Southern Rhodesia. Lonrho owned a pipeline from Mozambique to Rhodesia, which was thereupon closed. They alleged that the defendants and others had maintained the supply of oil to Rhodesia, thereby prolonging the period of unconstitutional government and lengthening the period of closure of the claimant's pipeline. One of the arguments related to liability for the breach of statutory duty arising from the order. Held: dismissing the appeal, that the order did not give rise to civil liability.

LORD DIPLOCK: The sanctions Order thus creates a statutory prohibition upon the doing of certain classes of acts and provides the means of enforcing the prohibition by prosecution for a criminal offence which is subject to heavy penalties including imprisonment. So one starts with the presumption laid down originally by Lord Tenterden CJ in *Doe d. Murray* v *Bridges* (1831) 1 B & Ad 847, 859, where he spoke of the 'general rule' that 'where an Act creates an obligation, and enforces the performance in a specified manner . . . that performance cannot be enforced in any other manner'— a statement that has frequently been cited with approval ever since, including on several occasions in speeches in this House. Where the only manner of enforcing performance for which the Act provides is prosecution for the criminal offence of failure to perform the statutory obligation or for contravening the statutory prohibition which the Act creates, there are two classes of exception to this general rule.

The first is where upon the true construction of the Act it is apparent that the obligation or prohibition was imposed for the benefit or protection of a particular class of individuals, as in the case of the Factories Acts and similar legislation. As Lord Kinnear put it in *Butler (or Black)* v *Fife Coal Co. Ltd* [1912] AC 149, 165, in the case of such a statute:

> There is no reasonable ground for maintaining that a proceeding by way of penalty is the only remedy allowed by the statute. . . . We are to consider the scope and purpose of the statute and in particular for whose benefit it is intended. Now the object of the present statute is plain. It was intended to compel mine owners to make due provision for the safety of the men working in their mines, and the persons for whose benefit all these rules are to be enforced are the persons exposed to danger. But when a duty of this kind is imposed for the benefit of particular persons there arises at common law a correlative right in those persons who may be injured by its contravention.

The second exception is where the statute creates a public right (i.e. a right to be enjoyed by all those of Her Majesty's subjects who wish to avail themselves of it) and a particular member of the public suffers what Brett J in *Benjamin* v *Storr* (1874) LR 9 CP 400, 407, described as 'particular, direct, and substantial' damage 'other and different from that which was common to all the rest of the public.' Most of the authorities about this second exception deal not with public rights created by statute but with public rights existing at common law, particularly in respect of use of highways. *Boyce* v *Paddington Borough Council* [1903] 1 Ch 109 is one of the comparatively few cases about a right conferred upon the general public by statute. It is in relation to that class of statute only that Buckley J's oft-cited statement at p. 114 as to the two cases in which a plaintiff, without joining the Attorney-General, could himself sue in private law for interference with that public right, must be understood. The two cases he said were: . . . first, where the interference with the public right is such as that some private right of his is at the same time interfered with . . . and, secondly, where no private right is interfered with, but the plaintiff, in respect of his public right, suffers special damage peculiar to himself from the interference with the public right.' The first case would not appear to depend upon the existence of a public right in addition to the private one; while to come within the second case at all it has first to be shown that the statute, having regard to its scope and language, does fall within that class of statutes which creates a legal right to be enjoyed by all of Her Majesty's subjects who wish to avail themselves of it. A mere prohibition upon members of the public generally from doing what it would otherwise be lawful for them to do, is not enough.

In agreement with all those present and former members of the judiciary who have considered the matter I can see no ground on which contraventions by Shell and BP of the sanctions Order though not amounting to any breach of their contract with Lonrho, nevertheless constituted a tort for which Lonrho could recover in a civil suit any loss caused to them by such contraventions.

## NOTES

1. In *X* v *Bedfordshire C.C.* [1995] 2 AC 633 (see Chapter 6), various claimants claimed that certain local authorities had failed in their statutory obligation as regards (a) the welfare of children and (b) the provision of special educational needs. It was said that usually a breach of statutory duty does not give rise to a private right of action, but may do so if as a matter of construction it can be shown that the statute was for the protection of a limited class of

the public and that impliedly a private right of action was intended. If the statute does not provide any means of enforcing the duty that will tend to suggest a private right, but the provision of means of enforcement does not necessarily rule out a private right, as the factory cases show. It was also said that usually regulatory or welfare legislation which involves the exercise of administrative discretion would not give rise to a private right, and the actions in this case were struck out.

2. A further example of welfare legislation not providing a private right is *O'Rourke* v *Camden LBC* [1998] AC 188 which involved the duty to house the homeless under the Housing Act 1985, s. 63(1). Lord Hoffmann said that the factors against a private right were that the Act is a scheme of social welfare intended to confer benefits at public expense on grounds of public policy. It was not simply a private matter between the claimant and the housing authority. Secondly provision of a benefit under the Act involved a good deal of judgement on the part of the authority. Finally, an adequate public law remedy was available.

3. An example of a civil action in a non-industrial sphere is *Rickless* v *United Artists* [1988] QB 40, where the Dramatic and Musical Performers' Protection Act 1958 made it an offence to make use of a film without the consent of the performers. The defendants made a film called *Trail of the Pink Panther*, which, after the death of Peter Sellers, incorporated 'out-takes' from his previous five Pink Panther films. It was held that the statute gave a civil remedy in addition to the fine of £400, and damages of $1,000,000 were granted to the personal representatives of Peter Sellers.

---

### *Gorris* v *Scott*
Court of Exchequer (1874) LR 9 Exch 125

The defendant owned a ship called *The Hastings*, on which he carried the claimant's sheep from Hamburg to Newcastle. On the voyage some of the sheep were washed overboard. The Animals Order 1871 required sheep and cattle to be kept in pens. If they had been, which they had not, they would not have been lost. Held: the defendants were not liable.

PIGOTT B: For the reasons which have been so exhaustively stated by the Lord Chief Baron, I am of opinion that the declaration shews no cause of action. It is necessary to see what was the object of the legislature in this enactment, and it is set forth clearly in the preamble as being 'to prevent the introduction into Great Britain of contagious or infectious diseases among cattle, sheep, or other animals,' and the 'spread of such diseases in Great Britain.' The purposes enumerated in s. 75 are in harmony with this preamble, and it is in furtherance of that section that the order in question was made. The object, then, of the regulations which have been broken was, not to prevent cattle from being washed overboard, but to protect them against contagious disease. The legislature never contemplated altering the relations between the owners and carriers of cattle, except for the purposes pointed out in the Act; and if the Privy Council had gone out of their way and made provisions to prevent cattle from being washed overboard, their act would have been ultra vires. If, indeed, by reason of the neglect complained of, the cattle had contracted a contagious disease, the case would have been different. But as the case stands on this declaration, the answer to the action is this: Admit there has been a breach of duty; admit there has been a consequent injury; still the legislature was not legislating to protect against such an injury, but for an altogether different purpose; its object was not to regulate the duty of the carrier for all purposes, but only for one particular purpose.

### ■ QUESTIONS

Which of the following provisions give rise to additional civil liability?

(a) A requirement to maintain water in the mains at a certain pressure, the claimant being a person whose house burnt down because of insufficient supply of water. (*Atkinson* v *Newcastle Waterworks Co.* (1877) LR 2 Ex D 441.)

(b) A duty on racetrack owners, so long as a 'totalisator' is being operated, to allow bookmakers onto the course, the claimant being a bookmaker who was excluded. (*Cutler* v *Wandsworth Stadium* [1949] AC 398.)

(c) A rule prohibiting a person from lending his car to a person who is not insured, the claimant being a person injured by the uninsured driver. (*Monk* v *Warbey* [1935] 1 KB 75.)

(d) An obligation on the Law Society to consider complaints by individuals against the conduct of solicitors, the claimant being a person who alleges that the Law Society failed to investigate her complaint adequately. (*Wood* v *The Law Society* (1993) 143 NLJ 1475.)

(e) Breach of a right of a person detained under terrorism provisions in Northern Ireland to consult a solicitor privately. (*Cullen* v *Chief Constable of the RUC* [2003] NI 375.)

# 17

## Product Liability

This chapter deals with damage caused by defective products, and the topic is covered by two separate legal regimes. The first is the ordinary law of negligence (with some qualifications) and the second is the system of strict liability introduced by the Consumer Protection Act 1987, as required by an EC Directive. The latter is limited to personal injuries and to damage to private property, so there will still be a number of cases where a claimant will have to rely on negligence—for example, where there is damage to goods used for commercial purposes. Also, the Act applies only to certain kinds of defendants ('producers'), and a claimant will need to use negligence if, for example, he is injured by a defectively repaired product.

One important point is that both systems apply only to damage to goods other than the defective product and not to damage which the defective product causes to itself: that is a matter solely for the law of contract.

---

### SECTION 1 LIABILITY FOR NEGLIGENCE

*Donoghue* v *Stevenson* was important, not only for establishing a general concept of duty of care in negligence (the wide rule) but also for laying down the qualifications of that broad concept when applied to liability for damage caused by a defective product (the narrow rule). The relevant passages are reproduced below.

---

### Donoghue v Stevenson
House of Lords [1932] AC 562; 147 LT 281; 48 TLR 494

The facts are given above in Chapter 2. Held: that a manufacturer owes a duty of care to the consumer of a product which he has produced negligently, even though there is no contractual relationship between them.

LORD ATKIN: There will no doubt arise cases where it will be difficult to determine whether the contemplated relationship is so close that the duty arises. But in the class of case now before the Court I cannot conceive any difficulty to arise. A manufacturer puts up an article of food in a container which he knows will be opened by the actual consumer. There can be no inspection by any purchaser and no reasonable preliminary inspection by the consumer. Negligently, in the course of preparation, he allows the contents to be mixed with poison. It is said that the law of England and Scotland is that the poisoned consumer has no remedy against the negligent manufacturer. If this were the result of the authorities, I should consider the result a grave defect in the law, and so contrary to principle that I should hesitate long before following any decision to that effect which had not the authority of this House. I would point out that, in the assumed state of the authorities, not only would the consumer have no remedy against the manufacturer, he would have none against any one else, for in the circumstances alleged there would be no evidence of negligence against any one other than the manufacturer; and, except in the case of a consumer who was also a purchaser, no contract and no warranty of fitness, and in the case of the purchase of a specific article under its patent or trade name, which might well be the case in the purchase of some articles of food or drink, no warranty protecting even the purchaser-consumer. There are other instances than of articles of food and drink where goods are sold intended to be used immediately by the consumer, such as many forms of goods sold for cleaning purposes, where the same liability must exist. The doctrine supported by the decision below would not only deny a remedy to the consumer who was injured by consuming bottled beer or chocolates poisoned by the negligence of the manufacturer, but also to the user of what should be a harmless proprietary medicine, an ointment, a soap, a cleaning fluid or cleaning powder. I confine myself to articles of common household use, where every one, including the manufacturer, knows that the articles will be used by other persons than the actual ultimate purchaser—namely, by members of his family and his servants, and in some cases his guests. I do not think so ill of our jurisprudence as to suppose that its principles are so remote from the ordinary needs of civilized society and the ordinary claims it makes upon its members as to deny a legal remedy where there is so obviously a social wrong.

It will be found, I think, on examination that there is no case in which the circumstances have been such as I have just suggested where the liability has been negatived. There are numerous cases, where the relations were much more remote, where the duty has been held not to exist. There are also dicta in such cases which go further than was necessary for the determination of the particular issues, which have caused the difficulty experienced by the Courts below. I venture to say that in the branch of the law which deals with civil wrongs, dependent in England at any rate entirely upon the application by judges of general principles also formulated by judges, it is of particular importance to guard against the danger of stating propositions of law in wider terms than is necessary, lest essential factors be omitted in the wider survey and the inherent adaptability of English law be unduly restricted. For this reason it is very necessary in considering reported cases in the law of torts that the actual decision alone should carry authority, proper weight, of course, being given to the dicta of the judges.

In my opinion several decided cases support the view that in such a case as the present the manufacturer owes a duty to the consumer to be careful. . . .

My Lords, if your Lordships accept the view that this pleading discloses a relevant cause of action you will be affirming the proposition that by Scots and English law alike a manufacturer of products, which he sells in such a form as to show that he intends them to reach the ultimate consumer in the form in which they left him with no reasonable possibility of intermediate examination, and with the knowledge that the absence of reasonable care in the preparation or putting up of the products will result in an injury to the consumer's life or property, owes a duty to the consumer to take that reasonable care.

LORD MACMILLAN: . . . The question is: Does he owe a duty to take care, and to whom does he owe that duty? Now I have no hesitation in affirming that a person who for gain engages in the business of manufacturing articles of food and drink intended for consumption by members of the public in the form in which he issues them is under a duty to take care in the manufacture of these articles. That duty, in my opinion, he owes to those whom he intends to consume his products. He manufactures his commodities for human consumption; he intends and contemplates that they shall be consumed. By reason of that very fact he places himself in a relationship with all the potential consumers of his commodities, and that relationship which he assumes and desires for his own ends imposes upon him a duty to take care to avoid injuring them. He owes them a duty not to convert by his own carelessness an article which he issues to them as wholesome and innocent into an article which is dangerous to life and health. It is sometimes said that liability can only arise where a reasonable man would have foreseen and could have avoided the consequences of his act or omission. In the present case the respondent, when he manufactured his ginger-beer, had directly in contemplation that it would be consumed by members of the public. Can it be said that he could not be expected as a reasonable man to foresee that if he conducted his process of manufacture carelessly he might injure those whom he expected and desired to consume his ginger-beer? The possibility of injury so arising seems to me in no sense so remote as to excuse him from foreseeing it. Suppose that a baker, through carelessness, allows a large quantity of arsenic to be mixed with a batch of his bread, with the result that those who subsequently eat it are poisoned, could he be heard to say that he owed no duty to the consumers of his bread to take care that it was free from poison, and that, as he did not know that any poison had got into it, his only liability was for breach of warranty under his contract of sale to those who actually bought the poisoned bread from him? Observe that I have said 'through carelessness,' and thus excluded the case of a pure accident such as may happen where every care is taken. I cannot believe, and I do not believe, that neither in the law of England nor in the law of Scotland is there redress for such a case. . . . . . . It must always be a question of circumstances whether the carelessness amounts to negligence, and whether the injury is not too remote from the carelessness. I can readily conceive that where a manufacturer has parted with his product and it has passed into other hands it may well be exposed to vicissitudes which may render it defective or noxious, for which the manufacturer could not in any view be held to be to blame. It may be a good general rule to regard responsibility as ceasing when control ceases. So, also, where between the manufacturer and the user there is interposed a party who has the means and opportunity of examining the manufacturer's product before he re-issues it to the actual user. But where, as in the present case, the article of consumption is so prepared as to be intended to reach the consumer in the condition in which it leaves the manufacturer, and the manufacturer takes steps to ensure this by sealing or otherwise closing the container so that the contents cannot be tampered with, I regard his control as remaining effective until the article reaches the consumer and the container is opened by him. The intervention of any exterior agency is intended to be excluded, and was in fact in the present case excluded. . . .

NOTES

1. The above principle was applied in *Grant* v *Australian Knitting Mills Ltd* [1936] AC 85, where the claimant contracted dermatitis from wearing underpants manufactured by the defendants and which contained an excess of sulphites. It was pointed out that the use of the word 'control' by Lord Macmillan was misleading ('I regard his control as remaining effective until the article reaches the consumer'). According to the Privy Council, all that was meant was that 'the consumer must use the article exactly as it left the maker, that is in all material features, and use it as it was intended to be used'.

2. The principle has been extended to repairers of goods (*Haseldine* v *Daw* [1941] 2 KB 343), and also to distributors where they might be expected to test the product before passing it on. Thus, in *Watson* v *Buckley, Osborne Garrett & Co. and Wyrovoys Products* [1940] 1 All ER 174 the claimant had his hair dyed by Mrs Buckley with dye that she had obtained from the distributors, Osborne Garrett & Co., who had bought it from Mr Wyrovoys ('a gentleman who had emerged unexpectedly from Spain'). The dye was delivered in carboys and packaged by Osborne Garrett. Stable J held Mrs Buckley liable in contract and Osborne Garrett in tort. Wyrovoys Products had ceased to exist. Liability was based on the fact that by packaging the dye the defendants had brought themselves into a relationship with the ultimate consumer. However, the principle is not limited to situations where the defendant has packaged the goods as his own, for it will extend to cases where the goods remain in the same form, but where it is expected that the distributor or retailer will have tested them. Thus, in *Andrews* v *Hopkinson* [1957] 1 QB 229 it was held that a commercial seller of a second-hand car was liable in negligence for not testing the car for safety before selling it.

■ QUESTION

In *Grant* (above) the harm could have been avoided if the underpants had been washed before use, but Lord Wright forthrightly pointed out that 'it was not contemplated that they should first be washed'. What if the packet said 'Warning: these underpants should be washed before use'? If the claimant had not done so, would that have been a complete defence to the manufacturer, or a matter of contributory negligence on the part of the claimant? What if it is shown that nobody takes any notice of such ultra-cautious notices, thinking they are only designed to remove the manufacturer's responsibility for producing safe goods?

NOTE

A defendant is liable only if the defective product damages property other than itself. The problem is, what is 'other property'? In *Aswan Engineering* v *Lupdine Ltd* [1987] 1 WLR 1, the claimants bought a quantity of waterproofing compound called Lupguard from the first defendants, Lupdine Ltd. The Lupguard was packed in pails which had been manufactured by the second defendants, Thurgar Bolle Ltd. The Lupguard was exported to Kuwait where the pails were stacked five high on the quayside in full sunshine, and the pails collapsed. The whole consignment was lost. It was held that there was no liability on the sellers in contract as the pails were of merchantable quality, and no liability in tort because the type of damage was unforeseeable. One issue was whether the product had merely damaged itself, or whether the pails (assuming they were defective, which they were not) had damaged other property of the claimant, i.e. the Lupguard in the pails. It was thought, obiter, that the contents of the pails were 'other property'.

A similar problem arises under s. 5(2) of the Consumer Protection Act 1987 (below), which says that there is no liability under the Act for damage to the product itself or to the whole or any part of any product which has been supplied with the product in question comprised in it.

## SECTION 2: STRICT LIABILITY

Strict liability for products has long been accepted in the United States (see Restatement 2nd, s. 402A), and there had been numerous recommendations, both in Britain and in Europe, for its adoption. These were the Law Commission Report No. 82, The Pearson Commission (Cmnd 70054, 1978 Ch. 22), The European Convention on Products Liability (The Strasbourg Convention), and finally the EEC Directive (85/374) on liability for defective products. As a result of the mandatory nature of the Directive, strict liability was finally adopted in this country by the Consumer Protection Act 1987.

This section reproduces The Consumer Protection Act 1987, which imposes strict liability in tort in certain limited circumstances, together with the EC Directive.

### CONSUMER PROTECTION ACT 1987

#### PART I PRODUCT LIABILITY

**1. Purpose and construction of Part I**

(1) This Part shall have effect for the purpose of making such provision as is necessary in order to comply with the product liability Directive and shall be construed accordingly.

(2) In this Part, except in so far as the context otherwise requires—

'dependant' and 'relative' have the same meaning as they have in, respectively, the Fatal Accidents Act 1976 and the Damages (Scotland) Act 1976; 'producer', in relation to a product, means—

(a) the person who manufactured it;

(b) in the case of a substance which has not been manufactured but has been won or abstracted, the person who won or abstracted it;

(c) in the case of a product which has not been manufactured, won or abstracted but essential characteristics of which are attributable to an industrial or other process having been carried out (for example, in relation to agricultural produce), the person who carried out that process;

'product' means any goods or electricity and (subject to subsection (3) below) includes a product which is comprised in another product, whether by virtue of being a component part or raw material or otherwise; and 'the product liability Directive' means the Directive of the Council of the European Communities, dated 25th July 1985, (No. 85/374/EEC) on the approximation of the laws, regulations and administrative provisions of the member States concerning liability for defective products.

(3) For the purposes of this Part a person who supplies any product in which products are comprised, whether by virtue of being component parts or raw materials or otherwise, shall not be treated by reason only of his supply of that product as supplying any of the products so comprised.

### 2. Liability for defective products

(1) Subject to the following provisions of this Part, where any damage is caused wholly or partly by a defect in a product, every person to whom subsection (2) below applies shall be liable for the damage.

(2) This subsection applies to—

(a) The producer of the product;

(b) any person who, by putting his name on the product or using a trade mark or other distinguishing mark in relation to the product, has held himself out to be the producer of the product;

(c) any person who has imported the product into a member State from a place outside the member States in order, in the course of any business of his, to supply it to another.

(3) Subject as aforesaid, where any damage is caused wholly or partly by a defect in a product, any person who supplied the product (whether to the person who suffered the damage, to the producer of any product in which the product in question is comprised or to any other person) shall be liable for the damage if—

(a) the person who suffered the damage requests the supplier to identify one or more of the persons (whether still in existence or not) to whom subsection (2) above applies in relation to the product;

(b) that request is made within a reasonable period after the damage occurs and at a time when it is not reasonably practicable for the person making the request to identify all those persons; and

(c) the supplier fails, within a reasonable period after receiving the request, either to comply with the request or to identify the person who supplied the product to him.

(4) [repealed]

(5) Where two or more persons are liable by virtue of this Part for the same damage, their liability shall be joint and several.

(6) This section shall be without prejudice to any liability arising otherwise than by virtue of this Part.

### 3. Meaning of 'defect'

(1) Subject to the following provisions of this section, there is a defect in a product for the purposes of this Part if the safety of the product is not such as persons generally are entitled to expect; and for those purposes 'safety', in relation to a product, shall include safety with respect to products comprised in that product and safety in the context of risks of damage to property, as well as in the context of risks of death or personal injury.

(2) In determining for the purposes of subsection (1) above what persons generally are entitled to expect in relation to a product all the circumstances shall be taken into account, including—

(a) the manner in which, and purposes for which, the product has been marketed, its get-up, the use of any mark in relation to the product and any instructions for, or warnings with respect to, doing or refraining from doing anything with or in relation to the product;

(b) what might reasonably be expected to be done with or in relation to the product; and

(c) the time when the product was supplied by its producer to another;

and nothing in this section shall require a defect to be inferred from the fact alone that the safety of a product which is supplied after that time is greater than the safety of the product in question.

## 4. Defences

(1) In any civil proceedings by virtue of this Part against any person ('the person proceeded against') in respect of a defect in a product it shall be a defence for him to show—

(a) that the defect is attributable to compliance with any requirement imposed by or under any enactment or with any Community obligation; or

(b) that the person proceeded against did not at any time supply the product to another; or

(c) that the following conditions are satisfied, that is to say—

   (i) that the only supply of the product to another by the person proceeded against was otherwise than in the course of a business of that person's; and

   (ii) that section 2(2) above does not apply to that person or applies to him by virtue only of things done otherwise than with a view to profit; or

(d) that the defect did not exist in the product at the relevant time; or

(e) that the state of scientific and technical knowledge at the relevant time was not such that a producer of products of the same description as the product in question might be expected to have discovered the defect if it had existed in his products while they were under his control; or

(f) that the defect

   (i) constituted a defect in a product ('the subsequent product') in which the product in question had been comprised; and

   (ii) was wholly attributable to the design of the subsequent product or to compliance by the producer of the product in question with instructions given by the producer of the subsequent product.

(2) In this section 'the relevant time', in relation to electricity, means the time at which it was generated, being a time before it was transmitted or distributed, and in relation to any other product, means—

(a) if the person proceeded against is a person to whom subsection (2) of section 2 above applies in relation to the product, the time when he supplied the product to another;

(b) if that subsection does not apply to that person in relation to the product, the time when the product was last supplied by a person to whom that subsection does apply in relation to the product.

## 5. Damage giving rise to liability

(1) Subject to the following provisions of this section, in this Part 'damage' means death or personal injury or any loss of or damage to any property (including land).

(2) A person shall not be liable under section 2 above in respect of any defect in a product for the loss of or any damage to the product itself or for the loss of or any damage to the whole or any part of any product which has been supplied with the product in question comprised in it.

(3) A person shall not be liable under section 2 above for any loss of or damage to any property which, at the time it is lost or damaged, is not—

(a) of a description of property ordinarily intended for private use, occupation or consumption; and

(b) intended by the person suffering the loss or damage mainly for his own private use, occupation or consumption.

(4) No damages shall be awarded to any person by virtue of this Part in respect of any loss of or damage to any property if the amount which would fall to be so awarded to that person, apart from this subsection and any liability for interest, does not exceed £275.

(5) In determining for the purposes of this Part who has suffered any loss of or damage to property and when any such loss or damage occurred, the loss or damage shall be regarded as having occurred at the earliest time at which a person with an interest in the property had knowledge of the material facts about the loss or damage.

(6) For the purposes of subsection (5) above the material facts about any loss of or damage to any property are such facts about the loss or damage as would lead a reasonable person with an interest in the property to consider the loss or damage sufficiently serious to justify his instituting proceedings for damages against a defendant who did not dispute liability and was able to satisfy a judgment.

(7) For the purposes of subsection (5) above a person's knowledge includes knowledge which he might reasonably have been expected to acquire—

    (a) from facts observable or ascertainable by him; or

    (b) from facts ascertainable by him with the help of appropriate expert advice which it is reasonable for him to seek;

but a person shall not be taken by virtue of this subsection to have knowledge of a fact ascertainable by him only with the help of expert advice unless he has failed to take all reasonable steps to obtain (and, where appropriate, to act on) that advice.

(8) Subsections (5) to (7) above shall not extend to Scotland.


**6. Application of certain enactments etc.**

(1) Any damage for which a person is liable under section 2 above shall be deemed to have been caused—

    (a) for the purposes of the Fatal Accidents Act 1976, by that person's wrongful act, neglect or default;

    (b) for the purposes of section 3 of the Law Reform (Miscellaneous Provisions) (Scotland) Act 1940 (contribution among joint wrongdoers), by that person's wrongful act or negligent act or omission;

    (c) for the purposes of section 1 of the Damages (Scotland) Act 1976 (rights of relatives of a deceased), by that person's act or omission; and

    (d) for the purposes of Part II of the Administration of Justice Act 1982 (damages for personal injuries, etc.—Scotland), by an act or omission giving rise to liability in that person to pay damages.

(2) Where—

    (a) a person's death is caused wholly or partly by a defect in a product, or a person dies after suffering damage which has been so caused;

    (b) a request such as mentioned in paragraph (a) of subsection (3) of section 2 above is made to a supplier of the product by that person's personal representatives or, in the case of a person whose death is caused wholly or partly by the defect, by any dependent or relative of that person; and

    (c) the conditions specified in paragraphs (b) and (c) of that subsection are satisfied in relation to that request,

this Part shall have effect for the purposes of the Law Reform (Miscellaneous Provisions) Act 1934, the Fatal Accidents Act 1976 and the Damages (Scotland) Act 1976 as if liability of the supplier to that person under that subsection did not depend on that person having requested the supplier to identify certain persons or on the said conditions having been satisfied in relation to a request made by that person.

(3) Section 1 of the Congenital Disabilities (Civil Liability) Act 1976 shall have effect for the purposes of this Part as if—

    (a) a person were answerable to a child in respect of an occurrence caused wholly or partly by a defect in a product if he is or has been liable under section 2 above in respect of any effect of the occurrence on a parent of the child, or would be so liable if the occurrence caused a parent of the child to suffer damage;

(b) the provisions of this Part relating to liability under section 2 above applied in relation to liability by virtue of paragraph (a) above under the said section 1; and

(c) subsection (6) of the said section 1 (exclusion of liability) were omitted.

(4)  Where any damage is caused partly by a defect in a product and partly by the fault of the person suffering the damage, the Law Reform (Contributory Negligence) Act 1945 and section 5 of the Fatal Accidents Act 1976 (contributory negligence) shall have effect as if the defect were the fault of every person liable by virtue of this Part for the damage caused by the defect.

(5)  In subsection (4) above 'fault' has the same meaning as in the said Act of 1945.

(6)  [omitted]

(7)  It is hereby declared that liability by virtue of this Part is to be treated as liability in tort for the purposes of any enactment conferring jurisdiction on any court with respect to any matter.

(8)  Nothing in this Part shall prejudice the operation of section 12 of the Nuclear Installations Act 1965 (rights to compensation for certain breaches of duties confined to rights under that Act).

### 7. Prohibition on exclusions from liability

The liability of a person by virtue of this Part to a person who has suffered damage caused wholly or partly by a defect in a product, or to a dependant or relative of such a person, shall not be limited or excluded by any contract term, by any notice or by any other provision.

### PART V

### 45. Interpretation

(1)  In this Act, except in so far as the context otherwise requires—

'aircraft' includes gliders, balloons and hovercraft;

'business' includes a trade or profession and the activities of a professional or trade association or of a local authority or other public authority;

'goods' includes substances, growing crops and things comprised in land by virtue of being attached to it and any ship, aircraft or vehicle;

'personal injury' includes any disease and any other impairment of a person's physical or mental condition;

'ship' includes any boat and any other description of vessel used in navigation;

'substance' means any natural or artificial substance, whether in solid, liquid or gaseous form or in the form of a vapour, and includes substances that are comprised in or mixed with other goods.

### 46. Meaning of 'supply'

(1)  Subject to the following provisions of this section, references in this Act to supplying goods shall be construed as references to doing any of the following, whether as principal or agent, that is to say—

(a) selling, hiring out or lending the goods;

(b) entering into a hire-purchase agreement to furnish the goods;

(c) the performance of any contract for work and materials to furnish the goods;

(d) providing the goods in exchange for any consideration (including trading stamps) other than money;

(e) providing the goods in or in connection with the performance of any statutory function; or

(f) giving the goods as a prize or otherwise making a gift of the goods; and, in relation to gas or water, those references shall be construed as including references to providing the service by which the gas or water is made available for use.

(2)  For the purposes of any reference in this Act to supplying goods, where a person ('the ostensible supplier') supplies to another person ('the customer') under a hire-purchase agreement,

conditional sale agreement or credit-sale agreement or under an agreement for the hiring of goods (other than a hire-purchase agreement) and the ostensible supplier—

(a) carries on the business of financing the provision of goods for others by means of such agreements; and

(b) in the course of that business acquired his interest in the goods supplied to the customer as a means of financing the provision of them for the customer by a further person ('the effective supplier'),

the effective supplier and not the ostensible supplier shall be treated as supplying the goods to the customer.

(3) Subject to subsection (4) below, the performance of any contract by the erection of any building or structure on any land or by the carrying out of any other building works shall be treated for the purposes of this Act as a supply of goods in so far as, but only in so far as, it involves the provision of any goods to any person by means of their incorporation into the building, structure or works.

(4) Except for the purposes of, and in relation to, notices to warn or any provision made by or under Part III of this Act, references in this Act to supplying goods shall not include references to supplying goods comprised in land where the supply is effected by the creation or disposal of an interest in the land.

---

## LIMITATION ACT 1980

### 11A. Actions in respect of defective products

(1) This section shall apply to an action for damages by virtue of any provision of Part I of the Consumer Protection Act 1987.

(2) None of the time limits given in the preceding provisions of this Act shall apply to an action to which this section applies.

(3) An action to which this section applies shall not be brought after the expiration of the period of ten years from the relevant time, within the meaning of section 4 of the said Act of 1987; and this subsection shall operate to extinguish a right of action and shall do so whether or not that right of action had accrued, or time under the following provisions of this Act had begun to run, at the end of the said period of ten years.

(4) Subject to subsection (5) below, an action to which this section applies in which the damages claimed by the plaintiff consist of or include damages in respect of personal injuries to the plaintiff or any other person or loss of or damage to any property, shall not be brought after the expiration of the period of three years from whichever is the later of—

(a) the date on which the cause of action accrued; and

(b) the date of knowledge of the injured person or, in the case of loss of or damage to property, the date of knowledge of the plaintiff or (if earlier) of any person in whom his cause of action was previously vested.

NOTES

1. In relation to s. 4(1)(e), the EC Commission instituted an action against the United Kingdom on the ground that this section did not comply with Article 7(e) of the Directive (below) but this was rejected (see below). In addition, the question whether any country should be allowed to use this defence is currently being considered by the EC.

2. It is uncertain whether computer software is 'goods' for the purposes of the 1987 Act. (Note, however, that the EC Directive speaks of 'movables', which may be wider than 'goods', and the EC Commission is clearly of the view that the Directive applies to software.) If defective software is incorporated into a machine it should be possible to regard the whole machine as defective. This at least will protect anybody injured by the machine and will leave the software manufacturer and the machine assembler to sort out liability between themselves on a contractual basis. For the purposes of the Sale of Goods Act 1979, software by itself is not goods but a disk containing it is (*St Albans DC* v *ICL* [1996] 4 All ER 481). If this applies to the

Consumer Protection Act 1987, it would mean that if you download software from the Net there would be no liability on the producer, but if you pick up a free software disk there would be. As software will normally be on something, that something will be goods, and so the problem will arise only where software is downloaded. In this situation the Directive probably does apply, but note that economic loss is not covered; neither is damage to things used by a business, so the issue is unlikely to arise.

## EC COUNCIL DIRECTIVE

### on the approximation of the laws, regulations and administrative provisions of the Member States concerning liability for defective products

OJ L 210/29 (25.7.1985), as amended by Directive 1999/34

*Article 1*

The producer shall be liable for damage caused by a defect in his product.

*Article 2*

For the purpose of this Directive 'product' means all movables even though incorporated into another movable or into an immovable. 'Product' includes electricity.

*Article 3*

1. 'Producer' means the manufacturer of a finished product, the producer of any raw material or the manufacturer of a component part and any person who, by putting his name, trade mark or other distinguishing feature on the product presents himself as its producer.

2. Without prejudice to the liability of the producer, any person who imports into the Community a product for sale, hire, leasing or any form of distribution in the course of his business shall be deemed to be a producer within the meaning of this Directive and shall be responsible as a producer.

3. Where the producer of the product cannot be identified, each supplier of the product shall be treated as its producer unless he informs the injured person, within a reasonable time, of the identity of the producer or of the person who supplied him with the product. The same shall apply, in the case of an imported product, if this product does not indicate the identity of the importer referred to in paragraph 2, even if the name of the producer is indicated.

*Article 4*

The injured person shall be required to prove the damage, the defect and the causal relationship between defect and damage.

*Article 5*

Where, as a result of the provisions of this Directive, two or more persons are liable for the same damage, they shall be liable jointly and severally, without prejudice to the provisions of national law concerning the rights of contribution or recourse.

*Article 6*

1. A product is defective when it does not provide the safety which a person is entitled to expect, taking all circumstances into account, including:

(a) the presentation of the product;
(b) the use to which it could reasonably be expected that the product would be put;
(c) the time when the product was put into circulation.

2. A product shall not be considered defective for the sole reason that a better product is subsequently put into circulation.

*Article 7*

The producer shall not be liable as a result of this Directive if he proves:

(a) that he did not put the product into circulation; or
(b) that, having regard to the circumstances, it is probable that the defect which caused the

damage did not exist at the time when the product was put into circulation by him or that this defect came into being afterwards; or

(c) that the product was neither manufactured by him for sale or any form of distribution for economic purpose nor manufactured or distributed by him in the course of his business; or

(d) that the defect is due to compliance of the product with mandatory regulations issued by the public authorities; or

(e) that the state of scientific and technical knowledge at the time when he put the product into circulation was not such as to enable the existence of the defect to be discovered; or

(f) in the case of a manufacturer of a component, that the defect is attributable to the design of the product in which the component has been fitted or to the instructions given by the manufacturer of the product.

### Article 8

1. Without prejudice to the provisions of national law concerning the right of contribution or recourse, the liability of the producer shall not be reduced when the damage is caused both by a defect in product and by the act or omission of a third party.

2. The liability of the producer may be reduced or disallowed when, having regard to all the circumstances, the damage is caused both by a defect in the product and by the fault of the injured person or any person for whom the injured person is responsible.

### Article 9

For the purpose of Article 1, 'damage' means:

(a) damage caused by death or by personal injuries;

(b) damage to, or destruction of, any item of property other than the defective product itself, with a lower threshold of 500 ECU, provided that the item of property:

   (i) is of a type ordinarily intended for private use or consumption, and

   (ii) was used by the injured person mainly for his own private use or consumption.

This Article shall be without prejudice to national provisions relating to non-material damage.

### Article 10

1. Member States shall provide in their legislation that a limitation period of three years shall apply to proceedings for the recovery of damages as provided for in this Directive. The limitation period shall begin to run from the day on which the plaintiff became aware, or should reasonably have become aware, of the damage, the defect and the identity of the producer.

2. The laws of Member States regulating suspension or interruption of the limitation period shall not be affected by this Directive.

### Article 11

Member States shall provide in their legislation that the rights conferred upon the injured person pursuant to this Directive shall be extinguished upon the expiry of a period of 10 years from the date on which the producer put into circulation the actual product which caused the damage, unless the injured person has in the meantime instituted proceedings against the producer.

### Article 12

The liability of the producer arising from the Directive may not, in relation to the injured person, be limited or excluded by a provision limiting his liability or exempting him from liability.

### Article 13

This Directive shall not affect any rights which an injured person may have according to the rules of the law of contractual or non-contractual liability or a special liability system existing at the moment when this Directive is notified.

## Commission of the European Communities v United Kingdom
European Court of Justice Case C–300/95 (29 May 1997); [1997] 3 CMLR 923; [1997] All ER (EC) 481

The European Commission had alleged that s. 4(1)(e) of the 1987 Act (the state of scientific knowledge defence) was not in compliance with the requirements of Article 7(e) of the Directive. Held: that the application was dismissed.

*Judgment of the Court*

In its application, the Commission argues that the United Kingdom legislature has broadened the defence under Article 7(e) of the Directive to a considerable degree and converted the strict liability imposed by Article 1 of the Directive into mere liability for negligence. In order to determine whether the national implementing provision at issue is clearly contrary to Article 7(e) as the Commission argues, the scope of the Community provision which it purports to implement must first be considered.

Several observations can be made as to the wording of Article 7(e) of the Directive. First, that provision refers to 'scientific and technical knowledge at the time when [the producer] put the product into circulation'; Article 7(e) is not specifically directed at the practices and safety standards in use in the industrial sector in which the producer is operating, but, unreservedly, at the state of scientific and technical knowledge, including the most advanced level of such knowledge, at the time when the product in question was put into circulation.

Second, the clause providing for the defence in question does not contemplate the state of knowledge of which the producer in question actually or subjectively was or could have been apprised, but the objective state of scientific and technical knowledge of which the producer is presumed to have been informed. However, it is implicit in the wording of Article 7(e) that the relevant scientific and technical knowledge must have been accessible at the time when the product in question was put into circulation.

It follows that, in order to have a defence under Article 7(e) of the Directive, the producer of a defective product must prove that the objective state of scientific and technical knowledge, including the most advanced level of such knowledge, at the time when the product in question was put into circulation 'was not such as to enable the existence of the defect to be discovered'. Further, in order for the relevant scientific and technical knowledge to be successfully pleaded as against the producer, that knowledge must have been accessible at the time when the product in question was put into circulation. On this last point, Article 7(e) of the Directive, contrary to what the Commission seems to consider, raises difficulties of interpretation which, in the event of litigation, the national courts will have to resolve, having recourse, if necessary, to Article 177 of the EC Treaty.

For the present, it is the heads of claim raised by the Commission in support of its application that have to be considered. The Commission takes the view that inasmuch as section 4(1)(e) of the Act refers to what may be expected of a producer of products of the same description as the product in question, its wording clearly conflicts with Article 7(e) of the Directive in that it permits account to be taken of the subjective knowledge of a producer taking reasonable care, having regard to the standard precautions taken in the industrial sector in question.

That argument must be rejected in so far as it selectively stresses particular terms used in section 4(1)(e) without demonstrating that the general legal context of the provision at issue fails effectively to secure full application of the Directive. Taking that context into account, the Commission has failed to make out its claim that the result intended by Article 7(e) of the Directive would clearly not be achieved in the domestic legal order.

The Court has consistently held that the scope of national laws, regulations or administrative provisions must be assessed in the light of the interpretation given to them by national courts. Yet in this case the Commission has not referred in support of its application to any national judicial decision which, in its view, interprets the domestic provision at issue inconsistently with the Directive.

There is nothing in the material produced to the Court to suggest that the courts in the United Kingdom, if called upon to interpret section 4(1)(e), would not do so in the light of the wording and the purpose of the Directive so as to achieve the result which it has in view and thereby comply with the third paragraph of Article 189 of the Treaty. Moreover, section 1 (1) of the Act expressly imposes such an obligation on the national courts.

NOTE

The point here is that the test is objective and that knowledge includes knowledge even at an advanced level. However, the Court also notes that the knowledge must be *accessible*, and presumably one way of establishing this is to show that other producers were or ought to have been aware of the knowledge. But that would not be the only way of showing that the knowledge was accessible, and therefore s. 4(1)(c) of the Act needs to be interpreted as meaning that the defence will apply only when the knowledge of the potential defect was not accessible and one way of showing that is to show that other producers would not be expected to have known of the problem, but the defendant may also need to show that there was no other way that the knowledge could be regarded as accessible.

---

### *A* v *National Blood Authority*
High Court [2001] 3 All ER 289; [2001] Lloyd's Rep Med 187

The claimants contracted Hepatitis C by transfusions of blood taken from infected donors. The claim was made under the Consumer Protection Act 1987 and it was conceded that blood was a 'product' and that its preparation involved an 'industrial process'. At the relevant time the risk of infection was known but it was not possible to test for the presence of the Hepatitis C virus in the blood of donors, and thus the risk of infection could not be avoided. Accordingly one issue was whether 'unavoidability' was a relevant circumstance in determining whether a product was defective under Article 6 of the Directive (s. 3 of the Act). Another issue was whether an unavoidable but known risk qualified for the defence under Article 7(e) (s. 4(1)(e) of the Act) that the state of scientific knowledge at the time was not such as to enable the existence of the defect to be discovered. (Note: as the Act implements the Directive, the judgment generally refers to the terms of the Directive.) Held: the defendants were liable.

BURTON J:

**Article 6**

[6.1 A product is defective when it does not provide the safety which a person is entitled to expect, taking all circumstances into account, including:

(a) the presentation of the product;
(b) the use to which it could reasonably be expected that the product would be put;
(c) the time when the product was put into circulation.]

*The Differences Between the Parties*

**32** Having set out what is common ground, I now summarise briefly the difference between the two parties, some of which is already apparent from my setting in context of the factual common ground:

(i) As to Article 6, the Claimants assert that, with the need for proof of negligence eliminated, consideration of the conduct of the producer, or of a reasonable or legitimately expectable producer, is inadmissible or irrelevant. Therefore questions of avoidability cannot and do not arise: what the Defendants could or should have done differently: whether there were any steps or precautions reasonably available: whether it was impossible to take any steps by way of prevention or avoidance, or impracticable or economically unreasonable. Such are not 'circumstances' falling to be considered within Article 6. Insofar as the risk was known to blood producers and the medical profession, it was not known to the public at large (save for those few patients who might ask their doctor, or read the occasional article about blood in a newspaper) and no risk that any percentage of transfused blood would be infected was accepted by them.

(ii) The Defendants assert that the risk was known to those who mattered, namely the medical profession, through whom blood was supplied. Avoiding the risk was impossible and unattainable, and it is not and cannot be legitimate to expect the unattainable. Avoidability or unavoidability is a circumstance to be taken into account within Article 6. The public did not and/or was not entitled to expect 100% clean blood. The most they could legitimately expect was that all legitimately expectable (reasonably available) precautions—or in this case tests— had been taken or carried out . . .

(iii) The Claimants respond that Article 7(e) does not apply to risks which are known before the supply of the product, whether or not the defect can be identified in the particular product; and there are a number of other issues between the parties in respect of Article 7(e) to which I shall return later.

*All Circumstances*

**35** The dispute therefore is as to what further, if anything, falls to be considered within 'all circumstances'. There is no dispute between the parties, as set out in paragraph 31(i) and (ii) above, that consideration of the fault of the producer is excluded; but does consideration of 'all circumstances' include consideration of the conduct to be expected from the producer, the level of safety to be expected from a producer of that product? The parties agree that the starting point is the particular product with the harmful characteristic, and if its inherent nature and intended use (e.g., poison) are dangerous, then there may not need to be any further consideration, provided that the injury resulted from that known danger. However, if the product was not intended to be dangerous, that is the harmful characteristic was not intended, by virtue of the intended use of the product, then there must be consideration of whether it was safe and the level of safety to be legitimately expected. At this stage, the Defendants assert that part of the investigation consists of what steps could have been taken by a producer to avoid that harmful characteristic. The Defendants assert that conduct is to be considered not by reference to identifying the individual producer's negligence, but by identifying and specifying the safety precautions that the public would or could reasonably expect from a producer of the product. The exercise is referred to as a balancing act; the more difficult it is to make safe, and the more beneficial the product, the less is expected and vice versa, an issue being whether a producer has complied with the safety precautions reasonably to be expected. . . .

*Non-Standard Products*

**36** In any event, however, the Claimants make a separate case in relation to the blood products here in issue: namely that they are what is called in the United States 'rogue products' or 'lemons', and in Germany '*Ausreisse*'—'escapees' or 'off the road' products. These are products which are isolated or rare specimens which are different from the other products of a similar series, different from the products as intended or desired by the producer. In the course of Mr Forrester QC's submissions, other more attractive or suitable descriptions were canvassed, and I have firmly settled on what I clearly prefer, namely the 'non-standard' product. Thus a *standard* product is one which is and performs as the producer intends. A *non-standard* product is one which is different, obviously because it is deficient or inferior in terms of safety, from the standard product; and where it is the harmful characteristic or characteristics present in the non-standard product, but not in the standard product, which has or have caused the material injury or damage. Some Community jurisdictions in implementing the Directive have specifically provided that there will be liability for 'non-standard' products, i.e., that such will automatically be defective within Article 6: Italy and Spain have done so by express legislation, and Dr Weber, in *Produkthaftung im Belgischen Recht* 1988 at 219–20, considers that that is now the position in Belgium also as a result of the implementation of the Directive.

**38** In a jurisdiction where, unlike Spain and Italy, and perhaps Belgium, no legislative distinction has been drawn between standard and non-standard products, the distinction, even if I were to conclude that the blood bags in this case are non-standard products, would not be absolute. Non-standard products would not be automatically defective. A product may be unsafe because it differs from the standard product, or because the standard product itself is unsafe, or at risk of being unsafe. It may however be easier to prove defectiveness if the product differs from the standard product.

### Article 7(e)

**47** I repeat, for the sake of convenience at this stage, Article 7(e):

The producer shall not be liable as a result of this Directive if he proves . . . that the state of scientific and technical knowledge at the time when he put the product into circulation was not such as to enable the existence of the defect to be discovered.

*The Issues Between the Parties*

**50** Must the producer prove that the defect had not been and could not be discovered in the product in question, as the Defendants contend, or must the producer prove that the defect had not been and could not be discovered generally, i.e., in the population of products? If it be the latter, it is common ground here that the existence of the defect in blood generally, i.e., of the infection of blood in some cases by hepatitis virus notwithstanding screening, was known, and indeed knwon to the Defendants. The question is thus whether, in order to take advantage of the escape clause, the producer must show that no objectively assessable scientific or technical information existed any-where in the world which had identified, and thus put producers potentially on notice of, the problem; or whether it is enough for the producer to show that, although the existence of the defect in such product was or should have been known, there was no objectively accessible information available anywhere in the world which would have enabled a producer to discover the existence of that known defect in the particular product in question . . .

### Conclusions on Article 6

**55** I do not consider it to be arguable that the consumer had an actual expectation that blood being supplied to him was not 100% clean, nor do I conclude that he had knowledge that it was, or was likely to be, infected with Hepatitis C. It is not seriously argued by the Defendants, notwithstand-ing some few newspaper cuttings which were referred to, that there was any public understanding or acceptance of the infection of transfused blood by Hepatitis C. Doctors and surgeons knew, but did not tell their patients unless asked, and were very rarely asked. It was certainly, in my judgment, not known and accepted by society that there was such a risk . . .

**56** I do not consider that the legitimate expectation of the public at large is that legitimately expectable tests will have been carried out or precautions adopted. Their legitimate expectation is as to the safeness of the product (or not) . . .

**57** In this context I turn to consider what is intended to be included within 'all circumstances' in Article 6. I am satisfied that this means all relevant circumstances. It is quite plain to me that (albeit that Professor Stapleton has been pessimistic about its success) the Directive was intended to eliminate proof of fault or negligence. I am satisfied that this was not simply a legal consequence, but that it was also intended to make it easier for claimants to prove their case, such that not only would a consumer not have to prove that the producer did not take reasonable steps, or all reasonable steps, to comply with his duty of care, but also that the producer did not take all legitimately expectable steps either. In this regard I note paragraph 16 of the Advocate General's Opinion in *Commission* v *UK* [1997] All ER (EC) 481 where, in setting out the background to the Directive, he pointed out that:

Albeit injured by a defective product, consumers were in fact and too often deprived of an effective remedy, since it proved very difficult procedurally to prove negligence on the part of the producer, that is to say, that he failed to take all appropriate steps to avoid the defect arising.

**63** I conclude therefore that *avoidability* is not one of the *circumstances* to be taken into account within Article 6. I am satisfied that it is not a relevant circumstance, because it is outwith the purpose of the Directive, and indeed that, had it been intended that it would be included as a derogation from, or at any rate a palliation of, its purpose, then it would certainly have been mentioned; for it would have been an important circumstance, and I am clear that, irrespective of the absence of any word such as *notamment* in the English language version of the Directive, it was intended that the most significant circumstances were those listed.

**64** This brings me to a consideration of Article 7(e) in the context of consideration of Article 6. Article 7(e) provides a very restricted escape route, and producers are, as emphasised in *Commission v UK* [1997] All ER (EC) 481 unable to take advantage of it, unless they come within its very restricted conditions, whereby a producer who has taken all possible precautions (certainly all legitimately expectable precautions, if the terms of Article 6, as construed by Mr Underhill QC, are to be cross-referred) remains liable unless that producer can show that 'the state of scientific and technical knowledge [anywhere and anyone's in the world, provided reasonably accessible] was not such as to enable the existence of the defect to be discovered'. The significance seems to be as follows. Article 7(e) is the escape route (if available at all) for the producer who has done all he could reasonably be expected to do (and more); and yet that route is emphatically very restricted, because of the purpose and effect of the Directive (see particularly paragraphs 26, 36 and 38 of the European Court's judgment). This must suggest a similarly restricted view of Article 6, indeed one that is even more restricted, given the availability of the (restricted) Article 7(e) escape route. If that were not the case, then if the Article 7(e) defence were excluded, an option permitted (and indeed taken up, in the case of Luxembourg and Finland) for those Member States who wish to delete this 'exonerating circumstance' as 'unduly restricting the protection of the consumer' (Recital 16 and Article 15), then, on the Defendants' case, an even less restrictive 'exonerating circumstance', and one available even in the case of risks known to the producer, would remain in Article 6; and indeed one where the onus does not even rest on the Defendant, but firmly on the Claimant.

**65** Further, in my judgment, the infected bags of blood were non-standard products. I have already recorded that it does not seem to me to matter whether they would be categorised in US tort law as manufacturing or design defects. They were in any event different from the norm which the producer intended for use by the public . . .

But I am satisfied, as I have stated above, that the problem was not *known* to the consumer. However, in any event, I do not accept that the consumer expected, or was entitled to expect, that his bag of blood was defective even if (which I have concluded was not the case) he had any knowledge of any problem. I do not consider, as Mr Forrester QC put it, that he was expecting or entitled to expect a form of Russian roulette. That would only arise if, contrary to my conclusion, the public took that as socially acceptable (*sozialadäquat*). For such knowledge and acceptance there would need to be at the very least publicity and probably express warnings, and even that might not, in the light of the no-waiver provision in Article 12 set out above, be sufficient.

**67** The first step must be to identify the harmful characteristic which caused the injury (Article 4). In order to establish that there is a defect in Article 6, the next step will be to conclude whether the product is standard or non-standard. This will be done (in the absence of admission by the producer) most easily by comparing the offending product with other products of the same type or series produced by that producer. If the respect in which it differs from the series includes the harmful characteristic, then it is, for the purpose of Article 6, non-standard. If it does not differ, or if the respect in which it differs does not include the harmful characteristic, but all the other products, albeit different, share the harmful characteristic, then it is to be treated as a standard product.

### Non-standard Products

**68** The circumstances specified in Article 6 may obviously be relevant—the product may be a second—as well as the circumstances of the supply. But it seems to me that the primary issue in relation to a non-standard product may be whether the public at large accepted the non-standard nature of the product—i.e., they accept that a proportion of the products is defective (as I have concluded they do not in this case). That, as discussed, is not of course the end of it, because the question is of *legitimate* expectation, and the Court may conclude that the expectation of the public is too high or too low. But manifestly questions such as warnings and presentations will be in the forefront. However I conclude that the following are not relevant:

(i) Avoidability of the harmful characteristic—i.e. impossibility or unavoidability in relation to precautionary measures.

(ii) The impracticality, cost or difficulty of taking such measures.

(iii) The benefit to society or utility of the product: (except in the context of whether—with full information and proper knowledge—the public does and ought to accept the risk).

*Standard Products*

**71** If a standard product is unsafe, it is likely to be so as a result of alleged error in design, or at any rate as a result of an allegedly flawed system. The harmful characteristic must be identified, if necessary with the assistance of experts. The question of presentation/time/circumstances of supply/social acceptability etc. will arise as above. The sole question will be safety for the foreseeable use. If there are any comparable products on the market, then it will obviously be relevant to compare the offending product with those other products, so as to identify, compare and contrast the relevant features. There will obviously need to be a full understanding of how the product works—particularly if it is a new product, such as a scrid, so as to assess its safety for such use. Price is obviously a significant factor in legitimate expectation, and may well be material in the comparative process. But again it seems to me there is no room in the basket for:

(i) what the producer could have done differently:

(ii) whether the producer could or could not have done the same as the others did.

**Conclusions on Article 7(e)**

**74** As to construction:

(i) I note (without resolving the question) the force of the argument that the *defect* in Article 7(b) falls to be construed as the defect in the particular product; but I do not consider that to be determinative of the construction of Article 7(e), and indeed I am firmly of the view that such is not the case in Article 7(e).

(ii) The analysis of Article 7(e), with the guidance of *Commission* v *UK* [1997] All ER (EC) 481 seems to me to be entirely clear. If there is a known risk, i.e., the existence of the defect is known or should have been known in the light of non-Manchurianly accessible information, then the producer continues to produce and supply at his own risk. It would, in my judgment, be inconsistent with the purpose of the Directive if a producer, in the case of a known risk, continues to supply products simply because, and despite the fact that, he is unable to identify in which if any of his products that defect will occur or recur, or, more relevantly in a case such as this, where the producer is obliged to supply, continues to supply without accepting the responsibility for any injuries resulting, by insurance or otherwise.

(iii) *The existence of the defect* is in my judgment clearly generic. Once the *existence of the defect* is known, then there is then the *risk* of that defect materialising in any particular product.

**76** The purpose of Article 7(e) was plainly not to discourage innovation, and to exclude development risks from the Directive, and it succeeds in its objective, subject to the very considerable restrictions that are clarified by *Commission* v *UK*: namely that the risk ceases to be a development risk and becomes a known risk not if and when the producer in question (or, as the CPA inappropriately sought to enact in Section 4(1)(e) 'a producer of products of the same description as the product in question') had the requisite knowledge, but if and when such knowledge were accessible anywhere in the world outside Manchuria. Hence it protects the producer in respect of the unknown (*inconnu*). But the consequence of acceptance of the Defendants' submissions would be that protection would also be given in respect of the known.

**77** The effect is, it seems to me . . . that non-standard products are incapable of coming within Article 7(e). Non-standard products may qualify once—i.e. if the problem which leads to an occasional defective product is (unlike the present case) not known: this may perhaps be more unusual than in relation to a problem with a standard product, but does not seem to me to be an impossible scenario. However once the problem is known by virtue of accessible information, then the non-standard product can no longer qualify for protection under Article 7(e).

### The Result in Law on Issue I

**78** Unknown risks are unlikely to qualify by way of defence within Article 6. They may however qualify for Article 7(e). Known risks do not qualify within Article 7(e), even if unavoidable in the particular product. They may qualify within Article 6 if fully known and socially acceptable.

**79** The blood products in this case were non-standard products, and were unsafe by virtue of the harmful characteristics which they had and which the standard products did not have.

**80** They were not *ipso facto* defective (an expression used from time to time by the Claimants) but were defective because I am satisfied that the public at large was entitled to expect that the blood transfused to them would be free from infection. There were no warnings and no material publicity, certainly none officially initiated by or for the benefit of the Defendants, and the knowledge of the medical profession, not materially or at all shared with the consumer, is of no relevance. It is not material to consider whether any steps or any further steps could have been taken to avoid or palliate the risk that the blood would be infected.

NOTES

1. This case is important not only for its interpretation of Articles 6 and 7, but also because it stresses the no-fault nature of the scheme. The question is not whether it is unfair to impose liability on a defendant who cannot avoid the loss, but given that some losses will occur ('accidents will happen') which of the two parties should bear the cost, or perhaps which of the two should insure against the risk. The purpose of the Directive is to prefer the consumer in this situation.

2. When does a risk become 'socially acceptable'? (See para. 65.) In other words when is it generally agreed that not every example of a product will be perfect? In *Richardson* v *LRC Products* [2000] Lloyd's Rep Med 280 the claimant's husband used one of the defendant's condoms which fractured and she became pregnant. The cause of the fracture was unexplained. The judge seems to have thought that there was no defect in the condom when it left the factory, but even if there was he said it would not be defective within the Act. He pointed out that while the expectation is that the condom will not fail, no method of contraception is 100 per cent effective and there will always be inexplicable failures. Thus, he seems to have thought that so long as the testing procedures were rigorous, that was all the public was entitled to expect. In *A* v *National Blood Authority* Burton J thought this case was unclear but in general the question is whether the public generally accept that condoms sometimes burst.

3. What is technical knowledge? In *Abouzaid* v *Mothercare* The Times, 20 February 2001, the claimant was injured in the eye by the recoil of an elastic strap on one of the defendants' products. They relied on the Department of Trade database which did not reveal any similar accidents having happened before and said that without such information they could not have discovered the defect. The Court of Appeal thought that such accident records were probably not 'technical knowledge' and found the defendants liable.

4. In para. 76 Burton J mentions 'Manchuria'. This relates to the accessibility of the technical knowledge—see *Commission* v *UK* (above). The argument is that it would be unrealistic to expect manufacturers in general to know of research which is not reasonably likely to circulate.

5. For further reading see Newdick, 'The development risk defence of the Consumer Protection Act 1987' (1988) 47 CLJ 455 and more generally Stapleton, *Product Liability* (1994).

# 18

## Occupiers' Liability

This chapter deals with the liability of an occupier to persons who are injured on his premises. (If the damage is caused by something on the premises but the damage occurs *off* the premises, that is dealt with by the law of negligence or nuisance.) The basis of liability is fault, and to visitors at least the duty differs little from the requirements of negligence, but there are sufficient differences to make it subject to a special chapter. These differences arise partly for historical reasons, but also because of the need to balance the rights of the occupier to deal with his property as he wishes and the need to protect entrants from injury. Property rights still make a difference.

The character of the entrant also makes a difference, and rather than subject this to the usual tests of proximity in negligence, a clear distinction is made between visitors and other entrants. The draconian rules relating to trespassers have been ameliorated, and the duty owed is now flexible enough to distinguish between kinds of trespassers, e.g. the burglar and the wandering child.

Some jurisdictions have abandoned these distinctions based on status. The Occupiers' Liability (Scotland) Act 1960 makes no distinction between trespassers and visitors, and in Australia the High Court has abandoned the separate rules of occupiers' liability altogether and has subjected all issues to the ordinary rules of negligence. In *Australian Safeway Stores* v *Zaluzna* (1987) 162 CLR 479 the court approved the view of Deane J in *Hackshaw* v *Shaw* (1984) 155 CLR 614, where he said:

> It is not necessary, in an action in negligence against an occupier, to go through the procedure of considering whether either one or other or both of a special duty *qua* occupier and an ordinary duty of care was owed. All that is necessary is to determine whether, in all the relevant circumstances including the fact of the defendant's occupation of premises and the manner of the plaintiff's entry upon them, the defendant owed a duty of care under the ordinary principles of negligence to the plaintiff. A prerequisite of any such duty is that there be the necessary degree of proximity of relationship.

That, however, is not a step which has been taken in this country, and the law is governed by the Occupiers' Liability Act 1957 in relation to visitors, and by the Occupiers' Liability Act 1984 in relation to trespassers and other non-visitors.

---

### OCCUPIERS' LIABILITY ACT 1957

#### 1. Preliminary

(1) The rules enacted by the two next following sections shall have effect, in place of the rules of the common law, to regulate the duty which an occupier of premises owes to his visitors in

respect of dangers due to the state of the premises or to things done or omitted to be done on them.

(2) The rules so enacted shall regulate the nature of the duty imposed by law in consequence of a person's occupation or control of premises and of any invitation or permission he gives (or is to be treated as giving) to another to enter or use the premises, but they shall not alter the rules of the common law as to the persons on whom a duty is so imposed or to whom it is owed; and accordingly for the purpose of the rules so enacted the persons who are to be treated as an occupier and as his visitors are the same (subject to subsection (4) of this section) as the persons who would at common law be treated as an occupier and as his invitees or licensees.

(3) The rules so enacted in relation to an occupier of premises and his visitors shall also apply, in like manner and to the like extent as the principles applicable at common law to an occupier of premises and his invitees or licensees would apply, to regulate—

(a) the obligations of a person occupying or having control over any fixed or moveable structure, including any vessel, vehicle or aircraft; and

(b) the obligations of a person occupying or having control over any premises or structure in respect of damage to property, including the property of persons who are not themselves his visitors.

(4) A person entering any premises in exercise of rights conferred by virtue of—

(a) section 2(1) of the Countryside and Rights of Way Act 2000, or

(b) an access agreement or order under the National Parks and Access to the Countryside Act 1949,

is not, for the purposes of this Act, a visitor of the occupier of the premises.

## 2. Extent of occupier's ordinary duty

(1) An occupier of premises owes the same duty, the 'common duty of care', to all his visitors, except in so far as he is free to and does extend, restrict, modify or exclude his duty to any visitor or visitors by agreement or otherwise.

(2) The common duty of care is a duty to take such care as in all the circumstances of the case is reasonable to see that the visitor will be reasonably safe in using the premises for the purposes for which he is invited or permitted by the occupier to be there.

(3) The circumstances relevant for the present purpose include the degree of care, and of want of care, which would ordinarily be looked for in such a visitor, so that (for example) in proper cases—

(a) an occupier must be prepared for children to be less careful than adults; and

(b) an occupier may expect that a person, in the exercise of his calling, will appreciate and guard against any special risks ordinarily incident to it, so far as the occupier leaves him free to do so.

(4) In determining whether the occupier of premises has discharged the common duty of care to a visitor, regard is to be had to all the circumstances, so that (for example)—

(a) where damage is caused to a visitor by a danger of which he had been warned by the occupier, the warning is not to be treated without more as absolving the occupier from liability, unless in all the circumstances it was enough to enable the visitor to be reasonably safe; and

(b) where damage is caused to a visitor by a danger due to the faulty execution of any work of construction, maintenance or repair by an independent contractor employed by the occupier, the occupier is not to be treated without more as answerable for the danger if in all the circumstances he had acted reasonably in entrusting the work to an independent contractor and had taken such steps (if any) as he reasonably ought in order to satisfy himself that the contractor was competent and that the work had been properly done.

(5) The common duty of care does not impose on an occupier any obligation to a visitor in respect of risks willingly accepted as his by the visitor (the question whether a risk was so accepted to be decided on the same principles as in other cases in which one person owes a duty of care to another).

(6) For the purposes of this section, persons who enter premises for any purpose in the exercise of a right conferred by law are to be treated as permitted by the occupier to be there for that purpose, whether they in fact have his permission or not.

### 3. Effect of contract on occupier's liability to third party

(1) Where an occupier of premises is bound by contract to permit persons who are strangers to the contract to enter or use the premises, the duty of care which he owes to them as his visitors cannot be restricted or excluded by that contract, but (subject to any provision of the contract to the contrary) shall include the duty to perform his obligations under the contract, whether undertaken for their protection or not, in so far as those obligations go beyond the obligations otherwise involved in that duty.

(2) A contract shall not by virtue of this section have the effect, unless it expressly so provides, of making an occupier who has taken all reasonable care answerable to strangers to the contract for dangers due to the faulty execution of any work of construction, maintenance or repair or other like operation by persons other than himself, his servants and persons acting under his direction and control.

(3) In this section 'stranger to the contract' means a person not for the time being entitled to the benefit of the contract as a party to it or as the successor by assignment or otherwise of a party to it, and accordingly includes a party to the contract who has ceased to be so entitled.

(4) Where by the terms or conditions governing any tenancy (including a statutory tenancy which does not in law amount to a tenancy) either the landlord or the tenant is bound, though not by contract, to permit persons to enter or use premises of which he is the occupier, this section shall apply as if the tenancy were a contract between the landlord and the tenant.

### 5. Implied term in contracts

(1) Where persons enter or use, or bring or send goods to, any premises in exercise of a right conferred by contract with a person occupying or having control of the premises, the duty he owes them in respect of dangers due to the state of the premises, or to things done or omitted to be done on them, in so far as the duty depends on a term to be implied in the contract by reason of its conferring that right, shall be the common duty of care.

(2) The foregoing subsection shall apply to fixed and moveable structures as it applies to premises.

(3) This section does not affect the obligations imposed on a person by or by virtue of any contract for the hire of, or for the carriage for reward of persons or goods in, any vehicle, vessel, aircraft or other means of transport, or by virtue of any contract of bailment.

### SECTION 1: OCCUPIERS' LIABILITY AND NEGLIGENCE

One consequence of adopting duties based on the status of the entrant is the need to distinguish between a person's duty under the *Donoghue* v *Stevenson* principle not to injure another and his duties under the Occupiers' Liability Act 1957. In practice the problem does not matter very much, as the two duties are very similar, but although there has been some doubt about the question, the usual view is that activity duties are dealt with by the rules of ordinary negligence, and occupancy duties by the special rules of occupiers' liability. The distinction is not easy, but it is usually asked whether the premises themselves have been rendered unsafe.

### New Zealand Insurance Co. v Prudential Assurance Ltd
Court of Appeal, New Zealand [1976] NZLR 84

Mrs Woods committed suicide by drinking arsenic. On the following day, after the body had been taken away, Mr Woods and his son Roger entered the house. In the kitchen Roger saw what appeared to be a glass of lemon juice and he drank some of it. The glass contained arsenic and Roger died. Mrs Woods was covered by an insurance policy: one clause dealt with personal liability and limited a claim to $10,000 whereas another clause (cl. 2C(1) ) dealt with liability as occupier and limited the claim to $50,000. The question therefore arose whether the liability of Mrs Woods was based on occupiers' liability or not. In a dispute concerning indemnities it was held: that the procedure adopted by the parties was inappropriate, but Richmond J also indicated, without deciding, that the matter probably was one of occupiers' liability.

RICHMOND J: I return now to the judgment of O'Regan J. He did not advert to any procedural difficulties, and I sympathise with his evident desire to assist the parties. He dealt with the case in the following way. First, and very importantly, he said that section 2C(1) 'has to do with the insured's legal liability "as occupier" '. He then referred to the distinction drawn by Denning LJ in *Dunster v Abbott* [1954] 1 WLR 58, 62; [1953] 2 All ER 1572, 1574, between duties arising out of the particular relationship between an occupier and an invitee or licensee, on the one hand, and the duties arising out of the general duty of care. Denning LJ thought that the former duty related only to the static condition of the premises and not to current operations on the premises. This distinction is often described as one between 'occupancy' duties and 'activity' duties. O'Regan J came to the conclusion that an 'activity' duty was outside the scope of the Occupiers' Liability Act 1962. He noted that s.3(1) prima facie appeared to relate to both duties, as it refers to the duty, which an occupier owes to his visitors in his capacity as an occupier, in respect of dangers 'due to the state of the premises or to *things done or omitted to be done on them*'. He thought, however, that s.3(2) made it clear that only 'occupancy' duties were covered because that subsection states that 'The rules so enacted shall regulate the nature of the duty imposed by law *in consequence of a person's occupation or control of premises*'. The Judge then said:

> Relating the view I have taken to the facts of the case, I consider that the liability in tort for the act of the elder Mrs Woods leaving a glass of poisonous substance on the sink bench is the same as if such act was done by a trespasser or an overnight guest in the house. Such liability is in no way dependent on her occupation of the premises; it arises *qua neighbour* and not *qua occupier*.

From what I have said it will be seen that the Judge really decided two things:

(1)  A question of construction of the policy, namely, that section 2C(1) 'has to do with the insured's legal liability "as occupier" '. Although he did not elaborate on this, or discuss any alternative construction, I think he meant that section 2C(1) is concerned only with cases where the fact of occupancy is an essential legal ingredient of the cause of action.

(2)  A question of liability as between the widow and the New Zealand Insurance Co. Ltd. He held, on such evidence as he had before him, and as a mixed question of fact and law, that the widow could not succeed in a claim under the Occupiers' Liability Act.

On the hearing of this appeal Mr Clark challenged both the foregoing conclusions. I propose to deal with them in reverse order.

In the passage from the judgment in *Dunster's* case upon which O'Regan J relied, Denning LJ appears to have treated dangers in the 'static condition of the premises' as the equivalent of dangers 'which have been present for some time in the physical structure of the premises'. It is probable that the Judge based his conclusion in the present case upon the fact that the presence of a glass of poison obviously did not affect the 'physical structure of the premises'. While sympathising with the position in which O'Regan J found himself I think that he allowed himself to become involved in a question of mixed fact and law which was quite outside the type of question which can be dealt with on an originating summons under the Declaratory Judgments Act. Accordingly, I do not myself propose to deal with this question by attempting a definite answer to it. I am inclined to think, however, that it is impossible to say that current operations which do not affect the physical structure of the premises are outside the scope of the Act. The problem may rather be to draw the line between those 'current operations' or 'activities' which do, and those which do not, result in a state of affairs falling within the scope of the Act. The point is discussed in *Street's Law of Torts* (5th ed) 180–181, and also in *North's Occupiers' Liability* (1971) 80–82. Both the learned authors are agreed that the Act is not limited in the way which I believe found favour with O'Regan J. This because of the words in subs (1), 'or to things done or omitted to be done on them'. Both also agree that the Act only replaces the common law in respect of duties consequent upon occupation. But because of the words in subs (1) to which I have just referred it is said in *Street* at p. 180: 'At the very least, then, the Act covers acts or omissions which have created a dangerous condition of a continuing nature which later causes harm'.

Likewise it is said in *North* at p. 80: 'This would include conduct on the land which causes a continuing source of danger and thereby renders the premises or structure unsafe'.

But it is clear that both authors find difficulty in drawing a satisfactory line between those activities which are relevant under the Act and those which are not. Professor Street thinks that an activity such as the shooting of arrows would be outside the Act 'for the duty of care is imposed on the actor because he is himself performing an act which is foreseeably likely to cause harm to others present on the premises, and not because the occupier occupies the land' (p. 181). In *North's Occupiers' Liability* at p. 81 it is suggested that an activity on the premises which does not affect the safety of the premises as a structure falls outside the Act.

These difficulties are also discussed in *Clerk & Lindsell on Torts* (13th ed) pp. 595–596. It is there said:

> It is clear that the duty under the Act covers dangers due to the static condition of the premises, and dangers due to the condition of the premises at the time of the visitor's entry, although the condition has been temporarily brought about by 'things done or omitted to be done' thereon. It is suggested that it does not cover 'superadded negligence' such as dropping a sack of sugar on the visitor from a crane, running into him in a car or locomotive, shooting him, or pouring tea over him, where these acts are done by the occupier or his servants.

*Roles* v *Nathan* [1963] 1 WLR 1117; [1963] 2 All ER 908 suggests that the presence of carbon monoxide gas in a building may be an occupiers' liability situation. Pearson LJ (at p. 1131; 917) seems to have regarded the lighting of the fire in that case as the breach of the occupier's duty. As to whether it may be possible to draw an analogy between the presence of carbon monoxide and the continuing presence of a glass of poison I express no opinion. But I have referred to the views of three textbook writers as being in agreement at least to the point that the Act extends to cover conduct which causes a continuing source of danger and thereby renders the premises unsafe. At the same time they are all in agreement that the Act does not extend to every activity of the occupier. As I have said, the present proceedings are quite inappropriate to enable the Court to express any final opinion on this question. But I am inclined to think that O'Regan J took too narrow a view of the scope of the Act.

NOTES

1. In *Fairchild* v *Glenhaven Funeral Services* [2002] 1 WLR 1052, in the Court of Appeal, Brooke LJ affirmed the distinction between occupancy and activity duties, being the distinction between the dangerous condition of premises and dangerous activities carried out on the premises. In *Dunster* v *Abbott* [1954] 1 WLR 58 Lord Denning distinguished between the static condition of premises and current operations. See also *Bottomley* v *Todmorden Cricket Club* [2003] EWCA Civ 1575 where an occupier was liable for the negligent letting off of fireworks by a contractor, not as a part of occupancy duty but for failing to engage a competent contractor.

2. In *Revill* v *Newbery* [1996] 1 All ER 291 an occupier shot an intruder trying to enter his allotment shed. It was said this was not a matter of occupiers' liability but rather was to be decided under the general tort of negligence. Occupiers' liability is limited to liability as occupier and the Occupiers' Liability Acts are concerned with only the safety of the premises and with dangers due to things done on the premises. However, it was also held that the special duty in the Occupiers' Liability Act 1984 was the appropriate level of duty for ordinary negligence in the circumstances. In the event, the defendant was liable as he had used greater force than was justified although the trespasser was held to be two-thirds contributorily negligent.

3. Some insurance policies provide cover for a person's liability 'as owner', and people might be misled into thinking that this provides cover for accidents occurring on their land. It does not: a person who is insured 'as owner' is not covered for liability as 'occupier'.

## SECTION 2: WHO IS AN OCCUPIER?

Liability is imposed on a person not because he is the owner of the land but because he is the occupier, and indeed, as will be seen, it may not be necessary for a person to have property rights over the land at all (see *Collier* v *Anglian Water Authority* below). Conversely, a person may be the occupier if he merely has the right to occupy (*Harris* v *Birkenhead Corporation* below). The principal test is one of control on the grounds that the person to be liable should be the person who could prevent the damage, and it is possible for two people to be occupiers of either different parts of the premises, or of the same part at the same time.

---

### *Wheat* v *E. Lacon & Co. Ltd*
House of Lords [1966] AC 552; [1966] 2 WLR 581; [1966] 1 All ER 582

Lacon & Co. owned the Golfers Arms at Great Yarmouth and employed Mr Richardson as their manager. He and his wife lived on the upper floor, and they had a lodger, Mr Wheat. One evening at about 9.00 p.m. Mr Wheat was coming down the stairs when he fell and was killed. The handrail on the stairs ended just above the third step from the bottom and there was no knob on the end of the rail. At the top of the stairs was a light fitting but it had no bulb and the stairs were dark. Held: dismissing the appeal, that Lacon & Co. owed a duty of care as occupiers of the stairs, but on the facts were not in breach of that duty.

LORD DENNING: The case raises this point of law: did the brewery company owe any duty to Mr Wheat to see that the handrail was safe to use or to see that the stairs were properly lighted? That depends on whether the brewery company was 'an occupier' of the private portion of the 'Golfers' Arms,' and Mr Wheat its 'visitor' within the Occupiers' Liability Act, 1957: for, if so, the brewery company owed him the 'common duty of care.'

In order to determine this question we must have resort to the law before the Act: for it is expressly enacted [in section 1(2)] that the Act

shall not alter the rules of the common law as to the persons on whom a duty is so imposed or to whom it is owed; and accordingly . . . the persons who are to be treated as an occupier and as his visitors are the same . . . as the persons who would at common law be treated as an occupier and as his invitees or licensees.

At the outset, I would say that no guidance is to be obtained from the use of the word 'occupier' in other branches of the law: for its meaning varies according to the subject-matter.

In the Occupiers' Liability Act, 1957, the word 'occupier' is used in the same sense as it was used in the common law cases on occupiers' liability for dangerous premises. It was simply a convenient word to denote a person who had a sufficent degree of control over premises to put him under a duty of care towards those who came lawfully on to the premises. Those persons were divided into two categories, invitees and licensees: and a higher duty was owed to invitees than to licensees. But by the year 1956 the distinction between invitees and licensees had been reduced to vanishing point. The duty of the occupier had become simply a duty to take reasonable care to see that the premises were reasonably safe for people coming lawfully on to them: and it made no difference whether they were invitees or licensees: see *Slater* v *Clay Cross Co. Ltd* [1956] 2 QB 264. The Act of 1957 confirmed the process. It did away, once and for all, with invitees and licensees and classed them all as 'visitors', and it put upon the occupier the same duty to all of them, namely, the common duty of care. This duty is simply a particular instance of the general duty of care which each man owes to his 'neighbour'. . . . Translating this general principle into its particular application to dangerous premises, it becomes simply this: wherever a person has a sufficient degree of control over premises that he ought to realise that any failure on his part to use care may result in injury to a person coming lawfully there, then he is an 'occupier' and the person coming lawfully there is his 'visitor': and the 'occupier' is under a duty to his 'visitor' to use reasonable care. In order to be an 'occupier' it is not necessary for a person to have entire control over the premises. He need not have exclusive occupation. Suffice it that he has some degree of control. He may share the control with others. Two or more may be 'occupiers.' And whenever this happens, each is under a duty to use care towards persons coming lawfully on to the premises, dependent on his degree of control. If each fails in his duty, each is liable to a visitor who is injured in consequence of his failure, but each may have a claim to contribution from the other.

In *Salmond on Torts*, 14th ed. (1965), p. 372, it is said that an 'occupier' is 'he who has the immediate supervision and control and the power of permitting or prohibiting the entry of other persons.' This definition was adopted by Roxburgh J in *Hartwell* v *Grayson, Rollo and Clover Docks Ltd*, [1947] KB 901, and by Diplock LJ in the present case. There is no doubt that a person who fulfils that test is an 'occupier.' He is the person who says 'come in.' But I think that test is too narrow by far. There are other people who are 'occupiers,' even though they do not say 'come in.' If a person has any degree of control over the state of the premises it is enough. . . .

. . . I ask myself whether the brewery company had a sufficient degree of control over the premises to put them under a duty to a visitor. Obviously they had complete control over the ground floor and were 'occupiers' of it. But I think that they had also sufficient control over the private portion. They had not let it out to Mr Richardson by a demise. They had only granted him a licence to occupy it, having a right themselves to do repairs. That left them with a residuary degree of control which was equivalent to that retained by the Chelsea Corporation in *Greene's* case [1954] 2 QB 127. They were in my opinion 'an occupier' within the Act of 1957. Mr Richardson, who had a licence to occupy, had also a considerable degree of control. So had Mrs Richardson, who catered for summer guests. All three of them were, in my opinion, 'occupiers' of the private portion of the 'Golfer's Arms.' There is no difficulty in having more than one occupier at one and the same time, each of whom is under a duty of care to visitors. The Court of Appeal so held in the recent case of *Crockfords Club* (*Fisher* v *CHT Ltd*) [1965] 1 WLR 1093.

What did the common duty of care demand of each of these occupiers towards their visitors? Each was under a duty to take such care as 'in all the circumstances of the case' is reasonable to see that the visitor will be reasonably safe. So far as the brewery company are concerned, the circumstances demanded that on the ground floor they should, by their servants, take care not only of the structure of the building, but also the furniture, the state of the floors and lighting, and so forth, at all hours of day or night when the premises were open. But in regard to the private portion, the circumstances did not demand so much of the brewery company. They ought to see that the structure was reasonably safe, including the handrail, and that the system of lighting was efficient. But I doubt whether they were bound to see that the lights were properly switched on or the rugs laid safely on the floor. The brewery company were entitled to leave those day-to-day matters to Mr and Mrs Richardson. They, too, were occupiers. The circumstances of the case demanded that Mr and Mrs Richardson should take care of those matters in the private portion of the house. And of other matters, too. If they had realised the handrail was dangerous, they should have reported it to the brewery company.

We are not concerned here with Mr and Mrs Richardson. The judge has absolved them from any negligence and there is no appeal. We are only concerned with the brewery company. They were, in my opinion, occupiers and under a duty of care. In this respect I agree with Sellers LJ and Winn J, but I come to a different conclusion on the facts. I can see no evidence of any breach of duty by the brewery company. So far as the handrail was concerned, the evidence was overwhelming that no one had any reason before this accident to suppose that it was in the least dangerous. So far as the light was concerned, the proper inference was that it was removed by some stranger shortly before Mr Wheat went down the staircase. Neither the brewery company nor Mr and Mrs Richardson could be blamed for the act of a stranger.

NOTES

1. In *Collier* v *Anglian Water Authority* The Times, 26 March 1983, the claimant tripped over an uneven paving slab on the promenade at Mablethorpe. The promenade was owned by the local authority who kept it clean and granted leases to shop owners on it, but they did no repair work on it. The repairs were conducted by the water authority (who appeared to have no property interest in the promenade) as part of their duty to maintain adequate sea defences. It was held that both the local authority and the water authority were occupiers, the latter because, by maintaining the promenade as part of their statutory duty, they exercised control over it.

2. In *Harris* v *Birkenhead Corporation* [1976] 1 All ER 279 the defendants were held to be occupiers, even though they had never exercised control over the property, because they had the *right* to do so. The defendants compulsorily purchased a house which was owned by Mrs Gledhill and let to Mrs Redmond. Mrs Redmond left without telling the defendants, and the house became vacant and derelict. The claimant, aged 4, entered the house and fell from the second floor. It was held that the defendants were occupiers, even though they had never entered the property, because the compulsory purchase order gave them the immediate right to enter.

■ QUESTION

A owns land on which buildings are to be demolished. He engages B to do the demolition work, and B subcontracts the work to C. Who occupies the land? (See *Ferguson* v *Welsh* [1987] 1 WLR 1553.)

---

**DEFECTIVE PREMISES ACT 1972**

**4. Landlord's duty of care in virtue of obligation or right to repair premises demised**

(1) Where premises are let under a tenancy which puts on the landlord an obligation to the tenant for the maintenance or repair of the premises, the landlord owes to all persons who might reasonably be expected to be affected by defects in the state of the premises a duty to take such care as is reasonable in all the circumstances to see that they are reasonably safe from personal injury or from damage to their property caused by a relevant defect.

(2) The said duty is owed if the landlord knows (whether as the result of being notified by the tenant or otherwise) or if he ought in all the circumstances to have known of the relevant defect.

(3) In this section 'relevant defect' means a defect in the state of the premises existing at or after the material time and arising from, or continuing because of, an act or omission by the landlord which constitutes or would if he had had notice of the defect, have constituted a failure by him to carry out his obligation to the tenant for the maintenance or repair of the premises; and for the purposes of the foregoing provision 'the material time' means—

(a) where the tenancy commenced before this Act, the commencement of this Act; and

(b) in all other cases, the earliest of the following times, that is to say—

> (i)   the time when the tenancy commences;
>
> (ii)  the time when the tenancy agreement is entered into;
>
> (iii) the time when possession is taken of the premises in contemplation of the letting.
>
> (4) Where premises are let under a tenancy which expressly or impliedly gives the landlord the right to enter the premises to carry out any description of maintenance or repair of the premises, then, as from the time when he first is, or by notice or otherwise can put himself, in a position to exercise the right and so long as he is or can put himself in that position, he shall be treated for the purposes of subsections (1) to (3) above (but for no other purpose) as if he were under an obligation to the tenant for that description of maintenance or repair of the premises; but the landlord shall not owe the tenant any duty by virtue of this subsection in respect of any defect in the state of the premises arising from, or continuing because of, a failure to carry out an obligation expressly imposed on the tenant by the tenancy.
>
> (5) For the purposes of this section obligation imposed or rights given by any enactment in virtue of a tenancy shall be treated as imposed or given by the tenancy.
>
> (6) This section applies to a right of occupation given by contract or any enactment and not amounting to a tenancy as if the right were a tenancy, and 'tenancy' and cognate expressions shall be construed accordingly.

NOTE

In *McCauley* v *Bristol City Council* [1991] 1 All ER 749, the claimant, a council tenant, fell and injured her ankle when an unstable concrete step in the garden moved under her. The council was only obliged to repair the structure and exterior of the house and the tenant was responsible, *inter alia*, for the garden. However, clause 6(c) of the tenancy agreement entitled the council to enter the premises for any purpose. The court held that for the purposes of s. 4(4) of the 1972 Act there was an implied right for the council to enter any part of the premises for the purpose of maintenance as they could insist on doing so if the tenant refused to maintain the property. Accordingly the council was liable under the Act. If the council had inserted in the tenancy agreement an express provision that they should have no right to do repairs to the garden they would not have been liable.

## SECTION 3: WHO IS A VISITOR?

Section 1 of the Occupiers' Liability Act 1957 merely defines a visitor as a person who could have been either an 'invitee' or a 'licensee' at common law. An invitee was a person you asked to come onto your land for your purposes, and a licensee was a person you permitted to enter. It is no longer necessary to distinguish between them, but it is still necessary to define the outer limits of the two categories. Thus, visitor = invitee + licensee. It does not include trespassers or those using rights of way.

---

### *Edwards* v *Railway Executive*
House of Lords [1952] AC 737; [1952] 2 All ER 430; [1952] 2 TLR 237

For a number of years children had been accustomed to climb through a fence beside a railway line and toboggan down the embankment. The defendants repaired the fence whenever they found it broken. The claimant was injured by a train when he was playing on the line. Held: dismissing the appeal, that the claimant was a trespasser and not an implied visitor.

LORD PORTER: The first matter for decision accordingly is whether there was any evidence from which it could be inferred that children from the recreation ground had become licensees to enter the respondents' premises and toboggan down the embankment.

The appellants support their claim on the authority of such cases as *Cooke* v *Midland Great Western Railway of Ireland* [1909] AC 229 and *Lowery* v *Walker* [1911] AC 10. I refrain from referring to the many cases which have not reached your Lordships' House inasmuch as the principle is, I think, clear—the application alone difficult. There must, I think, be such assent to the user relied upon as amounts to a licence to use the premises. Whether that result can be inferred or not must, of course, be a question of degree, but in my view a court is not justified in lightly inferring it. In *Cooke's* case [1909] AC 229 there was an open and well worn pathway leading to a turntable on which children could ride and which was an allurement to them. Apparently the whole station staff in that case knew of the practice of children to congregate there and ride upon the turntable and no attempt was made to stop them. Similar considerations apply to *Lowery* v *Walker* [1911] AC 10. The ground of the decision is best set out in the words of Lord Loreburn LC. The facts of the case were that the defendant put a dangerous horse into a field through which he knew the public were accustomed to pass as a short cut to the station. Lord Loreburn says: 'I think in substance it' (i.e., the county court judge's finding) 'amounts to this: that the plaintiff was not proved to be in this field of right; that he was there as one of the public who habitually used the field to the knowledge of the defendant; that the defendant did not take steps to prevent that user; and in those circumstances it cannot be lawful that the defendant should with impunity allow a horse which he knew to be a savage and dangerous beast to be loose in that field without giving any warning whatever, either to the plaintiff or to the public, of the dangerous character of the animal.'

I mention these cases because they deal with circumstances having some resemblance to the present case, but each case must be determined on its own facts. The onus is on the appellants to establish their licence, and in my opinion they do not do so merely by showing that, in spite of a fence now accepted as complying with the Act requiring the respondents to fence, children again and again broke their way through. What more, the appellants were asked, could the respondents do? Report to the corporation? But their caretaker knew already. Prosecute? First you have to catch your children and even then would that be more effective? In any case I cannot see that the respondents were under any obligation to do more than keep their premises shut off by a fence which was duly repaired when broken and obviously intended to keep intruders out.

It will be observed that in expressing this opinion I have assumed that the servants of the Railway Executive had knowledge that children were accustomed to go there. I am not convinced that they had this knowledge, but it may have been legitimate for the jury to find that the ganger who repaired the fence must have known, although I am not prepared to accept the proposition that any inference can be drawn from the fact that trains passed up or down, or to hold that their drivers ought or must be taken to have seen the children. However that may be, and even assuming that the respondents had knowledge of the intrusion of children onto the embankment, the suggestion that that knowledge of itself constitutes the children licensees, in my opinion, carries the doctrine of implied licence much too far, though no doubt where the owner of the premises knows that the public or some portion of it is accustomed to trespass over his land he must take steps to show that he resents and will try to prevent the invasion.

An open pathway, as in *Cooke* v *Midland Great Western Railway of Ireland* [1909] AC 229, or a knowledge that a track is and has long been constantly used, coupled with a failure to take any steps to indicate that ingress is not permitted, as in *Lowery* v *Walker* [1911] AC 10, may well amount to a tacit licence. But I do not accept the theory that every possible step to keep out intruders must be taken and, if it is not, a licence may be inferred. . . .

NOTES

1. Another way of trying to turn a trespasser into an implied visitor was the doctrine of allurement, whereby a person, usually a child, was tempted away from where he was allowed to be to somewhere where he was not. In *Glasgow Corporation* v *Taylor* [1922] 1 AC 44, a boy aged 7 entered the herb garden in the Botanic Gardens, Glasgow, where he picked berries from a belladonna bush and ate them. He died. The defendants were liable, although technically

permission to enter the gardens did not include permission to meddle with the plants. (Until recently there was a notice by the herb garden saying that children under 10 were not admitted unless accompanied by a responsible adult. Would this have made any difference as to the status of the entrant?)

2. Now that trespassers are owed a duty under the Occupiers' Liability Act 1984, the 'device' of implied permission may no longer be necessary, and the principles discussed above may no longer apply. See *Herrington* v *British Rlys Board* [1972] AC 877, at p. 933, per Lord Diplock.

■ QUESTION

In *The Calgarth* [1927] P 93, Scrutton LJ said 'When you invite a person into your house to use the staircase you do not invite him to slide down the bannisters'. From whose point of view is a limitation of what an entrant is allowed to do judged? The reasonable occupier, the reasonable entrant, or the reasonable bystander?

## SECTION 4: THE DUTY OWED TO VISITORS

The nature of the duty owed by an occupier to his visitors is dealt with in s. 2 of the Occupiers' Liability Act 1957, and this has generally been equated with the ordinary rules of negligence, subject to the particular conditions in s. 2(3) and (4), which relate to children and to skilled entrants and to the role of warnings. It should be noted that the statute does not require the premises themselves to be safe, but only that the visitor is enabled to be safe. This can be achieved not only by making the premises safe, but also by warning the entrant of dangers or otherwise enabling him to avoid them.

---

### *Roles* v *Nathan*
Court of Appeal [1963] 1 WLR 1117; [1963] 2 All ER 908

Donald and Joseph Roles were chimney sweeps who were working on the flues of the Manchester Assembly Rooms. There was a boiler with lengthy flues and, the fire being difficult to light, a boiler engineer was consulted. He advised that two vent holes should be sealed up, and warned the Roles brothers of the dangers of working on the flues with the fires lit and of the risk of carbon monoxide poisoning. One day the men were working on the flue (with the fire lit) in the presence of the engineer and the manager. The work had not been finished, and the two returned later that evening to complete it. They died of carbon monoxide poisoning, and at first instance the judge held the occupier liable for not having the fire drawn or at least damped down. Held: allowing the appeal, that the occupier was not liable.

LORD DENNING MR: The occupier now appeals and says that it is not a case of negligence and contributory negligence, but that, on the true application of the Occupiers' Liability Act, 1957, the occupier was not liable at all. This is the first time we have had to consider that Act. It has been very beneficial. It has rid us of those two unpleasant characters, the invitee and the licensee, who haunted the courts for years, and it has replaced them by the attractive figure of a visitor, who has so far given no trouble at all. The Act has now been in force six years, and hardly any case has come before the courts in which its interpretation has had to be considered. The draftsman expressed the hope that 'the Act would replace a principle of the common law with a new principle *of the common law*; instead of having the judgment of Willes J construed as if it were a statute, one is to have a statute which can be construed as if it were a judgment of Willes J.' It seems that his hopes are being fulfilled. All the fine distinctions about traps have been thrown aside and replaced by the common duty of care.

'The common duty of care,' the Act says, 'is a duty to take such care as in all the circumstances of the case is reasonable to see that the visitor'—note the visitor, not the premises—'will be reasonably safe in using the premises for the purposes for which he is invited or permitted by the occupier to be there.' That is comprehensive. All the circumstances have to be considered. But the Act goes on to give examples of the circumstances that are relevant. The particular one in question here is in subsection (3) of section 2:

> The circumstances relevant for the present purpose include the degree of care, and of want of care, which would ordinarily be looked for in such a visitor, so that (for example) in proper cases . . . (b) an occupier may expect that a person, in the exercise of his calling, will appreciate and guard against any special risks ordinarily incident to it, so far as the occupier leaves him free to do so.

. . . Likewise in the case of a chimney sweep who comes to sweep the chimneys or to seal up a sweep-hole. The householder can reasonably expect the sweep to take care of himself so far as any dangers from the flues are concerned. These chimney sweeps ought to have known that there might be dangerous fumes about and ought to have taken steps to guard against them. They ought to have known that they should not attempt to seal up a sweep-hole whilst the fire was still alight. They ought to have had the fire withdrawn before they attempted to seal it up, or at any rate they ought not to have stayed in the alcove too long when there might be dangerous fumes about. All this was known to these two sweeps; they were repeatedly warned about it, and it was for them to guard against the danger. It was not for the occupier to do it, even though he was present and heard the warnings. When a householder calls in a specialist to deal with a defective installation on his premises, he can reasonably expect the specialist to appreciate and guard against the dangers arising from the defect. The householder is not bound to watch over him to see that he comes to no harm. I would hold, therefore, that the occupier here was under no duty of care to these sweeps, at any rate in regard to the dangers which caused their deaths. If it had been a different danger, as for instance if the stairs leading to the cellar gave way, the occupier might no doubt be responsible, but not for these dangers which were special risks ordinarily incidental to their calling.

Even if I am wrong about this point, and the occupier was under a duty of care to these chimney sweeps, the question arises whether the duty was discharged by the warning that was given to them. This brings us to subsection (4) which states:

> In determining whether the occupier of premises has discharged the common duty of care to a visitor, regard is to be had to all the circumstances, so that (for example)—(a) where damage is caused to a visitor by a danger of which he had been warned by the occupier, the warning is not to be treated without more as absolving the occupier from liability, unless in all the circumstances it was enough to enable the visitor to be reasonably safe.

Apply subsection (4) to this case. I am quite clear that the warnings which were given to the sweeps were enough to enable them to be reasonably safe. The sweeps would have been quite safe if they had heeded these warnings. They should not have come back that evening and attempted to seal up the sweep-hole while the fire was still alight. They ought to have waited till next morning, and then they should have seen that the fire was out before they attempted to seal up the sweep-hole. In any case they should not have stayed too long in the sweep-hole. In short, it was entirely their own fault. The judge held that it was contributory negligence. I would go further and say that under the Act the occupier has, by the warnings, discharged his duty.

---

### *Phipps* v *Rochester Corporation*
Queen's Bench Division [1955] 1 QB 450; [1955] 2 WLR 23; [1955] 1 All ER 129

Yvonne Phipps, aged 7, and her brother Ian, aged 5, entered land which was being developed for building, in order to collect blackberries. On the site was a trench eight or nine feet deep and two feet wide, and Ian fell into it, breaking his leg. As children were known to play on the site the claimant was an implied visitor. Held: the occupier was not liable.

DEVLIN J: The cases which deal with the licensor's duty towards children in general are well known. The law recognizes for this purpose a sharp difference between children and adults. But there might well, I think, be an equally well-marked distinction between 'big children' and 'little children.' I shall use those broad terms to denote broadly the difference between children who know what they are about and children who do not. The latter are sometimes referred to in the cases as 'children of tender years.' Not having reached the age of reason or understanding, they present a special problem. When it comes to taking care of themselves, there is a greater difference between big and little children than there is between big children and adults, and much justification for putting little children into a separate category. Adults and big children can be guilty of contributory negligence; a little child cannot.

I have not been able to find in the cases which have been cited to me any clearly authoritative formulation of the licensor's duty towards little children. I think that the cases do show that judges have not allowed themselves to be driven to the conclusion that licensors must make their premises safe for little children; but they have chosen different ways of escape from that conclusion. . . . A third way is to treat the licence as being conditional upon the little child being accompanied by a responsible adult. That is a solution for which Mr O'Connor contends in the alternative. A fourth way is to frame the duty so as to compromise between the robustness that would make children take the world as they found it and the tenderness which would give them nurseries wherever they go. On this view the licensor is not entitled to assume that all children will, unless they are allured, behave like adults; but he is entitled to assume that normally little children will in fact be accompanied by a responsible person and to discharge his duty of warning accordingly.

I think that it would be an unjustifiable restriction of the principle if one were to say that although the licensor may in determining the extent of his duty have regard to the fact that it is the habit, and also the duty, of prudent people to look after themselves, he may not in that determination have a similar regard to the fact that it is the habit, and also the duty, of prudent people to look after their little children. If he is entitled, in the absence of evidence to the contrary, to assume that parents will not normally allow their little children to go out unaccompanied, he can decide what he should do and consider what warnings are necessary on that basis. He cannot then be made liable for the exceptional child that strays, nor will he be required to prove that any particular parent has been negligent. It is, I think, preferable that this result should be achieved by allowing the general principle to expand in a natural way rather than by restricting its influence and then having to give it artificial aids in order to make it work at all in the case of little children.

The principle I am seeking to express is that contained in the passage I have quoted from the speech of Lord Shaw in *Glasgow Corporation* v *Taylor*, [1922] 1 AC 44, where he says that the municipality is entitled to take into account that reasonable parents will not permit their children to be sent into danger without protection; that the guardians of the child and of the park must each act reasonably; and that each is entitled to assume of the other that he will. That passage was not spoken in reference to the English law of licence, but nevertheless it seems to me to express perfectly the way in which the English law can reasonably be applied. A licensor who tacitly permits the public to use his land without discriminating between its members must assume that the public may include little children. But as a general rule he will have discharged his duty towards them if the dangers which they may encounter are only those which are obvious to a guardian or of which he has given a warning comprehensible by a guardian. To every general rule there are, of course, exceptions. A licensor cannot divest himself of the obligation of finding out something about the sort of people who are availing themselves of his permission and the sort of use they are making of it. He may have to take into account the social habits of the neighbourhood. No doubt there are places where little children go to play unaccompanied. If the licensor knows or ought to anticipate that, he may have to take steps accordingly. But the responsibility for the safety of little children must rest primarily upon the parents; it is their duty to see that such children are not allowed to wander about by themselves, or at the least to satisfy themselves that the places to which they do allow their children to go unaccompanied are safe for them to go to. It would not be socially desirable if parents were, as a matter of course, able to shift the burden of looking after their children from their own shoulders to those of persons who happen to have accessible bits of land. Different considerations may well apply to public parks or to recognized playing grounds where parents allow their children to go unaccompanied in the reasonable belief that they are safe.

NOTE

In *Simkiss* v *Rhondda BC* (1983) 81 LGR 460, Catherine Simkiss, aged 7, and a friend, aged 10, went to picnic on a hillside occupied by the defendants. They came there as visitors, and the picnic spot was visible from Catherine's parents' flat. After the picnic they walked up the mountain and then slid down the slope on a blanket. The claimant fell down a natural bluff for some 30 feet and was injured. The defendants were not liable because (a) the occupiers were entitled to assume that parents would have warned their children of the dangers, and (b) the standard applicable to the occupier was that of a reasonably prudent parent, and they could not be expected to fence off every natural hazard which provided an opportunity to children to injure themselves.

■ QUESTION

In evidence in *Simkiss* v *Rhondda BC* Mr Simkiss was asked whether he, as a reasonably prudent parent, regarded the bluff as a danger. What are the legal consequences of his answering 'Yes' or 'No' to this question?

NOTE

Section 2(4)(b) involves the duty of an occupier to select a competent contractor to work on his land. In *Gwilliam* v *West Hertfordshire Hospitals NHS Trust* [2002] 3 WLR 1425 the hospital organized a fund-raising event in its grounds and engaged a contractor to operate a 'splat wall' where visitors bounced on a trampoline. The claimant was injured. The contractor had merely been selected from the telephone book, but the defendants had checked that the contractor was insured. Unfortunately, the insurance expired a few days before the event. The court held that by analogy with s. 2(4)(b) the defendants had a duty to see that the contractor was insured but that they had fulfilled that duty. Sedley LJ (although concurring in the result) disagreed with the idea that there was a duty to check insurance as it would be a step too far which would give rise to open-ended liability. Such a doctrine would also subvert the principle of vicarious liability whereby an 'employer' is not generally liable for the torts of his contractor. This view was adopted in *Payling* v *Naylor* [2004] EWCA Civ 560, *The Times* 2 June 2004, where Neuberger LJ said that in the absence of special circumstances there can be no liability on an employer for failing to check the insurance of his contractor.

## SECTION 5: THE DUTY OWED TO TRESPASSERS AND OTHER NON-VISITORS

The issue of the level of duty which should be owed to trespassers has had a turbulent history, but following the Law Commission Report No. 75 on Liability for Damage or Injury to Trespassers and Related Questions of Occupiers' Liability (Cmnd 6429, 1976), the matter was settled by the Occupiers' Liability Act 1984. However, it is important to realize the limits of the Act, and the position now is as follows:

(a) the 1984 Act applies only to personal injuries incurred by trespassers and other non-visitors, but the Act does not apply to highway users;

 (b) property damage to all non-visitors is covered, if at all, by the common law, as expressed in *Herrington* v *British Railways Board*;

 (c) users of *adopted* highways are covered by the Highways Act 1980, s. 41;

 (d) injury to users of *unadopted* highways is covered by the tort of public nuisance, or possibly the duty in *Herrington* v *British Railways Board*. However, an occupier of land over which such a public right of way runs is not under any obligation to maintain the path or road and thus is not liable in negligence for failure to maintain: see *McGeown* v *Northern Ireland Housing Executive* [1994] 3 All ER 53.

---

## OCCUPIERS' LIABILITY ACT 1984

### 1. Duty of occupier to persons other than his visitors

(1) The rules enacted by this section shall have effect, in place of the rules of the common law, to determine—

 (a) whether any duty is owed by a person as occupier of premises to persons other than his visitors in respect of any risk of their suffering injury on the premises by reason of any danger due to the state of the premises or to things done or omitted to be done on them; and

 (b) if so, what that duty is.

(2) For the purposes of this section, the persons who are to be treated respectively as an occupier of any premises (which, for those purposes, include any fixed or movable structure) and as his visitors are—

 (a) any person who owes in relation to the premises the duty referred to in section 2 of the Occupiers' Liability Act 1957 (the common duty of care), and

 (b) those who are his visitors for the purposes of that duty.

(3) An occupier of premises owes a duty to another (not being his visitor) in respect of any such risk as is referred to in subsection (1) above if—

 (a) he is aware of the danger or has reasonable grounds to believe that it exists;

 (b) he knows or has reasonable grounds to believe that the other is in the vicinity of the danger concerned or that he may come into the vicinity of the danger (in either case, whether the other has lawful authority for being in that vicinity or not); and

 (c) the risk is one against which, in all the circumstances of the case, he may reasonably be expected to offer the other some protection.

(4) Where, by virtue of this section, an occupier of premises owes a duty to another in respect of such a risk, the duty is to take such care as is reasonable in all the circumstances of the case to see that he does not suffer injury on the premises by reason of the danger concerned.

(5) Any duty owed by virtue of this section in respect of a risk may, in an appropriate case, be discharged by taking such steps as are reasonable in all the circumstances of the case to give warning of the danger concerned or to discourage persons from incurring the risk.

(6) No duty is owed by virtue of this section to any person in respect of risks willingly accepted as his by that person (the question whether a risk was so accepted to be decided on the same principles as in other cases in which one person owes a duty of care to another).

(6A) At any time when the right conferred by section 2(1) of the Countryside and Rights of Way Act 2000 is exercisable in relation to land which is access land for the purposes of Part I of that Act, an occupier of the land owes (subject to subsection (6C) below) no duty by virtue of this section to any person in respect of—

 (a) a risk resulting from the existence of any natural feature of the landscape, or any river, stream, ditch or pond whether or not a natural feature, or

 (b) a risk of that person suffering injury when passing over, under or through any wall, fence or gate, except by proper use of the gate or of a stile.

(6B) For the purposes of subsection (6A) above, any plant, shrub or tree, of whatever origin, is to be regarded as a natural feature of the landscape.

(6C)  Subsection (6A) does not prevent an occupier from owing a duty by virtue of this section in respect of any risk where the danger concerned is due to anything done by the occupier—

(a)  with the intention of creating that risk, or

(b)  being reckless as to whether that risk is created.

(7)  No duty is owed by virtue of this section to persons using the highway, and this section does not affect any duty owed to such persons.

(8)  Where a person owes a duty by virtue of this section, he does not, by reason of any breach of the duty, incur any liability in respect of any loss of or damage to property.

(9)  In this section—

'highway' means any part of a highway other than a ferry or waterway; 'injury' means anything resulting in death or personal injury, including any disease and any impairment of physical or mental condition; and 'movable structure' includes any vessel, vehicle or aircraft.

### 1A.  Special considerations relating to access land

In determining whether any, and if so what, duty is owed by virtue of section 1 by an occupier of land at any time when the right conferred by section 2(1) of the Countryside and Rights of Way Act 2000 is exercisable in relation to the land, regard is to be had, in particular, to—

(a)  the fact that the existence of that right ought not to place an undue burden (whether financial or otherwise) on the occupier,

(b)  the importance of maintaining the character of the countryside, including features of historic, traditional or archaeological interest, and

(c)  any relevant guidance given under section 20 of that Act.

---

## HIGHWAYS ACT 1980

### 41.  Duty to maintain highways maintainable at public expense

The authority who are for the time being the highway authority for a highway maintainable at the public expense are under a duty . . . to maintain the highway.

### 58.  Special defence in action against a highway authority for damages for non-repair of highway

(1)  In an action against a highway authority in respect of damage resulting from their failure to maintain a highway maintainable at the public expense it is a defence (without prejudice to any other defence or the application of the law relating to contributory negligence) to prove that the authority had taken such care as in all the circumstances was reasonably required to secure that the part of the highway to which the action relates was not dangerous for traffic.

(2)  For the purposes of a defence under subsection (1) above, the court shall in particular have regard to the following matters:—

(a)  the character of the highway, and the traffic which was reasonably to be expected to use it;

(b)  the standard of maintenance appropriate for a highway of that character and used by such traffic;

(c)  the state of repair in which a reasonable person would have expected to find the highway;

(d)  whether the highway authority knew, or could reasonably have been expected to know, that the condition of the part of the highway to which the action relates was likely to cause danger to users of the highway;

(e)  where the highway authority could not reasonably have been expected to repair that part of the highway before the cause of action arose, what warning notices of its condition had been displayed;

but for the purposes of such a defence it is not relevant to prove that the highway authority had arranged for a competent person to carry out or supervise the maintenance of the part of the highway to which the action relates unless it is also proved that the authority had given him proper instructions with regard to the maintenance of the highway and that he had carried out the instructions.

---

### British Railways Board v Herrington
House of Lords [1972] AC 877; [1972] 2 WLR 537; [1972] 1 All ER 749

The claimant, aged 6, went to play in Bunces Meadow, a National Trust property, near Mitcham in Surrey. Alongside the field was an electrified railway line protected by a chain link fence. The fence had fallen into disrepair and had been trodden down to about ten inches from the ground. The claimant went through the fence and was injured by touching the electrified rail. Held: dismissing the appeal, that the defendants were liable. (Note: liability to trespassers is now almost wholly governed by the Occupiers' Liability Act 1984, but this case is included for its potential residual liability in cases not covered by that Act and for the justification given by Lord Pearson for treating trespassers differently from visitors.)

LORD REID: Normally the common law applies an objective test. If a person chooses to assume a relationship with members of the public, say by setting out to drive a car or to erect a building fronting a highway, the law requires him to conduct himself as a reasonable man with adequate skill, knowledge and resources would do. He will not be heard to say that in fact he could not attain that standard. If he cannot attain that standard he ought not to assume the responsibility which that relationship involves. But an occupier does not voluntarily assume a relationship with trespassers. By trespassing they force a 'neighbour' relationship on him. When they do so he must act in a humane manner—that is not asking too much of him—but I do not see why he should be required to do more.

So it appears to me that an occupier's duty to trespassers must vary according to his knowledge, ability and resources. It has often been said that trespassers must take the land as they find it. I would rather say that they must take the occupier as they find him.

So the question whether an occupier is liable in respect of an accident to a trespasser on his land would depend on whether a conscientious humane man with his knowledge, skill and resources could reasonably have been expected to have done or refrained from doing before the accident something which would have avoided it. If he knew before the accident that there was a substantial probability that trespassers would come I think that most people would regard as culpable failure to give any thought to their safety. He might often reasonably think, weighing the seriousness of the danger and the degree of likelihood of trespassers coming against the burden he would have to incur in preventing their entry or making his premises safe, or curtailing his own activities on his land, that he could not fairly be expected to do anything. But if he could at small trouble and expense take some effective action, again I think that most people would think it inhumane and culpable not to do that. If some such principle is adopted there will no longer be any need to strive to imply a fictitious licence.

It would follow that an impecunious occupier with little assistance at hand would often be excused from doing something which a large organisation with ample staff would be expected to do.

LORD PEARSON: There are several reasons why an occupier should not have imposed upon him onerous obligations to a trespasser—

(1) There is the unpredictability of the possible trespasser both as to whether he will come on the land at all and also as to where he will go and what he will do if he does come on the land. I enlarged on this point in *Videan* v *British Transport Commission* [1963] 2 QB 650, 679, and I will only sum-marise it shortly here. As the trespasser's presence and movements are unpredictable, he is not within the zone of reasonable contemplation (*Bourhill* v *Young* [1943] AC 92) and he is not a 'neighbour' (*Donoghue* v *Stevenson*) to the occupier, and the occupier cannot reasonably be required to take precautions for his safety. Occupiers are entitled to farm lands, operate quarries and factories, run express trains at full speed through stations, fell trees and fire shots without regard to

the mere general possibility that there might happen to be in the vicinity a trespasser who might be injured. The occupiers do not have to cease or restrict their activities in view of that possibility, which is too remote to be taken into account and could not fairly be allowed to curtail their freedom of action.

(2) Even when his presence is known or reasonably to be anticipated, so that he becomes a neighbour, the trespasser is rightly to be regarded as an under-privileged neighbour. . . .

(3) . . . It would in many, if not most, cases be impracticable to take effective steps to prevent (instead of merely endeavouring to deter) trespassers from going into or remaining in situations of danger. The cost of erecting and maintaining an impenetrable and unclimbable or, as it has been put, 'boy-proof' fence would be prohibitive, if it could be done at all. . . .

(4) There is also a moral aspect. Apart from trespasses which are inadvertent or more or less excusable, trespassing is a form of misbehaviour, showing lack of consideration for the rights of others. It would be unfair if trespassers could by their misbehaviour impose onerous obligations on others. One can take the case of a farmer. He may know well from past experience that persons are likely to trespass on his land for the purpose of tearing up his primroses and bluebells, or picking his mushrooms or stealing his turkeys, or for the purpose of taking country walks in the course of which they will tread down his grass and leave gates open and watch their dogs chasing the farmer's cattle and sheep. It would be intolerable if a farmer had to take expensive precautions for the protection of such persons in such activities.

---

### Tomlinson v Congleton Borough Council
[House of Lords [2004] 1 AC 46; [2003] 3 All ER 1122; [2003] 3 WLR 1603; [2003] UKHL 47]

The Council owned the Brereton Heath Country Park near Congleton in Cheshire. In the park is a 14 acre lake with sandy beaches. After sunbathing, the claimant ran into the water and dived, but he struck his head on the sandy bottom and broke his neck. He became tetraplegic and is unable to walk. Notices around the lake stated 'Dangerous Water. No Swimming' but the Council knew that these were often ignored. The claimant conceded that he was a trespasser when he entered the water, but claimed that the defendants had failed to prevent him encountering danger. Held: the defendants were not liable.

LORD HOFFMANN

*A danger 'due to the state of the premises'*

**26** The first question, therefore, is whether there was a risk within the scope of the statute; a danger 'due to the state of the premises or to things done or omitted to be done on them'. The judge found that there was 'nothing about the mere at Brereton Heath which made it any more dangerous than any other ordinary stretch of open water in England'. There was nothing special about its configuration; there were no hidden dangers. It was shallow in some places and deep in others, but that is the nature of lakes. Nor was the Council doing or permitting anything to be done which created a danger to persons who came to the lake. No power boats or jet skis threatened the safety of either lawful windsurfers or unlawful swimmers. So the Council submits that there was no danger attributable to the state of premises or things done or omitted on them. In *Donoghue* v *Folkestone Properties Ltd* [2003] 2 WLR 1138, 1153 Lord Phillips of Worth Matravers MR expressed the same opinion. He said that he had been unable to identify the 'state of the premises' which carried with it the risk of the injury suffered by Mr Tomlinson:

> It seems to me that Mr Tomlinson suffered his injury because he chose to indulge in an activity which had inherent dangers, not because the premises were in a dangerous state.

**27** In making this comment, the Master of the Rolls was identifying a point which is in my opinion central to this appeal. It is relevant at a number of points in the analysis of the duties under the 1957 and 1984 Acts. Mr Tomlinson was a person of full capacity who voluntarily and without any pressure or inducement engaged in an activity which had inherent risk. The risk was that he might not execute his dive properly and so sustain injury. Likewise, a person who goes mountaineering incurs the risk that he might stumble or misjudge where to put his weight. In neither case can the risk be attributed to the state of the premises. Otherwise any premises can be said to be dangerous to someone who chooses to use them for some dangerous activity. In the present case, Mr Tomlinson knew the lake well and even if he had not, the judge's finding was that it contained no dangers which one would not have expected. So the only risk arose out of what he chose to do and not out of the state of the premises.

**28** Mr Braithwaite was inclined to accept the difficulty of establishing that the risk was due to the state of the premises. He therefore contended that it was due to 'things done or omitted to be done' on the premises. When asked what these might be, he said that they consisted in the attraction of the lake and the Council's inadequate attempts to keep people out of the water. The Council, he said, were 'luring people into a deathtrap'. Ward LJ said that the water was 'a siren call strong enough to turn stout men's minds'. In my opinion this is gross hyperbole. The trouble with the island of the Sirens was not the state of the premises. It was that the Sirens held mariners spellbound until they died of hunger. The beach, give or take a fringe of human bones, was an ordinary Mediterranean beach. If Odysseus had gone ashore and accidentally drowned himself having a swim, Penelope would have had no action against the Sirens for luring him there with their songs. Likewise in this case, the water was perfectly safe for all normal activities. In my opinion 'things done or omitted to be done' means activities or the lack of precautions which cause risk, like allowing speedboats among the swimmers. It is a mere circularity to say that a failure to stop people getting into the water was an omission which gave rise to a duty to take steps to stop people from getting into the water.

**29** It follows that in my opinion, there was no risk to Mr Tomlinson due to the state of the premises or anything done or omitted upon the premises. That means that there was no risk of a kind which gave rise to a duty under the 1957 or 1984 Acts. I shall nevertheless go on to consider the matter on the assumption that there was.

*The conditions for the existence of a duty*

*(i) Knowledge or foresight of the danger*

**30** Section 1(3) has three conditions which must be satisfied. First, under paragraph (a), the occupier must be aware of the danger or have reasonable grounds to believe that it exists. For this purpose, it is necessary to say what the relevant danger was . . . I accept that the Council must have known that there was a possibility that some boisterous teenager would injure himself by horseplay in the shallows and I would not disturb the concurrent findings that this was sufficient to satisfy paragraph (a). But the chances of such an accident were small. I shall return later, in connection with condition (c), to the relevance of where the risk comes on the scale of probability.

*(ii) Knowledge or foresight of the presence of the trespasser*

**31** Once it is found that the risk of a swimmer injuring himself by diving was something of which the Council knew or which they had reasonable grounds to believe to exist, paragraph (b) presents no difficulty. The Council plainly knew that swimmers came to the lake and Mr Tomlinson fell within that class.

*(iii) Reasonable to expect protection*

**32** That leaves paragraph (c). Was the risk one against which the Council might reasonably be expected to offer the claimant some protection? The judge found that 'the danger and risk of injury from diving in the lake where it was shallow were obvious.' In such a case the judge held, both as a matter of common sense and following consistent authority (*Staples* v *West Dorset District Council* [1995] PIQR 439; *Ratcliff* v *McConnell* [1999] 1 WLR 670; *Darby* v *National Trust* [2001] PIQR 372), that there was no duty to warn against the danger. A warning would not tell a swimmer anything he did not already know. Nor was it necessary to do anything else. 'I do not think', said the judge, 'that the defendants' legal duty to the claimant in the circumstances required them to take the extreme measures which were completed after the accident'. Even if Mr Tomlinson had been owed a duty under the 1957 Act as a lawful visitor, the Council would not have been obliged to do more than they did.

**33** The Court of Appeal disagreed. Ward LJ said that the Council was obliged to do something more. The gravity of the risk, the number of people who regularly incurred it and the attractiveness of the beach created a duty. The prohibition on swimming was obviously ineffectual and therefore it was necessary to take additional steps to prevent or discourage people from getting into the water. Sedley LJ said: 'It is only where the risk is so obvious that the occupier can safely assume that nobody will take it that there will be no liability.' Longmore LJ dissented. The majority reduced the damages by two-thirds to reflect Mr Tomlinson's contributory negligence, although Ward LJ said that he would have been inclined to reduce them only by half. The Council appeals against the finding of liability and Mr Tomlinson appeals against the apportionment, which he says should have been in accordance with the view of Ward LJ.

*The balance of risk, gravity of injury, cost and social value*

**34** My Lords, the majority of the Court of Appeal appear to have proceeded on the basis that if there was a foreseeable risk of serious injury, the Council was under a duty to do what was necessary to prevent it. But this in my opinion is an oversimplification. Even in the case of the duty owed to a lawful visitor under section 2(2) of the 1957 Act and even if the risk had been attributable to the state of the premises rather than the acts of Mr Tomlinson, the question of what amounts to 'such care as in all the circumstances of the case is reasonable' depends upon assessing, as in the case of common law negligence, not only the likelihood that someone may be injured and the seriousness of the injury which may occur, but also the social value of the activity which gives rise to the risk and the cost of preventative measures. These factors have to be balanced against each other.

*The 1957 and 1984 Acts contrasted*

**38** In the case of the 1984 Act, there is the additional consideration that unless in all the circumstances it is reasonable to expect the occupier to do something, that is to say, to 'offer the other some protection', there is no duty at all. One may ask what difference there is between the case in which the claimant is a lawful visitor and there is in principle a duty under the 1957 Act but on the particular facts no duty to do anything, and the case in which he is a trespasser and there is on the particular facts no duty under the 1984 Act. Of course in such a case the result is the same. But Parliament has made it clear that in the case of a lawful visitor, one starts from the assumption that there is a duty whereas in the case of a trespasser one starts from the assumption that there is none.

*The balance under the 1957 Act*

**39** My Lords, it will in the circumstances be convenient to consider first the question of what the position would have been if Mr Tomlinson had been a lawful visitor owed a duty under section 2(2) of the 1957 Act. Assume, therefore, that there had been no prohibition on swimming. What was the risk of serious injury? To some extent this depends upon what one regards as the relevant risk. As I have mentioned, the judge thought it was the risk of injury through diving while the Court of Appeal thought it was any kind of injury which could happen to people in the water. Although, as I have said, I am inclined to agree with the judge, I do not want to put the basis of my decision too narrowly. So I accept that we are concerned with the steps, if any, which should have been taken to prevent any kind of water accident. According to the Royal Society for the Prevention of Accidents, about 450 people drown while swimming in the United Kingdom every year (see *Darby* v *National Trust* [2001] PIQR 372, 374). About 25–35 break their necks diving and no doubt others sustain less serious injuries. So there is obviously some degree of risk in swimming and diving, as there is in climbing, cycling, fell walking and many other such activities.

**40**  I turn then to the cost of taking preventative measures. Ward LJ described it (£5,000) as 'not excessive'. Perhaps it was not, although the outlay has to be seen in the context of the other items (rated 'essential' and 'highly desirable') in the Borough Council budget which had taken precedence over the destruction of the beaches for the previous two years.

**41**  I do not however regard the financial cost as a significant item in the balancing exercise which the court has to undertake. There are two other related considerations which are far more important. The first is the social value of the activities which would have to be prohibited in order to reduce or eliminate the risk from swimming. And the second is the question of whether the Council should be entitled to allow people of full capacity to decide for themselves whether to take the risk.

**42**  The Court of Appeal made no reference at all to the social value of the activities which were to be prohibited. The majority of people who went to the beaches to sunbathe, paddle and play with their children were enjoying themselves in a way which gave them pleasure and caused no risk to themselves or anyone else. This must be something to be taken into account in deciding whether it was reasonable to expect the Council to destroy the beaches.

*Free will*

**44**  The second consideration, namely the question of whether people should accept responsibility for the risks they choose to run, is the point made by Lord Phillips of Worth Matravers MR in *Donoghue* v *Folkestone Properties Ltd* [2003] 2 WLR 1138, 1153 and which I said was central to this appeal. Mr Tomlinson was freely and voluntarily undertaking an activity which inherently involved some risk. By contrast, Miss Bessie Stone, to whom the House of Lords held that no duty was owed, was innocently standing on the pavement outside her garden gate at 10 Beckenham Road, Cheetham when she was struck by a ball hit for 6 out of the Cheetham Cricket Club ground. She was certainly not engaging in any activity which involved an inherent risk of such injury. So compared with *Bolton* v *Stone*, this is an a fortiori case.

**45**  I think it will be extremely rare for an occupier of land to be under a duty to prevent people from taking risks which are inherent in the activities they freely choose to undertake upon the land. If people want to climb mountains, go hang gliding or swim or dive in ponds or lakes, that is their affair. Of course the landowner may for his own reasons wish to prohibit such activities. He may be think that they are a danger or inconvenience to himself or others. Or he may take a paternalist view and prefer people not to undertake risky activities on his land. He is entitled to impose such conditions, as the Council did by prohibiting swimming. But the law does not require him to do so.

**46**  My Lords, as will be clear from what I have just said, I think that there is an important question of freedom at stake. It is unjust that the harmless recreation of responsible parents and children with buckets and spades on the beaches should be prohibited in order to comply with what is thought to be a legal duty to safeguard irresponsible visitors against dangers which are perfectly obvious. The fact that such people take no notice of warnings cannot create a duty to take other steps to protect them. I find it difficult to express with appropriate moderation my disagreement with the proposition of Sedley LJ (at para. 45) that it is 'only where the risk is so obvious that the occupier can safely assume that nobody will take it that there will be no liability'. A duty to protect against obvious risks or self-inflicted harm exists only in cases in which there is no genuine and informed choice, as in the case of employees, or some lack of capacity, such as the inability of children to recognise danger (*British Railways Board* v *Herrington* [1972] AC 877) or the despair of prisoners which may lead them to inflict injury on themselves (*Reeves* v *Commissioner of Police* [2000] 1 AC 360).

**47**  It is of course understandable that organisations like the Royal Society for the Prevention of Accidents should favour policies which require people to be prevented from taking risks. Their function is to prevent accidents and that is one way of doing so. But they do not have to consider the cost, not only in money but also in deprivation of liberty, which such restrictions entail. The courts will naturally respect the technical expertise of such organisations in drawing attention to what can be done to prevent accidents. But the balance between risk on the one hand and individual autonomy on the other is not a matter of expert opinion. It is a judgment which the courts must make and which in England reflects the individualist values of the common law.

**48**  As for the Council officers, they were obvious motivated by the view that it was necessary to take defensive measures to prevent the Council from being held liable to pay compensation. The

Borough Leisure Officer said that he regretted the need to destroy the beaches but saw no alterna-tive if the Council was not to be held liable for an accident to a swimmer. So this appeal gives your Lordships the opportunity to say clearly that local authorities and other occupiers of land are ordinarily under no duty to incur such social and financial costs to protect a minority (or even a majority) against obvious dangers. On the other hand, if the decision of the Court of Appeal were left standing, every such occupier would feel obliged to take similar defensive measures. Sedley LJ was able to say that if the logic of the Court of Appeal's decision was that other public lakes and ponds required similar precautions, 'so be it'. But I cannot view this prospect with the same equanimity. In my opinion it would damage the quality of many people's lives.

**50** My Lords, for these reasons I consider that even if swimming had not been prohibited and the Council had owed a duty under section 2(2) of the 1957 [Act], that duty would not have required them to take any steps to prevent Mr Tomlinson from diving or warning him against dangers which were perfectly obvious. If that is the case, then plainly there can have been no duty under the 1984 Act. The risk was not one against which he was entitled under section 1(3)(c) to protection. I would therefore allow the appeal and restore the decision of Jack J. It follows that the cross-appeal against the apportionment of damages must be dismissed.

### LORD HOBHOUSE

**81** The fourth point, one to which I know that your Lordships attach importance, is the fact that it is not, and should never be, the policy of the law to require the protection of the foolhardy or reckless few to deprive, or interfere with, the enjoyment by the remainder of society of the liberties and amenities to which they are rightly entitled. Does the law require that all trees be cut down because some youths may climb them and fall? Does the law require the coast line and other beauty spots to be lined with warning notices? Does the law require that attractive water side picnic spots be destroyed because of a few foolhardy individuals who choose to ignore warning notices and indulge in activities dangerous only to themselves? The answer to all these questions is, of course, no. But this is the road down which your Lordships, like other courts before, have been invited to travel and which the councils in the present case found so inviting. In truth, the arguments for the claimant have involved an attack upon the liberties of the citizen which should not be countenanced. They attack the liberty of the individual to engage in dangerous, but otherwise harmless, pastimes at his own risk and the liberty of citizens as a whole fully to enjoy the variety and quality of the landscape of this country. The pursuit of an unrestrained culture of blame and compensation has many evil consequences and one is certainly the interference with the liberty of the citizen. The discussion of social utility in the Illinois Supreme Court is to the same effect: *Bucheleres* v *Chicago Park District* 171 Ill 2d 435, at 457–8.

NOTES

1. This is an interesting attack on the 'compensation culture' and contains some unusually strong language. Note particularly the view of Lord Hobhouse that the arguments of the claimants were an attack on the civil liberties of the citizen, and Lord Hoffmann also stressed the relevance of social welfare. This suggests that we are becoming too risk averse and the House of Lords hopes to reverse this trend. Perhaps today we have got used to the idea that we can't do something (i.e. that our freedom should be curtailed) because of 'health and safety reasons' which may amount to little more than the fanciful imaginings of the paranoid. The modern era has greatly encouraged the 'jobsworth' whose only delight is to interfere with our pleasure, citing either safety or bureaucratic rules dressed up as such.

2. Paddling in the lake was allowed. Accordingly the claimant might have argued that when he entered the water he was a visitor. As his claim was that he was not adequately warned of the danger of swimming, did not that duty arise when he was a visitor? Lord Scott accepted this argument, but the majority said that he was a trespasser. The reason was that as his purpose on entering the water was to swim, he was there not as a paddler but as a potential swimmer. Lord Hoffmann said 'I can see no difference between a person who comes onto land without permission and one who, having come on with permission, does something he was not given permission to do'.

## SECTION 6: EXCLUSION OF LIABILITY

Section 2(1) of the Occupiers' Liability Act 1957 allows an occupier to exclude liability 'in so far as he is free to and does extend, restrict, modify or exclude his duty to any visitor or visitors by agreement or otherwise'. This, of course, is subject to the restrictions imposed by the Unfair Contract Terms Act 1977, for which see Chapter 15. As can be seen from *White v Blackmore* (below), it is necessary to distinguish between an exclusion notice, which is subject to the Unfair Contract Terms Act, and a warning notice, which is subject to the test of adequacy in s. 2(4) of the Occupiers' Liability Act 1957.

It is generally assumed that an exclusion clause is valid because it varies the terms of the licence granted to the visitor, but if this is the rationale, it is difficult to see how such a notice would restrict liability to trespassers. This creates an anomaly because it could mean that a non-business occupier could exclude liability to visitors but not to trespassers. See Mesher, 'Occupiers, Trespassers and The Unfair Contract Terms Act 1977' (1979) Conv 58.

---

### White v Blackmore
Court of Appeal [1972] 2 QB 651; [1972] 3 WLR 296; [1972] 3 All ER 158

Mr White was a member of a jalopy racing club. One morning he took his jalopy car to a field where races were to be held and signed on as a competitor. In the afternoon he went to the field with his family. At the entrance was a notice saying 'Warning to the Public: Motor Racing is Dangerous' and excluding liability to 'spectators or ticket holders'. Mr White paid for his family to enter, but he himself entered free as a competitor. On each programme was a notice excluding liability 'to you'.

After finishing his race Mr White went to stand by the ropes to watch other races. About one third of a mile away a car collided with the ropes, and the rear wheel acted as a winch and pulled all the safety ropes tight, pulling out the stakes. Mr White was catapulted into the air and later died. Held: dismissing the appeal, that the defendants were not liable.

LORD DENNING MR, *dissenting*: Section 2(4)(a) of the Occupiers' Liability Act 1957 says explicitly: 'where damage is caused to a visitor by a danger of which he had been warned by the occupier, the warning is not to be treated without more as absolving the occupier from liability, unless in all the circumstances it was enough to enable the visitor to be reasonably safe; . . .'

During the argument we were not referred to that subsection: nor was the judge below. But I think it is decisive. The warning notices in this case do not enable the visitor to be reasonably safe. They do not tell him anything about any danger except that 'motor racing is dangerous.' They do not tell him to avoid the danger by going away—for that is the very last thing the organisers want him to do. They want him to come and stay and see the races. By inviting him to come, they are under a duty of care to him: which they cannot avoid by telling him that it is dangerous.

I appreciate, of course, that the warning notices go on to say: 'The organisers will not be liable for any accident howsoever caused.' But that does not make any difference. Or, at any rate, it ought not to do so. It does no more than underline the warning about danger. It is just another attempt to avoid their responsibilities. Suppose there was a stream running through this field with a rotten footbridge across it. A warning 'This bridge is dangerous' would not exempt the occupiers from liability for negligence—see the illustration I gave in *Roles v Nathan* [1963] 1 WLR 1117, 1124. It follows that a warning 'Visitors cross this bridge at their own risk' equally does not exempt him. An occupier cannot get round the statute by such a change of wording. It is a warning still and within the statute.

BUCKLEY LJ: When the deceased returned with his family in the afternoon, the notice to which Lord Denning MR has referred was prominently displayed near the entrance to the ground. The judge found as a fact that the deceased saw that notice and appreciated that it was a notice governing the conditions under which people were to be admitted to watch the racing.

No argument was addressed to us based upon the Occupiers' Liability Act 1957, s. 2(4). This, I think, was right. To the extent that the notice at the entrance was a warning of a danger, I agree with Lord Denning MR that it did not enable a visitor to be reasonably safe, but the notice was more than a warning of danger: it was designed to subject visitors to a condition that the classes of persons mentioned in it should be exempt from liability arising out of accidents. Section 2(4) has, it seems to me, no application to this aspect of the notice.

What then was the effect of the situation which arose when the deceased returned to the field in the afternoon? It is clear that the occupier of land, who permits someone else to enter upon that land as his licensee, can by imposing suitable conditions limit his own liability to the licensee in respect of any risks which may arise while the licensee is on the land (*Ashdown* v *Samuel Williams & Sons Ltd* [1957] 1 QB 409). The Occupiers' Liability Act 1957, which in section 2(1) refers to an occupier excluding his duty of care to any visitor 'by agreement or otherwise' has not altered the law in this respect. Mr Griffiths concedes that in the present case the notice displayed at the entrance to the ground was sufficient to exclude liability on the part of the organisers of the meeting to all spectators properly so-called, but he contends that a distinction is to be drawn between competitors and spectators for this purpose. It is common ground that the deceased was not a ticket holder within the meaning of the notice, but, in my judgment, he was a spectator. The judge so held, and I think that he was right in doing so. The notice was, in my opinion, sufficiently explicit in its application to the deceased. I feel unable to accept the suggestion that the heading 'Warning to the Public' should be read in a restrictive sense excluding competitors.

NOTES

1. This case would now be decided differently, as under the Unfair Contract Terms Act 1977, the occupier of business premises is no longer permitted to exclude liability for personal injuries, but an occupier of private premises may do so.
2. In *Burnett* v *British Waterways Board* [1973] 1 WLR 700, the claimant worked on a barge on the River Thames, and was injured when a rope pulling his barge into a lock snapped. The defendants admitted this was due to the negligence of their staff, but claimed that liability was excluded by a notice at the entrance to the lock. Nevertheless, the defendants were held liable on the grounds that they could not exclude liability where the claimant had no choice whether to enter the lock, because he was bound to do so by his contract of employment. (He was not employed by the defendants but by another company.)

■ QUESTIONS

1. A is a postman delivering mail to a private house. On the gate is a notice saying 'Beware of falling slates. No liability is accepted under the Occupiers' Liability Act 1957 for any injury caused to any entrant.' A is hit by a falling slate. Is the occupier liable?

2. How would you deal with the question of whether an exclusion notice affects trespassers? If it does not, how would you resolve the anomaly thereby created in relation to visitors? Should the duty in the 1984 Act or in *Herrington* be an irreducible minimum?

# 19

## Nuisance

Private nuisance is an ancient wrong designed as an action between neighbouring landowners to protect a person's interest in land from being adversely affected by the activities of his neighbour. The harm is usually indirect, as the tort of trespass protects a person against direct invasion. The tort protects only a limited range of interests such as physical harm to the land or interference with quiet enjoyment of it, and generally a defendant's activity must be unreasonable. The tort therefore defines two things: first, what kinds of interests a person has in his land (e.g. does he have the right to receive television or to have an uninterrupted view) and, second, if such an interest has been interfered with, whether the level of the interference is unreasonable and has been caused by an unreasonable activity.

Confusion is sometimes caused by the analogous wrong of public nuisance, which has entirely different antecedents, but which covers similar subject matter. The distinction between public and private nuisance will be dealt with first, and public nuisance can then be left to one side.

### SECTION 1: PUBLIC AND PRIVATE NUISANCE

Private nuisance deals with the rights between two landowners, and generally the harm must affect private land. Public nuisance is a crime to which a civil remedy has been attached, and the harm need not emanate from or affect private land. However, a civil action will be allowed only where an individual has suffered harm over and above that experienced by the general public. The various heads of damage claimed in *Halsey* v *Esso Petroleum* (below) neatly illustrate which kinds of harm can be claimed in private and which in public nuisance.

---

### *Halsey* v *Esso Petroleum*
Queen's Bench Division [1961] 1 WLR 683; [1961] 2 All ER 145

The claimants owned a house in Fulham, opposite which the defendants operated an oil depot. The claimant complained of the following: (i) acid smuts from a boiler in the depot which damaged the claimant's washing; (ii) the same acid smuts which damaged his car standing in the road outside; (iii) the smell of oil, which was unpleasant but caused no damage to health; (iv) noise from the boilers; (v) noise from lorries in the depot; (vi) noise from lorries on the road entering the depot. Held: the defendants were liable. Heads (i), (iii), (iv) and (v) were private nuisance, and heads (ii) and (vi) were public nuisance.

VEALE J: So far as the present case is concerned, liability for nuisance by harmful deposits could be established by proving damage by the deposits to the property in question, provided of course that the injury was not merely trivial. Negligence is not an ingredient of the cause of action, and the character of the neighbourhood is not a matter to be taken into consideration. On the other hand, nuisance by smell or noise is something to which no absolute standard can be applied. It is always a question of degree whether the interference with comfort or convenience is sufficiently serious to constitute a nuisance. The character of the neighbourhood is very relevant and all the relevant circumstances have to be taken into account. What might be a nuisance in one area is by no means necessarily so in another. In an urban area, everyone must put up with a certain amount of discomfort and annoyance from the activities of neighbours, and the law must strike a fair and reasonable balance between the right of the plaintiff on the one hand to the undisturbed enjoyment of his property, and the right of the defendant on the other hand to use his property for his own lawful enjoyment. That is how I approach this case.

It may be possible in some cases to prove that noise or smell have in fact diminished the value of the plaintiff's property in the market. That consideration does not arise in this case, and no evidence has been called in regard to it. The standard in respect of discomfort and inconvenience from noise and smell which I have to apply is that of the ordinary reasonable and responsible person who lives in this particular area of Fulham. This is not necessarily the same as the standard which the plaintiff chooses to set up for himself. It is the standard of the ordinary man, and the ordinary man, who may well like peace and quiet, will not complain, for instance, of the noise of traffic if he chooses to live on a main street in an urban centre, nor of the reasonable noises of industry, if he chooses to live alongside a factory.

Nuisance is commonly regarded as a tort in respect of land. In *Read* v *J. Lyons & Co. Ltd* [1947] AC 156, Lord Simonds said: 'he alone has a lawful claim who has suffered an invasion of some proprietary or other interest in land.' In this connection the allegation of damage to the plaintiff's motor-car calls for special consideration, since the allegation is that when the offending smuts from the defendants' chimney alighted upon it, the motor-car was not actually upon land in the plaintiff's occupation, but was on the public highway outside his door. In my judgment the plaintiff is also right in saying that if the motor-car was damaged in this way while on the public highway, it is a public nuisance in respect of which he has suffered special damage. . . .

I approach this question [of the smell] with caution, as Mr Gardiner asked me to do, since there has been no injury to health, but injury to health is not a necessary ingredient in the cause of action for nuisance by smell, and authority for that proposition is to be found in the judgment of Lord Romilly MR in *Crump* v *Lambert* (1867) 3 Eq 409, 412. I reject the contention that the evidence for the plaintiff has been exaggerated by people who feel strongly against the defendants on other grounds. I accept the evidence for the plaintiff, and it is right to add that the description by the witnesses of the nature of the smell was confirmed by my own experience on the night of February 10. On that night, at half past eleven, there was in Rainville Road and Wingrave Road, clearly emanating from the defendants' depôt, a nasty smell, which could properly be described, as the plaintiff has described it in his further and better particulars, namely, 'a pungent, rather nauseating smell of an oily character.' The defendants in my judgment are liable for nuisance by smell.

I turn now to the question of nuisance by noise. This question relates to two distinct matters: the noise of the plant and the noise of the vehicles, the latter complaint including the noise of the vehicles themselves and the attendant noises made by drivers shouting and slamming doors and banging pipes. It is in connection with noise that, in my judgment, the operations of the defendants at night are particularly important. After all, one of the main objects of living in a house or flat is to have a room with a bed in it where one can sleep at night. Night is the time when the ordinary man takes his rest. No real complaint is made by the plaintiff so far as the daytime is concerned; but he complains bitterly of the noise at night. . . .

I accept the evidence of the plaintiff as to noise and I hold it is a serious nuisance, going far beyond a triviality, and one in respect of which the plaintiff is entitled to complain. Because of the noise made by the boilers, I think that the plaintiff is not so much, certainly since the throbbing of the steam pumps ceased, troubled by the noise of the electric pumps. But that is because the noise of the pumps is largely drowned by the noise of the boilers, and even if the noise of the boilers stopped, it might be that the plaintiff could justifiably complain of the noise of the pumps.

. . . But bearing in mind, I hope, all the relevant considerations, in my judgment the defendants are liable in nuisance for the noise of their plant, though only at night. Applying and adapting the well-known words of Knight-Bruce V-C in *Walter* v *Selfe*, 64 ER 849, this inconvenience is, as I find to be the fact, more than fanciful, more than one of mere delicacy or fastidiousness. It is an inconvenience materially interfering with the ordinary comfort physically of human existence, not merely according to elegant or dainty modes of living, but according to plain and sober and simple notions among ordinary people living in this part of Fulham.

But the question of noise does not stop there. At intervals through the night tankers leave and come to the defendants' depot. It has been urged upon me that the public highway is for the use of all, and that is true. But it must be borne in mind that these tankers are not ordinary motor-cars; they are not ordinary lorries which make more noise than a motor-car; they are enormous vehicles, some when laden weighing 24 tons, which, apart from the loud noise of the engine, may rattle as they go, particularly when empty and especially if they hit something in the road like a grating. They all enter the depot almost opposite the plaintiff's house, which involves a sharp turn in order to do so, often changing down into low great at the same time. They leave by the exit gate which is also close to the plaintiff's house. The noise of a tanker was 83 decibels—in the 'very loud' category. . . .

It is said by the defendants that since the public highway is for the use of everyone, the plaintiff cannot complain if all the defendants do is to make use of their right to use the public highway. I agree, if that is all that the defendants have done. If a person makes an unreasonable use of the public highway, for instance, by parking stationary vehicles on it, a member of the public who suffers special damage has a cause of action against him for public nuisance. Similarly, in my view, if a person makes an unreasonable use of the public highway by concentrating in one small area of the highway vehicles in motion and a member of the public suffers special damage, he is equally entitled to complain, although in most cases concentration of moving as opposed to stationary vehicles will be more likely to be reasonable. . . .

In the particular circumstances of this case I do not think it matters very much whether one regards the alleged nuisance by vehicular noise as a private or a public nuisance. The history of the cause of action for private nuisance is set out by Lord Wright in *Sedleigh-Denfield* v *O'Callaghan* [1940] AC 880. The ground of responsibility is the possession and control of the land from which the nuisance proceeds, though Lord Wright refers to 'possibly certain anomalous exceptions.' Public nuisance on the other hand, as Denning LJ said in the Court of Appeal in *Southport Corporation* v *Esso Petroleum Co.* [1954] 2 QB 182 can cover a multitude of sins, great and small. In this latter case Devlin J, whose judgment is reported as part of the report of the proceedings in the House of Lords [1956] AC 218, said:

> It is clear that to give a cause of action for private nuisance the matter complained of must affect the property of the plaintiffs. But I know of no principle that it must emanate from land belonging to the defendant. Mr Nelson cited *Cunard* v *Antifyre Ltd* [1933] 1 KB 551, and I think that the statement of the principle is put there as clearly and concisely as it can be. Talbot J said; 'Private nuisances, at least in the vast majority of cases, are interferences for a substantial length of time by owners or occupiers of property with the use of enjoyment of neighbouring property; and it would manifestly be inconvenient and unreasonable if the right to complain of such interference extended beyond the occupier, or (in the case of injury to the reversion) the owner, of such neighbouring property.' It is clear from that statement of principle that the nuisance must affect the property of the plaintiff; and it is true that in the vast majority of cases it is likely to emanate from the neighbouring property of the defendant. But no statement of principle has been cited to me to show that the latter is a prerequisite to a cause of action; and I can see no reason why, if land or water belonging to the public, or waste land, is misused by the defendant, or if the defendant as a licensee or trespasser misuses someone else's land, he should not be liable for the creation of a nuisance in the same way as an adjoining occupier would be.

NOTE

*Public nuisance*. An example of a person suffering damage over and above that suffered by the public at large is *Tate and Lyle* v *Greater London Council* [1983] 2 AC 509, where the claimants operated a sugar refinery which had a jetty in the River Thames. The defendants' predecessors had built a terminal for the Woolwich Ferry which caused the channel to the claimants' jetty to silt up. It was held that the claimants did not have any *private* rights which enabled them to insist on a certain depth of water round their jetty, so there was no liability in *private* nuisance. However, in relation to *public* nuisance it was held the siltation caused by the ferry terminals was an interference with the public right of navigation, and that the claimants had suffered particular damage over and above that caused to the public at large, and therefore the defendants were liable for public nuisance.

## SECTION 2: PRIVATE NUISANCE: THE INTERESTS PROTECTED

One of the issues which has come to the fore recently is whether a claimant in private nuisance must have an interest in land to be able to sue. The traditional view was that the function of nuisance was to protect a person who has an interest in land in the enjoyment of his property. This included not only freeholders, but also lesses and even tenants at will, but it excluded those with no property interest. For example, in *Malone* v *Laskey* [1907] 2 KB 141 it was said that a wife 'who had no interest in property, no right of occupation in the proper sense of the term' could not sue in nuisance for personal injuries arising out of a neighbour's activities. *Hunter* v *Canary Wharf* (below) has now confirmed this rule with the consequence that actions for personal injuries and damage to chattels (probably even if belonging to the owner) must now be brought in negligence. This allows negligence and nuisance to be properly separated and means that the issue of the role of fault in nuisance can be dealt with by relating it to the purpose of nuisance and without notions of duty spreading in from negligence. This may mean that nuisance will tend more towards strict liability, albeit protecting a narrower range of interests than before. The result is that we now have to determine what rights adhere to ownership of property rather than looking only at the benefits enjoyed by the occupier—for example, there is the issue of interference with television reception as discussed in *Hunter* itself.

Nuisance will protect only certain interests of the claimant, and whether he has a protectable interest is a matter of law. Physical damage and interference with quiet enjoyment of land are covered, but it is not clear the extent to which the law protects recreational or aesthetic interests. Probably the tort does not protect the value of the property itself as opposed to an invasion of a protectable interest which causes a diminution in value, but *Thompson-Schwab* v *Costaki* (below) comes dangerously close to simply protecting property values. If the interest is not regarded as protectable, neither unreasonableness nor malice on the defendant's part can make it protectable.

---

### *Hunter* v *Canary Wharf*

House of Lords [1997] AC 655; [1997] 2 WLR 684; [1997] 2 All ER 426

The claimants, of whom there were several hundred, complained that their television reception had been impaired by the presence of the Canary Wharf Tower, which is over 800 feet high. Some of the claimants were householders but others, such as spouses, children or lodgers, had no property interest in the houses where they lived. The case raised two issues: (1) Is a property interest necessary to be able to sue in private nuisance? (2) Is interference with television reception by a physical obstruction a nuisance? Held: the defendants were not liable.

LORD LLOYD OF BERWICK: . . . Private nuisances are of three kinds. They are (1) nuisance by encroachment on a neighbour's land; (2) nuisance by direct physical injury to a neighbour's land; and (3) nuisance by interference with a neighbour's quiet enjoyment of his land. In cases (1) and (2) it is the owner, or the occupier with the right to exclusive possession, who is entitled to sue. It has never, so far as I know, been suggested that anyone else can sue, for example, a visitor or a lodger; and the reason is not far to seek. For the basis of the cause of action in cases (1) and (2) is damage to the land itself, whether by encroachment or by direct physical injury.

In the case of encroachment the plaintiff may have a remedy by way of abatement. In other cases he may be entitled to an injunction. But where he claims damages, the measure of damages in cases (1) and (2) will be the diminution in the value of the land. This will usually (though not always) be equal to the cost of reinstatement. The loss resulting from diminution in the value of the land is a loss suffered by the owner or occupier with the exclusive right to possession (as the case may be) or both, since it is they alone who have a proprietary interest, or stake, in the land. So it is they alone who can bring an action to recover the loss.

Mr Brennan argues that the position is quite different when one comes to the third category of private nuisance, namely, interference with a neighbour's quiet enjoyment of his land. He submits that here the right to bring an action for nuisance is not confined to those with a proprietary interest, but extends to all those who occupy the property as their home. This would include not only the wife and children of the owner, as has been held by the Court of Appeal, but also, as Mr Brennan argues, a lodger with a contractual right to remain in the house as licensee, or a living-in servant or an au pair girl.

One can see the attraction in this approach. The wife at least, if not the children, should surely be regarded nowadays as sharing the exclusive possession of the home which she occupies, so as to give her an independent right of action. There is also a superficial logic in the approach. Suppose there are two adjoining properties, affected by smoke from a neighbouring factory. One of the properties is occupied by a bachelor, the other is occupied by a married man with two children. If they are all equally affected by the smoke, it would seem to follow that the damages recoverable by the married man and his family should be four times the damages recovered by the bachelor. Many of the textbooks favour this approach. In the current edition of *Clerk & Lindsell On Torts*, 17th ed. (1995), pp. 910–911, para. 18–39 it is said that such a conclusion would affect 'a degree of modernisation' in the law, 'while freeing it from undue reliance upon the technicalities of land law.'

Like, I imagine, all your Lordships, I would be in favour of modernising the law wherever this can be done. But it is one thing to modernise the law by ridding it of unnecessary technicalities; it is another thing to bring about a fundamental change in the nature and scope of a cause of action. It has been said that an actionable nuisance is incapable of exact definition. But the essence of private nuisance is easy enough to identify, and it is the same in all three classes of private nuisance, namely, interference with land or the enjoyment of land. In the case of nuisances within class (1) or (2) the measure of damages is, as I have said, the diminution in the value of the land. Exactly the same should be true of nuisances within class (3). There is no difference of principle. The effect of smoke from a neighbouring factory is to reduce the value of the land. There may be no diminution in the market value. But there will certainly be loss of amenity value so long as the nuisance lasts. If that be the right approach, then the reduction in amenity value is the same whether the land is occupied by the family man or the bachelor.

If the occupier of land suffers personal injury as a result of inhaling the smoke, he may have a cause of action in negligence. But he does not have a cause of action in nuisance for his *personal* injury, nor for interference with his *personal* enjoyment. It follows that the quantum of damages in private nuisance does not depend on the number of those enjoying the land in question. It also follows that the only persons entitled to sue for loss in amenity value of the land are the owner or the occupier with the right to exclusive possession.

Damages for loss of amenity value cannot be assessed mathematically. But this does not mean that such damages cannot be awarded. . . .

It was said that confining the right to sue would cause inconvenience. There might be a case, for example, where the owner was unwilling to bring proceedings because he was less sensitive to smoke than other members of his family. I find it difficult to visualise such a case in practice. In any event the inconvenience, such as it would be, does not justify a departure from principle.

As for authority, one need look no further than the dictum of Lord Simonds in *Read* v *J. Lyons & Co. Ltd* [1947] AC 156, 183:

> For if a man commits a legal nuisance it is no answer to his injured neighbour that he took the utmost care not to commit it. There the liability is strict, and there he alone has a lawful claim who has suffered an invasion of some proprietary or other interest in land.

No doubt Lord Simonds will have had in mind the decision of the Court of Appeal in *Malone* v *Laskey* [1907] 2 KB 141. There the plaintiff was injured by a falling bracket in the lavatory, caused by vibrations from the defendants' engine next door. The plaintiff occupied the house as her home, but neither she nor her husband had any proprietary interest in the house. They were mere licensees. The plaintiff sued in nuisance and negligence. As to nuisance, Sir Gorell Barnes P said, at p. 151:

> The main question, however, on this part of the case is whether the plaintiff can maintain this action on the ground of vibration causing the damage complained of, and in my opinion the plaintiff has no cause of action upon that ground. Many cases were cited in the course of the argument in which it had been held that actions for nuisance could be maintained where a person's rights of property had been affected by the nuisance, but no authority was cited, nor in my opinion can any principle of law be formulated, to the effect that a person who has no interest in property, no right of occupation in the proper sense of the term, can maintain an action for a nuisance arising from the vibration caused by the working of an engine in an adjoining house.

If *Malone* v *Laskey* was correctly decided, the decision below cannot stand.

LORD HOFFMANN: . . . *St Helen's Smelting Co.* v *Tipping* was a landmark case. It drew the line beyond which rural and landed England did not have to accept external costs imposed upon it by industrial pollution. But there has been, I think, some inclination to treat it as having divided nuisance into two torts, one of causing 'material injury to the property,' such as flooding or depositing poisonous substances on crops, and the other of causing 'sensible personal discomfort' such as excessive noise or smells. In cases in the first category, there has never been any doubt that the remedy, whether by way of injunction or damages, is for causing damage to the land. It is plain that in such a case only a person with an interest in the land can sue. But there has been a tendency to regard cases in the second category as actions in respect of the discomfort or even personal injury which the plaintiff has suffered or is likely to suffer. On this view, the plaintiff's interest in the land becomes no more than a qualifying condition or springboard which entitles him to sue for injury to himself.

If this were the case, the need for the plaintiff to have an interest in land would indeed be hard to justify. The passage I have quoted from Dillon LJ (*Khorasandjian* v *Bush* [1993] QB 727, 734) is an eloquent statement of the reasons. But the premise is quite mistaken. In the case of nuisances 'productive of sensible personal discomfort,' the action is not for causing discomfort to the person but, as in the case of the first category, for causing injury to the land. True it is that the land has not suffered 'sensible' injury, but its utility has been diminished by the existence of the nuisance. It is for an unlawful threat to the utility of his land that the possessor or occupier is entitled to an injunction and it is for the diminution in such utility that he is entitled to compensation.
. . .

It follows that damages for nuisance recoverable by the possessor or occupier may be affected by the size, commodiousness and value of his property but cannot be increased merely because more people are in occupation and therefore suffer greater collective discomfort. If more than one person has an interest in the property, the damages will have to be divided among them. If there are joint owners, they will be jointly entitled to the damages. If there is a reversioner and the nuisance has caused damage of a permanent character which affects the reversion, he will be entitled to damages according to his interest. But the damages cannot be increased by the fact that the interests in the land are divided; still less according to the number of persons residing on the premises. . . .

Once it is understood that nuisances 'productive of sensible personal discomfort' (*St Helen's Smelting Co.* v *Tipping* 11 HL Cas 642, 650) do not constitute a separate tort of causing discomfort to people but are merely part of a single tort of causing injury to land, the rule that the plaintiff must have an interest in the land falls into place as logical and, indeed, inevitable.

Is there any reason of policy why the rule should be abandoned? Once nuisance has escaped the bounds of being a tort against land, there seems no logic in compromise limitations, such as that proposed by the Court of Appeal in this case, requiring the plaintiff to have been residing on land as his or her home. This was recognised by the Court of Appeal in *Khorasandjian* v *Bush* [1993] QB 727 where the injunction applied whether the plaintiff was at home or not. There is a good deal in this case and other writings about the need for the law to adapt to modern social conditions. But the development of the common law should be rational and coherent. It should not distort its principles and create anomalies merely as an expedient to fill a gap.

The perceived gap in *Khorasandjian* v *Bush* was the absence of a tort of intentional harassment causing distress without actual bodily or psychiatric illness. This limitation is thought to arise out of cases like *Wilkinson* v *Downton* [1897] 2 QB 57 and *Janvier* v *Sweeney* [1919] 2 KB 316. The law of harassment has now been put on a statutory basis (see the Protection from Harrassment Act 1997) and it is unnecessary to consider how the common law might have developed. But as at present advised, I see no reason why a tort of intention should be subject to the rule which excludes compensation for mere distress, inconvenience or discomfort in actions based on negligence: see *Hicks* v *Chief Constable of the South Yorkshire Police* [1992] 2 All ER 65. The policy considerations are quite different. I do not therefore say that *Khorasandjian* v *Bush* was wrongly decided. But it must be seen as a case on *intentional* harassment, not nuisance.

So far as the claim is for personal injury, it seems to me that the only appropriate cause of action is negligence. It would be anomalous if the rules for recovery of damages under this head were different according as to whether, for example, the plaintiff was at home or at work. It is true, as I have said, that the law of negligence gives no remedy for discomfort or distress which does not result in bodily or psychiatric illness. But this is a matter of general policy and I can see no logic in making an exception for cases in which the discomfort or distress was suffered at home rather than somewhere else.

Finally there is the position of spouses. It is said to be contrary to modern ways of thinking that a wife should not be able to sue for interference with the enjoyment of the matrimonial home merely because she has no proprietary right in the property. To some extent, this argument is based upon the fallacy which I have already discussed, namely that the action in nuisance lies for inconvenience or annoyance caused to people who happen to be in possession or occupation of land. But so far as it is thought desirable that the wife should be able to sue for injury to a proprietary or possessory interest in the home, the answer in my view lies in the law of property, not the law of tort. The courts today will readily assume that a wife has acquired a beneficial interest in the matrimonial home. If so, she will be entitled to sue for damage to that interest. On the other hand, if she has no such interest, I think it would be wrong to create a quasi-proprietary interest only for the purposes of giving her locus standi to sue for nuisance. . . .

*Interference with television*

In the television action, the plaintiffs complain that Canary Wharf Tower has diminished the amenity of their houses by interfering with television reception. In *Bridlington Relay Ltd* v *Yorkshire Electricity Board* [1965] Ch 436, 447 Buckley J said, tentatively and obiter:

> For myself, however, I do not think that it can at present be said that the ability to receive television free from occasional, even recurrent and severe, electrical interference is so

important a part of an ordinary householder's enjoyment of his property that such interference should be regarded as a legal nuisance, particularly, perhaps, if such interference affects only one of the available alternative programmes.

The judge was plainly not laying down a general rule that interference with television can never be an actionable nuisance. In principle I do not see why in an appropriate case it should not. *Bridlington Relay*, was a case of alleged interference by electromagnetic radiation from high tension electric cables. The Court of Appeal left open the question of whether interference of such a kind could be actionable and so would I.

In this case, however, the defendants say that the type of interference alleged, namely by the erection of a building between the plaintiffs' homes and the Crystal Palace transmitter, cannot as a matter of law constitute an actionable nuisance. This is not by virtue of anything peculiar to television. It applies equally to interference with the passage of light or air or radio signals or to the obstruction of a view. The general principle is that at common law anyone may build whatever he likes upon his land. If the effect is to interfere with the light, air or view of his neighbour, that is his misfortune. The owner's right to build can be restrained only by covenant or the acquisition (by grant or prescription) of an easement of light or air for the benefit of windows or apertures on adjoining land.

That such has until now been the law of England seems to me indisputable. A right to an uninterrupted prospect cannot be acquired even by prescription: *Aldred's Case* 9 Co Rep 57b. The same is true of a right to the uninterrupted flow of undefined air to a chimney: *Bryant* v *Lefever* (1879) 4 CPD 172. In the absence of an easement, there is no right to light. . . .

In the absence of agreement, therefore, the English common law allows the rights of a landowner to build as he pleases to be restricted only in carefully limited cases and then only after the period of prescription has elapsed. In this case there is no claim to an easement of television by prescription. And in any event, on the reasoning in *Dalton* v *Angus* I do not think that such an easement can exist. The extent to which a building may interfere with television reception is far from obvious. Nor is its potential effect limited to immediate neighbours. The number of plaintiffs in the television action is itself enough to demonstrate how large a burden would be imposed on anyone wishing to erect a tall building.

Once again we must consider whether modern conditions require these well established principles to be modified. The common law freedom of an owner to build upon his land has been drastically curtailed by the Town and Country Planning Act 1947 and its successors. It is now in normal cases necessary to obtain planning permission. The power of the planning authority to grant or refuse permission, subject to such conditions as it thinks fit, provides a mechanism for control of the unrestricted right to build which can be used for the protection of people living in the vicinity of a development. In a case such as this, where the development is likely to have an impact upon many people over a large area, the planning system is, I think, a far more appropriate form of control, from the point of view of both the developer and the public, than enlarging the right to bring actions for nuisance at common law. It enables the issues to be debated before an expert forum at a planning inquiry and gives the developer the advantage of certainty as to what he is entitled to build.

In saying this, I am not suggesting that a grant of planning permission should be a defence to anything which is an actionable nuisance under the existing law. It would, I think, be wrong to allow the private rights of third parties to be taken away by a permission granted by the planning authority to the developer. The Court of Appeal rejected such an argument in this case and the point has not been pursued in your Lordships' House. But when your Lordships are invited to develop the common law by creating a new right of action against an owner who erects a building upon his land, it is relevant to take into account the existence of other methods by which the interests of the locality can be protected.

In this case, as I mentioned at the beginning of this speech, the normal protection offered to the community by the Act of 1971 was largely removed. Parliament authorised this to be done on the grounds that the national interest required the rapid regeneration of the Docklands urban development area. the plaintiffs may well feel that their personal convenience was temporarily sacrificed to the national interest. But this is not a good enough reason for changing the principles of the law of nuisance which apply throughout the country.

On the one hand, therefore, we have a rule of common law which, absent easements, entitles an owner of land to build what he likes upon his land. It has stood for many centuries. If an exception were to be created for large buildings which interfere with television reception, the developers would be exposed to legal action by an indeterminate number of plaintiffs, each claiming compensation in a relatively modest amount. Defending such actions, whatever their merits or demerits, would hardly be cost-effective. The compensation and legal fees would form an unpredictable additional cost of the building. On the other hand, the plaintiffs will ordinarily have been able to make their complaints at the planning stage of the development and, if necessary, secure whatever conditions were necessary to provide them with an alternative source of television signals. The interference in such a case is not likely to last very long because there is no technical difficulty about the solution. In my view the case for a change in the law is not made out.

### NOTES

1. *The requirement of a property interest.* This case puts nuisance on a proper jurisprudential basis and satisfactorily distinguishes it from negligence. It means that only invasions which affect a property owner *as owner* will found an action in nuisance, i.e. damage to the land itself or interference with *rights* of property. Accordingly, there can be no action for personal injuries in nuisance and maybe not even for damage to chattels. Such actions must now be based on negligence. This will also affect the interests that are protected by nuisance since damages can only be for injury to the amenity value of the land, and the issue raises the question of what rights a person has *as owner* rather than as occupier. See further, Kidner, 'Nuisance and Rights of Property' (1998) 62 Conveyancer 267.

2. In *Hunter* it was said that the right to sue in nuisance is limited to those with a proprietary interest in land and those with exclusive possession. Lord Hoffmann said that 'exclusive possession de jure or de facto, now or in the future, is the bedrock of English land law' and he pointed out that a potential adverse possessor could sue, whereas a mere trespasser could not as he would not have exclusive possession. This point arose in *Pemberton* v *Southwark Borough Council* [2000] All ER 924 where the claimant's flat had become infested with cockroaches. She had failed to pay her rent and her secure tenancy had come to an end, but as a 'tolerated trespasser' under the Housing Act 1985 she retained exclusive possession until such time as the landlord could obtain a court order to evict her. Accordingly she had sufficient interest to sue in nuisance.

3. *Interference with television reception.* The mere fact that an interference with rights of enjoyment reduces the value of a property should not by itself amount to a nuisance, although *Thompson-Schwab* (below) comes close to that. The question is whether freedom from electronic interference is a right which adheres to rights of property and it may be that in this modern age it should. *Hunter* v *Canary Wharf* did not say that it could never amount to a nuisance but only that if the interference is by physical obstruction there will be no nuisance because the right of a land owner to put up a building (subject to planning laws) overrides the interests of the neighbouring owner. This leaves open the question of whether interference with electronic reception by electrical means should be a nuisance. On this see *Bridlington Relay* v *Yorkshire Electricity Board* [1965] Ch 436 (against) and *Nor-Video Services* v *Ontario Hydro* (1978) 84 DLR 3d 221 (in favour).

4. As to 'extra-sensitive claimants' it was thought that an extra-sensitive claimant could sue only if a person of ordinary sensitivity could have sued. In other words, a person cannot impose a higher burden of care upon his neighbour by engaging in especially sensitive activities. In *Robinson* v *Kilvert* (1889) 41 ChD 88 the defendants manufactured paper boxes in the cellar of a building, and this required considerable heat which damaged the claimant's stock of brown paper on the floor above. It was found that the heat would not have injured normal paper, and therefore the defendant was not liable. However, this principle has been disapproved by the Court of Appeal in *Network Rail Infrastructure* v *Morris* [2004] Env LR 41 (at p. 861), [2004] EWCA Civ 172. In that case the claimant (Morris) operated a recording studio which was 80 metres from a railway line. In 1994 Network Rail installed new track circuits which interfered with the amplifiers in the studio, causing the claimant loss of business. It

was held that the defendants were not liable as it was not foreseeable that the track circuits would interfere with the amplifiers. Buxton LJ said that there was no longer any need for the principle of 'abnormal sensitiveness' in nuisance which was developed at a time when liability for nuisance was thought to be strict. What is now required is an 'analysis of the demands of reasonableness' which the court could assess in terms of foreseeability. Thus the test of liability is still reasonable user, but foreseeability now plays a major part in deciding this. Overall this judgment is a part of the continuing process of 'generalization' of the concepts of nuisance, which is bringing nuisance closer to negligence.

---

### *Thompson-Schwab* v *Costaki*
Court of Appeal [1956] 1 WLR 335; [1956] 1 All ER 652

The claimant owned 13 Chesterfield Street in London. The defendants, Blanche Marie Costaki and Carol Sullivan, were prostitutes who occupied 12 Chesterfield Street. The claimant complained of the existence of the brothel and of the fact that the prostitutes solicited in the street. He stated that Chesterfield Street was a good class residential street and that the existence of the brothel depreciated the value of his house and interfered with his comfortable enjoyment of it. Held: dismissing the appeal, that an interlocutory injunction would be granted on the grounds of nuisance.

LORD EVERSHED MR: The question raised by this appeal is a matter of some public interest and, I do not doubt, some public importance too . . . Mr Lindner and Mr Stenham, for the defendants, have put the first plank in their case boldly, thus: they say that the law of nuisance, as it has been developed from the ancient assize, has never comprehended activities of this kind which, they say, though possibly shocking to the susceptibilities of ordinary people, does not in any material, that is physical, way interfere with the land of the plaintiffs or their use of it. That such is their case—whether entirely of their own motion or not I do not pause to inquire—is perhaps made plainer by the circumstance that the defence which they have, as we were told, put in makes it clear that, according to their submission, they should be free (that is, without impinging upon the civil rights of any other person) to use these premises for the purposes of prostitution to their heart's content and in any way they like. That certainly seems a bold plea. But Mr Lindner has pointed out with truth that no case has come before the courts in which this kind of activity has been held to constitute a common law nuisance.

In *Sedleigh-Denfield* v *O'Callaghan* [1940] AC 880, Lord Wright said: 'It is impossible to give any precise or universal formula, but it may broadly be said that a useful test is perhaps what is reasonable according to the ordinary usages of mankind living in society, or more correctly in a particular society. The forms which nuisance may take are protean.'

In the years 1955 and 1956 I daresay that the activities of prostitutes are less taboo in ordinary polite conversation than they were a hundred years ago; and it is true that so far as the evidence in this case goes there is nothing about the activities of the two defendants which is shown to be unlawful in the sense of being illegal or criminal. But it does not, to my mind, follow at all that their activities should, therefore, be regarded as free from the risk or possibility that they cause a nuisance in the proper sense of that term to a neighbour merely because they do not impinge upon the senses—for example, the nose or the ear—as would the emanation of smells or fumes or noises. In other words, the test as it seems to me (and I adopt it for the purposes of this appeal) is that which I have stated, namely, whether what is being done interferes with the plaintiffs in the comfortable and convenient enjoyment of their land, regard being had, to borrow Lord Wright's language, to the usages in this matter of civilized society, and regard being also had to the character, as proved, of the neighbourhood.

The plaintiffs have shown, in my opinion, a sufficient prima facie case to the effect that the activities being conducted at No. 12 Chesterfield Street are not only open, but they are notorious, and such as force themselves upon the sense of sight at least of the residents in No. 13. The perambulations of the prostitutes and of their customers is something which is obvious, which is blatant, and which, as I think, the first plaintiff has shown prima facie to constitute not a mere hurt of his sensibilities as a fastidious man, but so as to constitute a sensible interference with the comfortable and convenient enjoyment of his residence, where live with him his wife, his son and his servants. . . .

Let me say one other thing which might have been said earlier. It is, I should have thought, obvious, having regard to the proximity of other streets with a less savoury reputation, that if this kind of use of houses is allowed to creep into Chesterfield Street, the whole character of the street might very soon and very seriously change for the worse. That, I think, is a circumstance which it is proper to bear in mind in considering whether, pending the trial, an injunction should be granted to protect the plaintiffs in their use of their own residences. . . .

■ QUESTION

What interest was being protected in this case? Would a centre for the rehabilitation of alcoholics or drug users be a nuisance? What about an AIDS hospice? Would a family of Eastenders be a nuisance in Belgravia?

NOTES

1. *Thompson-Schwab* was followed in *Laws* v *Florinplace* [1981] 1 All ER 659, where an interlocutory injunction was granted on the grounds of nuisance, preventing the use of premises in Pimlico in London as a sex shop. Vinelott J said that there was at least a triable issue for the purposes of whether an interlocutory injunction should be granted as to whether a sex shop is in itself a nuisance. It was also said that, even though 80 per cent of the customers may be mature and normal men, the risk of the other 20 per cent being unbalanced and a danger to residents could not be brushed aside. Do you think that if the case had gone to full trial a permanent injunction should have been granted? If so, what interest was being protected? What if the defendants had been granted a licence by the local authority to operate a sex shop? (In fact they had not and were operating in breach of planning regulations.)

2. If the interest invaded is not regarded as a protected interest in law, not even an intentional or malicious interference will ground an action. In other words, malice cannot change an unprotected interest into a protected one. In *Mayor of Bradford* v *Pickles* [1985] AC 587, the defendant owned land through which water percolated which ultimately was collected in the Corporation reservoirs. The defendant wanted the Corporation to buy his land, or at least his rights to the water, and he deliberately obstructed the flow of water to the reservoir by sinking a shaft. It was held that as the claimants had no right to receive percolating water, the fact that the defendant was acting maliciously could not convert into a nuisance what would otherwise not be a nuisance.

3. Malice can deprive a defendant of two arguments: first, that his use of land was reasonable and, second, that the claimant's user was extra-sensitive. In *Hollywood Silver Fox Farm* v *Emmett* [1936] 2 KB 468 the defendant objected to the claimant's development of his land as a mink farm, and accordingly he fired shotguns near the claimant's mink pens. Firing shotguns does not make an unreasonable noise and is a reasonable use of land in the country. However, mink are extra-sensitive, in that when subjected to loud noises they tend to devour their young. It was held that the defendant was liable. Intentionally causing harm is not a reasonable use of land, and if a person intends a consequence he cannot claim it is too remote or sensitive.

## SECTION 3: REASONABLE USER

The standard required of an occupier is that of reasonable use of land. This is quite different from reasonableness in negligence for it relates to a balance between what it is reasonable for a person to do on his land and what it is reasonable for his neighbour to put up with. This relates not only to the kind of activity but also to its gravity and both will be subject to society's view at the time as to what is reasonable, as well as to the utility of the defendant's conduct. *Halsey* v *Esso Petroleum* (above, section 1) is a good example of this balancing process.

### *St Helen's Smelting Co.* v *Tipping*
House of Lords (1865) 11 ER 1483

The claimant owned property near the defendants' smelting works, and he complained that noxious gases, vapours and other matter caused damage to hedges and trees and interfered with the beneficial use of his land. Held: the defendants were liable.

LORD WESTBURY LC: My Lords, in matters of this description it appears to me that it is a very desirable thing to mark the difference between an action brought for a nuisance upon the ground that the alleged nuisance produces material injury to the property, and an action brought for a nuisance on the ground that the thing alleged to be a nuisance is productive of sensible personal discomfort. With regard to the latter, namely, the personal inconvenience and interference with one's enjoyment, one's quiet, one's personal freedom, anything that discomposes or injuriously affects the senses or the nerves, whether that may or may not be denominated a nuisance, must undoubtedly depend greatly on the circumstances of the place where the thing complained of actually occurs. If a man lives in a town, it is necessary that he should subject himself to the consequences of those operations of trade which may be carried on in his immediate locality, which are actually necessary for trade and commerce, and also for the enjoyment of property, and for the benefit of the inhabitants of the town and of the public at large. If a man lives in a street where there are numerous shops, and a shop is opened next door to him, which is carried on in a fair and reasonable way, he has no ground for complaint, because to himself individually there may arise much discomfort from the trade carried on in that shop. But when an occupation is carried on by one person in the neighbourhood of another, and the result of that trade, or occupation, or business, is a material injury to property, then there unquestionably arises a very different consideration. I think, my Lords, that in a case of that description, the submission which is required from persons living in society to that amount of discomfort which may be necessary for the legitimate and free exercise of the trade of their neighbours, would not apply to circumstances the immediate result of which is sensible injury to the value of the property.

NOTES
1. In *Sturges* v *Bridgman* (1879) 11 ChD 852, at p. 865, Thesiger LJ said 'What would be a nuisance in Belgrave Square would not necessarily be so in Bermondsey'. Bermondsey was well known for its tanneries, which used urine and excreta in the tanning process.
2. With regard to interference with enjoyment, Knight-Bruce LJ said in *Walter* v *Selfe* (1851) 64 ER 849 that the question is:

ought this inconvenience to be considered in fact as more than fanciful, more than one of mere delicacy or fastidiousness, as an inconvenience materially interfering with the ordinary comfort physically of human existence, not merely according to elegant or dainty modes and habits of living, but according to plain and sober and simple notions among the English people?

SECTION 4: **WHO IS LIABLE?**

The creator of a nuisance is liable as is a person who is 'responsible' for its continuance. Thus, an occupier can be liable for a nuisance created by a trespasser if he 'adopts' or 'continues' that nuisance (*Sedleigh-Denfield*, below). Equally a person can be liable for a natural hazard which he ought to have removed and can be liable when he has authorized an act which in ordinary circumstances will amount to a nuisance, as in *Tetley* v *Chitty* [1986] 1 All ER 663, where a local authority authorized the use of its land in a residential area as a go-kart racing circuit.

---

*Sedleigh-Denfield* v *O'Callaghan*
House of Lords [1940] AC 880; [1940] 3 All ER 349; 164 LT 72

The Middlesex County Council had replaced a culvert with a pipe: the end of the pipe projected about two feet onto the defendant's land, and therefore the council were technically trespassing when they put the pipe there. The workmen placed a grating over the end of the pipe to prevent leaves blocking it, but this was done incorrectly, as the grating was placed directly onto the end of the pipe so the leaves would collect on the grating and block the pipe. The grating should have been placed a foot or two in front of the opening. After the pipe was in place the defendant's workers regularly cleaned out the ditch and the end of the pipe. In 1937 a severe storm blocked the pipe and caused flooding on the claimant's neighbouring land. Held: allowing the appeal, the defendant was liable for the nuisance.

LORD ATKIN: In this state of the facts the legal position is not I think difficult to discover. For the purposes of ascertaining whether as here the plaintiff can establish a private nuisance I think that nuisance is sufficiently defined as a wrongful interference with another's enjoyment of his land or premises by the use of land or premises either occupied or in some cases owned by oneself. The occupier or owner is not an insurer; there must be something more than the mere harm done to the neighbour's property to make the party responsible. Deliberate act or negligence is not an essential ingredient but some degree of personal responsibility is required, which is connoted in my definition by the word 'use.' This conception is implicit in all the decisions which impose liability only where the defendant has 'caused or continued' the nuisance. We may eliminate in this case 'caused.' What is the meaning of 'continued'? In the context in which it is used 'continued' must indicate mere passive continuance. If a man uses on premises something which he found there, and which itself causes a nuisance by noise, vibration, small or fumes, he is himself in continuing to bring into existence the noise, vibration, etc., causing a nuisance. Continuing in this sense and causing are the same thing. It seems to me clear that if a man permits an offensive thing on his premises to continue to offend, that is, if he knows that it is operating offensively, is able to prevent it, and omits to prevent it, he is permitting the nuisance to continue; in other words he is continuing it. The liability of an occupier has been carried so far that it appears to have been decided that, if he comes to occupy, say as tenant, premises upon which a cause of nuisance exists, caused by a previous occupier, he is responsible even though he does not know that either the cause or the result is in existence. . . .

In the present case, however, there is as I have said sufficient proof of the knowledge of the defendants both of the cause and its probable effect. What is the legal result of the original cause being due to the act of a trespasser? In my opinion the defendants clearly continued the nuisance for they come clearly within the terms I have mentioned above, they knew the danger, they were able to prevent it and they omitted to prevent it. In this respect at least there seems to me to be no difference between the case of a public nuisance and a private nuisance, and the case of *Attorney-General* v *Tod-Heatley* [1897] 1 Ch 560, is conclusive to show that where the occupier has knowledge of a public nuisance, has the means of remedying it and fails to do so, he may be enjoined from allowing it to continue. I cannot think that the obligation not to 'continue' can have a different meaning in 'public' and in 'private' nuisances. . . .

LORD WRIGHT: Though the rule has not been laid down by this House, it has I think been rightly established in the Court of Appeal that an occupier is not prima facie responsible for a nuisance created without his knowledge and consent. If he is to be liable a further condition is necessary, namely, that he had knowledge or means of knowledge, that he knew or should have known of the nuisance in time to correct it and obviate its mischievous effects. The liability for a nuisance is not, at least in modern law, a strict or absolute liability. If the defendant by himself or those for whom he is responsible has created what constitutes a nuisance and if it causes damage, the difficulty now being considered does not arise. But he may have taken over the nuisance, ready made as it were, when he acquired the property, or the nuisance may be due to a latent defect or to the act of a trespasser, or stranger. Then he is not liable unless he continued or adopted the nuisance, or, more accurately, did not without undue delay remedy it when he became aware if it, or with ordinary and reasonable care should have become aware of it. This rule seems to be in accordance with good sense and convenience. The responsibility which attaches to the occupier because he has possession and control of the property cannot logically be limited to the mere creation of the nuisance. It should extend to his conduct if, with knowledge, he leaves the nuisance on his land. The same is true if the nuisance was such that with ordinary care in the management of his property he should have realised the risk of its existence. . . .

NOTE

A person can be liable even for natural phenomena which cause a nuisance. In *Leakey* v *National Trust* [1980] QB 485, the claimants owned houses next to a large mound in Somerset called the Burrow Mump which was owned by the defendants. Part of the mound subsided and encroached on the claimants' houses. The defendants were held liable even though the mound was a natural one and the subsidence was caused by the forces of nature. It was said by the Court of Appeal that the defendant's obligation is what it is reasonable for him as an individual to do, taking account, for example, of his means, and the practicality of taking preventative measures.

■ QUESTION

Would the defendant in *Sedleigh-Denfield* v *O'Callaghan* have been liable if, although knowing of the existence of the ditch and the pipe, he completely ignored them and was unaware of how the pipe and grating had been put together?

---

### Holbeck Hall Hotel v Scarborough BC
Court of Appeal [2000] QB 836; [2000] 2 WLR 1396; [2000] 2 All ER 705

The Holbeck Hall Hotel stood 65 metres above sea level on South Cliff, Scarborough. The defendants owned the land between the hotel and the sea. On 3 June 1993, there was a massive landslip on the defendants' land and the hotel gardens disappeared and the ground collapsed under part of the hotel, which became unsafe and had to be demolished. There had been earlier, minor slips in 1982 and 1986 and some rather ineffective remedial steps had been taken, and it was said that the defendants knew that at some indeterminate time the slip might progress. However, nobody could have foreseen the catastrophic slip that did occur without further extensive geological investigation. The trial judge held the defendants liable for the total loss. Held: the defendants were under a duty to the claimants but were liable only for part of the loss.

STUART-SMITH LJ:

**31** In *Goldman* v *Hargrave* [1971] AC 645 the Privy Council extended the principle in *Sedleigh-Denfield's* case to a hazard caused on the Defendant's land by the operation of nature. In that case a tall redgum tree on the Defendant's land was struck by lightening and set on fire. The Defendant at first took reasonable steps to deal with the problem. He cleared and dampened the area round the tree and then cut it down. Having done so, however, the Defendant took no further steps to prevent the spread of fire, which he could readily have done by dousing it with water. Instead, he let the fire burn out. The wind got up and set light to the surrounding area from whence it spread to the Plaintiff's land and damaged his property. The Privy Council held the Defendant liable. There was no difference in principle between a nuisance created by a trespasser and one created by the forces of nature, provided the Defendant knew of the hazard. Lord Wilberforce, who delivered the advice of the Board, said in relation to the supposed distinction at p. 661:

> The fallacy of this argument is that, as already explained, the basis of the occupier's liability lies not in the use of his land: in the absence of 'adoption' there is no such use; but in the neglect of action in the face of something which may damage his neighbour. To this, the suggested distinction is irrelevant.

**32** In both *Sedleigh-Denfield's* case and *Goldman's* case the hazard arose entirely on the Defendant's land; the Plaintiff had no knowledge of it before the damage was done; the Defendant was liable for failing to take steps to stop the spread or escape to the Plaintiff's land, steps which he could reasonably take.

**33** In *Leakey* v *National Trust* [1980] QB 485 the Court of Appeal held that the law, as laid down in *Goldman's* case, correctly stated the law of England. In that case the Plaintiffs' houses had been built at the foot of a large mound on the Defendant's land. Over the years soil and rubble had fallen from the Defendant's land onto the Plaintiffs'. The falls were due to natural weathering and the nature of the soil. By 1968 the Defendant knew that there was a threat to the Plaintiffs' properties. After a very dry summer and wet autumn a large crack opened in the mound above the Plaintiffs' house. They drew the Defendant's attention to the danger to their houses; but the Defendant said it had no responsibility. A few weeks later a large quantity of earth and some stumps fell onto the Plaintiffs' land. In interlocutory proceedings the Defendant was ordered to carry out the necessary work to abate the nuisance. The Court of Appeal upheld the judge's decision in the trial of the action to the effect that the Defendant was liable.

**34** Megaw LJ, with whose judgment Cumming-Bruce LJ agreed, said at p. 523F:

> If, as a result of the working of the forces of nature, there is, poised above my land, or above my house, a boulder or a rotten tree, which is liable to fall at any moment of the day or night, perhaps destroying my house, and perhaps killing or injuring me or members of my family, am I without remedy? (Of course the standard of care required may be much higher where there is risk of life or limb as contrasted with mere risk to property, but can it be said that the duty exists in the one case and not in the other?) Must I, in such a case, if my protests to my neighbour go unheeded, sit and wait and hope that the worst will not befall? If it is said that I have in such circumstances a remedy of going on my neighbour's land to abate the nuisance, that would, or might, be an unsatisfactory remedy. But in any event, if there were such a right of abatement, it would, as counsel for the Plaintiffs rightly contended, be because my neighbour owed me a duty. There is, I think, ample authority that, if I have a right of abatement, I have also a remedy in damages if the nuisance remains unabated and causes me damage or personal injury. . . .

**35** . . . Mr Stow argued that the principle in the three cases of *Sedleigh-Denfield*, *Goldman* and *Leakey* should be confined to cases where there is an escape or encroachment of some noxious thing from the defendant's land to that of the claimant. He points to the repeated use of the word 'encroachment' in the judgment of Megaw LJ at p. 514B–D. On the other hand it is difficult to see what difference there is in principle between a danger caused by loss of support on the defendant's land and any other hazard or nuisance there which affects the claimant's use and enjoyment of land. Encroachment is simply one form of nuisance; interference causing physical damage to the neighbour's land and building as a result of activities on the Defendant's land is another form of nuisance.

There seems no reason why, where the Defendant does not create the nuisance, but the question is whether he had adopted or continued it, different principles should apply to one kind of nuisance rather than another. In each case liability only arises if there is negligence, the duty to abate the nuisance arises from the Defendant's knowledge of the hazard that will affect his neighbour.

. . .

*The extent of the Defendant's knowledge*

**39** In order to give rise to a measured duty of care, the Defendant must know or be presumed to know of the defect or condition giving rise to the hazard and must, as a reasonable man, foresee that the defect or condition will, if not remedied, cause damage to the Claimant's land. In *Goldman* [and] *Leakey* . . . the Defendant had actual knowledge of the defect or condition giving rise to the hazard or alleged hazard. In *Sedleigh-Denfield* the Defendant's responsible servant knew. In each case it was reasonably foreseeable that damage would occur to the Plaintiff's land if nothing was done.

. . .

**41** In *Leakey's* case Megaw LJ said at p. 518D:

So long as the defect remains 'latent' there is no duty on the occupier, whether the defect has been caused by a trespasser or by nature. Equally, once the latent becomes patent, a duty will arise, whether the causative agent of the defect is man or nature. But the mere fact that there is a duty does not necessarily mean that inaction constitutes a breach of the duty.

In that passage Megaw LJ referred to the defect. At p. 522D he said:

. . . the duty arising from a nuisance which is not brought about by human agency does not arise unless and until the defendant has, or ought to have had, knowledge of the existence of the defect and the danger thereby created.

Here the Lord Justice is referring both to the defect and the danger arising from it. And again at p. 524G when discussing the scope of the duty he posed this question:

Was there sufficient time for preventive action to have been taken, by persons acting reasonably in relation to the known risk, between the time when it became known to, or should have been realised by, the defendant, and the time when the damage occurred?

Here Megaw LJ refers to the risk or the danger.

**42** The duty arises when the defect is known and the hazard or danger to the Claimants' land is reasonably foreseeable, that is to say it is a danger which a reasonable man with knowledge of the defect should have foreseen as likely to eventuate in the reasonably near future. It is the existence of the defect coupled with the danger that constitutes the nuisance; it is knowledge or presumed knowledge of the nuisance that involves liability for continuing it when it could reasonably be abated. Mr Stow submits that the defect must be patent and not latent; that is to say that it is a defect which can be observed; it is no answer for the landowner to say that he did not observe it, if a responsible servant did so; or if as a reasonable landowner he, or the person to whom he entrusted the responsibility of looking after the land, should have seen it. But if the defect is latent, the landowner or occupier is not to be held liable simply because, if he had made further investigation, he would have discovered it. I accept Mr Stow's submission; in my judgment that is what is meant by the expression 'knowledge or presumed knowledge'.

**43** Mr Stow further submits that although Scarborough knew of a defect in their land, and that they realised that there was a risk of a slip, they did not know, and could not have known without the two stage geological investigation, of the defect; in particular, as Mr Clements said in his evidence in the passage I have cited, that they realised that over many years there might be progressive slips which eventually might affect the Plaintiffs' grounds, but they did not and could not have realised the serious extent of the slip plane or the fact that it extended so far into the Claimants' land as to affect the hotel. He submits that while Scarborough did foresee some damage to the Claimants' land, if nothing was done about the existing slip, they could not reasonably have foreseen the catastrophic danger that materialised. Mr Stow seeks to draw a distinction between a shallow slip, which is what the 1982 and 1986 slips were, and a rotational slide, which is what the 1993 slip was, and the 1893 and the other major slip, to which the judge refers, were. I am not sure that a differentiation between the nature of the slips is a critical one. But it is in my view clear that Scarborough did not foresee a danger of anything like the magnitude that eventuated. It was common ground that the GEN report gave no clue of such an eventuality; and it seems clear that they could not have appreciated the risk without further investigation by experts.

**44** The critical question is whether these distinctions affect Scarborough's liability. In most cases where physical injury either to the person or property of the Claimant is reasonably foreseeable, the Defendant will be under a duty of care and will be liable for all damage of the type which was foreseeable, whether the actual extent of the damage is foreseeable or not. This is so in cases where the Defendant's activity gives rise to the danger, whether it be the manner of his driving, the operations conducted on his land or in his business, or the treatment he gives as a professional undertaking the care of his patient. It matters not that he did not foresee the full extent of the injury in fact sustained. So too in cases of economic loss; if there is the necessary foreseeability of the type of damage sustained and proximity, subject to the need for it to be fair, just and reasonable for a duty to be imposed, the Defendant will be liable for all damage of the type foreseen, even if the full extent was not foreseen or reasonably foreseeable.

**45** Mr Symons submits that that principle is applicable here; provided Scarborough knew that there was a defect on their land, i.e. the existence of a slip plane and consequent risk of a slip, and provided they either did or ought as reasonable people to have foreseen that it might affect the Claimants' land more than to a trivial extent, they are liable for the full extent of the damage. Mr Symons relied on the well-known decision of *Hughes* v *Lord Advocate* [1963] AC 837 in support of his proposition. But there the duty of care existed, damage of the type which occurred, namely injury by burning, was foreseeable as a result of the Defendant's operations, it was merely that the source of danger acted in an unpredictable way. As Lord Morris of Borth-y-Guest put it at p. 853:

> My Lords, in my view, there was a duty owed by the defenders to safeguard the pursuer against the type or kind of occurrence which in fact happened and which resulted in his injuries, and the defenders are not absolved from liability because they did not envisage 'the precise concatenation of circumstances which "led up to the accident." . . .'

In my judgment this does not assist the Claimants in this case. It was an application of the ordinary rule which I have referred to in the previous paragraph; the unpredictable nature of the accident did not make the damage too remote.

**46** But the present is a case of non-feasance: Scarborough have done nothing to create the danger which has arisen by the operation of nature. And it is clear that the scope of the duty is much more restricted. It is defined in the cases of *Goldman* and *Leakey* as a measured duty of care. In the former case Lord Wilberforce said at p. 663A:

> So far it has been possible to consider the existence of a duty, in general terms. But the matter cannot be left there without some definition of the scope of his duty. How far does it go? What is the standard of the effort required? What is the position as regards expenditure? It is not enough to say merely that these must be 'reasonable,' since what is reasonable to one man may be very unreasonable, and indeed ruinous, to another: the law must take account of the fact that the occupier on whom the duty is cast has, *ex hypothesi*, had this hazard thrust upon him through no seeking or fault of his own. His interest, and his resources, whether physical or material, may be of a very modest character either in relation to the magnitude of the hazard, or as compared with those of his threatened neighbour. A rule which required of him in such unsought circumstances in his neighbour's interest a physical effort of which he is not capable, or an excessive expenditure of money, would be unenforceable or unjust. *One may say in general terms that the existence of a duty must be based upon knowledge of the hazard, ability to foresee the consequences of not checking or removing it, and the ability to abate it.* And in many cases, as, for example, in Scrutton LJ's hypothetical case of stamping out a fire, or the present case, where the hazard could have been removed with little effort and no expenditure, no problem arises. But other cases may not be so simple. In such situations the standard ought to be to require of the occupier what it is reasonable to expect of him in his individual circumstances. . . .

**47** In the passage which I have [emphasized] Lord Wilberforce refers expressly only to the existence of the duty; but the passage occurs in the middle of that part of the judgment dealing with the scope of the duty. It seems to me that Lord Wilberforce could equally have said 'existence and scope of the duty', especially as ability to abate it is related to the subjective characteristics of the Defendant.

**48** In *Leakey's* case Megaw LJ dealt with the scope of the duty at p. 524E:

The duty is a duty to do that which is reasonable in all the circumstances, and no more than what, if anything, is reasonable, to prevent or minimise the known risk of damage or injury to one's neighbour or to his property. The considerations with which the law is familiar are all to be taken into account in deciding whether there had been a breach of duty, and, if so, what that breach is, and whether it is causative of the damage in respect of which the claim is made. Thus, there will fall to be considered the extent of the risk; what, so far as reasonably can be foreseen, are the chances that anything untoward will happen or that any damage will be caused? *What is to be foreseen as to the possible extent of the damage if the risk becomes a reality*? Is it practicable to prevent, or to minimise, the happening of any damage? If it is practicable, how simple or how difficult are the measures which could be taken, how much and how lengthy work do they involve, and what is the probable cost of such work? Was there sufficient time for preventive action to have been taken, by persons acting reasonably in relation to the known risk, between the time when it became known to, or should have been realised by, the defendant, and the time when the damage occurred? Factors such as these, so far as they apply in a particular case, fall to be weighed in deciding whether the defendant's duty of care requires, or required, him to do anything, and, if so, what.

**49** In both these passages concentration tends to be upon the ease and expense of abatement and the ability of the Defendant to achieve it. But in the passage in Megaw LJ's judgment which I have [emphasized], the extent of the foreseen damage is said to be a relevant consideration. Moreover, I do not think either judge was purporting to give an exhaustive list of relevant considerations. While I agree with Megaw LJ (see p. 524B) that it would be a grievous blot on our law if there was no liability on the Defendants in those cases, I do not think justice requires that a Defendant should be held liable for damage which, albeit of the same type, was vastly more extensive than that which was foreseen or could have been foreseen without extensive further geological investigation; and this is particularly so where the defect existed just as much on the Claimant's land as on their own. In considering the scope of the measured duty of care, the courts are still in relatively uncharted waters. But I can find nothing in the two cases where it has been considered, namely *Goldman* and *Leakey* to prevent the Court reaching a just result.

. . .

**51** The cases of *Goldman* and *Leakey* were decided before the decision of the House of Lords in *Caparo Industries Ltd* v *Dickman* [1990] 2 AC 605, in which the three stage test for the existence of a duty of care was laid down, namely foreseeability, proximity and the need for it to be fair, just and reasonable. In *Marc Rich & Co.* v *Bishop Rock Ltd* [1996] 1 AC 211 it was held that the three stage *Caparo* test was appropriate whatever the nature of the damage. (See per Lord Steyn at p. 235 approving a dictum of Saville LJ.) The requirement that it must be fair, just and reasonable is a limiting condition where foreseeability and proximity are established. In my judgment very similar considerations arise whether the court is determining the scope of a measured duty of care or whether it is fair, just and reasonable to impose a duty or the extent of that duty. And for my part I do not think it is just and reasonable in a case like the present to impose liability for damage which is greater in extent than anything that was foreseen or foreseeable (without further geological investigation), especially where the defect and danger existed as much on the Claimants' land as the Defendants'.

. . .

**54** For the reasons I have given I conclude that the scope of Scarborough's duty was confined to an obligation to take care to avoid damage to the Claimants' land which they ought to have foreseen without further geological investigation. It may also have been limited by other factors, as the passages from *Goldman* and *Leakey* cited in paragraphs 46 and 48 make clear, so that it is not necessarily incumbent on someone in Scarborough's position to carry out extensive and expensive remedial work to prevent the damage which they ought to have foreseen; the scope of the duty may be limited to warning claimants of such risk as they were aware of or ought to have foreseen and sharing such information as they had acquired relating to it.

. . .

NOTES

1. Stuart-Smith LJ talks of a 'measured' duty in cases of omission by which the defendant will not be liable for all the damage even if it is of a type of damage that was foreseeable, where what actually happened was more extensive than expected. This is not a matter of remoteness of damage, but rather defines what it is that the defendant failed to do. Here the defendants were aware that the land was unstable and should have taken remedial steps to prevent that limited damage, or perhaps even only warn the claimants of the problem. The court said that the defendants were only liable for damage that might have been expected bearing in mind the previous minor slips, and held that this was limited to slips which would have affected the rose garden and some part of the lawn and did not extend to the collapse of the whole hotel.

2. An occupier of land can be liable for the acts of his licensees away from the land, either because he has created the nuisance or because he has allowed it to continue. In *Lippiatt* v *South Gloucestershire Council* [1999] 4 All ER 149, a number of travellers occupied Council land from 1991 until 1994, and during that time the travellers entered neighbouring land causing damage. It was held that the nuisance 'emanated' from the defendants' land and they were liable either because they had created the nuisance by allowing the travellers to occupy the land, or because they 'continued' or 'adopted' the nuisance. However, a landlord is not liable for the acts of his tenants unless he has authorized the nuisance (see *Hussain* v *Lancaster City Council* [1999] 4 All ER 125).

## SECTION 5: REMOTENESS OF DAMAGE

Substantive liability in nuisance does not depend on fault for as we have seen the controlling factor is reasonable use of land. In *Wagon Mound (No. 2)* [1967] 1 AC 617 Lord Reid said that 'negligence is not an essential element in nuisance' but nevertheless went on to say that foreseeability is relevant in relation to remoteness of damage. This has now been confirmed by the *Cambridge Water* case (below). Thus, an occupier who creates a nuisance will be liable if his acts are an unreasonable use of land, but will only be liable in so far as the kind of damage which occured was foreseeable. Hence 'fault' plays a different role in nuisance as it is only relevant at the remoteness stage and foreseeability for this purpose may be weaker than that required to establish a duty of care in negligence. Thus, it may be premature to regard nuisance as being wholly subsumed under negligence.

---

### Cambridge Water Co. v Eastern Counties Leather
House of Lords [1994] 1 All ER 53; [1994] 2 WLR 53

This case concerned contamination of the claimant's bore hole by a chemical which seeped into the ground water from the defendant's tannery. It was found that a reasonable supervisor at the tannery would not have foreseen that spillage of the chemical would cause contamination. For further facts see Chapter 22. During the course of discussing liability under the rule in *Rylands* v *Fletcher* Lord Goff made the following comments about the law of nuisance.

LORD GOFF:

*Foreseeability of damage in nuisance*

It is, of course, axiomatic that in this field we must be on our guard, when considering liability for damages in nuisance, not to draw inapposite conclusions from cases concerned only with a claim for an injunction. This is because, where an injunction is claimed, its purpose is to restrain further action by the defendant which may interfere with the plaintiff's enjoyment of his land, and ex hypothesi the defendant must be aware, if and when an injunction is granted, that such interference may be caused by the act which he is restrained from committing. It follows that these cases provide no guidance on the question whether foreseeability of harm of the relevant type is a prerequisite of the recovery of damages for causing such harm to the plaintiff. In the present case, we are not concerned with liability in damages in respect of a nuisance which has arisen through natural causes, or by the act of a person for whose actions the defendant is not responsible, in which cases the applicable principles in nuisance have become closely associated with those applicable in negligence: see *Sedleigh-Denfield* v *O'Callaghan* [1940] AC 880 and *Goldman* v *Hargrave* [1967] 1 AC 645. We are concerned with the liability of a person where a nuisance has been created by one for whose actions he is responsible. Here, as I have said, it is still the law that the fact that the defendant has taken all reasonable care will not of itself exonerate him from liability, the relevant control mechanism being found within the principle of reasonable user. But it by no means follows that the defendant should be held liable for damage of a type which he could not reasonably foresee; and the development of the law of negligence in the past 60 years points strongly towards a requirement that such foreseeability should be a prerequisite of liability in damages for nuisance, as it is of liability in negligence. For if a plaintiff is in ordinary circumstances only able to claim damages in respect of personal injuries where he can prove such foreseeability on the part of the defendant, it is difficult to see why, in common justice, he should be in a stronger position to claim damages for interference with the enjoyment of his land where the defendant was unable to foresee such damage. Moreover, this appears to have been the conclusion of the Privy Council in *Overseas Tankship (UK) Ltd* v *Miller Steamship Co. Pty (The Wagon Mound (No. 2))* [1967] 1 AC 617. The facts of the case are too well known to require repetition, but they gave rise to a claim for damages arising from a public nuisance caused by a spillage of oil in Sydney Harbour. Lord Reid, who delivered the advice of the Privy Council, considered that, in the class of nuisance which included the case before the Board, foreseeability is an essential element in determining liability. He then continued, at p. 640:

> It could not be right to discriminate between different cases of nuisance so as to make foreseeability a necessary element in determining damages in those cases where it is a necessary element in determining liability, but not in others. So the choice is between it being a necessary element in all cases of nuisance or in none. In their Lordships' judgment the similarities between nuisance and other forms of tort to which *The Wagon Mound (No. 1)* applies far outweigh any differences, and they must therefore hold that the judgment appealed from is wrong on this branch of the case. It is not sufficient that the injury suffered by the respondents' vessels was the direct result of the nuisance if that injury was in the relevant sense unforeseeable.

It is widely accepted that this conclusion, although not essential to the decision of the particular case, has nevertheless settled the law to the effect that foreseeability of harm is indeed a pre-requisite of the recovery of damages in private nuisance, as in the case of public nuisance. I refer in particular to the opinion expressed by Professor Fleming in *Fleming on the Law of Torts*, 8th ed. (1992), pp. 443–444. It is unnecessary in the present case to consider the precise nature of this principle; but it appears from Lord Reid's statement of the law that he regarded it essentially as one relating to remoteness of damage.

NOTES

1. The passage in *Fleming on Torts* referred to by Lord Goff is as follows:

The loss must, of course, not be too remote. Resolving all prior doubts, the Privy Council in *The Wagon Mound (No. 2)*, a case of public nuisance, held that this depended, as in negligence, on whether the injury was reasonably foreseeable rather than, as was once thought, on whether it was merely 'direct'. Admittedly, negligence in the narrow sense is not always essential to liability. It will be recalled that in *The Wagon Mound* the defendants had been found negligent with respect to the spillage of oil and it would have been Pickwickian to determine their liability for the subsequent fire by a different test in nuisance than in negligence. But the court went further and prescribed the same rule of remoteness for all cases of nuisance regardless of whether fault or negligence happened to be a necessary element of liability. Another important step was thus taken in consolidating the fault element in the modern law of nuisance and assimilating nuisance with the pervasive theory of negligence.

2. This principle will be important where a person knowingly does an unjustified act and can foresee some damage will follow but not damage of the kind that occurred. As Lord Goff pointed out, the control on 'substantive' liability is reasonable user and foreseeability only comes in as a matter of remoteness of damage. Thus, in the *Wagon Mound (No. 2)* the defendants could foresee that the oil they discharged would foul neighbouring slipways but not that it would cause a fire. This may limit common law liability for pollution, for example where a person unjustifiably discharges waste which he has no reason to believe is toxic but which is later found to have caused damage. See further discussion of the *Cambridge Water* case in Chapter 20 and Cross, 'Does only the careless polluter pay?' (1994) 111 LQR 445.

## SECTION 6: STATUTORY AUTHORITY AND PLANNING

Statutory authority to engage in activities can be a defence to any tort, but it most commonly arises in relation to nuisance. If Parliament has authorized the commission of a nuisance there can be no liability, but statutes are rarely explicit on the issue, and the question will often be whether an authorized act will necessarily amount to a nuisance. If it will there is no liability, but where the interference with the claimant's interests is greater than or different from the necessary consequences of the authorized act, there will be no defence.

Similar problems arise where the granting of planning permission might appear to authorize a nuisance. It appears that where 'zoning' issues are involved it may do so if the nuisance is an inevitable consequence of a change in character of the neighbourhood brought about by planning permission, but in other cases activities authorized by planning permission must be carried on in such a way as not to create a nuisance.

### *Allen* v *Gulf Oil Refining Ltd*
House of Lords [1981] AC 1001; [1981] 2 WLR 188; [1981] 1 All ER 353

The claimants sued for nuisances caused by the Gulf Oil refinery at Waterston in Wales. The Gulf Oil Refining Act 1965 authorized the company to compulsorily purchase land for the construction of a refinery, but said nothing about the use or operation of it. The House of Lords held that the power to purchase land for a refinery necessarily implied the operation of a refinery. Held: allowing the appeal, that the defence of statutory authority applied and the defendants were not liable.

LORD WILBERFORCE: We are here in the well charted field of statutory authority. It is now well settled that where Parliament by express direction or by necessary implication has authorised the construction and use of an undertaking or works, that carries with it an authority to do what is authorised with immunity from any action based on nuisance. The right of action is taken away: *Hammersmith and City Railway Co.* v *Brand* (1869) LR 4 HL 171, 215 *per* Lord Cairns. To this there is made the qualification, or condition, that the statutory powers are exercised without 'negligence'— that word here being used in a special sense so as to require the undertaker, as a condition of obtaining immunity from action, to carry out the work and conduct the operation with all reasonable regard and care for the interests of other persons: *Geddis* v *Proprietors of Bann Reservoir* (1878) 3 App Cas 430, 455 *per* Lord Blackburn. It is within the same principle that immunity from action is withheld where the terms of the statute are permissive only, in which case the powers conferred must be exercised in strict conformity with private rights: *Metropolitan Asylum District* v *Hill* (1881) 6 App Cas 193. . . .

My Lords, . . . Parliament considered it in the public interest that a *refinery*, not merely the works (jetties etc.), should be constructed, and constructed upon lands at Llandstadwell to be compulsorily acquired.

To show how this intention was to be carried out I need only quote section 5:

> (1) Subject to the provisions of this Act, the company may enter upon, take and use such of the lands delineated on the deposited plans and described in the deposited book of reference as it may require for the purposes of the authorised works or *for the construction of a refinery* in the parish of Llandstadwell in the rural district of Haverfordwest in the county of Pembroke or for purposes ancillary thereto or connected therewith. (2) The powers of compulsory acquisition of land under this section shall cease after the expiration of three years from October 1, 1965.

. . .

I cannot but regard this as an authority—whether it should be called express or by necessary implication may be a matter of preference—but an authority to construct and operate *a refinery* upon the lands to be acquired—a refinery moreover which should be commensurate with the facilities for unloading offered by the jetties (for large tankers), with the size of the lands to be acquired, and with the discharging facilities to be provided by the railway lines. I emphasize the words *a refinery* by way of distinction from *the refinery* because no authority was given or sought except in the indefinite form. But that there was authority to construct and operate *a* refinery seems to me indisputable. . . .

If I am right upon this point, the position as regards the action would be as follows. The respondent alleges a nuisance, by smell, noise, vibration, etc. The facts regarding these matters are for her to prove. It is then for the appellants to show, if they can, that it was impossible to construct and operate a refinery upon the site, conforming with Parliament's intention, without creating the nuisance alleged, or at least a nuisance. Involved in this issue would be the point discussed by Cumming-Bruce LJ in the Court of Appeal, that the establishment of an oil refinery, etc. was bound to involve some alteration of the environment and so of the standard of amenity and comfort which neighbouring occupiers might expect. To the extent that the environment has been changed from that of a peaceful unpolluted countryside to an industrial complex (as to which different standards apply—*Sturges* v *Bridgman* (1879) 11 ChD 852) Parliament must be taken to have authorised it. So far, I venture to think, the matter is not open to doubt. But in my opinion the statutory authority extends beyond merely authorising a change in the environment and an alteration of standard. It confers immunity against proceedings for any nuisance which can be shown (the burden of so showing being upon the appellants) to be the inevitable result of erecting a refinery upon the site—not, I repeat, the existing refinery, but any refinery—however carefully and with however great a regard for the interest of adjoining occupiers it is sited, constructed and operated. To the extent and only to the extent that the actual nuisance (if any) caused by the actual refinery and its operation exceeds that for which immunity is conferred, the plaintiff has a remedy. . . .

NOTE

An example of a case where a defendant did have statutory authority, but which did not provide a defence because the powers could have been exercised without causing a nuisance, is *Tate & Lyle* v *GLC* [1983] 2 AC 509, where the defendants built ferry terminals at Woolwich which caused siltation around the claimants' jetty. The terminals were authorized by statute, but it was shown that the choice of design caused additional siltation, which need not have occurred if a different design had been adopted. The House of Lords held that the statute did not absolve the defendants from the need to 'have all reasonable regard and care for the interests of other persons' and that as the damage could have been avoided they were liable.

---

### *Wheeler v Saunders*
Court of Appeal [1996] Ch 19; [1995] 3 WLR 466; [1995] 2 All ER 697

The claimant owned a house and holiday cottages adjacent to the defendants' pig farm. In 1989 and 1990 the defendants obtained planning permission for additional capacity by way of two 'Trowbridge' houses, each capable of holding 400 pigs. One of the houses was only 11 metres from the claimant's holiday cottage. The claimant sued for nuisance because of the smell and the defendants claimed that as they had planning permission they were not liable. Held: dismissing the appeal on this issue, that the defendants were liable.

STAUGHTON LJ: . . . What then was the effect of the planning permission for two Trowbridge houses? It was opposed by Dr and Mrs Wheeler, but nevertheless granted. Does that mean that they have lost any right which they had previously enjoyed to live their lives free from the smell of pigs on their doorstep? Surprisingly, there appears to have been no direct authority on the point until recently. There have however been cases dealing with the question of whether statutory authority is a defence to a claim in nuisance. One such was *Allen* v *Gulf Oil Refining Ltd* [1981] AC 1001, where Mrs Allen complained of nuisance from an oil refinery built with statutory authority. Lord Wilberforce said, at p. 1011:

> It is now well settled that where Parliament by express direction or by necessary implication has authorised the construction and use of an undertaking or works, that carries with it an authority to do what is authorised with immunity from any action based on nuisance.

However, he added, at p. 1114, that the immunity was confined to harm which was the inevitable result of what parliament had authorised. The Gulf company had to show that it was impossible to construct the refinery without creating the nuisance complained of.

I do not consider that planning permission necessarily has the same effect as statutory authority. Parliament is sovereign and can abolish or limit the civil rights of individuals. As Sir John May put it in the course of argument, Parliament cannot be irrational just as the Sovereign can do no wrong. The planning authority on the other hand has only the powers delegated to it by Parliament. It is not in my view self-evident that they include the power to abolish or limit civil rights in any or all circumstances. The process by which planning permission is obtained allows for objections by those who might be adversely affected, but they have no right of appeal if their objections are overruled. It is not for us to say whether the private bill procedure in Parliament is better or worse. It is enough that it is different.

In *Allen* v *Gulf Oil Refining Ltd* [1980] QB 156, before the Court of Appeal Cumming-Bruce LJ touched on the effect of planning permission on what would otherwise be a nuisance. He said, at p. 174: 'the planning authority has no jurisdiction to authorise a nuisance save (if at all) in so far as it has statutory power to permit the change of the character of a neighbourhood.'

One can readily appreciate that planning permission will, quite frequently, have unpleasant consequences for some people. The man with a view over open fields from his window may well be displeased if a housing estate is authorised by the planners and built in front of his house; the character of the neighbourhood is changed. But there may be nothing which would qualify as a nuisance and no infringement of his civil rights. What if the development does inevitably create what would otherwise be a nuisance? Instead of a housing estate the planners may authorise a factory which would emit noise and smoke to the detriment of neighbouring residents. Does that come within the first proposition of Cumming-Bruce LJ that a planning authority has no jurisdiction to authorise a nuisance? Or is it within the second, that the authority may change the character of a neighbourhood? The problem arose directly in *Gillingham Borough Council* v *Medway (Chatham) Dock Co. Ltd* [1993] QB 343. There planning permission had been granted for the development as a commercial port of part of the Bulmer Road dockyard in Chatham. This had the result that heavy goods vehicles in large numbers used roads in the neighbourhood for 24 hours a day, much to the harm of local residents. This was said to be an actionable public nuisance. Buckley J held that it was authorised by the grant of planning permission and so was not actionable. His reasoning closely followed the dictum of Cumming-Bruce LJ which I have quoted. He said, at p. 359:

> It has been said, no doubt correctly, that planning permission is not a licence to commit nuisance and that a planning authority has no jurisdiction to authorise nuisance. However, a planning authority can, through its development plans and decisions, alter the character of a neighbourhood.

He concluded at p. 361:

> In short, where planning consent is given for a development or change of use, the question of nuisance will thereafter fall to be decided by reference to a neighbourhood with that development or use and not as it was previously.

However, he did accept, at p. 360: 'it is only a nuisance inevitably resulting from the authorised works on which immunity is conferred.' . . .

What may matter is whether the subsequent nuisance flowed inevitably from the activity which was authorised by the two planning permissions. In my opinion it did. The Trowbridge houses were to contain 800 pigs based on slurry within 36 feet of the nearest holiday cottage. There was bound to be nuisance by smell. True the nuisance would be greater when the pigs were fed on whey, but there would inevitably be nuisance even if they were not. It follows that if this were a case where the buildings were authorised by statute, there would be immunity from any action based on nuisance. But, as I have already said, I consider that the case may be different where one is concerned with planning permission rather than statute.

I accept what was said by Cumming-Bruce LJ: first, that a planning authority has in general no jurisdiction to authorise a nuisance, and secondly, if it can do so at all, that is only by the exercise of its power to permit a change in the character of a neighbourhood. To the extent that those two propositions feature in the judgment of Buckley J, I agree with his decision, but I would not for the present go any further than that.

It would in my opinion be a misuse of language to describe what has happened in the present case as a change in the character of a neighbourhood. It is a change of use of a very small piece of land, a little over 350 square metres according to the dimensions on the plan, for the benefit of the applicant and to the detriment of the objectors in the quiet enjoyment of their house. It is not a strategic planning decision affected by considerations of public interest. Unless one is prepared to accept that any planning decision authorises any nuisance which must inevitably come from it, the argument that the nuisance was authorised by planning permission in this case must fail. I am not prepared to accept that premise. It may be—I express no concluded opinion—that some planning decisions will authorise some nuisances. But that is as far as I am prepared to go. There is no immunity from liability for nuisance in the present case. I would dismiss the second part of this appeal.

NOTES

1. As one of the other judges pointed out, the decision means that the defendants, having constructed the Trowbridge houses in accordance with planning permission, cannot now use them. But why should planning permission allow them to disregard other rules of law?

2. Sir John May said that apart from cases where the permission changes the character of the neighbourhood, even if the nuisance complained of was an inevitable consequence of

the permission, that could not license the nuisance. Furthermore, he said that permission which inevitably resulted in a nuisance would be subject to judicial review on the ground of irrationality.

## SECTION 7: THE EFFECT OF THE HUMAN RIGHTS ACT 1998

The provisions of the Human Rights Act relevant to nuisance are as follows:-

**EUROPEAN CONVENTION FOR THE PROTECTION OF HUMAN RIGHTS AND FUNDAMENTAL FREEDOMS**

### Article 8

Right to respect for private and family life

1. Everyone has the right to respect for his private and family life, his home and his correspondence.
2. There shall be no interference by a public authority with the exercise of this right except such as is in accordance with the law and is necessary in a democratic society in the interests of national security, public safety or the economic well-being of the country, for the prevention of disorder or crime, for the protection of health or morals, or for the protection of the rights and freedoms of others.

## THE FIRST PROTOCOL

### Article 1

Protection of property

Every natural or legal person is entitled to the peaceful enjoyment of his possessions. No one shall be deprived of his possessions except in the public interest and subject to the conditions provided for by law and by the general principles of international law. The preceding provisions shall not, however, in any way impair the right of a State to enforce such laws as it deems necessary to control the use of property in accordance with the general interest or to secure the payment of taxes or other contributions or penalties.

NOTE

It is not yet clear what effect these provisions will have, but they could affect nuisance in a number of ways. One relates to the rule that only a person with an interest in the property can sue—on this see the note on *McKenna* v *British Aluminium* (below). Another relates to the balance between public and private interests which is discussed in *Marcic* v *Thames Water*, of which extracts are printed below. In *Hatton* v *UK* (European Court of Human Rights Case No. 36022/97), which concerned noise from Heathrow Airport, the Court reiterated the fundamentally subsidiary role of the Convention, saying that the national authorities have direct democratic legitimation and are better placed than an international court to evaluate local needs and conditions and accordingly the role of the domestic policy maker should be given special weight. It was said that 'Article 8 may apply in environmental cases whether the pollution is directly caused by the State or whether State responsibility arises from the failure properly to regulate private industry. Whether the case is analysed in terms of a positive duty on the State to take reasonable and appropriate measures to secure the applicants' rights under paragraph 1 of Article 8 or in terms of an interference by a public authority to be justified in accordance with paragraph

2, the applicable principles are broadly similar. In both contexts regard must be had to the fair balance that has to be struck between the competing interests of the individual and of the community as a whole; and in both contexts the State enjoys a certain margin of appreciation in determining the steps to be taken to ensure compliance with the Convention.' The case below is an example of making that balance.

---

### *Marcic* v *Thames Water Utilities Limited*
House of Lords [2004] 2 AC 42 [2003] 3 WLR 1603; [2004] 1 All ER 135; [2003] UKHL 66]

The claimant had suffered a number of incidents of flooding from two sewers in Old Church Lane, Stanmore. The sewers were built in the 1930s but had become inadequate after later housing development. The Water Industry Act 1991 provides that the remedy for breach of a sewerage undertaker's obligations is an enforcement order issued by the Director General of Water Services and no direct statutory remedy is available to a member of the public affected by the breach. The claimant tried to sidestep this system by asserting claims in nuisance and for breach of the Human Rights Act 1998. The claim in nuisance was rejected because Thames Water was not an ordinary occupier of land but was a provider of public utilities and this raised questions of public interest which courts are not equipped to resolve in ordinary litigation. It was also said that the common law should not impose obligations inconsistent with the 1991 Act. The Human Rights Act claim was also rejected. Held: the defendants were not liable.

LORD NICHOLLS OF BIRKENHEAD

*The claim under the Human Rights Act 1998*

**37** I turn to Mr Marcic's claim under the Human Rights Act 1998. His claim is that as a public authority within the meaning of section 6 of the Human Rights Act 1998 Thames Water has acted unlawfully. Thames Water has conducted itself in a way which is incompatible with Mr Marcic's Convention rights under article 8 of the Convention and article 1 of the First Protocol to the Convention. His submission was to the following effect. The flooding of Mr Marcic's property falls within the first paragraph of article 8 and also within article 1 of the First Protocol. That was common ground between the parties. Direct and serious interference of this nature with a person's home is prima facie a violation of a person's right to respect for his private and family life (article 8) and of his entitlement to the peaceful enjoyment of his possessions (article 1 of the First Protocol). The burden of justifying this interference rests on Thames Water. At the trial of the preliminary issues Thames Water failed to discharge this burden. The trial judge found that the system of priorities used by Thames Water in deciding whether to carry out flood alleviation works might be entirely fair. The judge also said that on the limited evidence before him it was not possible to decide this issue, or to decide whether for all its apparent faults the system fell within the wide margin of discretion open to Thames Water and the Director: [2002] QB 929, 964, para 102.

**38** To my mind the fatal weakness in this submission is the same as that afflicting Mr Marcic's claim in nuisance: it does not take sufficient account of the statutory scheme under which Thames Water is operating the offending sewers. The need to adopt some system of priorities for building more sewers is self-evident. So is the need for the system to be fair. A fair system of priorities necessarily involves balancing many intangible factors. Whether the system adopted by a sewerage undertaker is fair is a matter inherently more suited for decision by the industry regulator than by a court. And the statutory scheme so provides. Moreover, the statutory scheme provides a remedy where a system of priorities is not fair. An unfair system of priorities means that a sewerage undertaker is not properly discharging its statutory drainage obligation so far as those who are being treated unfairly are concerned. The statute provides what should happen in these circumstances. The Director is charged with deciding whether to make an enforcement order in respect of a sewerage undertaker's failure to drain property properly. Parliament entrusted this decision to the Director, not the courts.

**39** What happens in practice accords with this statutory scheme. When people affected by sewer flooding complain to the Director he considers whether he should require the sewerage undertaker to take remedial action. Before doing so he considers, among other matters, the severity and history of the problem in the context of that undertaker's sewer flooding relief programme, as allowed for in its current price limits. In many cases the company agrees to take action, but sometimes he accepts that a solution is not possible in the short term.

**40** So the claim based on the Human Rights Act 1998 raises a broader issue: is the statutory scheme as a whole, of which this enforcement procedure is part, Convention-compliant? Stated more specifically and at the risk of over-simplification, is the statutory scheme unreasonable in its impact on Mr Marcic and other householders whose properties are periodically subjected to sewer flooding?

**41** The recent decision of the European Court of Human Rights, sitting as a Grand Chamber, in *Hatton v United Kingdom* Application No 36022/97, (unreported) 8 July 2003 confirms how courts should approach questions such as these. In *Hatton's* case the applicants lived near Heathrow airport. They claimed that the government's policy on night flights at Heathrow violated their rights under article 8. The court emphasised 'the fundamentally subsidiary nature' of the Convention. National authorities have 'direct democratic legitimation' and are in principle better placed than an international court to evaluate local needs and conditions. In matters of general policy, on which opinions within a democratic society may reasonably differ widely, 'the role of the domestic policy maker should be given special weight': see paragraph 97. A fair balance must be struck between the interests of the individual and of the community as a whole.

**42** In the present case the interests Parliament had to balance included, on the one hand, the interests of customers of a company whose properties are prone to sewer flooding and, on the other hand, all the other customers of the company whose properties are drained through the company's sewers. The interests of the first group conflict with the interests of the company's customers as a whole in that only a minority of customers suffer sewer flooding but the company's customers as a whole meet the cost of building more sewers. As already noted, the balance struck by the statutory scheme is to impose a general drainage obligation on a sewerage undertaker but to entrust enforcement of this obligation to an independent regulator who has regard to all the different interests involved. Decisions of the Director are of course subject to an appropriately penetrating degree of judicial review by the courts.

**43** In principle this scheme seems to me to strike a reasonable balance. Parliament acted well within its bounds as policy maker. In Mr Marcic's case matters plainly went awry. It cannot be acceptable that in 2001, several years after Thames Water knew of Mr Marcic's serious problems, there was still no prospect of the necessary work being carried out for the foreseeable future. At times Thames Water handled Mr Marcic's complaint in a tardy and insensitive fashion. But the malfunctioning of the statutory scheme on this occasion does not cast doubt on its overall fairness as a scheme. A complaint by an individual about his particular case can, and should, be pursued with the Director pursuant to the statutory scheme, with the long stop availability of judicial review. That remedial avenue was not taken in this case.

**44** I must add that one aspect of the statutory scheme as presently administered does cause concern. This is the uncertain position regarding payment of compensation to those who suffer flooding while waiting for flood alleviation works to be carried out. A modest statutory compensation scheme exists regarding internal flooding: see paragraph 7B of the Water Supply and Sewerage Services (Customer Service Standards) Regulations 1989, SI 1989/1159, as amended by SI 1993/500 and SI 2000/2301. There seems to be no statutory provision regarding external sewer flooding. Some sewerage undertakers make payments, others do not. They all provide a free clean up and disinfecting service, including removal of residual effluent.

**45** It seems to me that, in principle, if it is not practicable for reasons of expense to carry out remedial works for the time being, those who enjoy the benefit of effective drainage should bear the cost of paying some compensation to those whose properties are situated lower down in the catchment area and who, in consequence, have to endure intolerable sewer flooding, whether internal or external. As the Court of Appeal noted, the flooding is the consequence of the benefit provided to those making use of the system: [2002] QB 929, 1001, para 113. The minority who suffer damage and disturbance as a consequence of the inadequacy of the sewerage system ought not to be required to bear an unreasonable burden. This is a matter the Director and others should reconsider in the light of the facts in the present case.

**46** For these reasons I consider the claim under the Human Rights Act 1998 is ill founded. The scheme set up by the 1991 Act is Convention-compliant. The scheme provides a remedy for persons in Mr Marcic's unhappy position, but Mr Marcic chose not to avail himself of this remedy.

NOTES

1. In *Dennis* v *Ministry of Defence* [2003] EWHC 198 (decided before *Marcic*) the claimant complained of noise from RAF Wittering. At common law the noise was at such a level as to constitute a nuisance, but the public interest required the training of pilots and, as the airfield was operated responsibly, the nuisance was justified. However, the effect of the Human Rights Act was to require compensation as even though the public interest is greater than the individual private interests of the claimants, it is not 'proportionate' to give effect to the public interest without compensating the individuals affected. In *Hatton* v *UK* (referred to in *Marcic*) the issue was whether the system of limiting the number of night flights at Heathrow was fair, and the European Court accepted that national governments have a wide discretion on matters such as these and the scheme was held to be valid. In *Dennis* the view was that the choice was not simply between allowing or not allowing the flights, but rather whether the flights should continue albeit with compensation being paid.

2. *McKenna* v *British Aluminium* [2002] Env LR 30 was a case concerning pollution from a neighbouring factory where some of the claimants had no property interest in the affected land. In a striking out action Neuberger J thought there was a powerful case for saying that effect had not properly been given to Article 8 of the Convention if a person with no interest in the home, but who has lived there for some time, is at the mercy of the person who owns the home as the only person who may bring proceedings. He also thought it questionable whether it would be Article-8 compliant if damages are to be limited. This latter comment refers to the fact that damages are for interference with the land rather than for personal inconvenience. However, he also noted the argument that nuisance is a property based wrong and that it may not be appropriate to test it by Article 8, as that relates to personal rights.

## SECTION 8: REMEDIES

Remedies for nuisance include abatement (self help), injunctions and damages. Interim injunctions are commonly applied for in nuisance cases, and examples of the application of the principles in *American Cyanamid* v *Ethicon* [1975] AC 396 are *Hubbard* v *Pitt* [1975] ICR 308 and *Laws* v *Florinplace* [1981] 1 All ER 659. This section, however, will concentrate on whether a claimant should be awarded an injunction or be satisfied with damages. This is an area which has been subject to considerable economic analysis and raises wide questions of policy—for example, should a defendant be entitled to purchase a licence to commit an unlawful act by the payment of damages?

---

### Kennaway v Thompson
Court of Appeal [1981] QB 88; [1980] 3 WLR 311; [1980] 3 All ER 329

In 1969 the claimant built a house near a man-made lake, which for a number of years had been used for motor-boat racing. The defendants were held liable for the nuisance created by the noise, and at first instance the claimant was awarded damages of £16,000. Held: allowing the appeal, the claimant was entitled to an injunction limiting the use of the lake to certain days and to certain noise limits.

LAWTON LJ: Mr Kempster based his submissions primarily on the decision of this court in *Shelfer* v *City of London Electric Lighting Co.* [1895] 1 Ch 287. The opening paragraph of the headnote, which correctly summarises the judgment, is as follows:

> Lord Cairns' Act 1858, in conferring upon courts of equity a jurisdiction to award damages instead of an injunction, has not altered the settled principles upon which those courts interfered by way of injunction; and in cases of continuing actionable nuisance the jurisdiction so conferred ought only to be exercised under very exceptional circumstances.

In a much-quoted passage, Lindley LJ said, at pp. 315–316:

> . . . ever since Lord Cairns' Act was passed the Court of Chancery has repudiated the notion that the legislature intended to turn that court into a tribunal for legalising wrongful acts; or in other words, the court has always protested against the notion that it ought to allow a wrong to continue simply because the wrongdoer is able and willing to pay for the injury he may inflict. Neither has the circumstance that the wrongdoer is in some sense a public benefactor (e.g., a gas or water company or a sewer authority) ever been considered a sufficient reason for refusing to protect by injunction an individual whose rights are being persistently infringed.

A. L. Smith LJ, in his judgment, set out what he called a good working rule for the award of damages in substitution for an injunction. His working rule does not apply in this case. The injury to the plaintiff's legal rights is not small; it is not capable of being estimated in terms of money save in the way the judge tried to make an estimate, namely by fixing a figure for the diminution of the value of the plaintiff's house because of the prospect of a continuing nuisance—and the figure he fixed could not be described as small. The principles enunciated in *Shelfer's* case, which is binding on us, have been applied time and time again during the past 85 years. The only case which raises a doubt about the application of the *Shelfer* principles to all cases is *Miller* v *Jackson* [1977] QB 966, a decision of this court. The majority (Geoffrey Lane and Cumming-Bruce LJJ, Lord Denning MR dissenting) adjudged that the activities of an old-established cricket club which had been going for over 70 years, had been a nuisance to the plaintiffs by reason of cricket balls landing in their garden. The question then was whether the plaintiffs should be granted an injunction. Geoffrey Lane LJ was of the opinion that one should be granted. Lord Denning MR and Cumming-Bruce LJ thought other-wise. Lord Denning MR said that the public interest should prevail over the private interest. Cumming-Bruce LJ stated that a factor to be taken into account when exercising the judicial dis-cretion whether to grant an injunction was that the plaintiffs had bought their house knowing that it was next to the cricket ground. He thought that there were special circumstances which should inhibit a court of equity from granting the injunction claimed. Lord Denning MR's statement that the public interest should prevail over the private interest runs counter to the principles enunciated in *Shelfer's* case and does not accord with Cumming-Bruce LJ's reason for refusing an injunction. We are of the opinion that there is nothing in *Miller* v *Jackson* [1977] QB 966 binding on us, which qualifies what was decided in *Shelfer's* case. Any decisions before *Shelfer's* case (and there were some at first instance, as Mr Gorman pointed out) which give support for the proposition that the public interest should prevail over the private interest must be read subject to the decision in *Shelfer's* case.

It follows that the plaintiff was entitled to an injunction and that the judge misdirected himself in law in adjudging that the appropriate remedy for her was an award of damages under Lord Cairns's

Act. But she was only entitled to an injunction restraining the club from activities which caused a nuisance, and not all of their activities did. As the judge pointed out, and the plaintiff, by her counsel, accepted in this court, an injunction in general terms would be unworkable.

Our task has been to decide on a form of order which will protect the plaintiff from the noise which the judge found to be intolerable but which will not stop the club from organising activities about which she cannot reasonably complain.

When she decided to build a house alongside Mallam Water she knew that some motor-boat racing and water skiing was done on the club's water and she thought that the noise which such activities created was tolerable. She cannot now complain about that kind of noise provided it does not increase in volume by reason of any increase in activities. The intolerable noise is mostly caused by the large boats; it is these which attract the public interest.

Now nearly all of us living in these islands have to put up with a certain amount of annoyance from our neighbours. Those living in towns may be irritated by their neighbours' noisy radios or incompetent playing of musical instruments; and they in turn may be inconvenienced by the noise caused by our guests slamming car doors and chattering after a late party. Even in the country the lowing of a sick cow or the early morning crowing of a farmyard cock may interfere with sleep and comfort. Intervention by injunction is only justified when the irritating noise causes inconvenience beyond what other occupiers in the neighbourhood can be expected to bear. The question is whether the neighbour is using his property reasonably, having regard to the fact that he has a neighbour. The neighbour who is complaining must remember, too, that the other man can use his property in a reasonable way and there must be a measure of give and take, live and let live.

NOTES

1. For further discussion of this subject, see Ogus and Richardson, 'Economics of the Environment: a study of private nuisance' [1977] CLJ 2841; Tromans, 'Nuisance—prevention or payment?' [1982] CLJ 87; and Jolowicz, 'Damages in Equity—a study of Lord Cairns Act' [1975] CLJ 224.

2. This case also illustrates the principle that it is no defence that the claimant came to the nuisance, i.e. that the nuisance was already there and the claimant knew of it when she built the house. The rule was established in *Sturges* v *Bridgman* (1879) 11 ChD 852, where a doctor built a consulting room near the premises of a confectioner which had been used for many years. The claimant succeeded in his claim for nuisance arising from noise and vibrations caused by the defendant. In *Miller* v *Jackson* [1977] QB 966 the claimant bought a house in 1972 near a cricket ground which had been used since 1905. The cricket club was liable for the nuisance created by balls being hit out of the ground and Geoffrey Lane LJ said he was bound by *Sturges* v *Bridgman*, but he also commented that 'it does not seem just that a long-established activity—in itself innocuous—should be brought to an end because someone chooses to build a house nearby and so turn an innocent pastime into an actionable nuisance'. The court in that case refused to grant an injunction, but that may not now be a possible way to resolve the problem after *Kennaway* v *Thompson*. How can such conflicts of interest be resolved?

# 20

# Liability for the Escape of Dangerous Things

Many things are dangerous, more so today than in earlier times, but the approach of the law to such activities is haphazard. The general principle is that the more dangerous a thing is, the greater the obligation to take care to prevent it causing harm, and this is a matter for the law of negligence. In addition, there is statutory liability for injuries caused by some unsafe activities or things, as under the Health and Safety at Work Act 1974 or the Consumer Protection Act 1987. However, this chapter collects together those areas of the law where strict liability is imposed for escapes of dangerous things, and the subject is closely allied to nuisance.

The idea of strict liability is not new and has existed in the common law for centuries, and it was not until the rise and ultimate domination of the fault principle that strict liability was regarded as out of the ordinary. Today the fault principle is no longer seen as morally obvious, and the demands for strict liability for a range of activities is growing. This is usually achieved by statute and a few examples are given in section 3, but this is often done in response to a particular crisis or demand from a pressure group, and the liability for dangerous activities lacks coherence. The Pearson Commission was unable to formulate any satisfactory general principle and proposed an extension of strict liability by reference to particular activities, based on their propensity to create a high risk of injury or a risk of extensive injury.

As in the rest of the law of tort, the question of whether strict liability should be imposed is a matter of how best to allocate the risk created by an activity. The move from liability for fault to strict liability is often based on the idea that it is unreasonable to expect a potential victim to bear the risk where the defendant has created an exceptional hazard, either by way of increased risk of injury or by way of risk of greater injury. This involves economic as well as social questions, and the extension of strict liability is a matter of considerable debate.

## SECTION 1: THE RULE IN *RYLANDS* v *FLETCHER*

In 1866 when Blackburn J formulated the rule in *Rylands* v *Fletcher*, he believed he was creating nothing new, but was merely formulating a general principle by gathering together existing examples of strict liability. This may have been rather ingenuous, since a general principle has capacity for a much wider application than individual instances, but in the event the principle has had very little effect. That it was *capable* of transforming the law cannot be doubted and we might have had a tort of strict liability for hazardous activities, but the rise of the fault principle hampered the growth of the doctrine. In the event the rule has been restricted by its origins in trespass and nuisance, and is probably now incapable of judicial development beyond the area of liability for escapes from land.

---

### *Rylands* v *Fletcher*
House of Lords (1868) LR 3 HL 330; 37 LJ Ex 161; 19 LT 22

The defendant (Rylands) owned the Ainsworth Mill in Lancashire, and the claimant (Fletcher) owned the Red House Colliery nearby. In 1860 the defendant constructed a reservoir for his mill on land belonging to Lord Wilton and employed engineers and contractors to build it. During construction they found a number of old shafts, but it was not realized that these indirectly connected with the colliery. The contractors were negligent in not ensuring that the filled-in shafts could bear the weight of water, and on 11 December 1860 the partially filled reservoir burst through into the claimant's colliery. Held: dismissing the appeal, that the defendant was liable.

LORD CAIRNS LC: My Lords, the principles on which this case must be determined appear to me to be extremely simple. The defendants, treating them as the owners or occupiers of the close on which the reservoir was constructed, might lawfully have used that close for any purpose for which it might in the ordinary course of the enjoyment of land be used; and if, in what I may term the natural user of that land, there had been any accumulation of water, either on the surface or underground, and if, by the operation of the laws of nature, that accumulation of water had passed off into the close occupied by the plaintiff, the plaintiff could not have complained that that result had taken place. If he had desired to guard himself against it, it would have lain upon him to have done so, by leaving or by interposing, some barrier between his close and the close of the defendants in order to have prevented that operation of the laws of nature. . . .

On the other hand if the defendants, not stopping at the natural use of their close, had desired to use it for any purpose which I may term a non-natural use, for the purpose of introducing into the close that which in its natural condition was not in or upon it, for the purpose of introducing water either above or below ground in quantities and in a manner not the result of any work or operation on or under the land,—and if in consequence of their doing so, or in consequence of any imperfection in the mode of their doing so, the water came to escape and to pass off into the close of the plaintiff, then it appears to me that that which the defendants were doing they were doing at their own peril; and, if in the course of their doing it, the evil arose to which I have referred, the evil, namely, of the escape of the water and its passing away to the close of the plaintiff and injuring the plaintiff, then for the consequence of that, in my opinion, the defendants would be liable. . . .

My Lords, these simple principles, if they are well founded, as it appears to me they are, really dispose of this case.

The same result is arrived at on the principles referred to by Mr Justice Blackburn in his judgment, in the Court of Exchequer Chamber . . .

LORD CRANWORTH: My Lords, I concur with my noble and learned friend in thinking that the rule of law was correctly stated by Mr Justice Blackburn in delivering the opinion of the Exchequer Chamber. If a person brings, or accumulates, on his land anything which, if it should escape, may cause damage to his neighbour, he does so at his peril. If it does escape, and cause damage, he is responsible, however careful he may have been, and whatever precautions he may have taken to prevent the damage.

## Court of Exchequer Chamber
(1866) LR 1 Ex 265

BLACKBURN J: We think that the true rule of law is, that the person who for his own purposes brings on his lands and collects and keeps there anything likely to do mischief if it escapes, must keep it in at his peril, and, if he does not do so, is prima facie answerable for all the damage which is the natural consequence of its escape. He can excuse himself by shewing that the escape was owing to the plaintiff's default; or perhaps that the escape was the consequence of vis major, or the act of God; but as nothing of this sort exists here, it is unnecessary to inquire what excuse would be sufficient. The general rule, as above stated, seems on principle just. The person whose grass or corn is eaten down by the escaping cattle of his neighbour, or whose mine is flooded by the water from his neighbour's reservoir, or whose cellar is invaded by the filth of his neighbour's privy, or whose habitation is made unhealthy by the fumes and noisome vapours of his neighbour's alkali works, is damnified without any fault of his own; and it seems but reasonable and just that the neighbour, who has brought something on his own property which was not naturally there, harmless to others so long as it is confined to his own property, but which he knows to be mischievous if it gets on his neighbour's, should be obliged to make good the damage which ensues if he does not succeed in confining it to his own property. But for his act in bringing it there no mischief could have accrued, and it seems but just that he should at his peril keep it there so that no mischief may accrue, or answer for the natural and anticipated consequences. And upon authority, this we think is established to be the law whether the things so brought be beasts, or water, or filth, or stenches. . . .

The view which we take of the first point renders it unnecessary to consider whether the defendants would or would not be responsible for the want of care and skill in the persons employed by them, under the circumstances stated in the case.

NOTES
1. It may be that Lord Cairns in the House of Lords thought he was saying the same thing as Blackburn J, but the difference between 'which was not naturally there' in Blackburn's formulation and 'non-natural use' (Lord Cairns) is crucial and has enabled subsequent courts to limit the doctrine. It seems likely that the original point of the restriction was merely to exclude liability for natural lakes.
2. It is important to note that the claimant put forward two arguments for liability. The first was strict liability on the defendant for having constructed the reservoir, and the second was vicarious liability for the negligence of his independent contractor. The decision was based solely upon the first ground. For the vicarious liability point, see now *Honeywill & Stein Ltd* v *Larkin* [1934] 1 KB 191.
3. The facts of this case and the reasons for it have attracted enormous attention. For a description of the present site (near the Bury to Bolton road), see A. W. B. Simpson, *Leading Cases in the Common Law*, Chapter 8. For a discussion of the fact that only two Law Lords appear to have sat in the case (whereas the quorum is three), see (1970) 86 LQR 160 (Heuston) and 311 (Yale). For general studies see the judgment of Windeyer J in *Benning* v *Wong* (1969) 122 CLR 249, at p. 294; Linden, 'Whatever happened to *Rylands* v *Fletcher*?' in Klar, *Studies in Canadian Tort Law*; and Bohlen, 'The rule in *Rylands* v *Fletcher*' (1911) 59 U Pa L Rev 298 or his *Studies in the Law of Torts*, Chapter 7.

## Transco v Stockport Metropolitan Borough Council
House of Lords [2004] 2 AC 1 [2003] 3 WLR 1467; [2004] 1 All ER 589; [2003] UKHL 61]

The defendants owned an 11 storey tower block on the Brinnington Housing Estate near Stockport. This was provided with a high pressure water pipe which supplied large tanks in the basement which then pumped water to the flats. This pipe fractured and a considerable amount of water escaped before the break was discovered and repaired. The water had run into an old landfill and thence along an old railway formation. Transco had laid a gas main under the old railway line and where it became an embankment the water washed away the formation leaving the gas pipe suspended. Repairs by the claimants cost £93,681. Held : the defendants were not liable for the damage caused by the escape of the water.

LORD HOFFMANN

**27** *Rylands* v *Fletcher* was therefore an innovation in being the first clear imposition of liability for damage caused by an escape which was not alleged to be either intended or reasonably foreseeable. I think that this is what Professor Newark meant when he said in his celebrated article ('The Boundaries of Nuisance' (1949) 65 LQR 480, 488) that the novelty in *Rylands* v *Fletcher* was the decision that 'an isolated escape is actionable'. That is not because a single deluge is less of a nuisance than a steady trickle, but because repeated escapes such as the discharge of water in the mining cases and the discharge of chemicals in the factory cases do not raise any question about whether the escape was reasonably foreseeable. If the defendant does not know what he is doing, the plaintiff will certainly tell him. It is the single escape which raises the question of whether or not it was reasonably foreseeable and, if not, whether the defendant should nevertheless be liable. *Rylands* v *Fletcher* decided that he should.

*The social background to the rule*

**28** Although the judgment of Blackburn J is constructed in the traditional common law style of deducing principle from precedent, without reference to questions of social policy, Professor Brian Simpson has demonstrated in his article 'Legal Liability for Bursting Reservoirs. The Historical Context of *Rylands* v *Fletcher*' (1984) 13 J Leg Stud 209 that the background to the case was public anxiety about the safety of reservoirs, caused in particular by the bursting of the Bradfield Reservoir near Sheffield on 12 March 1864, with the loss of about 250 lives. The judicial response was to impose strict liability upon the proprietors of reservoirs. But, since the common law deals in principles rather than ad hoc solutions, the rule had to be more widely formulated.

**29** It is tempting to see, beneath the surface of the rule, a policy of requiring the costs of a commercial enterprise to be internalised; to require the entrepreneur to provide, by insurance or otherwise, for the risks to others which his enterprise creates. That was certainly the opinion of Bramwell B, who was in favour of liability when the case was before the Court of Exchequer: (1865) 3 H & C 774. He had a clear and consistent view on the matter: see *Bamford* v *Turnley* (1862) 3 B & S 62, 84–85 and *Hammersmith and City Railway Co* v *Brand* (1867) LR 2 QB 223, 230–231. But others thought differently. They considered that the public interest in promoting economic development made it unreasonable to hold an entrepreneur liable when he had not been negligent: see *Wildtree Hotels Ltd* v *Harrow London Borough Council* [2001] 2 AC 1, 8–9 for a discussion of this debate in the context of compensation for disturbance caused by the construction and operation of works authorised by statutory powers. On the whole, it was the latter view—no liability without fault—which gained the ascendancy. With hindsight, *Rylands* v *Fletcher* can be seen as an isolated victory for the internalisers. The following century saw a steady refusal to treat it as laying down any broad principle of liability. I shall briefly trace the various restrictions imposed on its scope.

*Restrictions on the rule*

*(a) Statutory authority*

**30** A statute which authorises the construction of works like a reservoir, involving risk to others, may deal expressly with the liability of the undertakers. It may provide that they are to be strictly liable, liable only for negligence or not liable at all. But what if it contains no express provision? If the principle of *Rylands* v *Fletcher* is that costs should be internalised, the undertakers should be liable in the same way as private entrepreneurs. The fact that Parliament considered the construction and operation of the works to be in the public interest should make no difference. As Bramwell B repeatedly explained, the risk should be borne by the public and not by the individual who happens to have been injured. But within a year of the decision of the House of Lords in *Rylands* v *Fletcher*,

Blackburn J advised the House that, in the absence of negligence, damage caused by operations authorised by statute is not compensatable unless the statute expressly so provides: see *Hammersmith and City Railway Co* v *Brand* (1869) LR 4 HL 171, 196. The default position is that the owner of land injured by the operations 'suffers a private loss for the public benefit'. In *Geddis* v *Proprietors of Bann Reservoir* (1878) 3 App Cas 430, 455 Lord Blackburn summed up the law:

> It is now thoroughly well established that no action will lie for doing that which the legislature has authorised, if it be done without negligence, although it does occasion damage to anyone.

**31** The effect of this principle was to exclude the application of the rule in *Rylands* v *Fletcher* to works constructed or conducted under statutory authority: see *Green* v *Chelsea Waterworks Co* (1894) 70 LT 547; *Dunne* v *North Western Gas Board* [1964] 2 QB 806.

*(b)  Acts of God and third parties*

**32** Escapes of water and the like are often the result of natural events—heavy rain or drains blocked by falling leaves—or the acts of third parties, like vandals who open taps or sluices. This form of causation does not usually make the damage any the less a consequence of the risk created by the presence of the water or other escaping substance. No serious principle of allocating risk to the enterprise would leave the injured third party to pursue his remedy against the vandal. But early cases on *Rylands* v *Fletcher* quickly established that natural events ('Acts of God') and acts of third parties excluded strict liability. In *Carstairs* v *Taylor* (1871) LR 6 Ex 217, 221 Kelly CB said that he thought a rat gnawing a hole in a wooden gutter box counted as an Act of God and in *Nichols* v *Marsland* (1876) 2 Ex D 1 Mellish LJ (who, as counsel, had lost *Rylands* v *Fletcher*) said that an exceptionally heavy rainstorm was a sufficient excuse. In *Rickards* v *Lothian* [1913] AC 263 the same was said of the act of a vandal who blocked a washbasin and turned on the tap. By contrast, acts of third parties and natural events are not defences to the strict criminal liability imposed by section 85(1) of the Water Resources Act 1991 for polluting controlled waters unless they are really exceptional events: *Environment Agency (formerly National Rivers Authority)* v *Empress Car Co (Abertillery) Ltd* [1999] 2 AC 22.

*(c)  Remoteness*

**33** *Rylands* v *Fletcher* established that, in a case to which the rule applies, the defendant will be liable even if he could not reasonably have foreseen that there would be an escape. But is he liable for all the consequences of the escape? In *Cambridge Water Co* v *Eastern Counties Leather plc* [1994] 2 AC 264 the House of Lords decided that liability was limited to damage which was what Blackburn J had called the 'natural', ie reasonably foreseeable, consequence of the escape. Lord Goff of Chieveley, in a speech which repays close attention, took the rule back to its origins in the law of nuisance and said that liability should be no more extensive than it would have been in nuisance if the discharge itself had been negligent or intentional. Adopting the opinion of Professor Newark, to which I have already referred, he said that the novel feature of *Rylands* v *Fletcher* was to create liability for an 'isolated' (ie unforeseeable) escape. But the rule was nevertheless founded on the principles of nuisance and should not otherwise impose liability for unforeseeable damage.

*(d)  Escape*

**34** In *Read* v *J Lyons & Co Ltd* [1947] AC 156 a radical attempt was made to persuade the House of Lords to develop the rule into a broad principle that an enterprise which created an unusual risk of damage should bear that risk. Mrs Read had been drafted into the Ministry of Supply and directed to inspect the manufacture of munitions at a factory operated by J Lyons & Company Ltd. In August 1942 she was injured by the explosion of a shell. There was no allegation of negligence; the cause of action was said to be the hazardous nature of the activity. But the invitation to generalise the rule was comprehensively rejected. The House of Lords stressed that the rule was primarily concerned with the rights and duties of occupiers of land. Escape from the defendant's land or control is an essential element of the tort.

*(e) Personal injury*

**35** In some cases in the first half of the 20th century plaintiffs recovered damages under the rule for personal injury: *Shiffman* v *St John of Jerusalem (Grand Priory in the British Realm of the Venerable Order of the Hospital)* [1936] 1 All ER 557; *Hale* v *Jennings Bros* [1938] 1 All ER 579 are examples. But dicta in *Read* v *J Lyons & Co Ltd* cast doubt upon whether the rule protected anything beyond interests in land. Lord Macmillan (at pp 170–171) was clear that it had no application to personal injury and Lord Simonds (at p 180) was doubtful. But I think that the point is now settled by two recent decisions of the House of Lords: *Cambridge Water Co* v *Eastern Counties Leather plc* [1994] AC 264, which decided that *Rylands* v *Fletcher* is a special form of nuisance and *Hunter* v *Canary Wharf Ltd* [1997] AC 655, which decided that nuisance is a tort against land. It must, I think, follow that damages for personal injuries are not recoverable under the rule.

*(f) Non-natural user*

**36** The principle in *Rylands* v *Fletcher* was widely expressed; the essence was the escape of something which the defendant had brought upon his land. Not surprisingly, attempts were immediately made to apply the rule in all kinds of situations far removed from the specific social problem of bursting reservoirs which had produced it. Leaks caused by a rat gnawing a hole in a wooden gutter-box (*Carstairs* v *Taylor* LR 6 Ex 217) were not at all what Blackburn J and Lord Cairns had had in mind. In some cases the attempt to invoke the rule was repelled by relying on Blackburn J's statement that the defendant must have brought whatever escaped onto his land 'for his own purposes'. This excluded claims by tenants that they had been damaged by escapes of water from plumbing installed for the benefit of the premises as whole. Another technique was to imply the claimant's consent to the existence of the accumulation. But the most generalized restriction was formulated by Lord Moulton in *Rickards* v *Lothian* [1913] AC 263, 280:

> It is not every use to which land is put that brings into play that principle. It must be some special use bringing with it increased danger to others, and must not merely be the ordinary use of the land or such a use as is proper for the general benefit of the community.

**37** The context in which Lord Moulton made this statement was a claim under *Rylands* v *Fletcher* for damage caused by damage to stock in a shop caused by an overflow of water from a wash-basin in a lavatory on a floor above. To exclude domestic use is understandable if one thinks of the rule as a principle for the allocation of costs; there is no enterprise of which the risk can be regarded as a cost which should be internalised. That would at least provide a fairly rational distinction. But the rather vague reference to 'the ordinary use of the land' and in particular the reference to a use 'proper for the general benefit of the community' has resulted in the rule being applied to some commercial enterprises but not others, the distinctions being sometimes very hard to explain.

**38** In the *Cambridge Water Co* case [1994] 2 AC 264, 308–309 Lord Goff of Chieveley noted these difficulties but expressed the hope that it would be possible to give the distinction 'a more recognisable basis of principle.' The facts of that case, involving the storage of substantial quantities of chemicals on industrial premises, were in his opinion 'an almost classic case of non-natural use'. He thought that the restriction of liability to the foreseeable consequences of the escape would reduce the inclination of the courts to find other ways of limiting strict liability, such as extension of the concept of natural use.

*Where stands the rule today?*

**39** I pause at this point to summarise the very limited circumstances to which the rule has been confined. First, it is a remedy for damage to land or interests in land. As there can be few properties in the country, commercial or domestic, which are not insured against damage by flood and the like, this means that disputes over the application of the rule will tend to be between property insurers and liability insurers. Secondly, it does not apply to works or enterprises authorised by statute. That means that it will usually have no application to really high risk activities. As Professor Simpson points out ([1984] 13 J Leg Stud 225) the Bradfield Reservoir was built under statutory powers. In the absence of negligence, the occupiers whose lands had been inundated would have had no remedy. Thirdly, it is not particularly strict because it excludes liability when the escape is for the most common reasons, namely vandalism or unusual natural events. Fourthly, the cases in which there is an escape which is not attributable to an unusual natural event or the act of a third party will, by the same token, usually give rise to an inference of negligence. Fifthly, there is a broad and ill-defined exception for 'natural' uses of land. It is perhaps not surprising that counsel could not find a reported case since the second world war in which anyone had succeeded in a claim under the rule. It is hard to escape the conclusion that the intellectual effort devoted to the rule by judges and writers over many years has brought forth a mouse.

### Is it worth keeping?

**40** In *Burnie Port Authority* v *General Jones Pty Ltd* (1994) 179 CLR 520 a majority of the High Court of Australia lost patience with the pretensions and uncertainties of the rule and decided that it had been 'absorbed' into the law of negligence. Your Lordships have been invited by the respondents to kill off the rule in England in similar fashion. It is said, first, that in its present attenuated form it serves little practical purpose; secondly, that its application is unacceptably vague ('an essentially unprincipled and ad hoc subjective determination' said the High Court (at p 540) in the *Burnie* case) and thirdly, that strict liability on social grounds is better left to statutory intervention.

**43** But despite the strength of these arguments, I do not think it would be consistent with the judicial function of your Lordships' House to abolish the rule. It has been part of English law for nearly 150 years and despite a searching examination by Lord Goff of Chieveley in the *Cambridge Water* case [1994] 2 AC 264, 308, there was no suggestion in his speech that it could or should be abolished. I think that would be too radical a step to take.

**44** It remains, however, if not to rationalise the law of England, at least to introduce greater certainty into the concept of natural user which is in issue in this case. In order to do so, I think it must be frankly acknowledged that little assistance can be obtained from the kinds of user which Lord Cairns must be assumed to have regarded as 'non-natural' in *Rylands* v *Fletcher* itself. They are, as Lord Goff of Chieveley said in the *Cambridge Water* case [1994] 2 AC 264, 308, 'redolent of a different age'. So nothing can be made of the anomaly that one of the illustrations of the rule given by Blackburn J is cattle trespass. Whatever Blackburn J and Lord Cairns may have meant by 'natural', the law was set on a different course by the opinion of Lord Moulton in *Rickards* v *Lothian* [1913] AC 263 and the question of what is a natural use of land or, (the converse) a use creating an increased risk, must be judged by contemporary standards.

**45** Two features of contemporary society seem to me to be relevant. First, the extension of statutory regulation to a number of activities, such as discharge of water (section 209 of the Water Industry Act 1991) pollution by the escape of waste (section 73(6) of the Environmental Protection Act 1990) and radio-active matter (section 7 of the Nuclear Installations Act 1965). It may have to be considered whether these and similar provisions create an exhaustive code of liability for a particular form of escape which excludes the rule in *Rylands* v *Fletcher*.

**46** Secondly, so far as the rule does have a residuary role to play, it must be borne in mind that it is concerned only with damage to property and that insurance against various forms of damage to property is extremely common. A useful guide in deciding whether the risk has been created by a 'non-natural' user of land is therefore to ask whether the damage which eventuated was something against which the occupier could reasonably be expected to have insured himself. Property insurance is relatively cheap and accessible; in my opinion people should be encouraged to insure their own property rather than seek to transfer the risk to others by means of litigation, with the heavy transactional costs which that involves. The present substantial litigation over £100,000 should be a warning to anyone seeking to rely on an esoteric cause of action to shift a commonplace insured risk.

**47** In the present case, I am willing to assume that if the risk arose from a 'non-natural user' of the council's land, all the other elements of the tort were satisfied. Transco complains of expense having to be undertaken to avoid damage to its gas pipe; I am willing to assume that if damage to the pipe would have been actionable, the expense incurred in avoiding that damage would have been recoverable. I also willing to assume that Transco's easement which entitled it to maintain its pipe in the embankment and receive support from the soil was a sufficient proprietary interest to enable it to sue in nuisance and therefore, by analogy, under the rule in *Rylands* v *Fletcher*. Although the council, as owner of Hollow End Towers, was no doubt under a statutory duty to provide its occupiers with water, it had no statutory duty or authority to build that particular tower block and it is therefore not suggested that the pipe was laid pursuant to statutory powers so as to exclude the rule. So the question is whether the risk came within the rule.

**48** The damage which eventuated was subsidence beneath a gas main: a form of risk against which no rational owner of a gas main would fail to insure. The casualty was caused by the escape of water from the council's land. But the source was a perfectly normal item of plumbing. The pipe was, it is true, considerably larger than the ordinary domestic size. But it was smaller than a water main. It was installed to serve the occupiers of the council's high rise flats; not strictly speaking a commercial purpose, but not a private one either.

**49** In my opinion the Court of Appeal was right to say that it was not a 'non-natural' user of land. I am influenced by two matters. First, there is no evidence that it created a greater risk than is normally associated with domestic or commercial plumbing. True, the pipe was larger. But whether that involved greater risk depends upon its specification. One cannot simply assume that the larger the pipe, the greater the risk of fracture or the greater the quantity of water likely to be discharged. I agree with my noble and learned friend Lord Bingham of Cornhill that the criterion of exceptional risk must be taken seriously and creates a high threshold for a claimant to surmount. Secondly, I think that the risk of damage to property caused by leaking water is one against which most people can and do commonly insure. This is, as I have said, particularly true of Transco, which can be expected to have insured against any form of damage to its pipe. It would be a very strange result if Transco were entitled to recover against the council when it would not have been entitled to recover against the Water Authority for similar damage emanating from its high pressure main.

NOTES

1. This case is an important restatement of the *Rylands* principle, but it is also important for what it does not do. In particular it restricts any move towards a more general tort of strict liability for hazardous activities and closely limits *Rylands* to its historical origins. The Supreme Court of India took a very much wider view in *Mehta* v *Union of India* 1987 AIR (SC) 1086, where there was a discharge of toxic gas from a factory in Delhi. The court rejected many of the traditional limitations of *Rylands*, adopting a more general tort of strict liability for engaging in hazardous activities. (See Bergman (1988) 138 NLJ 420.) That approach has now been rejected by the Law Commission (Report No. 32) and twice by the House of Lords, citing the uncertainties and practical difficulties of its application.

2. *Transco* also adopts a very strict interpretation of the elements of the tort, including the rules on escape from the premises, non-natural user and no liability for personal injuries. Non-natural user has been much discussed and in *Transco* Lord Bingham said that 'ordinary user is a preferable test to natural user, making it clear that the rule in *Rylands* v *Fletcher* is engaged only where the defendant's use is shown to be extraordinary and unusual'. It is not a question of reasonable user but rather whether the defendant has done something quite out of the ordinary in the place and time when he does it. The question is to what extent industrial activities might be ordinary user, and later Lord Bingham refers to an occupier who has brought onto his land an 'exceptionally dangerous or mischievous thing in extraordinary or unusual circumstances'. Is this too narrow an interpretation?

3. One particular problem with *Rylands* has been the issue of remoteness of damage but this seems to have been resolved in *Transco*. In *Cambridge Water* v *Eastern Counties Leather* [1994] 2 AC 264 the defendants operated a tannery which used a chemical called PCE. Over the years small quantities of this were spilled and soaked into the ground and then dissolved in

percolating groundwater. This eventually contaminated the claimant's water borehole over a mile away. It was not foreseeable that the chemical would create an environmental hazard. The House of Lords held that the use of the chemical was 'non-natural' but that the eventual damage was not a foreseeable kind of damage. It seems clear from *Transco* that the issue is whether *assuming* there is an escape, is the damage which has occurred of a foreseeable kind? (See Lord Hoffmann at para. 33.) There is no need to foresee the escape.

4. In *Burnie Port Authority* v *General Jones Pty Ltd* (1992) 179 CLR 520 (referred to in *Transco*) the High Court of Australia rejected *Rylands* v *Fletcher* altogether, saying that the situations envisaged by that doctrine can be dealt with by negligence. It was said that proximity would exist because of the special vulnerability and dependence of the claimant arising out of the hazardous activities of the defendant and that this would give rise to a non-delegable duty of care arising out of the defendant's control of the premises. It was also said that the standard of care would relate to the degree of danger and that it could even involve 'a degree of diligence so stringent as to amount practically to a guarantee of safety'. For a general discussion of the value of the tort see Nolan 'The Distinctiveness of Rylands v Fletcher' (2005) 121 LQR 421 where it is argued that the tort has become so emasculated that it no longer serves a useful function. Note however Murphy 'The Merits of Rylands v Fletcher' (2004) 24 OJLS 643 which seeks to defend the rule, arguing that it provides a useful residual mechanism for securing environmental protection by individuals affected by harmful escapes from polluting heavyweight industrialists.

## SECTION 2: LIABILITY FOR FIRES

Fires are dangerous, and from earliest times there has been a special form of liability upon occupiers for damage caused by 'their' fires, although of course other torts such as negligence or nuisance also apply. The form of the law is complicated because the ancient common law action, together with negligence and nuisance (but not liability based on *Rylands* v *Fletcher*), is subject to a statutory defence which relieves an occupier of liability for fires which 'accidentally' begin. The position, therefore, is that an occupier is liable for damage done by a fire for which he, or his guest or his contractor, was responsible except where the fire began by mere chance. There is a debate about whether the common law action is based on occupation or control, but it seems likely that both are required: see Ogus, 'Vagaries in liability for the escape of fire' [1969] CLJ 104.

---

### Balfour v Barty-King
Court of Appeal [1957] 1 QB 497; [1957] 2 WLR 84; [1957] 1 All ER 156

A large country house had been divided into separate houses, one of which was occupied by the defendants and another by the claimant. After a severe frost, pipes in the defendants' part were frozen, and two men were employed to unfreeze them. They used a blow lamp and in doing so they set fire to the lagging, and the fire spread to the claimant's house. Held: dismissing the appeal, that the defendants were liable.

LORD GODDARD CJ: The earliest case on the subject which the industry of counsel or our own researches have discovered is *Beaulieu* v *Finglam*, conveniently translated in Mr Fifoot's History of Sources of the Common Law, 1st ed. (1949), p. 166. It will be noticed that the writ was founded upon a common custom of the realm and alleges that the defendant so negligently kept his fire (ignem suum) that the goods and chattels of the plaintiff were burnt. The court held that a man shall answer to his neighbour for each person who enters his house by his leave or knowledge or is a guest if he does any act with a candle or aught else whereby his neighbour's house is burnt. But, said the court, if a man from outside my house and against my will starts a fire in the thatch of my house or elsewhere whereby my house is burned and my neighbour's house is burned as well, for this I shall not be held bound, for this cannot be said to be done by wrong on my part, but is against my will. . . .

Sir William Holdsworth, in his History of English Law, Vol. XI, p. 607, thinks that by the time [*Tuberville* v *Stamp* (1697) 91 ER 1072] was decided, 1698, lawyers were beginning to think it was anomalous that a man should be liable for fire damage not caused by negligence, and that this was one of the reasons for the Act of 1707, 6, Anne, c. 31, which provided that no action should lie against any person in whose house a fire should accidentally begin. This provision was re-enacted in the Fires Prevention (Metropolis) Act, 1774, s. 86, an Act which has been held to extend to the whole country. That it was necessary to give this measure of exemption to householders seems to show that by the common law there was an absolute duty to prevent the escape of fire, and this was the opinion of Blackstone, who says (Commentaries I, p. 431) that the common law was altered by the Statute of Anne. The two cases cited above, however, show that at common law the act of God and the act of a stranger were exceptions, and in *Musgrove* v *Pandelis* [1919] 2 KB 43, it was held that the statute which protects the householder in the case of an accidental fire leaves the other heads of liability at common law untouched. The citation in that case from the judgment of Lord Denman CJ in *Filliter* v *Phippard* (1847) 116 ER 506, shows that in his opinion the common law was that a person in whose house a fire originated and which afterwards spread to his neighbour's house was responsible for the damage, and it was to that liability that the statute was directed.

The precise meaning to be attached to 'accidentally' has not been determined, but it is clear from these last two cited cases that where the fire is caused by negligence it is not to be regarded as accidental. Although there is a difference of opinion among eminent text writers whether at common law the liability was absolute or depended on negligence, at the present day it can safely be said that a person in whose house a fire is caused by negligence is liable if it spreads to that of his neighbour, and this is true whether the negligence is his own or that of his servant or his guest, but he is not liable if the fire is caused by a stranger.

Who, then, is a stranger? Clearly a trespasser would be in that category, but if a man is liable for the negligent act of his guest, it is, indeed, difficult to see why he is not liable for the act of a contractor whom he has invited to his house to do work on it, and who does the work in a negligent manner. . . .

In the recent case of *Perry* v *Kendricks Transports Ltd* [1956] 1 All ER 154, Parker LJ referred to a stranger as a person over whom the defendant had no control. From one point of view it may be said that the test of an independent contractor is that he is left to carry out the work in his own way, but that is not, I think, the sense in which the Lord Justice is using the word 'control.' The defendants here had control over the contractor in that they chose him, they invited him to their premises to do work, and he could have been ordered to leave at any moment. It was left to the men who were sent how to do the work, and in our opinion the defendants are liable to the plaintiff for this lamentable occurrence, the more lamentable in that the persons ultimately responsible are insolvent.

NOTES

1. In *Beaulieu* v *Finglam* (1401) YB 2 Hen IV, f. 18, pl. 6 (see Fifoot, *History and Sources of the Common Law*, p. 166), which is referred to above, it was argued that if liability were imposed the defendant would be 'undone and impoverished all his days'. Thirning CJ vigorously replied 'What is that to us? It is better that he should be utterly undone than that the law be changed for him.'

2. For another example of liability for the act of another, see *H. & N. Emmanuel Ltd v GLC* [1971] 2 All ER 835, where the defendants were liable for a fire started by demolition contractors on their land, even though they had been instructed not to light fires. Lord Denning said that a

'stranger' is 'anyone who in lighting a fire or allowing it to escape acts contrary to anything which an occupier could anticipate that he would do'.

3. The common law action does not apply to fires escaping from chattels. In *Mayfair v Pears* [1987] 1 NZLR 459 the defendant unlawfully parked his car on the claimant's property. The car caught fire and the fire spread to the claimant's buildings. The court held the defendant was not liable, as such liability would place a chattel owner under a stricter liability than a landowner, who could have the benefit of the statutory defence in the Act of 1774 (below).

## FIRES PREVENTION (METROPOLIS) ACT 1774

### Section 86

And no action suit or process whatever shall be had, maintained or prosecuted against any person in whose house, chamber, stable, barn or other building, or in whose estate any fire shall accidentally begin . . .

NOTES

1. In *Filliter v Phippard* (1847) 11 QB 347; 116 ER 506 the defendant lit a fire on his land which spread to the claimant's fields. The defendant was held liable, the court pointing out that 'accidentally begin' means 'a fire produced by mere chance, or incapable of being traced to any cause, and so would stand opposed to the negligence of either servants or masters'. It was also pointed out that the Act extends to the whole of the country and not just to the metropolis. Note also that a fire which accidentally begins may be *continued* by carelessness, as in *Musgrove v Pandelis* [1919] 2 KB 43, where a fire 'accidentally began' in the carburettor of a car, but was carelessly continued because the chauffeur failed to turn off the petrol tap which was then fitted to all cars.

2. In *Johnson v BJW Property Developments* [2002] 3 All ER 574 the claimant's property was damaged by the escape of a fire which had been lit in the defendant's domestic grate, which was in the party wall which separated the two properties. The fire escaped because of negligent repair work by an independent contractor. The defendant was liable under the old common law principle and the 1774 Act was no defence since the fire had spread because of negligence—thus the fire in the claimant's property had not accidentally begun. The defendant was also vicariously liable for the negligence of the contractor as work on a party wall involved a special risk to the claimant's property.

3. *Negligence*. Liability for damage caused by fires can also be imposed in other torts. An example of negligence is *Goldman v Hargrave* [1967] 1 AC 645, where lightning set fire to a redgum tree in Australia. The defendant cut the tree down but failed to put water on it. The smouldering fire revived and spread. The defendant was held liable.

4. *Nuisance*. An example is *Spicer v Smee* [1946] 1 All ER 489, where a fire was caused by defective electrical wiring which was probably carelessly installed by a contractor. It was held that the state of the wiring constituted a nuisance, and that the 1774 Act did not apply where a nuisance was created by an occupier or his contractor.

5. *Rylands v Fletcher*. In *Mason v Levy Autoparts* [1967] 2 QB 530 the defendants brought onto the land large quantities of combustible materials which inexplicably caught fire. MacKenna J, in holding the defendants liable, adopted a principle analogous to *Rylands v Fletcher* but slightly different from it, in that it was not the thing brought onto the land which escaped. He said there would be liability if '(1) he brought onto his land things likely to catch fire, and kept them there in such conditions that if they did ignite the fire would be likely to spread to the plaintiff's [claimant's] land; (2) he did so in the course of some non-natural use; and (3) the things ignited and the fire spread'.

## SECTION 3: LIABILITY FOR NUCLEAR ESCAPES

The motives for imposing strict liability by statute are often mixed. These include the inability of the common law to deal with the problem, as in the case of oil pollution, the need to protect the public from hazardous activities, and the need to limit liability. The latter two reasons are often combined, as in the case of nuclear escapes, where strict liability is imposed but with a limit of £140 million arising out of any one occurrence. The insurance industry will not undertake unlimited liability and a compromise of some kind is necessary. Alternatively, the excess liability could be borne by the taxpayer or, as in the case of oil pollution, by a levy on the industry.

### NUCLEAR INSTALLATIONS ACT 1965

**7. Duty of licensee of licensed site**

(1) Subject to subsection (4) below where a nuclear site licence has been granted in respect of any site, it shall be the duty of the licensee to secure that—

(a) no such occurrence involving nuclear matter as is mentioned in subsection (2) of this section causes injury to any person or damage to any property of any person other than the licensee, being injury or damage arising out of or resulting from the radioactive properties, or a combination of those and any toxic, explosive or other hazardous properties, of that nuclear matter; and

(b) no ionising radiations emitted during the period of the licensee's responsibility
   (i) from anything caused or suffered by the licensee to be on the site which is not nuclear matter; or
   (ii) from any waste discharged (in whatever form) on or from the site, cause injury to any person or damage to any property of any person other than the licensee.

(2) The occurrences referred to in subsection (1)(a) of this section are—

(a) any occurrence on the licensed site during the period of the licensee's responsibility, being an occurrence involving nuclear matter;

(b) any occurrence elsewhere than on the licensed site involving nuclear matter which is not excepted matter and which at the time of the occurrence—
   (i) is in the course of carriage on behalf of the licensee as licensee of that site; or
   (ii) is in the course of carriage to that site with the agreement of the licensee from a place outside the relevant territories; and
   (iii) in either case, is not on any other relevant site in the United Kingdom;

(c) any occurrence elsewhere than on the licensed site involving nuclear matter which is not excepted matter and which—
   (i) having been on the licensed site at any time during the period of the licensee's responsibility; or
   (ii) having been in the course of carriage on behalf of the licensee as licensee of that site,

has not subsequently been on any relevant site, or in the course of any relevant carriage, or (except in the course of relevant carriage) within the territorial limits of a country which is not a relevant territory.

(3) In determining the liability by virtue of subsection (1) of this section in respect of any occurrence of the licensee of a licensed site, any property which at the time of occurrence is on that site, being—

(a) a nuclear installation; or

(b) other property which is on that site—

(i) for the purpose of use in connection with the operation, or the cessation of the operation, by the licensee of a nuclear installation which is or has been on that site; or

(ii) for the purpose of the construction of a nuclear installation on that site, shall, notwithstanding that it is the property of some other person, be deemed to be the property of the licensee.

(4) Section 8 of this Act shall apply in relation to sites occupied by the Authority.

## 8. Duty of Authority

[This section extends s. 7 to sites occupied by the United Kingdom Atomic Energy Authority.]

## 13. Exclusion, extension or reduction of compensation in certain cases

(4) The duty imposed by section 7, 8, 9, 10 or 11 of this Act—

(a) shall not impose any liability on the person subject to that duty with respect to injury or damage caused by an occurrence which constitutes a breach of that duty if the occurrence or the causing thereby of the injury or damage, is attributable to hostile action in the course of any armed conflict, including any armed conflict within the United Kingdom; but

(b) shall impose such a liability where the occurrence, or the causing thereby of the injury or damage, is attributable to a natural disaster, notwithstanding that the disaster is of such an exceptional character that it could not reasonably have been foreseen.

(6) The amount of compensation payable to or in respect of any person under this Act in respect of any injury or damage caused in breach of a duty imposed by section 7, 8, 9 or 10 of this Act may be reduced by reason of the fault of that person if, but only if, and to the extent that, the causing of that injury or damage is attributable to any act of that person committed with the intention of causing harm to any person or property or with reckless disregard for the consequences of his act.

## 15. Time for bringing claims under ss. 7 to 11

(1) Subject to subsection (2) of this section and to section 16(3) of this Act, but notwithstanding anything in any other enactment, a claim by virtue of any of sections 7 to 11 of this Act may be made at any time before, but shall not be entertained if made at any time after, the expiration of thirty years from the relevant date, that is to say, the date of the occurrence which gave rise to the claim or, where that occurrence was a continuing one, or was one of a succession of occurrences all attributable to a particular happening on a particular relevant site or to the carrying out from time to time on a particular relevant site of a particular operation, the date of the last event in the course of that occurrence or succession of occurrences to which the claim relates.

(2) Notwithstanding anything in subsection (1) of this section, a claim in respect of injury or damage caused by an occurrence involving nuclear matter stolen from, or lost, jettisoned or abandoned by, the person whose breach of a duty imposed by section 7, 8, 9 or 10 of this Act gave rise to the claim shall not be entertained if the occurrence takes place after the expiration of the period of twenty years beginning with the day when the nuclear matter in question was so stolen, lost, jettisoned or abandoned.

## 16. Satisfaction of claims by virtue of ss. 7 to 10

(1) The liability of any person to pay compensation under this Act by virtue of a duty imposed on that person by section 7, 8 or 9 thereof shall not require him to make in respect of any one occurrence constituting a breach of that duty payments by way of such compensation exceeding in the aggregate, apart from payments in respect of interest or costs, £140 million or, in the case of the licensees of such sites as may be prescribed, £10 million.

NOTE

By further provisions in s. 16, if a claim is made after ten years have elapsed from the date of the occurrence, it should be made to the appropriate government minister. A 'prescribed site' for the purposes of s. 16 is defined by the Nuclear Installations (Prescribed Site) Regulations 1983, SI 1983/919 as, subject to other conditions, a small nuclear reactor with a thermal output not exceeding 600 kw. By s. 12 all other forms of liability are excluded.

---

### *Blue Circle Industries* v *Ministry of Defence*
Court of Appeal [1999] Ch 289 [1999] 2 WLR 295; [1998] 3 All ER 385

Blue Circle Industries (BCL) owned a large house, gardens and marshland which adjoined the Atomic Weapons Establishment at Aldermaston. In July 1989, a storm caused ponds on the defendants' land to overflow and the claimants' marshland became contaminated with plutonium above the regulatory limits. Although the radioactivity was not such as to cause harm, regulations required that the soil be removed. Damages were claimed for the reduced chance of selling the estate and the cost of cleaning up. Held: the defendants were liable.

ALDOUS J: . . . Mr. Flint, who appeared for the MOD, accepted that the contamination of the marshland was an 'occurrence involving nuclear matter.' He submitted that before there could be a breach of the duty imposed by section 7(1)(a) there had to be 'damage to property' which 'arose out of or resulted from radioactive properties' namely the physical and chemical properties of radioactive substances. Thus there must be physical damage to BCL's property which arose out of or resulted from the physical or chemical properties of the radioactive material deposited in the marshland. That, he submitted, did not occur. To support that last submission he relied on the evidence given by the expert witnesses and the findings of the judge as to the effect of the radio-active material upon the marshland.

The judge had before him expert evidence as to the nature of the contamination and its effect. He said that the contamination consisted of the intermingling of plutonium, amongst other chemicals, with the soil in the marsh with the result that there was no practical process, other than excavation, which would remove it. That was a feature of the chemical properties of plutonium which was unrelated to any radioactive property. It was not a function of ionising radiation. The judge considered in depth the evidence as to the levels of radioactivity and the risk that was involved to plants and humans in the area of the marshland. He concluded:

> The overall conclusion of the evidence is not in dispute. The 1989 incident resulted in levels of radioactivity well above the normal background levels and above the regulatory threshold. However, even before any remedial work, and applying pessimistic assumptions, they were well below levels which would have posed any risk to health.

Mr Flint relied upon that conclusion to support his submission that the marshland had not been physically damaged by the radioactive properties of the plutonium. It physically was the same as before, albeit it had been mixed with a very small amount of plutonium. No doubt the plutonium emitted ionising radiations above the level set by the regulations, but the radioactivity was not such as to cause harm nor had it changed the properties of the soil. Removal of the soil was necessary because of the regulations, not because there was any damage to the marshland caused by radioactive properties. He asked—what was it that could have damaged the marshland? The answer was, he submitted, the emission of ionising radiations from the plutonium. But the radiations did not do any physical or chemical damage to the soil in the marsh nor did they pose any potential or actual risk to the vegetation or to humans. Thus there was no damage to the property arising out of or resulting from the radioactive properties of the plutonium. That result was, he submitted, consistent with the intention of the Act when subsection (1)(a) and (b)(ii) of section 7 were read together. Section 7(1)(b)(ii) applied to damage to property from ionising radiations from waste discharged from a site. BCL did not suggest that such damage had occurred in this case. It would therefore be odd if section 7(1)(a) went wider and permitted recovery, not in respect of the physical effect, but in respect of the economic effect of the intermingling of the plutonium with the soil in the marsh.

To support his submission, Mr Flint referred us to the judgment of Gatehouse J in *Merlin v British Nuclear Fuels Plc* [1990] 2 QB 557. In that case the plaintiffs claimed that their house had been damaged by radioactive material that had been discharged into the Irish Sea from Sellafield which had subsequently become deposited in their house as dust. The judge concluded that the Act of 1965 required them to establish that there had been damage to property, meaning tangible property. He went on to reject the plaintiffs' claim that the house included the air space within the walls, ceilings and floors and that it had been damaged by the presence of radioactive material which had resulted in the house being rendered less valuable. All that had happened was that the house had been contaminated and that did not amount to damage to property which was the type of damage for which the Act provided compensation. The fact that the house was less valuable was the economic result of the presence of radioactive material, not the result of damage to the house from the radioactive properties of the material.

In my view the judge was right to reject Mr. Flint's submissions. The physical damage to property contemplated in section 7(1)(a) is not limited to particular types of damage. Damage within the Act will occur provided there is some alteration in the physical characteristics of the property, in this case the marshland, caused by radioactive properties which render it less useful or less valuable: see *Hunter v Canary Wharf Ltd* [1997] AC 655, 676. I have no doubt that there was such an alteration in this case.

The plutonium intermingled with the soil in the marsh to such an extent that it could not be separated from the soil by any practical process. The marshland became radioactive with the result that it was 'radioactive waste' as defined in the Radioactive Substances Act 1960. The marshland was less valuable as was apparent from the valuation evidence given by the experts and the accepted fact that the estate was unsaleable until the contaminated soil had been removed. Further, the level of contamination was such that the topsoil of the marsh had to be excavated and removed from the site because the level of radioactivity exceeded that allowed by the regulations.

The educated reader of section 7(1)(a) of the Act of 1965 would realise that it imposed a duty to prevent damage to property from the radioactive properties of nuclear material. He would have no difficulty in concluding that the marshland, admixed with radioactive material, was damaged as the level of contamination was such as to reduce its market value. He would also realise that such damage was the result of the radioactive properties of the plutonium soil admixture. He would be very surprised to be told that the M.O.D. believed that there had been no damage to the property despite the fact that the level of contamination was such that the relevant regulations classified the topsoil of the marshland as 'radioactive waste' and required it to be excavated and removed.

I have no doubt that the addition of plutonium to the topsoil rendered the characteristics of the marshland different. Further, the result of the addition was that the marshland became less useful and less valuable. The facts in this case are different to those in the *Merlin* case [1990] 2 QB 557. In the *Merlin* case the dust was in the house and the judge did not hold that the house and the radioactive material were so intermingled as to mean that the characteristics of the house had in any way altered. It was therefore possible on those facts for the judge to hold that the cause of the reduction in the value of the plaintiffs' house resulted from stigma, not from damage to the house itself. There is no need to decide whether the *Merlin* case was rightly decided as this case is distinguishable on the facts.

The present case is more analogous to *Losinjska Plovidba v Transco Overseas Ltd (The Orjula)* [1995] 2 Lloyd's Rep 395 where a vessel was held to be damaged because it had to be decontaminated and *Hunter v Canary Wharf Ltd* [1997] AC 655 where the Court of Appeal held that dust could in certain circumstances cause damage to property, for example, where it was trampled into a carpet in such a way as to lessen the value of the fabric. The damage in the present case was not mere economic damage and therefore the reasoning in such cases as *Murphy v Brentwood District Council* [1991] AC 398 does not apply. The land itself was physically damaged by the radioactive properties of the plutonium which had been admixed with it. The consequence was economic, in the sense that the property was worth less and required the owner to expend money to remove the topsoil, but the damage was physical.

NOTES
1. In *Merlin* v *British Nuclear Fuels* [1990] 3 WLR 383 (distinguished in *Blue Circle*), the claimants owned a house in which dust showed high levels of contamination, and they had to sell the house for a substantially reduced amount. The defendants, who had caused the contamination, were not liable as there must be damage and the 'radionuclides cannot do any significant damage to persons or property externally, but when inhaled . . . they may induce cancers . . .'. It was said that the increase in risk of cancer was not by itself damage. Further, the reduction in the value of the house resulted from stigma and not from damage to the house. Is *Merlin* wrong, or properly distinguishable?
2. The point of the reference above to *Hunter* v *Canary Wharf* is that in the Court of Appeal in that case Pill LJ said that the deposit of dust could amount to damage, the test being whether the physical change renders the article less useful or valuable. (However, the fact that it costs money or labour to remove the dust will not necessarily mean that the property has been damaged.) In *Merlin*, did the change to the air and the dust in it render the air less useful?

# 21

## Animals

The modern statutory liability for animals replaces the ancient rules of the common law, but to a large extent follows its structure. While some aspects of the law may seem primitive in these days of the dominance of negligence, this is not so, for the law provides relatively simple and straightforward rules for what is often minor damage or injury (the Pearson Commission (1978) thought there were about 50,000 injuries caused by animals a year). However, some animals cause very serious injury, and the modern tendency to keep ferocious breeds of dog has led to the demand for more stringent laws, and this control has so far been effected by use of the criminal law. Nevertheless, it may be argued that there should be strict liability for injury caused by dogs, for not only do they cause a large number of injuries but also it seems strange that if a human being is attacked by a dog he must prove knowledge of this propensity on the part of the keeper, but if a sheep is attacked liability is strict. Why are sheep better protected than humans?

It is not only the statutory liability that can apply to animals, for other torts can also be relevant. For example, in *Draper* v *Hodder* [1972] 2 QB 556 the claimant, who was three years old, was savaged by a pack of Jack Russell terriers and he suffered over 100 bites, losing a large part of his scalp. The defendant was held liable in negligence because he ought to have realized that the dogs were liable to attack when they are in a pack. A further example of liability in negligence is the potential liability of a keeper or occupier of premises for damage done when an animal escapes onto the highway because of inadequate fencing (*Davies* v *Davies* [1975] QB 172, which discusses the exemption for common land in s. 8 of the 1971 Act).

The law of nuisance can also be relevant to liability for animals, for example for inconvenience caused by the crowing of cockerels (*Leeman* v *Montague* [1936] 2 All ER 1677) or the barking of dogs.

For a full study of the law on liability for animals, see North, *The Modern Law of Animals* (1972).

---

### ANIMALS ACT 1971

**2. Liability for damage done by dangerous animals**

(1) Where any damage is caused by an animal which belongs to a dangerous species, any person who is a keeper of the animal is liable for the damage, except as otherwise provided by this Act.

(2) Where damage is caused by an animal which does not belong to a dangerous species, a keeper of the animal is liable for the damage, except as otherwise provided by this Act, if—

    (a) the damage is of a kind which the animal, unless restrained, was likely to cause or which, if caused by the animal, was likely to be severe; and

(b) the likelihood of the damage or of its being severe was due to characteristics of the animal which are not normally found in animals of the same species or are not normally so found except at particular times or in particular circumstances; and

(c) those characteristics were known to that keeper or were at any time known to a person who at that time had charge of the animal as that keeper's servant or, where that keeper is the head of a household, were known to another keeper of the animal who is a member of that household and under the age of sixteen.

### 3. Liability for injury done by dogs to livestock

Where a dog causes damage by killing or injuring livestock, any person who is a keeper of the dog is liable for the damage, except as otherwise provided by this Act.

### 4. Liability for damage and expenses due to trespassing livestock

(1) Where livestock belonging to any person strays on to land in the ownership or occupation of another and—

(a) damage is done by the livestock to the land or to any property on it which is in the ownership or possession of the other person; or

(b) any expenses are reasonably incurred by that other person in keeping the livestock while it cannot be restored to the person to whom it belongs or while it is detained in pursuance of section 7 of this Act, or in ascertaining to whom it belongs;

the person to whom the livestock belongs is liable for the damage or expenses, except as otherwise provided by this Act.

(2) For the purposes of this section any livestock belongs to the person in whose possession it is.

### 5. Exceptions from liability under sections 2 to 4

(1) A person is not liable under sections 2 to 4 of this Act for any damage which is due wholly to the fault of the person suffering it.

(2) A person is not liable under section 2 of this Act for any damage suffered by a person who has voluntarily accepted the risk thereof.

(3) A person is not liable under section 2 of this Act for any damage caused by an animal kept on any premises or structure to a person trespassing there, if it is proved either—

(a) that the animal was not kept there for the protection of persons or property; or

(b) (if the animal was kept there for the protection of persons or property) that keeping it there for that purpose was not unreasonable.

(4) A person is not liable under section 3 of this Act if the livestock was killed or injured on land on to which it had strayed and either the dog belonged to the occupier or its presence on the land was authorised by the occupier.

(5) A person is not liable under section 4 of this Act where the livestock strayed from a highway and its presence there was a lawful use of the highway.

(6) In determining whether any liability for damage under section 4 of this Act is excluded by subsection (1) of this section the damage shall not be treated as due to the fault of the person suffering it by reason only that he could have prevented it by fencing; but a person is not liable under that section where it is proved that the straying of the livestock on to the land would not have occurred but for a breach by any other person, being a person having an interest in the land, of a duty to fence.

### 6. Interpretation of certain expressions used in sections 2 to 5

(1) The following provisions apply to the interpretation of sections 2 to 5 of this Act.

(2) A dangerous species is a species—

    (a)  which is not commonly domesticated in the British Islands; and

    (b)  whose fully grown animals normally have such characteristics that they are likely, unless restrained, to cause severe damage or that any damage they may cause is likely to be severe.

(3)  Subject to subsection (4) of this section, a person is a keeper of an animal if—

    (a)  he owns the animal or has it in his possession; or

    (b)  he is the head of a household of which a member under the age of sixteen owns the animal or has it in his possession;

and if at any time an animal ceases to be owned by or to be in the possession of a person, any person who immediately before that time was a keeper thereof by virtue of the preceding provisions of this subsection continues to be a keeper of the animal until another person becomes a keeper thereof by virtue of those provisions.

(4)  Where an animal is taken into and kept in possession for the purpose of preventing it from causing damage or of restoring it to its owner, a person is not a keeper of it by virtue only of that possession.

(5)  Where a person employed as a servant by a keeper of an animal incurs a risk incidental to his employment he shall not be treated as accepting it voluntarily.

### 8. Duty to take care to prevent damage from animals straying on to the highway

(1)  So much of the rules of the common law relating to liability for negligence as excludes or restricts the duty which a person might owe to others to take such care as is reasonable to see that damage is not caused by animals straying on to a highway is hereby abolished.

(2)  Where damage is caused by animals straying from unfenced land to a highway a person who placed them on the land shall not be regarded as having committed a breach of the duty to take care by reason only of placing them there if—

    (a)  the land is common land, or is land situated in an area where fencing is not customary, or is a town or village green; and

    (b)  he had a right to place the animals on that land.

### 10. Application of certain enactments to liability under sections 2 to 4

For the purposes of the Fatal Accidents Act 1846 to 1959, the Law Reform (Contributory Negligence) Act 1945 and the Limitation Act 1980 any damage for which a person is liable under sections 2 to 4 of this Act shall be treated as due to his fault.

### 11. General interpretation

In this Act—

'common land', and 'town or village green' have the same meanings as in the Commons Registration Act 1965;

'damage' includes the death of, or injury to, any person (including any disease and any impairment of physical or mental condition);

'fault' has the same meaning as in the Law Reform (Contributory Negligence) Act 1945;

'fencing' includes the construction of any obstacle designed to prevent animals from straying;

'livestock' means cattle, horses, asses, mules, hinnies, sheep, pigs, goats and poultry, and also deer not in the wild state and, in sections 3 and 9, also, while in captivity, pheasant, partridges and grouse;

'poultry' means the domestic varieties of the following, that is to say, fowls, turkeys, geese, ducks, guinea-fowls, pigeons, peacocks and quails; and

'species' includes sub-species and variety.

■ QUESTION

What is an animal? Presumably it must be able to move independently, but must it also be able to feel sensations? Are bacteria animals? The Animals (Scotland) Act 1987 states that 'animal' does not include viruses, bacteria, algae, fungi or protozoa.

## SECTION 1: STATUTORY LIABILITY FOR DANGEROUS SPECIES

See the Animals Act 1971, ss. 2(1) and 6(2) above. This form of liability derives from the common law rules relating to animals *ferae naturae* and is of ancient origin. Whether liability is strict depends not on the characteristics of the individual animal, but of the adults of that species. Thus, liability is strict whether the animals are young or tame. In *Behrens* v *Bertram Mills Circus* [1957] 2 QB 1, the claimants, husband and wife, were dwarfs who made a living by exhibiting themselves at fairs, and they had a booth at Olympia while the defendant's circus was on. Their manager was looking after a dog, called Simba, which escaped as some Burmese elephants, including one called Bullu, were near. The dog snapped and barked: Bullu took fright and chased and killed it, but in doing so knocked over the claimants' booth and injured them. It was held that the fact that the elephant was actually tame was irrelevant, as in law it was classified as a dangerous species. Devlin J also pointed out that the manner of the injury is irrelevant since liability is strict. He said (at p. 17) 'If a person wakes up in the middle of the night and finds an escaping tiger on top of his bed, and suffers a heart attack, it would be nothing to the point that the intentions of the tiger were entirely amiable. . . . It is not in my judgment practicable to introduce conceptions of mens rea and malevolence in the case of animals.'

Another example is *Tutin* v *Chipperfield* (1980) NLJ 807, where the actress Dorothy Tutin was taking part in a camel race for charity, when she fell off, injuring her back. The defendant was strictly liable under the Animals Act because, as camels are not domesticated in the British Isles, they are capable of being classed as a dangerous species. Are there any wild camels anywhere?

For criminal provisions relating to dangerous animals see the Dangerous Wild Animals Act 1976, which requires keepers of certain animals to obtain a licence from the local authority which can only be granted if the keeper has insurance against liability for any damage caused by the animal. The relevant animals are listed in the Dangerous Wild Animals (Modification) Order 1981 (SI 1981/1173), and they include camels, wolves, alligators, emus, cobras, adders and other snakes, tigers, gibbons, and ostriches.

For legislation controlling dangerous dogs, see the Dogs Acts 1871 and 1906, the Dogs (Protection of Livestock) Act 1953, the Guard Dogs Act 1975 and the Dangerous Dogs Acts 1989 and 1991.

See the Animals Act 1971, s. 2(2). This applies to any animal which is not defined as dangerous under s. 6 of the Act, and derives from the old *scienter* action, i.e. one based on the knowledge of the keeper as to the dangerous characteristics of the individual animal. One problem is to determine whether the likelihood of damage was due to characteristics of the animal which are not normally found in animals of the same species, but a particular difficulty is whether a keeper should be liable for the predictable (and thus normal) reaction of an animal to unusual circumstances.

### *Mirvahedy* v *Henley*
House of Lords [2003] 2 AC 491; [2003] 2 WLR 882; [2003] 2 All ER 401; [2003] UKHL 16

The defendants owned three horses which they kept in a field enclosed by a barbed wire fence. One night the horses were frightened by something or someone unknown and they trampled down the fence and escaped. They travelled just over a mile when they came to a main road. One of the horses ran into a car driven by the claimant who suffered personal injuries in the accident. The horses were normally docile and the fencing was adequate and it was assumed that something had caused them to panic. Held: the defendants were liable.

LORD NICHOLLS:

*Section 2 of the Animals Act 1971*

**14** Section 2(2) established a different regime where damage is caused by an animal not belonging to a dangerous species. This subsection applies, therefore, to all species of animals commonly domesticated here. It includes horses. The material part of section 2(2) provides:

> (2) Where damage is caused by an animal which does not belong to a dangerous species, a keeper of the animal is liable for the damage, except as otherwise provided by this Act, if—
> (a) the damage is of a kind which the animal, unless restrained, was likely to cause or which, if caused by the animal, was likely to be severe; and
> (b) the likelihood of the damage or of its being severe was due to characteristics of the animal which are not normally found in animals of the same species or are not normally so found except at particular times or in particular circumstances; and
> (c) those characteristics were known to that keeper?

**15** In the present case nothing turns on requirement (a). It is accepted that this pre-condition of liability is satisfied. Similarly with requirement (c): the judge found that this requirement was satisfied in this case, and his finding has not been challenged.

**16** The crucial requirement is requirement (b). Requirement (b) is concerned, in short, with the source of the animal's dangerousness. If requirement (b) is to be met, the dangerousness of the animal, as described in requirement (a), must be attributable to the animal having characteristics falling within one or other of two classes. The first limb of paragraph (b) identifies one class. The animal must have characteristics 'which are not normally found in animals of the same species'. The second limb of paragraph (b) identifies the other class of qualifying characteristics. The animal must have characteristics which are not normally found in animals of the same species 'except at particular times or in particular circumstances'.

**17** Both these classes, it can be noticed at once, are described in terms of abnormality. The first class is that the particular animal has characteristics not normally found in animals of the same species. Unless the relevant characteristic of the animal which caused the damage satisfies this test of abnormality, the case does not fall within the first class. Likewise, the case does not fall within the second class unless the relevant characteristic of the animal is one which, except at particular times or in particular circumstances, is abnormal. The characteristic of the particular animal must be a characteristic which, save on particular occasions, is not a characteristic of animals of the same species.

**18**  Thus, the first class embraces a case where animals of the species are normally docile but the particular animal is not. In such a case requirement (b) is met. However, there are many species of animals which are normally docile but which, in certain circumstances or at particular times, behave differently, even dangerously. Dogs are not normally prone to bite all and sundry. But a dog guarding its territory, or a bitch with a litter whose pups are being threatened, may well be vicious. The second class is directed at this type of case. A dog which is prone to bite is likely to fall within the second class. A dog with a general propensity to bite has a characteristic which, save in particular circumstances, is not normally found in dogs. Such a dog has an abnormal characteristic. In such a case requirement (b) is satisfied.

**19**  Thus far there is no difficulty. But what of the case where the dog which attacks and bites is at the time acting as a guard dog or is a bitch with pups? Such an animal is behaving dangerously but it is doing so in a manner characteristic of its species in the circumstances. Does such a case also fall within the second class of cases? On this there has been a difference of judicial opinion. This difference of view exists also in your Lordships' House on the instant appeal.

**20**  Some judges have held that such a case is within the second class of cases. It falls within the literal language of the statute. The likelihood that the guard dog or the bitch with pups will bite is due to a characteristic of the particular animal which is not normally found in members of the species except in the particular circumstances of guarding territory or protecting pups. To that extent the animal's behaviour was a departure from the normal behaviour of animals of the same species.

**21**  I shall call this interpretation of the second limb of section 2(2)(b) 'the Cummings interpretation'. This interpretation was adopted in *Cummings v Granger* [1977] QB 397. On this interpretation, Mr Mirvahedy's claim succeeds. Horses do not normally behave as did the horses of Dr and Mrs Henley during the night of 28 August 1996. They do so only in particular circumstances, namely, when seriously frightened.

**22**  Other judges have said that this type of case is outside the second class of cases identified in paragraph (b). The second limb of section 2(2)(b) does not treat as abnormal behaviour which is characteristic of the species in the circumstances in which it occurred. The object of the second limb is to provide that characteristics not normally found in the species do not cease to be abnormal because, in certain circumstances or at certain times, all animals of the species behave in that way. A dog prone to attack all strangers has an abnormal characteristic. It is an abnormal characteristic even though in some circumstances all dogs are liable to attack strangers.

**23**  I shall call this 'the *Breeden* interpretation'. This interpretation was favoured in the unreported decision of the Court of Appeal in *Breeden v Lampard* (21 March 1985). On this construction of the second limb of section 2(2)(b), Mr Mirvahedy's claim fails. The horse which escaped from the field and collided with his car was not behaving differently from the way any normal horse would have behaved in the circumstances.

*The interpretation of section 2(2)*

**31**  In common with all other judges who have had to wrestle with this question, I have found that the tortuous language of section 2(2)(b) renders its intended meaning peculiarly difficult to ascertain. I readily acknowledge that my mind has fluctuated between the two interpretations.

**32**  The starting point is to seek to identify the purpose of requirement (b). Stated in general terms the function of requirement (b) is not in doubt. The purpose of this paragraph is to limit the circumstances in which there will be strict liability for damage caused by an animal having the dangerous characteristics described in requirement (a). Possession of such characteristics by an animal (requirement (a)), together with the keeper's awareness that the animal has these characteristics (requirement (c)), is not enough. Meeting requirements (a) and (c) will not suffice. Something more is needed before strict liability arises.

**33** That this is the purpose of requirement (b) is self-evident. Requirement (b) is a pre-condition of liability additional to requirements (a) and (c). That this is the purpose of paragraph (b) is also confirmed by the background to the legislation.

**44** . . . on balance I prefer the *Cummings* interpretation of section 2(2)(b), for a combination of reasons. First, this interpretation accords more easily and naturally with the statutory language. Damage caused by an attack by a newly-calved cow or a dog on guard duty fits readily into the description of damage due to characteristics of a cow or a dog which are not normally found in cows or dogs except in particular circumstances. That is not so with the Breeden interpretation. The *Breeden* interpretation has the effect that these examples would fall outside both limbs of paragraph (b). This result makes sense only on the supposition that, by the references to abnormal character-istics in section 2(2)(b) (characteristics 'not normally found'), Parliament intended that strict liability should never arise if the animal's conduct was normal for the species in the circumstances in which it occurred. But the language of the paragraph provides no substantial support for this supposition.

**45** Secondly, the *Breeden* interpretation would depart radically from the legislative scheme recommended by the Law Commission. There is no evidence that any such departure was intended. Indeed, far from such a departure being intended, the wording of clause 2(2)(b) of the reformulated Animals Bill, subsequently enacted as section 2(2)(b) of the Animals Act, was plainly drawn from, and closely followed, the language of paragraphs 18(ii) and 91(iv) of the Law Commission's report.

**46** Thirdly, the 'lack of content' argument levelled against the *Cummings* interpretation cannot be pressed too far. The *Cummings* interpretation does not empty requirement (b) of all content. Some forms of accidental damage are instances where this requirement could operate. Take a large and heavy domestic animal such as a mature cow. There is a real risk that if a cow happens to stumble and fall onto someone, any damage suffered will be severe. This would satisfy requirement (a). But a cow's dangerousness in this regard may not fall within requirement (b). This dangerousness is due to a characteristic normally found in all cows at all times. The dangerousness results from their very size and weight. It is not due to a characteristic not normally found in cows 'except at particular times or in particular circumstances'.

**47** For these reasons I agree with the interpretation of section 2(2)(b) adopted in *Cummings* v *Granger* [1977] QB 397 and *Curtis* v *Betts* [1990] 1 WLR 459 and by the Court of Appeal in the instant case. The fact that an animal's behaviour, although not normal behaviour for animals of that species, was nevertheless normal behaviour for the species in the particular circumstances does not take the case outside section 2(2)(b).

**48** I also agree with the decision of the Court of Appeal on the facts in the present case. Horses are large and heavy animals. But it was not this innate physical characteristic of the defendants' horses which caused the road accident. The horses escaped because they were terrified. They were still not behaving ordinarily when they careered over the main road, crashing into vehicles rather than the other way about. Hale LJ concluded that it was precisely because they were behaving in this unusual way caused by their panic that the road accident took place: see [2002] 2 WLR 566, 571. That conclusion, on the evidence, seems to me irrefutable and to be fatal to the case of Dr and Mrs Henley. I would dismiss this appeal.

NOTES
1. The issue is whether a defendant should be liable for normal reactions in unusual circum-stances. The above is one example: another is *Curtis* v *Betts* [1990] 1 WLR 459 where a bull mastiff was in the back of a Land Rover. When approached by the 10-year-old claimant the dog jumped up and bit him. The court found that such dogs tended to defend their own territory and as the defendants were aware of such behaviour they were liable. For *Cummings* v *Granger* (referred to above) see section 3 below.
2. The result in *Mirvahedy* may seem harsh as the defendants could not have done anything to avoid the damage. However, the point is that the scheme for liability for animals is not based on the fault of the defendant but on the likelihood of the damage. Even normal animals can cause damage either in usual circumstances (dogs in cars) or in unpredictable circumstances (panicking horses). If the keeper is aware that in certain situations the animal may cause damage, he is liable if that behaviour is not the usual behaviour of the animal, even if it is a predictable reaction to unusual circumstances.

See the Animals Act 1971, s. 5. The provisions of s. 5(3) and the decision in *Cummings* v *Granger* (below) must be read in the light of the Guard Dogs Act 1975, which is discussed in note 3 below.

---

### *Cummings* v *Granger*
Court of Appeal [1977] 1 QB 397; [1976] 3 WLR 842; [1977] 1 All ER 104

The defendant was the keeper of an Alsatian which was used to guard a scrapyard in East London. One evening the claimant, who was a barmaid at a nearby pub, went into the yard with her friend, Mr Hobson, who wanted to collect some tools from his car. Mr Hobson had permission to enter the yard, but the claimant was a trespasser. She was attacked by the dog and her cheek was torn open. At the entrance to the yard was a notice saying 'Beware of the Dog.' The dog was allowed to roam free in the yard at night. Held: allowing the appeal, that the defendant was prima facie liable under s. 2(2) of the 1971 Act, but that ss. 5(2) and 5(3) both provided defences. He was thus not liable to the claimant.

LORD DENNING MR: The statutory liability for a tame animal, like a dog, is defined in section 2(2) of the Act, subject to exceptions contained in section 5. Now it seems to me that this is a case where the keeper of the dog is strictly liable unless he can bring himself within one of the exceptions. I say this because the three requirements for strict liability are satisfied. The section is very cumbrously worded and will give rise to several difficulties in future. But in this case the judge held that the three requirements were satisfied and I agree with him for the following reasons. Section 2(2)(*a*): this animal was a dog of the Alsatian breed; if it did bite anyone, the damage was 'likely to be severe.' Section 2(2)(*b*): this animal was a guard dog kept so as to scare intruders and frighten them off. On the defendant's own evidence, it used to bark and run round in circles, especially when coloured people approached. Those characteristics—barking and running around to guard its territory—are not normally found in Alsatian dogs except in circumstances where they are used as guard dogs. Those circumstances are 'particular circumstances' within section 2(2)(*b*). It was due to those circumstances that the damage was likely to be severe if an intruder did enter on its territory. Section 2(2)(*c*): those characteristics were known to the defendant. It follows that the defendant is strictly liable unless he can bring himself within one of the exceptions in section 5. Obviously section 5(1) does not avail. The bite was not *wholly* due to the fault of the plaintiff, but only *partly* so.

Section 5(3) may, however, avail the keeper. It says that if someone trespasses on property and is bitten or injured by a guard dog, the keeper of the guard dog is exempt from liability if it is proved 'that keeping it there for that purpose was not unreasonable.' The judge held that the defendant was unreasonable in keeping it in this yard. He said [1975] 1 WLR 1330, 1336–1337: 'It seems to me that it was unreasonable to keep an untrained dog, known to be ferocious and known to be likely to attack at least coloured people, if they came near the place, to protect a lot of old broken-down scrap motor cars in this yard, by night.'

I take a different view. This was a yard in the East End of London where persons of the roughest type come and go. It was a scrap-yard, true, but scrap-yards, like building sites, often contain much valuable property. It was deserted at night and at weekends. If there was no protection, thieves would drive up in a lorry and remove the scrap with no one to see them or to stop them. The only reasonable way of protecting the place was to have a guard dog. True it was a fierce dog. But why not? A gentle dog would be no good. The thieves would soon make friends with him. It seems to me that it was very reasonable—or, at any rate, not unreasonable—for the defendant to keep this dog there. Long ago in 1794 Lord Kenyon said in *Brock* v *Copeland* (1794) 1 Esp 203 that 'every man had a right to keep a dog for the protection of his yard or house.'

Alternatively there is another defence provided by section 5(2). It says that a person is not liable 'for any damage suffered by a person who has voluntarily accepted the risk thereof.' This seems to me to warrant a reference back to the common law. . . . The plaintiff certainly knew the animal was there. She worked next door. She knew all about it. She must have seen this huge notice on the door 'Beware of the Dog.' Nevertheless she went in, following her man friend. In the circumstances she must be taken voluntarily to have incurred this risk. So with any burglar or thief who goes on to premises knowing that there is a guard dog there. If he is bitten or injured, he cannot recover. He voluntarily takes the risk of it. Even if he does not know a guard dog is there, he might be defeated by the plea 'ex turpi causa non oritur actio.'

There is only one further point I would mention. This accident took place in November 1971 very shortly after the Animals Act 1971 was passed. In 1975 the Guard Dogs Act 1975 was passed. It does not apply to this case. But it makes it quite clear that in future a person is not allowed to have a guard dog to roam about on his premises unless the dog is under the control of a handler. If he has no handler, the dog must be chained up so that it is not at liberty to roam around. If a person contravenes the Act, he can be brought before a magistrate and fined up to £400. But it is only criminal liability. It does not confer a right of action in any civil proceedings. It may however have the effect in civil proceedings of making it unreasonable for the defendant to let a dog free in the yard at night (as this defendant did) and it may thus deprive the defendant of a defence under section 5(3)(*b*). But he might still be able to rely on the defence under section 5(2) of volenti non fit injuria.

Coming back to the present case, I think the defendant is not under any strict liability to the plaintiff because she was a trespasser and also because she voluntarily took the risk. . . .

NOTES
1. This case has been much discussed: see, for example, Ingman (1977) 127 NLJ 895; Jackson (1977) 40 MLR 590; Spencer [1977] CLJ 39.
2. It is important to note that the question of liability under s. 2 was determined not by the characteristics of dogs in general but by the characteristics of Alsatians, since 'species' in s. 2 is defined as including subspecies or variety by s. 11. Second, prima facie liability existed not because this Alsatian was ferocious and most are not, but because in the circumstances of roaming loose in what it regarded as its territory it was ferocious, whereas Alsatians in general are not.
3. The Guard Dogs Act 1975 was passed after public concern about guard dogs, especially Alsatians, attacking people and there had been considerable outrage about attacks on young children. The Act provides that it is a criminal offence to have a dog guarding premises unless it is under the control of a handler at all times or it is not at liberty to go freely about the premises. Although the Act creates only criminal and not civil liability, it surely could not be 'reasonable' to keep a guard dog for the purposes of s. 5(3) if it is unlawful to do so. Accordingly, the main ground for decision in *Cummings* v *Granger* would now be different. But suppose the existence of the dog was not unlawful because it was on a long lead, and the trespasser was a 5-year-old who was unable to run away from the dog in time?

# 22

# Trespass to the Person

Trespass is an ancient set of wrongs which mainly deals with the direct, and usually intentional, invasion of a claimant's interest in either his person, his land or his goods. The law of trespass today reveals much of its origins in the criminal law, and to some extent this is borne out by the fact that its function is more often deterrent than compensatory. For example, an action will lie in trespass, but not in negligence, even if the claimant has suffered no damage, and this shows its usefulness in protecting civil rights. It is the right itself which is protected, and not just the freedom from resulting damage, and much of the law of trespass is the basis of our civil liberties today.

This chapter covers the wrongs of assault, battery and false imprisonment, together with various defences. The principal use today of these torts relates not so much to the recovery of compensation but rather to the establishment of a right, or a recognition that the defendant acted unlawfully. For example, trespass to the person or false imprisonment will often be used to establish whether an arrest was lawful, but the special conditions applying to such cases, such as the powers of the police, will not be dealt with here. The point to note is that as these torts are actionable without proof of damage (or actionable *per se*), they can be used to protect civil rights, and also will protect a person's dignity, even if no physical injury has occurred (for example the taking of finger prints).

Also, in a number of cases which amount to trespass to the person it will not be necessary to bring an action, for where a criminal offence has been committed the courts have power under the Powers of Criminal Courts Act 1973, s. 35 (as amended) to make a compensation order.

## SECTION 1: TRESPASS AND NEGLIGENCE

While the technical distinction between trespass and negligence has no procedural effect today, there are still theoretical differences between the two subjects which have not yet been resolved, and probably never will be. The theoretical problem concerns the issue of negligent invasions of the claimant's interest, and while this was historically a trespass, there is a tendency today to say that in such cases only the tort of negligence, and not trespass, should be applied. However, the distinction does have some practical effects as in the issue of limitation periods which is dealt with in note 3 to the main case.

### *Letang* v *Cooper*
Court of Appeal [1965] 1 QB 232; [1964] 2 All ER 929; [1964] 3 WLR 573

Doreen Letang was sunbathing in the grounds of the Ponsmere Hotel at Perranporth in Cornwall when the defendant negligently drove over her legs with his Jaguar. The writ was issued more than three years later, and under the Law Reform (Limitation of Actions) Act 1954 a writ should have been issued within three years of the accident if it related to personal injuries and the claim was for 'negligence, nuisance or breach of duty'. The claimant admitted that an action in negligence was time barred, but claimed that she could sue for trespass (for which the general limitation period is six years) on the grounds that this did not come within the phrase 'breach of duty'. In the High Court this claim succeeded. Held: allowing the appeal, that the action was time barred and the defendant was not liable. [Note: in the judgment below Lord Denning refers to 'action on the case'. This would now be called an action for negligence.]

LORD DENNING MR: The argument, as it was developed before us, became a direct invitation to this court to go back to the old forms of action and to decide this case by reference to them. The statute bars an action on the case, it is said, after three years, whereas trespass to the person is not barred for six years. The argument was supported by reference to text-writers, such as *Salmond on Torts*, 13th ed. (1961), p. 790. I must say that if we are, at this distance of time, to revive the distinction between trespass and case, we should get into the most utter confusion. The old common lawyers tied themselves in knots over it, and we should do the same. Let me tell you some of their contortions. Under the old law, whenever one man injured another by the direct and immediate application of force, the plaintiff could sue the defendant in trespass to the person, without alleging negligence . . ., whereas if the injury was only consequential, he had to sue in case. You will remember the illustration given by Fortescue J in *Reynolds* v *Clarke* (1725) 93 ER 747: 'If a man throws a log into the highway, and in that act it hits me, I may maintain trespass because it is an immediate wrong; but if as it lies there I tumble over it, and receive an injury, I must bring an action upon the case; because it is only prejudicial in consequence.' Nowadays, if a man carelessly throws a piece of wood from a house into a roadway, then whether it hits the plaintiff or he tumbles over it the next moment, the action would not be trespass or case, but simply negligence. . . .

I must decline, therefore, to go back to the old forms of action in order to construe this statute. I know that in the last century Maitland said 'the forms of action we have buried, but they still rule us from their graves' (see Maitland, *Forms of Action* (1909), p. 296), but we have in this century shaken off their trammels. These forms of action have served their day. They did at one time form a guide to substantive rights; but they do so no longer. Lord Atkin, in *United Australia Ltd* v *Barclays Bank Ltd* [1941] AC 1, told us what to do about them: 'When these ghosts of the past stand in the path of justice clanking their mediaeval chains the proper course for the judge is to pass through them undeterred'.

The truth is that the distinction between trespass and case is obsolete. We have a different subdivision altogether. Instead of dividing actions for personal injuries into trespass (direct damage) or case (consequential damage), we divide the causes of action now according as the defendant did the injury intentionally or unintentionally. If one man intentionally applies force directly to another, the plaintiff has a cause of action in assault and battery, or, if you so please to describe it, in trespass to the person. 'The least touching of another in anger is a battery', *per* Holt CJ in *Cole* v *Turner* (1704) 87 ER 907. If he does not inflict injury intentionally, but only unintentionally, the plaintiff has no cause of action today in trespass. His only cause of action is in negligence, and then only on proof of want of reasonable care. If the plaintiff cannot prove want of reasonable care, he may have no cause of action at all. Thus, it is not enough nowadays for the plaintiff to plead that 'the defendant shot the plaintiff'. He must also allege that he did it intentionally or negligently. If intentional, it is the tort of assault and battery. If negligent and causing damage, it is the tort of negligence.

The modern law on this subject was well expounded by Diplock J in *Fowler* v *Lanning* [1959] 1 QB 426, with which I fully agree. But I would go this one step further: when the injury is not inflicted intentionally, but negligently, I would say that the only cause of action is negligence and not trespass. If it were trespass, it would be actionable without proof of damage; and that is not the law today.

In my judgment, therefore, the only cause of action in the present case, where the injury was unintentional, is negligence and is barred by reason of the express provision of the statute . . ..

I come, therefore, to the clear conclusion that the plaintiff's cause of action here is barred by the Statute of Limitations. Her only cause of action here, in my judgment, where the damage was unintentional, was negligence and not trespass to the person. It is therefore barred by the word 'negligence' in the statute.

NOTES

1.  It should not be assumed that Lord Denning's views on the distinction between trespass and negligence are necessarily accepted, and it may well be that the traditional distinction as referred to by Fortescue J in *Reynolds* v *Clarke* (above) between direct and indirect acts is still valid. It is unlikely that this theoretical problem will ever need to be resolved. However, in *Wilson* v *Pringle* [1987] QB 237, Croom-Johnson LJ did say that 'It has long been the law that claims arising out of an unintentional trespass must be made in negligence'. For all practical purposes, therefore, it can be said that trespass deals with direct intentional acts, and negligence with careless or indirect acts.

2.  In *Fowler* v *Lanning* [1959] 1 QB 426, the claimant merely alleged in his statement of claim that on 19 November 1957, at Vineyard Farm, Corfe Castle in the County of Dorset the defendant shot the claimant. Neither intention nor negligence was alleged, but the claimant argued that the statement of claim did allege a good cause of action on the grounds that in trespass the burden of disproving negligence was on the defendant. Diplock J rejected this argument, saying that 'trespass to the person does not lie if the injury to the plaintiff, although the direct consequence of the act of the defendant, was caused unintentionally and without negligence on the defendant's part' and that the onus of proving negligence lay on the claimant.

3.  The problem of whether an act is within the tort of negligence or not has given rise to considerable problems in relation to limitation periods, that is the period within which the claim must be brought. The general rule is that the limitation period for trespass is a fixed period of six years, whereas in negligence it is three years, but that may in certain circumstances be extended at the discretion of the court (Limitation Act 1980, ss. 2,11,14 and 33). In *Stubbings* v *Webb* [1993] AC 498, the claimant issued a writ many years after the event saying that she had been sexually abused by her father. The House of Lords held that the claim was out of time as the allegation could only amount to trespass and not to negligence or a breach of duty of care, so a fixed period of six years applied.

## SECTION 2: BATTERY AND ASSAULT

In common usage the word 'assault' is used to mean actual contact, but it is probably useful to keep the terms battery and assault separate. Battery occurs where there is contact with the person of another, and assault is used to cover cases where the claimant apprehends contact.

### *Wilson* v *Pringle*
Court of Appeal [1987] QB 237; [1986] 2 All ER 440; [1986] 3 WLR 1

Both Peter Wilson (the claimant) and Ian Pringle (the defendant) were aged 13 and attended Great Wyrley High School, Walsall. It was agreed that while in a corridor the claimant was carrying a hand grip type of bag, holding it over his shoulder with his right hand. The defendant admitted that as an act of ordinary horseplay he pulled the bag off the claimant's shoulder, and this caused the claimant to fall and injure his hip. The claimant applied for summary judgment on the ground that this admission amounted to a clear case of battery to which there was no defence. The trial judge accepted this view. Held: allowing the appeal, that the admitted facts did not automatically amount to a battery, and the defendant was given leave to defend the action.

CROOM-JOHNSON LJ: The first distinction between the two causes of action where there is personal injury is the element of contact between the plaintiff and defendant: that is, a touching of some sort. In the action for negligence the physical contact (where it takes place at all) is normally though by no means always unintended. In the action for trespass, to constitute a battery, it is deliberate. Even so it is not every intended contact which is tortious. Apart from special justifications (such as acting in self-defence) there are many examples in everyday life where an intended contact or touch is not actionable as a trespass. These are not necessarily those (such as shaking hands) where consent is actual or to be implied. They may amount to one of the instances had in mind in *Tuberville* v *Savage*, 1 Mod. 3 which take place in innocence. A modern instance is the batsman walking up the pavilion steps at Lord's after making a century. He receives hearty slaps of congratulation on his back. He may not want them. Some of them may be too heavy for comfort. No one seeks his permission, or can assume he would give it if it were asked. But would an action for trespass to the person lie?

Another ingredient in the tort of trespass to the person is that of hostility. The references to anger sufficing to turn a touch into a battery (*Cole* v *Turner*, (1704) 87 ER 907) and the lack of an intention to assault which prevents a gesture from being an assault are instances of this. If there is hostile intent, that will by itself be cogent evidence of hostility. But the hostility may be demonstrated in other ways.

The defendant in the present case has sought to add to the list of necessary ingredients. He has submitted that before trespass to the person will lie it is not only the touching that must be deliberate but the infliction of injury. The plaintiff's counsel, on the other hand, contends that it is not the injury to the person which must be intentional, but the act of touching or battery which precedes it: as he put it, what must be intentional is the application of force and not the injury. . . .

In our view, the submission made by counsel for the plaintiff is correct. It is the act and not the injury which must be intentional. An intention to injure is not essential to an action for trespass to the person. It is the mere trespass by itself which is the offence. . . .

What, then, turns a friendly touching (which is not actionable) into an unfriendly one (which is)? We have been referred to two criminal cases. *Reg* v *Sutton (Terrence)* [1977] 1 WLR 182 was decided in the Court of Appeal (Criminal Division). It was a case concerning alleged indecent assault on boys who consented in fact although in law they were too young to do so. They were asked to pose for photographs. The only touching of the boys by the appellant was to get them to stand in poses. It was touching on the hands, arms, legs or torso but only for the purpose of indicating how he wanted them to pose; it was not hostile or threatening. The court which was presided over by Lord Widgery CJ held these were therefore not assaults.

A more recent authority is *Collins* v *Wilcock* [1984] 1 WLR 1172. The case was not cited to the judge. It had not been reported at the time of the hearing of the Order 14 appeal. The facts were that a woman police officer, suspecting that a woman was soliciting contrary to the Street Offences Act 1959, tried to question her. The woman walked away, and was followed by the police officer. The officer took hold of her arm in order to restrain her. The woman scratched the officer's arm. She was arrested, charged with assaulting a police officer in the execution of her duty, and convicted. On appeal by case stated, the appeal was allowed, on the ground that the officer had gone beyond the scope of her duty in detaining the woman in circumstances short of arresting her. The officer had accordingly committed a battery.

The judgment of the Divisional Court was given by Robert Goff LJ. It is necessary to give a long quotation to do full justice to it. He said, at pp. 1177–1178:

> The law draws a distinction, in terms more easily understood by philologists than by ordinary citizens, between an assault and a battery. An assault is an act which causes another person to apprehend the infliction of immediate, unlawful, force on his person; a battery is the actual infliction of unlawful force on another person. Both assault and battery are forms of trespass to the person. Another form of trespass to the person is false imprisonment, which is the unlawful imposition of constraint upon another's freedom of movement from a particular place. The requisite mental element is of no relevance in the present case.
>
> We are here concerned primarily with battery. The fundamental principle, plain and incontestable, is that every person's body is inviolate. It has long been established that any touching of another person, however slight, may amount to a battery. So Holt CJ held in *Cole v Turner* (1704) 87 ER 907 that 'the least touching of another in anger is a battery.' The breadth of the principle reflects the fundamental nature of the interest so protected. As Blackstone wrote in his *Commentaries*, 17th ed. (1830), vol. 3, p. 120: 'the law cannot draw the line between different degrees of violence, and therefore totally prohibits the first and lowest stage of it; every man's person being sacred, and no other having a right to meddle with it, in any the slightest manner.' The effect is that everybody is protected not only against physical injury but against any form of physical molestation.
>
> But so widely drawn a principle must inevitably be subject to exceptions. For example, children may be subjected to reasonable punishment; people may be subjected to the lawful exercise of the power of arrest; and reasonable force may be used in self-defence or for the prevention of crime. But, apart from these special instances where the control or constraint is lawful, a broader exception has been created to allow for the exigencies of everyday life. Generally speaking, consent is a defence to battery; and most of the physical contacts of ordinary life are not actionable because they are impliedly consented to by all who move in society and so expose themselves to the risk of bodily contact. So nobody can complain of the jostling which is inevitable from his presence in, for example, a supermarket, an underground station or a busy street; nor can a person who attends a party complain if his hand is seized in friendship, or even if his back is, within reason, slapped: see *Tuberville v Savage* (1669) 86 ER 684. Although such cases are regarded as examples of implied consent, it is more common nowadays to treat them as falling within a general exception embracing all physical contact which is generally acceptable in the ordinary conduct of daily life. We observe that, although in the past it has sometimes been stated that a battery is only committed where the action is 'angry, revengeful, rude, or insolent' (see *Hawkins, Pleas of the Crown*, 8th ed. (1824), vol. 1, c. 15, section 2), we think that nowadays it is more realistic, and indeed more accurate, to state the broad underlying principle, subject to the broad exception.
>
> Among such forms of conduct, long held to be acceptable, is touching a person for the purpose of engaging his attention, though of course using no greater degree of physical contact than is reasonably necessary in the circumstances for that purpose . . .

It still remains to indicate what is to be proved by a plaintiff who brings an action for battery. Robert Goff LJ's judgment is illustrative of the considerations which underlie such an action, but it is not practicable to define a battery as 'physical contact which is not generally acceptable in the ordinary conduct of daily life'.

In our view, the authorities lead one to the conclusion that in a battery there must be an intentional touching or contact in one form or another of the plaintiff by the defendant. That touching must be proved to be a hostile touching. That still leaves unanswered the question 'when is a touching to be called hostile?' Hostility cannot be equated with ill-will or malevolence. It cannot be governed by the obvious intention shown in acts like punching, stabbing or shooting. It cannot be solely governed by an expressed intention, although that may be strong evidence. But the element of hostility, in the sense in which it is now to be considered, must be a question of fact for the tribunal of fact. It may be imported from the circumstances. Take the example of the police officer in *Collins* v *Wilcock* [1984] 1 WLR 1172. She touched the woman deliberately, but without an intention to do more than restrain her temporarily. Nevertheless, she was acting unlawfully and in that way was acting with hostility. She was acting contrary to the woman's legal right not to be physically restrained. We see no more difficulty in establishing what she intended by means of questions and answer, or by inference from the surrounding circumstances, than there is in establishing whether an apparently playful blow was struck in anger. The rules of law governing the legality of arrest may require strict application to the facts of appropriate cases, but in the ordinary give and take of everyday life the tribunal of fact should find no difficulty in answering the question 'was this, or was it not, a battery?' Where the immediate act of touching does not itself demonstrate hostility, the plaintiff should plead the facts which are said to do so.

Although we are all entitled to protection from physical molestation, we live in a crowded world in which people must be considered as taking on themselves some risk off injury (where it occurs) from the acts of others which are not in themselves unlawful. If negligence cannot be proved, it may be that an injured plaintiff who is also unable to prove a battery, will be without redress.

NOTES
1. In *Cole* v *Turner* (1704) 87 ER 907 (referred to above) Holt CJ said:

First, that the least touching of another in anger is a battery.

Secondly, if two or more meet in a narrow passage, and without any violence or design of harm, the one touches the other gently, it will be no battery.

Thirdly, if any of them use violence against the other, to force his way in a rude inordinate manner, it will be a battery; or any struggle about the passage to that degree as may do hurt, will be a battery.

2. In *Re F* [1990] 2 AC 1, at p. 73, Lord Goff said that he doubted whether it is correct to say that the touching must be hostile. He added that 'the suggested qualification is difficult to reconcile with the principle that any touching of another's body is, in the absence of lawful excuse, capable of amounting to a battery and a trespass'.

3. As in the criminal law, there must be both an act and intention. In *Fagan* v *Metropolitan Police* [1969] 1 QB 439 (a criminal case) Vincent Fagan unwittingly parked his car on a policeman's foot. Despite requests, he refused to move the car until some minutes later. It was held that he was rightly convicted as his actions could not be regarded as a mere omission. James J said Fagan remained in the car so that his body, through the medium of the car, was in contact with the policeman's foot. He switched off the ignition and maintained the car on the foot. Do you agree or do you prefer the dissenting view of Bridge J that he should have been acquitted because he actually did nothing?

4. An 'assault' occurs where the claimant apprehends imminent physical contact; but if the defendant is actually unable to deliver the blow, there is no assault (at least if the claimant should have realized that the attack was impossible). In *Thomas* v *NUM* [1986] Ch 20, pickets were jeering working miners who were being taken into a colliery by buses. It was held that there was no assault as the claimants were in buses and the pickets were being held back by police. See also *Stephens* v *Myers* (1830) 172 ER 735.

5. Traditionally words have not by themselves amounted to an assault. The reason may be that an assault must be a threat of an *immediate* battery and words, if delivered from a distance, do not do that, but rather give the recipient the chance to avoid the future battery. Nevertheless, words by themselves could induce fear and in *R* v *Ireland* [1996] 3 WLR 650 Lord Steyn said that words, even if not accompanied by any actions, could cause apprehension of immediate contact. But what if the threat is of a future battery? (If there is actual damage caused by the threat other torts might be available.) However, its clear that words may qualify an otherwise innocent act so as to make it intimidatory, or qualify an intimidatory act so as to make it innocent. In *Read* v *Coker* (1853) 138 ER 1437, the defendant's workers gathered around the claimant, rolling up their sleeves and threatening to break the claimant's neck if he did not leave. The words characterized the otherwise innocent act as one threatening imminent contact. On the other hand, in *Tuberville* v *Savage* (1669) 86 ER 684, Tuberville put his hand

on his sword and said 'If it were not assize time, I would not take such language from you.' In effect he was saying that he would not strike as the judges were in town, and this rendered the act innocent.

■ QUESTIONS

1. Is 'hostile' an appropriate word to use, especially in a civil case? Can you think of another word or phrase which expresses the point more clearly?

2. Is it an assault to point an unloaded gun at someone?

3. What is wrong with saying that a battery is an offensive conduct or one which is not generally acceptable in the ordinary conduct of daily life?

## SECTION 3: **FALSE IMPRISONMENT**

This tort protects a person in his or her interest in freedom from restraint, and is another example of trespass protecting important civil rights. The significance of *Bird* v *Jones*, below, is that the tort only protects a person against restraint and does not give a right to absolute choice in one's freedom of movement. That is a freedom or liberty and not a right.

### *Bird* v *Jones*
Court of Queen's Bench (1845) 7 QB 742; 15 LJQB 82; 115 ER 668

In August 1843 the Hammersmith Bridge Company cordoned off part of their bridge, placed seats on it, and charged spectators for viewing a regatta. The claimant objected to this and forced his way into the enclosure, where he was stopped by two police officers. He was prevented from proceeding across the bridge, but was allowed to go back the way he came. He refused, and in the course of proceedings for his arrest the question arose whether he had been imprisoned on the bridge. Held: this was not an 'imprisonment' and the defendant was not liable for the subsequent arrest.

COLERIDGE J: And I am of opinion that there was no imprisonment. To call it so appears to me to confound partial obstruction and disturbance with total obstruction and detention. A prison may have its boundary large or narrow, visible and tangible, or, though real, still in the conception only; it may itself be moveable or fixed: but a boundary it must have; and that boundary the party imprisoned must be prevented from passing; he must be prevented from leaving that place, within the ambit of which the party imprisoning would confine him, except by prison-breach. Some confusion seems to me to arise from confounding imprisonment of the body with mere loss of freedom: it is one part of the definition of freedom to be able to go whither-soever one pleases; but imprisonment is something more than the mere loss of this power; it includes the notion of restraint within some limits defined by a will or power exterior to our own . . .

LORD DENMAN [*dissenting*]: I had no idea that any person in these times supposed any particular boundary to be necessary to constitute imprisonment, or that the restraint of a man's person from doing what he desires ceases to be an imprisonment because he may find some means of escape.

It is said that the party here was at liberty to go in another direction. I am not sure that in fact he was, because the same unlawful power which prevented him from taking one course might, in case of acquiescence, have refused him any other. But this liberty to do something else does not appear to me to affect the question of imprisonment. As long as I am prevented from doing what I have a right to do, of what importance is it that I am permitted to do something else? How does the imposition of an unlawful condition shew that I am not restrained? If I am locked in a room, am I not imprisoned because I might effect my escape through a window, or because I might find an exit dangerous or inconvenient to myself, as by wading through water or by taking a route so circuitous that my necessary affairs would suffer by delay?

It appears to me that this is a total deprivation of liberty with reference to the purpose for which he lawfully wished to employ his liberty: and, being effected by force, it is not the mere obstruction of a way, but a restraint of the person. The case cited as occurring before Lord Chief Justice Tindal, as I understand it, is much in point. He held it an imprisonment where the defendant stopped the plaintiff on his road till he had read a libel to him. Yet he did not prevent his escaping in another direction.

### NOTE

Whether a person is restrained is a matter of fact, and there need not be actual physical restraint. For example, an arrest, even if executed by merely touching the claimant, is a restraint, as it would be if a person has the physical capacity to leave but it is unreasonable to expect him to do so because, for example, he has no clothes on or he is imprisoned in a first floor room with an open window.

---

### *Robinson* v *Balmain New Ferry*
Privy Council [1910] AC 295; 79 LJPC 84; 84 TLR 143

The defendants operated a ferry from Sydney to Balmain. On the Sydney side there were some turnstiles. A person travelling from Sydney to Balmain paid on the Sydney side (i.e. on entry), as did a person who travelled from Balmain to Sydney (i.e. he paid *after* using the ferry: the system was similar to that used on the Liverpool- Birkenhead ferry). By the turnstiles was a notice saying 'A fare of one penny must be paid on entering or leaving the wharf. No exception will be made to this rule, whether the passenger has travelled by the ferry or not.' The claimant entered on the Sydney side and paid one penny. Finding that no ferry was due to cross for 20 minutes, he decided to leave the wharf, whereupon he was asked to pay a further penny. He refused and for a short time was prevented from leaving. Held: dismissing the appeal, that the defendants were not liable for false imprisonment.

LORD LOREBURN LC: The plaintiff paid a penny on entering the wharf to stay there till the boat should start and then be taken by the boat to the other side. The defendants were admittedly always ready and willing to carry out their part of this contract. Then the plaintiff changed his mind and wished to go back. The rules as to the exit from the wharf by the turnstile required a penny for any person who went through. This the plaintiff refused to pay, and he was by force prevented from going through the turnstile. He then claimed damages for assault and false imprisonment.

There was no complaint, at all events there was no question left to the jury by the plaintiff's request, of any excessive violence, and in the circumstances admitted it is clear to their Lordships that there was no false imprisonment at all. The plaintiff was merely called upon to leave the wharf in the way in which he contracted to leave it. There is no law requiring the defendants to make the exit from their premises gratuitous to people who come there upon a definite contract which involves their leaving the wharf by another way; and the defendants were entitled to resist a forcible passage through their turnstile.

The question whether the notice which was affixed to these premises was brought home to the knowledge of the plaintiff is immaterial, because the notice itself is immaterial.

When the plaintiff entered the defendants' premises there was nothing agreed as to the terms on which he might go back, because neither party contemplated his going back. When he desired to do so the defendants were entitled to impose a reasonable condition before allowing him to pass through their turnstile from a place to which he had gone of his own free will. The payment of a penny was a quite fair condition, and if he did not choose to comply with it the defendants were not bound to let him through. He could proceed on the journey he had contracted for.

---

### Herd v Weardale Steel, Coal and Coke Co.
House of Lords [1915] AC 67; 30 TLR 620; 84 LJKB 121

The claimant miners entered the Thornley Colliery owned by the defendants at 9.30 a.m. on 30 May 1911. In the ordinary course of events their shift would have ended at 4.00 p.m. During the morning they believed the work they were being asked to do was unsafe and in breach of an agreement with the employers, and at about 11.00 a.m. they asked to be taken to the surface. The employers refused, and they were not given permission to use the cages to return to the surface until 1.30 p.m. The employers sued the miners in the County Court for breach of contract and were awarded five shillings. The claimants replied with an action for false imprisonment. Held: dismissing the appeal, that the defendants were not liable.

VISCOUNT HALDANE LC: My Lords, by the law of this country no man can be restrained of his liberty without authority in law. That is a proposition the maintenance of which is of great importance; but at the same time it is a proposition which must be read in relation to other propositions which are equally important. If a man chooses to go into a dangerous place at the bottom of a quarry or the bottom of a mine, from which by the nature of physical circumstances he cannot escape, it does not follow from the proposition I have enunciated about liberty that he can compel the owner to bring him up out of it. The owner may or may not be under a duty arising from circumstances, on broad grounds the neglect of which may possibly involve him in a criminal charge or a civil liability. It is unnecessary to discuss the conditions and circumstances which might bring about such a result, because they have, in the view I take, nothing to do with false imprisonment.

My Lords, there is another proposition which has to be borne in mind, and that is the application of the maxim volenti non fit injuria. If a man gets into an express train and the doors are locked pending its arrival at its destination, he is not entitled, merely because the train has been stopped by signal, to call for the doors to be opened to let him out. He has entered the train on the terms that he is to be conveyed to a certain station without the opportunity of getting out before that, and he must abide by the terms on which he has entered the train. So when a man goes down a mine, from which access to the surface does not exist in the absence of special facilities given on the part of the owner of the mine, he is only entitled to the use of these facilities (subject possibly to the exceptional circumstances to which I have alluded) on the terms on which he has entered. I think it results from what was laid down by the Judicial Committee of the Privy Council in *Robinson* v *Balmain New Ferry Co.*, [1910] AC 295 that that is so. There there was a pier, and by the regulations a penny was to be paid by those who entered and a penny on getting out. The manager of the exit gate refused to allow a man who had gone in, having paid his penny, but having changed his mind about embarking on a steamer, and wishing to return, to come out without paying his penny. It was held that that was not false imprisonment; volenti non fit injuria. The man had gone in upon the pier knowing that those were the terms and conditions as to exit, and it was not false imprisonment to hold him to conditions which he had accepted. So, my Lords, it is not false imprisonment to hold a man to the conditions he has accepted when he goes down a mine.

NOTE
The above two cases have caused a lot of controversy, and varying reasons have been given for the decisions. Although in *Robinson* the Privy Council thought the notice irrelevant, surely one answer is that the claimant was free to leave on the terms by which he had agreed to enter (either on the ferry, or by leaving the wharf on payment of one penny). Equally, he was not imprisoned at all as he had a reasonable means of escape by taking the next ferry. In *Herd*, again it could be said that the contract was crucial, and this is one of many areas where the difficult question of

the effect of a contract on duties in tort is raised. For a general discussion of the two cases see Tan, 'A misconceived issue in the law of tort' (1981) 44 MLR 166, where it is argued that the issue is one of consent and that in both cases the claimants were entitled to withdraw their consent to being held where they were and should have won their cases.

---

### *Murray* v *Ministry of Defence*
House of Lords [1988] 1 WLR 692; [1988] 2 All ER 521

The claimant was suspected of being involved in the collection of money for the purchase of arms for the IRA. Corporal Davies and five other soldiers went to her house at 7.00 a.m. The claimant opened the door and Corporal Davies and three others entered. The rest of the family were gathered in one room, and the claimant, accompanied by Corporal Davies, went upstairs to get dressed. When they returned downstairs at about 7.30 a.m., Corporal Davies said 'As a member of Her Majesty's forces, I arrest you.' In an action for false imprisonment the claimant alleged that she had been detained unlawfully from 7.00 a.m. until 7.30 a.m., and although the court was sure that the claimant did realise that she was being restrained during that time, the House of Lords nevertheless discussed whether a person can be 'imprisoned' without being aware of the fact. Held: dismissing the appeal, that the defendants were not liable as it was reasonable under the Northern Ireland (Emergency Provisions) Act 1978 to delay formal words of arrest until the premises had been searched. However, it was also indicated that a person can be restrained without being aware of it.

LORD GRIFFITHS: Although on the facts of this case I am sure that the plaintiff was aware of the restraint on her liberty from 7.00 a.m., I cannot agree with the Court of Appeal that it is an essential element of the tort of false imprisonment that the victim should be aware of the fact of denial of liberty. The Court of Appeal relied upon *Herring* v *Boyle* (1834) for this proposition which they preferred to the view of Atkin LJ to the opposite effect in *Meering* v *Grahame-White Aviation Co. Ltd*, 122 LT 44. *Herring* v *Boyle* is an extraordinary decision of the Court of Exchequer: a mother went to fetch her 10-year-old son from school on 24 December 1833 to take him home for the Christmas holidays. The headmaster refused to allow her to take her son home because she had not paid the last term's fees, and he kept the boy at school over the holidays. An action for false imprisonment brought on behalf of the boy failed. In giving judgment Bolland B said, at p. 381:

> as far as we know, the boy may have been willing to stay; he does not appear to have been cognisant of any restraint, and there was no evidence of any act whatsoever done by the defendant in his presence. I think that we cannot construe the refusal to the mother in the boy's absence, and without his being cognisant of any restraint, to be an imprisonment of him against his will; . . .

I suppose it is possible that there are schoolboys who prefer to stay at school rather than go home for the holidays but it is not an inference that I would draw, and I cannot believe that on the same facts the case would be similarly decided today. In *Meering* v *Grahame-White Aviation Co. Ltd*, the plaintiff's employers, who suspected him of theft, sent two of the works police to bring him in for questioning at the company's offices. He was taken to a waiting-room where he said that if he was not told why he was there he would leave. He was told he was wanted for the purpose of making inquiries about things that had been stolen and he was wanted to give evidence; he then agreed to stay. Unknown to the plaintiff, the works police had been instructed not to let him leave the waiting-room until the Metropolitan Police arrived. The works police therefore remained outside the waiting-room and would not have allowed the plaintiff to leave until he was handed over to the Metropolitan Police, who subsequently arrested him. The question for the Court of Appeal was whether on this evidence the plaintiff was falsely imprisoned during the hour he was in the waiting-room or whether there could be no 'imprisonment' sufficient to found a civil action unless the plaintiff was aware of the restraint on his liberty. Atkin LJ said, at pp. 53–54:

> It appears to me that a person could be imprisoned without his knowing it. I think a person can be imprisoned while he is asleep, while he is in a state of drunkenness, while he is unconscious, and while he is a lunatic. Those are cases where it seems to me that the person might properly complain if he were imprisoned, though the imprisonment began and ceased while he was in that state. Of course, the damages might be diminished and would be affected by the question whether he was conscious of it or not. So a man might in fact, to my mind, be imprisoned by having the key of a door turned against him so that he is imprisoned in a room in fact although he does not know that the key has been turned. It may be that he is being detained in that room by persons who are anxious to make him believe that he is not in fact being imprisoned, and at the same time his captors outside that room may be boasting to persons that he is imprisoned, and it seems to me that if we were to take this case as an instance supposing it could be proved that Prudence had said while the plaintiff was waiting: 'I have got him detained there waiting for the detective to come in and take him to prison'—it appears to me that that would be evidence of imprisonment. It is quite unnecessary to go on to show that in fact the man knew that he was imprisoned. If a man can be imprisoned by having the key turned upon him without his knowledge, so he can be imprisoned if, instead of a lock and key or bolts and bars, he is prevented from, in fact, exercising his liberty by guards and warders or policemen. They serve the same purpose. Therefore it appears to me to be a question of fact. It is true that in all cases of imprisonment so far as the law of civil liability is concerned that 'stone walls do not a prison make,' in the sense that they are not the only form of imprisonment, but any restraint within defined bounds which is a restraint in fact may be an imprisonment.

I agree with this passage. In the first place it is not difficult to envisage cases in which harm may result from unlawful imprisonment even though the victim is unaware of it. Dean William L. Prosser gave two examples in his article in the Columbia Law Review, vol. 55 (June 1955), p. 847 ('False Imprisonment: Consciousness of Confinement'), in which he attacked section 42 of the *Restatement of Torts* which at that time stated the rule that 'there is no liability for intentionally confining another unless the person physically restrained knows of the confinement.' Dean Prosser wrote, at p. 849:

> Let us consider several illustrations. A locks B, a child two days old, in the vault of a bank. B is, of course, unconscious of the confinement, but the bank vault cannot be opened for two days. In the meantime, B suffers from hunger and thirst, and his health is seriously impaired; or it may be that he even dies. Is this no tort? Or suppose that A abducts B, a wealthy lunatic, and holds him for ransom for a week. E is unaware of his confinement, but vaguely understands that he is in unfamiliar surroundings, and that something is wrong. He undergoes mental suffering affecting his health. At the end of the week, he is discovered by the police and released without ever having known that he has been imprisoned. Has he no action against B? . . . If a child of two is kidnapped, confined, and deprived of the care of its mother for a month, is the kidnapping and the confinement in itself so minor a matter as to call for no redress in tort at all?

The *Restatement of Torts* has now been changed and requires that the person confined 'is conscious of the confinement or is harmed by it' (*Restatement of the Law, Second, Torts 2d.* (1965), section 35, p. 52).

If a person is unaware that he has been falsely imprisoned and has suffered no harm, he can normally expect to recover no more than nominal damages, and it is tempting to redefine the tort in the terms of the present rule in the American *Restatement of Torts*. On reflection, however, I would not do so. The law attaches supreme importance to the liberty of the individual and if he suffers a wrongful interference with that liberty it should remain actionable even without proof of special damage.

■ QUESTIONS

1. Need the defendant know that if he or she does the act, imprisonment will follow? If a room has two doors and a person locks one door, believing the other door to be unlocked when in fact it is locked, is that person liable?

2. If a person locks the door to a room in which there is a man of 20 years old, knowing that there is an open window six feet above the ground, is that person liable for imprisoning him if the man has fragile bones and dares not jump?

## SECTION 4: SELECTED DEFENCES TO TRESPASS TO THE PERSON

## A: Consent

As we have seen from *Wilson* v *Pringle* (above), consent is not strictly a 'defence' to trespass to the person, but rather a denial that any tort was committed in the first place. This is so because if a trespass is defined as an offensive contact, a touching cannot be offensive to a person who has consented to it. Consent may be express or implied, so that, for example, a rugby player consents to contacts within the rules during a game. A particular problem concerns express consents, as in surgical operations, where the suggestion is that if the consent is to what is done, that absolves the defendant in trespass, whereas if the allegation is that the claimant did not fully consent because he was unaware or not fully informed of the consequences of the act, that is a matter for the tort of negligence.

### *Chatterton* v *Gerson*
Queen's Bench Division [1981] QB 432; [1980] 3 WLR 1003; [1981] 1 All ER 257

During an operation for a hernia the claimant's ileo-inguinal nerve was trapped and this caused her great pain. The defendant was a specialist in chronic intractable pain and he injected the claimant. This was unsuccessful in blocking the pain, but did render her right leg numb. She claimed in trespass on the ground that her consent to the injection was invalid as she had not been informed of the potential consequences, and in negligence on the ground that the defendant owed her a duty to warn her of the risks. Held: the defendant was not liable in either trespass or negligence.

BRISTOW J: It is clear law that in any context in which consent of the injured party is a defence to what would otherwise be a crime or a civil wrong, the consent must be real. Where for example a woman's consent to sexual intercourse is obtained by fraud, her apparent consent is no defence to a charge of rape. It is not difficult to state the principle or to appreciate its good sense. As so often, the problem lies in its application.

In my judgment what the court has to do in each case is to look at all the circumstances and say 'Was there a real consent?' I think justice requires that in order to vitiate the reality of consent there must be a greater failure of communication between doctor and patient than that involved in a breach of duty if the claim is based on negligence. When the claim is based on negligence the plaintiff must prove not only the breach of duty to inform, but that had the duty not been broken she would not have chosen to have the operation. Where the claim is based on trespass to the person, once it is shown that the consent is unreal, then what the plaintiff would have decided if she had been given the information which would have prevented vitiation of the reality of her consent is irrelevant.

In my judgment once the patient is informed in broad terms of the nature of the procedure which is intended, and gives her consent, that consent is real, and the cause of the action on which to base a claim for failure to go into risks and implications is negligence, not trespass. Of course if information is withheld in bad faith, the consent will be vitiated by fraud. Of course if by some accident, as in a case in the 1940's in the Salford Hundred Court where a boy was admitted to hospital for tonsilectomy [sic] and due to administrative error was circumcised instead, trespass would be the appropriate cause of action against the doctor, though he was as much the victim of the error as the boy. But in my judgment it would be very much against the interests of justice if actions which are really based on a failure by the doctor to perform his duty adequately to inform were pleaded in trespass.

In this case in my judgment even taking the plaintiff's evidence at its face value she was under no illusion as to the general nature of what an intrathecal injection of phenol solution nerve block would be, and in the case of each injection her consent was not unreal. I should add that getting the patient to sign a pro forma expressing consent to undergo the operation 'the effect and nature of which have been explained to me,' as was done here in each case, should be a valuable reminder to everyone of the need for explanation and consent. But it would be no defence to an action based on trespass to the person if no explanation had in fact been given. The consent would have been expressed in form only, not in reality.

## NOTES

1. This view was approved in *Sidaway* v *Governors of the Bethlem Royal Hospital* [1985] AC 871, which was discussed in Chapter 3. That case rejected the doctrine of informed consent, i.e. that a consent is not valid unless all the risks have been explained. Thus, the issue in trespass is whether the patient knew what was being done, and the issue in negligence is whether he or she ought to have been informed of the risks.

2. In relation to implied consent, in *Blake* v *Galloway* [2004] 1 WLR 2844, [2004] EWCA Civ 814, a group of 15-year-olds were engaging in horseplay by throwing twigs and bark at each other. The defendant threw a piece of bark which struck the claimant in the eye. The Court of Appeal held that there was no battery as the claimant must be taken to have consented to any missile being thrown more or less in accordance with the tacit understandings or conventions of the game. Nor was there liability in negligence as there was no failure to take reasonable care in the circumstances of the horseplay in which they were engaged. There would only be liability if there was recklessness.

3. If a person touches another (who has consented to being touched) with a metal bar, but fails to disclose that it is charged with electricity, is that person liable in trespass? Would it make any difference if he represents that the bar is not 'live'? The question is whether the consent is effective if the claimant knows the nature of the act but is misled about its quality. Compare the facts of *Hegarty* v *Shine* (1878) 14 Cox CC 145, where the defendant was sued for battery after he had sexual intercourse with his mistress without informing her that he had a venereal disease. The defendant was not liable: Ball C said 'We are not dealing with deceit as to the nature of the act done. . .'. However, in *R* v *Dica* [2004] QB 1257, a recent criminal case, it was said that where a man failed to inform his lover that he was HIV positive there was no reason for the woman to think that she was at risk from infection and therefore she did not consent to the disease, even though she did consent to the sexual intercourse.

4. *Duress*. Duress can vitiate consent to trespass, but it may be limited to threats of violent or unlawful acts. In *Latter* v *Braddell* (1880) 50 LJQB 166 and 448, the defendants suspected that their maid, the claimant, was pregnant, and asked a male doctor to examine her. The claimant protested but reluctantly submitted to the examination. In holding there was no liability Lindley J said, 'The plaintiff [claimant] had entirely in her own power physically to comply or not to comply with her mistress's orders . . . Should economic duress, such as this, vitiate consent? (In *Universe Tankships of Monrovia* v *ITF* [1981] ICR 129, shipowners were entitled to

recover payments they had made to a seamen's union welfare fund in order to have the blacking of their ship lifted, on the grounds that the payments had been made under economic duress.)

---

## B: Provocation and contributory negligence

---

### Lane v Holloway
Court of Appeal [1968] 1 QB 379; [1967] 3 WLR 1003; [1967] 3 All ER 129

Relations were strained between the claimant, Mr Lane, who was a retired gardener aged 64, and his neighbour, Mr Holloway (aged 23), a café proprietor in Dorchester. One night Mr Lane came back from the pub and was talking to a Mrs Brake. Mrs Holloway called out 'You bloody lot'. Mr Lane replied 'Shut up, you monkey faced tart'. Mr Holloway sprang up and said 'What did you say to my wife?' Mr Lane replied 'I want to see you on your own', and he later threw a light punch at Mr Holloway, whereupon the younger man punched him in the eye. The wound needed 19 stitches. Held: allowing the appeal, that the defendant was liable and no deduction from damages should be made for Mr Lane's provocation.

LORD DENNING MR: It is said that the judge ought not to have reduced the damages. The judge had cases before him, both in this country and New Zealand and Canada, where it was held that provocation could be used to reduce the damages. But most of these cases were considered by the High Court of Australia in 1962 in *Fontin* v *Katapodis*, (1962) 108 CLR 177. The plaintiff struck the defendant with a weapon, a wooden T-square. It broke on his shoulder. There was not much trouble from that. But then the defendant picked up a sharp piece of glass with which he was working and threw it at the plaintiff, causing him severe injury. The judge reduced the damages from £2,850 to £2,000 by reason of the provocation. But the High Court of Australia, including the Chief Justice, Sir Owen Dixon, held that provocation could be used to wipe out the element of exemplary or aggravated damages but could not be used to reduce the actual figure of pecuniary compensation. So they increased the damages to the full £2,850.

I think that the Australian High Court should be our guide. The defendant has done a civil wrong and should pay compensation for the physical damage done by it. Provocation by the plaintiff can properly be used to take away any element of aggravation. But not to reduce the real damages . . .

SALMON LJ: To say in circumstances such as those that ex turpi causa non oritur actio is a defence seems to me to be quite absurd. Academically of course one can see the argument, but one must look at it, I think, from a practical point of view. To say that this old gentleman was engaged jointly with the defendant in a criminal venture is a step which, like the judge, I feel wholly unable to take.

The defence of volenti non fit injuria seems to me to be equally difficult. It is inconceivable that the old man, full of beer as he was, was voluntarily taking the risk of having an injury of this kind inflicted upon him. I think the judge was quite right in rejecting the defence of volenti non fit injuria. . . .

There are many cases from the Commonwealth Law Reports in which the question has been considered as to whether or not the fact that the plaintiff behaved badly can diminish damages which are awarded as compensation for physical injury. Some of these decisions are conflicting. For my part I entirely accept what was said in the High Court of Australia in *Fontin* v *Katapodis*, (1962) 108 CLR 177. It was an exceptionally strong court consisting of Sir Owen Dixon CJ, McTiernan and Owen JJ. The case seems to me, for all practical purposes, indistinguishable from the present and it states in the plainest terms what, as I have already said, I should have been prepared to hold without any authority, namely, that on principle, when considering what damages a plaintiff is entitled to as compensation for physical injury, the fact that the plaintiff may have behaved badly is irrelevant. I think it is important to remember this. Some of the older English authorities and some of the Commonwealth cases appear to fall into the error, which until recently had by no means been eliminated, of thinking that damages for tort were partly to punish the defendant. We now know, certainly since *Rookes* v *Barnard* [1964] AC 1129, that they are nothing of the kind, that they are purely compensatory—with the exception, of course, of exemplary damages. And in the present case there was no question of exemplary damages being claimed or awarded.

The judge, however, was persuaded that he could take the plaintiff's conduct into account, and he obviously did so, and discounted a great deal on this account. To my mind, even if he was entitled to discount anything, which, in my view, he was not, he discounted much too much.

Mr O'Brien relied also upon contributory negligence to reduce the damages. At first he relied on a wider ground under the Law Reform (Contributory Negligence) Act, 1945, but in the end I think he restricted his argument under this Act to contributory negligence. As Winn LJ pointed out in the course of the argument, if the plaintiff on the facts of this case can be said to have been negligent, then before the statute what he did would have afforded the defendant a complete defence to the action—a somewhat surprising proposition. To my mind it is impossible to hold that what this old man did, however rude or silly or cantankerous, amounted to contributory negligence.

NOTES
1. This case is *not* about self defence, but about provocation.
2. *Contributory negligence*. Following *Lane* v *Holloway* it was suggested that if a person genuinely shows a lack of regard for his own safety (which on the facts was not so in *Lane* v *Holloway*), damages might be reduced for contributory negligence. Nevertheless, in the state of Victoria in *Horkin* v *North Melbourne Football Club* [1983] VR 153, Brooking J held that, on historical and public policy grounds, contributory negligence is not a defence in trespass. One of the functions of trespass is to repress wrongful behaviour and to preserve public order. The problem with applying the doctrine to trespass is the difficulty of balancing the defendant's intentional act against the claimant's careless act. If contributory negligence is based on cause, how can the defendant say that he did not wholly cause the damage which he intended? In *Quinn* v *Leathem* [1901] AC 495, Lord Lindley said 'the intention to injure negatives all excuses'. However, in *Barnes* v *Nayer* The Times, 19 December 1986, it was said that contributory negligence would be allowed as a defence. The defendant alleged that he and his family were subjected to constant abuse by their neighbours, and that on one occasion, after threats to his son, the defendant killed the deceased with a machete. The Court of Appeal held that contributory negligence is available as a defence to trespass to the person but it did not apply to the facts of this case. In *Standard Chartered Bank* v *PNSC* [2003] 1 All ER 173 Lord Rogers reserved his opinion on whether the doctrine would apply to trespass to the person, but he appeared to doubt whether it would. See also Hudson, 'Contributory negligence as a defence to battery' (1984) 4 LS 332, and also Childs, 'Pause for thought: contributory negligence and intentional trespass to the person' (1993) 44 NILQ 334.

# 23

# Trespass to Land

Trespass to land protects a person in possession of land against direct invasion of his property. (If the invasion is indirect, that is a matter for the law of nuisance.) The right to sue includes not only those with a proprietorial interest in the land, such as owners and tenants, but also those who have exclusive occupation such as squatters. In some cases even a licensee may have sufficient exclusive occupation to be able to sue. For example, in *Monsanto v Tilly* [2000] Env LR 313, the claimants had planted genetically modified crops on a farmer's land and the defendants entered and attacked the crops. The claimants were entitled to an injunction. (Incidentally, this case also decides that there is no defence of public interest in trespass to land.)

The fact that any invasion of land, however minute and whether it causes damage or not, is a trespass, indicates that the primary function of this tort is to protect rights in property, rather than simply to provide compensation. It is here that the question of remedies is important, as *Anchor Brewhouse* (below) indicates.

---

### Gregory v Piper
Court of King's Bench (1820) 9 B & C 591; 109 ER 220

The claimant occupied the Rising Sun in Newmarket, and he owned the wall which separated his yard from that of the defendant. In the course of a dispute about a right of way, the defendant ordered his employee, Stubbings, to dump rubbish so as to block the way but not to touch the wall. The rubbish was loose and as it dried out some of it rolled or settled against the wall. Held: the defendant was liable.

PARKE J: I think that the defendant is liable in this form of action. If a single stone had been put against the wall it would have been sufficient. Independently of Stubbings's evidence there was sufficient evidence to satisfy the jury that the rubbish was placed there by the defendant, for he expressed his determination not to remove it. It does not rest there. Stubbings says he was desired not to let the rubbish touch the wall. But it appeared to be of a loose kind, and it was therefore probable that some of it naturally might run against the wall. Stubbings said that some of it of course would go against the wall. Now the defendant must be taken to have contemplated all the probable consequences of the act which he had ordered to be done, and one of these probable consequences was, that the rubbish would touch the plaintiff's wall. If that was so, then the laying the rubbish against the wall was as much the defendant's act as if it had been done by his express command. The defendant, therefore, was the person who caused the act to be done, and for the necessary or natural consequence of his own act he is responsible as a trespasser.

NOTE
Compare *Esso Petroleum v Southport Corporation* [1956] AC 218, where it was doubted, without deciding, whether it would be trespass to discharge oil at sea which was then washed onto the

foreshore. The oil was 'committed to the action of wind and wave, with no certainty . . . how, when or under what conditions it might come to shore'.

---

### *Basely* v *Clarkson*
Court of Common Pleas (1682) 3 Lev 37; 83 ER 565

Trespass is a tort of intention and so there will be no liability for an involuntary act. The question in this case was whether a person could be liable if he intentionally entered land, but he believed the land was his—hence the heading below.

[Difference *inter* trespass involuntary, and *per* mistake]

Trespass for breaking his closs called the *balk* and the *hade*, and cutting his grass, and carrying it away. The defendant disclaims any title in the lands of the plaintiff, but says that he hath a *balk* and *hade* adjoining to the balk and hade of the plaintiff, and in mowing his own land he involuntarily and by mistake mowed down some grass growing upon the balk and hade of the plaintiff, intending only to mow the grass upon his own *balk* and *hade*, and carried the *grass, &c. quæ est eadem, &C. Et quod ante emanationem brevis* he tendered to the plaintiff 2s. in satisfaction, and that 2s. was a sufficient amends. Upon this the plaintiff demurred, and had judgement; for it appears the fact was voluntary, and his intention and knowledge are not traversable; they cannot be known.

NOTE

The point here is that the defendant did not mean to cut the claimant's grass, but rather he made a mistake about where the boundary was. He was liable because he intentionally did an act (albeit under a misapprehension) which in fact was an invasion of the claimant's land. This illustrates how trespass can be used to determine disputes between neighbouring landowners about where the proper boundary between them is.

---

### *League Against Cruel Sports* v *Scott*
Queen's Bench Division [1986] 1 QB 240; [1985] 3 WLR 400, [1985] 2 All ER 489

The claimants owned various areas of unfenced moorland around Exmoor for the purpose of establishing a sanctuary for deer. Accordingly they did not allow hunting on their land. The defendants were joint masters of the Devon and Somerset staghounds, and it was shown that on a number of occasions hounds belonging to the hunt had entered the claimants' property, and the claimants alleged trespass by the defendants, their servants or agents. No material damage was caused. Held: the defendants were liable. Damages were awarded and in respect of one property an injunction was granted.

PARK J: In my judgment the law as I take it to be may be stated thus: where a master of staghounds takes out a pack of hounds and deliberately sets them in pursuit of a stag or hind, knowing that there is a real risk that in the pursuit hounds may enter or cross prohibited land, the master will be liable for trespass if he intended to cause hounds to enter such land, or if by his failure to exercise proper control over them he caused them to enter such land.

In the present case, on each of the occasions on which the league alleges trespass by hounds the master (or on some occasions the masters) had taken out the pack and set hounds in pursuit of a stag or hind. On each occasion the master or masters knew that there was a real risk that one or more hounds might enter league land; on each occasion one or more hounds did, in fact, enter league land. The question is, therefore, whether on any, and if so which, of those occasions the trespass was caused either by the master intending that hounds should enter or by his failure to exercise proper control over them.

This is, in each case, a question of fact. The master's intention, or the intention of those servants or agents or followers of the hunt for whose conduct he is responsible, has to be inferred from his or their conduct in all the circumstances of the case. For example, whether he or they stood by and allowed hounds which were plainly about to enter prohibited land to do so, or allowed hounds which were plainly on the land to remain there; or whether, by making appropriate sounds vocally or on the horn, he encouraged hounds to go on to or to remain on such land.

Further, if it is virtually impossible, whatever precautions are taken, to prevent hounds from entering league land, such as Pitleigh for example, yet the master knowing that to be the case, nevertheless persists in hunting in its vicinity, with the result that hounds frequently trespass on the land, then the inference might well be drawn that his indifference to the risk of trespass amounted to an intention that hounds should trespass on the land.

The master's negligence, or the negligence of those servants or agents or followers of the hunt for whose conduct he is responsible, has also to be judged in the light of all the circumstances in which the trespass in question occurred.

It involves consideration of such questions as the stage in the chase at which it ought reasonably to have been foreseen that there was a risk that hounds might trespass on league land and what precautions, if any, were taken by the master at that stage to prevent trespass by heading off the hounds.

## Bernstein v Skyviews and General Ltd
Queen's Bench Division [1978] QB 479; [1977] 3 WLR 136; [1977] 2 All ER 962

The defendants flew above Lord Bernstein's country house and took a photograph of it, which they then offered to sell to him. The claimant claimed damages for trespass by invasion of his air space. Held: the defendants were not liable.

GRIFFITHS J: I turn now to the law. The plaintiff claims that as owner of the land he is also owner of the air space above the land, or at least has the right to exclude any entry into the air space above his land. He relies upon the old Latin maxim, cujus est solum ejus est usque ad coelum et ad inferos, a colourful phrase often upon the lips of lawyers since it was first coined by Accursius in Bologna in the 13th century. There are a number of cases in which the maxim has been used by English judges, but an examination of those cases shows that they have all been concerned with structures attached to the adjoining land, such as overhanging buildings, signs or telegraph wires, and for their solution it has not been necessary for the judge to cast his eyes towards the heavens; he has been concerned with the rights of the owner in the air space immediately adjacent to the surface of the land. . . .

I can find no support in authority for the view that a landowner's rights in the air space above his property extend to an unlimited height. In *Wandsworth Board of Works* v *United Telephone Co. Ltd*, 13 QBD 904 Bowen LJ described the maxim, usque ad coelum, as a fanciful phrase, to which I would add that if applied literally it is a fanciful notion leading to the absurdity of a trespass at common law being committed by a satellite every time it passes over a suburban garden. The academic writers speak with one voice in rejecting the uncritical and literal application of the maxim . . . I accept their collective approach as correct. The problem is to balance the rights of an owner to enjoy the use of his land against the rights of the general public to take advantage of all that science now offers in the use of air space. This balance is in my judgment best struck in our present society by restricting the rights of an owner in the air space above his land to such height as is necessary for the ordinary use and enjoyment of his land and the structures upon it, and declaring that above that height he has no greater rights in the air space than any other member of the public.

Applying this test to the facts of this case, I find that the defendants' aircraft did not infringe any rights in the plaintiff's air space, and thus no trespass was committed. It was on any view of the evidence flying many hundreds of feet above the ground and it is not suggested that by its mere presence in the air space it caused any interference with any use to which the plaintiff put or might wish to put his land. The plaintiff's complaint is not that the aircraft interfered with the use of his land but that a photograph was taken from it. There is, however, no law against taking a photograph, and the mere taking of a photograph cannot turn an act which is not a trespass into the plaintiff's air space into one that is a trespass.

My finding that no trespass at common law has been established is sufficient to determine this case in the defendants' favour. I should, however, deal with a further defence under the Civil Aviation Act 1949, section 40(1) of which provides:

> No action shall lie in respect of trespass or in respect of nuisance, by reason only of the flight of an aircraft over any property at a height above the ground, which, having regard to wind, weather and all the circumstances of the case is reasonable, or the ordinary incidents of such flight so long as the provisions of Part II and this Part of this Act and any Order in Council or order made under Part II or this Part of this Act are duly complied with.

It is agreed that all the statutory provisions have been complied with by the defendants, nor is there any suggestion that the aircraft was not flying at a reasonable height; but it is submitted by the plaintiff that the protection given by the subsection is limited to a bare right of passage over land analogous to the limited right of a member of the public to pass over the surface of a highway, and my attention has been drawn to a passage in *Shawcross & Beaumont on Air Law*, 3rd ed. (1966), p. 561 in which the editors express this view. I see nothing in the language of the section to invite such a restricted reading which would withdraw from its protection many very beneficial activities carried on from aircraft. For example, we heard during this case that Granada Television, a company of which Lord Bernstein is chairman, made a series of educational films called 'The Land' for educational purposes. To make the films helicopters flew far and wide over the country and photographed the land below in all its various aspects. Of course they had not obtained the permission of every occupier whose land they photographed—it would have been an impossible task. According to the plaintiff's contention that innocent activity would not be protected even if the helicopters were flying at a reasonable height and complying with all statutory requirements, for they would not be mere birds of passage but making use of the air space for the purpose of aerial photography or survey. As I read the section its protection extends to all flights provided they are at a reasonable height and comply with the statutory requirements. And I adopt this construction the more readily because subsection (2) imposes upon the owner of the aircraft a strict liability to pay damages for any material loss or damage that may be caused by his aircraft.

It is, however, to be observed that the protection given is limited by the words 'by reason only of the flight,' so although an owner can found no action in trespass or nuisance if he relies solely upon the flight of the aircraft above his property as founding his cause of action, the section will not preclude him from bringing an action if he can point to some activity carried on by or from the aircraft that can properly be considered a trespass or nuisance, or some other tort. For example, the section would give no protection against the deliberate emission of vast quantities of smoke that polluted the atmosphere and seriously interfered with the plaintiff's use and enjoyment of his property; such behaviour remains an actionable nuisance. Nor would I wish this judgment to be understood as deciding that in no circumstances could a successful action be brought against an aerial photographer to restrain his activities. The present action is not founded in nuisance for no court would regard the taking of a single photograph as an actionable nuisance. But if the circumstances were such that a plaintiff was subjected to the harassment of constant surveillance of his house from the air, accompanied by the photographing of his every activity, I am far from saying that the court would not regard such a monstrous invasion of his privacy as an actionable nuisance for which they would give relief. However, that question does not fall for decision in this case and will be decided if and when it arises.

On the facts of this case even if contrary to my view the defendants' aircraft committed a trespass at common law in flying over the plaintiff's land, the plaintiff is prevented from bringing any action in respect of that trespass by the terms of section 40(1) of the Civil Aviation Act 1949.

NOTES
1. The Civil Aviation Act 1949, s. 40(1) has been replaced by the Civil Aviation Act 1982, s. 75(1) which is in similar terms. The statute also imposes strict liability upon the owner of an

aircraft for any material damage caused by any article, animal or person falling from an aircraft in flight.

2. For invasion of air space by structures on neighbouring land, see *Anchor Brewhouse* v *Berkley House* (below).

---

### Anchor Brewhouse Developments Ltd v Berkley House Ltd
Chancery Division [1987] 2 EGLR 172

The defendants were developing a site in London and were using a tower crane in the construction work. The jib of the tower crane swung over the claimants' property, and this was held to be a trespass to the claimants' airspace. Another factor in the case was whether the claimants were limited to a remedy in damages or whether they could obtain an injunction, and, if so, whether that injunction could be temporarily suspended to allow the defendants to complete their building. Held: it was a trespass to the airspace and an injunction was granted.

SCOTT J: . . . What is complained of in the present case is infringement of air space by a structure positioned upon a neighbour's land. The defendant has erected tower cranes on its land. Attached to each tower crane is a boom which swings over the plaintiffs' land. The booms invade the air space over the plaintiffs' land. Each boom is part of the structure on the defendant's land. The tort of trespass represents an interference with possession or with the right to possession. A landowner is entitled, as an attribute of his ownership of the land, to place structures on his land and thereby to reduce into actual possession the air space above his land. If an adjoining owner places a structure on his (the adjoining owner's) land that overhangs his neighbour's land, he thereby takes into his possession air space to which his neighbour is entitled. That, in my judgment, is trespass. It does not depend upon any balancing of rights.

The difficulties posed by overflying aircraft or balloons, bullets or missiles seem to me to be wholly separate from the problem which arises where there is invasion of air space by a structure placed or standing upon the land of a neighbour. One of the characteristics of the common law of trespass is, or ought to be, certainty. The extent of proprietary rights enjoyed by landowners ought to be clear. It may be that, where aircraft or overflying missiles are concerned, certainty cannot be achieved. I do not wish to dissent at all from Griffiths J's approach to that problem in the *Bernstein* case. But certainty is capable of being achieved where invasion of air space by tower cranes, advertising signs and other structures are concerned. In my judgment, if somebody erects on his own land a structure, part of which invades the air space above the land of another, the invasion is trespass. . . .

That brings me to Mr Moss' second point. He submitted that if the trial were now, the plaintiffs would not succeed in obtaining a permanent injunction. So, he submitted, they should not get an interlocutory injunction either.

Mr Martin has submitted that if I am satisfied, as I am, that the oversailing booms of the cranes are committing trespass and if it is the case, as it is, that the trespass is threatened to be continued by the defendant, the plaintiffs are entitled to an injunction as of course. An injunction is a discretionary remedy, but it is well settled that the discretion must be exercised in accordance with judicial precedent and principle and there is authority for Mr Martin's submission that a trespass threatened to be continued will be restrained by injunction as of course.

In *Woollerton and Wilson* v *Costain* [1970] 1 WLR 411 Stamp J said at p. 413:

> It is the plaintiffs' case that the absence of any damage caused by the trespass, either present or apprehended, is no reason for refusing the injunction for which they ask. It is their further contention that since the tort of trespass is admitted and is threatened to be continued there is no good reason for refusing interlocutory relief on the ground of balance of convenience. In my judgment both these submissions are well founded.
>
> It is in my judgment well established that it is no answer to a claim for an injunction to restrain a trespass that the trespass does no harm to the plaintiff. Indeed, the very fact that no harm is done is a reason for rather than against the granting of an injunction: for if there is

no damage done the damage recovered in the action will be nominal and if the injunction is refused the result will be no more nor less than a licence to continue the tort of trespass in return for a nominal payment. . . .

Mr Moss pointed out, and it is common ground, that there is a flaw in that exposition of the law [in *Woollerton and Wilson v Costain*]. The learned judge proceeded on the footing that nominal damages only could be recovered for the trespass. He was not referred by counsel to the line of authority enabling damages to be awarded to represent the sum that on a 'willing grantor/grantee' basis the plaintiff might have charged the defendant for a licence to commit the trespass. Mr Moss fastened on that error in order to submit that Stamp J's conclusion that an injunction should be granted to restrain the trespass was unsound. I do not agree. Stamp J based himself upon firm early authority in the form of the decision of Lord Selborne in *Goodson v Richardson* [(1874) 9 Ch App 221] and of Sir George Jessel in *Eardley v Granville* [(1876) 3 Ch D 826]. Both these authorities justify the grant of injunctive relief to restrain trespass notwithstanding that the damage to the plaintiff may be trivial only. Lord Selborne and Sir George Jessel adopted a robust Victorian approach which might, perhaps, find less sympathy now. The ownership of property entitled the owner to license or refuse to license the use of it by others. If he is asked to license the use of it by others, he can charge whatever he chooses for the licence. The law will recognise and protect the monopoly that his ownership carries with it. That is the philosophy, as I read the two cases, underlying the judgments of Lord Selborne and of Sir George Jessel. The grant of the injunction by Stamp J was in accordance with the principle expressed in these two cases. It did not depend on the nominal damages point. It is to be noted that, having found that an injunction ought to be granted, Stamp J then proceeded to suspend the operation of it for the only period for which it could have been of any use. Some reservation as to the correctness of that suspension was subsequently expressed by the Court of Appeal in *Charrington v Simons & Co. Ltd* [1971] 1 WLR 598.

In *John Trenberth Ltd v National Westminster Bank Ltd* (1979) 39 P & CR 104 Walton J expressed the clear view that the suspension was wrong. . . .

What has troubled me about the plaintiffs' claim to an injunction is not any of the special circumstances relied on by Mr Moss but simply that it seems sensible that the defendant's building construction should be done by means of tower cranes. The injunctions which I feel obliged to grant in order to reflect the plaintiffs' proprietary rights will put the defendant in a position in which it must come to terms with the plaintiffs if it is going to continue to use its tower cranes.

It would in many respects be convenient if the court had power, in order to enable property developments to be expeditiously and economically completed, to allow, on proper commercial terms, some use to be made by the developers of the land of neighbours. But the court has no such power and ought not, in my view, to claim it indirectly by the withholding of injunctions in cases like the present. Some statutes have granted the court analogous powers: see eg the Medicines Act 1968, the Patents Act 1949, the Mines (Working Facilities and Support) Act 1966. There is a sense in which the grant of an injunction against trespass enables a landowner to behave like a dog in a manger. I am not suggesting that these plaintiffs are so behaving, but the conclusion that, even if they are, they are none the less entitled to their injunction sticks a little in my gullet. It would be possible for the law to be that the court should not grant an injunction to restrain a trifling trespass if it were shown to be reasonable and sensible that the trespass be allowed to continue for a limited period upon payment of substantial and proper damages. But I do not think it is open to me to proceed on that footing. There is too much authority in the way. The authorities establish, in my view, that the plaintiffs are entitled as of course to injunctions to restrain continuing trespass.

For these reasons, reached with some regret, I grant the injunctions as asked.

NOTES

1. The problem of whether to award damages or to grant an injunction also arises in nuisance, where again the preferred view is that a claimant whose interest is being invaded is generally entitled to an injunction. See for example *Kennaway v Thompson* [1981] QB 88. As Scott J admitted in *Anchor Brewhouse*, the effect is to dramatically alter the bargaining power of the claimant who may be tempted to charge an exorbitant sum for permission to use the airspace. In *LJP Investments v Howard Chia Investments* (1991) 24 NSWLR 499, where for

complicated reasons it was necessary to measure damages for trespass to airspace by scaffold-ing, Hodgson J held that where the space used has peculiar value for a defendant then damages should reflect that value rather than the general market value. Damages should reflect the price which the claimant and defendant would reasonably have negotiated having regard to the claimant's position and the defendant's wish to develop the site, and the judge said that one relevant factor in this would be the extra cost which the defendant would incur if he were not able to gain access to the claimant's air space.

Note also the Access to Neighbouring Land Act 1992 where a court may make an order allowing access but only where the entry is for the purpose of preservation and not for improvement or building a new structure.

2. In *Jaggard* v *Sawyer* [1995] 2 All ER 189, the Court of Appeal approved the dictum in *Shelfer* v *City of London Electric Lighting* [1895] 1 Ch 287 that an injunction may be refused where: (1) the injury to the claimant's legal rights is small; (2) it is one which is capable of being estimated in money; (3) it can be adequately compensated by a small money payment; and (4) it would be oppressive to the defendant to grant an injunction. In deciding whether it would be oppressive in relation to a permanent invasion of land (e.g. by erecting a building on the claimant's land) the court would take into account whether the defendant knew he was committing a trespass and completed the work in the hope of presenting a court with a fait accompli.

3. *Recovery of possession.* Part 55 of the Civil Procedure Rules provides an expeditious remedy when land is being occupied by trespassers. Apart from speed, the main advantage is that an order can be obtained against trespassers without knowing their names.

4. *Criminal trespass.* Trespass is not generally a crime, but several statutes make it so in particular circumstances. For example, the Criminal Law Act 1977, s. 6 makes it a crime (except for a displaced residential occupier) to use force to enter premises; and the Criminal Justice and Public Order Act 1994, s. 61 deals with the case of two or more persons entering land with a view to residing there, and causing damage or using abusive language or bringing six or more vehicles onto the land. Section 68 establishes an offence of aggravated trespass in relation to a person who trespasses on land in the open air and obstructs or disrupts a lawful activity on that or adjoining land. It is also a crime to trespass on specific kinds of land such as railways (Regulation of Railways Act 1868, s. 23), or airports (Civil Aviation Act 1982, s. 39).

■ QUESTIONS

1. If a person enters a shop and begins filming staff and customers, is that person liable for trespass? (See *Lincoln Hunt Australia* v *Willesee* (1986) 4 NSWLR 457 and *TV3* v *BSA* [1995] 2 NZLR 720 at 733.)

2. If a person is driven by another in a car onto the claimant's land when at the entrance there is a notice saying 'Private: no entry', is that person liable for trespass? If so, when?

---

### Burton v Winters

Court of Appeal [1993] 1 WLR 1077; [1993] 3 All ER 847

The defendant built a garage which encroached by 4½ inches onto the claimant's land. Having failed to obtain an injunction to have the garage removed, the claimant built a counter wall on the defendant's land which she refused to remove and was sentenced to 12 months' imprisonment for contempt. The claimant later damaged the garage and was sentenced to two years' imprisonment. On appeal from that order one issue was whether the claimant was entitled to use 'self help' (or exercise a right of abatement) in order to put an end to the trespass by the defendant's garage. Held: the claimant had no right of self help and was limited to damages; the sentence of two years was justified.

LLOYD LJ: There is a common law right of self-redress for trespass by encroachment, which was already regarded as an ancient remedy in the time of Bracton. It is similar to the common law right of abatement in the case of nuisance. But at an early stage of our history the right of abatement was supplemented by the assize of nuisance or 'quod permittat prosternere'. The action lay to have the nuisance abated by the defendants and to recover damages: see *Baten's Case* (1610) 9 Co Rep 536. If the plaintiff abated the nuisance himself, he lost his right to recover damages.

With the coming of equity, the common law action for abatement was supplanted by the mandatory injunction. But the remedy by way of self-help was still available . . .

Ever since the assize of nuisance became available, the courts have confined the remedy by way of self-redress to simple cases such as an overhanging branch, or an encroaching root, which would not justify the expense of legal proceedings, and urgent cases which require an immediate remedy. Thus, it was Bracton's view that where there is resort to self-redress, the remedy should be taken without delay. In *Blackstone's Commentaries on the Laws of England*, Book III, chapter 1, we find:

> And the reason why the law allows this private and summary method of doing one's self justice, is because injuries of this kind, which obstruct or annoy such things as are of daily convenience and use, require an immediate remedy; and cannot wait for the slow progress of the ordinary forms of justice.

The modern textbooks, both here and in other common law jurisdictions, follow the same line: see *Salmond & Heuston on Torts*, 20th ed. (1992) p. 485; *Clerk & Lindsell on Torts*, 16th ed. (1989), p. 36; *Fleming, The Law of Torts*, 7th ed. (1987), p. 415 and *Prosser & Keeton, The Law of Torts*, 4th ed. (1971), p. 641. In *Prosser & Keeton* we find:

> Consequently the privilege [of abatement] must be exercised within a reasonable time after knowledge of the nuisance is acquired or should have been acquired by the person entitled to abate; if there has been sufficient delay to allow resort to legal process, the reason for the privilege fails, and the privilege with it.

The authority cited for this proposition is *Moffett v Brewer* (1848) Iowa 1 Greene 348, 350, where Greene J said:

> This summary method of redressing a grievance, by the act of an injured party, should be regarded with great jealousy, and authorised only in cases of particular emergency, requiring a more speedy remedy than can be had by the ordinary proceedings at law.

Applying this stream of authority to the facts of the present case, it is obvious that it is now far too late for the plaintiff to have her remedy by way of abatement. The garage wall was built in 1975. Not only was there ample time for the plaintiff to 'wait for the slow progress of the ordinary forms of justice;' she actually did so.

But it is not only a question of delay. There is modern House of Lords authority for the proposition that the law does not favour the remedy of abatement: see *Lagan Navigation Co.* v *Lambeg Bleaching, Dyeing and Finishing Co. Ltd* [1927] AC 226, 244, *per* Lord Atkinson.

In my opinion, this never was an appropriate case for self-redress, even if the plaintiff had acted promptly. There was no emergency. There were difficult questions of law and fact to be considered and the remedy by way of self-redress, if it had resulted in the demolition of the garage wall, would have been out of all proportion to the damage suffered by the plaintiff.

But, even if there had ever been a right of self-redress, it ceased when Judge Main refused to grant a mandatory injunction. We are now in a position to answer the question left open by Chitty J in *Lane v Capsey* [1891] 3 Ch 411. Self-redress is a summary remedy, which is justified only in clear and simple cases, or in an emergency. Where a plaintiff has applied for a mandatory injunction and failed, the sole justification for a summary remedy has gone. The court has decided the very point in issue. This is so whether the complaint lies in trespass or nuisance. In the present case, the court has decided that the plaintiff is not entitled to have the wall on her side of the boundary removed. It follows that she has no right to remove it herself.

NOTE

Similar problems arise in relation to trespass to goods, especially in regard to wheel clamping. In *Lloyd* v *DPP* [1992] 1 All ER 982 (a criminal case), the defendant parked his car in a private car park (and so was trespassing) and the car was clamped. He refused to pay the £25 fee and removed his car by cutting two padlocks. He was found guilty of criminal damage. It was said that self help involving the use of force was only available where there was no reasonable alternative, and here the alternative was to pay the fee and sue in the civil courts. But was the use of a wheel clamp by the landowner a reasonable alternative to suing for trespass to land?

So far as civil actions are concerned, the issue is determined by whether the owner willingly accepted the risk of being clamped. In *Vine* v *Waltham Forest LBC* [2000] 4 All ER 169, the claimant was in a distressed state and left her car for three or four minutes in a private car park. The car was clamped and the claimant had to pay £108.68 to retrieve it. The court held that clamping a car is trespass to goods unless the owner consented or willingly accepted the risk. Normally clear signs would be effective, but here there was a finding of fact that the claimant had not seen the notice about clamping, and she was entitled to the return of what she had paid together with damages of £5 for loss of use of the car.

# 24

## Wrongful Interference with Goods

The wrongs in this chapter protect a person's interest in the integrity of his goods, and here there is a connection with both commercial law and contract. For example, many cases which deal with the passing of title in commercial law raise that issue by way of an action for conversion.

Although statute collects the various torts under the generic title 'wrongful interference with goods', in fact the substantive rules of trespass to goods and conversion are hardly affected. Trespass to goods deals with any direct interference with a person's possession, whereas conversion deals with more serious invasions of property rights, so as, in effect, to deprive the claimant of the benefits of ownership.

### TORTS (INTERFERENCE WITH GOODS) ACT 1977

**1. Definition of 'wrongful interference with goods'**

In this Act 'wrongful interference', or 'wrongful interference with goods', means—

    (a) conversion of goods (also called trover),

    (b) trespass to goods,

    (c) 'negligence so far as it results in damage to goods or to an interest in goods,

    (d) 'subject to section 2, any other tort so far as it results in damage to goods or to an interest in goods,

and references in this Act (however worded) to proceedings for wrongful interference or to a claim or right to claim for wrongful interference shall include references to proceedings by virtue of Part I of the Consumer Protection Act 1987 (product liability) in respect of any damages to goods or to an interest in goods or, as the case may be, to a claim or right to claim by virtue of that Part in respect of any such damage.

**2. Abolition of detinue**

    (1) Detinue is abolished.

    (2) An action lies in conversion for loss or destruction of goods which a bailee has allowed to happen in breach of his duty to his bailor (that is to say it lies in a case which is not otherwise conversion, but would have been detinue before detinue was abolished).

**3. Form of judgment where goods are detained**

    (1) In proceedings for wrongful interference against a person who is in possession or in control of the goods relief may be given in accordance with this section, so far as appropriate.

    (2) The relief is—

        (a) an order for delivery of the goods, and for payment of any consequential damages, or

        (b) an order for delivery of the goods, but giving the defendant the alternative of paying damages by reference to the value of the goods, together in either alternative with payment of any consequential damages, or

(c) damages.

(3) Subject to rules of court—

(a) relief shall be given under only one of paragraphs (a), (b) and (c) of subsection (2),

(b) relief under paragraph (a) of subsection (2) is at the discretion of the court, and the claimant may choose between the others.

(4) If it is shown to the satisfaction of the court that an order under subsection (2)(a) has not been complied with, the court may—

(a) revoke the order, or the relevant part of it, and

(b) make an order for payment of damages by reference to the value of the goods.

(5) Where an order is made under subsection (2)(b) the defendant may satisfy the order by returning the goods at any time before execution of judgment, but without prejudice to liability to pay any consequential damages.

(6) An order for delivery of the goods under subsection (2)(a) or (b) may impose such conditions as may be determined by the court, or pursuant to rules of court, and in particular, where damages by reference to the value of the goods would not be the whole of the value of the goods, may require an allowance to be made by the claimant to reflect the difference.

For example, a bailor's action against the bailee may be one in which the measure of damages is not the full value of the goods, and then the court may order delivery of the goods, but require the bailor to pay the bailee a sum reflecting the difference.

(7) Where under subsection (1) or subsection (2) of section 6 an allowance is to be made in respect of an improvement of the goods, and an order is made under subsection (2)(a) or (b), the court may assess the allowance to be made in respect of the improvement, and by the order require, as a condition for delivery of the goods, that allowance to be made by the claimant.

### 5. Extinction of title on satisfaction of claim for damages

(1) Where damages for wrongful interference are, or would fall to be, assessed on the footing that the claimant is being compensated—

(a) for the whole of his interest in the goods, or

(b) for the whole of his interest in the goods subject to a reduction for contributory negligence,

payment of the assessed damages (under all heads), or as the case may be settlement of a claim for damages for the wrong (under all heads), extinguishes the claimant's title to that interest.

### 6. Allowance for improvement of the goods

(1) If in proceedings for wrongful interference against a person (the 'improver') who has improved the goods, it is shown that the improver acted in the mistaken but honest belief that he had a good title to them, an allowance shall be made for the extent to which, at the time as at which the goods fall to be valued in assessing damages, the value of the goods is attributable to the improvement.

(2) If, in proceedings for wrongful interference against a person ('the purchaser') who has purported to purchase the goods—

(a) from the improver, or

(b) where after such a purported sale the goods passed by a further purported sale on one or more occasions, on any such occasion,

it is shown that the purchaser acted in good faith, an allowance shall be made on the principle set out in subsection (1).

For example, where a person in good faith buys a stolen car from the improver and is sued in conversion by the true owner the damages may be reduced to reflect the improvement, but if the person who bought the stolen car from the improver sues the improver for failure of consideration, and the improver acted in good faith, subsection (3) below will ordinarily make a comparable reduction in the damages he recovers from the improver.

(3) If in a case within subsection (2) the person purporting to sell the goods acted in good faith, then in proceedings by the purchaser for recovery of the purchase price because of failure of consideration, or in any other proceedings founded on that failure of consideration, an allowance shall, where appropriate, be made on the principle set out in subsection (1).

(4) This section applies, with the necessary modifications, to a purported bailment or other disposition of goods as it applies to a purported sale of goods.

### 8. Competing rights to the goods

(1) The defendant in an action for wrongful interference shall be entitled to show, in accordance with rules of court, that a third party has a better right than the plaintiff as respects all or any part of the interest claimed by the plaintiff, or in right of which he sues, and any rule of law (sometimes called jus tertii) to the contrary is abolished.

(2) Rules of court relating to proceedings for wrongful interference may—

   (a) require the plaintiff to give particulars of his title,
   (b) require the plaintiff to identify any person who, to his knowledge, has or claims any interest in the goods,
   (c) authorise the defendant to apply for directions as to whether any person should be joined with a view to establishing whether he has a better right than the plaintiff, or has a claim as a result of which the defendant might be doubly liable,
   (d) where a party fails to appear on an application within paragraph (c), or to comply with any direction given by the court on such an application, authorise the court to deprive him of any right of action against the defendant for the wrong either unconditionally, or subject to such terms or conditions as may be specified.

### 11. Minor amendments

(1) Contributory negligence is no defence in proceedings founded on conversion, or on intentional trespass to goods.

(2) Receipt of goods by way of pledge is conversion if the delivery of the goods is conversion.

(3) Denial of title is not of itself conversion.

NOTE

Despite the terms of s. 11, contributory negligence may be pleaded in certain circumstances by a bank which collects payment of a cheque: Banking Act 1979, s. 47.

---

## SECTION 1: TRESPASS TO GOODS AND CONVERSION

### *Fouldes* v *Willoughby*
Court of Exchequer (1841) 8 M&W 540; 151 ER 1153

The defendant operated a steam boat ferry from Birkenhead to Liverpool, and in October 1840 the claimant came on board with two horses. It was said that the claimant behaved improperly, and in order to induce him to go ashore the defendant took hold of his two horses and led them ashore and let them loose on the road. The claimant sued for conversion of the horses. Held: the defendant was not liable for conversion.

LORD ABINGER CB: It is a proposition familiar to all lawyers, that a simple asportation of a chattel, without any intention of making any further use of it, although it may be a sufficient foundation for an action of trespass, is not sufficient to establish a conversion. I had thought that the matter had been fully discussed, and this distinction established, by the numerous cases which have occurred on this subject; but, according to the argument put forward by the plaintiff's counsel today, a bare asportavit is a sufficient foundation to support an action of trover. I entirely dissent from this argument; and therefore I think that the learned Judge was wrong, in telling the jury that the simple fact of putting these horses on shore by the defendant, amounted to a conversion of them to his own use. In my opinion, he should have added to his direction, that it was for them to consider what was the intention of the defendant in so doing. If the object, and whether rightly or wrongfully entertained is immaterial, simply was to induce the plaintiff to go on shore himself, and the defendant, in furtherance of that object, did the act in question, it was not exercising over the horses any right inconsistent with, or adverse to, the rights which the plaintiff had in them. . . . In order to constitute a conversion, it is necessary either that the party taking the goods should intend some use to be made of them, by himself or by those for whom he acts, or that, owing to his act, the goods are destroyed or consumed, to the prejudice of the lawful owner. As an instance of the latter branch of this definition, suppose, in the present case, the defendant had thrown the horses into the water, whereby they were drowned, that would have amounted to an actual conversion; or as in the case cited in the course of the argument, of a person throwing a piece of paper into the water for, in these cases, the chattel is changed in quality, or destroyed altogether. But it has never yet been held, that the single act of removal of a chattel, independent of any claim over it, either in favour of the party himself or any one else, amounts to a conversion of the chattel. In the present case, therefore, the simple removal of these horses by the defendant, for a purpose wholly unconnected with any the least denial of the right of the plaintiff to the possession and enjoyment of them, is no conversion of the horses, and consequently the rule for a new trial ought to be made absolute . . .

NOTE

After the horses were left on the road, they were found to be in the stables of a hotel kept by the defendant's brother. The claimant refused to pay for their keep and they were sold at auction. Presumably it was accepted that their presence at the brother's hotel was mere coincidence, because if it had been the intention of the defendant to deprive the claimant of his horses that would have been conversion. The point is that the defendant was saying the opposite. He was saying simply 'these are your horses, get them and yourself off my ship'. He never intended to exercise any rights over them. Whether he would have been liable for trespass to goods depends on whether his holding of the horses was justified, but that point was not decided.

## SECTION 2: CONVERSION

Conversion is hard to define, but may generally be regarded as an interference with goods which is seriously inconsistent with the claimant's rights over the goods. In other words, have the goods been essentially lost to the claimant? Title to goods is often resolved by an action for conversion, and this may involve complicated questions of commercial law. For example if A's car is bought fraudulently by B who sells it to C, A may sue C in conversion, and the outcome will depend on rules of commercial law as to whether A passed title to B. However, such questions belong more appropriately in courses on commercial law and are not dealt with here. The object of this section is only to give examples of the basic rules of the tort of conversion, which may be committed in a variety of ways, some of which are discussed below.

---

### *Kuwait Airways Corporation* v *Iraqi Airways Company (Nos. 4 & 5)*
House of Lords [2002] AC 883; [2002] 2 WLR 1353; [2002] 3 All ER 209; [2002] UKHL 19

When Iraq invaded Kuwait in August 1990 they seized ten commercial aircraft belonging to Kuwait Airways Corporation (KAC) which were then removed to Iraq. In September the Iraqi government dissolved KAC and transferred all its property to the state-owned Iraqi Airways Co (IAC). KAC sued the Republic of Iraq and IAC, claiming damages of over $800 million. Four of the ten aircraft seized from KAC ('the Mosul Four') were destroyed by coalition bombing. Six aircraft ('the Iran Six') were evacuated by IAC to Iran and were later returned, but KAC had to pay Iran $20 million for the cost of keeping, sheltering and maintaining them. The proceedings involved difficult questions of private and public international law but the actions of IAC were held to be a conversion.

LORD NICHOLLS

**37** ... The relevant tort is conversion. But, so it was submitted, the acts done by IAC post-17 September 1990 did not constitute conversion. IAC did not *take* the aircraft. The aircraft had already been taken from KAC by the government of Iraq in the exercise of sovereign authority, before the crucial date of 17 September 1990. IAC did not *dispose* of the aircraft. KAC does not rely upon the removal of the Iran Six from Baghdad to Iran, which occurred after the issue of the writ on 11 January 1991, as an act of conversion. Nor is this a case of wrongfully *keeping* the aircraft. IAC had possession of the aircraft, but mere unauthorised possession or detention is not an act of conversion. Demand and refusal to deliver up are required, as under the old tort of detinue, which did not occur here. Anyway, such a demand would have been unreal: KAC could not have required delivery other than in Iraq and that would have been impossible.

**38** Nor, it was submitted, do the acts done by IAC after 17 September 1990 suffice, even if they constituted a denial of KAC's title. Denial of title is not of itself conversion: see section 11(3) of the Torts (Interference with Goods) Act 1977. To constitute conversion there must be a concomitant deprivation of use and possession. In support of this submission Mr Donaldson fastened upon a statement in *Clerk & Lindsell on Torts*, 17th ed (1995), p 636, paragraph 13–12:

> conversion is an act of deliberate dealing with a chattel in a manner inconsistent with another's right *whereby that other is deprived of the use and possession of it.* [Emphasis added]

A similar passage appears in Salmond and Heuston on the *Law of Torts*, 21st ed (1996), pages 97–98. In the present case, it was said, none of the acts of IAC deprived KAC of use or possession of the aircraft. Some of IAC's acts were entirely abstract, such as applying for certificates of airworthiness. Even the physical acts, such as repainting or flying the aircraft, had no impact on KAC's possession.

**39** In my view this line of argument was misconceived. I need not repeat the journey through the textbooks and authorities on which your Lordships were taken. Conversion of goods can occur in so many different circumstances that framing a precise definition of universal application is well nigh impossible. In general, the basic features of the tort are threefold. First, the defendant's conduct was inconsistent with the rights of the owner (or other person entitled to possession). Second, the conduct was deliberate, not accidental. Third, the conduct was so extensive an encroachment on the rights of the owner as to exclude him from use and possession of the goods. The contrast is with lesser acts of interference. If these cause damage they may give rise to claims for trespass or in negligence, but they do not constitute conversion.

**40** The judicially approved description of the tort in *Clerk and Lindsell* encapsulates, in different language, these basic ingredients. The flaw in IAC's argument lies in its failure to appreciate what is meant in this context by 'depriving' the owner of possession. This is not to be understood as meaning that the wrongdoer must himself actually take the goods from the possession of the owner. This will often be the case, but not always. It is not so in a case of successive conversions. For the purposes of this tort an owner is equally deprived of possession when he is excluded from possession, or possession is withheld from him by the wrongdoer.

**41** Whether the owner is excluded from possession may sometimes depend upon whether the wrongdoer exercised dominion over the goods. Then the intention with which acts were done may be material. The ferryman who turned the plaintiff's horses off the Birkenhead to Liverpool ferry was guilty of conversion if he intended to exercise dominion over them, but not otherwise: see *Fouldes* v *Willoughby* (1841) 8 M & W 540.

**42** Similarly, mere unauthorised retention of another's goods is not conversion of them. Mere possession of another's goods without title is not necessarily inconsistent with the rights of the owner. To constitute conversion detention must be adverse to the owner, excluding him from the goods. It must be accompanied by an intention to keep the goods. Whether the existence of this intention can properly be inferred depends on the circumstances of the case. A demand and refusal to deliver up the goods are the usual way of proving an intention to keep goods adverse to the owner, but this is not the only way.

**43** Here, on and after 17 September 1990 IAC was in possession and control of the ten aircraft. This possession was adverse to KAC. IAC believed the aircraft were now its property, just as much as the other aircraft in its fleet, and it acted accordingly. It intended to keep the goods as its own. It treated them as its own. It made such use of them as it could in the prevailing circumstances, although this was very limited because of the hostilities. In so conducting itself IAC was asserting rights inconsistent with KAC's rights as owner. This assertion was evidenced in several ways. In particular, in September 1990 the board of IAC passed a resolution to the effect that all aircraft belonging to the (dissolved) KAC should be registered in the name of IAC and that a number of ancillary steps should be taken in relation to the aircraft. In respect of nine aircraft IAC then applied to the Iraqi Directorate of Air Safety for certificates of airworthiness and reregistration in IAC's name. IAC effected insurance cover in respect of five aircraft, and a further four after the issue of the writ. Six of the aircraft were overpainted in IAC's livery. IAC used one aircraft on internal commercial flights between Baghdad and Basra and for training flights. The two Boeing 767s were flown from Basra to Mosul in mid-November 1990.

**44** Mance J concluded that in these circumstances IAC had wrongfully interfered with all ten aircraft. In the Court of Appeal Brooke LJ said, at p 1146, paragraph 74:

> The board resolution makes it completely clear that as soon as RCC resolution 369 came into effect IAC resolved to treat these ten aircraft as their own and to exercise dominion over them in denial of KAC's rights, and this continuing usurpation and conversion of KAC's aircraft subsisted right up to the issue of the writ in this action by which KAC demanded the return of all these aircraft.

I agree. IAC's acts would have been tortious if done in this country.

**77** I turn therefore to consider the purpose sought to be achieved by the tort of conversion. Conversion is the principal means whereby English law protects the ownership of goods. Misappropriation of another's goods constitutes conversion. Committing this tort gives rise to an obligation to pay damages. Payment of damages may have proprietary consequences. Payment of damages assessed on the footing that the plaintiff is being compensated for the whole of his interest in the goods extinguishes his title: see section 5 of the Torts (Interference with Goods) Act 1977. Further, when the defendant is in possession of the plaintiff's goods the remedies available to the plaintiff include a court order that the goods be delivered up: see section 3.

**78** Consistently with its purpose of providing a remedy for the misappropriation of goods, liability is strict. As Diplock LJ said in *Marfani & Co Ltd* v *Midland Bank Ltd* [1968] 1 WLR 956, 970–971, one's duty to one's neighbour is to refrain from doing any voluntary act in relation to his goods which is a usurpation of his property or possessory rights in them. Whether the defendant still has the goods or their proceeds matters not. Nor does it matter whether the defendant was a thief or acted in the genuine and reasonable belief the goods were his. Baron Cleasby's aphorism, uttered in 1872 in *Fowler* v *Hollins* LR 7 QB 616, 639, still represents the law: 'persons deal with the property in chattels or exercise acts of ownership over them at their peril'. This, he observed, was regarded as a salutary rule for the protection of property.

**79** Some aspects of this rule have attracted criticism. Vindication of a plaintiff's proprietary interests requires that, in general, all those who convert his goods should be accountable for *benefits* they receive. They must make restitution to the extent they are unjustly enriched. The goods are his, and he is entitled to reclaim them and any benefits others have derived from them. Liability in this regard should be strict subject to defences available to restitutionary claims such as change of position: see *Lipkin Gorman* v *Karpnale Ltd* [1991] 2 AC 548. Additionally, those who act dishonestly should be liable to make good any *losses* caused by their wrongful conduct. Whether those who act innocently should also be liable to make good the plaintiff's losses is a different matter. A radical re-appraisal of the tort of conversion along these lines was not pursued on these appeals. So I shall say nothing more about it.

**80** The existing principle of strict liability as described above is deeply ingrained in the common law. It has survived at least since the days of Lord Mansfield in *Cooper* v *Chitty* (1756) 1 Burr 20. The hardship it may cause to those who deal innocently with a person in possession of goods has long been recognised. Blackburn J noted this in the leading case of *Hollins* v *Fowler* (1875) LR 7 HL 757, 764. The hardship arises especially for innocent persons who no longer have the goods. There has been some statutory amelioration of the principle, in the Factors Acts and elsewhere, but in general the principle endures.

**81** Consistently with this principle, every person through whose hands goods pass in a series of conversions is himself guilty of conversion and liable to the owner for the loss caused by his misappropriation of the owner's goods. His liability is not diminished by reason, for instance, of his having acquired the goods from a thief as distinct from the owner himself. In such a case, it may be said, looking at the successive conversions overall, the owner is no worse off as a result of the acts of the person who acquired the goods from the thief. Such a person has not 'caused' the owner any additional loss.

**82** In one sense this is undoubtedly correct. The owner had already lost his goods. But that is really nothing to the point for the purposes of assessing damages for conversion. By definition, each person in a series of conversions wrongfully excludes the owner from possession of his goods. This is the basis on which each is liable to the owner. That is the nature of the tort of conversion. The wrongful acts of a previous possessor do not therefore diminish the plaintiff's claim in respect of the wrongful acts of a later possessor. Nor, for a different reason, is it anything to the point that, absent the defendant's conversion, someone else would wrongfully have converted the goods. The likelihood that, had the defendant not wronged the plaintiff, somebody would have done so is no reason for diminishing the defendant's liability and responsibility for the loss he brought upon the plaintiff.

NOTES

1. This case contains a useful summary of the principles of conversion but also deals with some interesting points. The defendants were liable as 'successive' converters as everybody in the chain can be liable even if their acts are done in good faith. So if A steals goods and sells them to B who sells to C, then A, B and C are all liable to the true owner (see *Hollins* v *Fowler*, below).

2. Lord Nicholls also said that in relation to *consequential* losses, a converter who acted in good faith is only liable for types of damage that can be expected to arise from the wrongful conduct (i.e. the type of damage must be foreseeable). But where a person *knowingly* converts another's goods he is liable for all damage flowing 'directly and naturally' from the wrongful act. Accordingly, IAC were liable for the cost of payments to Iran to recover the 'Iran Six' and for the cost of chartering substitute aircraft and for loss of profits.

3. One interesting point arose in relation to the 'Mosul Four'. It was found that these aircraft would have been destroyed anyway by coalition bombing even if they had not been seized by Iraq. Hence, under the 'but for' test (for which see Chapter 6) the defendants were not liable for the loss as it would have occurred anyway even without their wrongdoing. In relation to the 'Iran Six' it was found that they would not have been bombed as they were not wanted by Iraq and would have been parked out of the way of allied bombing.

4. The action began on 11 January 1991 and was still going on in 2005.

# A: Withholding possession

### *Perry* v *British Railways Board*
Chancery Division [1980] ICR 743; [1980] 1 WLR 13; [1980] 2 All ER 579

In 1980 there was a strike by steelworkers which was supported by members of the National Union of Railwaymen. The claimants were steel stockholders who owned 500 tons of steel which was lying in British Rail depots. For fear of exacerbating industrial relations, British Rail, while admitting that the steel belonged to the claimants, refused to give it up. Held: the defendants were liable for conversion.

MEGARRY V-C: The main thrust of Mr Gidley Scott's contentions was that as a mere refusal in response to a demand was not itself a conversion, though it could be evidence of a conversion (see *Clerk & Lindsell on Torts*, p. 678), and the defendants had at no stage denied the plaintiffs' title to the steel, or attempted to deal with it in any way inconsistent with the plaintiffs' rights, there had been no conversion within the true meaning of that term. There was no conversion, he said, if the reason for the refusal to release the goods was a genuine or reasonable fear, unless this meant that the owner could never have his goods. He accepted that there could be a conversion if the threat induced a withholding of the goods for a long period, measured in months or years, but not if it was merely a matter of days or week; and he said that the present case fell into this latter category, though he could not be persuaded to prophesy when the strike of steel workers would end. This contention was based to some extent, I think, on words of Bramwell B in *Hiort* v *Bott* (1874) LR 9 Ex 86, 89. The judge there said that a good description of what constituted a conversion was 'where a man does an unauthorized act which deprives another of his property permanently or for an indefinite time'; and I think that Mr Gidley Scott interpreted 'indefinite time' as meaning a period which was not only uncertain in length but also of substantial duration.

There seems to me to be considerable force in the observation in *Clerk & Lindsell on Torts*, p. 682 that 'It is perhaps impossible to frame a definition which will cover every conceivable case.' What I have to consider here is a case in which the defendants are in effect saying to the plaintiffs: 'We admit that the steel is yours and that you are entitled to possession of it. Yet because we fear that industrial action may be taken against us if we permit you to remove it, we have refused to allow you to collect it for some weeks now, despite your demands, and we will continue to refuse to allow you to collect it until our fears have been removed.' Looking at the matter as one of principle, I would conclude that this is a clear case of conversion. The defendants are denying the plaintiffs most of the rights of ownership, including the right to possession, for a period which clearly is indefinite. It may be short, or it may be long; but it is plainly uncertain. I do not think that a period which will not end until the defendants reach the conclusion that their fears no longer justify the withholding of the steel can very well be called 'definite.' There is a detention of the steel which is consciously adverse to the plaintiffs' rights, and this seems to me to be of the essence of at least one form of conversion. A denial of possession to the plaintiffs does not cease to be a denial by being accompanied by a statement that the plaintiffs are entitled to the possession that is being denied to them.

My conclusion is accordingly that this contention of the defendants fails. For the defendants to withhold the steel from the plaintiffs is a wrongful interference with goods within the Act of 1977 unless the reason for the withholding provides a justification. I cannot see that it does. This is no brief withholding made merely in order that the defendants may verify the plaintiffs' title to the steel, or for some other purpose to confirm that the delivery of the steel would be proper. This is a withholding despite the plain right of the plaintiffs to the ownership and possession of the steel, on the ground that the defendants fear unpleasant consequences if they do not deny the plaintiffs what they are entitled to.

NOTES
1. Following the order some of the steel was loaded onto British Rail lorries and taken to the claimants' premises. However, the steel was never delivered as there was not only a

picket of steelworkers but also members of the Transport and General Workers Union said that they would not unload the steel, which in the event was returned to the British Rail depots.

2. It is not a tort merely to be in possession of another's goods, for there may be many lawful reasons for possession. The usual way of establishing a conversion is by a 'demand and refusal', i.e. a demand by the owner for delivery and a refusal by the possessor. The point of *Perry* is that it is still a conversion if the possessor refuses to deliver even if he admits the owner's title.

# B: Wrongful disposition

### *Hollins* v *Fowler*

House of Lords (1875) LR 7 HL 757; 44 LJQB 169; 33 LT 73

Fowler & Co., the claimants, sold 13 bales of cotton to H. K. Bayley for a shilling a pound. Bayley never paid Fowler, but sold the cotton to the defendants Hollins & Co., for 11d. per pound, and they sold it on to Micholls & Co. who spun it into yarn. Thus, due to the fraud of Bayley the value of the cotton had been abstracted, and the question was which of two innocent parties (the person who sold the cotton to the rogue or the person who bought it from him) should bear the loss. Held: dismissing the appeal, that the defendants (the buyers) were liable for conversion.

LORD CHELMSFORD: The question upon the facts is whether the Defendants were guilty of a conversion. There can be no doubt that the property and legal right of possession of the cotton remained in the Plaintiffs; and *Bayley*, who had fraudulently obtained possession of it, could not give a title to any one to whom he transferred the possession, however ignorant the transferee might be of the means by which *Bayley* acquired it. A great deal of argument was directed to the question, What amounts in law to a conversion? I agree with what was said by Mr Justice *Brett* in the Court of Exchequer Chamber in this case: 'That in all cases where we have to apply legal principles to facts there are found many cases about which there can be no doubt, some being clear for the Plaintiff and some clear for the Defendant; and that the difficulties arise in doubtful cases on the border line between the two.' But to my mind the proposition which fits this case is, that any person who, however innocently, obtains possession of the goods of a person who has been fraudulently deprived of them, and disposes of them, whether for his own benefit or that of any other person, is guilty of a conversion.

LORD O'HAGAN: The result of your Lordships' consideration of this case will, I fear, inflict hardship upon the Defendants. They are innocent of any actual wrongdoing, but those with whom they are in conflict are as innocent as they, and we can only regard the liability attached to them by the law, without being affected in our judgment by its unpleasant consequences. They appear to me to have been guilty of a conversion in dealing with the Plaintiffs' property, and disposing of it to other persons, without any right or authority to do so. Confessedly, that property never passed from the Plaintiffs. *Bayley's* fraud vitiated the sale to him, and he could not convey to the Defendants what in no way belonged to himself. They paid for it, and sampled it, and then disposed of it to Mr *Micholls*, whom they reasonably expected to make the purchase, but who had not made it, and was not bound to make it, when the void sale was effected with *Bayley*, and the Defendants got possession of the Plaintiffs' cotton. They had it conveyed to the railway station and forwarded to the purchaser in *Stockport*, who paid for it and made yarn of it. It seems to me that this state of facts entitles the Plaintiffs to recover in an action of trover, which rests on a right of property, wrongfully interfered with, at the peril of the person interfering with it, and whether the interference be for his own use or that of anybody else.

NOTES

1. In *Bishopsgate Motor Finance Corp.* v *Transport Brakes Ltd* [1949] 1 KB 332, Denning LJ said:

> In the development of our law, two principles have striven for mastery. The first is for the protection of property; no one can give a better title than he himself possesses. The second is for the protection of commercial transactions: the person who takes in good faith and for value without notice should get a better title. The first principle has held sway for a long time, but it has been modified by the common law itself and by statute so as to meet the needs of our times.

2. A 'ministerial' act will not amount to conversion under the *Hollins* v *Fowler* principle. In *Marcq* v *Christie Manson and Woods Ltd* [2003] 3 All ER 561 the claimant was the true owner of a painting which had been stolen in 1979 and which years later was sent for auction by one S. The painting was not sold and the defendants returned it to S. While it is clear that an auctioneer who *sells* goods is liable for conversion, here the defendants were not liable as they had merely changed the position of the goods and not the property in them—it was only a 'ministerial' act. Simple receipt and re-delivery of goods in good faith and without notice of any adverse claim is not a conversion.

3. There have been a number of exceptions to the principle enunciated in *Hollins* v *Fowler* and these more properly belong to a course on commercial law. See, for example, Sale of Goods Act 1979, ss. 24 and 25 (sale by a buyer in possession with the consent of the seller, and sale by a seller in possession with the consent of the buyer). Also see Hire Purchase Act 1964, s. 27 (see Consumer Credit Act 1974, Sch. 4), which allows a person who sells a car in breach of a hire purchase agreement to give a good title to a private purchaser who acquires the car in good faith.

4. *Limitation periods.* Where there are successive conversions the owner must sue within six years of the *first* conversion. However, where the goods are stolen the thief can always be sued, as can any subsequent possessor except a bona fide purchaser for value, who must be sued within six years of his purchase (Limitation Act 1980, ss. 3 and 4). For an example see *Gotha City* v *Sotheby's* The Times, 8 October 1998, where a painting owned by the Saxe-Coburg-Gotha family was stolen by the Russians in 1946 and consigned for sale in 1989 by Cobert Finance Co. who did not claim that they were bona fide purchasers. It was held that the City was entitled to the painting.

■ QUESTION

In *Hollins* v *Fowler*, how did the rogue get away with the fraud? Who could have prevented it, and who should take the risk? A sells a car to a rogue, B, and accepts a cheque in payment which turns out to be worthless. B sells the car to C. How could the loss have been prevented? Who will bear the loss under the present law, and should it be changed? See *Shogun Finance* v *Hudson* [2004] 1 All ER 215 where the risk was placed on the buyer.

## C: Finders: finder *v* occupier

### *Parker* v *British Airways*
[1982] QB 1004; [1982] 2 WLR 50; [1982] 1 All ER 834

The defendants operated an 'executive' lounge at Heathrow Airport to which only holders of first class tickets or members of the Executive Club were admitted. While in this lounge the claimant found on the floor a gold bracelet which he handed to an official of the airline together with his name and address. When the true owner could not be found the defendants sold the bracelet for £850, but refused to pay the proceeds to the claimant. Held: dismissing the appeal, that the defendants were liable for conversion.

DONALDSON LJ: One of the great merits of the common law is that it is usually sufficiently flexible to take account of the changing needs of a continually changing society. Accordingly, Mr Desch rightly directed our attention to the need to have common law rules which will facilitate rather than hinder the ascertainment of the true owner of a lost chattel and a reunion between the two. In his submission the law should confer rights upon the occupier of the land where a lost chattel was found which were superior to those of the finder, since the loser is more likely to make inquiries at the place of loss. I see the force of this submission. However, I think that it is also true that if this were the rule and finders had no prospect of any reward, they would be tempted to pass by without taking any action or to become concealed keepers of articles which they found. Furthermore, if a finder is under a duty to take reasonable steps to reunite the true owner with his lost property, this will usually involve an obligation to inform the occupier of the land of the fact that the article has been found and where it is to be kept.

In a dispute of this nature there are two quite separate problems. The first is to determine the general principles or rules of law which are applicable. The second, which is often the more troublesome, is to apply those principles or rules to the factual situation. I propose to confront those two problems separately.

*Rights and obligations of the finder*

1. The finder of a chattel acquires no rights over it unless (a) it has been abandoned or lost and (b) he takes it into his care and control.
2. The finder of a chattel acquires very limited rights over it if he takes it into his care and control with dishonest intent or in the course of trespassing.
3. Subject to the foregoing and to point 4 below, a finder of a chattel, whilst not acquiring any absolute property or ownership in the chattel, acquires a right to keep it against all but the true owner or those in a position to claim through the true owner or one who can assert a prior right to keep the chattel which was subsisting at the time when the finder took the chattel into his care and control.
4. Unless otherwise agreed, any servant or agent who finds a chattel in the course of his employment or agency and not wholly incidentally or collaterally thereto and who takes it into his care and control does so on behalf of his employer or principal who acquires a finder's right to the exclusion of those of the actual finder.
5. A person having a finder's rights has an obligation to take such measures as in all the circumstances are reasonable to acquaint the true owner of the finding and present whereabouts of the chattel and to care for it meanwhile.

*Rights and liabilities of an occupier*

1. An occupier of land has rights superior to those of a finder over chattels in or attached to that land and an occupier of a building has similar rights in respect of chattels attached to that building, whether in either case the occupier is aware of the presence of the chattel.
2. An occupier of a building has rights superior to those of a finder over chattels upon or in, but not attached to, that building if, but only if, before the chattel is found, he has manifested an intention to exercise control over the building and the things which may be upon it or in it.
3. An occupier who manifests an intention to exercise control over a building and the things which may be upon or in it so as to acquire rights superior to those of a finder is under an obligation to take such measures as in all the circumstances are reasonable to ensure that lost chattels are found and, upon their being found, whether by him or by a third party, to acquaint the true owner of the finding and to care for the chattels meanwhile. The manifestation of intention may be express or implied from the circumstances including, in particular, the

circumstance that the occupier manifestly accepts or is obliged by law to accept liability for chattels lost upon his 'premises,' e.g., an innkeeper or carrier's liability.

4. An 'occupier' of a chattel, e.g., a ship, motor car, caravan or aircraft, is to be treated as if he were the occupier of a building for the purposes of the foregoing rules.

*Application to the instant case*

The plaintiff was not a trespasser in the executive lounge and, in taking the bracelet into his care and control, he was acting with obvious honesty. Prima facie, therefore, he had a full finder's rights and obligations. He in fact discharged those obligations by handing the bracelet to an official of the defendants, although he could equally have done so by handing the bracelet to the police or in other ways such as informing the police of the find and himself caring for the bracelet.

The plaintiff's prima facie entitlement to a finder's rights was not displaced in favour of an employer or principal. There is no evidence that he was in the executive lounge in the course of any employment or agency and, if he was, the finding of the bracelet was quite clearly collateral thereto. The position would have been otherwise in the case of most or perhaps all the defendants' employees.

The defendants, for their part, cannot assert any title to the bracelet based upon the rights of an occupier over chattels attached to a building. The bracelet was lying loose on the floor. Their claim must, on my view of the law, be based upon a manifest intention to exercise control over the lounge and all things which might be in it. The evidence is that they claimed the right to decide who should and who should not be permitted to enter and use the lounge, but their control was in general exercised upon the basis of classes or categories of user and the availability of the lounge in the light of the need to clean and maintain it. I do not doubt that they also claimed the right to exclude individual undesirables, such as drunks, and specific types of chattels such as guns and bombs. But this control has no real relevance to a manifest intention to assert custody and control over lost articles. There was no evidence that they searched for such articles regularly or at all.

Evidence was given of staff instructions which govern the action to be taken by employees of the defendants if they found lost articles or lost chattels were handed to them. But these instructions were not published to users of the lounge and in any event I think that they were intended to do no more than instruct the staff on how they were to act in the course of their employment.

It was suggested in argument that in some circumstances the intention of the occupier to assert control over articles lost on his premises speaks for itself. I think that this is right. If a bank manager saw fit to show me round a vault containing safe deposits and I found a gold bracelet on the floor, I should have no doubt that the bank had a better title than I, and the reason is the manifest intention to exercise a very high degree of control. At the other extreme is the park to which the public has unrestricted access during daylight hours. During those hours there is no manifest intention to exercise any such control. In between these extremes are the forecourts of petrol filling stations, unfenced front gardens of private houses, the public parts of shops and supermarkets as part of an almost infinite variety of land, premises and circumstances.

This lounge is in the middle band and in my judgment, on the evidence available, there was no sufficient manifestation of any intention to exercise control over lost property before it was found such as would give the defendants a right superior to that of the plaintiff or indeed any right over the bracelet. As the true owner has never come forward, it is a case of 'finders keepers.'

NOTES

1. What matters is control over the building and its contents. In *Parker* the result meant that although the airline controlled the premises they did not control the chattels within them — that is a matter of deduction from the facts. However, in the case of private domestic premises it may be presumed that the occupier intends to exert control over all the goods on the premises even if he does not know of the existence of the particular item in question. See *Flack* v *National Crime Authority* (1997) 150 ALR 153.

2. *Articles attached to or under land. Waverley Borough Council* v *Fletcher* [1995] 4 All ER 756 has reaffirmed the well-known principle that where an article is attached to land or is under the

soil, the occupier has the better title, and this is so even if the land is public open space. In that case the respondent used a metal detector to find a valuable medieval gold brooch some 9 inches under the soil, and it was held that even though it was a public park the local authority, as occupier, had the better title.

3. *Owner* v *Finder*. Where the dispute is between the true owner of the chattel and the finder, the true owner will always win. The only problem is usually to determine whether in fact the claimant is the true owner or whether, for example, he has abandoned the goods. For example, in *Moffat* v *Kazana* [1969] 2 QB 152 the claimant had owned a house in which he had hidden (in the chimney) a biscuit tin containing £1,987 in £1 notes. When he sold the house the claimant failed to take the tin with him and it was later discovered by the defendants. It was held that the conveyance of the house did not transfer title to the biscuit tin and therefore the claimant was still the true owner.

   If a golf ball is lost has it been abandoned? Is it conversion for (a) a trespasser, or (b) another golfer to pick up and keep a lost ball? If so, against whom? See *Hibbert* v *McKiernan* [1948] 2 KB 142.

4. *Finder* v *Stranger*. Title is relative and therefore the winner will be the person who can establish the earlier possession. Thus, in a dispute between a finder and a person who subsequently obtains possession, the finder will win. (But note that under the Torts Act 1977, s. 8 a defendant can now say, 'it may not be mine, but it's not yours either'.) See *Armory* v *Delamirie* (1721) 93 ER 664, where the claimant was a chimney sweep's boy who found a jewel: he showed it to the defendant who was a goldsmith's apprentice. The apprentice refused to return the jewel and he was liable for conversion. Pratt CJ said 'The finder of a jewel, though he does not by such finding acquire an absolute property or ownership, yet he has such a property as will enable him to keep it against all but the rightful owner, and consequently may maintain trover.' For a modern example of this principle see *Costello* v *Chief Constable of Derbyshire* [2001] 1 WLR 1437, where the police seized a car in the possession of the claimant which they believed to have been stolen. The true owner of the car could not be traced and when the powers to retain the car under the Police and Criminal Evidence Act 1984 ceased they refused to return the car. The claimant was entitled to the car as 'possession' means the same whether it has been obtained lawfully or not. Thus, a thief is protected against someone who takes from him, at least until someone with a better right to possession is identified.

5. *Treasure*. The Treasure Act 1996 abolishes treasure trove and replaces it by a new system whereby treasure is: (a) any object (other than a coin) which is at least 300 years old and has a gold or silver content of at least 10 per cent; (b) one of at least two coins in the same find at least 300 years old and with a silver or gold content of at least 10 per cent; (c) one of at least 10 coins in the same find at least 300 years old; (d) any object at least 200 years old of a class designated by the Secretary of State as being of outstanding historical, archaeological or cultural importance.

   The decision whether an object is treasure is made by a coroner and, if it is, it vests (subject to any prior rights) in the Crown. A reward is payable to the finder, the occupier or any other person with an interest in the land, and the amount of the total reward and the proportion payable to each is to be determined by the Secretary of State.

# 25

# Defamation

The law of defamation is at last undergoing change. For many years it was subjected to considerable criticism, especially in relation to the size of damages awards. The law was considered by the Faulks Committee in 1975 (Cmnd 5709) but nothing was done to reform it. However, in 1991 the courts themselves took steps to deal with the damages problem and the Defamation Act 1996 introduces a number of significant reforms. None of the reforms addresses fundamental issues and it may be that questions need to be asked about the extent to which the law should protect reputation itself in the absence of any provable economic loss flowing from the tort, and about the extent to which the law inhibits the exposure of wrongdoing.

A further criticism of defamation is its highly technical nature, and especially the great importance and complexity of the pleadings, which often look as if the nineteenth-century reforms of procedure never happened. For this reason it is sometimes difficult to select suitable cases to illustrate the law, for so often the judgments concentrate on procedure. This chapter omits statutes and cases on the distinction between libel and slander and on absolute privilege, in order to keep its length within reasonable bounds.

The Human Rights Act 1998 (incorporating the European Convention on Human Rights) is becoming increasingly important in defamation and in the protection of privacy (see Chapter 26). The task here is to balance freedom of speech with the interests of an individual in the protection of his reputation, and this is relevant not only for who can sue (section 1) and for what is defamatory (section 3) but also for qualified privilege (section 8).

## EUROPEAN CONVENTION FOR THE PROTECTION OF HUMAN RIGHTS AND FUNDAMENTAL FREEDOMS

### Article 9

Freedom of thought, conscience and religion

1. Everyone has the right to freedom of thought, conscience and religion; this right includes freedom to change his religion or belief and freedom, either alone or in community with others and in public or private, to manifest his religion or belief, in worship, teaching, practice and observance.

2. Freedom to manifest one's religion or beliefs shall be subject only to such limitations as are prescribed by law and are necessary in a democratic society in the interests of public safety, for the protection of public order, health or morals, or for the protection of the rights and freedoms of others.

*Article 10*

Freedom of expression

1. Everyone has the right to freedom of expression. This right shall include freedom to hold opinions and to receive and impart information and ideas without interference by public authority and regardless of frontiers. This Article shall not prevent States from requiring the licensing of broadcasting, television or cinema enterprises.

2. The exercise of these freedoms, since it carries with it duties and responsibilities, may be subject to such formalities, conditions, restrictions or penalties as are prescribed by law and are necessary in a democratic society, in the interests of national security, territorial integrity or public safety, for the prevention of disorder or crime, for the protection of health or morals, for the protection of the reputation or rights of others, for preventing the disclosure of information received in confidence, or for maintaining the authority and impartiality of the judiciary.

## HUMAN RIGHTS ACT 1998

### 12. Freedom of expression

(1) This section applies if a court is considering whether to grant any relief which, if granted, might affect the exercise of the Convention right to freedom of expression.

(2) If the person against whom the application for relief is made ('the respondent') is neither present nor represented, no such relief is to be granted unless the court is satisfied—

    (a) that the applicant has taken all practicable steps to notify the respondent; or

    (b) that there are compelling reasons why the respondent should not be notified.

(3) No such relief is to be granted so as to restrain publication before trial unless the court is satisfied that the applicant is likely to establish that publication should not be allowed.

(4) The court must have particular regard to the importance of the Convention right to freedom of expression and, where the proceedings relate to material which the respondent claims, or which appears to the court, to be journalistic, literary or artistic material (or to conduct connected with such material), to—

    (a) the extent to which—

        (i)   the material has, or is about to, become available to the public; or

        (ii)  it is, or would be, in the public interest for the material to be published;

    (b) any relevant privacy code.

(5) In this section—

'court' includes a tribunal; and

'relief' includes any remedy or order (other than in criminal proceedings).

### 13. Freedom of thought, conscience and religion

(1) If a court's determination of any question arising under this Act might affect the exercise by a religious organisation (itself or its members collectively) of the Convention right to freedom of thought, conscience and religion, it must have particular regard to the importance of that right.

(2) In this section 'court' includes a tribunal.

## SECTION 1: WHO CAN SUE?

Individuals can sue for the protection of their reputation, as can corporations because they too have reputations to protect. However the question has arisen whether public bodies and political parties are in the same position.

---

### *Derbyshire CC* v *Times Newspapers*
Court of Appeal [1992] QB 770; [1992] 3 WLR 28; [1992] 3 All ER 65

The defendants published an article questioning the propriety of certain investments made by the Council of money in its superannuation fund. The Council
claimed that it had been injured in its credit and reputation and had been brought
into public contempt. This raised the question whether a local authority could
claim for libel in respect of its administrative or governing reputation. Held: the
local authority could not sue.

BUTLER-SLOSS LJ: . . . The European Court of Human Rights has considered the application of
article 10 to contempt of court in *The Sunday Times* v *United Kingdom* (1979) 2 EHRR 245; to criminal
defamation in *Lingens* v *Austria* (1986) 8 EHRR 407 and to breach of confidential information in *The
Sunday Times* v *United Kingdom (No. 2)* (1991) 14 EHRR 229. In each case the court considered
whether the interference complained of was necessary in a democratic society. In the *Lingens* case it
said, at p. 418:

> 39. The adjective 'necessary,' within the meaning of article 10(2), implies the existence of a
> 'pressing social need'. . . . The contracting states have a certain margin of appreciation
> in assessing whether such a need exists . . . but it goes hand in hand with a European
> supervision, embracing both the legislation and the decisions applying it, even those given by
> an independent court. . . . 40. . . . The court must determine whether the interference at
> issue was 'proportionate to the legitimate aim pursued' and whether the reasons adduced by
> the Austrian courts to justify it are 'relevant and sufficient'. . . . 41. In this connection, the
> court has to recall that freedom of expression, as secured in paragraph 1 of article 10,
> constitutes one of the essential foundations of a democratic society and one of the basic
> conditions for its progress and for each individual's self-fulfilment. Subject to paragraph 2, it is
> applicable not only to 'information' or 'ideas' that are favourably received or regarded as
> inoffensive or as a matter of indifference, but also to those that offend, shock or disturb. Such
> are the demands of that pluralism, tolerance and broadmindedness without which there is no
> 'democratic society'. . . . These principles are of particular importance as far as the press is
> concerned. Whilst the press must not overstep the bounds set, inter alia, for the 'protection
> of the reputation of others', it is nevertheless incumbent on it to impart information and ideas
> on political issues just as on those in other areas of public interest. Not only does the press
> have the task of imparting such information and ideas: the public also has a right to receive
> them. . . .

. . .

   I also believe that the application of article 10 to local authorities is right in principle. A local
authority is a corporation. It is also an elected body, elected in local elections and often run in council
on party political lines, as is this council. Elected councillors are politicians in the public domain. They
are and expect to be exposed to criticism and comment from many quarters within their sphere of
activity. Such comment may, and no doubt does, from time to time overstep boundaries acceptable
to the individual or local authority so criticised. Although this appeal is only the third case ever
brought by a local authority to come before the courts, not only are there numerous local
authorities, we were also provided with a list of government departments which happen to be
bodies corporate and would, on the argument of Mr Newman for the council, equally have the right
to sue for libel. In *The Sunday Times* v *United Kingdom (No. 2)*, 14 EHRR 229, 241 the European Court
of Human Rights, following its decision in *Lingens* (1986) 8 EHRR 407, set out the principles enshrined
in article 10:

> (a) . . . Freedom of expression, as enshrined in article 10, is subject to a number of exceptions
> which, however, must be narrowly interpreted and the necessity for any restrictions must be
> convincingly established. (b) . . . Not only does the press have the task of imparting such

information and ideas: the public also has a right to receive them. Were it otherwise, the press would be unable to play its vital role of 'public watchdog'.

. . .

Before turning to the competing interests and engaging in the balancing exercise, it is necessary to consider who is the public authority who may be seen to be exercising the interference referred to in article 10(1). Mr Newman has urged us to treat the Derbyshire County Council as the public authority and leave it to the court in each individual libel action to undertake the balancing exercise of the competing interests. It is true that the Derbyshire County Council is a public authority and it is engaged in an attempt to discourage a national newspaper from critical comment about its affairs by an action for damages. But Mr Lester raises a more fundamental argument, with which I agree, that the effect of this court declaring the law in such a way as to enable the local authority to sue in libel, would be interference by a judicial authority with the right of freedom of expression of the press. Such a judicial interference is unacceptable unless it falls within the exceptions set out in article 10(2), which are to be narrowly interpreted and the necessity for any restrictions convincingly established. This issue involves a question of principle as to whether a local authority can sue for libel and not a decision to be made in respect of each individual action.

This court has to balance the competing interests of the freedom of the press to provide information, to comment, criticise, offend, shock or disturb, against the right of a governmental corporation to be protected against the false, or seriously inaccurate, or unjust accounts of its activities. I have already set out the dangers of allowing a governmental authority to have the right to sue. But in doing the balancing act it is necessary also to consider whether an injustice will be perpetrated if a local authority does not have the right to protect its governing reputation by an action for libel, and whether such an action, if available to a local authority, would be proportionate to the legitimate aim pursued. If a local authority was unable to sue in libel it would not, however, be without recourse to the courts. There seem to me to be three possible remedies: (1) an action for malicious falsehood; (2) a prosecution, with leave of the judge for criminal libel; and (3) an action for libel by an individual within the local authority.

. . .

In my view, the existing available protection is adequate and gives to a governmental body all such rights as are necessary in a democratic society for the protection of its governing reputation. To give it more would be out of proportion to the need shown and would entail too high a risk of unjustifiable interference with the freedom of expression of the press and public. In carrying out the balancing exercise I, for my part, come down in favour of the freedom of speech even though it may go beyond generally acceptable limits, since there is adequate alternative protection available to a council.

. . .

NOTES
1. This decision was affirmed by the House of Lords without recourse to the European Convention: [1993] AC 534.
2. For decisions of the European Court of Justice on Article 10 of the Convention, see *Lingens v Austria* (1986) 8 EHRR 407; *Oberschlick v Austria* (1991) 19 EHRR 389; *Goodwin v United Kingdom* (1996) 22 EHRR 123; *De Haes and Gijsels v Belgium* (1998) 25 EHRR 1.
3. The *Derbyshire* principle has now been extended to political parties. In *Goldsmith v Bhoyrul* [1998] 2 WLR 435 it was held that the Referendum Party was unable to bring an action for defamation. Buckley J said that 'the public interest in free speech and criticism in respect of those bodies putting themselves forward for office or to govern is also sufficiently strong to justify withholding the right to sue . . .'.
4. The *Derbyshire* case also affirms that a trading corporation may sue for libel: see *South Hetton Coal Co.* v *North Eastern News Association* [1894] 1 QB 133. However, for technical reasons a trade union cannot sue: *EETPU v The Times* [1980] QB 585.

## SECTION 2: WHO CAN BE LIABLE?

At common law any person who distributes a defamatory statement could be liable, and this includes not only the author but also the printer, the publisher, the wholesaler and the retailer, even if they were unaware that the statement was defarnatory. To some extent this extreme position was ameliorated by the Defamation Act 1952, s. 4 (innocent dissemination), but the provision was limited, complicated and generally regarded as unsatisfactory. This was especially so in the light of new technology both in printing (direct input) and electronic forms of communication. Accordingly, the Defamation Act 1996 provides a defence for those other than authors, editors or publishers who are only involved in distribution of material so long as they have shown reasonable care. It is also very significant for providers of access to electronic systems of communication.

### DEFAMATION ACT 1996

**1.**—(1) In defamation proceedings a person has a defence if he shows that—

(a) he was not the author, editor or publisher of the statement complained of,

(b) he took reasonable care in relation to its publication, and

(c) he did not know, and had no reason to believe, that what he did caused or contributed to the publication of a defamatory statement.

(2) For this purpose 'author', 'editor' and 'publisher' have the following meanings, which are further explained in subsection (3)—

'author' means the originator of the statement, but does not include a person who did not intend that his statement be published at all;

'editor' means a person having editorial or equivalent responsibility for the content of the statement or the decision to publish it; and

'publisher' means a commercial publisher, that is, a person whose business is issuing material to the public, or a section of the public, who issues material containing the statement in the course of that business.

(3) A person shall not be considered the author, editor or publisher of a statement if he is only involved—

(a) in printing, producing, distributing or selling printed material containing the statement;

(b) in processing, making copies of, distributing, exhibiting or selling a film or sound recording (as defined in Part I of the Copyright, Designs and Patents Act 1988) containing the statement;

(c) in processing, making copies of, distributing or selling any electronic medium in or on which the statement is recorded, or in operating or providing any equipment system or service by means of which the statement is retrieved, copied, distributed or made available in electronic form;

(d) as the broadcaster of a live programme containing the statement in circumstances in which he has no effective control over the maker of the statement;

(e) as the operator of or provider of access to a communications system by means of which the statement is transmitted, or made available, by a person over whom he has no effective control.

In a case not within paragraphs (a) to (e) the court may have regard to those provisions by way of analogy in deciding whether a person is to be considered the author, editor or publisher of a statement.

(4) Employees or agents of an author, editor or publisher are in the same position as their employer or principal to the extent that they are responsible for the content of the statement or the decision to publish it.

(5) In determining for the purposes of this section whether a person took reasonable care, or had reason to believe that what he did caused or contributed to the publication of a defamatory statement, regard shall be had to—

    (a) the extent of his responsibility for the content of the statement or the decision to publish it,

    (b) the nature or circumstances of the publication, and

    (c) the previous conduct or character of the author, editor or publisher.

(6) This section does not apply to any cause of action which arose before the section came into force.

**17.**—(1) In this Act—

'publication' and 'publish', in relation to a statement, have the meaning they have for the purposes of the law of defamation generally, but 'publisher' is specially defined for the purposes of section 1;

'statement' means words, pictures, visual images, gestures or any other method of signifying meaning; and

'statutory provision' means—

    (a) a provision contained in an Act or in subordinate legislation within the meaning of the Interpretation Act 1978,

    (aa) a provision contained in an Act of the Scottish Parliament or in an instrument made under such an Act, or

    (b) a statutory provision within the meaning given by section 1(f) of the Interpretation Act (Northern Ireland) 1954.

(2) [omitted]

---

### Godfrey v Demon Internet

Queen's Bench Division [2001] QB 201, [2000] 3 WLR 1020, [1999] 4 All ER 342

The defendant Internet Service Provider (ISP) carried a newsgroup called 'soc.culture.thai'. On 13 January 1997, an unknown person made a posting on that site from the United States which purported to have been posted by the claimant, but it was a forgery and defamatory of the claimant. It followed a path from the American ISP to the defendant's news server in England. On 17 January the claimant sent a fax to the defendant informing it of the forgery and requesting its removal. However, it was not removed and expired naturally on 27 January. Held: the defendant ISP was liable for losses arising after 17 January, the date the defendant was informed of the libel.

MORLAND J: ... The governing statute is the Defamation Act 1996. Section 1 is headed 'Responsibility for Publication'.

In my judgment the Defendants were clearly not the publisher of the posting defamatory of the Plaintiff within the meaning of Section 1(2) and 1(3) and incontrovertibly can avail themselves of Section 1(1)(a).

However the difficulty facing the Defendants is Section 1(1)(b) and 1(1)(c). After the 17th January 1997 after receipt of the Plaintiff's fax the Defendants knew of the defamatory posting but chose not to remove it from their Usenet news servers. In my judgment this places the Defendants in an insuperable difficulty so that they cannot avail themselves of the defence provided by Section 1.

I am fortified in this conclusion by the contents of the Consultation Document issued by the Lord Chancellor's Department in July 1995 and the words of Lord Mackay LC during debate on the Defamation Bill on the 2nd April 1996 (see Hansard Col. 214).

In the Consultation Document it is said:—

    2.4 The defence of innocent dissemination has never provided an absolute immunity for distributors, however mechanical their contribution. It does not protect those who knew that the material they were handling was defamatory, or who ought to have known of its nature. Those safeguards are preserved, so that the defence is not available to a defendant who knew that his act involved or contributed to publication defamatory of the plaintiff. It is available only if, having taken all reasonable care, the defendant had no reason to suspect that his act had that effect. Sub-sections (5) and (6) describe factors which will be taken into account in determining whether the defendant took all reasonable care.

2.5 Although it has been suggested that the defence should always apply unless the plaintiff is able to show that the defendant did indeed have the disqualifying knowledge or cause for suspicion, only the defendant knows exactly what care he has taken. Accordingly, as in most defences, it is for the defendant to show that the defence applies to him.

Lord Mackay LC said in moving rejection of an amendment of Lord Lester of Herne Hill:—

Clause 1 is intended to provide a defence for those who have unwittingly provided a conduit which has enabled another person to publish defamatory material. It is intended to provide a modern equivalent of the common law defence of innocent dissemination, recognising that there may be circumstances in which the unwitting contributor to the process of publication may have had no idea of the defamatory nature of the material he has handled or processed.

The amendment proposed by the noble Lord would, in effect, create an entirely new defence. It would give a defence to a person who was indeed aware, or on notice that he was contributing to a defamatory publication, but nevertheless chose to do so. . . .

It is imperative that we do not lose sight of the effect on plaintiffs of giving a defence to those who have in fact been instrumental in bringing material which has defamed the plaintiff to its audience. . . .

But in my submission it would not be right to deprive a plaintiff of his cause of action against a defendant who was aware that he might be wronging the plaintiff and misjudged the plaintiff's chances of succeeding in a defamation action.

Mr Barca, for the Defendants, submitted that at Common Law the Defendants did not publish the defamatory posting and there was no publication.

Section 17 of the 1996 Act reads:—

'Publication' and 'publish', in relation to a statement, have the meaning they have for the purposes of the law of defamation generally, but 'publisher' is specially defined for the purposes of section 1.

At Common Law liability for the publication of defamatory material was strict. There was still publication even if the publisher was ignorant of the defamatory material within the document. Once publication was established the publisher was guilty of publishing the libel unless he could establish, and the onus was upon him, that he was an innocent disseminator.

An early example of the application of this principle is *Day* v *Bream* (1837) 2 Moody and Robinson 54.

The facts were:—

The libel complained of was a printed handbill, containing imputations on the plaintiff clearly libellous. The plaintiff lived at Marlborough; the defendant was the porter of the coach-office at that place, and it was his business to carry out and deliver the parcels that came by the different coaches to the office. For the plaintiff it was shewn that the defendant had delivered on the same day paper parcels, tied up, and containing a large quantity of the handbills in question, to two or three inhabitants of the place, to whom the parcels were directed.

Patteson J, a great master of Common Law,

in summing up, left it to the jury to say whether the defendant delivered the parcels in the course of his business without any knowledge of their contents; if so, find for him, observing, that *prima facie* he was answerable, inasmuch as he had in fact delivered and put into publication the libel complained of, and was therefore called upon to shew his ignorance of the contents.

In the Golf Club notice board case *Byrne* v *Deane* [1937] 1 KB 818 Greene LJ said at page 837:—

Now on the substantial question of publication, publication, of course, is a question of fact, and it must depend on the circumstances in each case whether or not publication has taken place. It is said that as a general proposition where the act of the person alleged to have published a libel has not been any positive act, but has merely been the refraining from doing some act, he cannot be guilty of publication. I am quite unable to accept any such general proposition. It may very well be that in some circumstances a person, by refraining from removing or obliterating the defamatory matter, is not committing any publication at all. In other circumstances he may be doing so. The test it appears to me is this: having regard to all the facts of the case is the proper inference that by not removing the defamatory matter the defendant really made himself responsible for its continued presence in the place where it had been put?

In my judgment the Defendants, whenever they transmit and whenever there is transmitted from the storage of their news server a defamatory posting, publish that posting to any subscriber to their ISP who accesses the newsgroup containing that posting. Thus everytime one of the Defendants' customers accesses 'soc. culture. that' and sees that posting defamatory of the Plaintiff there is a publication to that customer.

I do not accept Mr Barca's argument that the Defendants were merely owners of an electronic device through which postings were transmitted. The Defendants chose to store 'soc.culture.thai' postings within their computers. Such postings could be accessed on that newsgroup. The Defendants could obliterate and indeed did so about a fortnight after receipt.

NOTES

1. In *Godfrey*, the defendants were liable only because they had been informed of the existence of the libel. The effect has been that ISPs have been removing sites from their servers when a complaint has been made, without investigating whether the site is libellous or not, as they have no incentive to fight a case. Some contentious sites have been moved abroad. Some people have argued that the analogy with *Godfrey* would be to argue that a telephone provider such as BT would be liable for messages sent down its lines. Is this analogy correct? Should an ISP be exempted from libel actions altogether?

2. For the application of the Limitation Act 1980 to Internet publications see *Loutchansky* v *The Times* (below) which decides that the limitation period of one year begins whenever the site is accessed, which means that a libel action will hardly ever be out of time for web sites.

3. Internet cases pose interesting problems for jurisdiction and choice of the applicable law. As to jurisdiction, if the defendant (whether the poster of the libel or the server) is domiciled in a European State, the Brussels Convention on Jurisdiction says that he may be sued either in his domicile, or where the act was done or where the damage occurred. In other cases a writ may be served out of the jurisdiction if the harm occurred here. Thus, generally, the poster of a libel or the server on which it is posted may be sued here for the damage sustained here. The law to be applied will be English law so long as the act was wrongful, either by civil or criminal law, in the place where it was done. An example is *Shevill* v *Presse Alliance* [1995] All ER 289 (EC), where the claimant English person was libelled by a newspaper published in France but also distributed in England. The European Court held that the claimant could either sue in France for his total damage, or in England for so much of the loss as was sustained here.

4. In *Godfrey* v *Demon Internet (No. 2)*, 23 April 1999 (unreported), Morland J allowed the defendants to enter an amended defence that 'the claimant has cynically pursued the tactic of deliberately posting provocative, offensive, obnoxious and frequently puerile comments about other countries, their citizens and cultures; and has done so with a view to provoking others to trade insults which he can claim are defamatory and seek to use as the basis for bringing vexatious libel actions against them and against access or service providers such as the Defendant'. This raises an interesting point about damages. The defendant cannot say that the claimant does not deserve the reputation he has by digging up the past, but he can

mitigate damages by saying that the libel is causally linked to his conduct. In other words, what is relevant is not the general conduct of the claimant but rather the activities of the claimant which are causally connected to the libel, or where the libel has been provoked by the language of the claimant. On this point see also *Burstein* v *Times Newspapers* [2001] 1 WLR 577, which suggests that mitigating factors may go beyond causally linked matters and may include 'evidence of directly relevant background context'.

## SECTION 3: THE MEANING OF 'DEFAMATORY'

It has never been easy to define what is meant by 'defamatory', and each attempt has met with criticism. The following case discusses the various possibilities.

### *Berkoff* v *Burchill*
Court of Appeal [1996] 4 All ER 1008

The claimant is a director, actor and writer. The defendant journalist wrote an article in which she said 'film directors, from Hitchcock to Berkoff, are notoriously hideous-looking people'. Following a further article the claimant sued for defamation claiming that the article meant that he was hideously ugly. The defendant claimed that the article was not capable of being defamatory as it could not affect the reputation of the claimant. Held: dismissing the appeal, that the action would not be struck out and the issue should be considered by the jury.

NEILL LJ:

*Definitions of 'defamatory'*

I am not aware of any entirely satisfactory definition of the word 'defamatory'. It may be convenient, however, to collect together some of the definitions which have been used and approved in the past.

(1) The classic definition is that given by Lord Wensleydale (then Parke B) in *Parmiter* v *Coupland* (1840) 6 M&W 105 at 108, 151 ER 340 at 341–342. He said that in cases of libel it was for the judge to give a legal definition of the offence which he defined as being:

> A publication, without justification or lawful excuse, which is calculated to injure the reputation of another, by exposing him to hatred, contempt, or ridicule . . .

It is to be noted that in *Tournier* v *National Provincial Union Bank of England Ltd* [1924] 1 KB 461 at 477, [1923] All ER Rep 550 at 557 Scrutton LJ said that he did not think that this 'ancient formula' was sufficient in all cases, because words might damage the reputation of a man as a business man which no one would connect with hatred, ridicule or contempt. Atkin LJ expressed a similar opinion ([1924] 1 KB 461 at 486–487, [1923] All ER Rep 550 at 561):

> I do not think that it is a sufficient direction to a jury on what is meant by 'defamatory' to say, without more, that it means: Were the words calculated to expose the plaintiff to hatred, ridicule or contempt, in the mind of a reasonable man? The formula is well known to lawyers, but it is obvious that suggestions might be made very injurious to a man's character in business which would not, in the ordinary sense, excite either hate, ridicule, or contempt— for example, an imputation of a clever fraud which, however much to be condemned morally and legally, might yet not excite what a member of a jury might understand as hatred, or contempt.

(2) In *Scott* v *Sampson* (1882) 8 QBD 491, [1881–5] All ER Rep 628 the Divisional Court was concerned with the question as to the evidence which might be called by a defendant relating to the

character of the plaintiff. Cave J explained the nature of the right which is concerned in an action for defamation (8 QBD 491 at 503, [1881–5] All ER Rep 628 at 634):

Speaking generally the law recognizes in every man a right to have the estimation in which he stands in the opinion of others unaffected by false statements to his discredit; and if such false statements are made without lawful excuse, and damage results to the person of whom they are made, he has a right of action.

But as was pointed out in the Faulks Committee *Report of the Committee on Defamation* (Cmnd 5909) para 62, the word 'discredit' is itself incapable of precise explication. Nevertheless, in *Youssoupoff* v *Metro-Goldwyn-Mayer Pictures Ltd* (1934) 50 TLR 581 Scrutton LJ said that he thought that it was difficult to improve upon the language of this definition.

(3)   In *Sim* v *Stretch* [1936] 2 All ER 1237 at 1240 Lord Atkin expressed the view that the definition in *Parmiter* v *Coupland* was probably too narrow and that the question was complicated by having to consider the person or class of persons whose reaction to the publication provided the relevant test. He concluded this passage in his speech:

. . . after collating the opinions of many authorities I propose in the present case the test: would the words tend to lower the plaintiff in the estimation of right-thinking members of society generally?

(4)   As I have already observed, both Scrutton and Atkin LJJ in *Tournier's* case drew attention to words which damage the reputation of a man as a business man. In *Drummond-Jackson* v *British Medical Association* [1970] 1 All ER 1094, [1970] 1 WLR 688 the Court of Appeal was concerned with an article in a medical journal which, it was suggested, impugned the plaintiff's reputation as a dentist. Lord Pearson said:

. . . words may be defamatory of a trader or business man or professional man, although they do not impute any moral fault or default of personal character. They [can] be defamatory of him if they impute lack of qualification, knowledge, skill, capacity, judgment or efficiency in the conduct of his trade or business or professional activity . . . (See [1970] 1 All ER 1094 at 1104, [1970] 1 WLR 688 at 698–699.)

It is therefore necessary in some cases to consider the occupation of the plaintiff.

(5)   In *Youssoupoff* v *Metro-Goldwyn-Mayer Pictures Ltd* (1934) 50 TLR 581 at 587 Slesser LJ expanded the *Parmiter* v *Coupland* definition to include words which cause a person to be shunned or avoided. He said:

. . . not only is the matter defamatory if it brings the plaintiff into hatred, ridicule, or contempt by reason of some moral discredit on [the plaintiff's] part, but also if it tends to make the plaintiff be shunned and avoided and that without any moral discredit on [the plaintiff's] part. It is for that reason that persons who have been alleged to have been insane, or to be suffering from certain diseases, and other cases where no direct moral responsibility could be placed upon them, have been held to be entitled to bring an action to protect their reputation and their honour.

Slesser LJ added, in relation to the facts in that case:

One may, I think, take judicial notice of the fact that a lady of whom it has been said that she has been ravished, albeit against her will, has suffered in social reputation and in opportunities of receiving respectable consideration from the world.

(6)   The Faulks Committee in their report recommended that for the purpose of civil cases the following definition of defamation should be adopted (para 65):

Defamation shall consist of the publication to a third party of matter which in all the circumstances would be likely to affect a person adversely in the estimation of reasonable people generally.

(7)   In the American Law Institute's Restatement of the Law of Torts (2nd edn, 1977) § 559 the following definition is given:

A communication is defamatory if it tends so to harm the reputation of another as to lower him in the estimation of the community or to deter third persons from associating or dealing with him.

(8) In some of the Australian states a definition of 'defamatory matter' is contained in the Code. In the Queensland Criminal Code § 366, the following definition is given:

Any imputation concerning any person, or any member of his family, whether living or dead, by which the reputation of that person is likely to be injured, or by which he is likely to be injured in his profession or trade, or by which other persons are likely to be induced to shun or avoid or ridicule or despise him . . .

It will be seen from this collection of definitions that words may be defamatory, even though they neither impute disgraceful conduct to the plaintiff nor any lack of skill or efficiency in the conduct of his trade or business or professional activity, if they hold him up to contempt, scorn or ridicule or tend to exclude him from society. On the other hand, insults which do not diminish a man's standing among other people do not found an action for libel or slander. The exact borderline may often be difficult to define.

. . .

## THE APPEAL

It was argued by counsel on behalf of the defendants that the defining characteristic of the tort of defamation is injury to reputation. The fact that a statement may injure feelings or cause annoyance is irrelevant to the question whether it is defamatory. He reminded us of Lord Atkin's words in *Sim* v *Stretch* [1936] 2 All ER 1237 at 1242 that though the freedom of juries to award damages for injury to reputation was one of the safeguards of liberty, the protection was undermined 'when exhibitions of bad manners or discourtesy are placed on the same level as attacks on character, and are treated as actionable wrongs'.

Counsel accepted that it was also defamatory to say of a man that he was suffering from certain disease. But he submitted that a distinction had to be drawn between an allegation that someone was physically unwholesome and an allegation that someone was physically aesthetically unpleasing. It could not be defamatory to say that an individual had a streaming cold or influenza, so the test of being 'shunned or avoided' cannot be applied without qualification. It was also to be noted that it was not suggested in *Youssoupoff's* case that there was no evidence on which it could be found that the passages complained of were defamatory of the princess (see (1934) 50 TLR 581 at 586 per Greer LJ).

Counsel for Mr Berkoff on the other hand, contended that the present case fell into the residual class where words may be defamatory even though they do not involve an attack on a plaintiff's reputation in the conventional sense. Mr Berkoff, it was said, is an actor and a person in the public eye. It was submitted that it was necessary to look at all the circumstances. If this were done it was a matter for the jury to decide whether the words complained of had passed beyond mere abuse and had become defamatory by exposing Mr Berkoff to ridicule or by causing him to be shunned or avoided. It was suggested that these two passages would reduce the respect with which he was regarded. The words complained of might affect Mr Berkoff's standing among the public, particularly theatre-goers, and among casting directors.

In his helpful submissions on behalf of the defendants, Mr Price QC rightly underlined the central characteristic of an action for defamation as being a remedy for publications which damage a person's reputation. But the word 'reputation', by its association with phrases such as 'business reputation', 'professional reputation' or 'reputation for honesty', may obscure the fact that in this context the word is to be interpreted in a broad sense as comprehending all aspects of a person's standing in the community. A man who is held up as a figure of fun may be defeated in his claim for damages by, for example, a plea of fair comment, or, if he succeeds on liability, the compensation which he receives from a jury may be very small. But nevertheless, the publication of which he complains may be defamatory of him because it affects in an adverse manner the attitude of other people towards him.

It was argued on behalf of Mr Berkoff that in considering whether words were capable of a defamatory meaning it was necessary to take into account every possible group of persons to whom the words might apply. Could the words be defamatory of anyone? In my opinion this is not the right test. Mr Price was, I think, correct when he submitted that the question has to be answered in relation to the claim by the plaintiff. But if this is done, one has to look at the words and judge them in the context in which they were published. Indeed, as I pointed out earlier, it is pleaded in the statement of claim that reliance will be placed on the context. It may be that in some contexts the words 'hideously ugly' could not be understood in a defamatory sense, but one has to consider the words in the surroundings in which they appear. This task is particularly important in relation to the second article.

It is trite law that the meaning of words in a libel action is determined by the reaction of the ordinary reader and not by the intention of the publisher, but the perceived intention of the publisher may colour the meaning. In the present case it would, in my view, be open to a jury to conclude that in the context the remarks about Mr Berkoff gave the impression that he was not merely physically unattractive in appearance but actually repulsive. It seems to me that to say this of someone in the public eye who makes his living, in part at least, as an actor, is capable of lowering his standing in the estimation of the public and of making him an object of ridicule.

I confess that I have found this to be a far from easy case, but in the end I am satisfied that it would be wrong to decide this preliminary issue in a way which would withdraw the matter completely from the consideration of a jury.

I would dismiss the appeal.

MILLETT LJ [dissenting]: Many a true word is spoken in jest. Many a false one too. But chaff and banter are not defamatory, and even serious imputations are not actionable if no one would take them to be meant seriously. The question, however, is how the words would be understood, not how they were meant, and that issue is pre-eminently one for the jury. So, however difficult it may be, we must assume that Miss Julie Burchill might be taken seriously. The question then is: is it defamatory to say of a man that he is 'hideously ugly'?

Mr Berkoff is a director, actor and writer. Physical beauty is not a qualification for a director or writer. Mr Berkoff does not plead that he plays romantic leads or that the words complained of impugn his professional ability. In any case, I do not think that it can be defamatory to say of an actor that he is unsuitable to play particular roles.

How then can the words complained of injure Mr Berkoff's reputation? They are an attack on his appearance, not on his reputation. It is submitted on his behalf that they would cause people 'to shun and avoid him' and would 'bring him into ridicule'. Ridicule, it will be recalled, is the second member of a well-known trinity.

The submission illustrates the danger of trusting to verbal formulae. Defamation has never been satisfactorily defined. All attempted definitions are illustrative. None of them is exhaustive. All can be misleading if they cause one to forget that defamation is an attack on reputation, that is on a man's standing in the world.

. . .

The line between mockery and defamation may sometimes be difficult to draw. When it is, it should be left to the jury to draw it. Despite the respect which is due to the opinion of Neill LJ, whose experience in this field is unrivalled, I am not persuaded that the present case could properly be put on the wrong side of the line. A decision that it is an actionable wrong to describe a man as 'hideously ugly' would be an unwarranted restriction on free speech. And if a bald statement to this effect would not be capable of being defamatory, I do not see how a humorously exaggerated observation to the like effect could be. People must be allowed to poke fun at one another without fear of litigation. It is one thing to ridicule a man; it is another to expose him to ridicule. Miss Burchill made a cheap joke at Mr Berkoff's expense; she may thereby have demeaned herself, but I do not believe that she defamed Mr Berkoff.

If I have appeared to treat Mr Berkoff's claim with unjudicial levity it is because I find it impossible to take it seriously. Despite the views of my brethren, who are both far more experienced than I am, I remain of the opinion that the proceedings are as frivolous as Miss Burchill's article. The time of the court ought not to be taken up with either of them. I would allow the appeal and dismiss the action.

NOTES

1. In *Byrne* v *Deane* [1937] 1 KB 818 a golf club had some 'fruit machines' in the club house, and someone informed the police of the existence of these gaming machines and they required them to be removed. Someone then posted a notice in verse saying 'But he who gave the game away, may he byrne in hell and rue the day.' The claimant claimed that this accused him of disloyalty to the club, but the court held that it could not be defamatory to say of a person that he put in motion machinery for the suppression of a crime.

2. Opinion in society generally may be sharply divided on whether a person would be regarded as having acted reprehensibly. For example, is it defamatory to say of a trade union member that he has refused to support an official strike? Other trade unionists would regard that as disloyalty, but other people might applaud his action. In *Myroft* v *Sleight* (1921) 37 TLR 646 McCardie J thought it would not be defamatory, for it would merely be alleging 'independence of thought or courage of opinion or speech or manliness of action', although he did decide that it would be defamatory to say that a person who had voted for the strike had refused to leave work, for that would be to allege hypocrisy or underhand disloyalty.

## SECTION 4: WHAT DO THE WORDS USED MEAN?

Words should be construed in their oridnary and natural meaning, but they may also have a hidden meaning—the innuendo. There are two kinds of innuendo, rather confusingly called a 'true' (or legal) innuendo and a 'false' (or popular) innuendo. A true innuendo occurs where there are facts known to the recipient of the information which gives the apparently innocuous statement a different meaning, for example 'to say of a man that he was seen entering a named house would contain a derogatory implication for anyone who knew that the house was a brothel but not for anyone who did not' (Lord Devlin in *Rubber Improvement* v *Daily Telegraph* [1964] AC 234). A false innuendo is where the statement itself carries with it an implied meaning.

---

### *Lewis* v *Daily Telegraph*
House of Lords [1964] AC 234; [1963] 2 WLR 1063; [1963] 2 All ER 151

The defendants published a story headed 'Inquiry on firm by City Police' which stated that the City of London Fraud Squad were inquiring into the affairs of Rubber Improvement Ltd, of which the claimant, John Lewis, was chairman. It was claimed that the story meant that the affairs of the company were conducted fraudulently or dishonestly, or in such a way that the police suspected that their affairs were so conducted. Held: dismissing the appeal, that the words could not mean that the claimant was actually guilty of fraud, and a new trial was ordered on the basis that the words were only capable of meaning that the police suspected fraud.

LORD REID: The essence of the controversy between the parties is that the appellants maintain that these passages are capable of meaning that they were guilty of fraud. The respondents deny this: they admit that the paragraphs are libellous but maintain that the juries ought to have been directed that they are not capable of the meaning which the appellants attribute to them. The learned judge directed the juries in such a way as to leave it open to them to accept the appellants' contention, and it is obvious from the amounts of the damages awarded that the juries must have done this.

The gist of the two paragraphs is that the police, the City Fraud Squad, were inquiring into the appellants' affairs. There is no doubt that in actions for libel the question is what the words would convey to the ordinary man: it is not one of construction in the legal sense. The ordinary man does not live in an ivory tower and he is not inhibited by a knowledge of the rules of construction. So he can and does read between the lines in the light of his general knowledge and experience of worldly affairs. . . .

What the ordinary man would infer without special knowledge has generally been called the natural and ordinary meaning of the words. But that expression is rather misleading in that it conceals the fact that there are two elements in it. Sometimes it is not necessary to go beyond the words themselves, as where the plaintiff has been called a thief or a murderer. But more often the sting is not so much in the words themselves as in what the ordinary man will infer from them, and that is also regarded as part of their natural and ordinary meaning. Here there would be nothing libellous in saying that an inquiry into the appellants' affairs was proceeding: the inquiry might be by a statistician or other expert. The sting is in inferences drawn from the fact that it is the fraud squad which is making the inquiry. What those inferences should be is ultimately a question for the jury, but the trial judge has an important duty to perform.

Generally the controversy is whether the words are capable of having a libellous meaning at all, and undoubtedly it is the judge's duty to rule on that. I shall have to deal later with the test which he must apply. Here the controversy is in a different form. The respondents admit that their words were libellous, although I am still in some doubt as to what is the admitted libellous meaning. But they sought and seek a ruling that these words are not capable of having the particular meaning which the appellants attribute to them. I think that they are entitled to such a ruling and that the test must be the same as that applied in deciding whether the words are capable of having any libellous meaning. I say that because it appears that when a particular meaning has been pleaded, either as a 'true' or a 'false' innuendo, it has not been doubted that the judge must rule on the innuendo. And the case surely cannot be different where a part of the natural and ordinary meaning is, and where it is not, expressly pleaded.

The leading case is *Capital and Counties Bank Ltd* v *Henry & Sons* (1882) 7 App Cas 741. In that case Lord Selborne LC said: 'The test, according to the authorities, is, whether under the circumstances in which the writing was published, reasonable men, to whom the publication was made, would be likely to understand it in a libellous sense.' Each of the four noble Lords who formed the majority stated the test in a different way, and the speeches of Lord Blackburn and Lord Watson could be read as imposing a heavier burden on the plaintiff. But I do not think that they should now be so read. In *Nevill* v *Fine Art & General Insurance Co. Ltd* [1897] AC 68 Lord Halsbury said: '. . . what is the sense in which any ordinary reasonable man would understand the words of the communication so as to expose the plaintiff to hatred, or contempt or ridicule . . . it is not enough to say that by some person or another the words *might* be understood in a defamatory sense.' These statements of the law appear to have been generally accepted and I would not attempt to restate the general principle.

In this case it is, I think, sufficient to put the test in this way. Ordinary men and women have different temperaments and outlooks. Some are unusually suspicious and some are unusually naïve. One must try to envisage people between these two extremes and see what is the most damaging meaning they would put on the words in question. So let me suppose a number of ordinary people discussing one of these paragraphs which they had read in the newspaper. No doubt one of them might say—'Oh, if the fraud squad are after these people you can take it they are guilty.' But I would expect the others to turn on him, if he did say that, with such remarks as—'Be fair. This is not a police state. No doubt their affairs are in a mess or the police would not be interested. But that could be because Lewis or the cashier has been very stupid or careless. We really must not jump to conclusions. The police are fair and know their job and we shall know soon enough if there is anything in it. Wait till we see if they charge him. I wouldn't trust him until this is cleared up, but it is another thing to condemn him unheard.'

What the ordinary man, not avid for scandal, would read into the words complained of must be a matter of impression. I can only say that I do not think that he would infer guilt of fraud merely because an inquiry is on foot.

LORD DEVLIN: My Lords, the natural and ordinary meaning of words ought in theory to be the same for the lawyer as for the layman, because the lawyer's first rule of construction is that words are to be given their natural and ordinary meaning as popularly understood. The proposition that ordinary words are the same for the lawyer as for the layman is as a matter of pure construction undoubtedly true. But it is very difficult to draw the line between pure construction and implication, and the layman's capacity for implication is much greater than the lawyer's. The lawyer's rule is that the implication must be necessary as well as reasonable. The layman reads in an implication much more freely; and unfortunately, as the law of defamation has to take into account, is especially prone to do so when it is derogatory.

In the law of defamation these wider sorts of implication are called innuendoes. The word explains itself and is very apt for the purpose. . . .

An innuendo had to be pleaded and the line between an ordinary meaning and an innuendo might not always be easy to draw. A derogatory implication may be so near the surface that it is hardly hidden at all or it may be more difficult to detect. If it is said of a man that he is a fornicator the statement cannot be enlarged by innuendo. If it is said of him that he was seen going into a brothel, the same meaning would probably be conveyed to nine men out of ten. But the lawyer might say that in the latter case a derogatory meaning was not a necessary one because a man might go to a brothel for an innocent purpose. An innuendo pleading that the words were understood to mean that he went there for an immoral purpose would not, therefore, be ridiculous. . . .

I have said that a derogatory implication might be easy or difficult to detect; and, of course, it might not be detected at all, except by a person who was already in possession of some specific information. Thus, to say of a man that he was seen to enter a named house would contain a derogatory implication for anyone who knew that that house was a brothel but not for anyone who did not. . . . De Grey CJ [in *Rex* v *Horne* 2 Cowp 672] distinguished between this sort of implication and the implication that is to be derived from the words themselves without extrinsic aid, and he treats the term 'innuendo' as descriptive only of the latter. Since then the term has come to be used for both sorts of implication. . . .

. . . [Ord. 19, r. 6(2)] reads: '(2) In an action for libel or slander if the plaintiff alleges that the words or matter complained of were used in a defamatory sense other than their ordinary meaning, he shall give particulars of the facts and matters on which he relies in support of such sense.'

The word 'innuendo' is not used. But the effect of the language is that any meaning that does not require the support of extrinsic fact is assumed to be part of the ordinary meaning of the words. Accordingly, an innuendo, however well concealed, that is capable of being detected in the language used is deemed to be part of the ordinary meaning.

This might be an academic matter if it were not for the principle that the ordinary meaning of words and the meaning enlarged by innuendo give rise to separate causes of action. This principle, which originated out of the old forms of pleading, seems to me in modern times to be of dubious value. But it is now firmly settled on the authority of *Sim* v *Stretch* 52 TLR 669 and the House was not asked to qualify it. How is this principle affected by the new rule? Are there now three causes of action? If there are only two, to which of them does the innuendo that is inherent in the words belong? In *Grubb* v *Bristol United Press Ltd* [1963] 1 QB 309 the Court of Appeal, disagreeing with some observations made by Diplock LJ in *Loughans* v *Odhams Press Ltd* [1963] 1 QB 299, decided in effect that there were only two causes of action and that the innuendo cause of action comprised only the innuendo that was supported by extrinsic facts.

My Lords, I think, on the whole, that this is the better solution, though it brings with it a consequence that I dislike, namely, that at two points there is a divergence between the popular and the legal meaning of words. Just as the popular and legal meanings of 'malice' have drifted apart, so the popular and legal meanings of 'innuendo' must now be separated. I shall in the rest of my speech describe as a legal innuendo the innuendo that is the subject-matter of a separate cause of action. I suppose that it does not matter what terminology is used so long as it is agreed. But I do not care for the description of the popular innuendo as a false innuendo; it is the law and not popular usage that gives a false and restricted meaning to the word. The other respect is that the natural and ordinary meaning of words for the purposes of defamation is not their natural and ordinary meaning for other purposes of the law. There must be added to the implications which a court is prepared to make as a matter of construction all such insinuations and innuendoes as could reasonably be read into them by the ordinary man.

The consequence of all this is, I think, that there will have to be three paragraphs in a statement of claim where previously two have served. In the first paragraph the defamatory words will be set out as hitherto. It may be that they will speak for themselves. If not, a second paragraph will set out those innuendoes or indirect meanings which go beyond the literal meaning of the words but which the pleader claims to be inherent in them. Thirdly, if the pleader has the necessary material, he can plead a secondary meaning or legal innuendo supported by particulars under Ord. 19, r. 6(2). Hitherto it has been customary to put the whole innuendo into one paragraph, but now this may easily result in the confusion of two causes of action and in consequent embarrassment. The essential distinction between the second and third paragraph will lie in the fact that particulars under the rule must be appended to the third. That is, so to speak, the hallmark of the legal innuendo. . . .

NOTES

1. Inherent in the decision in *Lewis* is the so-called 'repetition' rule—that is that it is no defence for the defendant to say that he was merely repeating what he has been told. In other words it is still defamatory for A to say 'I was told by X that Y is a thief'. It may be true that X said this but A would still need to prove that Y is a thief. In *Lewis* Lord Reid said, 'I can well understand that if you say there is a rumour that X is guilty you can only justify it by proving that he is guilty, because repeating someone else's libellous statement is just as bad as making the statement directly'. For examples, see *Truth (NZ) Ltd* v *Holloway* [1960] 1 WLR 997 and *Stern* v *Piper* [1996] 3 All ER 385.

2. In *Gillick* v *BBC* The Times, 20 October 1995, Neill LJ said that the court should give to the material the natural and ordinary meaning which it would have conveyed to the ordinary reasonable reader or viewer, and that the reasonable reader was not naive but nor was he unduly suspicious, and he could read between the lines. He could read in an implication more readily than a lawyer and might indulge in a certain amount of loose thinking. But he must be treated as a man who was not avid for scandal and someone who did not select one bad meaning where other non-defamatory meanings were available. The court should be cautious of over-elaborate analysis of the material in issue and should not be too literal in its approach. Finally, a statement should be taken to be defamatory if it would tend to lower the claimant in the estimation of right-thinking members of society generally, or be likely to affect a person adversely in the estimation of reasonable people generally.

3. An example of a true or legal innuendo is *Tolley* v *Fry* [1931] AC 333, where the defendants advertised their chocolate by a caricature of the claimant with a packet of their chocolate in his pocket, together with a doggerel verse which named him. This seems innocent enough, but the claimant was a well-known amateur golfer, and it was claimed that people would think he had prostituted his amateur status and it was said that such a person would be asked to resign from any respectable club. The claimant won.

4. If a true innuendo is pleaded it is not necessary to show that the people who knew the special facts which rendered the statement defamatory actually believed the story. In *Hough* v *London Express Newspaper* [1940] 2 KB 507 it was said of Frank Hough, a boxer, that his 'curly headed wife sees every fight'. The curly headed woman was not Frank Hough's wife, and the true wife said that the statement meant that she had been falsely claiming to be his wife and that she had had his children without being married to him. This was a libel, even though the people called to give evidence as to the special facts pleaded to support the innuendo did not believe that the claimant was not Mrs Hough. Other people might have thought differently. What if *all* the people who knew of the special facts did not believe the story?

---

### *Charleston* v *News Group Newspapers*
[1995] 2 AC 65; [1995] 2 WLR 450; [1995] 2 All ER 313

The claimants played Harold and Madge Bishop in 'Neighbours'. The defendants published an article with the headline 'Strewth! What's Harold up to with our

Madge?', below which was a picture of a man and a woman nearly naked in a pornographic pose with the faces of the claimants superimposed on the figures. The article below made it clear that the photographs had been produced by a computer game company without the knowledge of the claimants and went on to castigate the makers of the game. The claimants claimed on the basis that the article conveyed that they had been willing participants in the production of the photographs. However, it was conceded that the article as a whole was not defamatory and the question was whether the headline and the photographs could be considered in isolation. Held: dismissing the appeal, that the defendants were not liable.

LORD BRIDGE: . . . The theme of Mr Craig's argument runs on the following lines. All the earlier authorities, he submits, are explicable on the basis that the allegedly defamatory matter with which they were concerned was located somewhere in a document in which there was no likelihood that it would be read in isolation. In such a situation it is natural and proper to look for the meaning conveyed to the reader by considering the publication as a whole. The techniques of modern tabloid journalism, however, confront the courts with a novel situation with which the law has not hitherto had to grapple. It is plain that the eye-catching headline and the eye-catching photograph will first attract the reader's attention, precisely as they were intended to do, and equally plain that a significant number of readers will not trouble to read any further. This phenomenon must be well known to newspaper editors and publishers, who cannot, therefore, complain if they are held liable in damages for any libel thus published to the category of limited readers.

At first blush this argument has considerable attractions, but I believe that it falls foul of two principles which are basic to the law of libel. The first is that, where no legal innuendo is alleged to arise from extrinsic circumstances known to some readers, the 'natural and ordinary meaning' to be ascribed to the words of an allegedly defamatory publication is the meaning, including any inferential meaning, which the words would convey to the mind of the ordinary, reasonable, fair-minded reader. This proposition is too well established to require citation of authority. The second principle, which is perhaps a corollary of the first, is that, although a combination of words may in fact convey different meanings to the minds of different readers, the jury in a libel action, applying the criterion which the first principle dictates, is required to determine the single meaning which the publication conveyed to the notional reasonable reader and to base its verdict and any award of damages on the assumption that this was the one sense in which all readers would have understood it. The origins and the implications of this second principle are the subject of a characteristically penetrating analysis in the judgment of Diplock LJ in *Slim* v *Telegraph Ltd* [1968] 2 QB 157, 171–172, 173, 174, from which it will, I think, be sufficient to cite the following passages:

> Everyone outside a court of law recognises that words are imprecise instruments for communicating the thoughts of one man to another. The same words may be understood by one man in a different meaning from that in which they are understood by another and both meanings may be different from that which the author of the words intended to convey. But the notion that the same words should bear different meanings to different men and that more than one meaning should be 'right' conflicts with the whole training of a lawyer. Words are the tools of his trade. He uses them to define legal rights and duties. They do not achieve that purpose unless there can be attributed to them a single meaning as the 'right' meaning. And so the argument between lawyers as to the meaning of words starts with the unexpressed major premise that any particular combination of words has one meaning which is not necessarily the same as that intended by him who published them or understood by any of those who read them but is capable of ascertainment as being the 'right' meaning by the adjudicator to whom the law confides the responsibility of determining it. . . .
>
> Where, as in the present case, words are published to the millions of readers of a popular newspaper, the chances are that if the words are reasonably capable of being understood as bearing more than one meaning, some readers will have understood them as bearing one of those meanings and some will have understood them as bearing others of those meanings.

But none of this matters. What does matter is what the adjudicator at the trial thinks is the one and only meaning that the readers as reasonable men should have collectively understood the words to bear. That is 'the natural and ordinary meaning' of words in an action for libel. . . .

Juries, in theory, must be unanimous upon every issue on which they have to adjudicate; and since the damages that they award must depend upon the defamatory meaning that they attribute to the words, they must all agree upon a single meaning as being the 'right' meaning. And so the unexpressed major premise, that any particular combination of words can bear but a single 'natural and ordinary meaning' which is 'right,' survived the transfer from judge to jury of the function of adjudicating upon the meaning of words in civil actions for libel.

It is precisely the application of the principle so clearly expounded in these passages which, in a libel action where no legal innuendo is alleged, prevents either side from calling witnesses to say what they understood the allegedly defamatory publication to mean. But it would surely be even more destructive of the principle that a publication has 'the one and only meaning that the readers as reasonable men should have collectively understood the words to bear' to allow the plaintiff, without evidence, to invite the jury to infer that different groups of readers read different parts of the entire publication and for that reason understood it to mean different things, some defamatory, some not.

Whether the text of a newspaper article will, in any particular case, be sufficient to neutralise the defamatory implication of a prominent headline will sometimes be a nicely balanced question for the jury to decide and will depend not only on the nature of the libel which the headline conveys and the language of the text which is relied on to neutralise it but also on the manner in which the whole of the relevant material is set out and presented. But the proposition that the prominent headline, or as here the headlines plus photographs, may found a claim in libel in isolation from its related text, because some readers only read headlines, is to my mind quite unacceptable in the light of the principles discussed above.

I have no doubt that Mr Craig is right in his assertion that many 'News of the World' readers who saw the offending publication would have looked at the headlines and photographs and nothing more. But if these readers, without taking the trouble to discover what the article was all about, carried away the impression that two well known actors in legitimate television were also involved in making pornographic films, they could hardly be described as ordinary, reasonable, fair-minded readers.

NOTES

1. Compare the rule in the tort of passing off that 'it is not sufficient that the only confusion would be to a very small unobservant section of the public, or, as Foster J put it recently (1979 FSR 117) if the only person who would be misled would be a "moron in a hurry" ' (*BBC* v *Newsweek* [1979] RPC 441).

2. Is it right to say that words can only have one reasonable meaning, or rather that there is a single meaning which would be conveyed to the reasonable reader?

## SECTION 5: DO THE WORDS REFER TO THE CLAIMANT?

The defamatory statement must be reasonably capable of applying to the claimant, although it is not necessary for him to be specifically referred to. It is sufficient if reasonable people who are aware of the special facts (which must be proved by the claimant) would believe that he was the person being referred to.

One of the most controversial aspects of this area of the law is the principle in *Hulton & Co.* v *Jones* [1910] AC 20, where the defendants published a humorous article about the behaviour in Dieppe of a fictitious character named Artemus Jones, referring to his being accompanied by a woman who was not his wife. A barrister named Artemus Jones successfully sued, even though the defendants had not intended to refer to him. *Newstead v London Express* (below) goes further, holding a statement to be defamatory of A even though it is true of B. The Faulks Committee considered this principle, but ultimately decided that it should be retained. However, this principle may be doomed if Article 10 of the European Convention on Human Rights is held to apply: see *O'Shea v MGN*, noted after the next case.

---

### Newstead v London Express Newspapers
Court of Appeal [1940] 1 KB 377; [1939] 4 All ER 319; 1621 LT 17

Under the heading 'Why do people commit bigamy' the defendants published a story stating that 'Harold Newstead, a 30-year-old Camberwell man, who was jailed for nine months liked having two wives at once.' The allegation was true of a 30-year-old Camberwell bartender, but not true of the claimant of the same name, who was a hairdresser in Camberwell and of about the same age. At first instance the claimant won, and was awarded one farthing in damages. Held: dismissing the appeal, that the defendants were liable.

SIR WILFRED GREENE MR: If the words used when read in the light of the relevant circumstances are understood by reasonable persons to refer to the plaintiff, refer to him they do for all relevant purposes. Their meaning cannot be affected by the recklessness or honesty of the writer.

I do not propose to refer to the authorities which establish this proposition, except to quote the words of Lord Loreburn LC in *E. Hulton & Co.* v *Jones* [1910] AC 20, where he said: 'What does the tort consist in? It consists in using language which others knowing the circumstances would reasonably think to be defamatory of the person complaining of and injured by it.' In the case of libel, once it is held that the words are capable of referring to the plaintiff, it is, of course, for the jury to say whether or not they do so refer. Subject to this, the principle is in truth an illustration of the rule that the author of a written document is to be taken as having intended his words to have the meaning which they convey when understood in the light of the relevant surrounding circumstances. In the case of libel, the same words may reasonably convey different meanings to a number of different persons or groups of persons, and so be held to be defamatory of more persons than one.

After giving careful consideration to the matter, I am unable to hold that the fact that defamatory words are true of A, makes it as a matter of law impossible for them to be defamatory of B, which was in substance the main argument on behalf of the appellants. At first sight this looks as though it would lead to great hardship. But the hardships are in practice not so serious as might appear, at any rate in the case of statements which are ex facie defamatory. Persons who make statements of this character may not unreasonably be expected, when describing the person of whom they are made, to identify that person so closely as to make it very unlikely that a judge would hold them to be reasonably capable of referring to someone else, or that a jury would hold that they did so refer. This is particularly so in the case of statements which purport to deal with actual facts. If there is a risk of coincidence it ought, I think, in reason to be borne not by the innocent party to whom the words are held to refer, but by the party who puts them into circulation. In matters of fiction, there is no doubt more room for hardship. Even in the case of matters of fact it is no doubt possible to construct imaginary facts which would lead to hardship. There may also be hardship if words, not on their faces defamatory, are true of A, but are reasonably understood by some as referring to B, and as applied to B are defamatory. But such cases must be rare. The law as I understand it is well settled, and can only be altered by legislation. . . .

MACKINNON LJ: If A publishes to another . person, or persons, words which upon their reasonable meaning refer to B, if those words are defamatory as holding B up to hatred, ridicule, or contempt, and if the words so referring to B cannot be justified as true, A may be liable for damages to B.

Secondly, the reasonable meaning of the words, upon the question whether they refer to B must be tested objectively and not subjectively. The question is what do the words mean as words, not what did A in his own mind mean by them or intend them to mean.

Thirdly, A cannot plead as a defence that he was unaware of B's existence.

Fourthly, A cannot plead as a defence that the words are, in their reasonable meaning, equally capable of referring to C, and that when referring to C they are true.

Fifthly, there has been in some of the cases (notably by Farwell LJ in *Jones* v *Hulton & Co.*, [1909] 2 KB 444) reference to negligence or recklessness on the part of A in making the publication. If the words, on their reasonable meaning, do refer to B, I think it is immaterial whether A was either negligent or reckless in not ascertaining the existence of B, or guarding against the applicability to him of the words. If B establishes his claim, the jury in assessing his damages may take into account all the circumstances of the publication. The negligence or recklessness of A may well be among such circumstances. Further or otherwise negligence or recklessness on the part of A is immaterial.

It is hardly necessary to add, sixthly, the rule which is elementary, namely, that it is the primary duty of the judge to decide whether the words complained of are capable of a meaning that is defamatory of B, and only if he answers that question in the affirmative to leave to the jury the questions whether they are in fact defamatory of B, and, if so, what damages he shall be awarded.

In a case in which there is no question that the words are defamatory of him, if they refer to B, and the contest is only whether they do so refer, this preliminary question for the judge must be: 'Are these words on their reasonable meaning capable of referring to the plaintiff?' And if he answers that affirmatively I think that, properly, the first question to be left to the jury should be: 'Could the words used by the defendant be reasonably interpreted by those to whom they were published as referring to the plaintiff?'

NOTES

1. The principle does not mean that any person with the same name as the person mentioned can sue, for the rule is that reasonable people must believe the story in fact refers to the claimant. Thus, in *Blennerhasset* v *Novelty Sales Service* (1933) 175 LTJo 393 the defendants advertised their yo-yo by saying that a Mr Blennerhasset had become obsessed by it and was under 'sympathetic surveillance' in the country. A stockbroker of the same name failed in his action for defamation because no reasonable person would think it applied to him.

2. *O'Shea* v *MGN* [2001] EMLR 40 deals with the application of the strict liability principle to 'look alike' photographs. In that case the defendants published a pornographic advertisement for a web site using the photograph of a model, Miss E, which looked very much like a picture of the claimant. The claim failed even though it was said that a jury, looking at the matter objectively, could decide that the photograph and accompanying text could refer to the claimant. Morland J said that at common law the strict liability principle would apply, but Article 10 of the European Convention on Human Rights (see above) meant that to apply the rule would be an unjustifiable interference with the right of freedom of expression and would be disproportionate to the legitimate aim of protecting the reputations of 'look alikes'. *Hulton* and *Newstead* could be distinguished on the ground that the real claimants involved there could have been discovered by the defendants but it would be impossible to discover whether a 'look alike' existed. However, it seems more likely that the *Hulton* v *Jones* principle will succumb to Article 10 of the Convention.

## SECTION 6: JUSTIFICATION

It is a defence to show that the words are true 'in substance and in fact'. The main problem with this area of the law is that it is for the defendant to prove that the words are true: the claimant merely has to establish that the words are defamatory and have been published. However, the Faulks Committee recommended that the burden of proving truth should remain with the defendant.

---

### *Sutherland* v *Stopes*
House of Lords [1925] AC 47; 132 LJ 550; 94 LJKB 166

Marie Stopes advocated the use of birth control and had established a clinic in London. The defendant wrote a book in which he alleged that the claimant was taking advantage of the poor, and he referred to her 'monstrous' campaign. The jury found the statements true in fact, but added that they were not fair comment. Held: that there was no evidence to support the finding that the comments were unfair, and Lord Shaw made the following comments about justification.

LORD SHAW: It remains to be considered what are the conditions and breadth of a plea of justification on the ground of truth. The plea must not be considered in a meticulous sense. It is that the words employed were true in substance and in fact. I view with great satisfaction the charge of the Lord Chief Justice when he made this point perfectly clear to the jury, that all that was required to affirm that plea was that the jury should be satisfied that the sting of the libel or, if there were more than one, the stings of the libel should be made out. To which I may add that there may be mistakes here and there in what has been said which would make no substantial difference to the quality of the alleged libel or in the justification pleaded for it. If I write that the defendant on March 6 took a saddle from my stable and sold it the next day and pocketed the money all without notice to me, and that in my opinion he stole the saddle, and if the facts truly are found to be that the defendant did not take the saddle from the stable but from the harness room, and that he did not sell it the next day but a week afterwards, but nevertheless he did, without my knowledge or consent, sell my saddle so taken and pocketed the proceeds, then the whole sting of the libel may be justifiably affirmed by a jury notwithstanding these errors in detail.

In the second place, however, the allegation of fact must tell the whole story. If, for instance, in the illustration given, the facts as elicited show what my writing had not disclosed—namely, that the defendant had a saddle of his own lying in my harness room, and that he took by mistake mine away instead of his own and, still labouring under that mistake, sold it—then the jury would properly declare that the libel was not justified on the double ground that there were facts completely explaining in a non-criminal sense anything that was done, and the jury would disaffirm the truth of the libel because, although meticulously true in fact, it was false in substance.

Then, as to the breadth of the justification. When a plea of truth in substance and in fact is made it affirms not only in the sense I have mentioned the facts, but it affirms all that attaches to them as their natural and reasonable meaning.

---

## DEFAMATION ACT 1952

### 5. Justification

In an action for libel or slander in respect of words containing two or more distinct charges against the plaintiff, a defence of justification shall not fail by reason only that the truth of every charge is not proved if the words not proved to be true do not materially injure the plaintiff's reputation having regard to the truth of the remaining charges.

NOTES
1. *Wakley* v *Cooke* (1849) 154 ER 1316 is an example of defining the meaning of the defamatory words and then deciding whether that meaning is true. The claimant was a coroner, and the defendants wrote that 'there can be no court of justice unpolluted which this libellous journalist, this violent agitator and sham humanitarian is allowed to disgrace with his presidentship'. The defendants attempted to justify 'libellous journalist' by saying that as

proprietor of *The Lancet* he had in fact published one libel. It was held that justification was not made out: Rolfe B said that the words either meant that the claimant was habitually publishing libels in his paper, or that he had published them from sordid motives. Neither was made out.

2. In *Bookbinder* v *Tebbit* [1989] 1 All ER 1169, the Derbyshire County Council overprinted all school stationery with the words 'Support Nuclear Free Zones'. The claimant, who was leader of the Council, sued Norman Tebbit, then chairman of the Conservative Party, over a statement which he claimed meant that he had acted irresponsibly in squandering money on the overprinting. The defendant sought to justify on the grounds that there were a number of occasions when the Council had squandered money. It was held that the defence of general squandering of public money should be struck out. In other words, the defendant must justify the specific charge.

## SECTION 7: FAIR COMMENT

'Fair comment' is probably a misnomer, as it is not necessary that the comment be reasonable or 'fair' in the usual sense, but rather the question is whether the opinion is honestly held. The Faulks Committee defined the defence as one where the defendant must show:

(a) that the facts alleged are true (subject to the Defamation Act 1952, s. 6 below);

(b) the expression of opinion is such that an honest man holding strong, exaggerated or even prejudiced views could have made;

(c) the subject matter of the comment is of public interest; and

(d) the facts relied on as founding the comment were in the defendant's mind when he made it.

---

### Merivale v Carson
Court of Appeal (1887) 20 QBD 275; 58 LJ 331; 4 TLR 125

The claimant and his wife were authors of a play called 'The Whip Hand'. The defendant was editor of *The Stage*, which published a critical review of which the innuendo was said to be that the play was of an immoral tendency. The defendants claimed the review was honest and there was no attack on the character of the authors. The jury awarded the claimants one shilling damages. Held: that the appeal was dismissed.

LORD ESHER MR: What is the meaning of a 'fair comment'? I think the meaning is this: is the article in the opinion of the jury beyond that which any fair man, however prejudiced or however strong his opinion may be, would say of the work in question? Every latitude must be given to opinion and to prejudice, and then an ordinary set of men with ordinary judgment must say whether any fair man would have made such a comment on the work. It is very easy to say what would be clearly beyond that limit; if, for instance, the writer attacked the private character of the author. But it is much more difficult to say what is within the limit. That must depend upon the circumstances of the particular case. I think the right question was really left by Field J, to the jury in the present case. No doubt you can find in the course of his summing-up some phrases which, if taken alone, may seem to limit too much the question put to the jury. But, when you look at the summing-up as a whole, I think it comes in substance to the final question which was put by the judge to the jury: 'If it is no more than fair, honest, independent, bold, even exaggerated, criticism, then your verdict will be for the defendants.' He gives a very wide limit, and, I think, rightly. Mere exaggeration, or even gross exaggeration, would not make the comment unfair. However wrong the opinion expressed may be in point of truth, or however prejudiced the writer, it may still be within the prescribed limit. The question which the jury must consider is this—would any fair man, however prejudiced he may be, however exaggerated or obstinate his views, have said that which this criticism has said of the work which is criticised? If it goes beyond that, then you must find for the plaintiff; if you are not satisfied that it does, then it falls within the allowed limit, and there is no libel at all. I cannot doubt that the jury were justified in coming to the conclusion to which they did come, when once they had made up their minds as to the meaning of the words used in the article, viz. that the plaintiffs had written an obscene play, and no fair man could have said that. There was therefore a complete misdescription of the plaintiffs' work, and the inevitable conclusion was that an imputation was cast upon the characters of the authors. Even if I had thought that the right direction had not been given to the jury, I should have declined to grant a new trial, for the same verdict must inevitably have been found if the jury had been rightly directed.

Another point which has been discussed is this. It is said that if in some other case the alleged libel would not be beyond the limits of fair criticism, and it could be shewn that the defendant was not really criticising the work, but was writing with an indirect and dishonest intention to injure the plaintiffs, still the motive would not make the criticism a libel. I am inclined to think that it would, and for this reason, that the comment would not then really be a criticism of the work. The mind of the writer would not be that of a critic, but he would be actuated by an intention to injure the author.

NOTES

1. In *Turner* v *MGM Pictures* [1950] 1 All ER 449, at p. 461, Lord Parker approved the dictum of Lord Esher, but saying that he would 'substitute "honest" for "fair" lest some suggestion of reasonableness instead of honesty should be read in', and in *Branson* v *Bower* [2002] 2 WLR 452 at para. 28 Eady J said that the only requirements were (1) that a defendant should have expressed the opinions honestly and (2) that he should have done so upon facts accurately stated.

2. The relationship between malice and fair comment was discussed by the House of Lords in *Telnikoff* v *Matusevitch* [1991] 4 All ER 817, where it was said that if the defendant can show as an objective matter that the opinion was one which could be honestly held, he does not have to prove that he in fact held it. Rather, it is then for the claimant to prove as part of his allegation of malice that the defendant did not in fact honestly hold that view. Hence, the test of 'fair comment' is wholly objective, and the issue of the subjective state of the defendant's mind is a matter for the test of malice.

3. Malice will destroy the privilege of fair comment, and this is so even where the comment might have been made honestly and fairly, but was in fact activated by malice. In *Thomas* v *Bradbury Agnew Ltd* [1906] 2 KB 627 the defendants had published a critical review in *Punch* to which they pleaded fair comment. There was extrinsic evidence of ill will between the reviewer and the author. This evidence was admitted, and the jury found for the claimants. On appeal the defendants contended that the article itself did not go beyond the bounds of fair comment, and therefore extrinsic evidence of malice was irrelevant. Lord Collins MR said that this amounted to saying that fair comment was an absolute and not a relative standard, and he rejected that view, saying that it was quite immaterial that somebody else might without malice have written an equally damnatory criticism.

## DEFAMATION ACT 1952

### 6. Fair comment

In an action for libel or slander in respect of words consisting partly of allegations of fact and partly of expression of opinion, a defence of fair comment shall not fail by reason only that the truth of every allegation of fact is not proved if the expression of opinion is fair comment having regard to such of the facts alleged or referred to in the words complained of as are proved.

## SECTION 8: QUALIFIED PRIVILEGE

The defence of qualified privilege is not as wide as is sometimes imagined, and in particular it is no defence for a newspaper to publish information which it believes to be in the public interest and which it believes to be true, and the Faulks Committee recommended that no change be made in this rule. The rule contributes to secrecy and the difficulty of exposing wrongdoing, whether of public bodies, companies, or individuals. The breadth of the defence of privilege is an important element in the extent of free speech and the European Convention on Human Rights (above) will play an important part in this, for which see *Reynolds* v *Times Newspapers* (below).

### *Watt* v *Longsdon*
Court of Appeal [1930] 1 KB 130; 142 LT 4; 45 TLR 619

Longsdon was the liquidator of the Scottish Petroleum Company, which carried on business in Morocco and elsewhere. Watt, a managing director, and Browne, a manager, were in Casablanca. Browne wrote a letter to Longsdon, the liquidator, stating that Watt had left Casablanca, leaving behind an unpaid bill for £88 for whisky, and that he had been 'in immoral relations' with his housemaid, who was described as an old woman, stone deaf, almost blind and with dyed hair. Longsdon gave a copy of the letter to Mr Singer, the chairman of the board of directors, and to Mrs Watt. Longsdon also wrote a letter defamatory of Watt to Browne. The defendants claimed qualified privilege. Held: that there was evidence of malice which ought to be left to a jury and a new trial was ordered. It was also stated that the publication by Longsdon to Singer and Browne was privileged, but not the publication to Mrs Watt.

SCRUTTON LJ: Lord Esher MR says in *Pullman* v *Hill & Co.* [1891] 1 QB 524: 'An occasion is privileged when the person who makes the communication has a moral duty to make it to the person to whom he does make it, and the person who receives it has an interest in hearing it. Both these conditions must exist in order that the occasion may be privileged.' Lord Atkinson in *Adam* v *Ward* [1917] AC 309 expresses it thus: 'It was not disputed, in this case on either side, that a privileged occasion is, in reference to qualified privilege, an occasion where the person who makes a communication has an interest or a duty, legal, social, or moral, to make it to the person to whom it is made, and the person to whom it is so made has a corresponding interest or duty to receive it. This reciprocity is essential.' With slight modifications in particular circumstances, this appears to me to be well established law, but, except in the case of communications based on common interest, the principle is that either there must be interest in the recipient and a duty to communicate in the speaker, or an interest to be protected in the speaker and a duty to protect it in the recipient. Except in the case of common interest justifying intercommunication, the correspondence must be between duty and interest. There may, in the common interest cases, be also a common or reciprocal duty. It is not every interest which will create a duty in a stranger or volunteer. This appears to fit in with the two statements of Parke B already referred to . . . that the communication was made in the discharge of some social or moral duty, or on the ground of an interest in the party making or receiving it. This is approved by Lindley LJ in *Stuart* v *Bell* [1891] 2 QB 341, but I think should be expanded into:

> either (1) a duty to communicate information believed to be true to a person who has a material interest in receiving the information, or (2) an interest in the speaker to be protected by communicating information, if true, relevant to that interest, to a person honestly believed

> to have a duty to protect that interest, or (3) a common interest in and reciprocal duty in respect of the subject matter of the communication between speaker and recipient.
>
> . . . In my opinion Horridge J went too far in holding that there could be privileged occasion on the ground of interest in the recipient without any duty to communicate on the part of the person making the communication. But that does not settle the question, for it is necessary to consider, in the present case, whether there was, as to each communication, a duty to communicate, and an interest in the recipient.
>
> First as to the communication between Longsdon and Singer, I think the case must proceed on the admission that at all material times Watt, Longsdon and Browne were in the employment of the same company, and the evidence afforded by the answer to the interrogatory put in by the plaintiff that Longsdon believed the statements in Browne's letter. In my view on these facts there was a duty, both from a moral and a material point of view, on Longsdon to communicate the letter to Singer, the chairman of his company, who, apart from questions of present employment, might be asked by Watt for a testimonial to a future employer. Equally, I think Longsdon receiving the letter from Browne, might discuss the matter with him, and ask for further information, on the ground of a common interest in the affairs of the company, and to obtain further information for the chairman. . . .
>
> The communication to Mrs Watt stands on a different footing. I have no intention of writing an exhaustive treatise on the circumstances when a stranger or a friend should communicate to husband or wife information he receives as to the conduct of the other party to the marriage. I am clear that it is impossible to say he is always under a moral or social duty to do so; it is equally impossible to say he is never under such a duty. It must depend on the circumstances of each case, the nature of the information, and the relation of speaker and recipient. . . . Using the best judgment I can in this difficult matter, I have come to the conclusion that there was not a moral or social duty in Longsdon to make this communication to Mrs Watt such as to make the occasion privileged, and that there must be a new trial so far as it relates to the claim for publication of a libel to Mrs Watt. . . .

### NOTE

The general principles adopted by Scrutton LJ in this case were applied in *Beach* v *Freeson* [1971] 2 All ER 860 in the area of communication to public bodies. The MP Reg Freeson received a complaint from one of his constituents about the claimant solicitors, and the constituent asked him to write to the Law Society believing that the involvement of an MP would add weight to his complaint. The defendant did so, and added that he had received other complaints about the claimants in the past. He sent the letter to the Law Society, and also a copy to the Lord Chancellor. On the question of privilege, the Court of Appeal said that the MP had a duty to pass on the complaint to the Law Society and a duty to make additional comments which he thought should be investigated. The Law Society, as the relevant disciplinary body, had a reciprocal interest in receiving the complaint. That letter was therefore privileged. The same was true of the letter to the Lord Chancellor, who had an interest in the proper administration of justice, but the court pointed out that the recipient must, as the Lord Chancellor did, have an actual interest in receiving the information, and it would not be enough merely for the sender mistakenly to believe that such an interest existed.

---

### *Reynolds* v *Times Newspapers*
House of Lords [2001] 2 AC 127; [1999] 3 WLR 1010; [1999] 4 All ER 609

The claimant was the Prime Minister of Ireland, and a few days after he resigned the *Sunday Times* published an article with the headline 'Goodbye gombeen man' with the sub-heading 'Why a fib too far proved fatal for the political career of Ireland's peacemaker and Mr Fixit'. The claimant claimed that the article meant that he had dishonestly misled the Dail by suppressing information. The jury found that the allegations were untrue and that there was no malice on the part of the defendants.

The claimant was awarded damages of one penny. The defendants claimed qualified privilege on the ground that information of political significance attracted a special privilege. Held: the article was not privileged.

LORD NICHOLLS: . . . As highlighted by the Court of Appeal judgment in the present case, the common law solution is for the court to have regard to all the circumstances when deciding whether the publication of particular material was privileged because of its value to the public. Its value to the public depends upon its quality as well as its subject matter. This solution has the merit of elasticity. As observed by the Court of Appeal, this principle can be applied appropriately to the particular circumstances of individual cases in their infinite variety. It can be applied appropriately to all information published by a newspaper, whatever its source or origin.

Hand in hand with this advantage goes the disadvantage of an element of unpredictability and uncertainty. The outcome of a court decision, it was suggested, cannot always be predicted with certainty when the newspaper is deciding whether to publish a story. To an extent this is a valid criticism. A degree of uncertainty in borderline cases is inevitable. This uncertainty, coupled with the expense of court proceedings, may 'chill' the publication of true statements of fact as well as those which are untrue. The chill factor is perhaps felt more keenly by the regional press, book publishers and broadcasters than the national press. However, the extent of this uncertainty should not be exaggerated. With the enunciation of some guidelines by the court, any practical problems should be manageable. The common law does not seek to set a higher standard than that of responsible journalism, a standard the media themselves espouse.

*Conclusion*

My conclusion is that the established common law approach to misstatements of fact remains essentially sound. The common law should not develop 'political information' as a new 'subject matter' category of qualified privilege, whereby the publication of all such information would attract qualified privilege, whatever the circumstances. That would not provide adequate protection for reputation. Moreover, it would be unsound in principle to distinguish political discussion from discussion of other matters of serious public concern. The elasticity of the common law principle enables interference with freedom of speech to be confined to what is necessary in the circumstances of the case. This elasticity enables the court to give appropriate weight, in today's conditions, to the importance of freedom of expression by the media on all matters of public concern.

Depending on the circumstances, the matters to be taken into account include the following. The comments are illustrative only. 1. The seriousness of the allegation. The more serious the charge, the more the public is misinformed and the individual harmed, if the allegation is not true. 2. The nature of the information, and the extent to which the subject matter is a matter of public concern. 3. The source of the information. Some informants have no direct knowledge of the events. Some have their own axes to grind, or are being paid for their stories. 4. The steps taken to verify the information. 5. The status of the information. The allegation may have already been the subject of an investigation which commands respect. 6. The urgency of the matter. News is often a perishable commodity. 7. Whether comment was sought from the plaintiff. He may have information others do not possess or have not disclosed. An approach to the plaintiff will not always be necessary. 8. Whether the article contained the gist of the plaintiff's side of the story. 9. The tone of the article. A newspaper can raise queries or call for an investigation. It need not adopt allegations as statements of fact. 10. The circumstances of the publication, including the timing.

This list is not exhaustive. The weight to be given to these and any other relevant factors will vary from case to case. Any disputes of primary fact will be a matter for the jury, if there is one. The decision on whether, having regard to the admitted or proved facts, the publication was subject to qualified privilege is a matter for the judge. This is the established practice and seems sound. A balancing operation is better carried out by a judge in a reasoned judgment than by a jury. Over time, a valuable corpus of case law will be built up.

In general, a newspaper's unwillingness to disclose the identity of its sources should not weigh against it. Further, it should always be remembered that journalists act without the benefit of the clear light of hindsight. Matters which are obvious in retrospect may have been far from clear in the heat of the moment. Above all, the court should have particular regard to the importance of freedom of expression. The press discharges vital functions as a bloodhound as well as a watchdog. The court should be slow to conclude that a publication was not in the public interest and, therefore, the public had no right to know, especially when the information is in the field of political discussion. Any lingering doubts should be resolved in favour of publication.

. . .

LORD STEYN: . . . Counsel submitted that the House should recognise a qualified privilege extending to the publication by a newspaper to the public at large of factual information, opinions and arguments concerning government and political matters that affect the people of the United Kingdom. For convenience, I will call this a generic qualified privilege of political speech. A distinctive feature of political speech published by a newspaper is that it is communicated to a large audience. And this characteristic must be kept in mind in weighing the arguments in the present case. It is further essential not to lose sight of the factual framework in which the question arises, namely a defamatory and factually incorrect statement which the newspaper believed to be true.

It is now necessary to explain what is meant by a generic qualified privilege. It is to be contrasted with each case being considered in the light of its own particular circumstances, that is, in an ad hoc manner, in the light of the concrete facts of the case, and balancing in each case the gravity of the damage to the plaintiff's reputation against the value of publication on the particular occasion. A generic privilege, on the other hand, uses the technique of applying the privilege to a category or categories of cases. An example is the rule in the *Sullivan* case, which requires proof of malice in all defamation actions by public officials and public figures. In the present case counsel for the newspaper argues for a generic test not applicable to a category of victim (such as public figures) but dependent on the subject matter (political speech). . . .

On balance two particular factors have persuaded me to reject the generic test. First, the rule and practice in England is not to compel a newspaper to reveal its sources: see section 1 of the Contempt of Court Act 1981; RSC, Ord. 82, r. 6; and *Goodwin* v *United Kingdom* (1996) 22 EHRR 123, 143, at para. 39. By contrast a plaintiff in the United States is entitled to a pre-trial enquiry into the sources of the story and editorial decision-making: *Herbert* v *Lando* (1979) 441 US 153. Without such information a plaintiff suing for defamation in England will be substantially handicapped. Counsel for the newspaper observed that the House could recommend a reform of the procedural rule. This is an unsatisfactory basis to embark on a radical development of the law. Given the procedural restrictions in England I regard the recognition of a generic qualified privilege of political speech as likely to make it unacceptably difficult for a victim of defamatory and false allegations of fact to prove reckless disregard of the truth. Secondly, a test expressed in terms of a category of cases, such as political speech, is at variance with the jurisprudence of the European Court of Human Rights which in cases of competing rights and interests requires a balancing exercise in the light of the concrete facts of each case. While there is as yet no decision directly in point, it seems to me that Professor John Fleming is right in saying that the basic approach of the European Court of Human Rights has been close to the German approach by insisting on individual evaluation of each case rather than categories: 'Libel and Constitutional Free Speech,' in *Essays for Patrick Atiyah*, ed. Cane and Stapleton (1991), pp. 333, 337 and 345. Our inclination ought to be towards the approach that prevails in the jurisprudence on the Convention. In combination these two factors make me sceptical of the value of introducing a rule dependent on general categorisation, with the attendant sacrifice of individual justice in particular cases.

I would answer question (1) by saying that there is no generic qualified privilege of political speech in England.

*Issue (2): soundness of the circumstantial test*

My Lords, it is important to appreciate that the judgment of the Court of Appeal marked a development of English law in favour of freedom of expression. In the context of political speech the judgment recognised a qualified privilege, dependent on the particular circumstance of the case, provided that three requirements are fulfilled. The first and second are the familiar requirements of duty and interest. The Court of Appeal then stated a third and separate requirement. The passage in the judgment [1998] 3 WLR 862, 899–900 reads:

> Were the nature, status and source of the material, and the circumstances of the publication, such that the publication should in the public interest be protected in the absence of proof of express malice? (We call this the circumstantial test.) We make reference to 'status' bearing in mind the use of that expression in some of the more recent authorities to denote the degree to which information on a matter of public concern may (because of its character and known provenance) command respect . . . The higher the status of a report, the more likely it is to meet the circumstantial test. Conversely, unverified information from unidentified and unofficial sources may have little or no status, and where defamatory statements of fact are to be published to the widest audience on the strength of such sources, the publisher undertakes a heavy burden in showing that the publication is 'fairly warranted by any reasonable occasion or exigency.'

. . .

. . . On balance however, I am satisfied that the support for it [the circumstantial test] in the authorities is not great. Except for obiter dicta in *Blackshaw* v *Lord* [1984] QB 1, 42 the other decisions relied on by the Court of Appeal (see [1998] 3 WLR 862, 894–899) are cases of institutional reporting which are materially different from reports resulting from investigative journalism. And *Blackshaw* v *Lord* predates the *Derbyshire* case [1993] AC 534.

. . . I would not accept the circumstantial test is soundly based. Having reached this point I would not wish to be taken to reject entirely the reasoning of the Court of Appeal. It will be recalled that the Court of Appeal had observed, at p. 910:

> While those who engage in public life must expect and accept that their public conduct will be the subject of close scrutiny and robust criticism, they should not in our view be taken to expect or accept that their conduct should be the subject of false and defamatory statements of fact *unless the circumstances of the publication are such as to make it proper, in the public interest, to afford the publisher immunity from liability in the absence of malice.* (Emphasis supplied.)

After all, this is the core of the reasoning of the Court of Appeal.

I would however rule that the circumstantial test should not be adopted.

*Issue (3): the alternative tests of duty and interest*

If both the generic test and the circumstantial test are rejected, as I have done, the only sensible course is to go back to the traditional twofold test of duty and interest. These tests are flexible enough to embrace, depending on the occasion and the particular circumstances, a qualified privilege in respect of political speech published at large.

. . .

The context in which the qualified privilege of free speech should be applied is all important. It was said by counsel for the newspaper that the English courts have not yet recognised that the press has a general duty to inform the public of political matters and that the public has a right to be so informed. If there is any doubt on the point this is the occasion for the House to settle the matter. It is an open space in the law which can be filled by the courts. It is true that in our system the media have no specially privileged position not shared by individual citizens. On the other hand, it is necessary to recognise the 'vital public watchdog role of the press' as a practical matter: see *Goodwin* v *The United Kingdom*, 22 EHRR 123, 143, para. 39. The role of the press, and its duty, was well described by the European Court of Human Rights in *Castells* v *Spain* (1992) 14 EHRR 445, 476, para. 43:

> the pre-eminent role of the press in a state governed by the rule of law must not be forgotten. Although it must not overstep various bounds set, *inter alia*, for the prevention of disorder and the protection of the reputation of others, it is nevertheless incumbent on it to impart information and ideas on political questions and on other matters of public interest. Freedom of the press affords the public one of the best means of discovering and forming an opinion of

the ideas and attitudes of their political leaders. In particular, it gives politicians the opportunity to reflect and comment on the preoccupations of public opinion; it thus enables everyone to participate in the free political debate which is at the very core of the concept of a democratic society.

In *De Haes and Gijsels* v *Belgium*, 25 EHRR 1 the European Court of Human Rights again emphasised that the press plays an essential role in a democratic society. The court trenchantly observed, at p. 53, para. 39: 'It is incumbent on the press to impart information and ideas of public interest. Not only does the press have the task of imparting such information and ideas: the public also has a right to receive them.' This principle must be the foundation of our law on qualified privilege of political speech.

The correct approach to the line between permissible and impermissible political speech was indicated by the European Court of Human Rights in *Lingens* v *Austria*, 8 EHRR 407, 419, para. 42:

The limits of acceptable criticism are accordingly wider as regards a politician as such than as regards a private individual. Unlike the latter, the former inevitably and knowingly lays himself open to close scrutiny of his every word and deed by both journalists and the public at large, and he must consequently display a greater degree of tolerance. No doubt article 10(2) enables the reputation of others—that is to say, of all individuals—to be protected, and this protection extends to politicians too, even when they are not acting in their private capacity; but in such cases the requirements of such protection have to be weighed in relation to the interests of open discussion of political issues.

. . .

In the result I would uphold qualified privilege of political speech, based on a weighing of the particular circumstances of the case.

. . .

NOTES

1. The House of Lords discussed three possible approaches to reform:
   (a) *Special political or public figure privilege (the generic test).* This would allow privilege for information and opinions concerning government and political matters and stems from the US decision in *New York Times* v *Sullivan* (1964) 376 US 254, and this has now been extended to public figures. It has also been adopted in Australia in *Lange* v *Australian Broadcasting Corporation* (1997) 145 ALR 96, but rejected in Canada (*Hill* v *Church of Scientology of Toronto* (1995) 126 DLR 3rd 129, a non-political case). None of their Lordships was in favour of this proposal (see especially the speech of Lord Steyn).
   (b) *The circumstantial test.* This was adopted by the Court of Appeal, the test being whether the nature, status and source of the material and the circumstances of publication were such that publication should in the public interest be protected in the absence of malice. This was done on the grounds that those who engage in public life must expect and accept that their conduct will be the subject of close scrutiny. This test was rejected by Lord Steyn and Lord Hope but accepted in a varied form by Lord Nicholls and Lord Hobhouse. Lord Cooke also seemed to accept it, but thought that it should not be treated as something apart from the duty-interest theory.
   (c) *The duty-interest test.* This is the traditional test that there must be a duty to impart the information and a right to receive it. Lord Nicholls and Lord Cooke thought the circumstantial test was merely a development or variation of this. Lord Steyn preferred a more liberal test based on the role of the press in a modern democratic society as expressed in the European Convention on Human Rights.

2. As the claimant was awarded only 1 penny in damages the dispute was wholly about who should pay the costs. The actual decision that the article was not privileged was based on the view that although it was a matter of public concern, the paper had made serious allegations without mentioning the claimant's explanation. Lords Steyn and Hope dissented.

3. For further elaboration of the *Reynolds* test see *Loutchansky* v *The Times* (below). In that case it was clearly stated that *Reynolds* was a striking departure from the earlier approach to qualified

privilege and that '*Reynolds* privilege' although built upon an orthodox foundation is in reality *sui generis*. Note, however, that the New Zealand courts have rejected the *Reynolds* doctrine, saying that it adds to uncertainty and to the chilling effect in this area of the law and reduces the role of the jury: see *Lange* v *Atkinson* [2000] 3 NZLR 385.

4. Should *Reynolds*-type qualified privilege apply where a journalist responsibly believes that an article is not defamatory (when in fact it is) and that the subject matter should be published in the public interest? This issue is addressed by cases in the Privy Council and in the Court of Appeal. In *Bonnick* v *Morris* [2003] 1 AC 300, [2002] UKPC 31, the Privy Council, on appeal from Jamaica, held that the defence did apply. In other words where there is doubt about what an article means or there are several possible meanings, the test would be whether a journalist acted responsibly in publishing the article, believing the non-defamatory meaning to be one which reasonable people would draw from the article. However in *Jameel* v *Wall Street Journal Europe* [2005] QB 904, [2005] EWCA Civ 74, the Court of Appeal drew attention to some difficulties with this idea and expressed no view as to whether it formed part of the law of England and Wales. The problems are that subjective belief in the truth of a statement or in its true meaning is only relevant to the issue of malice and not until now to the issue of privilege. There is also the problem that the jury may believe the statement to be defamatory, but it would be privileged if some people, including the author, could reasonably believe it to be non-defamatory. In the case itself the court sidestepped the issue by saying that no reasonable journalist could have ignored the fact that the article was *capable* of bearing a defamatory meaning. Is this now the test? What if the journalist realizes that there *might* be a defamatory meaning, but believes a non-defamatory meaning to be a reasonable interpretation? Leave to appeal to the House of Lords has been granted.

5. For an example of the application of Lord Nicholls' ten-point test see *Grobbelaar* v *News Group Newspapers* [2001] 2 All ER 437 where the defendants printed a story alleging that the claimant had engaged in fixing matches. After a full discussion of the ten points it was held that this was not privileged. Simon Brown LJ said 'the ultimate question is whether the public was entitled to receive the information contained in these publications irrespective of whether it proved to be true or false. Who, in other words, is to bear the risk that allegations of this sort, convincing though no doubt they appear to the newspaper when published, may finally turn out to be false?' He pointed out that given the commercial benefits of this style of journalism and the reduced level of damages now awarded, newspapers would not be discouraged from their investigatory role by the lack of protection by qualified privilege. Indeed he thought that if they were protected investigations would become less thorough and the results more sensationally promoted.

---

### *Loutchansky* v *The Times Newspapers (No. 2)*
Court of Appeal [2002] QB 783; [2002] 2 WLR 640; [2002] 1 All ER 652; [2001] EWCA Civ 1805

The defendants had alleged that the claimant was a leading member of the Russian mafia, but later admitted that this was defamatory. There were two actions; the first was based on articles published in the newspaper itself and the second related to the publication of back numbers on the Internet. The defendants pleaded qualified privilege in both actions and in the second claimed that the action, which was begun more than a year after publication of the original newspaper, was out of time. Held: that the first action should be remitted to the High Court but that the defendants were liable in the second action.

LORD PHILLIPS MR:

*The First Action Liability appeal*

**33** Whereas previously it could truly be said of qualified privilege that it attaches to the occasion of the publication rather than the publication. *Reynolds* privilege attaches, if at all, to the publication itself: it is impossible to conceive of circumstances in which the occasion of publication could be privileged but the article itself not so. Similarly, once *Reynolds* privilege attaches, little scope remains for any subsequent finding of malice. Actual malice in this context has traditionally been recognised to consist either of recklessness i.e. not believing the statement to be true or being indifferent as to its truth, or of making it with the dominant motive of injuring the claimant. But the publisher's conduct in both regards must inevitably be explored when considering Lord Nicholls' ten factors i.e. in deciding whether the publication is covered by qualified privilege in the first place. As May LJ observed in *GKR Karate (UK) Limited v Yorkshire Post Limited* [2000] 1 WLR 2571, at 2580:

> If the judge decides that the occasion is not privileged, the issue of malice does not arise. If the judge decides that the occasion was privileged, he must have decided that, in all the circumstances, at the time of the publication, including the extent of . . . enquiries, the public was entitled to know the particular information available . . . without [the journalist] making further enquiries. It is a little difficult to see how the same enquiries which objectively sustained the occasion as privileged would be capable of contributing to a conclusion that subjectively she was recklessly indifferent to the truth or falsity of her publication.

**35** The relevance of these observations to the present appeal is this. Once *Reynolds* privilege is recognised, as it should be, as a different jurisprudential creature from the traditional form of privilege from which it sprang, the particular nature of the 'interest' and 'duty' which underlie it can more easily be understood.

**36** The interest is that of the public in a modern democracy in free expression and, more particularly, in the promotion of a free and vigorous press to keep the public informed. The vital importance of this interest has been identified and emphasised time and again in recent cases and needs no restatement here. The corresponding duty on the journalist (and equally his editor) is to play his proper role in discharging that function. His task is to behave as a responsible journalist. He can have no duty to publish unless he is acting responsibly any more than the public has an interest in reading whatever may be published irresponsibly. That is why in this class of case the question whether the publisher has behaved responsibly is necessarily and intimately bound up with the question whether the defence of qualified privilege arises. Unless the publisher is acting responsibly privilege cannot arise. That is not the case with regard to the more conventional situations in which qualified privilege arises. A person giving a reference or reporting a crime need not act responsibly: his communication will be privileged subject only to relevance and malice.

**39** This court in *Al-Fagih* v *Saudi Research and Marketing* (unreported) adopted the approach suggested by Lord Hobhouse in *Reynolds* at p. 239E, namely to ask:

> . . . what it is in the public interest that the public should know and what the publisher could properly consider that he is under a public duty to tell the public.

**40** Simon Brown LJ suggested that that approach seemed:

> . . . properly to reflect on the one hand the importance of keeping the public informed and on the other the need for responsible journalism to guard against needless misinformation. A publisher could not properly consider that he was under a public duty to communicate the information to the public unless in deciding to do so he reasonably believed that he was acting responsibly.

It may be that the words 'reasonably believed that he' towards the end of that formulation are best omitted: they were intended, perhaps unnecessarily, to emphasise the objective nature of the test. In the final analysis it must be for the court, not the journalist, to decide whether he was acting responsibly. That appears clearly from several passages in *Reynolds*: in rejecting the newspaper's commended 'reliance upon the ethics of professional journalism', Lord Nicholls at p. 202B referred to 'the sad reality . . . that the overall handling of these matters by the national press, with its own commercial interests to serve, does not always command general confidence'. Lord Cooke at p. 220D–E suggested that 'experience of libel litigation is apt to generate a suspicion that' the restriction of freedom of speech thought necessary to give reasonable protection to personal reputation tends rather to chill the publication of untruths than of material which may be true but cannot be proved to be true. Lord Hope too spoke of situations in which the 'chilling' effect of the law 'is a necessary protection for the individual'. Perhaps one need look no further than Lord Nicholls' dictum in *Reynolds* at p. 202E–F:

> The common law does not seek to set a higher standard than that of responsible journalism, a standard the media themselves espouse. An incursion into press freedom which goes no further than this would not seem to be excessive or disproportionate.

**41** In deciding in any given case whether the standard of responsible journalism has been satisfied, the following considerations are likely to feature prominently in the court's thinking:

(i) If the publication is held privileged, that, to all intents and purposes, will provide the publishers with a complete defence. In this class of case, as already observed, a finding of privilege will effectively pre-empt a finding of malice. Lord Nicholls described malice as 'notoriously difficult to prove' (p. 201G), Lord Cooke as 'a dubious safeguard' (p. 219H), and Lord Hope as 'very difficult, if not impossible, [to prove] if the sources of the information cannot be identified'. Accordingly, if the defence is established, that, as Gray J pointed out in paragraph 16 of his judgment below, has 'the effect of denying any remedy, whether by way of compensation or other vindication to a person who has been libelled'. The damaging consequences of that, not merely for the aggrieved individual but for society at large, are highlighted by Lord Nicholls in *Reynolds* at p. 201 A–C:

Reputation is an integral and important part of the dignity of the individual. It also forms the basis of many decisions in a democratic society which are fundamental to its well-being: whom to employ or work for, whom to promote, whom to do business with or vote for. Once besmirched by an unfounded allegation in a national newspaper, a reputation can be damaged for ever, especially if there is no opportunity to vindicate one's reputation. When this happens, society as well as the individual is the loser. For it should not be supposed that protection of reputation is a matter of importance only to the affected individual and his family. Protection of reputation is conducive to the public good. It is in the public interest that the reputation of public figures should not be debased falsely.

(ii) Setting the standard of journalistic responsibility too low would inevitably encourage too great a readiness to publish defamatory matter. Journalists should be rigorous, not lax, in their approach. It is in the interests of the public as well as the defamed individual that, wherever possible, truths and not untruths should be told. This is in the interests of the media too: once untruths can be published with impunity, the public will cease to believe any communications, true or false.

(iii) Setting the standard too high, however, would be no less damaging to society. This would deter newspapers from discharging their proper function of keeping the public informed. When determining in respect of any given article whether or not it should attract qualified privilege, the court must bear in mind the likely impact of its ruling not only upon the case in hand but also upon the media's practices generally. Qualified privilege ordinarily falls to be judged as a preliminary issue and before, therefore, the truth or falsity of the communication is established. The question to be posed is accordingly whether it was in the public interest to publish the article, true or false, rather than whether it was in the public interest to publish an untruth. Even, moreover, when the untruth of the article *is* established (or when, as here, it is not formally disputed), it is important to remember that the defence of qualified privilege tolerates factual inaccuracy for two purposes: first so as not to deter the publication sued upon (which might have been true); and secondly so as not to deter future publications of truthful information.

*The Internet Single Publication appeal*

**57** It is a well established principle of the English law of defamation that each individual publication of a libel gives rise to a separate cause of action, subject to its own limitation period. *Duke of Brunswick* v *Harmer* (1849) 14 QB 185 provides a striking illustration of this principle. On 19 September 1830 an article was published in the *Weekly Dispatch*. The limitation period for libel was then six years. The article defamed the Duke of Brunswick. Seventeen years after its publication an agent of the Duke purchased a back number containing the article from the *Weekly Dispatch's* office. Another copy was obtained from the British Museum. The Duke sued on those two publications. The defendant contended that the cause of action was time barred, relying on the original publication date. The Court of Queen's Bench held that the delivery of a copy of the newspaper to the plaintiff's agent constituted a separate publication in respect of which suit could be brought.

**58** In *Godfrey* v *Demon Internet Limited* [2001] QB 201 the respondent brought an action in defamation against the appellants who were internet service providers. They had received and stored on their news server an article, defamatory of the respondent, which had been posted by an unknown person using another service provider. The issue was whether the appellants had a defence under s. 1(1) of the Defamation Act 1996. The Judge held that they did not. He observed at p. 208:

> In my judgment the defendants, whenever they transmit and whenever there is transmitted from the storage of their news server a defamatory posting, publish that posting to any subscriber to their ISP who accesses the newsgroup containing that posting. Thus every time one of the defendants' customers accesses soc.culture.thai and sees that posting defamatory of the plaintiff there is a publication to that customer.

**63** How is it that the appellants suggest that the law should evolve? They focus on the provision of s. 4A of the Limitation Act 1980 that no action shall be brought after the expiration of one year from the date on which *the cause of action accrued*. They contend that the words italicised should be interpreted to mean the date of the *initial publication*. The route by which they seek to achieve this is explained in the next paragraph of their skeleton argument as follows:

> The defendant seeks to adapt to an English context the rule known in the US as the 'single publication rule', whereby the distribution of a work involves only one publication, on the date of its first publication in a particular format. Hence, for example, the statute of limitations would start running on a libel in a book on the date of its first publication, even if it continued to be sold for months afterwards. Only one action for damages could be maintained, all damage suffered in all jurisdictions could be recovered in one action, and a judgment on the merits would bar any other actions for damages between the same parties in all jurisdictions. However, if a new edition is published, or a softback edition, or even a reprinting, time starts to run again.

**67** The reasons advanced by the appellants for introducing this novel concept into our law are very similar to those adumbrated in the passage from *Gregoire* v *Putnam's Sons* (1948) 81 NE 2d 45 which we have cited above. Section 4A of the Limitation Act 1980 imposes an unusually short limitation period in defamation cases. The object of this is to ensure that defamation claims are initiated promptly. If claims are brought within a year of the initial publication, the appellants will be able to marshal any available defence and data available. Lord Lester argued that these benefits will be defeated if, long after the initial publication, a respondent can base a claim on access by a single person to a copy of the publication in question.

**70** Lord Lester buttressed these arguments by reference to the Human Rights Act 1998 and the Convention. He submitted that to permit defamation actions to be commenced more than a year after the initial publication was a restriction on the writer's freedom of expression enshrined in Article 10 of the Convention. Section 12 of the Act required the Court to have particular regard to the importance of the Convention right to freedom of expression. To be justified, any curtailment of freedom of expression has to be convincingly established by a compelling countervailing consideration, and the means employed had to be necessary and proportionate to the ends sought to be achieved.

**71** Maintaining an archive of past press publications was a valuable public service. If a newspaper defendant which maintained a website of back numbers was to be indefinitely vulnerable to claims in defamation for years and even decades after the initial hard copy and Internet publication, such a rule was bound to have an effect on the preparedness of the media to maintain such websites, and thus to limit freedom of expression.

**72** In answer to these submission Mr Browne started by emphasising that the principle in the *Duke of Brunswick* that every publication of a libel gives rise to a separate cause of action is a well established principle of English law that was recognised by the House of Lords in *Berezovsky* v *Michaels* [2000] 1 WLR 1004. He submitted that this principle was not at odds with the Human Rights Convention. Article 10 recognised that the right of freedom of expression could properly be restricted 'for the protection of the reputation or rights of others'. The rule in the *Duke of Brunswick* was part of the system of English law that balanced the right of freedom of expression against the entitlement to protection of one's reputation. If the appellants were exposed to liability in the second action they had only themselves to blame for persisting in retaining the offending articles on their website without qualifying these in any way.

*Our conclusion*

**74** We do not accept that the rule in the *Duke of Brunswick* imposes a restriction on the readiness to maintain and provide access to archives that amounts to a disproportionate restriction on freedom of expression. We accept that the maintenance of archives, whether in hard copy or on the Internet, has a social utility, but consider that the maintenance of archives is a comparatively insignificant aspect of freedom of expression. Archive material is stale news and its publication cannot rank in importance with the dissemination of contemporary material. Nor do we believe that the law of defamation need inhibit the responsible maintenance of archives. Where it is known that archive material is or may be defamatory, the attachment of an appropriate notice warning against treating it as the truth will normally remove any sting from the material.

**75** Turning to the appellants' wider argument, it is true that to permit an action to be based on a fresh dissemination of an article published long ago is at odds with some of the reasons for the introduction of a 12 month limitation period for defamation. But the scale of such publication and any resulting damage is likely to be modest compared with that of the original publication. In the present case, as the Judge observed, the action based on the Internet publication is subsidiary to the main action.

**76** The change in the law of defamation for which the appellants contend is a radical one. In our judgment they have failed to make out their case that such a change is required. The Internet Single Publication appeal is therefore dismissed.

*The Internet Qualified Privilege appeal*

**79** . . . A subsidiary reason given by the Judge for striking out the defence was that the appellants had repeatedly republished on the Internet defamatory material that was the subject of a defamation action in which they were not seeking to justify the truth of the allegations without publishing any qualification to draw to the reader's attention the fact that the truth of the articles was hotly contested. The Judge considered that the republication of back numbers of *The Times* on the Internet was made in materially different circumstances from those obtaining at the time of the publication of the original hard copy versions in September and October 1999. We agree. The failure to attach any qualifications to the articles published over the period of a year on *The Times'* website could not possibly be described as responsible journalism. We do not believe that it can be convincingly argued that the appellants had a *Reynolds* duty to publish those articles in that way without qualification. It follows that we consider that the Judge was right to strike out the qualified privilege defence in the second action although not for the primary reason that he gave for so doing. For these reasons the Internet Single Publication appeal is also dismissed.

NOTE

This case is a useful elucidation of the *Reynolds* doctrine especially in its relationship to malice but it is also of great importance to archivists. The decision that (1) time begins to run whenever the web archive is accessed and (2) that a 'disclaimer' should be added to any document which is known to be defamatory (even if originally privileged) will lead to severe practical problems. Furthermore the refusal to adopt the 'single publication rule' for the application of the Limitation Act 1980 means that a libel action will hardly ever be out of time for web publications.

## DEFAMATION ACT 1996

**14.**—(1) A fair and accurate report of proceedings in public before a court to which this section applies, if published contemporaneously with the proceedings, is absolutely privileged.

(2) A report of proceedings which by an order of the court, or as a consequence of any statutory provision, is required to be postponed shall be treated as published contemporaneously if it is published as soon as practicable after publication is permitted.

(3) This section applies to—

(a) any court in the United Kingdom;

(b) the European Court of Justice or any court attached to that court;

(c) the European Court of Human Rights, and

(d) any international criminal tribunal established by the Security Council of the United Nations or by an international agreement to which the United Kingdom is a party.

In paragraph (a) 'court' includes any tribunal or body exercising the judicial power of the state.

(4) [omitted]

**15.**—(1)The publication of any report or other statement mentioned in Schedule 1 to this Act is privileged unless the publication is shown to be made with malice, subject as follows.

(2) In defamation proceedings in respect of the publication of a report or other statement mentioned in Part II of that Schedule, there is no defence under this section if the plaintiff shows that the defendant—

(a) was requested by him to publish in a suitable manner a reasonable letter or statement by way of explanation or contradiction, and

(b) refused or neglected to do so.

For this purpose 'in a suitable manner' means in the same manner as the publication complained of or in a manner that is adequate and reasonable in the circumstances.

(3) This section does not apply to the publication to the public, or a section of the public, of matter which is not of public concern and the publication of which is not for the public benefit.

(4) Nothing in this section shall be construed—

(a) as protecting the publication of matter the publication of which is prohibited by law, or

(b) as limiting or abridging any privilege subsisting apart from this section.

### SCHEDULE 1  QUALIFIED PRIVILEGE

### PART I    STATEMENTS HAVING QUALIFIED PRIVILEGE WITHOUT EXPLANATION OR CONTRADICTION

1.   A fair and accurate report of proceedings in public of a legislature anywhere in the world.

2.   A fair and accurate report of proceedings in public before a court anywhere in the world.

3.   A fair and accurate report of proceedings in public of a person appointed to hold a public inquiry by a government or legislature anywhere in the world.

4.   A fair and accurate report of proceedings in public anywhere in the world of an international organisation or an international conference.

5.   A fair and accurate copy of or extract from any register or other document required by law to be open to public inspection.

6.   A notice or advertisement published by or on the authority of a court, or of a judge or officer of a court, anywhere in the world.

7.   A fair and accurate copy of or extract from matter published by or on the authority of a government or legislature anywhere in the world.

8.   A fair and accurate copy of or extract from matter published anywhere in the world by an international organisation or an international conference.

## PART II  STATEMENTS PRIVILEGED SUBJECT TO EXPLANATION OR CONTRADICTION

9.—(1)  A fair and accurate copy of or extract from a notice or other matter issued for the information of the public by or on behalf of—

(a)  a legislature in any member State or the European Parliament;

(b)  the government of any member State, or any authority performing governmental functions in any member State or part of a member State, or the European Commission;

(c)  an international organisation or international conference.

(2)  In this paragraph 'governmental functions' includes police functions.

10.  A fair and accurate copy of or extract from a document made available by a court in any member State or the European Court of Justice, or any court attached to that court, or by a judge or officer of any such court.

11.—(1)  A fair and accurate report of proceedings at any public meeting or sitting in the United Kingdom of—

(a)  a local authority, local authority committee or in the case of a local authority which are operating executive arrangements the executive of that authority or a committee of that executive;

(b)  a justice or justices of the peace acting otherwise than as a court exercising judicial authority;

(c)  a commission, tribunal, committee or person appointed for the purposes of any inquiry by any statutory provision, by Her Majesty or by a Minister of the Crown, a member of the Scottish Executive or a Northern Ireland Department;

(d)  a person appointed by a local authority to hold a local inquiry in pursuance of any statutory provision;

(e)  any other tribunal, board, committee or body constituted by or under, and exercising functions under, any statutory provision.

(1A)  In the case of a local authority which are operating executive arrangements, a fair and accurate record of any decision made by any member of the executive where that record is required to be made and available for public inspection by virtue of section 22 of the Local Government Act 2000 or of any provision in regulations made under that section.

(2)  In sub-paragraphs (1) (a) and (1A)—

'executive' and 'executive arrangements' have the same meaning as in Part II of the Local Government Act 2000;

'local authority' means—

(a)  in relation to England and Wales, a principal council within the meaning of the Local Government Act 1972, any body falling within any paragraph of section 100J(1) of that Act or an authority or body to which the Public Bodies (Admission to Meetings) Act 1960 applies,

(b)  in relation to Scotland, a council constituted under section 2 of the Local Government etc. (Scotland) Act 1994 or an authority or body to which the Public Bodies (Admission to Meetings) Act 1960 applies,

(c)  in relation to Northern Ireland, any authority or body to which sections 23 to 27 of the Local Government Act (Northern Ireland) 1972 apply; and

'local authority committee' means any committee of a local authority or of local authorities, and includes—

(a)  any committee or sub-committee in relation to which sections 100A to 100D of the Local Government Act 1972 apply by virtue of section 100E of that Act (whether or not also by virtue of section 100J of that Act), and

(b)  any committee or sub-committee in relation to which sections 50A to 50D of the Local Government (Scotland) Act 1973 apply by virtue of section 50E of that Act.

(3)  A fair and accurate report of any corresponding proceedings in any of the Channel Islands or the Isle of Man or in another member State.

12.—(1)  A fair and accurate report of proceedings at any public meeting held in a member State.

(2)   In this paragraph a 'public meeting' means a meeting bona fide and lawfully held for a lawful purpose and for the furtherance or discussion of a matter of public concern, whether admission to the meeting is general or restricted.

13.—(1)   A fair and accurate report of proceedings at a general meeting of a UK public company.

(2)   A fair and accurate copy of or extract from any document circulated to members of a UK public company—

(a)  by or with the authority of the board of directors of the company,

(b)  by the auditors of the company, or

(c)  by any member of the company in pursuance of a right conferred by any statutory provision.

(3)   A fair and accurate copy of or extract from any document circulated to members of a UK public company which relates to the appointment, resignation, retirement or dismissal of directors of the company.

(4)   In this paragraph 'UK public company' means—

(a)  a public company within the meaning of section 1(3) of the Companies Act 1985 or Article 12(3) of the Companies (Northern Ireland) Order 1986, or

(b)  a body corporate incorporated by or registered under any other statutory provision, or by Royal Charter, or formed in pursuance of letters patent.

(5)   A fair and accurate report of proceedings at any corresponding meeting of, or copy of or extract from any corresponding document circulated to members of, a public company formed under the law of any of the Channel Islands or the Isle of Man or another member State.

14.—A fair and accurate report of any finding or decision of any of the following descriptions of association, formed in the United Kingdom or another member State, or of any committee or governing body of such an association—

(a)  an association formed for the purpose of promoting or encouraging the exercise of or interest in any art, science, religion or learning, and empowered by its constitution to exercise control over or adjudicate on matters of interest or concern to the association, or the actions or conduct of any person subject to such control or adjudication;

(b)  an association formed for the purpose of promoting or safeguarding the interests of any trade, business, industry or profession, or of the persons carrying on or engaged in any trade, business, industry or profession, and empowered by its constitution to exercise control over or adjudicate upon matters connected with that trade, business, industry or profession, or the actions or conduct of those persons;

(c)  an association formed for the purpose of promoting or safeguarding the interests of a game, sport or pastime to the playing or exercise of which members of the public are invited or admitted, and empowered by its constitution to exercise control over or adjudicate upon persons connected with or taking part in the game, sport or pastime;

(d)  an association formed for the purpose of promoting charitable objects or other objects beneficial to the community and empowered by its constitution to exercise control over or to adjudicate on matters of interest or concern to the association, or the actions or conduct of any person subject to such control or adjudication.

15.—(1)   A fair and accurate report of, or copy of or extract from, any adjudication, report, statement or notice issued by a body, officer or other person designated for the purposes of this paragraph—

(a)  for England and Wales or Northern Ireland, by order of the Lord Chancellor, and

(b)  for Scotland, by order of the Secretary of State.

(2)   An order under this paragraph shall be made by statutory instrument which shall be subject to annulment in pursuance of a resolution of either House of Parliament.

**PART III   SUPPLEMENTARY PROVISIONS**

16.—(1)   In this Schedule—

'court' includes any tribunal or body exercising the judicial power of the State;

'international conference' means a conference attended by representatives of two or more governments;

'international organisation' means an organisation of which two or more governments are members, and includes any committee or other subordinate body of such an organisation; and

'legislature' includes a local legislature.

(2)   References in this Schedule to a member State include any European dependent territory of a member State.

(3)   In paragraphs 2 and 6 'court' includes—

(a)   the European Court of Justice (or any court attached to that court) and the Court of Auditors of the European Communities,

(b)   the European Court of Human Rights,

(c)   any international criminal tribunal established by the Security Council of the United Nations or by an international agreement to which the United Kingdom is a party, and

(d)   the International Court of Justice and any other judicial or arbitral tribunal deciding matters in dispute between States.

(4)   In paragraphs 1, 3 and 7 'legislature' includes the European Parliament.

NOTE

For the purposes of what is now paragraph 12 above, a press conference will be regarded as a 'public meeting'. In *McCartan Turkington Breen* v *The Times* [2000] 4 All ER 913 Lord Bingham said that 'a meeting is public if those who organise it or arrange it open it to the public or, by issuing a general invitation to the press, manifest an intention or desire that the proceedings of the meeting should be communicated to a wider public. Press representatives may be regarded as members of the public . . . or as the eyes and ears of the public to whom they report.' Furthermore a press release, even if not read out at the meeting, will be regarded as part of the proceedings.

---

**FREEDOM OF INFORMATION ACT 2000**

**1.**—(1)   Any person making a request for information to a public authority is entitled—

(a)   to be informed in writing by the public authority whether it holds information of the description specified in the request, and

(b)   if that is the case, to have that information communicated to him.

**79.**—Where any information communicated by a public authority to a person ('the applicant') under section 1 was supplied to the public authority by a third person, the publication to the applicant of any defamatory matter contained in the information shall be privileged unless the publication is shown to have been made with malice.

## SECTION 9: DAMAGES

Damages for defamation are 'at large', and there has been considerable concern recently at the high level of awards in some cases. The record award so far is £1,500,000 in favour of Lord Aldington, awarded against Count Tolstoy and Mr Watts for allegations concerning the repatriation of Yugoslavs at the end of the war, but in view of its size this award was held to be contrary to Article 10 of the European Convention on Human Rights (see above).

Damages, with the exception of exemplary damages which are discussed below, are intended to be compensatory, but in the words of Windeyer J in *Uren* v *John Fairfax* (1967) 117 CLR 118:

a man defamed does not get damages *for* his damaged reputation. He gets damages *because* he was injured in his reputation, that is simply because he was publicly defamed. For this reason, compensation by damages operates in two ways—as a vindication of the plaintiff to the public and as a consolation to him for a wrong done. Compensation is here a solatium rather than a monetary recompense for a harm measurable in money.

Damages can include compensation for injury to feelings, and 'aggravated' damages can be awarded for the subsequent conduct of the defendant, including a failure to make a sufficient apology; a repetition of the libel; conduct calculated to deter the claimant from proceeding; persistence in a plea of justification which is bound to fail; and persecution of the claimant by other means. However, awards in this area are not split up into their component parts, but rather the jury will name a global sum, and it is the overall level of these sums which has caused concern.

Exemplary damages are awarded to 'punish' the defendant where he knew that he was committing a tort (or was reckless) but went ahead anyway because he expected to profit from the tort. For an example see *Cassell* v *Broome* [1972] AC 1027, where the defendants had published a book called *The Destruction of Convoy PQ 17* which wrongly blamed Commander Broome for the disaster. He was awarded £25,000 exemplary damages. See also *John* v *MGN* below.

An offer of amends under the Defamation Act 1996 can either provide a complete defence or act to reduce the damages substantially. This is dealt with at the end of this section.

---

### John v MGN Ltd
Court of Appeal [1997] QB 586; [1996] 3 WLR 593; [1996] 2 All ER 35

In 1992 the *Sunday Mirror* published a story that 'rock superstar Elton John is hooked on a bizarre new diet which doctors have warned could kill him'. It stated that Elton John had been observed at a party in California chewing snacks and then disposing of them in his napkin. The story was completely false and at first instance the claimant was awarded compensatory damages of £75,000 and exemplary damages of £275,000. Held: allowing the appeal, that compensatory damages should be £25,000 and exemplary damages £50,000.

SIR THOMAS BINGHAM MR: . . .

*Compensatory damages*

The successful plaintiff in a defamation action is entitled to recover, as general compensatory damages, such sum as will compensate him for the wrong he has suffered. That sum must compensate him for the damage to his reputation; vindicate his good name; and take account of the distress, hurt and humiliation which the defamatory publication has caused. In assessing the appropriate damages for injury to reputation the most important factor is the gravity of the libel; the more closely it touches the plaintiff's personal integrity, professional reputation, honour, courage, loyalty and the core attributes of his personality, the more serious it is likely to be. The extent of publication is also very relevant: a libel published to millions has a greater potential to cause damage than a libel published to a handful of people. A successful plaintiff may properly look to an award of damages to vindicate his reputation: but the significance of this is much greater in a case where the defendant asserts the truth of the libel and refuses any retraction or apology than in a case where the defendant acknowledges the falsity of what was published and publicly expresses regret that the libellous publication took place. It is well established that compensatory damages may and should compensate for additional injury caused to the plaintiff's feelings by the defendant's conduct of the action, as when he persists in an unfounded assertion that the publication was true, or refuses to apologise, or cross-examines the plaintiff in a wounding or insulting way. Although the plaintiff has been referred to as 'he', all this of course applies to women just as much as men.

A series of jury awards in sums wildly disproportionate to any damage conceivably suffered by the plaintiff has given rise to serious and justified criticism of the procedures leading to such awards. This has not been the fault of the juries. Judges, as they were bound to do, confined themselves to broad directions of general principle, coupled with injunctions to the jury to be reasonable. But they gave no guidance on what might be thought reasonable or unreasonable, and it is not altogether surprising that juries lacked an instinctive sense of where to pitch their awards. They were in the position of sheep loosed on an unfenced common, with no shepherd.

While the Court of Appeal reaffirmed the fundamental soundness of the traditional approach in *Sutcliffe v Pressdram Ltd* [1990] 1 All ER 269, [1991] 1 QB 153, the court did in that case recommend trial judges to draw the attention of juries to the purchasing power of the award they were minded to make, and of the income it would produce (see [1990] 1 All ER 269 at 283–284, 289, 293, [1991] 1 QB 153 at 178–179, 185–186, 190). This was thereafter done, and juries were reminded of the cost of buying a motor car, or a holiday, or a house. But judges were still constrained by authority from steering the jury towards any particular level of award.

Following the enactment of s. 8(2) of the Courts and Legal Services Act 1990 and the introduction of RSC Ord 59, r. 11(4) in its present form, the Court of Appeal was for the first time empowered, on allowing an appeal against a jury's award of damages, to substitute for the sum awarded by the jury such sum as might appear to the court to be proper . . .

In *Rantzen v Mirror Group Newspapers (1986) Ltd* [1993] 4 All ER 975, [1994] QB 670 the newspaper appealed against a jury's award of £250,000, contending that the size of the award was wholly disproportionate to the damage done to the plaintiff's reputation. The court concluded that at that time it would not be right to allow reference to be made to awards by juries in previous cases. But it took the view that awards made by the Court of Appeal stood on a different footing: over a period of time awards made by the Court of Appeal would provide a corpus to which reference could be made in subsequent cases (see [1993] 4 All ER 975 at 995, [1994] QB 670 at 694) . . .

. . .

We are persuaded by Mr Gray's argument that this subject deserves reconsideration, despite the short period since the *Rantzen* ruling was given. Any legal process should yield a successful plaintiff appropriate compensation, that is, compensation which is neither too much nor too little. That is so whether the award is made by judge or jury. No other result can be accepted as just. But there is continuing evidence of libel awards in sums which appear so large as to bear no relation to the ordinary values of life. This is most obviously unjust to defendants. But it serves no public purpose to encourage plaintiffs to regard a successful libel action, risky though the process undoubtedly is, as a road to untaxed riches. Nor is it healthy if any legal process fails to command the respect of lawyer and layman alike, as is regrettably true of the assessment of damages by libel juries. We are persuaded by the arguments we have heard that the subject should be reconsidered. This is not a field in which we are bound by previous authority (*Sutcliffe v Pressdram Ltd* [1990] 1 All ER 269 at 283, [1991] 1 QB 153 at 178) but it is necessary for us to review the arguments which have found favour in the past.

*Other awards in actions for defamation*

We wholly agree with the ruling in *Rantzen* that juries should not at present be reminded of previous libel awards by juries. Those awards will have been made in the absence of specific guidance by the judge and may themselves be very unreliable markers.

The position may change in the future if the additional guidance which we propose later in this judgment is given and proves to be successful. As was pointed out in the course of argument, however, comparison with other awards is very difficult because the circumstances of each libel are almost bound to be unique. Furthermore, the corpus of such awards will be likely to become unwieldy and time would be expended on the respective parties pointing to features which were either similar or dissimilar in the other cases.

### Awards approved or substituted by the Court of Appeal

We agree with the ruling in *Rantzen* that reference may be made to awards approved or made by the Court of Appeal. As and when a framework of awards is established this will provide a valuable pointer to the appropriate level of award in the particular case. But it is plain that such a framework will not be established quickly: it is now five years since s. 8(2) of the 1990 Act and Ord 59, r. 11(4) came into force, and there is no case other than *Gorman*, *Rantzen* and *Houston* in which the court has itself fixed the appropriate level of award.

It is true that awards in this category are subject to the same objection that time can be spent by the parties on pointing to similarities and differences. But, if used with discretion, awards which have been subjected to scrutiny in the Court of Appeal should be able to provide *some* guidance to a jury called upon to fix an award in a later case.

### Reference to damages in actions for personal injuries

. . .

It has often, and rightly, been said that there can be no precise correlation between a personal injury and a sum of money. The same is true, perhaps even more true, of injury to reputation. There is force in the argument that to permit reference in libel cases to conventional levels of award in personal injury cases is simply to admit yet another incommensurable into the field of consideration. There is also weight in the argument, often heard, that conventional levels of award in personal injury cases are too low and therefore provide an uncertain guide. But these awards would not be relied on as any exact guide, and of course there can be no precise correlation between loss of a limb, or of sight, or quadriplegia, and damage to reputation. But if these personal injuries respectively command conventional awards of, at most, about £52,000, £90,000 and £125,000 for pain and suffering and loss of amenity (of course excluding claims based on loss of earnings, the cost of care and other specific financial claims), juries may properly be asked to consider whether the injury to his reputation of which the plaintiff complains should fairly justify any greater compensation. The conventional compensatory scales in personal injury cases must be taken to represent fair compensation in such cases unless and until those scales are amended by the courts or by Parliament. It is in our view offensive to public opinion, and rightly so, that a defamation plaintiff should recover damages for injury to reputation greater, perhaps by a significant factor, than if that same plaintiff had been rendered a helpless cripple or an insensate vegetable. The time has in our view come when judges, and counsel, should be free to draw the attention of juries to these comparisons.

### Reference to an appropriate award and an appropriate bracket

It has been the invariable practice in the past that neither counsel nor the judge may make any suggestion to the jury as what would be an appropriate award. This practice was in line with the practice followed in actions for personal injuries when such actions were tried with a jury. In *Ward* v *James* [1965] 1 All ER 563 at 576, [1966] 1 QB 273 at 302 the Court of Appeal gave reasons as to why no figures should be mentioned. It was said:

> If the judge can mention figures to the jury, then counsel must be able to mention figures to them. Once that happened, we get into the same trouble again. Each counsel would, in duty bound, pitch the figures as high or as low as he dared. Then the judge would give his views on the rival figures. The proceedings would be in danger of developing into an auction.

. . .

We have come to the conclusion, however, that the reasons which have been given for prohibiting any reference to figures are unconvincing. Indeed, far from developing into an auction (and we do not see how it could), the process of mentioning figures would, in our view, induce a mood of realism on both sides.

In personal injury actions it is now commonplace for the advocates on both sides to address the judge in some detail on the quantum of the appropriate award. Any apprehension that the judge might receive a coded message as to the amount of any payment into court has not to our knowledge been realised. The judge is not in any way bound by the bracket suggested, but he finds it helpful as a check on his own provisional assessment. We can for our part see no reason why the parties' respective counsel in a libel action should not indicate to the jury the level of award which they respectively contend to be appropriate, nor why the judge in directing the jury should not give a similar indication. The plaintiff will not wish the jury to think that his main object is to make money rather than clear his name. The defendant will not wish to add insult to injury by underrating the seriousness of the libel. So we think the figures suggested by responsible counsel are likely to reflect the upper and lower bounds of a realistic bracket. The jury must, of course, make up their own mind and must be directed to do so. They will not be bound by the submission of counsel or the indication of the judge. If the jury make an award outside the upper or lower bounds of any bracket indicated and such award is the subject of appeal, real weight must be given to the possibility that their judgment is to be preferred to that of the judge.

The modest but important changes of practice described above would not in our view undermine the enduring constitutional position of the libel jury. Historically, the significance of the libel jury has lain not in their role of assessing damages, but in their role of deciding whether the publication complained of is a libel or no. The changes which we favour will, in our opinion, buttress the constitutional role of the libel jury by rendering their proceedings more rational and so more acceptable to public opinion.

### Exemplary damages

A summary of the existing English law on exemplary damages in actions for defamation, accepted by the Court of Appeal in *Riches* v *News Group Newspapers Ltd* [1985] 2 All ER 845 at 850, [1986] QB 256 at 269 as concise, correct and comprehensive, appears in *Duncan and Neill on Defamation* (2nd edn., 1983) para. 18.27. The passage remains a correct summary of the relevant law. So far as relevant to this case, and omitting footnotes and references, the passage reads:

> (a) Exemplary damages can only be awarded if the plaintiff proves that the defendant when he made the publication knew that he was committing a tort or was reckless whether his action was tortious or not, and decided to publish because the prospects of material advantage outweighed the prospects of material loss. 'What is necessary is that the tortious act must be done with guilty knowledge for the motive that the chances of economic advantage outweigh the chances of economic, or perhaps physical, penalty'. (b) The mere fact that a libel is committed in the course of a business carried on for profit, for example the business of a newspaper publisher, is not by itself sufficient to justify an award of exemplary damages. (c) If the case is one where exemplary damages *can* be awarded the court or jury should consider whether the sum which it proposes to award by way of compensatory damages is sufficient not only for the purpose of compensating the plaintiff but also for the purpose of punishing the defendant. It is only if the sum proposed by way of compensatory damages (which may include an element of aggravated damages) is insufficient that the court or jury should add to it enough 'to bring it up to a sum sufficient as punishment'. (d) The sum awarded as damages should be a single sum which will include, where appropriate, any elements of aggravated or exemplary damages . . . (f) A jury should be warned of the danger of an excessive award. (g) The means of the parties, though irrelevant to the issue of compensatory damages, can be taken into account in awarding exemplary damages . . . This summary of the law was not challenged in argument before us, and it was not seriously argued that we could rule (even if we wished) that exemplary damages are not recoverable in defamation if the conditions required by authority for making such an award are established to the proper satisfaction of a jury. We were, however, reminded by the newspaper that in English law the award of exemplary damages is regarded as exceptional and in some ways

anomalous. Authority, it was said, does not encourage any broadening of the categories of case in which such awards may be made nor any relaxation of the conditions for making them. Since art. 10 of the European Convention on Human Rights requires any restriction on freedom of expression to be prescribed by law and necessary in a democratic society for the protection of reputation, it was argued that the conditions for making an exemplary award should be closely scrutinised and rigorously applied. Our attention was accordingly drawn to certain aspects of the conditions established by authority.

First, the state of mind of the defendant publisher. Little difficulty arises in the straightforward but relatively rare case in which it can be shown that the defendant actually knew that he was committing a tort when he published. The alternative state of mind—recklessness—is not so easy . . .

Lord Kilbrandon referred to a publisher knowing or not caring whether his material is libellous and to a publisher knowing or having reason to believe that publication would subject him to compensatory damages (see [1972] 1 All ER 801 at 876, [1972] AC 1027 at 1133).

Where actual knowledge of unlawfulness is not in issue, a jury direction based on reference to 'reckless, not caring whether the publication be true or false' is sanctioned by long usage and is not incorrect. The crucial ingredient of this state of mind is, however, a lack of honest or genuine belief in the truth of what is published. That is what makes the publisher's conduct so reprehensible (or 'wicked') as to be deserving of punishment. Carelessness alone, however extreme, is not enough unless it properly justifies an inference that the publisher had no honest belief in the truth of what he published.

It seems to us therefore that the phrase 'not caring whether the publication be true or false', though an accurate formulation of the test of recklessness, is capable of leading to confusion because the words 'not caring' may be equated in the jury's minds with 'mere carelessness'. We therefore consider that where exemplary damages are claimed the jury should in future receive some additional guidance to make it clear that before such damages can be awarded the jury must be satisfied that the publisher had no genuine belief in the truth of what he published. The publisher must have suspected that the words were untrue and have deliberately refrained from taking obvious steps which, if taken, would have turned suspicion into certainty.

Secondly, the publisher must have acted in the hope or expectation of material gain. It is well established that a publisher need not be shown to have made any precise or arithmetical calculation. But his unlawful conduct must have been motivated by mercenary considerations: the belief that he would be better off financially if he violated the plaintiff's rights than if he did not. Mere publication of a newspaper for profit is not enough.

We do not accept, as was argued, that in seeking to establish that the conditions for awarding exemplary damages have been met the plaintiff must satisfy the criminal, rather than the civil, standard of proof. But a jury should in our judgment be told that as the charge is grave, so should the proof be clear. An inference of reprehensible conduct and cynical calculation of mercenary advantage should not be lightly drawn. In *Manson* v *Associated Newspapers* [1965] 2 All ER 954 at 959, [1965] 1 WLR 1038 at 1044 Widgery J directed the jury that they could draw inferences from proved facts if those inferences were 'quite inescapable', and he repeatedly directed that they should not draw an inference adverse to the publisher unless they were sure that it was the only inference to be drawn (see [1965] 2 All ER 954 at 959, 960, [1965] 1 WLR 1038 at 1045).

It is plain on the authorities that it is only where the conditions for making an exemplary award are satisfied, and only when the sum awarded to the plaintiff as compensatory damages is not itself sufficient to punish the defendant, show that tort does not pay and deter others from acting similarly, that an award of exemplary damages should be added to the award of compensatory damages. Since the jury will not know, when making their decision, what costs order will be made, it would seem that no account can be taken of the costs burden which the unsuccessful defendant will have to bear, although this could in itself have a punitive and deterrent effect. It is clear that the means of the defendant are relevant to the assessment of damages. Also relevant are his degree of fault and the amount of any profit he may be shown actually to have made from his unlawful conduct.

The authorities give judges no help in directing juries on the quantum of exemplary damages. Since, however, such damages are analogous to a criminal penalty, and although paid to the plaintiff play no part in compensating him, principle requires that an award of exemplary damages should never exceed the minimum sum necessary to meet the public purpose underlying such damages, that of punishing the defendant, showing that tort does not pay and deterring others. The same result is achieved by the application of art. 10. Freedom of speech should not be restricted by awards of exemplary damages save to the extent shown to be strictly necessary for the protection of reputations.

NOTES

1. Section 8 of the Courts and Legal Services Act 1990 permits the court to vary a jury's award which is 'excessive or inadequate'. In *Kiam* v *MGN (No. 1)* [2002] 2 All ER 219 the Court of Appeal held that 'excessive' means an award which substantially exceeds the most that any jury could reasonably have thought appropriate, and that in varying such an award the court should not substitute what it regards as proper but rather should award the highest damages which the jury could reasonably have thought necessary. In the same case Sedley LJ said that he regarded the general level of compensatory libel damages to be indefensible.

2. In *Rantzen* v *Mirror Group Newspapers* [1993] 4 All ER 975, the defendants falsely stated that Esther Rantzen had knowingly protected a teacher who had sexually abused children. The jury awarded her £250,000 and this was reduced on appeal to £110,000. In *Hunt* v *Severs* [1994] AC 350, the claimant suffered from paraplegia below the seventh vertebra; spinal fusion; pulmonary embolus; paralysis of bowel; perforation of bowel; and muscle spasm. She was awarded general damages of £90,000. If personal injury awards are to be referred to in defamation actions, could the award in *Rantzen* stand? However, for a criticism of the use of personal injury awards as a yardstick see Lord Hoffmann in *The Gleaner* v *Abrahams* [2003] 3 WLR 1038 (PC) where he points out that one of the functions of defamation damages is to act as a deterrent.

3. In *Tolstoy Miloslavsky* v *United Kingdom* (1995) 20 EHRR 442 the applicant had been ordered to pay damages of £1,500,000 to Lord Aldington for a libel concerning the repatriation of Yugoslavs at the end of the Second World War. The European Court of Human Rights held this to be contrary to Article 10 of the convention as not being 'necessary in a democratic society'; and said that the law provided no adequate safeguards against a disproportionately large award.

4. Defamation trials are usually held before juries: the Senior Courts Act 1981 (formerly the Supreme Court Act 1981), s. 69 states that in respect of libel or slander 'the action shall be tried with a jury unless the court is of the opinion that the trial requires any prolonged examination of documents or accounts or any scientific or local investigation which cannot conveniently be made with a jury'. For the meaning of this section, see *Beta Construction* v *Channel 4 TV* [1990] 1 WLR 1042.

---

## DEFAMATION ACT 1996

**2.**—(1) A person who has published a statement alleged to be defamatory of another may offer to make amends under this section.

(2) The offer may be in relation to the statement generally or in relation to a specific defamatory meaning which the person making the offer accepts that the statement conveys ('a qualified offer').

(3) An offer to make amends—

(a) must be in writing.

(b) must be expressed to be an offer to make amends under section 2 of the Defamation Act 1996, and

(c) must state whether it is a qualified offer and, if so, set out the defamatory meaning in relation to which it is made.

(4) An offer to make amends under this section is an offer—

    (a) to make a suitable correction of the statement complained of and a sufficient apology to the aggrieved party,

    (b) to publish the correction and apology in a manner that is reasonable and practicable in the circumstances, and

    (c) to pay to the aggrieved party such compensation (if any), and such costs, as may be agreed or determined to be payable.

The fact that the offer is accompanied by an offer to take specific steps does not affect the fact that an offer to make amends under this section is an offer to do all the things mentioned in paragraphs (a) to (c).

(5) An offer to make amends under this section may not be made by a person after serving a defence in defamation proceedings brought against him by the aggrieved party in respect of the publication in question.

(6) An offer to make amends under this section may be withdrawn before it is accepted; and a renewal of an offer which has been withdrawn shall be treated as a new offer.

**3.**—(1) If an offer to make amends under section 2 is accepted by the aggrieved party, the following provisions apply.

(2) The party accepting the offer may not bring or continue defamation proceedings in respect of the publication concerned against the person making the offer, but he is entitled to enforce the offer to make amends as follows.

(3) If the parties agree on the steps to be taken in fulfilment of the offer, the aggrieved party may apply to the court for an order that the other party fulfil his offer by taking the steps agreed.

(4) If the parties do not agree on the steps to be taken by way of correction, apology and publication, the party who made the offer may take such steps as he thinks appropriate, and may in particular—

    (a) make the correction and apology by a statement in open court in terms approved by the court, and

    (b) give an undertaking to the court as to the manner of their publication.

(5) If the parties do not agree on the amount to be paid by way of compensation, it shall be determined by the court on the same principles as damages in defamation proceedings.

The court shall take account of any steps taken in fulfilment of the offer and (so far as not agreed between the parties) of the suitability of the correction, the sufficiency of the apology and whether the manner of their publication was reasonable in the circumstances, and may reduce or increase the amount of compensation accordingly.

(6) If the parties do not agree on the amount to be paid by way of costs, it shall be determined by the court on the same principles as costs awarded in court proceedings.

(7) The acceptance of an offer by one person to make amends does not affect any cause of action against another person in respect of the same publication, subject as follows.

(8) In England and Wales or Northern Ireland, for the purposes of the Civil Liability (Contribution) Act 1978—

    (a) the amount of compensation paid under the offer shall be treated as paid in bona fide settlement or compromise of the claim; and

    (b) where another person is liable in respect of the same damage (whether jointly or otherwise), the person whose offer to make amends was accepted is not required to pay by virtue of any contribution under section 1 of that Act a greater amount than the amount of the compensation payable in pursuance of the offer.

(9) [omitted]

(10) Proceedings under this section shall be heard and determined without a jury.

**4.**—(1) If an offer to make amends under section 2, duly made and not withdrawn, is not accepted by the aggrieved party, the following provisions apply.

(2) The fact that the offer was made is a defence (subject to subsection (3) ) to defamation proceedings in respect of the publication in question by that party against the person making the offer.

A qualified offer is only a defence in respect of the meaning to which the offer related.

(3) There is no such defence if the person by whom the offer was made knew or had reason to believe that the statement complained of—

    (a) referred to the aggrieved party or was likely to be understood as referring to him, and

    (b) was both false and defamatory of that party;

but it shall be presumed until the contrary is shown that he did not know and had no reason to believe that was the case.

(4) The person who made the offer need not rely on it by way of defence, but if he does he may not rely on any other defence.

If the offer was a qualified offer, this applies only in respect of the meaning to which the offer related.

(5) The offer may be relied on in mitigation of damages whether or not it was relied on as a defence.

## NOTES

1. The effect of an offer of amends is illustrated by *Nail* v *News Group Newspapers* [2005] 1 All ER 1040 where the *News of the World* made a number of untrue allegations about the sexual history of the actor Jimmy Nail. The defendants accepted that the stories were untrue and made an offer of amends. The parties agreed the terms of an appropriate apology but were unable to agree on compensation. Under s. 3(5) of the Act the court may reduce the amount of compensation which would normally be payable. Here the court held that certain factors would reduce the damages by 50%. These factors were (1) an early offer of amends and an agreed apology (2) an early offer to compensate and (3) the claimant knows that his reputation has been repaired as far as possible and is relieved from the stress and anxiety of a court case.

2. Section 4 of the Act provides a complete defence if the offer of amends is rejected, except where the defendant 'knew or had reasonable grounds to believe' that the statement complained of was untrue. In *Milne* v *Express Newspapers* [2005] 1 All ER 1021 the Court of Appeal held that this meant recklessness in the sense that the defendant must know of a fact and then have reasonable grounds for positively believing that the words complained of were false. The phrase does not import negligence or constructive knowledge.

# 26

# Privacy and the Intentional Infliction of Distress

The protection of privacy has long been a problem for the common law but no general tort has yet been developed, partly because it has not been possible to define adequately the interests which deserve to be protected and partly because of the need to protect freedom of speech (see *Wainwright* in section 2). This chapter contains three linked sections each dealing with an aspect of privacy. The first deals with a very particular aspect of 'the right to be let alone'. It covers the limited tort of the intentional infliction of emotional distress which is now largely supplanted by the statutory tort of protection from harassment. The second section shows that there is no general common law right to protection from invasion of privacy, although it may be that the Human Rights Act 1998 does provide such a right against public authorities. The third section, on the equitable right of breach of confidence is the most interesting and shows the greatest potential for development. Arising from an equitable (not tortious) duty this has now been developed so that no prior relationship of confidence is required to obtain the right. When combined with the Human Rights Act 1998 this is a powerful tool. However it should be noted that this is rather different from the 'right to be let alone' as discussed in the second section, but rather deals with the protection of personal information.

---

## SECTION 1: THE INTENTIONAL INFLICTION OF DISTRESS

In 1897 Wright J 'invented' a new tort which came to be called the intentional infliction of emotional distress, but although it had great potential it was rarely used. In *Wong* v *Parkside Health Trust* [2003] 3 All ER 932 the court refused to develop a general tort of harassment from it and *Wainwright* (below) shows that whatever was thought in 1897, there must now be both actual harm and an intent to do damage, thus severely restricting the scope of this wrong. However, much of the ground is now covered by the Protection from Harassment Act 1997.

---

**PROTECTION FROM HARASSMENT ACT 1997**

**Prohibition of harassment**

    **1.**—(1)  A person must not pursue a course of conduct—
        (a)  which amounts to harassment of another, and
        (b)  which he knows or ought to know amounts to harassment of the other.
    (1A)  A person must not pursue a course of conduct—

(a) which involves harassment of two or more persons, and

(b) which he knows or ought to know involves harassment of those persons, and

(c) by which he intends to persuade any person (whether or not one of those mentioned above)—

    (i)   not to do something that he is entitled or required to do, or

    (ii)  to do something that he is not under any obligation to do.

(2) For the purposes of this section, the person whose course of conduct is in question ought to know that it amounts to or involves harassment of another if a reasonable person in possession of the same information would think the course of conduct amounted to or involved harassment of the other.

(3) Subsection (1) or (1A) does not apply to a course of conduct if the person who pursued it shows—

(a) that it was pursued for the purpose of preventing or detecting crime,

(b) that it was pursued under any enactment or rule of law or to comply with any condition or requirement imposed by any person under any enactment, or

(c) that in the particular circumstances the pursuit of the course of conduct was reasonable.

### Civil remedy

**3.**—(1) An actual or apprehended breach of section 1(1) may be the subject of a claim in civil proceedings by the person who is or may be the victim of the course of conduct in question.

(2) On such a claim, damages may be awarded for (among other things) any anxiety caused by the harassment and any financial loss resulting from the harassment.

(3)–(9) [omitted]

### 3A Injunctions to protect persons from harassment within section 1(1A)

(1) This section applies where there is an actual or apprehended breach of section 1(1A) by any person ('the relevant person').

(2) In such a case—

(a) any person who is or may be a victim of the course of conduct in question, or

(b) any person who is or may be a person falling within section 1(1A)(c),

may apply to the High Court or a county court for an injunction restraining the relevant person from pursuing any conduct which amounts to harassment in relation to any person or persons mentioned or described in the injunction.

(3) [omitted]

### Interpretation of this group of sections

**7.**—(1) This section applies for the interpretation of sections 1 to 5.

(2) References to harassing a person include alarming the person or causing the person distress.

(3) A 'course of conduct' must involve—

(a) in the case of conduct in relation to a single person (see section 1(1)), conduct on at least two occasions in relation to that person, or

(b) in the case of conduct in relation to two or more persons (see section 1(1A)), conduct on at least one occasion in relation to each of those persons.

(4) 'Conduct' includes speech.

(5) References to a person, in the context of the harassment of a person, are references to a person who is an individual.

NOTES

1. This Act was amended by the Serious Organized Crime and Police Act 2005 which inserted ss. 1(1A) and 3A and amended s. 7. The result is that an action for damages is *only* available for breach of s. 1 (harassment of an individual on at least two occasions). Where there is

harassment of two or more individuals on only one occasion (s. 1(1A)) damages are not available but an injunction is.

2. The remedy provided by this Act will often apply in cases which might have been covered by *Wilkinson* v *Downton* (below). The advantage is that damages may be awarded for anxiety and emotional distress but the disadvantage is that there must be a 'course of conduct' involving at least two episodes. For an example where it might have applied (had it been in force at the time) see *Wong* v *Parkside Health NHS Trust* [2003] 3 All ER 932 where the claimant was subjected to harassment by her colleagues at work. This included locking her out of her office, interfering with her personal effects and hiding things she needed. She claimed that she suffered a post-traumatic stress reaction but she lost her claim under *Wilkinson* v *Downton* on the ground that there was no intention to cause her harm (as opposed to distress). The case occurred before the Protection from Harassment Act 1997 which might now apply to such a situation if there is a 'course of conduct'.

3. In *Daiichi* v *Stop Huntingdon Animal Cruelty* [2004] 1 WLR 1503 the defendants' objective was the closure of Huntingdon Life Sciences which conducted research on animals. Accordingly they targeted the claimant and others who were customers of Huntingdon. Owen J held that the Act did not protect corporations from harassment (this is now covered by s. 7(5)) but he did issue injunctions in favour of the employees of the company, including the imposition of an exclusion zone.

4. In *Majrowski* v *Guy's and St Thomas's NHS Trust* [2005] QB 848; [2005] EWCA Civ 251, the Court of Appeal held that an employer can be vicariously liable for breach by an employee of this Act.

---

### *Wilkinson* v *Downton*
Queen's Bench Division [1897] 2 QB 57; 66 LJQB 493; 76 LT 495

The claimant's husband had gone to the races for the day, and the defendant came to her house and as a practical joke falsely told her that her husband had had an accident and was lying with both his legs broken at The Elms public house at Leytonstone. The claimant went to fetch her husband and later became ill from nervous shock. Held: the defendant was liable.

WRIGHT J: The defendant has, as I assume for the moment, wilfully done an act calculated to cause physical harm to the plaintiff—that is to say, to infringe her legal right to personal safety, and has in fact thereby caused physical harm to her. That proposition without more appears to me to state a good cause of action, there being no justification alleged for the act. This wilful injuria is in law malicious, although no malicious purpose to cause the harm which was caused nor any motive of spite is imputed to the defendant.

It remains to consider whether the assumptions involved in the proposition are made out. One question is whether the defendant's act was so plainly calculated to produce some effect of the kind which was produced that an intentioin to produce it ought to be imputed to the defendant, regard being had to the fact that the effect was produced on a person proved to be in an ordinary state of health and mind. I think that It was. It is difficult to imagine that such a statement, made suddenly and with apparent seriousness, could fail to produce grave effects under the circumstances upon any but an exceptionally indifferent person, and therefore an intention to produce such an effect must be imputed, and it is no answer in law to say that more harm was done than was anticipated, for that is commonly the case with all wrongs. The other question is whether the effect was, to use the ordinary phrase, too remote to be in law regarded as a consequence for which the defendant is answerable. Apart from authority, I should give the same answer and on the same ground as the last question, and say that it was not too remote . . . .

### *Wainwright* v *Home Office*

[House of Lords [2004] 2 AC 406 [2003] 3 WLR 1137; [2003] 4 All ER 969; [2003] UKHL 53]

Mrs Wainwright and her son went to Armley prison, Leeds, to visit another son, where they were strip searched in a procedure which breached Prison Rules. (Hence their consent was ineffective.) Both claimed for breach of privacy and the intentional infliction of harm. Held: the Home Office was not liable.

LORD HOFFMANN

**36** I turn next to the alternative argument based upon *Wilkinson* v *Downton* [1897] 2 QB 57. This is a case which has been far more often discussed than applied. Thomas Wilkinson, landlord of the Albion public house in Limehouse, went by train to the races at Harlow, leaving his wife Lavinia behind the bar. Downton was a customer who decided to play what he would no doubt have described as a practical joke on Mrs Wilkinson. He went into the Albion and told her that her husband had decided to return in a horse-drawn vehicle which had been involved in an accident in which he had been seriously injured. The story was completely false and Mr Wilkinson returned safely by train later that evening. But the effect on Mrs Wilkinson was dramatic. Her hair turned white and she became so ill that for some time her life was thought in danger. The jury awarded her £100 for nervous shock and the question for the judge on further consideration was whether she had a cause of action.

**37** The difficulty in the judge's way was the decision of the Privy Council in *Victorian Railway Comrs* v *Coultas* (1888) 13 App Cas 222, in which it had been said that nervous shock was too remote a consequence of a negligent act (in that case, putting the plaintiff in imminent fear of being run down by a train) to be a recoverable head of damages. RS Wright J distinguished the case on the ground that Downton was not merely negligent but had intended to cause injury. Quite what the judge meant by this is not altogether clear; Downton obviously did not intend to cause any kind of injury but merely to give Mrs Wilkinson a fright. The judge said, however, at p. 59, that as what he said could not fail to produce grave effects 'upon any but an exceptionally indifferent person', an intention to cause such effects should be 'imputed' to him.

**41** Commentators and counsel have nevertheless been unwilling to allow *Wilkinson* v *Downton* to disappear beneath the surface of the law of negligence. Although, in cases of actual psychiatric injury, there is no point in arguing about whether the injury was in some sense intentional if negligence will do just as well, it has been suggested (as the claimants submit in this case) that damages for distress falling short of psychiatric injury can be recovered if there was an intention to cause it. This submission was squarely put to the Court of Appeal in *Wong* v *Parkside Health NHS Trust* [2001] EWCA Civ 1721; [2003] 3 All ER 932 and rejected. Hale LJ said that before the passing of the Protection from Harassment Act 1997 there was no tort of intentional harassment which gave a remedy for anything less than physical or psychiatric injury. That leaves *Wilkinson* v *Downton* with no leading role in the modern law.

**44** I do not resile from the proposition that the policy considerations which limit the heads of recoverable damage in negligence do not apply equally to torts of intention. If someone actually intends to cause harm by a wrongful act and does so, there is ordinarily no reason why he should not have to pay compensation. But I think that if you adopt such a principle, you have to be very careful about what you mean by intend. In *Wilkinson* v *Downton* RS Wright J wanted to water down the concept of intention as much as possible. He clearly thought, as the Court of Appeal did afterwards in *Janvier* v *Sweeney* [1919] 2 KB 316, that the plaintiff should succeed whether the conduct of the defendant was intentional or negligent. But the *Victorian Railway Comrs* case 13 App Cas 222 prevented him from saying so. So he devised a concept of imputed intention which sailed as close to negligence as he felt he could go.

**45** If, on the other hand, one is going to draw a principled distinction which justifies abandoning the rule that damages for mere distress are not recoverable, imputed intention will not do. The defendant must actually have acted in a way which he knew to be unjustifiable and intended to cause harm or at least acted without caring whether he caused harm or not. Lord Woolf CJ, as I read his judgment, at [2002] QB 1334, 1350, paras 50–51, might have been inclined to accept such a principle. But the facts did not support a claim on this basis. The judge made no finding that the prison officers intended to cause distress or realized that they were acting without justification in asking the Wainwrights to strip. He said, at paragraph 83, that they had acted in good faith and, at paragraph 121, that:

> The deviations from the procedure laid down for strip-searches were, in my judgment, not intended to increase the humiliation necessarily involved but merely sloppiness.

**46** Even on the basis of a genuine intention to cause distress, I would wish, as in *Hunter's* case [1997] AC 655, to reserve my opinion on whether compensation should be recoverable. In institutions and workplaces all over the country, people constantly do and say things with the intention of causing distress and humiliation to others. This shows lack of consideration and appalling manners but I am not sure that the right way to deal with it is always by litigation. The Protection from Harassment Act 1997 defines harassment in section 1(1) as a 'course of conduct' amounting to harassment and provides by section 7(3) that a course of conduct must involve conduct on at least two occasions. If these requirements are satisfied, the claimant may pursue a civil remedy for damages for anxiety: section 3(2). The requirement of a course of conduct shows that Parliament was conscious that it might not be in the public interest to allow the law to be set in motion for one boorish incident. It may be that any development of the common law should show similar caution.

**47** In my opinion, therefore, the claimants can build nothing on *Wilkinson* v *Downton* [1897] 2 QB 57. It does not provide a remedy for distress which does not amount to recognized psychiatric injury and so far as there may a tort of intention under which such damage is recoverable, the necessary intention was not established. I am also in complete agreement with Buxton LJ, at [2002] QB 1334, 1355–1356, paras 67–72, that *Wilkinson* v *Downton* has nothing to do with trespass to the person.

NOTES

1. This case (and *Wong* v *Parkside Health Trust* referred to above) severely restricts the potential of the principle in *Wilkinson* v *Downton*. It is clear that it can no longer be developed into a tort for the protection of privacy (see below). The malicious infliction of distress by a single incident is not tortious and there now seems little scope for the principle.

2. One issue remains unresolved. What happens if the defendant only intends distress but recklessly causes harm? Lord Hoffmann says that it is uncertain whether the recklessness as to harm should be subjective or objective (i.e. whether the defendant should actually be aware of the risk of the harm). In the Court of Appeal Buxton LJ thought that only subjective recklessness would be sufficient.

## SECTION 2: PRIVACY

It might have been thought that *Wilkinson* v *Downton* could have been developed into a tort of privacy, but *Wainwright* prevents this. Nor, as is clear from *Kaye* v *Robertson* [1991] FSR 62, is there any other general tort to protect privacy. There are really two kinds of privacy problem: the first relates to invasion of the claimant's space either physically or mentally and the other is an abuse of position by the defendant which can be protected by an action in equity for breach of confidence as in *Campbell* v *MGN* [2004] 2 AC 457 (see section 3 below). The courts seem resolute that no common law protection for protection of privacy can be developed, and the Calcutt Committee on Privacy recommended against a statutory tort relating to privacy. However it is now clear that the Human Rights

Act 1998 will provide a right against the state for failing to protect its citizens (*von Hannover* v *Germany* below), and also a right against public bodies, as was acknowledged in *Campbell* v *MGN* [2004] 2 AC 457.

### *Wainwright* v *Home Office*

[House of Lords [2004] 2 AC 406 [2003] 3 WLR 1137; [2003] 4 All ER 969; [2003] UKHL 53]

Mrs Wainwright and her son went to Armley prison, Leeds, to visit another son, where they were strip searched in a procedure which breached Prison Rules. (Hence their consent was ineffective.) Both claimed for breach of privacy and the intentional infliction of harm. Held: the Home Office was not liable.

LORD HOFFMANN

**15** My Lords, let us first consider the proposed tort of invasion of privacy. Since the famous article by Warren and Brandeis (*The Right to Privacy* (1890) 4 Harvard LR 193) the question of whether such a tort exists, or should exist, has been much debated in common law jurisdictions. Warren and Brandeis suggested that one could generalise certain cases on defamation, breach of copyright in unpublished letters, trade secrets and breach of confidence as all based upon the protection of a common value which they called privacy or, following Judge Cooley (*Cooley on Torts*, 2nd ed. (1888), p. 29) the right to be let alone. They said that identifying this common element should enable the courts to declare the existence of a general principle which protected a person's appearance, sayings, acts and personal relations from being exposed in public.

**16** Courts in the United States were receptive to this proposal and a jurisprudence of privacy began to develop. It became apparent, however, that the developments could not be contained within a single principle; not, at any rate, one with greater explanatory power than the proposition that it was based upon the protection of a value which could be described as privacy. Dean Prosser, in his work on *The Law of Torts*, 4th ed. (1971), p. 804, said that:

> What has emerged is no very simple matter . . . it is not one tort, but a complex of four. To date the law of privacy comprises four distinct kinds of invasion of four different interests of the plaintiff, which are tied together by the common name, but otherwise have almost nothing in common except that each represents an interference with the right of the plaintiff 'to be let alone'.

**17** Dean Prosser's taxonomy divided the subject into (1) intrusion upon the plaintiff's physical solitude or seclusion (including unlawful searches, telephone tapping, long-distance photography and telephone harassment) (2) public disclosure of private facts and (3) publicity putting the plaintiff in a false light and (4) appropriation, for the defendant's advantage, of the plaintiff's name or likeness. These, he said, at p. 814, had different elements and were subject to different defences.

**18** The need in the United States to break down the concept of 'invasion of privacy' into a number of loosely-linked torts must cast doubt upon the value of any high-level generalisation which can perform a useful function in enabling one to deduce the rule to be applied in a concrete case. English law has so far been unwilling, perhaps unable, to formulate any such high-level principle. There are a number of common law and statutory remedies of which it may be said that one at least of the underlying values they protect is a right of privacy. Sir Brian Neill's well known article 'Privacy: a challenge for the next century' in *Protecting Privacy* (ed B. Markesinis, 1999) contains a survey. Common law torts include trespass, nuisance, defamation and malicious falsehood; there is the equitable action for breach of confidence and statutory remedies under the Protection from Harassment Act 1997 and the Data Protection Act 1998. There are also extra-legal remedies under Codes of Practice applicable to broadcasters and newspapers. But there are gaps; cases in which the courts have considered that an invasion of privacy deserves a remedy which the existing law does not offer. Sometimes the perceived gap can be filled by judicious development of an existing principle. The law of breach of confidence has in recent years undergone such a process: see in particular the judgment of Lord Phillips of Worth Matravers MR in *Campbell* v *MGN Ltd* [2003] QB 633. On the other hand, an attempt to create a tort of telephone harassment by a radical change in the basis of the action for private nuisance in *Khorasandjian* v *Bush* [1993] QB 727 was held by the House of Lords in *Hunter* v *Canary Wharf Ltd* [1997] AC 655 to be a step too far. The gap was filled by the 1997 Act.

**19** What the courts have so far refused to do is to formulate a general principle of 'invasion of privacy' (I use the quotation marks to signify doubt about what in such a context the expression would mean) from which the conditions of liability in the particular case can be deduced. The reasons were discussed by Sir Robert Megarry V-C in *Malone* v *Metropolitan Police Comr* [1979] Ch 344, 372–381. I shall be sparing in citation but the whole of Sir Robert's treatment of the subject deserves careful reading. The question was whether the plaintiff had a cause of action for having his telephone tapped by the police without any trespass upon his land. This was (as the European Court of Justice subsequently held in *Malone* v *United Kingdom* (1984) 7 EHRR 14) an infringement by a public authority of his right to privacy under article 8 of the Convention, but because there had been no trespass, it gave rise to no identifiable cause of action in English law . . .

**23** The absence of any general cause of action for invasion of privacy was again acknowledged by the Court of Appeal in *Kaye* v *Robertson* [1991] FSR 62, in which a newspaper reporter and photographer invaded the plaintiff's hospital bedroom, purported to interview him and took photographs. The law of trespass provided no remedy because the plaintiff was not owner or occupier of the room and his body had not been touched. Publication of the interview was restrained by interlocutory injunction on the ground that it was arguably a malicious falsehood to represent that the plaintiff had consented to it. But no other remedy was available. At the time of the judgment (16 March 1990) a Committee under the chairmanship of Sir David Calcutt QC was considering whether individual privacy required statutory protection against intrusion by the press. Glidewell L J said, at p. 66:

> The facts of the present case are a graphic illustration of the desirability of Parliament considering whether and in what circumstances statutory provision can be made to protect the privacy of individuals.

**24** Bingham LJ likewise said, at p. 70:

> The problems of defining and limiting a tort of privacy are formidable but the present case strengthens my hope that the review now in progress may prove fruitful.

**25** Leggatt LJ, at p. 71, referred to Dean Prosser's analysis of the development of the law of privacy in the United States and said that similar rights could be created in England only by statute: 'it is to be hoped that the making good of this signal shortcoming in our law will not be long delayed.'

**26** All three judgments are flat against a judicial power to declare the existence of a high-level right to privacy and I do not think that they suggest that the courts should do so. The members of the Court of Appeal certainly thought that it would be desirable if there was legislation to confer a right to protect the privacy of a person in the position of Mr Kaye against the kind of intrusion which he suffered, but they did not advocate any wider principle. And when the Calcutt Committee reported in June 1990, they did indeed recommend that 'entering private property, without the consent of the lawful occupant, with intent to obtain personal information with a view to its publication' should be made a criminal offence: see *Report of the Committee on Privacy and Related Matters* (1990) Cm. 1102, para. 6.33. The Committee also recommended that certain other forms of intrusion, like the use of surveillance devices on private property and long-distance photography and sound recording, should be made offences.

**27** But the Calcutt Committee did not recommend, even within their terms of reference (which were confined to press intrusion) the creation of a generalised tort of infringement of privacy: paragraph 12.5. This was not because they thought that the definitional problems were insuperable. They said that if one confined the tort to 'publication of personal information to the world at large' (paragraph 12.12) it should be possible to produce an adequate definition and they made some suggestions about how such a statutory tort might be defined and what the defences should be. But they considered that the problem could be tackled more effectively by a combination of the more sharply-focused remedies which they recommended: paragraph 12.32. As for a 'general wrong of infringement of privacy', they accepted, at paragraph 12.12, that it would, even in statutory form, give rise to 'an unacceptable degree of uncertainty'. There is nothing in the opinions of the judges in

*Kaye* v *Robertson* [1991] FSR 62 which suggests that the members of the court would have held any view, one way or the other, about a general tort of privacy.

NOTES

1. This case is a comprehensive rejection of a general right of privacy at common law. While there has been considerable sympathy for such a right, problems of definition and the balance of privacy against freedom of expression have suggested that judicial creativity is not appropriate. So far no statutory version has been forthcoming and indeed in 1990 the Calcutt Committee on Privacy (Cm. 1102) recommended against any statutory tort of infringement of privacy, preferring to rely on the system of self-regulation.

2. In *Campbell* v *MGN* [2004] 2 AC 457 (see section 3 below) it was said that if the Human Rights Act had been in force Mrs Wainwright would have been able to sue as she suffered at the hands of a public authority. Apart from that what remains to be seen is how the equitable principle of breach of confidence can protect privacy. As pointed out in *Wainwright* that doctrine deals with a rather different problem (i.e. the abuse of position by a person with a duty to respect a confidence). The problem here is rather (see *Wainwright*, para. 17) 'intrusion upon the plaintiff's physical solitude or seclusion' or, as it has been put elsewhere, the right to be let alone. Now that celebrities court publicity do they have a choice about when they should be let alone?

3. For the current position in New Zealand see *Hosking* v *Runting* (New Zealand Court of Appeal, [2005] NZLR 1, where the defendant photographed in a public street the two children of the claimants who were celebrities. Although the claimants lost, the majority of the court did accept a limited form of the privacy tort. Gault P said (para 117) that the two requirements for a successful action were (1) the existence of facts in respect of which there is a reasonable expectation of privacy and (2) that the publicity given to private facts would be considered highly offensive to an objective reasonable person. This is subject to a defence enabling publication to be justified by a legitimate public concern in the information as the scope of the privacy action should not exceed such limits on the freedom of expression as is justified in a free and democratic society. Finally the harm to be protected against is in the nature of humiliation and distress. On the other hand Anderson J roundly declared that 'this new liability, created by a sidewind, is amorphous, unnecessary, a disproportionate response to rare, almost hypothetical circumstances, and falls manifestly short of justifying its limitation on the right to freedom of expression . . .'

---

## HUMAN RIGHTS ACT 1998

*Public authorities*

**Acts of public authorities**

**6.**—(1) It is unlawful for a public authority to act in a way which is incompatible with a Convention right.

   (2) Subsection (1) does not apply to an act if—
   (a) as the result of one or more provisions of primary legislation, the authority could not have acted differently; or
   (b) in the case of one or more provisions of, or made under, primary legislation which cannot be read or given effect in a way which is compatible with the Convention rights, the authority was acting so as to give effect to or enforce those provisions.

   (3) In this section 'public authority' includes—
   (a) a court or tribunal, and
   (b) any person certain of whose functions are functions of a public nature, but does not include either House of Parliament or a person exercising functions in connection with proceedings in Parliament.

   (4) [repealed]

(5)  In relation to a particular act, a person is not a public authority by virtue only of subsection (3)(b) if the nature of the act is private.

(6)  'An act' includes a failure to act but does not include a failure to—

(a)  introduce in, or lay before, Parliament a proposal for legislation; or

(b)  make any primary legislation or remedial order.

## Proceedings

**7.**—(1)  A person who claims that a public authority has acted (or proposes to act) in a way which is made unlawful by section 6(1) may—

(a)  bring proceedings against the authority under this Act in the appropriate court or tribunal, or

(b)  rely on the Convention right or rights concerned in any legal proceedings,

but only if he is (or would be) a victim of the unlawful act.

(2)  In subsection (1)(a) 'appropriate court or tribunal' means such court or tribunal as may be determined in accordance with rules; and proceedings against an authority include a counterclaim or similar proceeding.

(3)  If the proceedings are brought on an application for judicial review, the applicant is to be taken to have a sufficient interest in relation to the unlawful act only if he is, or would be, a victim of that act.

(4)  If the proceedings are made by way of a petition for judicial review in Scotland, the applicant shall be taken to have title and interest to sue in relation to the unlawful act only if he is, or would be, a victim of that act.

(5)  Proceedings under subsection (1)(a) must be brought before the end of—

(a)  the period of one year beginning with the date on which the act complained of took place; or

(b)  such longer period as the court or tribunal considers equitable having regard to all the circumstances,

but that is subject to any rule imposing a stricter time limit in relation to the procedure in question.

(6)  In subsection (1)(b) 'legal proceedings' includes—

(a)  proceedings brought by or at the instigation of a public authority; and

(b)  an appeal against the decision of a court or tribunal.

(7)  For the purposes of this section, a person is a victim of an unlawful act only if he would be a victim for the purposes of Article 34 of the Convention if proceedings were brought in the European Court of Human Rights in respect of that act.

(8)  Nothing in this Act creates a criminal offence.

(9)–(13)  [omitted]

## Judicial remedies

**8.**—(1)  In relation to any act (or proposed act) of a public authority which the court finds is (or would be) unlawful, it may grant such relief or remedy, or make such order, within its powers as it considers just and appropriate.

(2)  But damages may be awarded only by a court which has power to award damages, or to order the payment of compensation, in civil proceedings.

(3)  No award of damages is to be made unless, taking account of all the circumstances of the case, including—

(a)  any other relief or remedy granted, or order made, in relation to the act in question (by that or any other court), and

(b)  the consequences of any decision (of that or any other court) in respect of that act,

the court is satisfied that the award is necessary to afford just satisfaction to the person in whose favour it is made.

(4)  In determining—

(a)  whether to award damages, or

(b)  the amount of an award,

the court must take into account the principles applied by the European Court of Human Rights in relation to the award of compensation under Article 41 of the Convention.

 (5) A public authority against which damages are awarded is to be treated—

  (a) in Scotland, for the purposes of section 3 of the Law Reform (Miscellaneous Provisions) (Scotland) Act 1940 as if the award were made in an action of damages in which the authority has been found liable in respect of loss or damage to the person to whom the award is made;

  (b) for the purposes of the Civil Liability (Contribution) Act 1978 as liable in respect of damage suffered by the person to whom the award is made.

 (6) In this section—

'court' includes a tribunal;

'damages' means damages for an unlawful act of a public authority; and

'unlawful' means unlawful under section 6(1).

### Freedom of expression

**12.**—(1) This section applies if a court is considering whether to grant any relief which, if granted, might affect the exercise of the Convention right to freedom of expression.

 (2) If the person against whom the application for relief is made ('the respondent') is neither present nor represented, no such relief is to be granted unless the court is satisfied—

  (a) that the applicant has taken all practicable steps to notify the respondent; or

  (b) that there are compelling reasons why the respondent should not be notified.

 (3) No such relief is to be granted so as to restrain publication before trial unless the court is satisfied that the applicant is likely to establish that publication should not be allowed.

 (4) The court must have particular regard to the importance of the Convention right to freedom of expression and, where the proceedings relate to material which the respondent claims, or which appears to the court, to be journalistic, literary or artistic material (or to conduct connected with such material), to—

  (a) the extent to which—

   (i) the material has, or is about to, become available to the public; or

   (ii) it is, or would be, in the public interest for the material to be published;

  (b) any relevant privacy code.

 (5) In this section—

'court' includes a tribunal; and

'relief' includes any remedy or order (other than in criminal proceedings).

### THE CONVENTION

### *Article 8*

Right to respect for private and family life

 1. Everyone has the right to respect for his private and family life, his home and his correspondence.

 2. There shall be no interference by a public authority with the exercise of this right except such as is in accordance with the law and is necessary in a democratic society in the interests of national security, public safety or the economic well-being of the country, for the prevention of disorder or crime, for the protection of health or morals, or for the protection of the rights and freedoms of others.

### *Article 10*

Freedom of expression

 1. Everyone has the right to freedom of expression. This right shall include freedom to hold opinions and to receive and impart information and ideas without interference by public authority

and regardless of frontiers. This Article shall not prevent States from requiring the licensing of broadcasting, television or cinema enterprises.

2. The exercise of these freedoms, since it carries with it duties and responsibilities, may be subject to such formalities, conditions, restrictions or penalties as are prescribed by law and are necessary in a democratic society, in the interests of national security, territorial integrity or public safety, for the prevention of disorder or crime, for the protection of health or morals, for the protection of the reputation or rights of others, for preventing the disclosure of information received in confidence, or for maintaining the authority and impartiality of the judiciary.

NOTES

1. The effect of the Human Rights Act 1998 incorporating the European Convention on Human Rights is uncertain. Article 8 states that 'Everyone has the right to respect for his private and family life . . .' and that 'There shall be no interference by a public authority with the exercise of this right . . .'. As pointed out in *Wainwright* the main difficulty is that this does not give a remedy against a private individual but only against the State. A good example is *Peck v UK* [2003] EHRR 79 where the applicant was filmed by CCTV walking around the town centre of Brentwood. He had a knife in his hand and attempted suicide by cutting his wrists. Brentwood Council released stills from the tape and one of these appeared in the local paper in an article extolling the benefits of CCTV. The applicant was awarded damages. It seems to have been essential that it was a public body that released the tape and the issue now is whether the Convention can be used to build a right against corporate bodies or individuals. For the view that that will not happen see Buxton, 'The Human Rights Act and Private Law' (2000) 116 LQR 48 at 64. For a thorough survey see Phillipson, 'Transforming Breach of Confidence? Towards a Common Law Right of Privacy under The Human Rights Act' (2003) 66 MLR 726. Also, in *Wainwright* Lord Hoffmann said that the Act does not 'require that the courts should provide an alternative remedy which distorts the principles of the common law'.

2. In *Wainwright* (above) Lord Hoffmann said that 'Article 8 may justify a monetary remedy for an intentional invasion of privacy by a public authority, even if no damage is suffered other than distress for which damages are not ordinarily recoverable. It does not follow that a merely negligent act should, contrary to general principle, give rise to a claim for damages for distress because it affects privacy rather than some other interest like bodily safety.' Thus, the Home Office did not wish to humiliate the Wainwrights and there had been no more than 'sloppiness' in failure to comply with the rules.

---

### Von Hannover v Germany
European Court of Human Rights (2005) 40 EHRR 1; Case No. 59320/00

The applicant was Princess Caroline of Monaco who complained of the publication of photographs of her in her daily life, albeit in public places, such as when walking out or leaving a restaurant. The German courts had refused a remedy on the grounds of freedom of the press (even the entertainment press) and the public interest in knowing how she behaved outside her representative function. The ECHR however said that there was a breach of Article 8.

THE COURT:

56. In the present case the applicant did not complain of an action by the State, but rather of the lack of adequate State protection of her private life and her image.

57. The Court reiterates that although the object of Article 8 is essentially that of protecting the individual against arbitrary interference by the public authorities, it does not merely compel the State to abstain from such interference: in addition to this primarily negative undertaking, there may be positive obligations inherent in an effective respect for private or family life. These obligations may involve the adoption of measures designed to secure respect for private life even in the sphere of the

relations of individuals between themselves . . . That also applies to the protection of a person's picture against abuse by others.

The boundary between the State's positive and negative obligations under this provision does not lend itself to precise definition. The applicable principles are, nonetheless, similar. In both contexts regard must be had to the fair balance that has to be struck between the competing interests of the individual and of the community as a whole; and in both contexts the State enjoys a certain margin of appreciation . . .

58. That protection of private life has to be balanced against the freedom of expression guaranteed by Article 10 of the Convention. In that context the Court reiterates that the freedom of expression constitutes one of the essential foundations of a democratic society. Subject to paragraph 2 of Article 10, it is applicable not only to 'information' or 'ideas' that are favourably received or regarded as inoffensive or as a matter of indifference, but also to those that offend, shock or disturb. Such are the demands of that pluralism, tolerance and broadmindedness without which there is no 'democratic society' . . .

In that connection the press plays an essential role in a democratic society. Although it must not overstep certain bounds, in particular in respect of the reputation and rights of others, its duty is nevertheless to impart—in a manner consistent with its obligations and responsibilities—information and ideas on all matters of public interest . . . Journalistic freedom also covers possible recourse to a degree of exaggeration, or even provocation . . .

59. Although freedom of expression also extends to the publication of photos, this is an area in which the protection of the rights and reputation of others takes on particular importance. The present case does not concern the dissemination of 'ideas', but of images containing very personal or even intimate 'information' about an individual. Furthermore, photos appearing in the tabloid press are often taken in a climate of continual harassment which induces in the person concerned a very strong sense of intrusion into their private life or even of persecution.

60. In the cases in which the Court has had to balance the protection of private life against the freedom of expression it has always stressed the contribution made by photos or articles in the press to a debate of general interest . . .

### c. Application of these general principles by the Court

61. The Court points out at the outset that in the present case the photos of the applicant in the various German magazines show her in scenes from her daily life, thus engaged in activities of a purely private nature such as practising sport, out walking, leaving a restaurant or on holiday. The photos, in which the applicant appears sometimes alone and sometimes in company, illustrate a series of articles with such anodyne titles as 'Pure happiness', 'Caroline . . . a woman returning to life', 'Out and about with Princess Caroline in Paris' and 'The kiss. Or: they are not hiding anymore . . .' (see paragraphs 11–17 above).

62. The Court also notes that the applicant, as a member of the Prince of Monaco's family, represents the ruling family at certain cultural or charitable events. However, she does not exercise any function within or on behalf of the State of Monaco or one of its institutions (see paragraph 8 above).

63. The Court considers that a fundamental distinction needs to be made between reporting facts—even controversial ones—capable of contributing to a debate in a democratic society relating to politicians in the exercise of their functions, for example, and reporting details of the private life of an individual who, moreover, as in this case, does not exercise official functions. While in the former case the press exercises its vital role of 'watchdog' in a democracy by contributing to 'impart[ing] information and ideas on matters of public interest' it does not do so in the latter case.

64. Similarly, although the public has a right to be informed, which is an essential right in a democratic society that, in certain special circumstances, can even extend to aspects of the private life of public figures, particularly where politicians are concerned, this is not the case here. The situation here does not come within the sphere of any political or public debate because the published photos and accompanying commentaries relate exclusively to details of the applicant's private life.

65. As in other similar cases it has examined, the Court considers that the publication of the photos and articles in question, of which the sole purpose was to satisfy the curiosity of a particular readership regarding the details of the applicant's private life, cannot be deemed to contribute to any debate of general interest to society despite the applicant being known to the public . . .

66. In these conditions freedom of expression calls for a narrower interpretation . . .

67. In that connection the Court also takes account of the resolution of the Parliamentary Assembly of the Council of Europe on the right to privacy, which stresses the 'one-sided interpretation of the right to freedom of expression' by certain media which attempt to justify an infringement of the rights protected by Article 8 of the Convention by claiming that 'their readers are entitled to know everything about public figures' . . .

68. The Court finds another point to be of importance: even though, strictly speaking, the present application concerns only the publication of the photos and articles by various German magazines, the context in which these photos were taken—without the applicant's knowledge or consent—and the harassment endured by many public figures in their daily lives cannot be fully disregarded (see paragraph 59 above).

In the present case this point is illustrated in particularly striking fashion by the photos taken of the applicant at the Monte Carlo Beach Club tripping over an obstacle and falling down (see paragraph 17 above). It appears that these photos were taken secretly at a distance of several hundred metres, probably from a neighbouring house, whereas journalists and photographers' access to the club was strictly regulated (see paragraph 33 above).

69. The Court reiterates the fundamental importance of protecting private life from the point of view of the development of every human being's personality. That protection—as stated above—extends beyond the private family circle and also includes a social dimension. The Court considers that anyone, even if they are known to the general public, must be able to enjoy a 'legitimate expectation' of protection of and respect for their private life . . .

70. Furthermore, increased vigilance in protecting private life is necessary to contend with new communication technologies which make it possible to store and reproduce personal data . . . This also applies to the systematic taking of specific photos and their dissemination to a broad section of the public.

71. Lastly, the Court reiterates that the Convention is intended to guarantee not rights that are theoretical or illusory but rights that are practical and effective . . .

72. The Court has difficulty in agreeing with the domestic courts' interpretation of section 23(1) of the Copyright (Arts Domain) Act, which consists in describing a person as such as a figure of contemporary society 'par excellence'. Since that definition affords the person very limited protection of their private life or the right to control the use of their image, it could conceivably be appropriate for politicians exercising official functions. However, it cannot be justified for a 'private' individual, such as the applicant, in whom the interest of the general public and the press is based solely on her membership of a reigning family whereas she herself does not exercise any official functions.

In any event the Court considers that, in these conditions, the Act has to be interpreted narrowly to ensure that the State complies with its positive obligation under the Convention to protect private life and the right to control the use of one's image.

73. Lastly, the distinction drawn between figures of contemporary society 'par excellence' and 'relatively' public figures has to be clear and obvious so that, in a state governed by the rule of law, the individual has precise indications as to the behaviour he or she should adopt. Above all, they need to know exactly when and where they are in a protected sphere or, on the contrary, in a sphere in which they must expect interference from others, especially the tabloid press.

74. The Court therefore considers that the criteria on which the domestic courts based their decisions were not sufficient to protect the applicant's private life effectively. As a figure of contemporary society 'par excellence' she cannot—in the name of freedom of the press and the public interest—rely on protection of her private life unless she is in a secluded place out of the public eye and, moreover, succeeds in proving it (which can be difficult). Where that is not the case, she has to accept that she might be photographed at almost any time, systematically, and that the photos are

then very widely disseminated even if, as was the case here, the photos and accompanying articles relate exclusively to details of her private life.

75. In the Court's view, the criterion of spatial isolation, although apposite in theory, is in reality too vague and difficult for the person concerned to determine in advance. In the present case merely classifying the applicant as a figure of contemporary society '*par excellence*' does not suffice to justify such an intrusion into her private life.

### d. Conclusion

76. As the Court has stated above, it considers that the decisive factor in balancing the protection of private life against freedom of expression should lie in the contribution that the published photos and articles make to a debate of general interest. It is clear in the instant case that they made no such contribution since the applicant exercises no official function and the photos and articles related exclusively to details of her private life.

77. Furthermore, the Court considers that the public does not have a legitimate interest in knowing where the applicant is and how she behaves generally in her private life even if she appears in places that cannot always be described as secluded and despite the fact that she is well known to the public.

Even if such a public interest exists, as does a commercial interest of the magazines in publishing these photos and these articles, in the instant case those interests must, in the Court's view, yield to the applicant's right to the effective protection of her private life.

78. Lastly, in the Court's opinion the criteria established by the domestic courts were not sufficient to ensure the effective protection of the applicant's private life and she should, in the circumstances of the case, have had a 'legitimate expectation' of protection of her private life.

79. Having regard to all the foregoing factors, and despite the margin of appreciation afforded to the State in this area, the Court considers that the German courts did not strike a fair balance between the competing interests.

80. There has therefore been a breach of Article 8 of the Convention.

NOTES

1. This decision is fairly restrictive as it seems to take the view that freedom of expression would normally be limited to the role of the press as a 'watchdog' in protecting the public interest (para 63). The Court noted that the princess did not exercise any official function on behalf of Monaco and that details of her daily life could not contribute to any debate of general interest to society despite her being well known to the public. However in a concurring judgment Judge Barreto said that 'the applicant is a public figure and the public does have a right to be informed about her life' and that the test is whether a person has a 'legitimate expectation' of being safe from the media. Perhaps the answer is that those who seek publicity can only expect limited protection and cannot always choose the nature of that publicity, but a person who has no official position and who seeks privacy will be better protected at least in relation to places and functions where they would not expect to be exposed to the press.

2. In the event Princess Caroline was awarded £7,000 against the German government for their failure to protect her interests.

## SECTION 3: BREACH OF CONFIDENCE

The action for breach of confidence derives from principles of equity rather than the common law. In *Ashburton* v *Pape* [1913] 2 Ch 469 Swinfen-Eady J said 'The principle upon which the Court of Chancery has acted for many years has been to restrain the publication of confidential information improperly or surreptitiously obtained or of information imparted in confidence which ought not to be divulged.' Thus, the claimant must show that the information was 'confidential' and that the person disclosing it had a duty to respect the confidentiality of the information. In *Argyll* v *Argyll* [1967] Ch 302 it was made clear that the obligation of confidence could be implied (here arising from marriage) and also that an injunction may be granted to restrain publication by anybody into whose hands the information has improperly come. The action is often used to protect trade secrets but has lately been used to prevent the press publishing details of a celebrity's private life. This has been an important development because it is now clear that no previous relationship of confidence need exist between the parties, but rather there is a general obligation to protect information where there is 'a reasonable expectation' of privacy, subject to the countervailing public interest in the freedom of speech. It is at this point that the Human Rights Act 1998 becomes relevant and it is clear that the provisions of the European Convention on Human Rights will guide the courts in constructing a balance between privacy and freedom of speech.

---

### *Campbell* v *MGN Ltd*
House of Lords [2004] 2 AC 457; [2004] 2 WLR 1232; [2004] 2 All ER 995; [2004] UKHL 22.

The *Daily Mirror* published an article (with photographs) about the model Naomi Campbell (who had previously denied that she took drugs) and this contained the following elements—(1) the fact that Miss Campbell was a drug addict; (2) the fact that she was receiving treatment for her addiction; (3) the fact that the treatment which she was receiving was provided by Narcotics Anonymous; (4) details of the treatment—for how long, how frequently and at what times of day she had been receiving it, the nature of it and extent of her commitment to the process; and (5) a visual portrayal by means of photographs of her when she was leaving the place where treatment had been taking place. The majority of the House held by 3 to 2 that the defendants were liable for elements 3, 4, and 5 and the claimant was awarded £3,500.

Note: Although the judges differed as to how the competing interests of privacy and free speech should be balanced on the facts of this case, Lord Hoffmann stated that they were unanimous on the general principles.

LORD HOFFMANN

46. In recent years, however, there have been two developments of the law of confidence, typical of the capacity of the common law to adapt itself to the needs of contemporary life. One has been an acknowledgement of the artificiality of distinguishing between confidential information obtained through the violation of a confidential relationship and similar information obtained in some other way. The second has been the acceptance, under the influence of human rights instruments such as Article 8 of the European Convention, of the privacy of personal information as something worthy of protection in its own right.

47. The first development is generally associated with the speech of Lord Goff of Chieveley in *Attorney-General v Guardian Newspapers Ltd (No 2)* [1990] 1 AC 109, 281, where he gave, as illustrations of cases in which it would be illogical to insist upon violation of a confidential relationship, the 'obviously confidential document . . . wafted by an electric fan out of a window into a crowded street' and the 'private diary . . . dropped in a public place'. He therefore formulated the principle as being that

'a duty of confidence arises when confidential information comes to the knowledge of a person . . . in circumstances where he has notice, or is held to have agreed, that the information is confidential, with the effect that it would be just in all the circumstances that he should be precluded from disclosing the information to others.'

48. This statement of principle, which omits the requirement of a prior confidential relationship, was accepted as representing current English law by the European Court of Human Rights in *Earl Spencer* v *United Kingdom* (1998) 25 EHRR CD 105 and was applied by the Court of Appeal in *A v B plc* [2003] QB 195, 207. It is now firmly established.

49. The second development has been rather more subtle. Until the Human Rights Act 1998 came into force, there was no equivalent in English domestic law of article 8 the European Convention or the equivalent articles in other international human rights instruments which guarantee rights of privacy. So the courts of the United Kingdom did not have to decide what such guarantees meant. Even now that the equivalent of article 8 has been enacted as part of English law, it is not directly concerned with the protection of privacy against private persons or corporations. It is, by virtue of section 6 of the 1998 Act, a guarantee of privacy only against public authorities. Although the Convention, as an international instrument, may impose upon the United Kingdom an obligation to take some steps (whether by statute or otherwise) to protect rights of privacy against invasion by private individuals, it does not follow that such an obligation would have any counterpart in domestic law.

50. What human rights law has done is to identify private information as something worth protecting as an aspect of human autonomy and dignity. And this recognition has raised inescapably the question of why it should be worth protecting against the state but not against a private person. There may of course be justifications for the publication of private information by private persons which would not be available to the state—I have particularly in mind the position of the media, to which I shall return in a moment—but I can see no logical ground for saying that a person should have less protection against a private individual than he would have against the state for the publication of personal information for which there is no justification. Nor, it appears, have any of the other judges who have considered the matter.

51. The result of these developments has been a shift in the centre of gravity of the action for breach of confidence when it is used as a remedy for the unjustified publication of personal information. It recognises that the incremental changes to which I have referred do not merely extend the duties arising traditionally from a relationship of trust and confidence to a wider range of people. As Sedley LJ observed in a perceptive passage in his judgment in *Douglas v Hello! Ltd* [2001] QB 967, 1001, the new approach takes a different view of the underlying value which the law protects. Instead of the cause of action being based upon the duty of good faith applicable to confidential personal information and trade secrets alike, it focuses upon the protection of human autonomy and dignity—the right to control the dissemination of information about one's private life and the right to the esteem and respect of other people.

52. These changes have implications for the future development of the law. They must influence the approach of the courts to the kind of information which is regarded as entitled to protection, the extent and form of publication which attracts a remedy and the circumstances in which publication can be justified.

BARONESS HALE

132. Neither party to this appeal has challenged the basic principles which have emerged from the Court of Appeal in the wake of the Human Rights Act 1998. The 1998 Act does not create any new cause of action between private persons. But if there is a relevant cause of action applicable, the court as a public authority must act compatibly with both parties' Convention rights. In a case such as this, the relevant vehicle will usually be the action for breach of confidence, as Lord Woolf CJ held in *A v B plc* [2002] EWCA Civ 337, [2003] QB 195, 202, para 4:

'[Articles 8 and 10] have provided new parameters within which the court will decide, in an action for breach of confidence, whether a person is entitled to have his privacy protected by the court or whether the restriction of freedom of expression which such protection involves cannot be justified. The court's approach to the issues which the applications raise has been modified because, under section 6 of the 1998 Act, the court, as a public authority, is required not to "act in a way which is incompatible with a Convention right". The court is able to achieve this by absorbing the rights which Articles 8 and 10 protect into the long-established action for breach of confidence. This involves giving a new strength and breadth to the action so that it accommodates the requirements of these articles.'

133. The action for breach of confidence is not the only relevant cause of action: the inherent jurisdiction of the High Court to protect the children for whom it is responsible is another example: see *In re S (a child) (identification: restrictions on publication)* [2003] EWCA Civ 963[2003] 3 WLR 1425. But the courts will not invent a new cause of action to cover types of activity which were not previously covered: see *Wainwright v Home Office* [2003] 3 WLR 1137. Mrs Wainwright and her disabled son suffered a gross invasion of their privacy when they were strip-searched before visiting another son in prison. The common law in this country is powerless to protect them. As they suffered at the hands of a public authority, the Human Rights Act would have given them a remedy if it had been in force at the time, but it was not. That case indicates that our law cannot, even if it wanted to, develop a general tort of invasion of privacy. But where existing remedies are available, the court not only can but must balance the competing Convention rights of the parties.

134. This begs the question of how far the Convention balancing exercise is premissed on the scope of the existing cause of action. Clearly outside its scope is the sort of intrusion into what ought to be private which took place in *Wainwright*. Inside its scope is what has been termed the protection of the individual's informational autonomy' by prohibiting the publication of confidential information. How does the scope of the action for breach of confidence accommodate the Article 8 rights of individuals? As Randerson J summed it up in *Hosking v Runting* [2003] 3 NZLR 385, 403, para 83 at p 403:

'[The English Courts] have chosen to develop the claim for breach of confidence on a case by case basis. In doing so, it has been recognised that no pre-existing relationship is required in order to establish a cause of action and that an obligation of confidence may arise from the nature of the material or may be inferred from the circumstances in which it has been obtained.'

The position we have reached is that the exercise of balancing article 8 and article 10 may begin when the person publishing the information knows or ought to know that there is a reasonable expectation that the information in question will be kept confidential. That is the way in which Lord Woolf CJ put it in *A v B plc*, at paras 11(ix) and (x) (in which he also referred to the approach of Dame Elizabeth Butler-Sloss P in *Venables v News Group Newspapers Ltd* [2001] Fam 430). It is, as I understand it, also the way in which it is put by my noble and learned friends, Lord Nicholls of Birkenhead (at paragraph 21) and Lord Hope of Craighead (at paragraph 84) in this case.

137. It should be emphasised that the 'reasonable expectation of privacy' is a threshold test which brings the balancing exercise into play. It is not the end of the story. Once the information is identified as 'private' in this way, the court must balance the claimant's interest in keeping the information private against the countervailing interest of the recipient in publishing it. Very often, it can be expected that the countervailing rights of the recipient will prevail.

138. The parties agree that neither right takes precedence over the other. This is consistent with Resolution 1165 (1998) of the Parliamentary Assembly of the Council of Europe, para 10:

'The Assembly reaffirms the importance of everyone's right to privacy, and of the right to freedom of expression, as fundamental to a democratic society. These rights are neither absolute nor in any hierarchical order, since they are of equal value.'

139. Each right has the same structure. Article 8(1) states that 'everyone has the right to respect for his private and family life, his home and his correspondence'. Article 10(1) states that 'Everyone has the right to freedom of expression. This right shall include freedom to hold opinions and to receive and impart information and ideas without interference by public authorities and regardless of frontiers. . . .' Unlike the Article 8 right, however, it is accepted in Article 10(2) that the exercise of this right 'carries with it duties and responsibilities.' Both rights are qualified. They may respectively be interfered with or restricted provided that three conditions are fulfilled:

(a) The interference or restriction must be 'in accordance with the law'; it must have a basis in national law which conforms to the Convention standards of legality.

(b) It must pursue one of the legitimate aims set out in each article. Article 8(2) provides for 'the protection of the rights and freedoms of others'. Article 10(2) provides for 'the protection of the reputation or rights of others' and for 'preventing the disclosure of information received in confidence'. The rights referred to may either be rights protected under the national law or, as in this case, other Convention rights.

(c) Above all, the interference or restriction must be 'necessary in a democratic society'; it must meet a 'pressing social need' and be no greater than is proportionate to the legitimate aim pursued; the reasons given for it must be both 'relevant' and 'sufficient' for this purpose.

140. The application of the proportionality test is more straightforward when only one Convention right is in play: the question then is whether the private right claimed offers sufficient justification for the degree of interference with the fundamental right. It is much less straightforward when two Convention rights are in play, and the proportionality of interfering with one has to be balanced against the proportionality of restricting the other. As each is a fundamental right, there is evidently a 'pressing social need' to protect it. The Convention jurisprudence offers us little help with this. The European Court of Human Rights has been concerned with whether the state's interference with privacy (as, for example, in Z v Finland (1997) 25 EHRR 371) or a restriction on freedom of expression (as, for example, in Jersild v Denmark (1994) 19 EHRR 1, Fressoz and Roire v France (2001) 31 EHRR 2, and Tammer v Estonia (2001) 37 EHRR 857) could be justified in the particular case. In the national court, the problem of balancing two rights of equal importance arises most acutely in the context of disputes between private persons.

141. Both parties accepted the basic approach of the Court of Appeal in In re S [2003] 3 WLR 1425, 1451–2, at paras 54–60. This involves looking first at the comparative importance of the actual rights being claimed in the individual case; then at the justifications for interfering with or restricting each of those rights; and applying the proportionality test to each. The parties in this case differed about whether the trial judge or the Court of Appeal had done this, the appellant arguing that the Court of Appeal had assumed primacy for the Article 10 right while the respondent argued that the trial judge had assumed primacy for the Article 8 right.

(Note: as to the balancing of the interests it was generally agreed that the newspaper could publish the fact that the claimant had taken drugs but there was a difference of opinion concerning the link to Narcotics Anonymous and the publication of the photographs. On the latter issue Baroness Hale said 'But here the accompanying text made it plain that these photographs were different. They showed her coming either to or from the NA meeting. They showed her in the company of others, some of whom were undoubtedly part of the group. They showed the place where the meeting was taking place, which will have been entirely recognisable to anyone who knew the locality. A picture is "worth a thousand words" because it adds to the impact of what the words convey; but it also adds to the information given in those words. If nothing else, it tells the reader what everyone looked like; in this case it also told the reader what the place looked like. In context, it also added to the potential harm, by making her think that she was being followed or betrayed, and deterring her from going back to the same place again.)'

NOTES

1. In *Douglas v Hello Ltd* [2005] 4 All ER 128, [2005] EWCA Civ 595, Michael Douglas and Catherine Zeta Jones agreed with *OK!* magazine that on payment of £500,000 to each of them *OK!* was to have the exclusive rights to photographs of their wedding which took place in New York. Guests were told that no photographs were to be taken. The wedding reception was infiltrated by a paparazzo who took a number of photographs of which six were eventually sold for £125,000 to *Hello!* magazine. It was assumed that *Hello!* must have known of the arrangement with OK!, that it would have included a clause about exclusivity and that no unauthorized photographs were to be taken. At first instance (*Douglas v Hello! (No. 3)* [2003] 3 All ER 996) the defendants were held liable and the claimants were awarded damages of £3,750 each for personal distress.

In the Court of Appeal the Douglases held on to their claim for liability but lost their appeal on damages. The result seems to be as follows:

(1)  Photographs of the wedding fell within the protection of the law of confidentiality as now extended to cover private or personal information. On the relevance of the Human Rights Convention Lord Phillips said at para 53 'We conclude that, in so far as private information is concerned, we are required to adopt, as the vehicle for performing such duty as falls on the courts in relation to Convention rights, the cause of action formerly described as breach of confidence. As to the nature of that duty, it seems to us that sections 2, 3, 6 and 12 of the Human Rights Act all point in the same direction. The court should, insofar as it can, develop the action for breach of confidence in such a manner as will give effect to both Article 8 and Article 10 rights. In considering the nature of those rights, account should be taken of the Strasbourg jurisprudence. In particular, when considering what information should be protected as private pursuant to Article 8, it is right to have regard to the decisions of the ECtHR.' There was no appeal from the award of £3,750 for distress, but the court said that even though the damages were low the claimants should have been granted an interlocutory injunction to prevent publication.

(2)  This is not an action in tort. Arising from an issue relating to the conflict of laws (i.e. did it matter that the wedding was in New York?), the court held that an action for breach of confidence should not be categorized as a tort.

(3)  The Douglases' commercial rights were infringed. Lord Phillips said at para 118 'Where an individual ("the owner") has at his disposal information which he has created or which is private or personal and to which he can properly deny access to third parties, and he reasonably intends to profit commercially by using or publishing that information, then a third party who is, or ought to be, aware of these matters and who has knowingly obtained the information without authority, will be in breach of duty if he uses or publishes the information to the detriment of the owner.' However the court rejected the idea that damages should be based on a notional license fee—i.e. what the claimants might have charged *Hello!* to use the photographs.

(4)  *OK!* Did not obtain the protection of the law of confidence by virtue of their contract with the Douglases. Nor was *Hello!* liable for unlawful interference with business. Accordingly *Hello!* was not liable to *OK!*.

(5)  Leave to appeal to the House of Lords has been granted.

2.  Both the *Campbell* and *Douglas* cases are most important as they consolidate recent developments of this equitable principle, but much is yet to be worked out. The essential point is that the wrong will protect 'personal information', but as the cases show it is difficult to decide when a person has a 'reasonable expectation' of privacy. Why, for example, could the press disclose that Naomi Campbell was a drug addict but not that she was being treated by Narcotics Anonymous? How are pictures different from other forms of information? The other issue yet to be developed is the countervailing public interest in the freedom of speech, for which see the guidelines in *A* v *B and C* (below).

3.  For a thorough study of privacy see Moreham, 'Privacy in the Common Law: a Doctrinal and Theoretical Analysis' (2005) 121 LQR 628, which supports the 'reasonable expectation' of privacy test.

4.  Costs are a serious problem in defamation and privacy cases. The risk of having to pay huge costs can have a 'chilling' effect and inhibit a person from saying what he is entitled to say, and thus can act as a bar to freedom of speech. On the other hand Conditional Fee Agreements (no win, no fee) are a means by which the impecunious may pursue the protection of their reputation. After the decision in *Campbell*, Ms Campbell's solicitors served bills of costs on the defendants amounting to £1,086.295. The defendants failed in their claim before the House of Lords (*Campbell* v *MGN No. 2* [2005] 4 All ER 793; [2005] UKHL 61) that they should not have to pay the 'success fee' of the appeal to the House which was conducted under a conditional fee agreement. (The success fee was £279,981 and almost doubled the actual cost). The defendants argued that the threat of large fees was contrary to their freedom of

expression under Article 10 of the European Convention, but this was rejected. (However the House did point out that the claimant was only awarded damages of £3,500 and that of nine judges who considered the case five thought she should get nothing). Nevertheless Lord Hoffmann did say that finding ways of moderating costs would be in the interests of all and that legislation may be necessary to find a way of complying with Article 10.

---

### A v B and C

Court of Appeal [2003] QB 195; [2002] 2 All ER 545; [2002] 3 WLR 542; [2002] EWCA Civ 237

A, a football player, sought an injunction against a newspaper to prevent them publishing stories about his extra-marital affairs. The injunction was not granted.

LORD WOOLF

**4** The applications for interim injunctions have now to be considered in the context of articles 8 and 10 of the European Convention of Human Rights ('ECHR'). These articles have provided new parameters within which the court will decide, in an action for breach of confidence, whether a person is entitled to have his privacy protected by the court or whether the restriction of freedom of expression which such protection involves cannot be justified. The court's approach to the issues which the applications raise has been modified because under section 6 of the 1998 Act, the court, as a public authority, is required not to act 'in a way which is incompatible with a Convention right'. The court is able to achieve this by absorbing the rights which articles 8 and 10 protect into the long-established action for breach of confidence. This involves giving a new strength and breadth to the action so that it accommodates the requirements of those articles.

**5** The court is assisted in achieving this because the equitable origins of the action for breach of confidence mean that historically the remedy for breach of confidence will only be granted when it is equitable for this to happen. As the headnote makes clear, in *Argyll* v *Argyll* [1967] Ch 302 Ungoed Thomas J decided that 'a contract or obligation of confidence need not be express, but could be implied, and a breach of contract or trust or faith could arise independently of any right to property or contract (other than any contract which the imparting of the confidence might itself create); and that the court in the exercise of its equitable jurisdiction would restrain a breach of confidence independently of any right at law'. In *Stephens* v *Avery* [1988] 1 Ch 449, Sir Nicholas Browne-Wilkinson V-C made it clear that this approach could be extended to other relationships apart from that between husband and wife, though it would not necessarily apply in the same way.

**6** The manner in which the two articles operate is entirely different. Article 8 operates so as to extend the areas in which an action for breach of confidence can provide protection for privacy. It requires a generous approach to the situations in which privacy is to be protected. Article 10 operates in the opposite direction. This is because it protects freedom of expression and to achieve this it is necessary to restrict the area in which remedies are available for breaches of confidence. There is a tension between the two articles which requires the court to hold the balance between the conflicting interests they are designed to protect. This is not an easy task but it can be achieved by the courts if, when holding the balance, they attach proper weight to the important rights both articles are designed to protect. Each article is qualified expressly in a way which allows the interests under the other article to be taken into account.

*The guidelines*

**11** . . .

iv)  The fact that if the injunction is granted it will interfere with the freedom of expression of others and in particular the freedom of the press is a matter of particular importance. This well-established common law principle is underlined by section 12 (4) [of the Human Rights Act 1998]. Any interference with the press has to be justified because it inevitably has some effect on the ability of the press to perform its role in society. This is the position irrespective of whether a particular publication is desirable in the public interest. The existence of a free press is in itself desirable and so any interference with it has to be justified. Here we would endorse the approach of Hoffmann LJ in *R* v *Central Independent Television PLC* [1994] Fam 192 at p. 201–204, where he said:

> publication may cause needless pain, distress and damage to individuals or harm to other aspects of the public interest. But a freedom which is restricted to what Judges think to be responsible or in the public interest is no freedom. Freedom means the right to publish things which Government and Judges, however well motivated, think should not be published. It means the right to say things which 'right thinking people' regard as dangerous or irresponsible. This freedom is subject only to clearly defined exceptions laid down by common law or statute . . . the principle that the press is free from both Government and judicial control is more important than the particular case.

v) The fact that under section 12 (4) the court is required to have particular regard to whether it would be in the public interest for the material to be published does not mean that the court is justified in interfering with the freedom of the press where there is no identifiable special public interest in any particular material being published. Such an approach would turn section 12 (4) upside down. Regardless of the quality of the material which it is intended to publish *prima facie* the court should not interfere with its publication. Any interference with publication must be justified.

vi) It is most unlikely that any purpose will be served by a judge seeking to decide whether there exists a new cause of action in tort which protects privacy. In the great majority of situations, if not all situations, where the protection of privacy is justified, relating to events after the Human Rights Act came into force, an action for breach of confidence now will, where this is appropriate, provide the necessary protection. This means that at first instance it can be readily accepted that it is not necessary to tackle the vexed question of whether there is a separate cause of action based upon a new tort involving the infringement of privacy.

ix) The need for the existence of a confidential relationship should not give rise to problems as to the law. The difficulty will be as to the relevant facts. A duty of confidence will arise whenever the party subject to the duty is in a situation where he either knows or ought to know that the other person can reasonably expect his privacy to be protected. (See Lord Goff of Chieveley, in *Attorney General* v *Guardian Newspapers Ltd* [No. 2] [1990] 1 AC 109 at 281.) The range of situations in which protection can be provided is therefore extensive. Obviously, the necessary relationship can be expressly created. More often its existence will have to be inferred from the facts. Whether a duty of confidence does exist which courts can protect, if it is right to do so, will depend on all the circumstances of the relationship between the parties at the time of the threatened or actual breach of the alleged duty of confidence.

x) If there is an intrusion in a situation where a person can reasonably expect his privacy to be respected then that intrusion will be capable of giving rise to liability in an action for breach of confidence unless the intrusion can be justified. (See the approach of Dame Elizabeth Butler-Sloss P. in *Venables* v *Newsgroup Newspapers Ltd* [2001] 1038 at para. 81.) The bugging of someone's home or the use of other surveillance techniques are obvious examples of such an intrusion. But the fact that the information is obtained as a result of unlawful activities does not mean that its publication should necessarily be restrained by injunction on the grounds of breach of confidence (see the *Lenah Game* decision). Dependent on the nature of the unlawful activity there may be other remedies. On the other hand, the fact that unlawful means have been used to obtain the information could well be a compelling factor when it comes to exercising discretion.

xi) More difficult is the situation where the alleged intrusion into privacy is as a result of the reporting of the information to a third party by a party to the relationship which creates the privacy. This is a material factor in situations where two people have shared a sexual relationship outside marriage. If one wishes to exercise his or her article 10 rights that must impact on the other's right to maintain confidentiality. For example the information may relate, as in this case, to a situation where there is a sexual relationship between two parties and one of the parties informs the media about the relationship without the consent of the other party. Here the conflict between one party's right to privacy and the other party's right of freedom of expression is especially acute. In situations where the parties are not married (when they are, special considerations may arise) the fact that the confidence was a shared confidence which only one of the parties wishes to preserve does not extinguish the other party's right to have the confidence respected, but it does undermine that right. While recognising the special status of a lawful marriage under our law, the courts, for present purposes, have to recognise and give appropriate weight to the extensive range of relationships which now exist. Obviously, the more stable the relationship the greater will be the significance which is attached to it.

xii) Where an individual is a public figure he is entitled to have his privacy respected in the appropriate circumstances. A public figure is entitled to a private life. The individual, however, should recognise that because of his public position he must expect and accept that his actions will be more closely scrutinised by the media. Even trivial facts relating to a public figure can be of great interest to readers and other observers of the media. Conduct which in the case of a private individual would not be the appropriate subject of comment can be the proper subject of comment in the case of a public figure. The public figure may hold a position where higher standards of conduct can be rightly expected by the public. The public figure may be a role model whose conduct could well be emulated by others. He may set the fashion. The higher the profile of the individual concerned the more likely that this will be the position. Whether you have courted publicity or not you may be a legitimate subject of public attention. If you have courted public attention then you have less ground to object to the intrusion which follows. In many of these situations it would be overstating the position to say that there is a public interest in the information being published. It would be more accurate to say that the public have an understandable and so a legitimate interest in being told the information. If this is the situation then it can be appropriately taken into account by a court when deciding on which side of the line a case falls. The courts must not ignore the fact that if newspapers do not publish information which the public are interested in, there will be fewer newspapers published, which will not be in the public interest. The same is true in relation to other parts of the media . . .

xiii) In drawing up a balance sheet between the respective interests of the parties courts should not act as censors or arbiters of taste. This is the task of others. If there is not a sufficient case for restraining publication the fact that a more lurid approach will be adopted by the publication than the court would regard as acceptable is not relevant. If the contents of the publication are untrue the law of defamation provides prohibition. Whether the publication will be attractive or unattractive should not affect the result of an application if the information is otherwise not the proper subject of restraint.

xiv) Section 12 (4) requires the court to take into account 'any relevant privacy code' but it is only one of a number of factors to be taken into account. The Press Complaints Commission Code of Practice provides that:

> It is essential to the workings of an agreed code that it be honoured not only to the letter but in the full spirit. The code should not be interpreted so narrowly as to compromise its commitment to respect the rights of the individual, nor so broadly that it prevents publication in the public interest.

> Privacy

> (i)  Everyone is entitled to respect for his or her private and family life, home, health and correspondence. A publication will be expected to justify intrusions into any individual's private life without consent.
> (ii) The use of long lens photography to take pictures of people in private places without their consent is unacceptable.

> Note—Private places are public or private property where there is a reasonable expectation of privacy.

Harassment

They must not photograph individuals in private places (as defined by the note to clause 3) without their consent; must not persist in telephoning, questioning, pursuing or photographing individuals after having been asked to desist; must not remain on their property after having been asked to leave and must not follow them.

The public interest

1. The public interest includes:

(i)   Detecting or exposing crime or a serious misdemeanour.
(ii)  Protecting public health and safety.
(iii) Preventing the public from being misled by some statement or action of an individual or organisation.

Courts may well find this statement of practice of assistance. While recognising that section 12 (4) was primarily concerned with preserving the freedom of the press regard should be had to the guidance given by Lord Justice Brooke in *Douglas* v *Hello! Ltd* at paragraph 94, where he says;

94. It appears to me that the existence of these statutory provisions, coupled with the current wording of the relevant privacy code, mean that in any case where the court is concerned with issues of freedom of expression in a journalistic, literary or artistic context, it is bound to pay particular regard to any breach of the rules set out in clause 3 of the code, especially where none of the public interest claims set out in the preamble to the code is asserted. A newspaper which flouts clause 3 of the code is likely in those circumstances to have its claim to an entitlement to freedom of expression trumped by article 10(2) considerations of privacy. Unlike the court in *Kaye* v *Robertson* [1991] FSR 62, Parliament recognised that it had to acknowledge the importance of the article 8(1) respect for private life, and it was able to do so untrammelled by any concerns that the law of confidence might not stretch to protect every aspect of private life.

xv)  However, the court should discourage advocates seeking to rely on individual decisions of the Press Commission which at best are no more than illustrative of how the Press Commission performs its different responsibilities.

# INDEX